THE New York Intellectuals READER

THE New York Intellectuals

Intellectuals

READER

NEIL JUMONVILLE

EDITOR

Routledge
Taylor & Francis Group
New York   London

Routledge
Taylor & Francis Group
270 Madison Avenue
New York, NY 10016

Routledge
Taylor & Francis Group
2 Park Square
Milton Park, Abingdon
Oxon OX14 4RN

© 2007 by Taylor & Francis Group, LLC
Routledge is an imprint of Taylor & Francis Group, an Informa business

Printed in the United States of America on acid-free paper
10 9 8 7 6 5 4 3 2 1

International Standard Book Number-10: 0-415-95265-4 (Softcover) 0-415-95264-6 (Hardcover)
International Standard Book Number-13: 978-0-415-95265-1 (Softcover) 978-0-415-95264-4 (Hardcover)

Library of Congress Cataloging-in-Publication Data

The New York intellectuals reader / edited by Neil Jumonville.
    p. cm.
   ISBN 0-415-95264-6 (alk. paper) -- ISBN 0-415-95265-4 (alk. paper)
    1. Intellectuals--New York (State)--New York--Biography. 2. New York
(N.Y.)--Intellectual life--20th century. 3. New York (N.Y.)--Biography. 4.
United States--Intellectual life--20th century. 5. United States--Politics and
government--1933-1945. 6. United States--Politics and government--1945-1989. I.
Jumonville, Neil.

F128.5.N5595 2007
974.7'043--dc22
                                       2006033880

Visit the Taylor & Francis Web site at
http://www.taylorandfrancis.com

and the Routledge Web site at
http://www.routledge.com

Karen Marie Jumonville,
true companion

Contents

Neoconservatism

Preface

As in any volume of this kind, the reader is welcome to complain about what essays I've chosen to include. I hope, however, there is some small forbearance about what I have had to leave out, which is a great amount. I thank Routledge for its commitment to putting out this book, which puts it among a rare group of commercial houses that will reprint American critical essays. In this collection, I included three different types of essays. First, and representing the greatest number, are essays that are important because they are excellent and have shaped opinion. The second group, a small fraction of the first, represent essays that are famous enough to be part of the cultural landscape of the New York Intellectuals. Third, there are a handful of essays here that help tell the story of the group. I could have doubled the number of essays and not dropped the level of excellence at all, but there was no more room in a volume that was meant as a book for the interested public. The reader will find no poetry or stories in this collection. Although there were good poems and fiction in their magazines, the New York Intellectuals were strongest in criticism, and that is what is represented here.

Essays by Lewis Coser, Leslie Fiedler, Elizabeth Hardwick, Murray Hausknecht, Gertrude Himmelfarb, Norman Mailer, Bernard Rosenberg, Delmore Schwartz, Ben B. Seligman, Diana Trilling, Dennis Wrong, and a dozen others would have improved this volume. Figures such as Reinhold Niebuhr, David Riesman, Michael Harrington, James Baldwin, and Edward Shils, while important, were left out because although they wrote occasionally for the New York Intellectuals' magazines they were not central members of the group. Similarly, Richard Hofstadter, missing here, was a friend of many in the group but rarely wrote for their publications. There are no European cousins of the group represented: no Raymond Aron or Arthur Koestler, no Stephen Spender or Andre Malraux, no Ignazio Silone or Nicola Chiaromonte. The central magazines of the group in this period were *Partisan Review, Commentary, Dissent, The Menorah Journal, politics, The New Leader, Encounter* (England), and *The Public Interest*. Most of the essays in this volume are from these magazines.

The essays I chose cover a forty-five year period, from 1934 when the first rendition of *Partisan Review* began until Irving Kristol published his reflection on the adversary culture in 1979. Within a few years of that time many of the New York Intellectuals had died and their magazines were past their prime—although several of them are still influential today, including *Commentary* and *Dissent*.

I have capitalized the spelling of *New York Intellectuals* to indicate to the casual reader of this book that the name refers to a *specific* group of individuals instead of intellectuals in New York generally.

Tallahassee
October 2006

Acknowledgments

Sincere thanks to Robert Tempio, my editor for the first half of this project, who believed there was a need for an anthology of the New York Intellectuals' essays, and who asked me to assemble it for Routledge. Rob, now at Princeton University Press, is a co-editor with Robert Talisse of *Sidney Hook on Pragmatism, Democracy, and Freedom* (2002). He knew that a volume of the New York Intellectuals' essays did not yet exist and also was aware that most of their books of essays were out of print, an unfortunate comment about American culture and publishing.

David McBride, an excellent editor, guided this project through its third quarter. Kimberly Guinta who replaced him for the fourth quarter—the hardest assignment—has been kind enough to help me finish all the details and difficult work very professionally, and I appreciate her very much. I am particularly grateful for the help of Sylvia Wood, my copy editor, with whom I worked closely and happily. Brendan O'Neill, my contact person on the editorial team, made my life easy. Thanks also to Charlotte Roh and Zoe Arey.

For important advice and counsel on this volume I thank Alexander Bloom, Howard Brick, George Cotkin, Michael Kimmage, John Rodden, Gerald Sorin, and Harvey Teres. Cutler Edwards and Sterling Coleman gave me essential research assistance on this volume, and William Modrow in Strozier Library at Florida State University helped me acquire copies of several hard to find essays. Donald J. Foss, Joseph Travis, and Larry Abele afforded me research semesters to work on this project while I was a department chair, showing again that Florida State University is an excellent place to work on research. I thank members of the history department for putting up with my negligence and absences as chair while completing this volume, and thank Vicky Bernal for filling in for me during these frequent disappearances.

I would like to acknowledge the influence of Daniel Aaron, with whom I had the privilege to work as a graduate student a quarter of a century ago.

Every step I took in this book my wife Karen took, too, over lunch, an evening drink, or dinner. She is my life, my true companion. I am also indebted to Jean Lafitte, Bonnie, McKellar, and Riley Bob for their companionship, boosting my morale, sleeping on my office floor, and keeping me safe when UPS brought packages.

Introduction

The past twenty years have seen an upsurge in Americans' interest in public intellectuals. The increasing attention has been prompted primarily by two conflicting trends: rising concern that they are disappearing due to increasing specialization and intellectuals' elevated cultural status in the expanding knowledge-based economy. The term *public intellectual* describes one who is a generalist knowledgeable about cultural and political matters and whose ideas reach a substantial public. Their writings cross disciplines, and although they know much about the past and often address it directly, they train their analysis on contemporary debates. The intellectual role is different from that of scholars. Intellectuals usually write in periodicals for a general educated public while scholars write for their professional peers in books or refereed scholarly journals. Because they often address contemporary issues, intellectuals tend to write book reviews, columns, and articles partly because the pace of cultural debate requires a rapid response not available through the long gestation period of books.[1] In the cultural courtroom intellectuals resemble lawyers instead of judges because they are partisan advocates instead of neutral referees.

The group known as the New York Intellectuals was neither the first nor the last appearance of this species in America, but it remains among the best known and the most highly regarded. It followed a tradition set by figures such as Benjamin Franklin, one of the first public intellectuals in American culture. Franklin learned his craft by following the example of Englishman Joseph Addison's writing in the *Spectator*. He then produced his own pieces—under the pseudonym Silence Dogood, for his own paper and for his brother James Franklin's *New England Courant* in the 1720s—in which he pronounced on politics and culture and spoke as a generalist.

Like Franklin, the first American critics took their cues from the earlier British tradition of the literary reviewer. In the nineteenth century, this tradition of generalist cultural criticism grew slowly in the United States. Often referred to as the *letters tradition*, from the French pursuit called *belle lettres*, it was populated by such luminaries as Washington Irving (who sometimes wrote as Jonathan Oldstyle), Ralph Waldo Emerson, Elizabeth Palmer Peabody, Margaret Fuller, Henry David Thoreau, Theodore Parker, Nathaniel Hawthorne, David Walker, Frederick Douglass, Mark Twain, Henry Adams, and Henry James.

The term *intellectual* wasn't employed to mean a cultural critic until the Dreyfus Affair in France in the 1890s, when Emile Zola's *J'Accuse* set the new standard. By 1899, the term already had steamed across the Atlantic to Massachusetts, where William James referred to "American intellectuals."[2] In the first decades of the twentieth century, intellectual culture in the U.S. grew quickly, partly because America itself was becoming more important internationally. Writers central to the development of the tradition in the U.S. in this era included Van Wyck Brooks, Harold Stearns, Max Eastman, John Reed, Floyd Dell, Randolph Bourne, Walter Lippmann, Herbert Croly, Lewis Mumford, Edmund Wilson, and Malcolm Cowley. Almost without exception, before 1930 the tradition of cultural criticism in America was stocked by those from Harvard and a few other Ivies. Typically born in Boston, New York, or Chicago, they were largely patrician voices representing old Protestant America.

But that slowly began to change in the 1930s. Many of the immigrants who arrived in great numbers at Ellis Island in the 1890s were Jews from Russia or Eastern Europe who carted with them their socialism, trade unionism, respect for literary culture, and familiarity with ideological battles. By the mid-1920s and early 1930s, they had children of college age who, though schooled in America, had been raised at home in a European cultural tradition that proved vital to the development of a critical intellect.

These second-generation New York Jews took years to cohere into a recognizably intellectual group, and only a tiny percentage of the larger Jewish population became members. The price of admission was a talent for ideas, writing essays in a recognizable style, and an audacious ambition to succeed as an intellectual. Many of them attended City College in New York, where they met not only in classes but afterward in the political clubs and groups that had proliferated in the 1930s. They congregated at City College for two basic reasons: their families had little money and as Jews they were not welcome at more prestigious universities. There were a few exceptions: Lionel Trilling attended Columbia, Dwight Macdonald went to Yale, and Mary McCarthy to Vassar.

When they graduated from City College, many of these aspiring intellectuals found that the American university system, still highly elitist and not yet pried opened by the GI Bill of Rights of 1944, had little desire to hire Jews. As Irving Howe said later, "When intellectuals can do nothing else, they start a magazine."[3] A number of them did just that, founding some of the most important periodicals of the twentieth century, including *The Menorah Journal, Partisan Review, Commentary, politics, Dissent, Encounter* (in England), and *The Public Interest.*

Until Howe's 1968 *Commentary* piece, "The New York Intellectuals: A Chronicle and a Critique," though, the group was known only as the *Partisan Review* crowd (*PR* was the group's best known early magazine).[4] Occasionally, members of the *Partisan* circle would deny their membership, and nearly always because they did not want their own intellectual and scholarly work to be simply subsumed into that of the larger circle.

How do we know who actually belonged to the group? Of course, we can't determine any exact membership, partly because membership wasn't formal, and partly because group boundaries were porous. But this doesn't mean the group was a fiction, because the same problem arises for almost all groups in history: the abolitionists, the suffragists, the progressives, the New Left. In all such cases, it's easier to define those at the core than those on the periphery, and that is how it should be. For this particular group, it is relatively easy to identify the core members. The clearest signal is whether one edited or prominently wrote for their magazines. Next is whether one shared their anti-Stalinist socialism or, later, their anti-communist liberalism.

Members in the first cohort were born between 1900 and 1910, and representatives included Sidney Hook (1902), Meyer Schapiro (1904), Lionel Trilling (1905), Dwight Macdonald (1906), Philip Rahv (1908), and Clement Greenberg (1909). The second, born generally from 1915 to 1925, featured members such as Alfred Kazin (1915), Daniel Bell (1919), Irving Howe (1920), Irving Kristol, (1920), and Nathan Glazer (1923). The two members most associated with the third generation were Norman Podhoretz (1930) and Susan Sontag (1933).

As socialists and Jews, in their youth they maintained an uneasy relationship with America. Like Trotsky, who many of them admired, they felt homeless—proudly so. A few flirted with communism in their younger years but most of them adhered to one of the varieties of socialism in the 1930s. As World War II edged closer, Sidney Hook encouraged the *Partisan Review* editors to press for American support for the Allies and opposition to totalitarian forces. Hook's socialist critics called it a "lesser evil" strategy of selecting the best of two distasteful sides in the war, but Hook felt it was a reasonable choice for a pragmatist to make. Philip Rahv and William Phillips, two of *Partisan Review*'s editors, initially ignored Hook's suggestion, and two other editors, Dwight Macdonald and Clement Greenberg, rejected Hook's position as not radical enough. Like other socialist followers of Trotsky, Macdonald and Greenberg refused to support either the Allies or the Axis powers in the war and instead maintained a "third camp" position that opposed involvement in the war in the hope there would be a democratic socialist alternative to both sides after the war.

When American involvement in World War II became increasingly likely in 1941—the same year that Henry Luce wrote his famous *Life* editorial "The American Century"—Macdonald and Greenberg decided to put their position about the war into the *Partisan Review*. In their essay "10 Propositions on the War," the two emphasized that a large war effort by the United States would only make the U.S. fascist, too, and wouldn't produce the needed democratic revolution in America, which only a revolutionary socialist "mass action" of the people could create. Opposing American entry into the war and working in the U.S. for a democratic socialism would be a third-camp strategy, a potential third way between a fascist Europe and totalitarian Soviet Union on one side and the depression-era commercial capitalism of the U.S. on the other.

In response, Philip Rahv wrote "10 Propositions and 8 Errors," which disputed the suggestion of Macdonald and Greenberg for the U.S to sit out the war and hope for a "third-camp" alternative afterward. Instead, Rahv endorsed Hook's "lesser evil" approach that supported U.S. entry into the war. The disagreement among the editors was enough to drive Macdonald and Greenberg out of *Partisan Review*. Macdonald began his own magazine, *politics*, and Greenberg soon joined the editorial staff of *Commentary*. *Partisan Review's* support of American involvement in the war showed the *PR* group's growing identification with America itself.

The absolutist doctrines of fascism and Stalinist communism in the 1930s and 1940s influenced the group profoundly. These grim ideological spectacles nudged them out of the political left, in fact out of what they considered to be ideological politics generally, and prompted their gradual acceptance of a mildly reformist and pragmatic Deweyean liberalism, advocated by Sidney Hook, Dewey's most prominent student. God died in the nineteenth century, Irving Howe once observed, and utopia died in the twentieth. Although many of them only very slowly and grudgingly acknowledged that they were liberals, some of them became quite important articulators of liberal values and commitments. Even such unlikely figures as the democratic socialist Irving Howe, the rather diffident literary critic Lionel Trilling, and the neoconservative social and economic thinker Irving Kristol helped articulate the core values of liberalism from the late 1940s to the 1970s.

The New York Intellectuals comprised some of the key American essayists of the mid-twentieth century. Indeed, they were cultural and political *critics*—reviewers, analysts, and commentators—and most of them wrote analytical essays instead of fiction or poetry. Criticism fueled their magazines. In their pieces, they debated, argued, criticized, evaluated, adjudicated, explained, denounced, praised, revised, reevaluated, chose sides, sniffed out enemies, suggested future strategies, and buried outdated beliefs and commitments; they quibbled over scriptures whether religious, political, or literary; broke from their intellectual parents and chastised their cultural children; and fought and refought the last war. Raised on the Talmud, and considering Marxist theoretical disputations a sport, it was natural for them to feel at home in debate. They interpreted stories but rarely told them, deciphered paintings but seldom held a brush.

They not only lived the life of intellectuals but also had a hand in defining what that term meant. After encountering the absolutist societies of Germany, the Soviet Union, and other nations where intellectuals were expected to uphold and justify the policies of repressive totalitarian societies, American intellectuals in the *Partisan Review* circle began to make independent judgment a central part of the definition of an intellectual. Moreover, they believed those who adopted zealous, fanatical, or messianic mindsets disqualified themselves as real intellectuals. After World War II, the *Partisan Review* crowd began to define *ideology* itself as akin to fanaticism, and from this they argued that overly ideological thinkers were not truly intellectuals. They had taken stock of the frightening perversions that had plagued socialism, and following the war, treated intellectual freedom as a bulwark against absolutism in all of its guises.

Because the group stood at the crossroads of politics and culture, throughout their careers they waged their battles in those two arenas. Having grown up in depression-era New York, they first defined their cultural focus as proletarian realism in literature and painting. After only a few years, though—and partly as a result of their facing up to Stalinism—they shifted their allegiance to modernist literature and painting. They remained faithful to high modernism for the remainder of their careers.

Their initial enthusiasm for proletarian culture is understandable. After all, they came from proletarian neighborhoods and—more often than not—working class families. And when many of these young writers wanted to join the literary life, it was the Communist Party's John Reed writers clubs that offered them the best opportunity. *Partisan Review* itself was initially the magazine of the New York City branch of the John Reed Club. Through their essays on proletarian novels in the magazine's first two years, *Partisan Review* writers gleaned what was still usable from the socialist culture of their parents. The proletarian style itself focused on a shattered capitalism and suggested what might replace it. It allowed the profession of literature—such as it was—to put the bourgeoisie and the American dream on trial. But the magazine lost the support of the Communist Party when Stalin decided to drop proletarian culture in favor of creating a Popular Front with famous liberal writers in America who could urge their country to support the Soviet fight against fascism in the 1930s.

When Philip Rahv and William Phillips were left with a magazine without funding, it closed for a year and then reopened with new funding and a new cultural and political orientation. Gone were both proletarian literature and communist politics.[5] For intellectuals who valued independent cultural judgment, proletarian culture had become too limiting. Moreover, the Moscow Trials had brought to light Soviet totalitarianism and duplicity. The *Partisan Review* editors instead wanted to create an *independent* radical tradition and, as a result, they began to embrace an anti-Stalinist socialism. Proletarian realism seemed too close to Soviet culture and in addition it had no intellectual edge, but they quickly saw that cultural modernism provided no such limitations.

The importance they placed on modernism beginning in the 1940s was reasonable because it represented the European cultural although not the class roots of their parents. The *Partisan* crowd could interpret modernism at least partly as a championing of European values over those of America. From the platform of modernism they could also attack the culture of progressivism, represented by such writers as Theodore Dreiser, Vernon Parrington, and Van Wyck Brooks, as well as artists the *Partisans* thought were too earnest and too willing to champion the culture of the common American—and who therefore seemed too near to the proletarian sympathies the *Partisans* were trying to shed. In contrast, modernists embraced cultural alienation, produced a high art led by a vanguard of writers suspicious of mainstream values, celebrated technical experimentation, resented conformism, and wrote about the social and institutional pressure that crushed the spirit of the individual. In the abstract expressionist painting of the 1940s and 1950s, high-art modernism was especially evident. Abstract expressionists claimed that their canvases were so simple that anyone could view them, while in reality, they were explained in a coded and theoretical language known only to the initiated few.

The New York Intellectuals in the 1950s slowly began to prosper, finding jobs writing for the *New Yorker* and other magazines, or finding academic positions in a rapidly expanding university system. Their resulting move into the middle class presented problems for these former opponents of capitalism, becoming another of their cultural struggles. Could they still call themselves intellectuals and "critics" if they held professorships and lived in gracious surroundings? Philip Rahv spoke of the *embourgeoisement* of the intellectuals.[6] Did intellectuals need to maintain an adversarial relationship to mainstream society, as Irving Howe suggested? If so, as Granville Hicks and Sidney Hook asked, was automatic opposition to the dominant culture any more intelligent than automatic conformity? The writers for *Dissent* magazine in the 1950s answered this question differently from those at *Commentary*, who the *Dissent*ers considered to be cultural affirmers.

Members of the New York Intellectuals had disagreements. From the outside, it was clear they shared a respect for cultural modernism, high culture, and representative democracy. Less evident were the disagreements, particularly those between *Commentary* and *Dissent*. Those at *Commentary* drew writers who were more conservative, pro-capitalist, supportive of American culture, more enthusiastically anticommunist, against McCarthyism although their opposition was sometimes hard to detect, and more supportive of the Cold War. *Dissent*'s editors and writers had never entirely relinquished their socialism, were critical of American economic and social policies, believed that it was important to criticize American mass culture and conformity, were anticommunist, were loudly critical of Joe McCarthy, and worried that an excessively strong foreign policy could prompt a tragic nuclear exchange. Those at *Commentary* were critical of America, but they also affirmed its successes. Those at *Dissent* were, well, dissenters.

But clearly the group, even the dissenters, believed that not all opposition to society was equally good. The Beats in the 1950s, for example, were romantics, and romantics who depended on intuition, the New York Intellectuals believed, were not clear thinkers. In addition, the Beats, disdainful of mass consumerist society, turned their backs on the middle class and the values of the bourgeoisie to embrace authenticity, which they found in bucolic pastoralism and among the socially marginalized. The New York Intellectuals thought the Beats foolish and undereducated. Like Marx, the *Partisan Review* circle considered the bourgeoisie quite talented—particularly at creating wealth—and instead of denigrating the middle class and its values, they simply wanted economic and political benefits to be spread more equitably.

A disproportionate number of the New York Intellectuals counted themselves literary critics. Influenced by the sociology and politics they read as adolescents—of Marx, Weber, Durkheim, and the countless thinkers they argued over—literary criticism for the *Partisan* circle consisted mainly of history and biography. Like the work of Edmund Wilson before them, who was so admired by members of the group, the history they employed could be literary history or a wider general intellectual history of which biography and class and region were important parts. A book, in the view of the New York Intellectuals, was a social text, whether it was a novel or a nonfiction account such as Alfred Kinsey's report on sexuality.

The contextualism of the New York Intellectuals' literary criticism was not embraced universally by other critics. Consider their contemporaries known as the New Critics, whose ideas contrasted markedly with those of Irving Howe, Alfred Kazin, or Lionel Trilling. The New Critics, whose ranks included Kenneth Burke, Yvor Winters, R. P. Blackmur, Cleanth Brooks and others, considered biographical and social influences unimportant in literary works. A work of fiction or poetry, the New Critics believed, could be evaluated only through its own formal properties. Even the poststructuralist literary criticism of the last quarter of the twentieth century has little to do with the contextualism of the New York Intellectuals. In fact, the New York Intellectuals' criticism is apparently so unfashionable now that M. A. R. Habib's recent 848-page anthology of literary criticism from Plato to the present, simply entitled *A History of Literary Criticism*, contains no essays from the New York Intellectuals.[7]

The group also had several prominent political fights. Their major conflict, as we've seen, pitted them against the communists and fascists. Those Americans born after World War II who read of the excesses of McCarthyism sometimes concluded that, because there was no grave danger from domestic communism, there was no danger from international communism. The New York Intellectuals viewed matters quite differently. They had been closely connected to these issues since even before the founding of *Partisan Review* in 1934. Early in their lives, Sidney Hook, Lionel Trilling, Meyer Schapiro, and others knew communists and were sympathetic to some of their social justice and proletarian values. Thus, during the ensuing decades, members of the group were particularly sensitive to the consequences of centrally planned societies, messianic movements and nations, anti-Semitism and anti-intellectualism, utopian visions, mass societies, total solutions, religious orthodoxy, and secret or unaccountable government actions. Totalitarianism and absolutism were unacceptable in any form.

By the end of the 1940s, most members of the New York Intellectuals had either given up on socialism or, like those at *Dissent*, insisted that it be leavened with a strong measure of liberal values. Many of them knew individuals who, for thinking independently, had been murdered in Russia or Eastern Europe by Stalin's assassins. A person had to be a nonentity to survive in such a society, as Hannah Arendt pointed out. Merely to endure, one had to quietly worship government's decrees, pledge one's faith in the prevailing ideology, and never be noticed for any reason.

Because of their preoccupation with the threat of absolutist governments, foreign policy became a staple of the essays of some of the New York Intellectuals. Sidney Hook in the 1940s and 1950s was especially prolific on this topic, as were many other writers for *Partisan Review, Commentary, politics, Dissent, Encounter,* and the *New Leader.* Ultimately, these former socialists would begin to help outline the basic tenets of American Cold War foreign policy—at a time when some Americans still thought of them as dangerous socialist radicals.

By the 1950s, the world seemed very different from what it had been during their socialist college years. Now, instead of calling for labor justice, socialism, and equality, the *Partisan Review* group became more interested in intellectual freedom. They realized that the liberty to speak and act was vital to both intellectuals and radicals. Some of the most enduring arguments among the group in the 1950s and 1960s therefore were about what it meant to be a proper radical or a proper intellectual. In the 1980s, when Ronald Reagan inhabited the White House, some *Commentary* neoconservatives were invited into the circle of power. Jeanne Kirkpatrick became the American ambassador to the United Nations, and Norman Podhoretz was invited to visit Pennsylvania Avenue and make policy suggestions. The decades-old conversation about what it meant to be a proper intellectual began again: how close could an intellectual get to power—the White House—and still be properly independent?

A generational fault split the liberal left, beginning in the 1960s. The New Left was influenced by the romanticism of the decade's counterculture and that effect produced a radicalism different from that of both the Old Left and the New York Intellectuals. The New Leftists embraced revolution in virtually every social sphere: on campuses, in bedrooms, in poor neighborhoods, and in the segregated South. Moreover, they believed in learning through experience, not merely books. To their Old Left professors, they were anti-intellectuals who ignored the essential lessons from a generation before—the dangers of communism as well as the benefits of modernism and representative democracy. The younger generation spurned the anticommunism of the New York Intellectuals, which led to a notable divide between Old Left professors and New Left students over the Vietnam War. A more painful break between generations on the left could hardly have been devised.

By 1970, as the New York Intellectuals began to define themselves as part of the liberal political spectrum—with members spread out from left of center to right of center—they increasingly faced the problems that liberalism itself was encountering. With race and multiculturalism now dominating cultural politics, these former socialists tried to decide whether affirmative action, meritocracy, or some combination of the two would act as the best policy. Those at *Commentary* decided that America should remain committed to colorblind liberal integration instead of endorsing affirmative action and multicultural identity politics. Ultimately, *Dissent* supported a multiculturalism and affirmative action.

The story of the New York Intellectuals above might be summarized with a different emphasis. The generation of Americans that came to political age in the 1930s Depression was shaped by an economic agenda. Consequently, many liberals, leftists, and reformers were driven by the issues of equality, stability, poverty, economic growth, labor union activism, and—to a lesser degree—the socialist agenda. Beginning in the 1930s, the Democratic Party promoted this New Deal agenda, and continued to do so even into the 1950s and 1960s, a time of relatively broad affluence. The radicals of this New Deal economic–political era—those New York Intellectuals at *Dissent*, and other members of the Old Left, for example—had earlier in their educations drawn inspirational lessons from the later work of Karl Marx in *Capital* that argued against capitalist exploitation. Their proposals, consequently, were for a more equal distribution of economic and political power.

Their children, however, reached political consciousness in the mid-1960s. Those children, baby boomers, were raised in an affluent, postindustrial society, and were not haunted by the fears of the Great Depression. They discarded the *economic*-political motivations of their parents' New Deal agenda and instead produced a new *cultural*-political agenda. These radicals of a later generation were not shaped by economic deprivation but rather by the civil rights movement, the women's movement, and the burgeoning mass media, especially television. They developed their passions at a time when the communications revolution, along with momentous world events, brought diverse elements of the population into a truly national conversation. Concomitant to this was a revival of national civic religion. When they were influenced by Marx at all, radicals of this later generation—the New Left and others—chose his earlier gospels: the economic and philosophical manuscripts of 1844, whose emphasis on alienation and commodification fit well with the new importance of culture.

The New York Intellectuals, of course, belonged to the earlier, economically oriented group when it came to politics. And while it is true that many members of the New York group specialized in culture—in literature, art criticism, and sociology—the prevailing definition of culture changed in the mid-1960s. The New York Intellectuals adhered to the earlier definition of culture: Matthew Arnold's definition that culture was the best that civilization had yet produced, reflected in high art, high thought, and high expression—a kind of museum and symphony-hall definition of culture.

In the cultural watershed of the mid-1960s—caused by the civil rights and sexual revolutions along with a genuinely vital and creative popular culture—the younger generation adhered instead to an anthropological view of culture. It defined culture as rising from the bottom of society, a view that had been around on the periphery for decades and had been promoted by figures as diverse as Constance Rourke, Zora Neale Hurston, Margaret Mead, E. P. Thompson, Clifford Geertz, and Claude Levi-Strauss. This anthropological view of culture focused on the practices and beliefs of ordinary people who didn't necessarily leave written records; on stories and jokes; on ceremonies and rituals; on the configuration of houses; or, for example, on slave songs.

The New York Intellectuals, like so many of their generation, were part of an earlier and different world. *Après moi, le deluge.* They were not of an era in which the prevailing questions were about racial diversity, or gender equality, or sexual experimentation; where elements of low culture were thought more important to study than dense novels or the history of painting; where manners and graciousness were considered inauthentic; or where youth and energy was more important than experience and education. The minor exception to their disparagement of the young popular values was when, in the mid-1960s, a new generation of writers such as Susan Sontag and Richard Poirier began writing for their magazines. By the 1990s, *Partisan Review* was a different magazine, almost unrecognizable to its early readers, written by a different generation that had been suffused with 1960s culture. By then it had lost its stamp of the New York Intellectuals.

The *Partisan* circle's influence, then, began in the 1930s, peaked in the 1950s, and was swept aside by the 1960s revolution. Their remaining influence can be found in what, after the mid-1970s, became neoconservatism, a very influential outlook originally identified with the more conservative *Commentary* wing of the group. At this writing, most of New York Intellectuals' essays are out of print.

Yet their ideas are now more relevant than they have been for forty years—because liberals no longer know what *liberal* means, and the West has real self-proclaimed enemies again. Both of these issues—the meaning of liberalism and the presence of dangerous enemies—are matters that the group addressed. I am not suggesting that we now should adopt what the New York Intellectuals thought a half-century ago. But unless we turn to our own intellectual past, revisit and weigh the ideas of the New York Intellectuals and other relevant groups of thinkers before we continue on into the rest of the twenty-first century, our future will be more impoverished.

Notes

1. Neil Jumonville, "The Role of the Intellectual," *Encyclopedia of American Cultural and Intellectual History* (New York: Scribners' Sons, 2001), vol. 3, 225–236.
2. *The Letters of William James* (Boston, 1920), vol. 2, 100–101, quoted in Richard Hofstadter, *Anti-Intellectualism in American Life* (New York: Knopf, 1963), 39.
3. Irving Howe, *Twenty-Five Years of Dissent* (New York: Methuen, 1979), xv.
4. Irving Howe, "The New York Intellectuals: A Chronicle and a Critique," *Commentary* vol. 46, no. 4, October 1968, 29-51,.
5. For the early history of *Partisan Review* see Daniel Aaron, *Writers on the Left* (New York: Harcourt, Brace & World, 1961), chapter 11; and James Burkhart Gilbert, *Writers and Partisans* (New York: Wiley, 1968), chapters 4–5.
6. Philip Rahv, "Our Country and Our Culture," *Partisan Review* vol. 19, no. 3, May–June, 1952, 306.
7. M. A. R. Habib, *A History of Literary Criticism* (Malden, MA: Blackwell, 2005).

I
Finding Native Grounds

1
Alfred Kazin (1915–1998)
Starting Out in the Thirties (1962)

Editor's Introduction

Alfred Kazin might have been the first member of the New York Intellectuals to think of America, at least to consider it out loud in print, as his country and culture. In the preface to his first book, *On Native Grounds* (1942), a study of realism and naturalism from Howells to Faulkner written when he was only twenty seven, he referred to his subject sociably as "our modern life in America," "our society" and "our alienation *on* native grounds—the interwoven story of our need to take up our life on our own grounds, and the irony of our possessions." Casting American cultural figures as *ours* would not yet have occurred to other members of the New York Intellectuals. Members of his circle—still feeling rootless and homeless like their hero Leon Trotsky—might have asked, "On *native* grounds, Alfred?" But Kazin, since his early days growing up in the Brownsville neighborhood of New York, felt a connection with the country. As a boy he walked through the Metropolitan Museum of Art and was especially drawn to paintings of New York City from a century earlier. He searched those canvases for buildings or bridges he knew, streets he walked, snowstorms he braved.

If Kazin was among the earliest in the group to embrace American culture and its pantheon of figures, the following selections from the first two chapters of his autobiographical *Starting Out in the Thirties* (1962) show the even more pervasive influence of the Jewish immigrant experience in Brownsville into which he was born. Much of his young life was spent in the kitchen of his family's apartment, where his mother was a tailor and made dresses for neighborhood women. There, as she worked, he saw a daily progression of customers, relatives, sales representatives and neighbors crowd into the tiny space. In addition, how many American children had been raised as socialists? Part of his immigrant family and community life, socialism was so deeply embedded in him that he hardly thought about its presence. He later realized, "my socialism, though I felt it deeply, did not require any conscious personal assent or decision on my part; I was Socialist as so many Americans were 'Christians'; I had always lived in a Socialist atmosphere." The same would have been said by most other members of the New York Intellectuals. In these selections from his book Kazin tells of working his way into literary journalism. In the process of doing so, he understands how foreign his family seems to some of his friends—even as he was beginning to write about the native grounds of American culture.

Alfred Kazin was born in New York City and received his bachelor's degree from the College of the City of New York in 1935 and his masters from Columbia in 1938. He was a noted American literary and cultural critic in the mold of Edmund Wilson and Malcolm Cowley, a style in which one would review a book not only, perhaps not even primarily, for its literary meaning, plot and symbolism, but rather for its wider cultural and political significance, with the reviewer serving as a historian, a sociologist and an interpreter of cultural scriptures for a national congregation.

Source

Alfred Kazin, *Starting Out in the Thirties*. 1962; reprint, New York: Vintage, 1980. (Abridged.)

Selected Readings

Ted Solotaroff, *Alfred Kazin's America* (New York: HarperCollins, 2003). Alfred Kazin, ed., *A Lifetime Burning in Every Moment: From the Journals of Alfred Kazin* (New York: HarperCollins, 1996); *A Walker in the City* (New York: Harcourt, Brace and World, 1951).

* * * * *

One hot June afternoon in 1934, deep in the depression, I had just completed my college course for the year and was desolately on my way home to Brooklyn when a book review in the *New York Times* aroused me. I was just nineteen years old, my briefcase was full of college essays on Henry Vaughan, T. S. Eliot, Thomas Traherne, John Donne and other Anglo-Catholic poets who had come into fashion, and I had no prospects whatever. Although I was a "Socialist," like everyone else I knew, I thought of socialism as orthodox Christians might think of the Second Coming—a wholly supernatural event which one might await with perfect faith, but which had no immediate relevance to my life. "Socialism" was a way of life, since everyone else I knew in New York was a Socialist, more or less; but I was remarkably detached from it intellectually, and spent my days reading Blake and Lawrence and Whitman. I felt moral compulsions to be a Socialist, since the society in which sixteen million people were jobless that summer and a million on strike did not seem to admit saving except by a Socialist government. But my socialism, though I felt it deeply, did not require any conscious personal assent or decision on my part; I was a Socialist as so many Americans were "Christians"; I had always lived in a Socialist atmosphere. But if anyone who had thought his own way into socialism had questioned me sharply as to what I accepted or did not accept of Marxism, he

would have discovered very little to please him except my violent class prejudice. I was a literary radical, indifferent to economics, suspicious of organization, planning, Marxist solemnity and intellectual system-building; it was the
rebels of literature, the great wrestlers-with-God, Thor with his mighty ham-
mer, the poets of unlimited spiritual freedom, whom I loved—Blake, Emerson, Whitman, Nietzsche, Lawrence. I had watched Communists break up
Socialist meetings and in February I had seen them throwing chairs from the
balconies of Madison Square Garden down on the decent trade unionists who
had met to honor the Socialists of Vienna hanged by Dollfuss; for three years
I had the law on every possible subject handed down to me by classmates who
were interested less in the Revolution than in demonstrating their intellectual
grasp of everything at once, and just then I was sick of Communists. I had the
deepest contempt for those middle-class and doctrinaire radicals who, after
graduating from Harvard or Yale in the Twenties, had made it a matter of
personal honor to become Marxists, and who now worried in the *New Masses*
whether Proust should be read after the Revolution and why there seemed to
be no simple proletarians in the novels of André Malraux.

I felt myself to be a radical, not an ideologue; I was proud of the revolutionary yet wholly literary tradition in American writing to which I knew that I
belonged, and would say over to myself, from *Axel's Castle*, the last, woven
sentence of Edmund Wilson's chapter on Proust: "Proust is perhaps the last
great historian of the loves, the society, the intelligence, the diplomacy, the literature and the art of the Heartbreak House of capitalist culture; and the little
man with the sad appealing voice, the metaphysician's mind, the Saracen's
beak, the ill-fitting dress-shirt and the great eyes that seem to see all about
him like the many-faceted eyes of a fly, dominates the scene and plays host
in the mansion where he is not long to be master." I lived in the Heartbreak
House of capitalist culture, waiting for it to stand accused by all writers worthy of the name. I looked to literature for strong social argument, intellectual
power, human liberation. If anyone had bothered to point out the inconsistencies in my intellectual affections, I would not have been ashamed. Salvation
would come by the word, the long-awaited and fatefully exact word that only
the true writer would speak. After three years of City College in the depths of
the depression—engulfed by Socialists who were Norman Thomas Socialists,
old-line Social Democrats, Austro-Marxists; Communists who were Stalinist
centrists, Trotskyite leftists, Lovestoneite right-wingers, Musteites and Fieldites; Zionists who were Progressive Labor Zionists, left Socialist Zionists and
Religious Zionists—all the most accomplished philosophers ever born to the
New York streets, tireless virtuosi who threw radical argument at each other
morning, noon and night with the same curves and smashes with which they
played ping-pong at each other in the college basement that smelled of the oily
sandwiches that we brought from home—I was not worshipful of ideologists.
Yet I believed in socialism, if not in the savage "proletarian" exclusiveness of

the Communists at this time—before the growing power of Hitler and the Spanish Civil War induced a united front. I thought of socialism simply as a moral idea, an invocation of History in all its righteous sweep. At the moment this sweep, this eventual deliverance of mankind from material hardship, seemed very far from the realities of my life. A bleak New York summer was before me, I had no job and simply no idea what to do with myself.

It was the militant, too knowing sociological emphasis of the *Times* review that aroused me. The reviewer was John Chamberlain, who had become important to many of us for the brilliance and liveliness with which he had inaugurated a daily literary column in the staid old *Times*. Chamberlain had been reporting a recent book on America's youth by a professional youth leader who had been a Fascist and was presently (I guessed this from the review) a Communist. I knew all about professional youth leaders; the city college saw many of them, four and five years after graduation, still holding forth at street corners just outside the college walls. Youth leaders never seemed to graduate out of the class of youth. There was one of them, expelled from college because he had led a physical attack on Italian students, supposedly all Fascists, touring American colleges, whom one could see any day of the week, either at City College or Columbia—he was literally a professional agitator—working on a circle of students with a look of detached and professional hauteur. His personal arrogance had always infuriated me; he was always on podiums, street-corner platforms, in front of the statue of Alma Mater at Columbia, looking *down*. And it was this arrogance and knowingness, which had oozed out of the professional youth leader into the review by John Chamberlain, whom I usually admired, that woke me from my torpor that hot afternoon in the subway. I hated all abstract talk of youth and the problems of youth; *I* was youth, afraid to go home without a job. Chamberlain's programmatic remarks seemed to me condescending, his manner unfeeling; I was convinced that he knew nothing about the subject; even his bothering to review such a book showed a highly abstract mind. *I* was youth—out of college for the year, useless, driven as an alley cat. What the hell does this fellow know about it anyway?

On a sudden impulse I got off at Times Square and made my way up to the *Times*—and to my utter astonishment found Chamberlain in and perfectly willing to hear me out. Chamberlain was just over thirty then, but he looked twenty, and was so boyish and unpretentious in his manner that all my anger at his inhuman "progressivism" quickly vanished in the glow of that afternoon's talk. To be able to talk to him was so unexpected that I tumbled over in my excitement, went deliriously from subject to subject, but always returned the talk to "youth" for fear that he might think I had exhausted my reason for coming. Chamberlain astounded me; in those days, he astounded everyone. He looked young, ingenuous, carelessly one of the boys, with his tousled blond hair and his torn white shirt; he made radicalism seem as American as baseball. It was not until I got to know him better that I realized how abstract his mind was—before the decade's flames were out, Chamberlain's reaction against Communism was to make him an apologist for the American businessman; with him one cause led to another. He lived on ideas, "notions" of things, so completely missing the color and emotion of the human crisis behind them that it was possible to talk to him about anything, to talk to him all the time, without his entertaining the slightest curiosity about the human beings we discussed.

Chamberlain was the golden boy of a generation of ideologues; he was surrounded by radical intellectuals, he had even published a radical critique of the progressive movement called *Farewell to Reform*, "Being a History of the Rise, Life and Decay of the Progressive Mind in America," which ended with the declaration: "However we look at it, eventual constriction stares us in the face. And that is why a contemplation of 'reform' ... is productive of no further hopes in its tenets. The situation, looked upon with intelligence and considered as a long-range proposition, can lead to but one of two personal conclusions: it can make one either a cynic or a revolutionist." Chamberlain looked like Charles Augustus Lindbergh shyly starting out alone for Paris, like Gary Cooper at the end of a western modestly warding off a kiss. He was lean, handsome, kindly and awkward—while his conversation was all Veblen, Marx, Pareto, Beard, Sorokin, Spengler and William Graham Sumner. He never seemed to tire of turning over "ideas," for like many another middle-class American who had learned to resent capitalist society, he was looking hard for alternatives. His father was a wholesale furniture dealer in New Haven. The Chamberlains had been battered by the depression. His unprecedented and much-admired success as the "radical" first daily book critic of the *Times*—in no period but the early Thirties could Chamberlain's reviews have been a daily feature of the *Times*—was due to a stimulating, unorthodox, generous interest in ideas that made people grateful for his good faith in considering every social idea without lending himself abjectly to any one, Intellectuals in the subway would open the *Times* first to Chamberlain's book column; our unrest had reached as far as Forty-third Street. Chamberlain even looked like a Yale man's idea of a Yale man, and except for his careless clothes, like his classmates on Madison Avenue who spent their days thinking up slogans designed to make you buy toothpaste, soap and deodorants. His casualness impressed me deeply. Though he looked the all-American amateur in the company of highbrows whose opinions he respectfully listened to as he browsed through the social ideologies, Chamberlain, while always firmly rejecting Marxism as a panacea, associated himself with the radical cause as much as any writer did in the accelerating crisis that led full smash into the Nazi-Soviet pact and the outbreak of war. He seemed perpetually in search of new ideas and had become an intellectual journalist, a type as peculiar to the Thirties as Mencken had been to the Twenties; he personified to himself the crisis of the American middle class, of the old bourgeois certainties. The chilling deliberateness with which John Chamberlain was able to consider the formation of a radical party interested in more than reform, the possibilities of taking power, the confiscation of inherited wealth, all demonstrated the bankruptcy of normal middle-class standards, the crisis of middle-class Americans from small towns, of Yale graduates. The new style was Chamberlain's rambling flirtation with radical ideas, a willingness to consider *anything*, so long as it kept alive the possibility of creating a new society.

Chamberlain was interested in me that afternoon because I seemed to have an idea; at least I talked about ideas. As I was to learn later, one could never talk to Chamberlain about imaginative literature, music, painting, women; he never talked anything but social ideas. He was so absorbed in our talk that he still had his daily piece to finish, and when it became urgent for him to send his copy down, I watched with awe as he banged out his review for the day, rattling over the keys like a man who never had to stop for a moment. When the thing was done and he had sent it off, he eagerly leaned back in his chair to finish the point about Veblen that he had been making. It was only when evening came on and he realized that it was time for him to go home that it occurred to me to ask him for some help in getting a job. He looked at me with a puzzled frown when I showed him my college essays on Henry Vaughan and John Donne, laughed, and then sent me down to the *New Republic* with a scribbled recommendation—"here's an intelligent radical"—that I be given a chance to review.

•••

What made the *New Republic* really vivid to me was [Malcolm] Cowley's assistant, Otis Ferguson, a sandy, caustic, wild ex-sailor from Worcester, Massachusetts. Ferguson had been in the Navy before going to college, and having won a *New Republic* "college contest" came to New York, parked himself on the steps of West Twenty-first Street, and refused to budge until he was given a job. Ferguson was mad about jazz and movies, on which he wrote regularly for the paper, and whenever he had to review a "serious" book, he practiced a tone of bristling irony, of just barely veiled obscenity, that overturned the literary idealism, the note of High Culture, that had been traditional on the *New Republic*.

•••

In order to interest him in myself, I had promised Ferguson an "exotic" meal; I had tried to suggest that in our Jewish cuisine there were mysterious delights which he would never discover for himself, and after a good many postponements I had finally been able to pin him down and to get him to come out with me. All through the long subway ride to Brooklyn on that hot, hazy summer night, while the fans in the subway cars whirred round and round in the too brightly lighted cars, and chewing-gum wrappers and dust blew through the open windows, I seemed to see everything as if I were Ferguson, for I superstitiously thought of him as a visitor from the great literary world. As so often happened with me whenever I was lucky enough to meet anyone who seemed so positive about everything, I automatically tried to switch my mind to his—not because I really valued his opinions, but out of gratitude for my new friend.

It was August, August in New York, and brutally hot. The long subway ride, to which I had always submitted like an Arab slowly toiling through the desert, seemed to me unendurable for Ferguson's sake; and as we finally made our way out into the open and walked through the crowded dark streets of Brownsville to my home, I found myself desperately chattering in order to make up for the silence—and, it seemed to me, the obvious distaste—which Ferguson had put on just getting down the Elevated stairs. I was eager not only to interest Ferguson, but to impress my mother, who with her usual anxiety about our ability to reach the great world wanted concrete evidence, in the shape of a "boss" at dinner, that I was on to something at last. She was nervous about Ferguson's coming, for she was not sure that a Gentile would like our food and that she would be able even to communicate with him. We were all nervous; it was a big night for us. My mother's unmarried cousin Sophie, who had always lived with us, had hysterically threatened not to appear at all, for as soon as she had learned that the distinguished visitor I was bringing home was not Jewish and still in his twenties, she had miserably eliminated all thought of him as a suitor; the evening had begun to figure in her mind as an unnecessary ordeal; she could have nothing to say to him. But her little bedroom was just off the "dining room" where, for once, we were going to dine, and as she said, it would have been impossible for her to spend the evening cooped up in her room while we were all eating and gabbing away outside her door.

• • •

The dinner was not a success. I kept trying to see everything through Ferguson's eyes, and I felt that everything looked very strange to him. For the first time, I had brought into our home someone from "outside," from the great literary world, and as Ferguson patiently smiled away, interrupted only by my mother's bringing in more and more platters and pleading with him to *eat something*, I tried to imagine his reactions. We all sat around him at the old round table in the dining room—my father, my little sister, and myself—and there poor Ferguson, his eyes bulging with the strain and the harsh bright lights from the overhead lamp, his cheeks red with effort, kept getting shoveled into him cabbage and meatballs, chicken, meat loaf, endless helpings of seltzer and cherry soda; and all the while I desperately kept up a line of chatter to show him that he was not completely isolated, our cousin Sophie sat at the table silently staring at him, taking him in. In our boxlike rooms, where you could hear every creak, every cough, every whisper, while the Brooklyn street boiled outside, there was a strangled human emotion that seemed to me unworthy of Ferguson's sophistication, his jazz, his sardonic perch on Union Square. But as Sophie sat at the table in her withdrawn silence, my sister stared wide-eyed at the visitor, my mother bustlingly brought in more platters, and my father explained that he had always followed and admired the *New Republic*—oh, ever since the days of Walter Lippmann and Herbert Croly!—I felt, through Ferguson's razor-sharp eyes, how dreary everything was. My father kept slurping the soup and reaching out for the meat with his own fork; since I had warned him that Ferguson would expect a drink, he self-consciously left the bottle of whiskey on the table and kept urging our visitor all through the meal to take another drink. My mother, who did not have even her personal appreciation of the *New Republic* to regale Ferguson with, had nothing to do but bring food in, and after a while Sophie took to her room and barricaded herself in.

So the meal which I had so much advertised in advance—which I had allowed Ferguson to believe would be exotic, mysterious, vaguely Levantine—passed at last, and after he had charmingly said good-by to my parents and I walked him back to the subway at Rockaway Avenue, he studied me quietly for a moment and said, "What the hell was so exotic about that?" In order to interest Ferguson in us, I had painted such delights of Brooklyn and the strange Jewish cuisine that it now shocked me to realize that from his point of view we were, as a group, no more exotic or picturesque than anybody else. My effort to interest him in me by painting us all as if we wore fezzes, and lived near a palm tree, had plainly not gone down with Ferguson, who in the office often played the clown in order to get over the gap he felt between himself and "literary" people, but who in the ordinary affairs of life had a common sense that, when I had lost my self-consciousness with him, more and more impressed me.

As I said good-by to Ferguson at the subway station and walked through the dark Friday night streets, it unnerved me to realize that he found us as a group so commonplace. My first instinct was to seek out a girl I used to walk around with on Friday nights and find some comfort in her, but she was out and I walked by myself. In my effort to compass my own family, to bridge the wall of silence between us, I had always thought of them as requiring a certain effort to reach. We were a peculiar set. I was haunted by the lack of intimacy between my mother and father, and my father's sobs that Saturday night long ago on the East Side had become my own terror of being lost. But detached and strained as we all were with each other—which made every member of my family so "interesting" to me because we were so unreachable—it seemed to me that we were specially interesting because we were among the dispossessed of history; I saw us as the downtrodden, the lonely, the needy, in a way that fitted my faith in a total redemption.

There are times in history when a group feels that it is at the center of events. Poor as we were, anxious, lonely, it seemed to me obvious that everywhere, even in Hitler Germany, to be outside of society and to be Jewish was to be at the heart of things. History was preparing, in its Jewish victims and through them, some tremendous deliverance and revelation. I hugged my aloneness, our apartness, my parents' poverty, as a sign of our call to create the future. I identified everything good with a distant period in time, when my class, my people, myself, would be finally justified. Starting out in the Thirties under people who were "radical," like Chamberlain and Cowley and Ferguson, I could never identify myself with them, for they were so plainly with the haves, with the people who so mysteriously sat in positions of power, for which they had been chosen by—whom? Ferguson's boredom with us, with the crudity that had seemed to me positively sacramental in its significance for the future, with the worldly insignificance of poor Jews from whom had sprung the early passion of Christianity itself, shocked me; it seemed to send us all spinning into a world of actual dullness and tawdriness, where poverty was graceless and Jewishness merely a bore. I did not mind being poor, Jewish, excluded, for I knew that history was on the side of such things; what I could not understand was Ferguson's finding us dull.

At the same time I had a sense of unreality, of doubleness, almost of duplicity, about the daily contrast of my personal life, my friends, my life in Brownsville, with those literary personages in mid-Manhattan who were so exciting and unreal to me that I would come home from a lunch with Chamberlain, or an afternoon at the *New Republic*, in nervous exhaustion. There was a curious parallel for me here with Ferguson, the ex-sailor, who protected himself against the heavily literary tradition of the *New Republic* by emphasizing the boy from Worcester. Ferguson would toss around the new review books as they came in, making visceral puns on the names of literary gentlefolk like Mary Colum, or attacking the Van Dorens—who were his special butt, and whom he never tired of lampooning in his jealousy of Columbia professors who wrote so much and edited so much and knew so much about literature.

I was just then taking Mark Van Doren's graduate course at Columbia in the art of the long poem, and in the late afternoons would listen with gratitude to lectures on the *Aeneid* that brought home, under Van Doren's smiling touch, Virgil's eloquence and melancholy. Van Doren was unforgettably the poet in the classroom, direct, full of the most concrete feeling about Virgil's lines, which he would read with a shy, straight, Midwestern pleasantness. As the early winter twilight crept over the Columbia campus, Van Doren's craggy face looked as if he expected the sun to come out because he was teaching Virgil. He was in such pleasant relation to his text, his teaching, his students— after the lecture several of them regularly joined him on the Seventh Avenue local in order to hear more—he spoke in such accord with the fall of the lines and the fall of winter outside, that he embodied all the harmony and smiling charm and love of beauty which I associated with the writers of every generation and place but my own. All Van Dorens had this particular, "American" and rhythmical charm, but no one more than Mark at his teaching. Everything smiled. America was a sweet revolution in itself. Even in these informal lectures beauty came out of beauty, and poetry gave birth to poetry; the voice of the poet's eloquence and of the poet's nobility was calm, easy, undismayed by any terror outside Philosophy Hall.

For Otis, however, Mark Van Doren was just a softy out of that lying world before the depression. Otis had a whole gallery of the Twenties to shoot at— Benéts, Canbys, Van Dorens, Christopher Morleys, Alexander Woollcotts, Isabel Pattersons—cozy, Algonquin-lunching people, people who looked very individual and literary on book jackets as they were posed with their croquet mallets against their Connecticut houses. The more books they published, the more quietly superior the literary judgments they delivered in their chatty literary columns, the more Otis hated them with all the righteous fury of the sans-culotte who feels that his hour has come. Otis allied himself to the toughness of the times, to the militant new wind, to the anger which was always in the air, and in whose name you had only to point to a soup kitchen, a picket line, the Dust Bowl, the Memorial Day Massacre in Chicago, to shame those who had not been sailors like himself, who had not afterwards worked their way through college like himself, who as writers were not uncertain, angry and spasmodic like himself. Those writers of the Twenties, whose faces on book jackets were so "interesting," picturesque and comfortable, somehow made books as if they had always lived in books; from childhood on there had been a protective membrane between them and the surly crowded streets; they had tidy lives, and so could afford to despair of the universe at large.

Though I was far more "literary" than Ferguson, I understood this protectiveness. For me, too, all these critics in power—Cowley, the Van Dorens, Canby, Chamberlain—were outsiders. Although many of them were also politically left, it would never have occurred to me then to feel common cause with someone like Cowley, or to feel particularly close to Chamberlain, for writers from the business and professional class could only interpret in an abstract and literary way the daily struggle that was so real to me in Brownsville. No matter how radical these critics were, they seemed as alien as J. Donald Adams on the *Times* or Canby on the *Saturday Review*. I sensed that with them I would have to conceal what I felt most, for they would have been puzzled by anything personal that was outside their literary categories. Whenever I got out after the long subway ride, excitedly clutching a few new books, and walked over to see my neighborhood friends, I felt that I was leaving the stiff world behind, that I was coming home to my own.

2
Irving Howe (1920–1993)
New York in the Thirties (1961)

Editor's Introduction

Irving Howe, one of the most political of the major figures in the New York Intellectuals—illustrated by his status as founder and co-editor (with Lewis Coser) of the liberal socialist magazine *Dissent*—spent his early life in the Bronx, graduated from City College in New York in 1940 and then served in the U.S Army during World War II. A member of the Young People's Socialist League as a youth, in the early 1950s he gradually became a more moderate liberal socialist who was willing to work in what he felt was the realm of the politically possible on the far left of the Democratic party. Like several others among the New York Intellectuals, he gravitated to literary criticism as an academic field and wrote contextual biographical criticism that set a book's author and characters within the social and political currents of their time. His notable critical talents filling in for his lack of a graduate degree, Howe taught at Brandeis soon after it was founded, and later became Distinguished Professor of Literature at the City University of New York and a MacArthur Fellow in 1987. In 1983 Howe, along with Michael Harrington, helped form the Democratic Socialists of America. Not least, Howe was a recognized historian of Yiddish history and literature.

Howe's autobiographical fragment published here was one of the first reflections produced by the group, along with Mary McCarthy's *The Oasis* (1949), Alfred Kazin's *A Walker in the City* (1951) and *Starting Out in the Thirties* (1962) and Dwight Macdonald's introduction to *The Memoirs of a Revolutionist* (1957). The continuing importance to Howe of what he called the political "movement," and the extent to which it shaped much of what he became, is clear in this searching essay. Propelled throughout his life by a strong ambition and a lethal polemical edge, by middle age he directed his considerable energy pragmatically toward socialist politics and liberal democracy, values he thought were interconnected and mutually dependent. In this essay Howe revealed that he and his teen friends—poor, powerless, Jewish, leftist and alienated—felt themselves, in their Marxist divining of history, to be "on the rim of heroism." Their lives were imaginative theater that prepared them for important political and cultural roles later in life. Their adolescent years in the

Depression-era Bronx sharpened their literary and ideological skills so they later could play leadership roles in cultural and political magazines and in university departments. The social and philosophical questions that preoccupied them even as children were issues that continued to fascinate and frighten Europeans, Soviets and Americans for much of the twentieth century.

Source

Irving Howe, "New York in the Thirties: Some Fragments of Memory," *Dissent* vol. 8, no. 3, Summer 1961.

Selected Readings

Irving Howe, *A Margin of Hope* (New York: Harcourt, Brace, Jovanovich, 1982); "The New York Intellectuals: A Chronicle and a Critique," *Commentary* vol. 46, no. 4, October 1968; "Strangers," *Celebrations and Attacks* (New York: Horizon Press, 1979).
Gerald Sorin, *Irving Howe: A Life of Passionate Dissent* (New York: New York University Press, 2002).

* * * * *

New York in the Thirties
Some Fragments of Memory

Growing up in New York during the thirties meant, for me, the Jewish slums of the East Bronx, endless talk about Hitler, money worries of my parents migrating to my own psyche, public schools that really were schools and devoted teachers whose faces lived in memory longer than their names, fantasies of heroism drawn from Austria and Spain to excite my imagination, the certainty bordering on comfort that I would never find a regular job, and above all, the Movement. At the age of 14 I wandered into the ranks of the socialist youth, as much from loneliness as conviction, and from then on, all through my teens and twenties, the Movement was my home and passion, the Movement as it ranged through the various left-wing, anti-Communist groups.

From the chilling distance of time I now ask myself: what did it mean, what do I really feel about those years in New York? And to my dismay I hardly know, there does not seem to be a total and assured perspective upon the past. Annoyed by those who have made a virtue out of scoffing at the generosities of their youth, one part of me would cry out that despite all the fanaticism and absurdity, it was good, vibrant with hope, an opening to vision. Another part, involved beyond retreat with the style of the problematic, cannot help remembering in terms of uneasiness and dismay. As I rummage through the past, all I can find are bits and pieces of that chaos which forms the true substance of life.

1

New York did not really exist for us as a city, a defined place we felt to be our own. Too many barriers intervened, too many kinds of anxiety. In the thirties New York was not merely the vital metropolis, brimming with politics and contention, that has since become a sentimental legend; it was also brutal, ugly, frightening, the foul-smelling jungle that Celine would later evoke in *Journey to the End of the Night*. New York was the embodiment of that alien world which every boy raised in a Jewish immigrant home had been taught, whether he realized it or not, to look upon with suspicion. It was "their" city in ways that one's parents could hardly have explained, and hardly needed to; and later, once I had absorbed the values of the Movement, it became "their" city in a new and, as it seemed to me, deeper sense.

If someone had asked me in 1939 what I thought of New York, I would have been puzzled, for that was not the kind of question one worried in those days. It was quite as if I had been asked what I thought about my family: there seemed no choice but to accept the one I had, lamentable as it may sometimes have been, and I no more imagined that I would ever live—or be able to live— anywhere but in New York than that I could find myself a more fashionable set of parents. Provinciality breeds a determinism of its own, and the provincial- ity of New York in the thirties, which tended to regard a temporary meeting of ethnic cultures and social crises as if it were an unalterable fact of history, led us to suppose that only here, in New York, could one bear to live at all, yet that unless one were in total revolt the life of the city was mean, constricted, intol- erable. For the city in its own right, as it actually was, we had little concern or sensitivity. Only in the mythology of the Movement did New York figure significantly for us, and there it took on a glamorous cast: for New York was always "the party center," no matter which party it was; here you could listen to the leaders and intellectuals, and here it was possible, usually, to fill a fair- sized hall so as to soften our awareness of how small and futile we were.

Yet there were places I knew intimately. In our very distance from the city—caused, I suspect, less by a considered "alienation" than by a difficulty of access, a puritanical refusal of possibilities, and an unacknowledged shyness beneath our pose of bravado—we made for ourselves a kind of underground city consisting of a series of stopping-places where we could ease the strain of restlessness and feel indifferent to our lack of money. In the winter there were the numberless "socials" given by branches of the Movement to raise funds for their headquarters, evenings I remember, perhaps inaccurately, as drab and awkward. There were the movies on 42nd Street where amid clouds of steam and stench our political virtue was compromised by sophisticated European art films. There were the free concerts at the Metropolitan Musum where—it was a matter of pride to know—the music was poor but one found a sort of comfort in sitting on the marble floors, snuggling together in a chosen arc of relaxation, and allowing our romanticism to find a sanctioned outlet in Beethoven and Schubert.

In retrospect what strikes me as remarkable is that while we thought of ourselves as exposed to the coldest winds of the coldest capitalist city—and in many, many ways we were—we still lived in a somewhat sheltered world. Not only because the Movement had a way of turning in upon itself, becoming detached and self-contained, and finding a security in that isolation which all its speeches bemoaned. But more. Only now do I see the extent to which our life, for all that we had decided to cut ourselves off from official society, was shaped first by the fact that many of us came from immigrant Jewish families and second by the fact that in New York the Jews still formed a genuine community reaching half-unseen into a dozen neighborhoods and a multitude of institutions, within the shadows of which we found protection of a kind.

Attitudes of tolerance and permissiveness, feelings that one had to put up with and indulge one's cranks, eccentrics, idealists and extremists, affected the Jewish community to an extent that those profiting from them did not always stop to appreciate. And the Jewish labor movement, ranging from the garment workers unions to the large fraternal societies and small political groups, had established a tradition of protest, controversy and freedom, so that even when such organizations violated this tradition, it still exerted an enormous moral power in the Jewish community and provided cover for the left-wing parties. Trotskyist street meetings were sometimes broken up, but only upon the decision of the Communist party, which until the Popular Front prided itself on standing outside the spectrum of Jewish ideological life. In the garment center things were of course different, and there, in the bitter struggles between left and right unions, knives were wielded with a supreme indifference to race, creed, color or size. But the Jewish neighborhood was prepared to listen to almost anyone, with its characteristic mixture of skepticism, interest and amusement.

Even among the Stalinists the fact of Jewishness counted in surprising ways. I remember one evening when a street meeting was being harassed by a gang of Jewish Stalinists, and a screeching lady heckler jostled a friend of mine, causing her glasses to fall and break. My friend started bawling that her mother would beat her for breaking the glasses, and the Jewish lady, suddenly sympathetic, took the girl to a store and bought her a new pair. For the Communist lady my friend had a few minutes earlier been a "fascist" but when trouble came and the glasses were broken, she also must have seemed like a nice Jewish girl. ...

It was not only the Jewish labor movement that provided a protective aura; the Jewish community did the same thing, though less from political principle than from what I would hesitantly call ethnic shrewdness. In the thirties the ordinary New York Jew realized that Jewishness was not something one had much choice about, and in this respect his instincts were sounder, both morally and practically, than that of the radicals who chose for their "party names" almost anything that did not sound Jewish. You might be shouting at the top of your lungs against reformism or Stalin's betrayals, but for the middle-aged garment worker strolling along Southern Boulevard you were just a bright and cocky Jewish boy, a talkative little *pisher*.

The Jewish community enclosed one, not through choice as much as through experience and instinct, and often not very gently or with the most refined manners. What you believed, or said you believed, did not matter nearly as much as what you were, and what you were was not nearly so much a matter of choice as you might care to suppose. If you found a job, it was likely to be in a "Jewish industry" and if you went to college it was still within an essentially Jewish milieu. We did not realize then how sheltering it was to grow up in this world, just as we did not realize how the "bourgeois democracy" at which we railed was the medium making it possible for us to speak and survive. It was all part of our mania for *willing* a new life, our tacit wish to transform deracination from a plight into a program.

Thinking about it now, I am struck by how little I saw as boy in the thirties of hunger and suffering, though surely there was no lack of either in New York and I was quite prepared to notice both. I knew, of course, the shacks of Hooverville on Riverside Drive, the lines of people waiting before store-fronts rented by the welfare agencies, the piles of furniture on top of which sat the children of evicted tenants, the panhandlers slouching on Fourteenth Street, the idle men standing day after day near the rowboats of Crotona Park. But while the East Bronx was a place of poverty, it kept an inner discipline: Jews felt obligated to look after each other, they fought desperately to avoid going on relief, they would treat with the outer world only under extreme duress.

I have said that the movement was my home and passion. Yes; but the forces that shaped one, the subtle enveloping conditions that slowly did their work on character and disposition, were not really matters of choice. The world I never made, made me.

2

There never seemed any place to go. The thought of bringing my friends home was inconceivable, for I would have been as ashamed to show them to my parents as to show my parents to them. I had enough imagination to suppose that each could see through the shams and limitations of the other, but not enough courage to defend one against the other. Besides, where would people sit in those cramped apartments? The worldly manner, the *savoir faire* of Monroe High School and then of the city colleges, that was affected by some of my friends would have stirred flames of suspicion in the eyes of my father; the sullen immigrant kindliness of my parents would have struck my friends as all too similar to that of their own fathers and mothers; and my own self-consciousness, which in relation to my parents led me into a maze of superfluous lies and trivial deceptions, made it difficult for me to believe in the possibility of a life grounded in simple good-faith. I could not imagine bringing together the life that was given, with its sweet poignancy and embittered conflicts, and the life one had chosen, with its secret fellowship and sectarian vocabulary.

So we walked the streets, never needing to tell one another why we chose this neutral setting for our escape at evening. In the winter, when the Bronx is grey and icy, there were cafeterias in which the older comrades, those who had jobs or were on WPA, bought coffee while the rest of us filled the chairs. In the summer, after meetings, we would parade across the middle bulge of the Bronx from the tenements on Wilkins Avenue in the East to the forbidding apartment houses of the Grand Concourse on the West. I remember those night walks as carefree and relaxed, away from the pressures of family and politics, though always with some secret anxiety that I would get home too late—for my parents, in their sweet blind innocence, were more distressed by my irregular hours than my irregular opinions.

The streets would be empty, the summer nights cool, a kind of expansiveness would come over us. Our enemies slept, the world was ours. We would listen with pleasure to our professional jokester, full of panting malice as he raked every friend who happened not to be along, or to the brilliant leader who warmed us with his confidence. We would glide away in our Melvillian freedom, away from the frustrations of the Movement and the dreary thought of the next morning when, with mama's quarter in my pocket for carfare and lunch, I would be taking the subway to City College, prepared once again to cut the classes that had, I was entirely confident, nothing to teach me.

3

Someone always had a little money. I remember my friend M., who had a gift for picking up odd jobs and a passion for consuming ice cream sodas. Late one night, in the drab center of the Bronx, we passed by a little candy store whose owner had been sitting up in wait for a "sale." We went in, M. treated me to a soda and then returned to the storekeeper for a little more seltzer in his glass. The man stared at him in dismay, and M., no longer a budding Marxist theoretician but a nice roly-poly Jewish boy, said in great earnestness, "But I *always* get more seltzer with my sodas. ..." The storekeeper turned wearily to his fountain, shrugging his Jewish shoulders as if his fragment of profit, the reward of his vigil, had just been dissolved in the bubbling glass.

4

To be poor is something that happens; to experience poverty is to gain an idea as to what is happening. Once my father's grocery store went bankrupt in 1930 and he became a "customer peddler" trudging from door to door with sheets and linens, we were often very poor, living together with uncles, aunts and grandmother to save rent. Yet I had no very acute sense of being deprived, or any notions that I was the victim of social injustice. It was simply that, for reasons beyond my comprehension or probing, things had changed unpleasantly. Only after I had begun to go to high school did the idea of poverty start creeping into my consciousness, and I learned to regard it with the familiar blend of outrage, shame and ambition. When I was thirteen or fourteen I began to buy a magazine that was printing Sherwood Anderson's reports about hunger in the North Carolina textile towns, and I would read these articles with tears of indignation, barely aware of the extent to which I was really feeling sorry for myself. The realization of what it meant to be poor I had first to discover through writings about poverty; the sense of my own handicap became vivid to me only after I had learned about the troubles of people I did not know. And surely this experience was typical.

5

Why did the Movement prove so attractive to young people? Or perhaps more to the point, why have those who left it found themselves romanticizing their youthful time as radicals?

It was not merely the power of ideology which bound one to the Movement. Ideology mattered, of course, but only the more ambitious among us really tried to master the intricacies of Marxist economics or Trotsky's critique of Soviet industrial policy. (In economics I was a complete bust, and to this day feel somewhat queasy when trying to remember the formulas of *Capital*, perhaps because they were taught in the Movement with the same talmudic rote which, years earlier, had characterized my disastrous Hebrew lessons. For a young Marxist in the thirties, the greatest ploy was a claim to be learned in economics, the science we faithfully praised as basic and secretly regarded as dismal.) Nor was it merely the magnetic pull of group life, with its enormous yet curiously satisfying demands upon our time and loyalty, that drew us so closely to the Movement. Almost all of us rebelled, at one point or another, against the exhausting routine of political activism—so much of it meaningless and calculated to force upon us an understanding of our distance from American politics.

No, what I think held young people to the Movement was the sense that they had gained, not merely a "purpose" in life, but far more important, a coherent perspective upon everything that was happening to us. And this perspective was something rather different from, a good deal more practical and immediate than, Marxist ideology; it meant the capacity for responding quickly and with a comforting assurance to events. The Movement gave us a language of response and gesture, the security of a set orientation—perhaps impossible to a political tendency that lacked an ideology but not quite to be identified with ideology as such. It felt good "to know." One revelled in the innocence and arrogance of knowledge, for even in our inexpert hands Marxism could be a powerful analytic tool and we could nurture the feeling that, whether other people realized it or not, we enjoyed a privileged relationship to history. The totalism of the Marxist system seemed attractive not merely because we wanted a key to all the doors of knowledge (most of which we never tried to open), but also because there was a keen pleasure in picking up a copy of the *New York Times* and reading it with that critical superiority, that presumptive talent for giving a "basic" interpretation to events, which our commitment enabled us to command. And if we were often mistaken, we were surely no more so than most other people.

But there is a more fundamental reason for the appeal of the Movement. Marxism involves a profoundly *dramatic* view of human experience. With its stress upon inevitable conflicts, apocalyptic climaxes, ultimate moments, hours of doom and shining tomorrows, it appealed deeply to our imaginations. We felt that we were always on the rim of heroism, that the mockery we might suffer at the moment would turn to vindication in the future, that our loyalty to principle would be rewarded by the grateful masses of tomorrow. The principle of classic drama, *peripetia* or the sudden reversal of fortune, we stood upon its head quite as Marx was supposed to have done to Hegel; and then it became for us a crux of our political system. The moment would come, our leaders kept assuring us and no doubt themselves, if only we did not flinch, if only we were ready to remain a tiny despised minority, if only we held firm to our sense of destiny. It was this pattern of drama which made each moment of our participation seem so rich with historical meaning.

6

Were we so entirely wrong? The ways in which we were, are now obvious and if there is one middle-aged literary man or journalist who has failed to point them out I do not know his name. Our hopes and expectations were not realized, and concerning those that were crudely tainted by power-hunger it is perhaps just as well that they were not. But this is not at all to say, as so many people now do, that the radical outlook of the thirties was a mere fantasy or rested upon a failure to apprehend the realities of American society. There *were* millions of people desperate, hungry, hopeless; the society *was* sick and inhumane; people who cared nothing about ideology also shared the desire for profound social and moral change. When we fought against the Stalinist theory of "social reformism" we were partly responding to ideological disputes in Russia but also trying to cope with a form of political adventurism that threatened to destroy the trade unions of New York. When we endlessly debated "the class nature of Soviet Russia" in Webster Hall and Irving Plaza we were partly succumbing to a Marxist scholasticism but also trying to cope with the problem of a new kind of society, a problem that still bedevils serious students of politics. And when we thought in terms of catastrophe and apocalypse ... well, how many years did it take before catastrophe and apocalypse came to blacken the globe?

7

A Movement that raises in the imagination of its followers the vision of historical drama, must find ways of realizing the dramatic in the course of history. And so we lived in hopes of a reenactment that would be faithful to the severities of the Marxist myth and would embody once more in action the idea of October. Since we had, meanwhile, to suffer the awareness of our limitations, we found excitement—that poor substitute for drama—in the ceaseless round of faction rights.

Often enough these disputes concerned issues of genuine importance, in which the Movement found itself groping toward problems that most political analysts had not even begun to consider. Occasionally these disputes produced some vivid writing and speaking, in which the talents of the leaders, unable to find a public outlet, were expressed inwardly through polemic, wit and invective. But I think the factions fights had another purpose that we could not then acknowledge: they were charades of struggle, substitute rituals for the battles we could not join, ceremonies of "acting out." Through them we created our own drama in our own world.

Once these dialectical tournaments began, the opposing factions would line up their squads of speakers, like knights arrayed at both ends of the field. They would then batter away at each other to the point of exhaustion and hoarseness, and continue to enact the whole combat pageant even after everyone had firmly taken his stand. One's capacity for endurance played an extraordinary role in these political war-games, and there were old timers who prided themselves on battle scars from the legendary faction fights—the days of the titans—in the old days, just as there were party leaders whose prestige rested not on their achievements as organizers or gifts as writers but on their reputed shrewdness in faction maneuvers. It was a somewhat specialized skill.

If at a discussion meeting there happened to be a maverick who wished to speak apart from the lists of the two factions, the decorum of democracy required that he be given the floor. The sophisticated adherents of both sides shared, however, an impatience to get him out of the way, so that unless he were an important member whom it was advisable to court, the orderly buffeting of dispute could be resumed quite as if he had never spoken at all. Both sides gained a kind of pleasure from watching these disputes move forward step by step, from jocular argument to fierce attack, from amiable preparation to split or near-split:—a drama in which the main fighters held to their fixed roles and seemed bound by the fatalities of an action quite as much as the protagonists of a classical play. Later it would all be repeated, a bit more crudely, in the local branches and then in the youth organization. One of my least happy recollections is that of meetings where eighteen- and nineteen-year-olds would hector each other with pat formulas as to whether Russia was "state capitalist" or "bureaucratic collectivist," hardly aware of the semantic and analytic difficulties in which they had become entangled, so puffed up were they with the vanity of rhetoric.

Years later, one hot night in Indiana, I had a bitter quarrel with Alfred Kazin about the intellectual quality of this life. He had used the phrase "sodden brilliance" to describe it and I had reacted with irritation, making the point that his phrase was a contradiction in terms. I must have been wounded by the accuracy of Kazin's thrust and by what I took to be his piety of manner; but now I cannot help seeing that "sodden brilliance" was a good description. For while the debates were frequently brilliant, there was also a heavy-handed sarcasm, a nasty and unexamined personal violence, and a lumbering scholasticism that would warrant the qualifying "sodden."

8

The Movement was a school in both politics and life, and much of what we know, both good and bad, we learned there. It made us sensitive to the decay and brutality of the modern world. It taught us to look upon social problems in terms extending beyond local or even national interests. It imbued us with an intense fascination for the *idea* of history, and if that brought intellectual dangers, they were probably worth facing. It trained us to think on our feet, and opened to us the pleasures of thrust and parry. And not entirely by intention, it led us to a strong feeling for democracy, if only because the harassments and persecutions to which we were subjected by the Communists persuaded us to value freedom of thought more than we quite knew we did.

Yes, the Movement taught us to think, but "only along too well-defined and predictable lines." (I repeat this phrase from a comment a City College teacher once wrote on a Marxistic composition of mine. The phrase burnt itself into my consciousness, and hearing it can still make me blush. Later, having become a teacher myself, I found it a consoling memory when dealing with narrow-minded students.) What passed for thought among us was often no more than facility: we were clever and fast in responding to familiar cues, especially in arguments with Communists, but had little capacity for turning back with a critical eye upon our own assumptions. Against opponents who shared our essential beliefs we could argue well—too often confusing arguing well with thinking well—but against those who dared question our essential beliefs we were not nearly so effective. We were trained in agility rather than reflection, dialectic rather than investigation. We had a strong sense of intellectual honor, but only a feeble appetite for intellectual risk. And that is why we seldom became disturbed when a member questioned a tactical or strategic "line" of the Movement, but felt uneasy, as if sensing the threat of heresy, when he began to wonder about the more abstract and fundamental Marxist tenets. In my own case, a fleeting encounter with Robert Michels' book on political parties left me with a permanent feeling of uneasiness, which time and exposure sharpened into doubt.

At least as crippling as its refusal to examine first principles was the attitude of the Movement toward what we called "bourgeois thought." Perhaps the most insidious doctrine afflicting the radical world was the Leninist theory of the "vanguard party," the notion that we possessed the political truth, held the key to the future, and had, so to say, signed a pact with history for a 99-year lease on the privilege. Pride in belonging to the "vanguard" was an expression of, as also an incitement toward, a naive authoritarianism: I recall one youth leader riding on a Fifth Avenue bus and pointing to the skyscrapers with the remark: "Some day that will all belong to us. ..." Such historic arrogance had its intellectual equivalents: a barely disguised contempt for the thought and learning of the past, an intolerance of divergent thought, a condescension toward "bourgeois scholars" who, it is true, occasionally accumulated valuable material but who lacked the depth interpretation that "only Marxism" could provide. It was a heady brew for young people, and some suffered a hangover for years.

9

Still, life had a way of asserting itself, and the reality was always far more complex and diverse than any possible description. Life would break through the crevices of our ideology and prompt us to unpolitical happiness and spontaneous feelings, it would tempt us with the delights of *avant garde* writing—I read *Axel's Castle* at 15, understood little of it, and profited greatly—and lure us to the discoveries of romantic love. Some of the leaders were intellectuals *manqué,* full of pomp and pretension; others were serious and gifted men, at least as serious and gifted as the writers and professors I later came to know. When I try to summon an image of human goodness in its more public aspect, I still find myself remembering an ill-favored curmudgeon in the Bronx as selfless as he was grumpy, a girl in Brooklyn who poured the purity of her soul into the hope for socialism, a peculiarly mixed group of people whom I knew well or barely at all, yet who survive dimly as faces, those who enjoyed talking to "outsiders" about politics and those who were shy and would mail newspapers or fold leaflets in the office. For some the Movement was a mere stepping-stone to careers, a training school for political advisors to trade-union leaders, academic sociologists, free wheeling literary critics; for most it was an experience both liberating and crippling, beautiful and ugly....

Well, that was the New York I grew up in. It was neither typical of the city nor of American radicalism, it was simply mine.

10

It is all gone, and I do not want it back. There is nothing I desire more than a revival of American radicalism, but the past is done with, and I have no wish to recreate it nor any belief in the possibility of doing so. With time I hope that it will yet settle into coherence for me—more coherence than these notes reveal—and that I will learn to look back with peace and good feeling. There are moments now and again when I recall the life of New York in the thirties, and see it through the lens of affection; and then it all seems pure in the light of time, I feel with pleasure the old stirrings of faith and conviction, that love for the unborn future which may redeem the past.

3
Irving Kristol (1920—)
Memoirs of a Trotskyist (1977)

Editor's Introduction

Since the end of World War II, Irving Kristol has been one of the most recognized editors and writers in high journalism, first in the world of little political and cultural journals such as *Commentary* and *Encounter*, then, beginning in the late 1960s and 1970s, in *The Public Interest* and the *Wall Street Journal*. In his essays he wrote about anticommunism, the moral challenges to American culture and society, the impact of the 1960s radicalism and the American political and party systems. Kristol also focused on economics, particularly in its broad context once known as political economy, which he employed to address the contest between large systems of political values.

Although Howe and Kristol, the two Irvings (Howe said Sidney Hook always called him "Oiving"), inhabited very different political camps as adults, with Howe on the left and Kristol on the right, they began in college in the same ideological circle—marked by their spot, their alcove, in the City College lunchroom. Kristol's story of the lunchtime debates is the classic version of the alcoves tale. In these two memoirs (Howe's is essay #2) the Irvings relate the situations and experiences that impelled them into the life of the mind and shaped them to be a particular kind of thinker, to be intellectuals who were more interested in debate and criticism than in the creative act of fiction or poetry.

Here, eating modest lunches at City College, they sharpened the intellectual tools they used for the rest of their lives. They battled over doctrines, systems of thought, political strategies, ideologies, academic reputations, philosophical standing, global challenges, inevitabilities, inexorable conflicts, logistics of distribution, matters of identity. They could not have chosen a larger theater to inhabit at their age than the one on whose stage they rehearsed the ideological clashes of the globe. Their youthful experience echoed for decades in their work in the size of the problems they wrestled and the seriousness with which they confronted ideas. The lunchroom alcoves bred a European style of disputation, a form of choreographed positions played out and rehearsed in a debating style not common in America. Conventional debate teams prepared adolescents for law jobs some day. The City College alcoves shaped a talent for debating ideology, systems and culture, a set of skills that were welcome in opinion journals, book reviewing, publishing and academic jobs in cultural or ideological fields.

Irving Kristol graduated from City College in 1940, served in the army in World War II, was managing editor of *Commentary* from 1947 to 1952, co-founder and editor of *Encounter* (in England) from 1953 to 1958, edited *The Reporter* for two years, worked as vice president of Basic Books from 1961 to 1969, co-founded and co-edited *The Public Interest* with Daniel Bell in 1965 and served as Professor of Social Thought at New York University from 1969 to 1985. Kristol is a Fellow of the American Academy of Arts and Sciences. Like many of the New York Intellectuals, he is almost exclusively a writer of essays. Irving Kristol is father of William Kristol (1952–), founder and editor of the *Weekly Standard,* and is married to Gertrude Himmelfarb (1922), who until her retirement was Distinguished Professor of History at the Graduate Center of the City University of New York.

Source

Irving Kristol, "Memoirs of a Trotskyist," *New York Times Magazine,* Jan 23, 1977.

Selected Readings

Seymour Martin Lipset, "Out of the Alcoves," *The Wilson Quarterly* vol. 23, Winter 1999.
Irving Kristol, *Neoconservatism: The Autobiography of an Idea* (New York: Free Press, 1999).

* * * * *

Not long ago, I passed through the Loeb Student Center, at New York University's Washington Square campus. It is a modern and luxurious building—to my eyes, definitely "posh"—with comfortable sofas and chairs, ample space and light and all those little amenities that correspond to our middle-class notions of "gracious living." On that particular day, the main lounge was half-empty; a few students were slumped in armchairs, reading or dozing, while here and there groups of two or three were chatting over cups of coffee. As I stood there gazing with wonder at the opulence of it all, and with puzzlement at the languor of it all, I was prompted once again to remember the physical squalor and mental energy of Alcove No. 1 at C.C.N.Y.

Such memories had been provoked more than once during the turbulent 1960's. Anyone who had been a student radical in the 1930's was bound to be moved to compare his own experiences (or the recollections of his own experiences) with the rebellions he observed a generation later. The danger of such an exercise, in the heat of the tumult, is the natural temptation toward the fogy's lament: "Why can't they be as we were?" In truth, that is a legitimate question—if it is meant seriously as a question, and not merely as a reproach.

Perhaps now that the wave of student radicalism has subsided, to be succeeded (temporarily at least) by a kind of sullen resignation, one can put those memories to paper without seeming patronizing or self-serving. The student radicalism of the 30's was indeed different from that of the 60's, and different in ways that tell us something important, I think, about what happened to American society (and to the rebels against that society) in the intervening decades. And if the comparison is to the advantage of the earlier radicalism— as I admit right off it will be—it is because, in my opinion, the United States in the 30's was in many ways a healthier (if materially far less prosperous) society than it has become, so that rebellion was healthier, too.

I was graduated from City College in the spring of 1940, and the honor I most prized was the fact that I was a member in good standing of the Young People's Socialist League (Fourth International). This organization was commonly, and correctly, designated as Trotskyist (not "Trotskyite," which was a term used only by the official Communists, or "Stalinists" as we called them, of the day). I have not set foot on the City College campus since my commencement. The present president of the college, Robert Marshak, has amiably urged me to come and see the place again—it's very different but still recognizable, he says. I have promised to go, but somehow I think I may never find the time.

It is not that my memories of C.C.N.Y. are disagreeable. On the contrary: When I think back to those years, it is with a kind of nostalgia. It was at that place, and in that time, that I met the young men—there were no women at the uptown campus then—who became my lifelong friends. The education I got was pretty good, even if most of it was acquired outside the classroom. My personal life was no messier or more troubled than any adolescent's. True, I was poor—but so was everyone else, and I was by no means the poorest. True, too, it wasn't fun commuting by subway for more than an hour each way from and to Brooklyn, where I lived. But the memory of poverty and those tedious subway rides has faded with time, whereas what I now recollect most vividly is the incredible vivacity with which we all confronted the dismal 30's.

Is it then perhaps my radical past, now so firmly disowned, that bothers me and makes C.C.N.Y. unhallowed ground? I think not. I have no regret about that episode in my life. Joining a radical movement when one is young is very much like falling in love when one is young. The girl may turn out to be rotten, but the experience of love is so valuable it can never be entirely undone by the ultimate disenchantment.

But my feelings toward those radical days are even more positive than this kind of general reflection suggests. For the truth is that being a young radical was not simply part of my college experience; it was practically the whole of it. If I left City College with a better education than did many students at other and supposedly better colleges, it was because my involvement in radical politics put me in touch with people and ideas that prompted me to read and think and argue with a furious energy. This was not a typical experience—I am talking about a relatively small group of students, a particular kind of student radical. Going to City College meant, for me, being a member of this group. It was a privileged experience, and I know of no one who participated in it who does not look back upon it with some such sentiment.

So why have I never returned to visit the place? Perhaps because I know it is impossible. *That* place no longer exists. It has vanished with the time of which it was so integral a part. Whatever is now happening at City College, I doubt that I am likely to comprehend, much less enjoy, it. For what I have seen of student radicalism on various campuses over the past dozen years baffles and bothers me. It seems to be more a psychological than a truly political phenomenon. There is a desperate quest for self-identity, an evident and acute involvement of one's political beliefs with all kinds of personal anxieties and neuroses, a consequent cheerlessness and truculence.

The changing connotation of the term "alienated" tells us much. At City College in the 30's we were familiar enough with the word and the idea behind it. But for us it was a sociological category and referred to the condition of the working class. We were not alienated. By virtue of being radical intellectuals, we had "transcended" alienation (to use another Marxist term). We experienced our radicalism as a privilege of rank, not as a burden imposed by a malignant fate. It would never have occurred to us to denounce anyone or anything as "elitist." The elite was us—the "happy few" who had been chosen by History to guide our fellow creatures toward a secular redemption.

Alcove No. 1 was located in the City College lunchroom, a vast ground-floor space which even we, who came from slums or near-slums, judged to be an especially slummy and smelly place. There was a small semicircular counter where one could buy franks or milk or coffee. I suppose they also sold some sandwiches, but I certainly never bought one, and I do not remember anyone else ever committing such an act of unmitigated profligacy. The less poor among us purchased a frank or two; the rest brought their lunches from home—hard-boiled egg sandwiches, cream-cheese sandwiches, peanut-butter sandwiches, once in a while even a chicken sandwich—and there was always a bit of sandwich swapping to enliven one's diet. There was also some sandwich scrounging by those who were *really* poor; one asked and gave without shame or reservation.

The center of the lunchroom, taking up most of the space, consisted of chest-high, wooden tables under a low, artificial ceiling. There, most of the students ate their lunches, standing up. (I looked upon this as being reasonable, since at Boys' High, in Brooklyn, we had had the same arrangement. To this day I find it as natural to eat a sandwich standing up as sitting down.) Around this central area there was a fairly wide and high-ceilinged aisle; and bordering the aisle, under large windows with small panes of glass that kept out as much light as they let in, were the alcoves—semicircular (or were they rectangular?), each with a bench fitted along the wall and a low, long refectory table in the middle. The first alcove on the right, as you entered the lunchroom, was Alcove No. 1, and this soon became most of what City College meant to me. It was there one ate lunch, played Ping-Pong (sometimes with a net, sometimes without), passed the time of day between and after classes, argued incessantly and generally devoted oneself to solving the ultimate problems of the human race. The penultimate problems we figured could be left for our declining years, after we had graduated.

I would guess that, in all, there were more than a dozen alcoves, and just how rights of possession had been historically established was as obscure as the origins of the social contract itself. Once established, however, they endured, and in a manner typical of New York's "melting pot," each religious, ethnic, cultural and political group had its own little alcove. There was a Catholic alcove, the "turf" of the Newman Society, a Zionist alcove, an Orthodox Jewish alcove; there was a black alcove for the handful of blacks then at C.C.N.Y., an alcove for members of the athletic teams, etc. But the only alcoves that mattered to me were No. 1 and No. 2, the alcoves of the anti-Stalinist left and pro-Stalinist left, respectively. It was between these two alcoves that the war of the worlds was fought, over the faceless bodies of the mass of students, whom we tried desperately to manipulate into "the right position" but about whom, to tell the truth, we knew little and cared less.

City College was known at the time as a "radical" institution, and in an era when most college students identified themselves as Republicans the ascription was not incorrect. If there were any Republicans at City—and there must have been some—I never met them, or even heard of their existence. Most of the students, from Jewish working-class or lower-middle-class backgrounds with a socialist tint, were spontaneously sympathetic to the New Deal and F.D.R. The really left-wing groups, though larger than elsewhere, were a distinct minority. Alcove No. 2, by far the most populous of the "political" alcoves, could rarely mobilize more than 400 or 500 out of a total enrollment of perhaps 20,000 students for a protest rally, or "action;" we in Alcove No. 1 numbered about 30 "regulars" and were lucky to get an audience of 50 to 100 for one of ours. But then, as now, student government and student politics were a minority affair, and what the passive majority thought really didn't matter. What "happened" on campus was determined by *them*—the denizens of Alcove No. 2—or *us*. In truth, very little did happen; but at the time what did seemed terribly important. During my first three years, *they* controlled the college newspaper: in my last year, we got control. It was a glorious victory, and I do think that we went on to publish a slightly less mendacious newspaper—but I haven't even a vague remembrance of what we were slightly less mendacious about.

I shall not say much about Alcove No. 2—the home of the pro-Stalinist left—but, Lord, how dreary a bunch they seemed to be! I thought then, with a sectarian snobbery that comes so easily to young radicals, that they really didn't and never would amount to much. And I must say—at the risk of being accused of smugness—that in all these intervening decades, only two names from Alcove No. 2 have come to my attention. One is now a scientist at a major university. The other was Julius Rosenberg.

I do believe their dreariness was a fact, and that this dreariness in turn had something to do with the political outlook they took it upon themselves to espouse. These were young college students who, out of sympathy with Communism as officially established in the Soviet Union, had publicly to justify the Moscow trials and the bloody purge of old Bolsheviks; had publicly to accept the self-glorification of Joseph Stalin as an exemplar of Communist virtue and wisdom; had publicly to deny that there were concentration camps in the Soviet Union, etc., etc. Moreover, since this was the period of the popular front, they had for the time to repudiate (by way of reinterpretation) most of the Marxist–Leninist teachings on which their movement was ostensibly founded.

Though I had no trouble understanding how a young man at that time could have joined the Young Communist League, or one of its "fronts," I did find it hard to imagine how he stayed there. Not everyone did stay, of course;many of the members of Alcove No. 1 had had their first political experience with a Stalinist group and had left in disillusionment. But those who did stay on for any length of time—well, it had to have deleterious effects on their quality of mind. After all, members of the congregation of Alcove No. 2 were actually forbidden, under pain of ostracism and exile, from entering into conversation or even argument with any member of Alcove No. 1! This prohibition was dutifully obeyed, and such mindless obedience could not fail to have its costs.

Which brings me to Alcove No. 1, where pure intellect—a certain kind of intellect, anyway—reigned unchallenged.

Alcove No. 1 was the place you went to if you wanted to be radical *and* have a theory as to the proper kind of radical you should be. When I say "theory," I mean that in the largest sense. We in Alcove No. 1 were terribly concerned with being "right" in politics, economics, sociology, philosophy, history, anthropology, etc. It was essential to be "right" in all of these fields of knowledge, lest a bit of information from one should casually collide with a theoretical edifice and bring the whole structure tumbling down. So all the little grouplets that joined together to make Alcove No. 1 their home were always in keen competition to come up with startling bits of information—or, better yet, obscure and disorienting quotations from Marx or Engels or Lenin or Trotsky—that would create intellectual trouble for the rest of the company.

The Trotskyists, with perhaps a dozen members, were one of the largest grouplets and unquestionably the most feverishly articulate. Almost as numerous, though considerably less noisy, were the Socialists, or "the Norman Thomas Socialists" as one called them, to distinguish them from other kinds of socialists. Among these other kinds, none of which ever had more than two or three representatives in Alcove No. 1, were the Social Democrats (or "right-wing socialists") who actually voted for F.D.R., and the "revolutionary socialists" who belonged to one or another "splinter group"—the Ohlerites, the Marlinites, the Fieldites, the Lovestonites, and the who-can-remember-what-other-ites—which, finding itself in "principled disagreement" with every other sect, had its own little publication (usually called a "theoretical organ") and its own special prescription for achieving *real* socialism. In addition, and finally, there were a handful of "independents"—exasperating left-wing individualists who either could not bring themselves to join any group or else insisted on joining them all in succession. What held this crazy conglomeration together was, quite simply, the powerful presence of Alcove No. 2, and, beyond that, the looming shadow of Stalinism with its threat of so irrevocably debasing the socialist ideal as to rob humanity of what we were certain was its last, best hope.

Obviously, in such a milieu certain intellectual qualities tended to be emphasized at the expense of others. We were strongly inclined to celebrate the analytical powers of mind rather than the creative, and we paid more heed to public philosophies than to private ones. It cannot be an accident that so many graduates of Alcove No. 1 went on to become professors of social science; in a sense, what Alcove No. 1 provided was a peculiarly intense undergraduate education in what is now called social science but which we then called (more accurately, I sometimes think) political ideology. Nor can it be an accident that none of the graduates of Alcove No. 1—none who were there in my time, anyway—subsequently achieved any kind of distinction in creative writing or the arts; in that ideological hothouse, the personal vision and the personal accent withered for lack of nourishment.

So I do not want to be misunderstood as claiming superlative merits for Alcove No. 1 as an educational milieu. On the other hand, it *was* an authentic educational milieu. And this, I suppose, is why so many went on to become professors—getting paid, as it were, for continuing to be interested in the things they had always been interested in.

In some respects the quintessential representative of this milieu was Seymour Martin Lipset, now professor of sociology and political science at Stanford—a kind of intellectual bumblebee, whose function it was to spread the pollen of ideological doubt and political consternation over all Alcove No. 1's flowering ideologies. Irving Howe, in contrast, was a pillar of ideological rectitude. Thin, gangling, intense, always a little distant, his fingers incessantly and nervously twisting a cowlick as he enunciated sharp and authoritative opinions, Irving was the Trotskyist leader and "theoretician." In the years since, he has gone on to become a famous literary critic and a professor of literature at the City University. But he has remained politically *engagé*, though slowly moving "right" from Trotskyism to democratic socialism (as represented in his journal, *Dissent*). Since I have abandoned my socialist beliefs altogether, I feel that I am still ahead of him politically.

Daniel Bell, now professor of sociology at Harvard, was at the opposite pole from Irving. He was that rarity of the 30's: an honest-to-goodness social-democratic intellectual who believed in "a mixed economy," a two-party system based on the British model and other liberal heresies. His evident skepticism toward all our ideologies would ordinarily have disqualified him from membership in Alcove No. 1. But he had an immense intellectual curiosity, a kind of amused fondness for sectarian dialectics, knew his radical texts as thoroughly as the most learned among us and enjoyed "a good theoretical discussion" the way some enjoy a Turkish bath—so we counted him in. Over the years, his political views have probably changed less than those of the rest of us, with the result that, whereas his former classmates used to criticize him from the left, they now criticize him from all points of the ideological compass.

Others who later found, to their pleasant surprise, that what they had been doing in Alcove No. 1 was what the academic world would come to recognize and generously reward as "social science" were: Nathan Glazer (Harvard), Philip Selznick (Berkeley), Peter Rossi (Johns Hopkins), Morroe Berger (Princeton), I. Milton Sacks (Brandeis). Lawrence Krader and Bernard Bellush (City University), Seymour Melman (Columbia), Melvin J. Lasky (now editor of *Encounter*)—and others who may be just as pleased not to read their names in this context.

Bellush, a calm, and obstinately moderate socialist of the Norman Thomas persuasion, was a most unlikely candidate to serve as a central symbol of student radicalism, and yet at one point he did. During an anti-R.O.T.C. demonstration, Bernie was arrested for punching a police officer. The ensuing trial was a field day for us, as we "mobilized" the student body to attend protest rallies ("Cops off the campus!"), pack the courtroom, etc. Bernie was acquitted, and it was a moment of triumph. I must confess, however, that to this day I cannot honestly say whether or not he actually did punch that police officer; with typical radical disingenuousness, we studiously avoided asking either him or ourselves that question. Strange as it may sound to today's radical student, we really would have been disturbed had he been guilty as charged. At the very least, we would have been plunged into an endless debate on the finer points of "revolutionary morality." With the experience of Stalinism constantly in mind, we were extremely sensitive to the possibility that radical means could corrupt radical ends.

I certainly do not mean to suggest that membership in Alcove No. 1 was any kind of prerequisite for subsequent academic distinction. Kenneth Arrow, for instance, now a Nobel Prize-winning professor of economics at Harvard, and David Landes, now professor of history at Harvard, were contemporaries of mine at City who kept their distance from Alcove No. 1 and found other useful things (like studying) to do with their time. Nevertheless, it does seem clear to me that there was an academic impulse at work in Alcove No. 1, even if none of us understood its shaping force at the time. I mention this simply to emphasize the connection which was then possible—in many instances, probable—between student radicalism and intellectual vitality, a connection which seems to have been attenuated over the succeeding years.

Alcove No. 1 was, as I have said, where our real college education took place. Being a professor at City in those days was not a very attractive job. True, you had tenure and this counted for much in the 30's. But you taught 15 hours a week, had no private office, no faculty club, no library where you could do research; you commuted to the campus by subway, and, if you were a younger faculty member, your pay amounted to little more than pocket money. As a result, the very best professors left, if they could.

The Depression made it more difficult for many to do this, and the students benefited from their misfortune. But the fact remains that, for the bright, inquiring student, City College was a pretty dull educational place. The student who came seeking an intellectual community, in which the life of the mind was strenuously lived, had to create such a community and such a life for himself.

That an authentic educational process could exist outside of such a political community I discovered, to my amazement, at the University of Chicago, a couple of years after I left City. My wife had a graduate fellowship in history there, and I hung around the campus as a "nonstudent" for the better part of a year, working part time as a freight-handler on the Illinois Central while waiting for my draft records to be transferred from New York. I still see that year as through a golden haze—and I have never met a Chicago alumnus of that period who does not see it likewise. Under the powerful leadership of Robert M. Hutchins and Mortimer J. Adler, undergraduate education at Chicago centered on reading "great books," thinking about them, arguing about them. And the students did read, did think, did argue passionately. True, Chicago also had its share of young anti-Stalinist radicals who constituted a counterpart—much more literary, much less political—to Alcove No. 1. (Saul Bellow, Isaac Rosenfeld, Oscar Tarcov, H. T. Kaplan and Leslie Fiedler were members of that group.) But the point is that, at Chicago, you didn't *have* to be political to lead a vigorous intellectual life and be a member of an authentic intellectual community.

Though the specifically political radicalism or Alcove No. 1 was conventional and coarse enough, what gave it its special quality was the fact that it was intertwined with an intense interest in, and deference to, the "highbrow" in culture, philosophy and the arts. The two most influential journals in Alcove No. 1 were *The New International* and *Partisan Review*. The first was the Trotskyist "theoretical organ" and, confined by dogma though it certainly was, it was also full of a Marxist scholasticism that was as rigorous and learned, in its way, as the Jesuit scholasticism it so strikingly paralleled. Its contributors—Trotsky himself, Max Schachtman, James Burnham, Dwight Macdonald, C. L. R. James—were Marxist intellectuals. There were many important things one could not learn from reading *The New International*; but one most emphatically did learn how to read an intellectual discourse and several of us learned how to write one.

Partisan Review, the journal of the anti-Stalinist, left-wing, cultural avant-garde, was an intimidating presence in Alcove No. 1. Even simply to under-stand it seemed a goal beyond reach. I would read each article at least twice, in a state of awe and exasperation—excited to see such elegance of style and profundity of mind, depressed at the realization that a commoner like myself could never expect to rise into that intellectual aristocracy, an aristocracy that included Lionel Trilling, Philip Rahv, William Phillips, Sidney Hook, Mary McCarthy, Paul Goodman, Clement Greenberg, Harold Rosenberg, Meyer Schapiro and F. W. Dupee. I have recently had occasion to reread some of these issues of *Partisan Review* and, though I now see limitations then not visible to me, I also must affirm that it was a most remarkable magazine. The particular mission it set itself—to reconcile a socialist humanism with an indi-vidualistic "modernism" in the arts (the latter frequently being, in the 1930's, associated with "reactionary" political attitudes)—established a dialectic of challenge and response that released the finest creative energies. The effort at reconciliation eventually failed, in a quite unpredictable way, as the emerging "counter-culture" gradually abolished the category of "the highbrow" alto-gether. But it was a bold, imaginative effort, and *Partisan Review* in its heyday was unquestionably one of the finest American cultural periodicals ever pub-lished—perhaps even the very finest.

In addition, there were the frequent debates which we attended. The term "debate" as used today, really doesn't do them justice. To begin with, they ignored all conventional time limits. A speaker like Max Schachtman, the Trotskyist leader, or Gus Tyler of the Socialist Party, could argue at a high pitch of moral and intellectual and rhetorical intensity for two, three, even four hours. (Since the Stalinists refused to debate with other left-wing groups, we were always debating among ourselves.) When, in 1940, the Trotskyists split into two factions, it was after a debate among four speakers that contin-ued for two whole days. (The most succinct presentation, by James Burnham, lasted only two hours, and caused many of those present to question his "seri-ousness.") And, incredible as it may seem, the quality of the presentations was in all respects up to the quantity. They were—within the limits imposed by their socialist preconceptions—learned, witty, articulate, intellectually rigor-ous. I have never since seen or heard their equal, and, as a learning experience for college students, they were beyond comparison.

So far as I can see, universities today are not significantly better or worse than they were in the 30's; they are not—as they were not—intellectual communities. But the rebellion against the "merely academic" has tended to take the form of a secession from the life of the mind altogether.

The radicalism of the 30's was decidedly an adult movement, in which young people were permitted to participate. We young Trotskyists were as numerous as the adult party, but we unquestioningly accepted the authority of the latter. In contrast, the radicalism of the 60's was a generational movement, bereft of adult models and adult guidance. It is not easy to understand just how this came about, but one thing is certain: The radicals of the 60's were what they were because American society and American culture—which means we, the adults—permitted them (sometimes encouraged them) to grow up to be what they were. It is not, as some think, that we failed to impose our adult *beliefs* upon our children. That would be an absurd enterprise. What we failed to do is to transmit adult *values* to them—values affecting the way one holds beliefs which would have encouraged them to take their own and others' beliefs seriously, and to think coherently about them. And precisely because we adults encouraged our 20-year-old children to be "kids," their rebellion so often resembled a bewildering and self-destructive tantrum.

As to why American adults failed their children in this way—well, since some of my best friends are now social scientists, I'll leave that for them to figure out.

4

Mary McCarthy (1912–1989)
Philip Rahv 1908–1973 (1974)

Editor's Introduction

Born in Seattle, Mary McCarthy was orphaned at age six when her parents died in the flu epidemic of 1918. Afterward, she was raised mostly by her maternal grandparents, one Jewish and the other Protestant, in Seattle. As a girl she attended Annie Wright Seminary in Tacoma and then studied at Vassar, where she received her degree in 1933, the year before *Partisan Review* was founded. When she graduated she married immediately and left for New York City, but the marriage was short lived and by the mid-thirties she was sharing an apartment with Philip Rahv. After *Partisan Review* folded briefly and then was resuscitated in 1937, McCarthy was its drama editor. The next year she married the influential literary critic Edmund Wilson, and her only child was a product of that stormy union. Over the course of her days she married twice more and peopled her fiction with her life's intellectual and romantic figures.

McCarthy knew Rahv as few people did, both as a romantic partner and an editorial colleague at a particularly exciting time and place in American literary journalism. In this evocative remembrance of him at his death, she catches for posterity the depth of both foreign and American cultural instincts combined in one of the most important figures in the early years of the New York Intellectuals. Alfred Kazin, Irving Howe and Irving Kristol, for all the poverty and alienation of the immigrant neighborhoods of their youth, were born in the United States. A first-generation immigrant, Rahv escaped the turmoil of Russia, but as a child in Rhode Island who arrived at school awkwardly dressed in the costume of an unassimilated foreigner, he could not pretend to be anything but an outsider. After high school he found himself in the rainy little town of Newberg, Oregon, only a couple of streets wide, writing advertising copy and educating himself without any of the sustenance or training provided by City College's lunchroom alcoves. Yet Rahv and William Phillips were bright and ambitious enough to help shape American literary and political culture as the founding editors at *Partisan Review,* beginning in 1934.

Source

Mary McCarthy, "Philip Rahv, 1908–1973," *New York Times Book Review,* February 17, 1974.

Selected Readings

Mary McCarthy, *Intellectual Memoirs: New York, 1936–1938* (New York: Harcourt Brace Jovanovich, 1992); *Occasional Prose* (New York: Harcourt Brace Jovanovich, 1985); *Sights and Spectacles* (New York: Farrar, Straus and Cudahy, 1956); *The Oasis* (New York: Random House, 1949); *Cast a Cold Eye* (New York: Harcourt, Brace, 1950); *Memories of a Catholic Girlhood* (New York: Harcourt, Brace, World, 1957).

Carol Brightman, *Writing Dangerously: Mary McCarthy and Her World* (New York: Potter, 1992).

* * * * *

So he's gone, that dear phenomenon. If no two people are alike, he was less like anybody than anybody. A powerful intellect, a massive, overpowering personality and yet shy, curious, susceptible, confiding. All his life he was sternly faithful to Marxism, for him both a tool of analysis and a wondrous cosmogony; but he loved Henry James and every kind of rich, shimmery, soft texture in literature and in the stuff of experience. He was a resolute modernist, which made him in these recent days old-fashioned. It was as though he came into being with the steam engine: for him, literature began with Dostoevsky and stopped with Joyce, Proust and Eliot; politics began with Marx and Engels and stopped with Lenin. He was not interested in Shakespeare, the classics, Greek city states; and he despised most contemporary writing and contemporary political groups, being grumblingly out of sorts with fashion, except where he felt it belonged, on the backs of good-looking women and girls.

This did not overtake him with age or represent a hardening of his mental arteries. He was always that way. It helped him be a Trotskyite (he was a great admirer of the Old Man, though never an inscribed adherent) when Stalinism was chic. Whatever was "in" he threw out with a snort. Late in his life, serendipity introduced him to the word "swingers," which summed up everything he was against. With sardonic relish he adopted it as his personal shorthand. If he came down from Boston to New York and went to a literary party and you asked him "Well, how was it?" he would answer "Nothing but swingers!" and give his short soft bark of a laugh.

Yet he had a gift for discovering young writers. I think of Saul Bellow, Elizabeth Hardwick, Randall Jarrell, John Berryman, Bernard Malamud. There were many others. He was quickly aware of Bob Silvers, editor of *The New York Review of Books*, and became his close friend—counselor, too, sometimes. To the end of his life, he remained a friend of young people. It was middle-aged and old swingers he held in aversion; young ones, on the whole, he did not mind.

He had a marvelous sensitivity to verbal phrasing and structure. What art dealers call "quality" in painting he would recognize instantly in literature, even of a kind that, in principle, ought to have been foreign to him. I remember when I first knew him, back in the mid-thirties, at a time when he was an intransigent (I thought), pontificating young Marxist, and I read a short review he had done of *Tender Is the Night*—the tenderness of the review, despite its critical stance, startled me. I would not have suspected in Rahv that power of sympathetic insight into a writer so glamorized by rich Americans on the Riviera. Fitzgerald, I must add, was "out" then and not only for the disagreeable crowd at the *New Masses*.

That review was delicately, almost poetically written, and this too was a surprise. I would have expected him to write as he talked, pungently, harshly, drivingly, in a heavy Russian accent. It was as though another person had written the review. But as those who knew him discovered, there were two persons in Rahv, but solidly married to each other in a long-standing union—no quarrels. It would be simplifying to say that one was political, masculine and aggressive, one feminine, artistic and dreamy, but those contrasts were part of it.

Perhaps there were more than two, the third being an unreconstructed child with a child's capacity for wonder and amazement. Philip marveled constantly at the strangeness of life and the world. Recounting some story, seizing on some item in a newspaper, he would be transported, positively enraptured, with glee and offended disbelief. His black eyes with their large almost bulging whites would roll, and he would shake his head over and over, have a short fit of chuckling, nudge you, if you were a man, squeeze your arm, if you were a woman—as though you and he, together, were watching a circus parade of monstrosities and curious animals (in the form of human behavior) pass through your village.

His own childhood in the Russian Ukraine had stayed fast in his mind. He used to tell me how his grandmother (his parents were Jewish shopkeepers living in the midst of a peasant population) ran into the shop one day saying, "The Czar has fallen," and to him it was as if she had said, "The sky has fallen"; he hid behind the counter. Then, when the Civil War began, he remembered staying in the shop for weeks, it seemed, with the blinds pulled down, as Red and White troops took and retook the village.

His parents were early Zionists, and after the Civil War they emigrated to Palestine, where in the little furniture factory his father opened he got to know those strange people—Arabs. In 1922 he went to America, alone, to live with his older brother. There, in Providence, R.I., already quite a big boy, he went to grade school still dressed in the old-fashioned European schoolboy style, in long black trousers and black stockings, looking like a somber little man among the American kids. Starting to work early, as a junior advertising copywriter for a small firm out in Oregon, he had no time for college and got his education, alone, in public libraries. In the Depression, he migrated to New York. Standing in breadlines and sleeping on park beaches, he became a Marxist.

This education—Russia, the Revolution, Palestine, books read in libraries, hunger—shaped him. He read several languages: Russian, German (his family on its way to Palestine had spent a year or two in Austria), probably some Hebrew, and French, which he picked up by himself. He had a masterly sense of English and was a masterful copy-editor—the best, I am told by friends, they ever knew. American literature became a specialty with him, and he came to it curious and exploratory like a pioneer. Hawthorne, Melville, James, these were the main sources that fed his imagination. His insights, never random but tending to crystallize in theory, led him to make a series of highly original formulations, including the now famous distinction between redskins and palefaces among our literary men. He himself, being essentially a European, was neither.

Though he knew America intimately, he remained an outsider. He never assimilated, not to the downtown milieu of New York Jewish intellectuals he moved in during his early days, not to the university, although in time he occupied a professor's chair. When he lived in the country, which he did for long stretches, he was an obstinate city man and would hold forth darkly on the theme of "rural idiocy." He never learned to swim. This metaphorically summed up his situation: he would immerse his body in the alien element (I have nice pictures of him in bathing trunks by the waterside) but declined or perhaps feared to move with it. His resistance to swimming with the tide, his mistrust of currents, were his strength.

Remaining outside the American framework, his mind had a wider perspective, and at three critical junctures in our national intellectual life, its reflections were decisive. First, at the time of the Moscow trials, when he and William Philips broke with the Communists and "stole" *Partisan Review*, which they had edited as an organ of the John Reed Club. Second, during the war, when he broke with his former collaborators Dwight Macdonald and Clement Greenberg on the issue of whether the war against Hitler should be supported by American radicals or not. We had all been affirming the negative, but Rahv in a long meditative article moved toward the opposite position: I remember the last sentence, with which I did not agree at the time but which struck on my mind nevertheless and reverberated: "And yet in a certain sense it is our war." Third, in the McCarthy time, when so many of his old friends in the anti-Stalinist left were either defending McCarthy or "postponing judgment," Rahv, alone in his immediate circle, came out, in print, with an unequivocal condemnation and and contemptuous dismissal. On Vietnam, so far as I remember, he did not pronounce at any length; his characteristic voice is lost to my recollection, having mingled with so many others.

The words "radical' and "modern" had a wonderful charm for Philip; when he spoke them, his sometimes grating tone softened, became reverent, loving, as though touching prayer beads. He was also much attached to the word "ideas." "He has no *ideas*," he would declare, dismissing some literary claimant; to be void of ideas was, for him, the worst disaster that could befall an intellectual. He found this deficiency frequent, almost endemic, among us. That may be why he did not wish to assimilate.

I said, just now, that he was unlike anybody, but now I remember that I have seen someone like him—on the screen. Like the younger Rahv anyway: Serge Bondarchuck, the director of *War and Peace*, playing the part of Pierre. An uncanny resemblance in every sense and unsettling to preconceived notions. I had always pictured Pierre as blond, pink, tall and fat; nor could I picture Philip as harboring Pierre's ingenuous, embarrassed, puzzled, placid soul—they were almost opposites, I should have thought. And yet that swarthy Russian actor was showing us a different interior Philip and a different exterior Pierre. Saying good-bye to my old friend, I am moved by that and remember his tenderness for Tolstoy (see the very Rahvian and beautiful essay "The Green Twig and the Black Trunk") and Tolstoy's sense of Pierre as the onlooker, the eternal civilian, as out of place at the Battle of Borodino in his white hat and green swallow-tail coat as the dark little man in his long dark East European clothes eyeing the teacher from behind his grammar-school desk in Providence.

Partisan Review Editors
Editorial Statement (1934)

Editor's Introduction

By 1934 the Great Depression was already profoundly affecting American social and cultural life. The nation, two years earlier, had shifted from twelve years of Republicans in the White House to the beginning of a twenty-year Democratic dominance. The New Deal was already under way. It was not only immigrants from Europe who turned to socialism and communism to address the country's problems. The sons of privilege from Princeton (Edmund Wilson) and Harvard (Malcolm Cowley), and the daughters of influence from schools such as Vassar (Mary McCarthy), enlisted for a few years or more in the world of radical politics that they hoped might help design a new, more equitable, intelligent and rational society. The Soviet Union and its ideas were not yet discredited, and its apparent idealism and brave vision of the future drew the admiration of young American intellectuals in the thirties as once an untested set of American political and cultural ideas gained the approval of French Enlightenment philosophes.

Although *The New Masses* already had existed as a magazine of the Communist party since 1925, it was mainly political, and many on the left believed there was a need for a literary outlet. Philip Rahv and William Phillips convinced the party that *The New Masses* wasn't cultural enough to lead proletarian art, but a new party magazine devoted only to culture and with a Communist perspective could do the job. *Partisan Review* began in 1934 as the magazine of the New York chapter of the John Reed Club, the literary arm of the Communist party in the United States. Especially in its early years, in the decade or so before the end of World War II, the magazine was antagonistic toward American values and skeptical about the country's intentions. Those who ran the magazine and published in it were mostly Jewish, socialist, anti-capitalist and class conscious and were in America but felt they were not of it—much of which is evident in their opening lines of their first issue.

Philip Rahv and Phillips were the founding and central editors of the publication for decades after its inception. Their beginning editorial complains of the failure of capitalism, a criticism many Americans would have endorsed, but the editors go on to denounce racism, fascism, imperialist war and "debilitating liberalism." Most telling, the editors' statement proclaims the success of socialism in the Soviet Union and vows to defend that country as the future of the world. For an avowedly literary publication, *Partisan Review* obviously was intently interested in ideology and philosophy—a hallmark of many literary camps in the West throughout the twentieth century. When it began publishing in 1934 the proletarian revolution seemed imminent enough to them that the magazine focused on literature's role in this long-awaited uprising. The editors believed that writing about fiction and poetry could influence the future systems of the world, and that idea seemed tenable partly because fiction exercised far greater influence than it does today.

Source

"Editorial Statement," *Partisan Review*, vol. 1, no. 1, February–March 1934.

Selected Readings

Daniel Aaron, *Writers on the Left* (New York: Harcourt, Brace and World, 1961).

James Burkhart Gilbert, *Writers and Partisans* (New York: John Wiley and Sons, 1968).

* * * * *

Partisan Review appears at a time when American literature is undergoing profound changes. The economic and political crisis of capitalism, the growth of the revolutionary movement the world over, and the successful building of socialism in the Soviet Union have deeply affected American life, thought and art. They have had far-reaching effects not only upon the political activities of writers and artists, but upon their writing and thinking as well. For the past four years the movement to create a revolutionary art, which for a decade was confined to a small group, has spread throughout the United States. A number of revolutionary magazines has sprung up which publish revolutionary fiction, poetry and criticism. Some of these are issued by the John Reed Clubs.

Partisan Review is the organ of the John Reed Club of New York, which is the oldest and largest Club in the country. As such it has a specific function to fulfill. It will publish the best creative work of its members as well as of non-members who share the literary aims of the John Reed Club.

We propose to concentrate on creative and critical literature, but we shall maintain a definite viewpoint—that of the revolutionary working class. Through our specific literary medium we shall participate in the struggle of the workers and sincere intellectuals against imperialist war, fascism, national and racial oppression, and for the abolition of the system which breeds these evils. The defense of the Soviet Union is one of our principal tasks.

We shall combat not only the decadent culture of the exploiting classes but also the debilitating liberalism which at times seeps into our writers through the pressure of class-alien forces. Nor shall we forget to keep our own house in order. We shall resist every attempt to cripple our literature by narrow-minded, sectarian theories and practices.

We take this opportunity to greet the various magazines of revolutionary literature already in the field, especially the *New Masses* whose appearance as a weekly, like the present issuance of *Partisan Review*, is evidence of the growth of the new within the old.

6
Partisan Review Editors
Editorial Statement (1937)

Editor's Introduction

In April 1935, the year after *Partisan Review* began, and in the midst of the magazine's enthusiasm to perfect proletarian literature, instructions from the Soviet Union prompted American communists to adopt the Popular Front Against Fascism (which the critic Malcolm Cowley said he preferred to translate as "the people's front"), a friendship and united effort among communists, socialists, Marxists, and liberals to form a common bulwark against the spread of fascism worldwide. The directive from Moscow ordered American communists to join with liberals as a way to encourage America to save the Soviets from being overrun by European fascist nations. As a result, the party shut down the exclusively communist and proletarian John Reed Clubs and instead embraced the less strident and more ecumenical League of American Writers, a group that featured higher-profile authors whose reputations could add clout to the Soviet Union's plea for help. In this move, *Partisan Review*, the offspring of the New York John Reed Club, found itself without patronage and abandoned by its party. To keep from collapsing, during the rest of 1935 *Partisan Review* combined with the magazine *Anvil* and then was independent during 1936 until it folded temporarily in October of that year.

If the Communist party had been an unreliable sponsor by unceremoniously dropping its communist American writers, *PR*'s editors had other signs, too, that the leaders in Moscow would make dangerous long-term partners. In the Moscow Trials of 1936 the editors, like the rest of the world, learned that many of the original leaders of the Russian revolution were being put on trial for sedition by Stalin's lieutenants for no greater reason than that his terrible misdeeds could be performed easier without former leaders watching him. The examples of Stalin's tyranny of terror could not be ignored, and as a consequence *Partisan Review*—during the time between October 1936, when it ceased publication and December 1937, when William Phillips and Philip Rahv revived it—shifted consciously away from its Russian romance. The magazine still admired Leon Trotsky and some other socialists who were not in power, but its affair with official communism was now over and it began searching for a more independent radical position.

When *Partisan Review* began publishing again in December 1937 there were four new editors in addition to Philip Rahv and William Phillips: Mary McCarthy, Dwight Macdonald, Clement Greenberg and George L. K. Morris. This brief unsigned editorial, announced at the start of the magazine's revival (it would not fold again until volume 70, number 2, in the spring of 2003) its rejection of both its former alliance with the Communist party and its early embrace of proletarian literature. Instead, over the course of the next decade or so, *Partisan Review* politically supported an anti-Stalinist radicalism, and culturally for several more decades it promoted a high avant-garde modernism.

Source

"Editorial Statement," *Partisan Review*, vol. 4, no. 1, December 1937.

Selected Readings

Irving Howe and Lewis Coser, *The American Communist Party* (Boston: Beacon Press, 1957).
Judy Kutulas, *The Long War: The Intellectual People's Front and Anti-Stalinism, 1930–1940* (Durham: Duke University Press, 1995).
Steven Biel, *Independent Intellectuals in the United States, 1910–1945* (New York: New York University Press, 1995).

* * * * *

As our readers know, the tradition of aestheticism has given way to a literature which, for its origin and final justification, looks beyond itself and deep into the historic process. But the forms of literary editorship, at once exacting and adventurous, which characterized the magazines of the aesthetic revolt, were of definite cultural value; and these forms *Partisan Review* will wish to adapt to the literature of the new period.

Any magazine, we believe, that aspires to a place in the vanguard of literature today, will be revolutionary in tendency; but we are also convinced that any such magazine will be unequivocally independent. *Partisan Review* is aware of its responsibility to the revolutionary movement in general, but we disclaim obligation to any of its organized political expressions. Indeed we think that the cause of revolutionary literature is best served by a policy of no commitments to any political party. Thus our underscoring of the factor of independence is based, not primarily on our differences with any one group, but on the conviction that literature in our period should be free of all factional dependence.

There is already a tendency in America for the more conscious social writers to identify themselves with a single organization, the Communist Party; with the result that they grow automatic in their political responses but increasingly less responsible in an artistic sense. And the Party literary critics, equipped with the zeal of vigilantes, begin to consolidate into aggressive political-literary amalgams as many tendencies as possible and to outlaw all dissenting opinion. This projection on the cultural field of factionalism in politics makes for literary cleavages which, in most instances, have little to do with literary issues, and which are more and more provocative of a ruinous bitterness among writers. Formerly associated with the Communist Party, *Partisan Review* strove from the first against its drive to equate the interests of literature with those of factional politics. Our reappearance on an independent basis signifies our conviction that the totalitarian trend is inherent in that movement and that it can no longer be combatted from within.

But many other tendencies exist in American letters, and these, we think, are turning from the senseless disciplines of the official Left to shape a new movement. The old movement will continue and, to judge by present indications, it will be reënforced more and more by academicians from the universities, by yesterday's celebrities and today's philistines. Armed to the teeth with slogans of revolutionary prudence, its official critics will revive the petty-bourgeois tradition of gentility, and with each new tragedy on the historic level they will call the louder for a literature of good cheer. Weak in genuine literary authority but equipped with all the economic and publicity powers of an authentic cultural bureaucracy, the old regime will seek to isolate the new by performing upon it the easy surgery of political falsification. Because the writers of the new grouping aspire to independence in politics as well as in art, they will be identified with fascism, sometimes directly, sometimes through the convenient medium of "Trotskyism." Every effort, in short, will be made to excommunicate the new generation, so that their writing and their politics may be regarded as making up a kind of diabolic totality; which would render unnecessary any sort of rational discussion of the merits of either.

Do we exaggerate? On the contrary, our prediction as to the line the old regime will take is based on the first maneuvers of a campaign which has already begun. Already, before it has appeared, *Partisan Review* has been subjected to a series of attacks in the Communist Party press; already, with no regard for fact—without, indeed, any relevant facts to go by—they have attributed gratuitous political designs to *Partisan Review* in an effort to confuse the primarily literary issue between us.

But *Partisan Review* aspires to represent a new and dissident generation in American letters; it will not be dislodged from its independent position by any political campaign against it. And without ignoring the importance of the official movement as a sign of the times we shall know how to estimate its authority in literature. But we shall also distinguish, wherever possible, between the tendencies of this faction itself and the work of writers associated with it. For our editorial accent falls chiefly on culture and its broader social determinants. Conformity to a given social ideology or to a prescribed attitude or technique, will not be asked of our writers. On the contrary, our pages will be open to any tendency which is relevant to literature in our time. Marxism in culture, we think, is first of all an instrument of analysis and evaluation; and if, in the last instance, it prevails over other disciplines, it does so through the medium of democratic controversy. Such is the medium that *Partisan Review* will want to provide in its pages.

7
Dwight Macdonald (1906–1982)
I Choose the West (1952)

Editor's Introduction

As World War II edged closer, philosopher Sidney Hook, who held no position at *Partisan Review*, encouraged the editors to endorse American involvement in the conflict. Hook's critics called it a "lesser evil" strategy of selecting the best of two distasteful sides in the war, but he felt it was a reasonable choice for a pragmatist to make. Editors Phillip Rahv and William Phillips ignored Hook's advice, and editors Dwight Macdonald and Clement Greenberg rejected Hook's stance as not radical enough. Like other socialist followers of Trotsky, Macdonald refused to support either the Allies or the Axis powers in the war and instead maintained a "third camp" position that opposed involvement in the war in the hope that when it was over there would be a democratic socialist alternative to both sides. But after the Pearl Harbor attack, Rahv and Phillips decided to endorse Hook's lesser-evil choice of American involvement, which they considered sane. Thus the *Partisan* editors chose different war policies. Rahv and Phillips supported American entry, while Macdonald and Greenberg opposed it. The disagreement was enough to drive Macdonald and Greenberg out of *Partisan Review*. Macdonald began his own magazine, *politics*, and Greenberg later joined the editorial staff of *Commentary*.

The movement of *Partisan Review* from communism in 1934 to anti-Stalinist radicalism by the late thirties and then a support of the American war effort in the early forties represented a geological shift toward a more democratic radicalism. Naturally, that political shift slowly moved the New York Intellectuals closer to American values. Members of the New York group were still radicals after World War II, and that placed them outside the mainstream, but they gradually took an interest in American policies and social structures that once had seemed to them oppressive and alienating. Now the *Partisans* supported some aspects of American political culture because it prevented a Stalin from growing and prospering in the United States.

Dwight Macdonald surely didn't fit the profile most Americans envisioned for a radical. A graduate of Exeter and Yale, a management trainee at Macy's who later joined the staff of *Fortune* magazine, Macdonald was a son of privilege, and who would expect him to be alienated like those immigrant socialists arguing in the City College alcoves? Yet, as an intellectual, Macdonald was radicalized by the leftist ideas of the thirties, helped edit and then broke with *Partisan Review*, and next, in 1944, founded *politics*, a highly moral and pacifist publication that had more influence than its small subscriber list suggested. In his *politics* articles he still detested Soviet communism but also found much in American politics and culture to fault. He continued to urge a third-camp model for those in the United States and Europe.

It was thus surprising in 1952 when Dwight Macdonald acknowledged that he had "chosen the West." He dropped his insistence on a third-camp position between the Soviets and the West, and, as Rahv and Hook certainly must have said to themselves, he accepted the "lesser-evil" option. At the time of his announcement there was still a small crowd of the New York Intellectuals who felt it a shame that Macdonald had embraced the West. Those, such as Irving Howe, Lewis Coser, Harold Rosenberg and the rest who ended up writing for *Dissent* after 1954, must have thought so, although, through the succeeding decades, they slowly made their own peace with America, a small step at a time. Besides, Dwight remained irreverent, skeptical, fun, and loudly nonconformist, so it was easy to overlook his rather public profession.

Nonetheless, it was a significant moment, if only as a time when the group could be startled into an awareness that political and cultural attitudes among them had evolved. The very existence of the group itself was based on a radical rejection of what America stood for politically. In the intervening years since 1934 the gravitational realignment produced by the war had refigured the group's attitude. Increasingly, it believed that the liberal democratic foundation of the country, despite its obvious flaws and weaknesses, served as a protection from the fanatical ideological forces that produced such grisly results in Germany, the Soviet Union and other areas. In addition to their appreciation of physical safety, members of the New York group also valued the protection in the democratic West of their intellectual vocation. In the fascist and totalitarian countries, intellectuals were mistrusted and driven from their profession—because the ideal of an intellectual is to question the truth, and in closed societies questioning is punished.

In the almost two decades from the founding of *Partisan Review* to Dwight Macdonald's debate against Norman Mailer at Mt. Holyoke College where he—perhaps somewhat reluctantly—chose the West, a great and important tide had shifted. When Alfred Kazin published his book *On Native Grounds* in 1942, most of the New York Intellectuals could not have imagined America as their native sustaining cultural soil. A decade later, when Macdonald dropped his third-camp ideal and supported the West, it would not be so difficult for members of the New York group to envision America as a native ground, despite their conviction that it still contained considerable flaws.

Source

Dwight Macdonald, "I Choose the West," (1952) *Memoirs of a Revolutionist* (NY: Farrar, Straus and Cudahy, 1957).

Selected Readings

Gregory D. Sumner, *Dwight Macdonald and the* politics *Circle* (Ithaca: Cornell University Press, 1996).
Michael Wreszin, *A Rebel in Defense of Tradition* (New York: Basic Books, 1994).

* * * * *

I choose the West–the US and its allies–and reject the East–the Soviet Union and its ally, China, and its colonial provinces, the nations of Eastern Europe. By "choosing" I mean that I support the political, economic, and military struggle of the West against the East. I support it critically—I'm against the Smith and McCarran Acts, French policy in Indo-China, etc.—but in general I *do* choose, I support Western policies.

During the last war, I did not choose, at first because I was a revolutionary socialist of Trotskyist coloration, later because I was becoming, especially after the atom bomb, a pacifist. Neither of these positions now appear valid to me.

The revolutionary socialist position assumes there is a reasonable chance that some kind of popular revolution, a Third Camp independent of the warring sides and hostile to both, will arise during or after the war, as was the case in Russia in March, 1917. Nothing of the sort happened in the last war, despite even greater destruction and chaos than in 1917–18, because the power vacuum was filled at once by either Soviet or American imperialism. The Third Camp of the masses just doesn't exist any more, and so Lenin's "revolutionary defeatism" now becomes simply defeatism: it helps the enemy win and that's all.

As for pacifism, it assumes some degree of ethical similarity in the enemy, something in his heart that can be appealed to—or at least something in his traditions. Gandhi found this in the British, so his passive resistance movement could succeed, since there were certain repressive measures, such as executing him and his chief co-workers, which the British were inhibited from using by their traditional moral code, which is that of Western civilization in general. But the Soviet Communists are not so inhibited, nor were the Nazis. So I conclude that pacifism does not have a reasonable chance of being effective against a totalitarian enemy. Pacifism as a matter of individual conscience, as a *moral* rather than a *political* question, is another thing, and I respect it.

I choose the West because I see the present conflict not as another struggle between basically similar imperialisms as was World War I but as a fight to the death between radically different cultures. In the West, since the Renaissance and the Reformation, we have created a civilization which puts a high value on the individual, which has to some extent replaced dogmatic authority with scientific knowledge, which since the 18th century has progressed from slavery and serfdom to some degree of political liberty, and which has produced a culture which, while not as advanced as that of the ancient Greeks, still has some appealing features. I think Soviet Communism breaks sharply with this evolution, that it is a throwback not to the relatively humane middle ages but to the great slave societies of Egypt and the Orient.

Nor are the Communists content, or indeed able, to confine this 20th-century slave system to Russia or even to the vast new provinces in Asia and Eastern Europe added since 1945. Like Nazism, Soviet Communism is a young, aggressive, expansive imperialism (as against, for instance, the elderly British imperialism, which since 1945 has permitted India, Egypt, and Iran to escape from its grip). Also like Nazism, it represses its own population so brutally that it must always be "defending" itself against alleged foreign enemies—else its subjects would ask why such enormous sacrifices are needed. The rulers of Soviet Russia will consider they are encircled by threatening invaders so long as a single country in the world is left that is independent of them. A reader asked the Moscow *Bolshevik* recently: "Now that we control a third of the world, can we still speak of capitalist encirclement?" The editors replied: "Capitalist encirclement is a political term. Comrade Stalin has stated that capitalist encirclement cannot be considered a geographical notion." (Thus the existence of a UN army on the Korean peninsula constitutes a *political* encirclement of Communist China.) Furthermore, precisely because the bourgeois West is so obviously superior, in most of the spiritual and material things that people value, to the Communized East, the mere *existence* of a non-Communist country is a danger to Communism. This was shown in 1945–46 when the Red Army troops returned from their contact with Europe "infected with bourgeois ideology"—i.e., they had seen how much more free the masses outside Russia are and how much higher their standard of living is—and had to be quarantined in remote districts for a while.

In choosing the West, I must admit that already the effects on our own society of the anti-Communist struggle are bad: Senator McCarthy and his imitators are using lies to create hysteria and moral confusion in the best Nazi-Communist pattern; building a great military machine cannot but extend the power of the State and so encroach on freedom. In short, we are becoming to some extent like the totalitarian enemy we are fighting. But (1) being on the road is not the same thing as being there already (though one might think it was from certain Marxist and pacifist statements), and (2) this malign trend can be to some extent resisted.

After all, here and in Western Europe there still exist different political parties, free trade unions and other social groupings independent of the State; varied and competing intellectual and artistic tendencies; and the protection, by law and by tradition, of those individual civil rights on which all the rest depend. Ours is still a living, developing society, open to change and growth, at least compared to its opposite number beyond the Elbe.

When Ulysses made his journey to the Elysian Fields, he saw among the shades his old comrade-in-arms, Achilles, and asked him how are things? Achilles' answer was: "I would rather be the slave of a landless man in the country of the living than the ruler of the kingdom of the dead." This is my feeling. I prefer an imperfectly living, open society to a perfectly dead, closed society. We may become like Russia, but we may not—the issue is not settled so long as we are independent of Moscow. If Moscow wins, the door is slammed shut, and to open it again would be a more difficult and brutal business than is now required by the measures to keep it open.

[The following was written in 1953.] If it comes to another world war, I think we are done for, all of us. In supporting measures of opposition, including military ones as in Korea, against the Communists, I reason that the best chance of postponing war and perhaps avoiding it altogether is for the West to keep up its military strength and to be prepared to counter force with force. Appeasement didn't work with the Nazis and it won't work with the Communists. I admit that the results of the Korean war have been disastrous, especially for the Korean people; if I were a South Korean, I'm not sure I should have not preferred to have just let the North Koreans take over peacefully. Yet perhaps, in terms of world politics, the results of not making a fight to defend the Korean Republic would have been even more disastrous, like the results of letting Hitler absorb the Rhineland, Austria and Czechoslovakia without a fight.

Perhaps there is no solution any longer to these agonizing problems. Certainly the actual workings of history today yield an increasing number of situations in which *all* the real alternatives (as against the theoretically possible ones) seem hopeless. The reason such historical problems are insoluble now is that there have been so many crimes, mistakes, and failures since 1914, and each one making the solution of the next problem that much more difficult, that by now there are no uncorrupted, unshattered forces for good left with which to work. A decent social order in Europe after the first world war, for instance, would have made Hitler's rise impossible; even after he took power, a Loyalist victory in the Spanish Civil War or some radical reforms in France by Leon Blum's *Front Populaire* would have made his position very difficult. But none of these things happened, and when the *Reichswehr* marched into Poland, what solution was possible? Some of us felt it was our duty as socialists to "oppose the war," i.e., to refuse to fight the Nazis under the flags of existing governments; we also had illusions about the historical possibility of a "third camp" of the common people arising and making it possible to fight the Nazis with clean hands, so to speak. But this alternative, it is now clear, existed only on the ethical and ideological plane; it had no existence on the historical level. The only historically real alternatives in 1939 were to back Hitler's armies, to back the Allies' armies, or to do nothing. But none of these alternatives promised any great benefit for mankind, and the one that finally triumphed has led simply to the replacing of the Nazi threat by the Communist threat, with the whole ghastly newsreel flickering through once more in a second showing.

This is one reason I am less interested in politics than I used to be.

II
Against Absolutism

8

Sidney Hook (1902–1989)

The New Failure of Nerve (1943)

Editor's Introduction

Sidney Hook was a prominent early member of the New York Intellectuals equipped with a logical mind and an appetite for rough debate. After graduating from City College in 1923, where he studied with Morris Cohen and won the Ward Medal in Logic, Hook became a graduate student of John Dewey at Columbia University and received his Ph.D. in philosophy in 1927. Almost immediately he was one of the most recognized pragmatists of the twentieth century.

By the early 1930s many regarded Hook as the country's most authoritative Marxist voice, and, although he never joined the Communist Party he was friendly with many who did and was a "fellow traveler" for several years. But, alarmed by the Moscow Trials in 1936, he adopted a leading position as an independent radical intellectual, which meant that he was formally unaligned and outspokenly anti-Stalinist. From that time, he devoted the rest of his career to an active anticommunist campaign in periodicals and public appearances. After midcentury, Hook focused almost entirely on global foreign policy issues, and thereafter was unmoved by most American domestic policy debates except in those areas, such as McCarthyism and the student radicalism of the 1960s, that had foreign policy repercussions.

"I am a democrat. I am a socialist," he wrote in 1947 in *Partisan Review*. "And I am still a Marxist in the sense in which one may speak of a modern biologist as still a Darwinian" (Sidney Hook, "The Future of Socialism," *Partisan Review* 14, no. 1, January–February 1947, 24). Some of those closest to him in 1947 and after believed Hook was a democrat, his socialist commitment had vanished, and he was a Marxist not in allegiance but only in his scholarly background. Yet Hook was very clearly a pragmatist, and that remained a strong tie to his Marxist past. As a philosopher, Hook stumped through political and intellectual circles trying to alter the world instead of only dissecting it scholastically. Marx himself had propounded in his famous eleventh thesis on Feuerbach that "the philosophers have only interpreted the world; the point, however, is to change it," a claim that any pragmatist from William James to John Dewey to Sidney Hook would have been happy to endorse. As Hook said of himself, he was still a Marxist in a historical sense as a modern biologist is a Darwinian, and much of that Marxist connection for Hook as he got older was through his commitment to be an intellectual instead of a scholar, an intellectual who changed the world through pragmatic argument and action. He spread his pragmatic ideas not through scholarly journals of philosophy, but instead through the *Partisan Review*, the *New Leader*, and the popular press, in articles aimed at politics, foreign policy, religion, and society.

Finally, Hook's greatest ambition, as is clear in this essay, was not simply to oppose a political system such as communism, but to fight absolutist thought. He analyzed not only absolutist political and social systems but religion and all types of *a priori* thinking. Hook worried about the tendency during World War II for people everywhere to embrace mystical revelation in a time of crisis, an intellectual panic that turned to spiritual revival. It troubled him to witness an assault on the scientific method, a rejection of "the common variety truths of science and good sense." To choose religion over science as a guide for our actions, Hook believed to be a frightening failure of nerve. Operating by faith in a divine doctrine could not replace rational scientific analysis based on observation, testing and then weighing the consequences of actions. To follow the latter course would be pragmatic. To do otherwise would be to embrace a path that leads to a lack of choices. His protracted liberal struggle against absolutism gives Hook a continuing relevance in American culture.

Source

Sidney Hook, "The New Failure of Nerve," *Partisan Review* vol. 10, no. 1, January–February 1943.

Selected Readings

Sidney Hook, *Out of Step* (New York: Carroll and Graf, 1987), chapter 20.

* * * * *

In the famous third chapter of his *Four Stages of Greek Religion* Gilbert Murray characterizes the period from 300 B.C. through the first century of the Christian era as marked by "a failure of nerve." This failure of nerve exhibited itself in "a rise of asceticism, of mysticism, in a sense, of pessimism; a loss of self-confidence, of hope in this life and of faith in normal human efforts; a despair of patient inquiry, a cry for infallible revelation: an indifference to the welfare of the state, a conversion of the soul to God."

A survey of the cultural tendencies of our own times shows many signs pointing to a new failure of nerve in Western civilization. Its manifestations are more complex and sophisticated than in any previous time. It speaks in a modern idiom and employs techniques of expression and persuasion that reflect the ways of a secular culture. But at bottom it betrays, except in one respect, the same flight from responsibility, both on the plane of action and on the plane of belief, that drove the ancient world into the shelters of pagan and Christian supernaturalism.

There is hardly a field of theoretical life from which these signs of intellectual panic, heralded as portents of spiritual revival, are lacking. No catalogue can do justice to the variety of doctrines in which this mood appears. For purposes of illustration we mention the recrudescence of beliefs in the original depravity of human nature; prophecies of doom for western culture, no matter who wins the war or peace, dressed up as laws of social-dynamics; the frenzied search for a center of value that transcends human interests; the mystical apotheosis of "the leader" and élites; contempt for all political organizations and social programs because of the obvious failure of some of them, together with the belief that good will is sufficient to settle thorny problems of economic and social reconstruction; posturing about the cultivation of spiritual purity; the refurbishing of theological and metaphysical dogmas about the infinite as necessary presuppositions of knowledge of the finite; a concern with mystery rather than with problems, and the belief that myth and mysteries are modes of knowledge; a veritable campaign to "prove" that without a belief in God and immortality, democracy—or even plain moral decency—cannot be reasonably justified.

Liberalism—not the 19th century ideology or social theology of laissez-faire which was already moribund before the First World War—but liberalism as an intellectual temper, as faith in intelligence, as a tradition of the free market in the world of ideas is everywhere on the defensive. Before the onrush of cataclysmic social and historical changes, large sections of the intellectuals and clerks of the Western world are abandoning the hard-won critical positions of the last few centuries. In the schools, the churches, and in the literary arts, the tom-tom of theology and the bagpipes of transcendental metaphysics are growing more insistent and shrill. We are told that our children cannot be properly educated unless they are inoculated with "proper" religious beliefs; that theology and metaphysics must be given a dominant place in the curriculum of our universities; that churchmen should cultivate sacred theology before applying the social gospel; that business needs an inspired church that speaks authoritatively about absolutes,—this by the editors of *Fortune;* that what is basically at stake in this war is Christian civilization despite our gallant Chinese, Moslem, and Russian allies; that the stability of the state depends on an *unquestioned* acceptance of a unifying dogma, sometimes identified with the hierarchial authoritarianism of Catholicism, sometimes with democracy; that none of the arts and no form of literature can achieve imaginative distinction without "postulating a transcendental reality." *Obscurantism is no longer apologetic; it has now become precious and wilful. Fundamentalism is no longer beyond the pale; it has donned a top hat and gone high church.*

Philosophy and the Assault Against Scientific Method

The primary evidence of the new failure of nerve is to be found in an attitude underlying all of the views and movements enumerated, and many others as well. It exhibits itself as a loss of confidence in scientific method, and in varied quests for a "knowledge" and "truth" which, although they give us information about the world, are uniquely different from those won by the processes of scientific inquiry. Often, with no great regard for consistency, these uniquely different truths are regarded as "superior" to the common garden variety truths of science and good sense. They are the self-proclaimed governors of the moral and theoretical economy. Their function is to point to man's natural and supernatural end and to prevent science, competent to deal only with means, from stepping out of bounds.

This distrust of scientific method is often concealed by statements to the effect that science, of course, has a certain validity in its restricted sphere and that only the pretensions of scientific philosophy, naturalism, empiricism, positivism—not to speak of materialism,—are being criticized. Yet it is not to the actual procedures of scientific inquiry that such critics go to correct this or that formulation of scientific philosophy. Instead they invoke the claims of some rival method to give us knowledge of what is beyond the competence of scientific method. Occasionally they boldly assert that their substitute method gives a more reliable and completer knowledge of the matters that the sciences report on, particularly about the behavior of man and the history of society. What an eloquent revelation is contained in Reinhold Niebuhr's words: "Science which is only science cannot be scientifically accurate."[1]

Distrust of scientific method is transformed into open hostility whenever some privileged, "private" truth pleads for exemption from the tests set up to safeguard the intelligence from illusion. The pleas for exemption take many forms. They are rarely open and direct as in the frenzy of Kierkegaard who frankly throws overboard his intelligence in order to make those leaps of despairing belief which convert his private devils into transcendent absolutes. Usually these pleas are presented as corrolaries of special *theories* of knowledge, being, or experience. There are some who interpret science and discursive knowledge generally as merely a method of confirming what we *already* know in a dim but sure way by other modes of experience. If the methods of scientific inquiry do not yield this confirmation, they are held to be at fault; some other way must be found of validating and communicating primal wisdom. Others maintain that scientific method can give us only partial truths which become less partial not by subjecting them to more careful scrutiny but by incorporating them into a theological or metaphysical system whose cardinal principles are true but not testable by any method known to science. Still others openly declare it to be axiomatic that every experience, every feeling and emotion, directly reports a truth that cannot be warranted, and does not need to be warranted, by experiment or inference.

These, bluntly put, are gateways to intellectual and moral irresponsibility. They lay down roads to a happy land where we can gratify our wishes without risking a veto by stubborn fact. But of the view that every mode of experience gives direct authentic knowledge, it would be more accurate to say that it carries us far beyond the gateways. For in effect it is a defense of obscurantism. It starts from the assumption that *every* experience gives us an authentic report of the objective world instead of material for judgment. It makes our viscera an organ of knowledge. It justifies violent prejudice in its claims that if only we feel deeply enough about anything, the feeling declares some truth about the object which provokes it. This "truth" is regarded as possessing the same legitimacy as the considered judgment that finds no evidence for the feeling and uncovers its root in a personal aberration. After all is it not the case that every heresy-hunting bigot and hallucinated fanatic is convinced that there is a truth in the feelings, visions, and passions that run riot within him? Hitler is not the only one for whom questions of evidence are incidental or impertinent where his feelings are concerned. If the voice of feeling cannot be mistaken, differences would be invitations to battle, the ravings of an insane mind could legitimately claim to be prophecies of things to come. It is not only as a defense against the marginally sane that we need the safeguards of critical scientific method. Every vested interest in social life, every inequitable privilege, every "truth" promulgated as a national, class or racial truth, likewise denies the competence of scientific inquiry to evaluate its claims.

Those who hold this view sometimes seek to avoid its consequences by admitting that not every experience or feeling is as valid as every other, any more than every scientific judgment is as valid as every other. But this does not alter the logic of their position. The relative validity of different scientific judgments is established by methods of public verification open to all who submit themselves to its discipline, whereas the relative validity of feelings is decided by another private feeling.

Not infrequently the demand that the revelations of feeling, intuition or emotion about the world meet scientific canons of evidence is rejected as an arbitrary legislative decree concerning what visions are permissible and what may or may not exist. The complaint is made that such a demand impoverishes imaginative resources and blights the power to see new and fresh visions without which preoccupation with method is nothing but a word-game of sterile minds. As far as the seeing of visions and the winning of new truths are concerned, such an interpretation is nothing short of grotesque. The essential point, when the question of knowledge or truth arises, is whether we have seen a vision or been a victim of a delusion; or, to avoid the appearance of question-begging, whether we have beheld a trustworthy or untrustworthy vision. Some people claim to see what we know is not there. If seeing were believing, or if all seeing were evidence of what could be believed, independently of the conditions under which the seeing took place, it would be easy to keep men perpetually duped.

The intelligent demand for evidence need not paralyze the pioneers of truth who catch glimpses of what until then may be undreamed of. Nor does the progress of science demand complete and exact confirmation of an hypothesis at the very outset, but only enough to institute further inquiries. The history of the sciences is sufficient evidence that the discipline of its method, far from being a bar to the discovery of new knowledge, is a positive aid in its acquisition. What other discipline can point to the acquisition of new knowledge or to truths about existence that command the universal assent of all investigators?

Nor is it true that scientific method or the philosophy of naturalism, which whole-heartedly accepts scientific method as the only reliable way of reaching truths about man, society, and nature, decrees what may or may not exist. It concerns itself only with the responsibility of the assertions that proclaim the existence of anything. It does not forbid but explores and tests. It does not jeer at the mystical swoon of dumb rapture; it denies only the mystic's retrospective cognitive claim for which no evidence is offered except the fact of a trance. It does not rule out on *a priori* grounds the existence of supernatural entities and forces. The existence of God, immortality, disembodied souls or spirits, cosmic purpose or design, as these have customarily been interpreted by the great institutional religions, are denied by naturalists for the same generic reasons that they deny the existence of fairies, elves, leprechauns, and an invisible satellite revolving between the earth and moon. There is no plausible evidence to warrant belief in them or to justify a probable inference on the basis of partial evidence.

There are other conceptions of God, to be sure, and provided they are not self-contradictory, the naturalist would be unfaithful to his own philosophy if he refused to examine the evidence for their validity. All he asks is that the conception be sufficiently determinate to make possible specific inferences of the *how*, *when*, and *where* of His operation. The trouble with most conceptions of God which differ from the conventional ones is that either they are so vague that no one can tell what they mean, or else they designate something in experience for which a perfectly suitable term already exists.

Unfortunately, for all their talk of appeal to experience, direct or indirect, religious experientialists dare not appeal to any experience of sufficiently determinate character to permit of definite tests. There is a certain wisdom in this reluctance. For if experience can confirm a belief, it can also disprove it. But to most supernaturalists the latter is an inadmissable possibility. We therefore find that the kind of experience to which reference is made is not only unique but uniquely self-authenticating. Those who are not blessed by these experiences are regarded as blind or deaf and, under certain circumstances, dangerous to the community. But is it not odd that those who worship

Zeus on the ground of a unique experience should deny to others the right to worship Odin on the ground of a different unique experience?

Scientific method cannot deny that the secular and religious spokesmen of the supernatural hear voices, but it cannot accept these voices, as they are reported, as valid testimony about the world of fact or the world of value. It judges the truth of what is heard by what it logically leads to in the realm of empirical behavior. It seeks to draw what is reported about this world or any other into some community with the limited but precious store of responsible assertions that constitute knowledge. The attack upon scientific method, in order to be free to believe whatever voice speaks to us, is a flight from responsibility. This is the dominant characteristic of the failure of nerve.

Social Crisis and Metaphysical Hunger

The causes of the failure of nerve in our time are multiple and obvious. Economic crises, world war, a bad peace, tragically inept statesmanship, the tidal waves of totalitarianism, tell the story of the twentieth century. These are the phenomena that are behind the interrupted careers, the frustrated hopes, the anxiety, the sense of being lost and alone, the growing bewilderment, fear and horror—that feed the theology of despair and the politics of wish. It is important to remember this. The "arguments" of those who have been panicked into embracing the new varieties of transcendental consolation may be met a thousand times over. But not until a democratic, freedom-and-welfare-planning economy is built out of what is left of our world, in which stable traditions can absorb the conventions of revolt of political man and the experiments of growth of individual men, will these intellectual excesses subside from epidemic to episodic proportions. Until then it is necessary to prevent intellectual hysteria from infecting those who still cling to the principles of rational experiment and analysis.

There is still another source of the new fusion of super-agony and superstition. This is the inability of those liberal, labor, and socialist movements which have prided themselves on being scientific and which have lost one social campaign after another, to supply a positive philosophy, that would weld emotion and scientific intelligence, as a new rallying ground. Wilsonian idealism is dead although some do not know it, syndicalism is a fascist changeling, and orthodox Marxism is bankrupt. The grand visions of the socialist prophets have given way to petty political horse-trading and fixations on the good will of bourgeois statesmen. The left lives from day to day in a world going from worse to worse.

Into the breach has stepped the motley array of religionists filled with the *élan* of salvation and burdened with the theological baggage of centuries. *This is the one respect in which the new failure of nerve basically differs from the old.* The failure of nerve of the early Christian era sought to convert the soul to God in order to withdraw it from all concern with the world. Today the churches are so much of this world that their other worldliness is only a half-believed prophecy of man's inescapable destination rather than an ideal of personal and social life. As interpreters of divine purpose, they have now become concerned with social healing, with the institutions of society and with the bodies of men, as necessarily involved in the healing of individual souls. The world-order is to become a moral and religious order. Plans for the post-war world and for social reconstruction are coming from the Pope as well as from the humblest Protestant sect. They are now at flood-tide. The Churches bid well to replace political parties as sounding boards, if not instruments, of social reform.

It is characteristic of the tendencies hostile to scientific method that they reject the view that the breakdown of capitalism and the rise of totalitarianism are primarily the result of a conjunction of material factors. Rather do they allege that the bankruptcy of Western European civilization is the direct result of the bankruptcy of the scientific and naturalistic spirit. The attempt to live by science resulted in chaos, relativism, Hitlerism and war. The latter are treated as superficial evils destined to pass like all of God's trials. But the radical evil is a scientific attitude which sacrificed true understanding for prediction and individual salvation for social control.

That science was king in the social life of the Western world, that modern ills are the consequences of our attempt to live by scientific theory and practice—these assumptions border on fantasy. No convincing evidence has ever been offered for them. On the contrary, the chief causes of our maladjustments are to be found precisely in these areas of social life *in which the rationale of scientific method has not been employed.* Where is the evidence that any Western State ever attempted to meet scientifically the challenge of poverty, unemployment, distribution of raw materials, the impact of technology? Attempts to grapple with these problems in relation to human needs in a rational and scientific spirit have run squarely against class interests and privileges which cut savagely short any inquiry into their justification. What has controlled our response to basic social problems have been principles drawn from the outworn traditions or opportunist compromises that reflect nothing but the shifting strength of the interests behind them. In either case the procedure has had little to do with the ethics and logic of scientific method. It is only by courtesy that we can call them principles at all. Drift and improvisation have been the rule. Enthusiasm for the bare *results* of the physical sciences—which undoubtedly did reach a high pitch in the 19th century—does not betoken an acceptance of a scientific or experimental philosophy of life in which all values are tested by their causes and consequences. The cry that a set of "laboratory techniques" cannot determine values in a philosophy of life betrays the literary man's illusion that the laboratory procedures of the natural sciences are the be-all and end-all of scientific method instead of restricted applications of it in special fields.

The truth is that scientific method has until now been regarded as irrelevant in testing the values embodied in social institutions. *If* one accepted the religionists' assumption that values can be grounded only on a true religion and metaphysics, together with their views about the ideal causation of events, it could be legitimately urged against them that the bankruptcy of civilization testifies to the bankruptcy of *their* metaphysics. For if science is irrelevant to values, it cannot corrupt them; and if theology and metaphysics are their sacred guardian, they are responsible for the world we live in.

Theology in a Crisis

The social principles of Christianity have had almost two thousand years in which to order the world on a moral basis. It is not likely that anything new can be discovered from its principles or that its social gospel will succeed better in eliminating war, social distress, and intense factional strife, than it did during the historical periods in which religious institutions enjoyed chief authority. And when we examine the behavior and doctrines of different religious groups as they meet the trials of our world today, the impression is reinforced that there is no more unity of purpose among them, no more agreement in program and direction of effort, than among their secular brethren. But whereas the latter *may* rely upon a method by which to limit, adjudicate and negotiate the differences among them, the former *must* absolutize their differences if they are consistent.

It is an obvious fact that all religious groups, with the exception of some Protestant churches in America, have been able to find support of their own national governments in prosecuting the war compatible with the sacred principles of Christianity. Some of them have even professed to be able to derive the necessity of such support from sacred doctrine. Cardinal Verdier of France and Cardinal Hinsley of England have declared the war to be a religious crusade; so have some of the German bishops on the other side who have blessed Hitler's arms and prayed for his victory; while the Pope himself is still neutral in respect to it. M. Maritain at the time of the Nazi-Soviet Pact declared that the war against Hitler was a just war but not a religious one. He also asserted "it is entirely understandable" that the German bishops should support their government; indeed, that it was naive to be scandalized by the divisions among religious groups on the war. Today the just war has become transformed in M. Maritain's eyes into a "religious" war. Yet no matter how they characterize the war, religious groups do not contest the validity of opposite statements made about the war by other national religious groups who take their point of departure from the *same* religious premises.

Now this is extremely odd. No one would tax theologians with insincerity. But if it is true that a religious principle or dogma is compatible with two contradictory positions in respect to the defeat of Hitlerism, then the principle or dogma in question is irrelevant to the nature of the war. And since it is true that the defeat of Hitlerism is of the very first importance for the social reconstruction of Europe, we are justified in entertaining a lively suspicion of the relevance of Christian principles to such reconstruction, if at the same time they can reconcile themselves equally well to Hitler's victory or defeat.

The only implication that can be drawn from this strange state of affairs is that religious groups are seeking, as they always have, to make of God an instrument of national policy. One of two things: Either national policy can be defended as good or just without theological sanctions or dogmas, in which case the interposition of religion obscures issues: or the defense presupposes religious dogmas, in which case, to countenance a different national policy, is to betray *religious* dogma. The German Bishops who admonished the Catholic soldiers in a Pastoral Letter to give their lives "*in obedience to the Fuehrer*" should have been denounced as bad Catholics. Before Catholics, Protestants and Jews urge the acceptance of their dogmas as necessary preconditions for intelligent belief in democracy and anti-Hitlerism, let them convert their own churches to democracy, and denounce religious neutrality before Hitlerism for what it is, connivance with the enemy. This is their sector of the battle. But, better still, let them take their theology out of politics.

On the very question of the war itself the Protestant Churches of America are split wide open although this is somewhat concealed by the unanimity of interest in problems of post-war reconstruction. Yet no matter with what voice the Churches speak on the issues of the day, they do so not as other associations of citizens who must face demands of empirical evidence, but as guardians of a revelation which gives them unique knowledge of man and his destiny.

Religion can escape showing its credentials concerning the inspiration of its knowledge but not concerning its validity. For the reliability of any knowledge is tested in the necessities of intelligent action. That test, together with the varying counsel of the Churches on specific social policies, is sufficient to indicate that there is no unique religious knowledge or religious guidance. When Church pronouncements about the nature of the world are not irrelevant or clearly false, they can be more plausibly derived from positions that Churches usually characterize as unbelieving. When the claims to unique knowledge are exploded, the last resort of religionists is the assertion that religious beliefs, and only religious beliefs, can supply that dynamic faith without which secular defence of the good society is ineffectual, unable to implement its own humanist ideals.

Faith, Sin, and Good Sense

The defense of religious faith takes many forms. Most of them are variations on the theme that if the beliefs of faith were false, the world would be a terrible place: therefore they must be true. Or since the beliefs of faith are consoling, they cannot be false. Sometimes the argument rises a little higher. Because not everything can be proved, since even science must make assumptions, some faith in something is unavoidable if one is to believe or do anything. Therefore faith in the absurd is justifiable. But only our faith, not the other fellow's! On its most sophisticated level, faith is defended not as a specific belief but as an attitude of wisdom and resignation towards the human situation. When it is realized that such faith is not distinctively religious at all, either there is a relapse into metaphysical double-talk about faith also being a form of knowledge or religion is defined so that all people who have faith or passion, i.e., who are not yet dead, are regarded as religious and committed to religious beliefs. But when religious belief is a universal coefficient of all other beliefs, it is irrelevant to them. This may be seen most clearly in the theology of Reinhold Niebuhr.

Reinhold Niebuhr is one of those men of whom Emerson said they were better than their theology. A radical and honest intelligence, he brings to bear upon specific problems of social change a scientific attitude and rare courage, that make his discussions always illuminating. But not a single one of the positions that Niebuhr takes on the momentous issues of social and political life is dependent on his theology. One may accept his rather reactionary theology, which is an eloquent combination of profound disillusionment in human action and a violent belief in human ideals, and deny all his secular views. Or one may accept the latter, as so many of his friends do, and regard the former as moving rhetoric that breathes passionate conviction about something whose very sense is in doubt. Indeed, if we look closely at Niebuhr's theology, and take it out of the language of myth and paradox, we find that whatever is acceptable in it to critical thought is an obscure retelling of what was known to the wiser unbelievers of the past.

Consider, for example, Niebuhr's conception of religion. It is "the primary and ultimate act of faith by which life is endowed with meaning. Without that act of faith life cannot be lived at all."[2] To be alive is to be religious, and the atheists, the irreligious, the agnostics, have been converted by definition: they all have religion. This is innocent enough so long as we never lose sight of the differences between religions or *what* men believe in, and so long as we realize that although life cannot be lived without some acts of faith, death may be the consequence of other acts of faith, e.g., faith that pneumonia can be cured by absent treatment. What Niebuhr must now show as a theologian is that the faith necessary for life is necessarily faith in God. This he completely fails to do. Instead by another essay in redefinition—one not so innocent—he equates the meaning which is the object or reference of *any* faith, with God. "There is no action without religious orientation and no religion without God."[3] To be alive is not only to be religious, it is to have faith in God even if we deny his existence. This is still not the end. Niebuhr must now as a *Christian* theologian show that the God we affirm in action is the God of revealed Christianity who is transcendent to the world and yet intimately connected with it. This is accomplished in his Gifford Lectures by describing man as a "self-transcendent spirit" consumed by a metaphysical anxiety and hunger which can only be appeased by belief in the symbolical (not literal!) truth of the Incarnation. Insofar as arguments are employed instead of exhortation they are fallacious. For example: what is unique about the human spirit cannot be derived from man's animal nature; nor is it an expression of reason. Therefore, infers Niebuhr, man is a child of God who can only comprehend himself "by a principle of comprehension which is beyond his comprehension." One mystery calls to another and the plain fact that what is distinctive about human traits has its origin and fruit in the social and cultural matrix, is not so much as considered.

Man, Niebuhr asserts, is not only a creature of God, he is a sinner. He is an inevitable sinner and yet cannot escape responsibility for his sins. He is a sinner because he forgets that he is a creature of God, because he thinks he is more than he is, knows more than he does, because, in short, he is not God. When he is contritely aware of his sinfulness, of its inevitability and his responsibility for it, grace descends upon his soul and he receives remission from sin.

There is a simple moral homily that can be tortured out of this oxymoronic language but it is completely spoiled by Niebuhr's theology.

What Niebuhr is telling us is that every effort, every movement of man in warding off evil or achieving good, leads him to "the sin of imperialism in action." Whether we are selfish or righteous, the tincture of sin is present. For we absolutize the relative, dogmatize insight, eternalize the fleeting, take the part for the whole. Man deludes himself into believing that he sees the infinite from a finite perspective, and that he transcends self-interest and selfishness in his conceptions of impartial justice. All of his ideals, including his God, he makes in his own image. In his struggle to achieve his limited ideals, as if they were absolute, he consequently is guilty of fanaticism whose evils may be not less than those he set out to rectify. Man must therefore accept some supernatural standard to curb the conflicts of partial truths, each claiming to be the whole truth.

What is here correctly perceived as a problem still remains a problem, for Niebuhr's solution is stultifying. The conflict of absolutes is to be settled by appeal to another absolute which on Niebuhr's own theology is necessarily injected with human finitude! This is a romantic and violent solution of a human predicament already violently distorted to begin with. Niebuhr writes as if all men were naturally romantic theologians, victims of a fantastic logic according to which, if God did not exist, *they* must be God. He ignores the entire tradition of scientific and naturalistic philosophy that has never claimed divinity for man nor infallibility for his judgment. The doctrine of original sin turns out to be nothing more than the discovery that man is a limited creature. But this is no more justification for believing he is essentially evil than that he is essentially good. For these are qualities that depend upon the use man makes of his limitations. Naturalist philosophers have urged men to understand the causes of their limitations, so that by reducing the margins of ignorance and increasing their scientific knowledge, they may be less limited. The whole enterprise of scientific method with its self-corrective procedures cuts under the dogmatism, absolutism and fanaticism of Niebuhr's theological man at the same time as it gives us conclusions that are sufficiently reliable to overcome some specific limitations. Niebuhr would frighten men out of their mistaken belief in omnipotence by a fairy tale about a creature that is absolutely omnipotent. The humility it induces is one of fear, not the humility which is fostered by knowledge of human limitations and ignorance. His wisdom does not carry further than the caution that no claim is completely justified, but he is helpless before the problem of determining the degree and extent of its justification, so necessary in order to get on with the problems in hand. Whenever Niebuhr tackles these problems, he deserts his theology.

It is true that intellectual pride is an expression of "original sin" insofar as we make a claim to know what we do not know and overlook the natural and historical origins of reason. Niebuhr is very eloquent about the dangers of intellectual pride. "Fanaticism is always a partly conscious, partly unconscious attempt to hide the fact of ignorance and to obscure the problem of skepticism." And again: "The real fact is that all the pretensions of final knowledge and ultimate truth are partly prompted by the uneasy feeling that the truth is not final and also by an uneasy conscience which realizes that the interests of the ego are compounded with this truth."[4] True, but Niebuhr should address these words not to naturalists but to theologians, for in the history of thought it has been the naturalists who have exposed the pretensions of final truths and who have uncovered the nerve of interest behind the absolute values of church, state, and conscience. Science has known its dogmatism, too. But the cure of bad science is better science, not theology.

On many specific issues of scientific inquiry Niebuhr is one with us. Despite his extravagant rhetoric, he does not believe in blowing out the candle-light of intelligence and wallowing in the dark night of the soul in an effort to make mysteries more mysterious. The only point at which Niebuhr seems to use his theology is in situations where values and partial interests are locked in mortal combat.

But does an appeal to the absolute really help us here? Is any war so fanatical and bestial as a religious war in which the conditioned values of social and personal interests take on the awful authority of unconditioned claims? Is might right when it is divine might? Is not the God of faith always the God of limited, erring and partial men? If we must have an absolute, let us look for it elsewhere. Against Niebuhr's myth of a private and mysterious absolute, we counterpose the public and self-critical absolute of scientific method. By evaluating claims in the light of their causes and consequences, it makes clear the interests from which they spring, and the meaning of what they propose.

By guiding us to the construction of a social order whose institutions provide for the negotiation and compromise of claims on the basis of the completest knowledge available, it promises not absolute security but greater security. It does not pretend to make men gods but to treat more intelligently the problem always at hand. It is not incompatible with action, even with revolutionary action on a large scale. Nothing is won forever but something is always won. How to get men to accept this absolute method—and to test it by its fruits, not only in the realm of nature but of human affairs—is a specific problem of scientific politics and education concerning which theology can tell us nothing.[5]

The Tail Sting of Eternity

Niebuhr's theology has a grand irrelevance to the specific patterns and problems of social life, although psychologically it breathes a defeatism more congenial to Toryism than to his own political progressivism. The same cannot be said of other varieties of theological doctrine which are tied up with a Church as Niebuhr's is not and which take the historical content of revelation more literally than he does. This is most evident in the social and political implications of Roman Catholicism.

Political events bearing on the prospects of its survival have made it necessary for the Catholic Church to strike a new tune in democratic countries. Its leading spokesmen are seizing every occasion to assure us that the last and best defence of democracy and freedom is a Christian social order. By "freedom," they explain, is meant "freedom in its true Christian sense," and by "Christian," they are careful not to explain, is always meant "Catholic." Any catalogue of Church activities in these countries will reveal that it is increasing in power and influence. It is in the van of attack against the best liberal traditions of American culture and education, particularly in the field of education.[6] What is not understood so well is the fact that its official *doctrinal* teachings, although compatible with a "hierarchial, authoritarian democracy," are incompatible with the specific freedoms in the Bill of Rights, including religious toleration, which are essential to the democracy we know. Christian morality is Catholic morality and the Christian state is bound before God and man to carry out the precepts of morality as interpreted by the Church, which insists that the salvation of the soul is its chief concern, and that outside of the Church there is no salvation. Insofar as it is weak and its communicants in a minority, the Church tolerates modern freedoms and liberties. Where it is strong enough, it suppresses them, particularly the propagation of "false" religious teachings by other groups that may undermine "true" Catholic belief.

That these are not recondite inferences of a suspicious critic of church history is shockingly evident in the Papal Encyclical, *Libertas*, of Leo XIII. That American churchmen are faithful to this doctrine is just as clear. Fathers Ryan and Boland in their authoritative *Catholic Principles of Politics* explicitly say that if professing Catholics constituted a majority of the population in the

United States, the state they would set up "could not permit non-Catholic sects to carry on general propaganda nor accord their organizations certain privileges that had formerly been extended to all religious corporations, for example, exemption from taxation." (p. 200)[7]

This doctrine testifies not to a failure of nerve but just to plain nerve—brazen and provocative. To match it we must go to the literature of the Communist Party which, demanding unabridged civil rights for itself under existing society, tells us that under the proletarian dictatorship, "all the capitalist parties—Republican, Democratic, Progressive, Socialist, etc.—will be liquidated, the Communist Party functioning alone as the Party of the toiling masses."[8]

As the self-constituted shepherd of all men's souls, the Catholic Church demands as great a control over social and political life as any totalitarian party; for as Pope Leo XIII made abundantly clear, it alone can determine what is subject to the power and judgment of the Church as affecting the salvation of the human soul. Consequently, when the Catholic Bishops who constitute the Administrative Board of the National Catholic Welfare Conference list the chief evils that imperil supernatural religion in this country as "false doctrine, immorality, disbelief, and reborn paganism," it is not hard to see what they refer to. False doctrine is Protestantism, or any religious faith except the true one; immorality is civil marriage, divorce, birth control, any civil freedom that violates a sacrament; disbelief is modern philosophy, any heresy that contradicts the heresies canonized as *philosophia perennis;* reborn paganism is any morality which is not grounded on revelation and any political theory that advocates the separation of church and state. There is a sting of death to the free spirit in every measure the Church proposes to take to safeguard its dogmas.

Partly as a result of Catholic agitation and partly as an expression of spiritual despair, many influential Protestant groups have echoed the call for a society organized on Christian foundations. It is questionable whether all who employ the phrase know what they mean by a Christian society. But whatever it means, it must refer either to Christian organization or Christian dogma. Would a Christian society based on Protestant dogmas, assuming the Protestant sects could agree on any, lead to a state similar in anti-democratic outline to Catholic clericalism? This is not so clear but the evidence of history and the logic of the position make it likely. At most, it would tolerate different religious beliefs but not *the freedom of disbelief.* The state could no longer be regarded as neutral to religion. Education would have to be purged of all freethinkers to prevent them from examining the "truths" of religion as critically as the truths of other branches of knowledge. This conclusion is implicit in the recent writing of Professor Hocking. The new orthodoxy would find new ways to implement its sway over the minds and allegiances of citizens. Whatever methods it employed would require the contraction, if not the proscription, of the scientific temper in order to diminish the hazards of belief. The social usefulness of ideas to those who possessed power, and their comfort and consolation to those who did not, would become the criteria of accepted truth. The Protestant Reformation would have succumbed to the Counter-Reformation whose secular form already prevails in totalitarian Europe.

Democracy and the Hebraic-Christian Tradition

These new currents of Protestantism which profess sincere acceptance of present day democracy employ arguments whose force is drawn from a key assumption. It asserts that modern democracy has been derived from, and can only be justified by, the theological dogmas of Hebraic-Christianity according to which all men are created by God and equal before Him. This assumption is the common ground of unity of all religious and metaphysical rationalizations of democracy. It is the rallying point of the much publicized Conference on Science, Philosophy and Religion in their Relation to the Democratic Way of Life, whose pronouncements indicate that it has officially accepted Maritain's Catholic conception of a pluralistic, hierarchially organized culture, crowned by religion, as "the cornerstone on which human civilization must be erected in our day." Scientific inquiry has a place in it: it will meet the "need for men to attain that increased measure of knowledge, which, according to Francis Bacon, brings men back to God." This Hebraic-Christian philosophy of democracy and culture is presented to a world in which a false conception of scientific knowledge has made it "peculiarly resistant to the teachings of religion. ..."[9]

It can be briefly demonstrated that the derivation of modern democracy from the dogma that all men are created by God and equal before Him is (1) logically invalid (2) historically false and (3) irrelevant to the pressing problem of democratic defense and reconstruction.

(1) From the alleged fact that all men are equal before God, it does not at all follow logically that they are, or should be, equal before the state or enjoy equal rights in the community. This must be justified by other considerations. Even on the theological scheme, although God is equally the creator of angels, men, animals and things, they are not all equal in value before him. Men are also equal before death, pain, disease and the tax-collector. But how they should be treated often depends upon their relative state of health, their efforts, the consequences of their efforts, and other *differential* features of their behavior. Some Christians have held—with as much logic as their brethren who drew contrary conclusions—that because all men are equally sinners in the sight of the Lord, their social and political inequalities in this transitory life are unimportant. Not infrequently, pious Christians have believed that these inequalities are our punishment for the sins of our fathers. If men have a common origin, biological or theological, that in itself is not logically sufficient for asserting that they must or should have common opportunities or common education or common citizenship. If we believe that they should have, as we

do, then we believe it on grounds whose validity would be unaffected whether they had a common origin or not.

Nor is the alleged fact that man was created by God a logical ground for honoring him. We are told both by the Pope and the Archbishop of Canterbury and the American Institute of Judaism that the dignity of man lies not in himself but in that he is a child of God. In the course of a typical Catholic denunciation of "atheistic saboteurs" who would keep the idea of God separate from our government, Professor Manion of Notre Dame, at a public meeting sponsored by the Conference, proclaims: "The only reason why we have to respect this so-called dignity of man is because it is God-created."[10] The logic would be just as bad even if the rhetoric were better. As well say that the only reason we have for not lying is that it is forbidden by God. Or that the only reason for appreciating the beauty of a landscape is that it is God's handiwork. The origin of a thing may have a bearing upon its nature. But the value of a thing cannot be inferred from its origin. It is not putative original nature but what emerges in the course of developing nature which is relevant to normative judgment. To judge people not by their origins, for which they are not responsible, but by their efforts, fruits, and achievements is a sound democratic maxim.[11]

(2) There is little warrant for the view that the theological dogmas of Hebraic-Christianity are the historical source of modern democracy. Judaism contenanced slavery while Christianity never condemned it in principle. The Church was one of the mainstays of feudalism; until its real-estate holdings were raided by absolute monarchs, it furnished the chief theoretical justification of the divine right of kings. Ideologically, modern democratic theory owes more to Stoic philosophy and Roman law than to Christian Dogma.

Religious institutions based on supernatural dogmas tend towards theocracy. Priesthoods have often been hereditary, and when not tightly closed corporations, rarely subject to democratic influences. It has sometimes been urged as a mitigating feature of the hierarchical, authoritarian structure of the Church that "a peasant might become a Pope." True, but so can an Austrian housepainter or the son of a Georgian cobbler become a Dictator. Does that alter the character of totalitarianism?

(3) We are asked to accept religious dogmas as true mainly on the grounds of their effectiveness in combatting Hitlerism. This in turn rests, as we have seen, upon the notion that Fascism is the consequence not of economic conditions, nationalist tradition, and disastrous political policies inside Germany and out, but of the spread of positivism, secularism, and humanism. Why Fascism should then have arisen in such strongly religious and metaphysical countries as Italy and Germany and not in such scandalously heretical and positivistic countries as England and America, is something that the neo-Thomists and their fellow-travellers do not explain.

None of the specific proposals of social reform that issue from religious conclaves, or even the principles sometimes offered to justify them, follow from the theological dogmas that preface their announcement. This is no more surprising than the absence of connection between the pleas for divine guidance which since the war stud the speeches of *all* statesmen of belligerent countries, except those of Stalin,[12] and the content of the speeches. Specific proposals to insure peace, security and freedom warrant attentive consideration no matter from what quarter they come. But their value in effecting what they claim to accomplish depends not on pious faith and good will but upon their consequences which can be adequately explored only by rigorous scientific thought without benefit of theology. To the extent that the scope of scientific thinking is restricted or limited to judgments of bare fact, the new social consciousness of the Christian churches will have just as little relevance to the future as their old consolatory ideals to the past. At best it will take flight from power politics; at worst it will act as a cover for it.

The new failure of nerve in contemporary culture is compounded of unwarranted hopes and unfounded beliefs. It is a desperate quest for a quick and all-inclusive faith that will save us from the trouble of thinking about difficult problems. These hopes, beliefs and faiths pretend to a knowledge which is not knowledge and to a superior insight not responsible to the checks of intelligence. The more fervently they are held the more complete will be their failure. Out of them will grow a disillusion in the possibility of intelligent human effort so profound that even if Hitler is defeated, the blight of Hitlerism may rot the culture of his enemies.

Notes

1. *The Nature and Destiny of Man*, Vol. I, p. 73, N. Y. 1941.
2. *Modern Monthly*, Vol. 8, p. 712.
3. "Religion and Action," *Religion in the Modern World*, University of Pennsylvania Bicentennial Conference (1941) p. 91.
4. *The Nature and Destiny of Man*, p. 196.
5. For a more extended critique of Niebuhr, cf. my *Social Change and Original Sin*, *New Leader*, Nov. 11, 1941.
6. For a detailed examination see *The Bertrand Russell Case*, edited by John Dewey and H. M. Kallen, N. Y. (1941) 227 pp. This almost completely unreviewed book contains articles, in addition to those of the editors, by Morris R. Cohen, Walton Hamilton, Emory Guy Shipler, Richard McKeon, Carleton Washburne and others.
7. It is interesting to note that taxation was one of the means used by the Soviet State to wipe out Russian churches. The curious reasoning by which Msgr. Ryan justifies this position is detailed in another book:
   "As we have already pointed out, the men who defend the principle of toleration for all varieties of religious opinion, assume either that all religions are equally true or that the true cannot be distinguished from the false. On no other ground is it logically possible to accept the theory of indiscriminate and universal toleration (sic!).

"To the objection that the foregoing argument can be turned against Catholics by a non-Catholic State, there are two replies. First, if such a State should prohibit Catholic worship or preaching on the plea that it was wrong and injurious to the community, the assumption would be false; therefore the two cases are not parallel. Second, a Protestant State could not logically take such an attitude (although many of them did so in former centuries) because no Protestant sect claims to be infallible. Besides, the Protestant principle of private judgment logically implies that Catholics may be right in their religious convictions, and that they have a right to hold and preach them without molestation.

"Such in its ultimate rigor and complete implications is the Catholic position concerning the alliance that should exist between the Church and a Catholic State." Ryan and Miller *The State and Church*, Macmillan 1937, pp.36–37.

8. William Z. Foster, *Toward Soviet America*, p. 275 (1932).

9. All quotations from the official statement of the Third Annual Conference, *New York Times*, September 1, 1942.

10. Proceedings of Third Conference, p. 538.

11. For a more detailed refutation of the attempts to ground democracy upon theological and metaphysical foundations, cf. "The Philosophical Presuppositions of Democracy," *Ethics*, April, 1942, pp. 275–296.

12. For Stalin the dialectic takes the place of Providence. And since June 22nd, 1941, the Soviet radio has discovered that Nazism is a movement which seeks to destroy Christianity.

9
Hannah Arendt (1906–1975)
Total Domination (1951)

Editor's Introduction

Born in Germany, Hannah Arendt studied at the University of Marburg with Rudolph Bultmann and Martin Heidegger, and at the University of Heidelberg with Karl Jaspers. After being jailed by the Nazis and then escaping, Arendt spent most of the 1930s in Paris, where she helped save Jewish children. There she met Heinrich Blücher, whom she married in 1940. When the Nazis invaded France, the two were held separately, and when they were able to escape they fled together to New York until the war was over.

Arendt's work following World War II addressed the Jewish experience and the problems incident to mass societies, particularly in Germany and in the concentration camps there, a circumstance she described with the words *terror* and *totalitarian*. During this time she wrote *The Origins of Totalitarianism* (1951), and soon after the term *totalitarian* began to be used to describe a condition of total control and domination imposed by a state on its citizens, an experience very different from those of liberal democratic countries that allowed their citizens individual autonomy and self-created identity. A decade later, Arendt attended the trial of Adolf Eichmann and wrote a series of *New Yorker* articles that became *Eichmann in Jerusalem* (1963), a book that prompted painful arguments both among Jews and among many other interested readers about the nature of guilt and the banality of evil.

Arendt's ideas about totalitarianism shared many concerns with Sidney Hook's "The New Failure of Nerve." They were tied by a common fear, arising from the clashes and ashes of the thirties and forties, that absolutist ideologies in the name of progress and equality would suffocate independent thinking and action. The traits that frightened them were related: absolutism, totalitarianism, fanaticism, racism, anti-Semitism, zealotry, superstition, faith, mysticism, ideology and utopia. Arendt claimed that "the nature of total domination might serve to invalidate all obsolete political differentiations from right to left and to introduce beside and above them the politically most important yardstick for judging events in our time, namely: whether they serve totalitarian domination or not."

Most frightening of all, perhaps, was the totalitarian practice of "organized oblivion." Whereas ancient rulers allowed their victims to write their own histories and keep the memories of their martyrs alive, concentration camps "took away the individual's own death, proving that henceforth nothing belonged to him and he belonged to no one. His death merely set a seal on the fact that he had never really existed." Reality was outlawed and erased with a frightening coat of indelible paint. In a world where rulers increasingly forced policies to work in pursuit of some grand vision, despite the aggravated misery of the population, people were right to be fearful. Arendt emphasized that "the fearful imagination has the great advantage to dissolve the sophistic-dialectical interpretations of politics which are based on the superstition that something good might result from evil."

Source

Hannah Arendt, "Total Domination," (abridged) *The Origins of Totalitarianism* (New York: Harcourt Brace, 1951), 419-428.

Selected Readings

Social Research vol. 69, no. 2, Summer 2002.

* * * * *

The first essential step on the road to total domination is to kill the juridical person in man. This was done, on the one hand, by putting certain categories of people outside the protection of the law and forcing at the same time, through the instrument of denationalization, the nontotalitarian world into recognition of lawlessness; it was done, on the other, by placing the concentration camp outside the normal penal system, and by selecting its inmates outside the normal judicial procedure in which a definite crime entails a predictable penalty. Thus criminals, who for other reasons are an essential element in concentration-camp society, are ordinarily sent to a camp only on completion of their prison sentence. Under all circumstances totalitarian domination sees to it that the categories gathered in the camps—Jews, carriers of diseases, representatives of dying classes—have already lost their capacity for both normal or criminal action. Propagandistically this means that the "protective custody" is handled as a "preventive police measure,"[140] that is, a measure that deprives people of the ability to act. Deviations from this rule in Russia must be attributed to the catastrophic shortage of prisons and to a desire, so far unrealized, to transform the whole penal system into a system of concentration camps.[141]

The inclusion of criminals is necessary in order to make plausible the propagandistic claim of the movement that the institution exists for asocial elements.[142] Criminals do not properly belong in the concentration camps, if only because it is harder to kill the juridical person in a man who is guilty of some crime than in a totally innocent person. If they constitute a permanent category among the inmates, it is a concession of the totalitarian state to the prejudices of society, which can in this way most readily be accustomed to the existence of the camps. In order, on the other hand, to keep the camp system itself intact, it is essential as long as there is a penal system in the country that criminals should be sent to the camps only on completion of their sentence, that is when they are actually entitled to their freedom. Under no circumstances must the concentration camp become a calculable punishment for definite offenses.

The amalgamation of criminals with all other categories has moreover the advantage of making it shockingly evident to all other arrivals that they have landed on the lowest level of society. It soon turns out, to be sure, that they have every reason to envy the lowest thief and murderer; but meanwhile the lowest level is a good beginning. Moreover it is an effective means of camouflage: this happens only to criminals and nothing worse is happening than that what deservedly happens to criminals.

The criminals everywhere constitute the aristocracy of the camps. (In Germany, during the war, they were replaced in the leadership by the Communists, because not even a minimum of rational work could be performed under the chaotic conditions created by a criminal administration. This was merely a temporary transformation of concentration camps into forced-labor camps, a thoroughly atypical phenomenon of limited duration.)[143] What places the criminals in the leadership is not so much the affinity between supervisory personnel and criminal elements—in the Soviet Union apparently the supervisors are not, like the SS, a special elite trained to commit crimes[144]—as the fact that only criminals have been sent to the camp in connection with some definite activity. They at least know why they are in a concentration camp and therefore have kept a remnant of their juridical person. For the politicals this is only subjectively true; their actions, insofar as they were actions and not mere opinions or someone else's vague suspicions, or accidental membership in a politically disapproved group, are as a rule not covered by the normal legal system of the country and not juridically defined.[145]

To the amalgam of politicals and criminals with which concentration camps in Russia and Germany started out, was added at an early date a third element which was soon to constitute the majority of all concentration-camp inmates. This largest group has consisted ever since of people who had done nothing whatsoever that, either in their own consciousness or the consciousness of their tormenters, had any rational connection with their arrest. In Germany, after 1938, this element was represented by masses of Jews, in Russia by any groups which, for any reason having nothing to do with their actions, had incurred the disfavor of the authorities. These groups, innocent in every sense, are the most suitable for thorough experimentation in disfranchisement and destruction of the juridical person, and therefore they are both qualitatively and quantitatively the most essential category of the camp population. This principle was most fully realized in the gas chambers which, if only because of their enormous capacity, could not be intended for individual cases but only for people in general. In this connection, the following dialogue sums up the situation of the individual: "For what purpose, may I ask, do the gas chambers exist?"—"For what purpose were you born?"[146] It is this third group of the totally innocent who in every case fare the worst in the camps. Criminals and politicals are assimilated to this category; thus deprived of the protective distinction that comes of their having done something, they are utterly exposed to the arbitrary. The ultimate goal, partly achieved in the Soviet Union and clearly indicated in the last phases of Nazi terror, is to have the whole camp population composed of this category of innocent people.

Contrasting with the complete haphazardness with which the inmates are selected are the categories, meaningless in themselves but useful from the standpoint of organization, into which they are usually divided on their arrival. In the German camps there were criminals, politicals, asocial elements, religious offenders, and Jews, all distinguished by insignia. When the French set up concentration camps after the Spanish Civil War, they immediately introduced the typical totalitarian amalgam of politicals with criminals and the innocent (in this case the stateless), and despite their inexperience proved remarkably inventive in creating meaningless categories of inmates.[147] Originally devised in order to prevent any growth of solidarity among the inmates, this technique proved particularly valuable because no one could know whether his own category was better or worse than someone else's. In Germany this eternally shifting though pedantically organized edifice was given an appearance of solidity by the fact that under any and all circumstances the Jews were the lowest category. The gruesome and grotesque part of it was that the inmates identified themselves with these categories, as though they represented a last authentic remnant of their juridical person. Even if we disregard all other circumstances, it is no wonder that a Communist of 1933 should have come out of the camps more Communistic than he went in, a Jew more Jewish, and, in France, the wife of a Foreign Legionary more convinced of the value of the Foreign Legion; it would seem as though these categories promised some last shred of predictable treatment, as though they embodied some last and hence most fundamental juridical identity.

While the classification of inmates by categories is only a tactical, organizational measure, the arbitrary selection of victims indicates the essential principle of the institution. If the concentration camps had been dependent on the existence of political adversaries, they would scarcely have survived the first years of the totalitarian regimes. One only has to take a look at the number of inmates at Buchenwald in the years after 1936 in order to understand how absolutely necessary the element of the innocent was for the continued existence of the camps. "The camps would have died out if in making its arrests the Gestapo had considered only the principle of opposition,"[148] and toward the end of 1937 Buchenwald, with less than 1,000 inmates, was close to dying out until the November pogroms brought more than 20,000 new arrivals.[149] In Germany, this element of the innocent was furnished in vast numbers by the Jews since 1938; in Russia, it consisted of random groups of the population which for some reason entirely unconnected with their actions had fallen into disgrace.[150] But if in Germany the really totalitarian type of concentration camp with its enormous majority of completely "innocent" inmates was not established until 1938, in Russia it goes back to the early thirties, since up to 1930 the majority of the concentration-camp population still consisted of criminals, counterrevolutionaries and "politicals" (meaning, in this case, members of deviationist factions). Since then there have been so many innocent people in the camps that it is difficult to classify them—persons who had some sort of contact with a foreign country, Russians of Polish origin (particularly in the years 1936 to 1938), peasants whose villages for some economic reason were liquidated, deported nationalities, demobilized soldiers of the Red Army who happened to belong to regiments that stayed too long abroad as occupation forces or had become prisoners of war in Germany, etc. But the existence of a political opposition is for a concentration-camp system only a pretext, and the purpose of the system is not achieved even when, under the most monstrous terror, the population becomes more or less voluntarily co-ordinated, *i.e.,* relinquishes its political rights. The aim of an arbitrary system is to destroy the civil rights of the whole population, who ultimately become just as outlawed in their own country as the stateless and homeless. The destruction of a man's rights, the killing of the juridical person in him, is a prerequisite for dominating him entirely. And this applies not only to special categories such as criminals, political opponents, Jews, homosexuals, on whom the early experiments were made, but to every inhabitant of a totalitarian state. Free consent is as much an obstacle to total domination as free opposition.[151] The arbitrary arrest which chooses among innocent people destroys the validity of free consent, just as torture—as distinguished from death—destroys the possibility of opposition.

Any, even the most tyrannical, restriction of this arbitrary persecution to certain opinions of a religious or political nature, to certain modes of intellectual or erotic social behavior, to certain freshly invented "crimes," would render the camps superfluous, because in the long run no attitude and no opinion can withstand the threat of so much horror; and above all it would make for a new system of justice, which, given any stability at all, could not fail to produce a new juridical person in man, that would elude the totalitarian domination. The so-called *"Volksnutzen"* of the Nazis, constantly fluctuating (because what is useful today can be injurious tomorrow) and the eternally shifting party line of the Soviet Union which, being retroactive, almost daily makes new groups of people available for the concentration camps, are the only guaranty for the continued existence of the concentration camps, and hence for the continued total disfranchisement of man.

The next decisive step in the preparation of living corpses is the murder of the moral person in man. This is done in the main by making martyrdom, for the first time in history, impossible: "How many people here still believe that a protest has even historic importance? This skepticism is the real masterpiece of the SS. Their great accomplishment. They have corrupted all human solidarity. Here the night has fallen on the future. When no witnesses are left, there can be no testimony. To demonstrate when death can no longer be postponed is an attempt to give death a meaning, to act beyond one's own death. In order to be successful, a gesture must have social meaning. There are hundreds of thousands of us here, all living in absolute solitude. That is why we are subdued no matter what happens."[152]

The camps and the murder of political adversaries are only part of organized oblivion that not only embraces carriers of public opinion such as the spoken and the written word, but extends even to the families and friends of the victim. Grief and remembrance are forbidden. In the Soviet Union a woman will sue for divorce immediately after her husband's arrest in order to save the lives of her children; if her husband chances to come back, she will indignantly turn him out of the house.[153] The Western world has hitherto, even in its darkest periods, granted the slain enemy the right to be remembered as a self-evident acknowledgment of the fact that we are all men (and *only* men). It is only because even Achilles set out for Hector's funeral, only because the most despotic governments honored the slain enemy, only because the Romans allowed the Christians to write their martyrologies, only because the Church kept its heretics alive in the memory of men, that all was not lost and never could be lost. The concentration camps, by making death itself anonymous (making it impossible to find out whether a prisoner is dead or alive) robbed death of its meaning as the end of a fulfilled life. In a sense they took away the individual's own death, proving that henceforth nothing belonged to him and he belonged to no one. His death merely set a seal on the fact that he had never really existed.

This attack on the moral person might still have been opposed by man's conscience which tells him that it is better to die a victim than to live as a bureaucrat of murder. Totalitarian terror achieved its most terrible triumph when it succeeded in cutting the moral person off from the individualist escape and in making the decisions of conscience absolutely questionable and equivocal. When a man is faced with the alternative of betraying and thus murdering his friends or of sending his wife and children, for whom he is in every sense responsible, to their death; when even suicide would mean the immediate murder of his own family—how is he to decide? The alternative is no longer between good and evil, but between murder and murder. Who could solve the moral dilemma of the Greek mother, who was allowed by the Nazis to choose which of her three children should be killed?[154]

Through the creation of conditions under which conscience ceases to be adequate and to do good becomes utterly impossible, the consciously organized complicity of all men in the crimes of totalitarian regimes is extended to the victims and thus made really total. The SS implicated concentration-camp inmates—criminals, politicals, Jews—in their crimes by making them responsible for a large part of the administration, thus confronting them with the hopeless dilemma whether to send their friends to their death, or to help murder other men who happened to be strangers, and forcing them, in any event, to behave like murderers.[155] The point is not only that hatred is diverted from those who are guilty (the *capos* were more hated than the SS), but that the distinguishing line between persecutor and persecuted, between the murderer and his victim, is constantly blurred.[156]

Once the moral person has been killed, the one thing that still prevents men from being made into living corpses is the differentiation of the individual, his unique identity. In a sterile form such individuality can be preserved through a persistent stoicism, and it is certain that many men under totalitarian rule have taken and are each day still taking refuge in this absolute isolation of a personality without rights or conscience. There is no doubt that this part of the human person, precisely because it depends so essentially on nature and on forces that cannot be controlled by the will, is the hardest to destroy (and when destroyed is most easily repaired).[157]

The methods of dealing with this uniqueness of the human person are numerous and we shall not attempt to list them. They begin with the monstrous conditions in the transports to the camps, when hundreds of human beings are packed into a cattle-car stark naked, glued to each other, and shunted back and forth over the countryside for days on end; they continue upon arrival at the camp, the well-organized shock of the first hours, the shaving of the head, the grotesque camp clothing; and they end in the utterly unimaginable tortures so gauged as not to kill the body, at any event not quickly. The aim of all these methods, in any case, is to manipulate the human body—with its infinite possibilities of suffering—in such a way as to make it destroy the human person as inexorably as do certain mental diseases of organic origin.

It is here that the utter lunacy of the entire process becomes most apparent. Torture, to be sure, is an essential feature of the whole totalitarian police and judiciary apparatus; it is used every day to make people talk. This type of torture, since it pursues a definite, rational aim, has certain limitations: either the prisoner talks within a certain time, or he is killed. To this rationally conducted torture another, irrational, sadistic type was added in the first Nazi concentration camps and in the cellars of the Gestapo. Carried on for the most part by the SA, it pursued no aims and was not systematic, but depended on the initiative of largely abnormal elements. The mortality was so high that only a few concentration-camp inmates of 1933 survived these first years. This type of torture seemed to be not so much a calculated political institution as a concession of the regime to its criminal and abnormal elements, who were thus rewarded for services rendered. Behind the blind bestiality of the SA, there often lay a deep hatred and resentment against all those who were socially, intellectually, or physically better off than themselves, and who now, as if in fulfillment of their wildest dreams, were in their power. This resentment, which never died out entirely in the camps, strikes us as a last remnant of humanly understandable feeling.[158]

The real horror began, however, when the SS took over the administration of the camps. The old spontaneous bestiality gave way to an absolutely cold and systematic destruction of human bodies, calculated to destroy human dignity; death was avoided or postponed indefinitely. The camps were no longer amusement parks for beasts in human form, that is, for men who really belonged in mental institutions and prisons; the reverse became true: they were turned into "drill grounds," on which perfectly normal men were trained to be full-fledged members of the SS.[159]

The killing of man's individuality, of the uniqueness shaped in equal parts by nature, will, and destiny, which has become so self-evident a premise for all human relations that even identical twins inspire a certain uneasiness, creates a horror that vastly overshadows the outrage of the juridical-political person and the despair of the moral person. It is this horror that gives rise to the nihilistic generalizations which maintain plausibly enough that essentially all men alike are beasts.[160] Actually the experience of the concentration camps does show that human beings can be transformed into specimens of the human animal, and that man's "nature" is only "human" insofar as it opens up to man the possibility of becoming something highly unnatural, that is, a man.

After murder of the moral person and annihilation of the juridical person, the destruction of the individuality is almost always successful. Conceivably some laws of mass psychology may be found to explain why millions of human beings allowed themselves to be marched unresistingly into the gas chambers, although these laws would explain nothing else but the destruction of individuality. It is more significant that those individually condemned to death very seldom attempted to take one of their executioners with them, that there were scarcely any serious revolts, and that even in the moment of liberation there were very few spontaneous massacres of SS men. For to destroy individuality is to destroy spontaneity, man's power to begin something new out of his own resources, something that cannot be explained on the basis of reactions to environment and events.[161] Nothing then remains but ghastly marionettes with human faces, which all behave like the dog in Pavlov's experiments, which all react with perfect reliability even when going to their own death, and which do nothing but react. This is the real triumph of the system: "The triumph of the SS demands that the tortured victim allow himself to be led to the noose without protesting, that he renounce and abandon himself to the point of ceasing to affirm his identity. And it is not for nothing. It is not gratuitously, out of sheer sadism, that the SS men desire his defeat. They know that the system which succeeds in destroying its victim before he mounts the scaffold … is incomparably the best for keeping a whole people in slavery. In submission. Nothing is more terrible than these processions of human beings going like dummies to their death. The man who sees this says to himself: 'For them to be thus reduced, what power must be concealed in the hands of the masters,' and he turns away, full of bitterness but defeated."[162]

If we take totalitarian aspirations seriously and refuse to be misled by the common-sense assertion that they are utopian and unrealizable, it develops that the society of the dying established in the camps is the only form of society in which it is possible to dominate man entirely. Those who aspire to total domination must liquidate all spontaneity, such as the mere existence of individuality will always engender, and track it down in its most private forms, regardless of how unpolitical and harmless these may seem. Pavlov's dog, the human specimen reduced to the most elementary reactions, the bundle of reactions that can always be liquidated and replaced by other bundles of reactions that behave in exactly the same way, is the model "citizen" of a totalitarian state; and such a citizen can be produced only imperfectly outside of the camps.

The uselessness of the camps, their cynically admitted anti-utility, is only apparent. In reality they are most essential to the preservation of the regime's power than any of its other institutions. Without concentration camps, without the undefined fear they inspire and the very well-defined training they offer in totalitarian domination, which can nowhere else be fully tested with all of its most radical possibilities, a totalitarian state can neither inspire its nuclear troops with fanaticism nor maintain a whole people in complete apathy. The dominating and the dominated would only too quickly sink back into the "old bourgeois routine"; after early "excesses," they would succumb to everyday life with its human laws; in short, they would develop in the direction which all observers counseled by common sense were so prone to predict. The tragic fallacy of all these prophecies, originating in a world that was still safe, was to suppose that there was such a thing as one human nature established for all time, to identify this human nature with history, and thus to declare that the idea of total domination was not only inhuman but also unrealistic. Meanwhile we have learned that the power of man is so great that he really can be what he wishes to be.

It is in the very nature of totalitarian regimes to demand unlimited power. Such power can only be secured if literally all men, without a single exception, are reliably dominated in every aspect of their life. In the realm of foreign affairs new neutral territories must constantly be subjugated, while at home ever-new human groups must be mastered in expanding concentration camps, or, when circumstances require liquidated to make room for others. The question of opposition is unimportant both in foreign and domestic affairs. Any neutrality, indeed any spontaneously given friendship, is from the standpoint of totalitarian domination just as dangerous as open hostility, precisely because spontaneity as such, with its incalculability, is the greatest of all obstacles to total domination over man. The Communists of non-Communist countries, who fled or were called to Moscow, learned by bitter experience that they constituted a menace to the Soviet Union. Convinced Communists are in this sense, which alone has any reality today, just as ridiculous and just as menacing to the regime in Russia, as, for example, the convinced Nazis of the Röhm faction were to the Nazis.

What makes conviction and opinion of any sort so ridiculous and dangerous under totalitarian conditions is that totalitarian regimes take the greatest pride in having no need of them, or of any human help of any kind. Men insofar as they are more than animal reaction and fulfillment of functions are entirely superfluous to totalitarian regimes. Totalitarianism strives not toward despotic rule over men, but toward a system in which men are superfluous. Total power can be achieved and safeguarded only in a world of conditioned reflexes, of marionettes without the slightest trace of spontaneity. Precisely because man's resources are so great, he can be fully dominated only when he becomes a specimen of the animal-species man.

Therefore character is a threat and even the most unjust legal rules are an obstacle; but individuality, anything indeed that distinguishes one man from another, is intolerable. As long as all men have not been made equally superfluous—and this has been accomplished only in concentration camps—the ideal of totalitarian domination has not been achieved. Totalitarian states strive constantly, though never with complete success, to establish the superfluity of man—by the arbitrary selection of various groups for concentration camps, by constant purges of the ruling apparatus, by mass liquidations. Common sense protests desperately that the masses are submissive and that all this gigantic apparatus of terror is therefore superfluous; if they were capable of telling the truth, the totalitarian rulers would reply: The apparatus seems superfluous to you only because it serves to make men superfluous.

The totalitarian attempt to make men superfluous reflects the experience of modern masses of their superfluity on an overcrowded earth. The world of the dying, in which men are taught they are superfluous through a way of life in which punishment is meted out without connection with crime, in which exploitation is practiced without profit, and where work is performed without product, is a place where senselessness is daily produced anew. Yet, within the framework of the totalitarian ideology, nothing could be more sensible and logical; if the inmates are vermin, it is logical that they should be killed by poison gas; if they are degenerate, they should not be allowed to contaminate the population; if they have "slave-like souls" (Himmler), no one should waste his time trying to re-educate them. Seen through the eyes of the ideology, the trouble with the camps is almost that they make too much sense, that the execution of the doctrine is too consistent.

While the totalitarian regimes are thus resolutely and cynically emptying the world of the only thing that makes sense to the utilitarian expectations of common sense, they impose upon it at the same time a kind of supersense which the ideologies actually always meant when they pretended to have found the key to history or the solution to the riddles of the universe. Over and above the senselessness of totalitarian society is enthroned the ridiculous supersense of its ideological superstition. Ideologies are harmless, uncritical, and arbitrary opinions only as long as they are not believed in seriously. Once their claim to total validity is taken literally they become the nuclei of logical systems in which, as in the systems of paranoiacs, everything follows comprehensibly and even compulsorily once the first premise is accepted. The insanity of such systems lies not only in their first premise but in the very logicality with which they are constructed. The curious logicality of all isms, their simple-minded trust in the salvation value of stubborn devotion without regard for specific, varying factors, already harbors the first germs of totalitarian contempt for reality and factuality.

Common sense trained in utilitarian thinking is helpless against this ideological supersense, since totalitarian regimes establish a functioning world of no-sense. The ideological contempt for factuality still contained the proud assumption of human mastery over the world; it is, after all, contempt for reality which makes possible changing the world, the erection of the human artifice. What destroys the element of pride in the totalitarian contempt for reality (and thereby distinguishes it radically from revolutionary theories and attitudes) is the supersense which gives the contempt for reality its cogency, logicality, and consistency. What makes a truly totalitarian device out of the Bolshevik claim that the present Russian system is superior to all others is the fact that the totalitarian ruler draws from this claim the logically impeccable conclusion that without this system people never could have built such a wonderful thing as, let us say, a subway; from this, he again draws the logical conclusion that anyone who knows of the existence of the Paris subway is a suspect because he may cause people to doubt that one can do things only in the Bolshevik way. This leads to the final conclusion that in order to remain a loyal Bolshevik, you have to destroy the Paris subway. Nothing matters but consistency.

With these new structures, built on the strength of supersense and driven by the motor of logicality, we are indeed at the end of the bourgeois era of profits and power, as well as at the end of imperialism and expansion. The aggressiveness of totalitarianism springs not from lust for power, and if it feverishly seeks to expand, it does so neither for expansion's sake nor for profit, but only for ideological reasons: to make the world consistent, to prove that its respective supersense has been right.

It is chiefly for the sake of this supersense, for the sake of complete consistency, that it is necessary for totalitarianism to destroy every trace of what we commonly call human dignity. For respect for human dignity implies the recognition of my fellow-men or our fellow-nations as subjects, as builders of worlds or cobuilders of a common world. No ideology which aims at the explanation of all historical events of the past and at mapping out the course of all events of the future can bear the unpredictability which springs from the fact that men are creative, that they can bring forward something so new that nobody ever foresaw it.

What totalitarian ideologies therefore aim at is not the transformation of the outside world or the revolutionizing transmutation of society, but the transformation of human nature itself. The concentration camps are the laboratories where changes in human nature are tested, and their shamefulness therefore is not just the business of their inmates and those who run them according to strictly "scientific" standards; it is the concern of all men. Suffering, of which there has been always too much on earth, is not the issue, nor is the number of victims. Human nature as such is at stake, and even though it seems that these experiments succeed not in changing man but only in destroying him, by creating a society in which the nihilistic banality of *homo homini lupus* is consistently realized, one should bear in mind the necessary limitations to an experiment which requires global control in order to show conclusive results.

Until now the totalitarian belief that everything is possible seems to have proved only that everything can be destroyed. Yet, in their effort to prove that everything is possible, totalitarian regimes have discovered without knowing it that there are crimes which men can neither punish nor forgive. When the impossible was made possible it became the unpunishable, unforgivable absolute evil which could no longer be understood and explained by the evil motives of self-interest, greed, covetousness, resentment, lust for power, and cowardice; and which therefore anger could not revenge, love could not endure, friendship could not forgive. Just as the victims in the death factories or the holes of oblivion are no longer "human" in the eyes of their executioners, so this newest species of criminals is beyond the pale even of solidarity in human sinfulness.

It is inherent in our entire philosophical tradition that we cannot conceive of a "radical evil," and this is true both for Christian theology, which conceded even to the Devil himself a celestial origin, as well as for Kant, the only philosopher who, in the word he coined for it, at least must have suspected the existence of this evil even though he immediately rationalized it in the concept of a "perverted ill will" that could be explained by comprehensible motives. Therefore, we actually have nothing to fall back on in order to understand a phenomenon that nevertheless confronts us with its overpowering reality and breaks down all standards we know. There is only one thing that seems to be discernible: we may say that radical evil has emerged in connection with a system in which all men have become equally superfluous. The manipulators of this system believe in their own superfluousness as much as in that of all others, and the totalitarian murderers are all the more dangerous because they do not care if they themselves are alive or dead, if they ever lived or never were born. The danger of the corpse factories and holes of oblivion is that today, with populations and homelessness everywhere on the increase, masses of people are continuously rendered superfluous if we continue to think of our world in utilitarian terms. Political, social, and economic events everywhere are in a silent conspiracy with totalitarian instruments devised for making men superfluous. The implied temptation is well understood by the utilitarian common sense of the masses, who in most countries are too desperate to retain much fear of death. The Nazis and the Bolsheviks can be sure that their factories of annihilation which demonstrate the swiftest solution to the problem of overpopulation, of economically superfluous and socially rootless human masses, are as much of an attraction as a warning. Totalitarian solutions may well survive the fall of totalitarian regimes in the form of strong temptations which will come up whenever it seems impossible to alleviate political, social, or economic misery in a manner worthy of man.

Notes

140. Theodor Maunz, *Gestalt und Recht der Polizei* (Hamburg, 1943), p. 50, insists that criminals should never be sent to the camps for the time of their regular sentences.

141. The shortage of prison space in Russia has been such that in the year 1925–26, only 36 per cent of all court sentences could be carried out. See David J. Dallin and Boris I. Nicolaevsky, *Forced Labor In Russia*, (1947), p. 158 ff.

142. "Gestapo and SS have always attached great importance to mixing the categories of inmates in the camps. In no camp have the inmates belonged exclusively to one category" (Eugen Kogon, *Der SS-Staat, Munich*, 1946, p. 19).

   In Russia, it has also been customary from the beginning to mix political prisoners and criminals. During the first ten years of Soviet power, the Left political groups enjoyed certain privileges; only with the full development of the totalitarian character of the regime "after the end of the twenties the politicals were even officially treated as inferior to the common criminals" (Dallin. and Nicolaevsky, p. 177 ff.).

143. Rousset's book suffers from his overestimation of the influence of the German Communists, who dominated the internal administration of Buchenwald during the war. (David Rousset, *Univers Concentrationnaire*, 1947)

144. See for instance the testimony of Mrs. Buber-Neumann (former wife of the German Communist Heinz Neumann), who survived Soviet and German concentration camps: "The Russians never … evinced the sadistic streak of the Nazis. … Our Russian guards were decent men and not sadists, but they faithfully fulfilled the requirements of the inhuman system" (Margarete Buber-Neumann, *Under Two Dictators*, 1949).

145. Bruno Bettelheim, "Behavior in Extreme Situations," in *Journal of Abnormal and Social Psychology*, Vol. XXXVIII, No. 4, 1943, describes the self-esteem of the criminals and the political prisoners as compared with those who have not done anything. The latter "were least able to withstand the initial shock," the first to disintegrate. Bettelheim blames this on their middle-class origin.

146. Rousset, *op. cit.*, p. 71.

147. For conditions in French concentration camps, see Arthur Koestler, *Scum of the Earth*, 1941.

148. Kogon, *op. cit.*, p. 6.

149. See *Nazi Conspiracy*, IV, 800 f.

150. Beck and Godin, *op. cit.*, stale explicitly that "opponents constituted only a relatively small proportion of the [Russian] prison population" (p. 87), and that there was no connection whatever between "a man's imprisonment and any offense" (p. 95).

151. Bruno Bettelheim, "On Dachau and Buchenwald," when discussing the fact that most prisoners "made their peace with the values of the Gestapo," emphasizes that "this was not the result of propaganda ... the Gestapo insisted that it would prevent them from expressing their feelings anyway" (pp. 834–35).

    Himmler explicitly prohibited propaganda of any kind in the camps. "Education consists of discipline, never of any kind of instruction on an ideological basis." "On Organization and Obligation of the SS and the Police," in *Nationalpolitischer Lehrgang der Wehrmacht*, 1937. Quoted from *Nazi Conspiracy*, IV, 616 ff.

152. Rousset, *op. cit.*, p. 464.

153. See the report of Sergei Malakhov in David J. Dallin and Boris I. Nicolaevsky, *Forced Labor in Russia*, 1947.

154. See Albert Camus in *Twice A Year*, 1947.

155. Rousset's book, *op. cit.*, consists largely of discussions of this dilemma by prisoners.

156. Bettelheim, *op. cit.*, describes the process by which the guards as well as the prisoners became "conditioned" to the life in the camp and were afraid of returning to the outer world.

    Rousset, therefore, is right when he insists that the truth is that "victim and executioner are alike ignoble; the lesson of the camps is the brotherhood of abjection" (p. 588).

157. Bettelheim, *op cit.*, describes how "the main concern of the new prisoners seemed to be to remain intact as a personality" while the problem of the old prisoners was "how to live as well as possible within the camp."

158. Rousset, *op. cit.*, p. 390, reports an SS-man haranguing a professor as follows: "You used to be a professor. Well, you're no professor now. You're no big shot any more. You're nothing but a little runt now. Just as little as you can be. I'm the big fellow now."

159. Kogon, *op. cit.*, p. 6, speaks of the possibility that the camps will be maintained as training and experimental grounds for the SS. He also gives a good report on the difference between the early camps administered by the SA and the later ones under the SS. "None of these first camps had more than a thousand inmates. ... Life in them beggared all description. The accounts of the few old prisoners who survived those years agree that there was scarcely any form of sadistic perversion that was not practiced by the SA men. But they were all acts of individual bestiality, there was still no fully organized cold system, embracing masses of men. This was the accomplishment of the SS" (p. 7).

    This new mechanized system eased the feeling of responsibility as much as was humanly possible. When, for instance, the order came to kill every day several hundred Russian prisoners, the slaughter was performed by shooting through a hole without seeing the victim. (See Ernest Feder, "Essai sur la Psychologie de la Terreur," in *Synthèses*. Brussels, 1946.) On the other hand, perversion was artificially produced in otherwise normal men. Rousset reports the following from a SS guard: "Usually I keep on hitting until I ejaculate. I have a wife and three children in Breslau I used to be perfectly normal. That's what they've made of me. Now when they give me a pass out of here, I don't go home. I don't dare look my wife in the face" (p. 273).—The documents from the Hitler era contain numerous testimonials for the average normality of those entrusted with carrying out Hitler's program of extermination. A good collection is found in Léon Poliakov's "The Weapon of Antisemitism," published by UNESCO in *The Third Reich*, London, 1955. Most of the men in the units used for these purposes were not volunteers but had been drafted from the ordinary police for these special assignments. But even trained SS-men found this kind of duty worse than front-line fighting. In his report of a mass execution by the SS, an eyewitness gives high praise to this troop which had been so "idealistic" that it was able to bear "the entire extermination without the help of liquor."

    That one wanted to eliminate all personal motives and passions during the "exterminations" and hence keep the cruelties to a minimum is revealed by the fact that a group of doctors and engineers entrusted with handling the gas installations were making constant improvements that were not only designed to raise the productive capacity of the corpse factories but also to accelerate and ease the agony of death.

160. This is very prominent in Rousset's work. "The social conditions of life in the camps have transformed the great mass of inmates, both the Germans and the deportees, regardless of their previous social position and education ... into a degenerate rabble, entirely submissive to the primitive reflexes of the animal instinct" (p. 183).

161. In this context also belongs the astonishing rarity of suicides in the camps. Suicide occurred far more often before arrest and deportation than in the camp itself, which is of course partly explained by the fact that every attempt was made to prevent suicides which are, after all, spontaneous acts. From the statistical material for Buchenwald (*Nazi Conspiracy*, IV, 800 ff.) it is evident that scarcely more than one-half per cent of the deaths could be traced to suicide, that frequently there were only two suicides per year, although in the same year the total number of deaths reached 3,516. The reports from Russian camps mention the same phenomenon. Cf., for instance, Starlinger, *op. cit.*, p. 57.

162. Rousset, *op. cit.*, p. 525.

10
Philip Rahv (1908–1973)
The Sense and Nonsense of Whittaker Chambers (1952)

Editor's Introduction

When Philip Rahv reviewed Whittaker Chambers' massive and important *Witness* in 1952, he employed many of the same arguments against absolutism and for pragmatism that the New York Intellectuals as a whole were beginning to use more frequently after World War II. But where Sidney Hook's and Hannah Arendt's political sense originated in philosophy, Rahv brought a literary temperament to the evaluation of Chambers' story.

It was no accident that Rahv chose to compare Chambers to the Russian novelist Dostoevsky. Chambers, while still in college at Columbia, fell under the spell of the dramatic predictions made in the Soviet Union about the inevitable future of world history, and when he placed a bet on the outcome of that forecast he cast himself into a role that befit a dark and dedicated Dostoevskean character. He lived his role as a member of the Communist underground in the early 1930s, and so he described his journey in *Witness*. Chambers, as Rahv phrased it, displayed "that peculiar note of personal intensity and spiritual truculence, of commitment to the 'Idea' so absolute as to suggest that life had no meaning apart from it." Chambers' sin was not that he lived in an apocalyptic world, not that he saw so clearly and so much earlier than others the potential doom of freedom and conscience represented in the ideologies of the 1930s. Instead, his error, as the New York Intellectuals witnessed, was that he became fused with that fanatical world and only fed its most zealous and absolute tendencies.

After his affair with Soviet Communism ended, Chambers turned against not only Communism but everything to the left of patriotic small-government Americanism. Incensed, Rahv defended the liberal New Deal and even the integrity of socialism against Chambers' portrayal of tyranny, and he accused Chambers of standing on the dangerous fanatical ground of a Dostoevskean character when he "refuses to distinguish in principle between liberals, socialists, and party-line Communists, whatever the divergences among them. Regardless of their political practice at any given time, in theory they are all equally committed to unbelief, to the elevation of man above God," and thus all are to be opposed equally forcefully as a supreme danger.

In *Witness*, Chambers proudly walks out of the dark forest marked *absolutist ideology* and follows the road marked *religious faith*, which takes him not to the moderate center but, according to Rahv, simply loops him back into fanaticism and mystery, back into an only slightly less dangerous part of the wood. If only Chambers had been more attentive to the lesson of the Grand Inquisitor in Dostoevsky's *Notes from Underground*. "In that legend," Rahv explains, "Dostoevsky tells us that religion too, yes, even the religion of Christ, can be transformed into an instrument of power in the hands of a self-chosen elite bent on depriving men of their freedom and organizing a 'universal human antheap.'"

Rahv's fear of Chambers' replacing the mystery, authority and prerogative of the Party with that of the Church echoes Hook's anxiety, a decade earlier, about the new failure of nerve. It takes courage, according to the New York Intellectuals, to live in a tentative world, one without the assurance of the truth. Chambers at one point in his book, Rahv complains, hopes "to answer once [*and*] for all two questions: Can a man go on living in a world that is dying? If he can, what should he do in the crisis of the twentieth century?" Rahv takes these questions as evidence of Chambers' "thoroughly ideologized" view of life. "Essentially," Rahv warns, "it is the idea that in order to live at all one must first ascertain the answer to the ultimate questions—an idea so utterly unpragmatic that one is almost tempted to call it 'un-American.'"

Source

Philip Rahv, "The Sense and Nonsense of Whittaker Chambers," *Partisan Review* vol.19, no. 4, July–August 1952.

Selected Readings

Whittaker Chambers, *Witness* (New York: Random House, 1952).
Lionel Trilling, *The Middle of the Journey* (New York: Viking, 1947).

∗ ∗ ∗ ∗ ∗

What chiefly caught my interest when I first encountered Whittaker Chambers, back in the early thirties not long before the "underground" claimed him, was something in his talk and manner, a vibration, an accent, that I can only describe as Dostoevskyean in essence. I thought at the time that he was far from unconscious of the effect he produced. He had the air of a man who took more pleasure in the stylized than in the natural qualities of his personality. Still, whether aware or not, it was distinctly the Dostoevskyean note that he struck—that peculiar note of personal intensity and spiritual truculence, of commitment to the "Idea" so absolute as to suggest that life had no meaning apart from it, all oddly combined with a flair for mystification and melodrama. That early impression, since confirmed by other people, is now re-affirmed in his book.

Witness is in the main a fully convincing account of the role its author played in the Hiss case. It is also a heady mixture of autobiography, politics, and apocalyptic prophecy; and it contains a good many of the characteristic elements of a production à la Dostoevsky, above all the atmosphere of scandal and monstrous imputation, the furtive meetings and the secret agents, the spies, informers, and policemen, desperate collisions, extreme ideas, suffering, pity, and remorse, the entire action moving inexorably toward the typical *dénouement* of a judicial trial, in the course of which heroes and victims alike are exposed as living prey to the crowds and all the secrets come tumbling out.

The influence of the Russian novelist is literally everywhere in the book, in the action as in the moral import, in the plot no less than in the ideology. And Chambers goes in for ideology without stint or limit. Even his Maryland farm, of which he writes at great length, is at once a real place and a piece of ideology pure and simple. And the ideology is fashioned in accordance with the precepts of the Russian master, from whom he borrows some of his key terms and characteristic turns of thought. Thus Chambers seems to have appropriated, lock, stock, and barrel, the entire Dostoevskyean polemic against socialism as the culminating movement of Western rationalism and secularism, leading through the rejection of God to the deification of man. He accuses the radicals of worshiping "Almighty man," just as the creator of Ivan Karamazov accused them of worshiping the "man-god," and refuses to distinguish in principle between liberals, socialists, and party-line communists, whatever the divergences among them. Regardless of their political practice at any given time, in theory they are all equally committed to unbelief, to the elevation of man above God—the supreme act of rebellion converting man into a monster.

That is exactly the approach of Dostoevsky, who also saw no reason to discriminate among the varieties of free thought. (He did not hesitate, for instance, to lay the blame for the criminal acts of Nechayev—the model for the sinister figure of Pyotr Verhovensky in *The Possessed*—not only upon such revolutionary theorists as Belinsky and Herzen but also upon the far more moderate liberal idealists of the type of Granovsky, a Moscow professor who taught his students scarcely anything more virulent than that man was a creature endowed with a mind and that it was his duty to use it.) Science and reason are the enemy. And what is socialism? According to Dostoevsky it is "not merely the labor question, it is before all else the atheistic question, the question of the form taken by atheism today, the question of the tower of Babel built without God, not to mount from earth to Heaven, but to set up Heaven on earth." This, indeed, is the *locus classicus*. It is the pivotal thought of Chambers' book. But there are other ideas in Dostoevsky which he entirely ignores; and with good reason, for they emphatically call into question his view of religion as the one secure basis of freedom. Perhaps he would not be so certain of their "indivisible" union if he had been more attentive to the important historical lesson contained in the legend of the Grand Inquisitor—a lesson which belies the national-religious thesis of Dostoevsky's work as a whole and which is a deadly critique of the shallow doctrine that if men but believed they would soon enter the promised spiritual kingdom. In that legend Dostoevsky tells us that religion too, yes, even the religion of Christ, can be transformed into an instrument of power in the hands of a self-chosen elite bent on depriving men of their freedom and organizing a "universal human antheap." And it is precisely men's readiness to believe and their irresistible craving for "community of worship," the principal source of bigotry and intolerance, that induces them to accept the total claims of their rulers.

The Russian writer's influence on Chambers is one-sided but very real. In the biographical chapters, too, the story is sometimes given a Dostoevskyean twist. Consider the following brief passage in which, while recalling his student days at Columbia, Chambers portrays himself for all the world as if he were writing not about a boy from Long Island but a blood brother of Shatov or Raskolnikov, brooding in the Russian cold about the ultimate problems of existence. "One day, early in 1925, I sat down on a concrete bench on the Columbia campus, facing a little Greek shrine and the statue of my old political hero, Alexander Hamilton. The sun was shining, but it was chilly, and I sat huddled in my overcoat. I was there to answer once for all two questions: Can a man go on living in a world that is dying? If he can, what should he do in the crisis of the twentieth century?" The "huddled in my overcoat" is a good touch; but the peremptory "to answer *once for all* two questions" (and what questions!) is really priceless. Here, histrionics aside, it is not only the inflection of the narrative line which reminds us of the author of *Crime and Punishment*; even more suggestive is the thoroughly *ideologized* conceptions of life it reveals. Essentially it is the idea that in order to live at all one must first ascertain the answer to the ultimate questions—an idea so utterly unpragmatic that one is almost tempted to call it "unAmerican."

However, in spite of Chambers' wonderful aptitude for turning ideas into dramatic motives, in its lack of humor and irony his book is anything but Dostoevskyean. His seriousness is of that portentous kind which in a novelist we would at once recognize as a failure of sensibility. For Chambers eliminates from his account anything that might conceivably be taken as ambiguous or incongruous in his own motives and convictions, and this permits him to bear down all the more heavily on those of his opponents. No sense of humor or irony can survive that sort of attack. He is a splendid satirist; the mordant phrase, manipulated with ease and perfect timing, is ever at his disposal; but of that true irony, which implicates the person writing no less than other people, the subject as well as the object, there is not a trace in his pages. This deficiency makes it hard for him both to modulate his ideas and to relate himself to them without pomposity and self-conceit. Perhaps that will explain the occasional lapses in taste and the tone of heroic self-dramatization which is sometimes indistinguishable from sheer bathos, as when he writes that at issue in the

Hiss case was "the question whether this sick society, which we call Western civilization, could in its extremity still cast up a man whose faith in it was so great that he would voluntarily abandon those things which men hold good, including life, to defend it."

And his prose is open to criticism on related grounds. He is a born writer, greatly accomplished in a technical sense. Yet his prose, for all its unusual merit, is not very adaptable to confessional writing. Tightly organized and controlled, even streamlined, though in the best sense of that much-abused word, it is hardly an appropriate medium for the expression of intimate personal truth or the exploration of inner life. It shuns the spontaneous and repels subjectivity.

The fact is that when we are through reading this enormously long book, with its masses of detail, we are still left with very little knowledge of the author as a person. We have been instructed in his politics and in his philosophy; we have learned much about his childhood years, so fearfully depressing and ill-making; and we have learned to know him in his successive adult roles—Communist Party member, Soviet agent, editor of *Time*, Maryland farmer, convert, and witness. None the less he remains shielded from us to the very end, encased in his "character-armor." We communicate almost exclusively with the externalized Chambers, a man apparently bent on transforming his life into a public destiny, incapable of projecting himself on any level but that of objectified meaning, and possessed by a lust for the Absolute (the ultimate and unqualified pledge of objective Being). He is certain of its existence; and he finds it—invariably. First History, now God. For he repented of his unbelief even before he openly emerged from the Communist underground, thus insuring himself of uninterrupted contact with the Absolute.

One wishes that Chambers had absorbed less of Dostoevsky's political ideology—a sphere in which he is assuredly a false guide—and had instead absorbed more of his insight into unconscious motivation and the cunning maneuvers of the battered ego in reaching out for self-esteem, pleasure, and power. He might then not be quite so intent on dissolving the concrete existence of men in their specific conditions of life into the abstractions of the impersonal Idea, whether in its idealist or materialist version. (The difference between the two versions is not half so great as the devotees of metaphysics imagine.) Nor would he take it for granted, as he now does, that behavior can be directly deduced from ideology, thus overlooking the fact that the relation between them is frequently not only indirect but devious and thoroughly distorted.

But to Chambers the Idea is everything; men nothing. The role of personality in history is abolished. For instance, he absolves Stalin of responsibility for any and all of the evils of Communism, and even goes so far as to characterize him as a "revolutionary statesman" for carrying through the Great Purge. ("From the Communist viewpoint, Stalin could have taken no other course, so long as he believed he was right. ... That was the horror of the Purge—that acting as a Communist, Stalin had acted rightly.") This is sheer fantasy. What evidence is there that the Purge advanced the cause of Communism, that it was in any sense "objectively necessary," or that Stalin was under any illusions as to its effect? It should be obvious that the Purge strengthened Stalin's personal dictatorship at the cost of considerably weakening the Communist movement the world over. It shook the faith of millions in the Soviet myth. (For that matter, Chambers himself might still be numbered among the faithful if not for the Purge, the direct cause of his break.) After all, no policy that Stalin promulgated *after* the Purge could have been seriously resisted, let alone blocked, by the abject and beaten Old Guard of the Revolution. Not the necessities, real or imaginary, of the revolutionary cause but the drive for unlimited power on the part of Stalin and his faction, who have never hesitated to sacrifice the good of the cause for their own advantage, is the one plausible explanation of the Purge.

Chambers appears to have quit the Communist Party cherishing some of the same illusions with which he entered it. He was certainly close enough to the Stalinist oligarchy to have learned that it has long ago ceased to regard power merely as a means—least of all as a means of bringing to realization "the vision of man," as he calls it—but as an end in itself. The present Stalinist elite, which raised its leader to the supreme heights and which he, in turn, organized and disciplined in his own inimitable fashion, no longer cares to remember the socialist idealism of the generation that made the Revolution. It has been taught to despise that idealism; and Chambers' portrait of Colonel Bykov, his Russian superior in the "apparatus," is perfectly illustrative of this psychology. Whatever the nature of their rationalizations, those people now act more and more like the totalitarians in George Orwell's novel, *1984*, whose program comes to only one thing: power entirely for its own sake. "Power is not a means; it is an end. ... The object of persecution is persecution. The object of torture is torture. The object of power is power."

The original idea of Communism accounts for the behavior of real live Communists no more and no less than the original idea of Christianity can account for the behavior of real live Christians in the centuries when they wielded temporal power; the Great Purge, the slave-labor camps and the other horrors of the Soviet system can no more be deduced from the classic texts of socialism than the murderous Albigensian Crusade and the practices of the Holy Inquisition can be deduced from the Sermon on the Mount. Chambers denies that there is any phase or single event in the history of Bolshevism, like the Kronstadt rebellion for example, that can be taken as a turning point in its degeneration. Its fascist character, he writes, was "inherent in it from the beginning." That is true in a sense, but scarcely in a meaningful way. It is equally true that besides the totalitarian potential a good many other things were inherent in the Revolution which came to nothing by reason of the power in the hands of certain men and the irreducibly tragic nature of the circumstances under which they exercised it, such as Russia's isolation and ruinous poverty and the fusion of the absolutist element in the Marxist dialectic with the caesaro-papist heritage of the Russian mind. Chambers is so obsessed with the "atheistic question" that he is willing to absolve the very worst men of responsibility for their crimes in order all the more justifiably to implicate the values and ideas they profess. He forgets that men in general, not only the worst among them, tend to honor such values and ideas more in the breach than in the observance. At one time Lenin warned his followers that there is no idea or movement that cannot be turned into its exact opposite. If that is true, it is because ideas and movements have no reality except insofar as they derive it from living men. No ideology, whether secular or religious, exists in some ghostlike fashion apart from the men who believe in it or merely use it for their own ends; and since its one lodging place is in the power-mongering human mind, it can never be immune to corruption.

Though disappointing in its character as a work of ideas, *Witness* is still of the first importance as an authentic expression of historical crisis and as a presentation of crucial facts. And by far the most crucial is the fact that the Soviet Military Intelligence, by winning to its service men of the type of Harry Dexter White and Alger Hiss, came very close to penetrating the top headquarters of the U. S. Government: "It was not yet in the Cabinet room, but it was not far outside the door." The stealing of secret documents was, of course, of little consequence compared to the power that the infiltrators acquired to influence policy. This infiltration was not simply the exploit of clever spies; the spy-thriller aspect of their performance is of negligible interest. What is of commanding interest is the lesson it enforces; and that lesson is that the infiltration, which was more extensive, probably, than we shall ever know, was intrinsically the result of the political attitudes that prevailed in this country for a whole decade, if not longer, at the very least between 1938 and 1948.

Chambers may be exaggerating in saying that in those years it was the Popular Front mind that dominated American life, but he is hardly exaggerating when he specifies that it was that mind which then dominated most "avenues of communication between the intellectuals and the nation. It told the nation what it should believe; it made up the nation's mind for it. The Popular Fronters had made themselves the 'experts.' They controlled the narrows of news and opinion. ... The nation ... could not grasp or believe that a conspiracy on the scale of Communism was possible or that it had already made so deep a penetration. ..." And the fierce resistance which Chambers encountered when he finally broke through with his testimony to the nation at large was essentially a symptom of the anguish of the Popular Front mind and its unreasoning anger at being made to confront the facts of political life. The importance of the Hiss case was precisely that it dramatized that mind's struggle for survival and its vindictiveness under attack. That mind is above all terrified of the disorder and evil of history, and it flees the harsh choices which history so often imposes. It fought to save Hiss in order to safeguard its own illusions and to escape the knowledge of its gullibility and chronic refusal of reality.

Where Chambers goes wrong, I think, is in his attempt to implicate that mind in the revolutionary ethos. Hence his distorted picture of the New Deal as a "genuine revolution, whose deepest purpose was not simply reform within existing conditions, but a basic change in the social and, above all, the power relationships within the nation." The proof? The New Deal was bent on replacing the power of business with that of politics. But this notion is altogether too narrow, too one-sided. Of course the New Deal was bound to increase the power of government in its effort to pull the economy out of depression and to save business from its own follies. The New Deal is unrecognizable in Chambers' description of it. Here again he proceeds in accordance with the method of pure ideological deduction, this time deducing the New Deal from the revolutionary intention he imputes to the Popular Front mind. He is in error, it seems to me, in his evaluation of that mind. I see that mind not only as unrevolutionary but as profoundly bourgeois in its political amorphousness, evasion of historical choice, and search for formulas of empty reassurance. It is the bourgeois mind in its mood of good will and vague liberal aspiration, the mind of degenerated humanism glowing with the false militancy of universal political uplift. It wishes to maintain its loyalty to free institutions and at the same time to accommodate itself to the Communists, particularly so when the latter oblige by playing the game of not being "real Communists" at all but democrats of the extreme Left. It wanted to be and was duly sold on the theory of Chinese Stalinism as a movement of agrarian reform; and it never wanted to know the truth about Soviet Russia, even though for many years now, certainly since the Great Purge in the mid-thirties, it has not been very difficult to discover what that truth was. The Communist mind, on the other hand, while Utopian in its faith in the "science of history" and the materialist dogmas, is crassly realistic to the point of cynicism in its grasping sense of power and in the choice of means to attain it; its will is always armed and, whenever feasible, it prefers constraint to compromise in settling issues. If the New Dealers, insofar as they can be identified with the Popular Front mind (and the identification is by no means complete), failed to recognize the Communists in their midst, it was not, as Chambers asserts, because they lived in the same mental world with them but because at bottom they had almost nothing in common with the agents of the police state.

The dynamism of the New Deal in its early years should not mislead us as to its objectives, which were in reality very limited. Chambers invests that indigenous reform movement with sinister qualities, thus justifying his present allegiance to the far Right. I do not believe that the explanation for his political behavior is to be sought in any love he has of late acquired for laissez-faire economics and the division of society into warring classes. It must be his dread and hatred of Communism that impel him to reject precipitantly all ideas of social reform and innovation. But if Communism is so overwhelming an issue, what does the far Right actually offer by way of leadership in the struggle against it? As I see it, it provides neither a fundamental understanding of Communism nor the moral, intellectual, or political weapons with which to conduct that struggle to a successful conclusion. That withered conservatism, which invariably mistakes all social adjustments, however necessary and belated, for wild plunges into the sinful economics of "statism," and which looks to a reduction in taxes and a balanced budget for salvation, has simply ceased to count in the world of today. It is really another form of nihilism, by far the most mediocre and boring of all. Whatever the material force which this withered conservatism may still command in some countries, the Stalinist aggressors know well that it presents no serious obstacle to their world-wide sweep. Chambers, who can hardly be called an optimist, surely understands that this is the case, as he virtually despairs of "the world outside Communism, which lacks a faith and a vision." What, then, is the answer? His answer is religion.

It is at this juncture that Chambers ceases to think politically, giving in entirely to his mystic proclivities. One doubts that he has ever been really at home in politics, if we take politics to be a delimited form of social thought and action. It was in the course of his search for wholeness and identity that he joined the Communists, reading a transcendent meaning into their political passions. He admits that while in the Party he avoided reading all "books critical of Communism" and also that he had never sought to influence policy. Nor did his activity as spy-courier in the Party's secret apparatus make any urgent claims upon his political sense. Unconcerned with politics in its hard empirical aspects, he is essentially a mystic swept into the world of parties and movements by the crazy pressures of the age.

What he is unable to see in his present mood is that the appeal to religion, however valid in its own sphere, turns into the merest surrogate when made to do the work of politics. It is well known that the religious consciousness is reconcilable to so many contradictory and even antagonistic concepts of society that the attempt to hold it to any particular social or political orientation is nearly useless. There is no substitute for politics, just as for those who must have it there is no substitute for religion. It is true that religious believers have every reason to be hostile to Communism; yet the motive of belief forms but one strand in a complex of motives. Believers, like all men, live in the real world of varied and pressing needs and interests, of which the material interest is surely the last that we can afford to underrate; and all too frequently the predominant concerns of men are such that the acknowledged duty to their faith is easily thrust aside. In 1917 the Russian peasants, though traditionally far from irreligious, backed the Bolsheviks despite all churchly admonition—the petitions of orthodoxy counted as nothing against the promise of peace, bread, and land. Clearly, Lenin's professed atheism in no way deterred the peasants in their support of the Revolution; and now large sections of the peasantry of Italy and other countries show the same lack of inhibition in voting the Communist ticket. The breakup of traditional societies is a salient feature of our time, and no impromptu summons can recall these societies to the ancient faith. Of what relevance are the propositions of Christian theology in China or India, or in areas like the Middle East, where the crumbling of the social order unlooses the rage of masses and Stalinist ambition feeds on hunger and despair?

It is futile to expect religion to undertake the radical task of reorganizing the world. Its institutional practices are remote from such aims, and its doctrines have hardened in the mold of otherworldliness. In truth, we have nothing to go on but the rational disciplines of the secular mind as, alone and imperiled, it confronts its freedom in a universe stripped of supernatural sanctions. Chambers' melodramatic formula—God or Stalin?—is of no help to us in our modern predicament. He reproaches Western civilization for its "three centuries of rationalism." Now rationalism has its fallacies, to be sure, but is it fair to hold it to account for the horrors of the Russian police state, which has behind it not even one, much less three centuries, of rationalism? Soviet society bears the indelible stamp of the long Russian past of feudal-bureaucratic rule, an absolutist rule of the mind as of the body. Of course, the Marxist teaching is not exempt from censure for the consequences of the Revolution. It should be added, however, that this teaching, Western in its main origins and holding a heavy charge of Judaeo-Christian ethics, has suffered a strange metamorphosis in its Muscovite captivity. And now, in its movement deeper into the East, it is seized upon, with all the fervor of native absolutism, by the backward, semi-mendicant intelligentsia of the Asian countries. This intelligentsia, untrained in habits of social responsibility and unformed in the traditions of humanist and rationalist thought, has converted Marxism into a dogma of nothing less than incendiary content. Its detachment from the West is virtually complete.

Chambers allows for no modulations in his attacks on the rationalist and naturalist trends in Western culture. For him the only issue is atheism, even where the disorder is patently economic and social. His religious-political plea is made unconvincing by the very terms it is cast in, terms belonging to that type of religious conservatism which ordinarily finds its complement in political reaction. It may well be that the religious mind has a significant part to play in "the crisis of history," but the intervention of that mind will do religion no good if the Christian credentials are used to no better purpose than to consecrate, as the late Emmanuel Mounier put it, "the appeal to pre-existing ideas and established powers."

Mounier, a French Catholic thinker of radical tendency, saw with uncommon lucidity the dangers that threaten the religious mind in its turn to political projects. He protested against the idealist habit of thought by which the activity of men in nature and society is reduced to no more than a reflection of the spirit, and he warned against enlisting the religious tradition in defense of the conservative cult of the past—a defense by prestige which sooner or later exposes the defenders to vengeful blows. Not at all alarmed by the fact that his analysis of the present crisis coincided in some respects with that of the secular radicals, he kept a tight hold on the obvious truth which religionists generally appear to have great difficulty in keeping in mind—the inescapable truth that economic and social ills can only be cured by economic and social means, even if not by those means exclusively. "Christianity no longer holds the field," he wrote in his last book, *Personalism*. "There are other massive realities; undeniable values are emerging apparently without its help, arousing moral forces, heroisms, and even kinds of saintliness. It does not seem, for its own part, able to combine with the modern world … in a marriage such as it consummated with the medieval world. Is it, indeed, approaching its end? … Perhaps the decomposing hulk of a world that Christianity built, that has now slipped its moorings, is drifting away, and leaving behind it the pioneers of a new Christianity. …"

Whether Mounier's hope for a "new Christianity" will be historically justified or not we do not know, but that he had a deep understanding of the discords experienced by the modern consciousness in relating itself to religious life there can be no doubt. He corrects the excesses of a writer like Chambers, whose illusion it is that he is serving religion by pulling down the image of man.

III
Life and Culture at Midcentury

11
Meyer Schapiro (1904–1996)
Nature of Abstract Art (1937)

Editor's Introduction

Meyer Schapiro brought the interdisciplinary nature of the New York Intellectuals in politics and culture to the realm of painting and of art broadly speaking. Actually, he glided beyond that level to become the very personification of the interdisciplinary intellectual in the group. Politically engaged with socialism, he wrote as a Marxist in the 1930s like many in the *Partisan* group, but like Irving Howe he remained a socialist throughout his life and became a founding member of *Dissent* magazine, although he almost never wrote for it.

While many in the group were excellent interdisciplinary writers of one style or another—Dwight Macdonald, Irving Howe, Harold Rosenberg—nearly all members acknowledged Schapiro as the best intellectual speaker in the group. Schapiro, who wrote less than most of the New York Intellectuals, although not as little as is sometimes suggested, became a legend in the group for his spoken brilliance and talent. While a student at Columbia in the mid-1960s, the critic Marshall Berman sat in on a Schapiro lecture and found that "he projected an amazing flood of images, modern and medieval, paintings and newspaper photographs and blueprints and cartoons, representational and abstract … . He made dazzling jumpcuts into the past, into radically different cultures, into visions of the future." After Schapiro stopped, Berman realized "It was like sex, or music, or a few other peak experiences: He had shown us the richness of being." (Marshall Berman, "Meyer Schapiro: The Presence of the Subject," *New Politics*, vol. 5, no. 4 (new series), whole no. 20, Winter 1996). Irving Howe, never easily impressed, said that only Isaiah Berlin could speak as eloquently as Schapiro. "Luminously handsome, playful in his seriousness," Howe noted, "he became for us a legendary figure." (Irving Howe, *A Margin of Hope* (Harcourt Brace Jovanovich, 1982), 237–38.) The art critic Arthur Danto described a Schapiro lecture as filled with "whole shimmering architectures, gothic in the audacity with which arch sprang from arch, vaults opened onto vaults still higher, as his lectures spun themselves into something vast, ethereal, brilliant." (Arthur Danto, "The Prophet in Profile," *New Republic*, November 18, 1996.)

Although even his admirers agreed that Schapiro did not have such magic in the confines of the printed page, the reader can still feel the dizzying turns from one field to another as Schapiro races through his explanations. In the accompanying essay below, for example—in a single short paragraph on the artist Seurat—Schapiro speaks of economic development, the moral consequences of capitalism, the painters of the Symbolist and Synthetist groups, lower class recreation, commercialized entertainment, monumentalized art, the progressive technical side of the engineer and the latest findings of science. Elsewhere in this piece he discusses music, architecture, design, the impact of non-Euclidian geometry on the view that mathematics is independent of experience, cultural history, the advance of monopoly capitalism, primitive geometric styles of ornament, magic and fetishism, ethnology, myth, fate, movements in literature and philosophy, fascism, Nietzsche, ideologies, technology, textures, materials, revolutions, socialism and wars.

Yet this is hardly to suggest that he ignored the painted canvas in his criticism. Consider his discussion of Van Gogh's painting "The Poet's Garden," in which he talks about the blues and greens of the tree, the vitality expressed by "the fervour of the brushwork," particularly the colored lines of the tree's vegetation drawn in "diagonals and convergences" that highlight the "larger diagonals of the work" in the path and the legs of the couple walking beneath the tree. Or consult Schapiro's description of the coiled background of Van Gogh's final self-portrait, which he describes not as the work of a mental patient but the calculated and composed expression of a painter trying to convey the vertigo of a mind in distress. "As we shift our attention from the man to his surroundings and back again, the analogies are multiplied; the nodal points, or centres, in the background ornament begin to resemble more the eyes and ear and buttons of the figure," Schapiro notes carefully. "In all this turmoil and congested eddying motion, we sense the extraordinary firmness of the painter's hand …. all these point to a superior mind, however disturbed and apprehensive the artist's feelings."

Meyer Schapiro was born in Lithuania, arrived in the United States in 1907, and grew up in the Brownsville section of Brooklyn. At age sixteen he won scholarships to Columbia College, remained there for graduate school, and received his Ph.D. in 1929. His dissertation was a study of Romanesque art, but throughout his career he lectured and celebrated art from various periods and styles. He taught art history at Columbia beginning in 1928, and during his career he also lectured at various other universities in New York and elsewhere. Throughout his life he sketched, painted and sculpted.

Source

Meyer Schapiro, "Nature of Abstract Art," *Marxist Quarterly*, vol. 1, January 1937, 77–98; reprinted in Meyer Schapiro, *Modern Art: 19th and 20th Centuries* (New York: George Braziller, 1978), 185–211 .

Selected Readings

Joseph Leo Koerner. "Theory and Philosophy of Art: Style, Artists, and Society, Selected Papers, vol. IV," *The New Republic* vol. 212, no. 2-3, January 9, 1995.

Marshall Berman, "Meyer Schapiro: The Presence of the Subject," New Politics, vol. 5, no. 4 (new series), whole no. 20, Winter 1996).

* * * * *

Before there was an art of abstract painting, it was already widely believed that the value of a picture was a matter of colors and shapes alone. Music and architecture were constantly held up to painters as examples of a pure art which did not have to imitate objects but derived its effects from elements peculiar to itself. But such ideas could not be readily accepted, since no one had yet seen a painting made up of colors and shapes, representing nothing. If pictures of the objects around us were often judged according to qualities of form alone, it was obvious that in doing so one was distorting or reducing the pictures; you could not arrive at these paintings simply by manipulating forms. And in so far as the objects to which these forms belonged were often particular individuals and places, real or mythical figures, bearing the evident marks of a time, the pretension that art was above history through the creative energy or personality of the artist was not entirely clear. In abstract art, however, the pretended autonomy and absoluteness of the esthetic emerged in a concrete form. Here, finally, was an art of painting in which only esthetic elements seem to be present.

Abstract art had therefore the value of a practical demonstration. In these new paintings the very processes of designing and inventing seemed to have been brought on to the canvas; the pure form once masked by an extraneous content was liberated and could now be directly perceived. Painters who do not practice this art have welcomed it on just this ground, that it strengthened their conviction of the absoluteness of the esthetic and provided them a discipline in pure design. Their attitude toward past art was also completely changed. The new styles accustomed painters to the vision of colors and shapes as disengaged from objects and created an immense confraternity of works of art, cutting across the barriers of time and place. They made it possible to enjoy the remotest arts, those in which the represented objects were no longer intelligible, even the drawings of children and madmen, and especially primitive arts with drastically distorted figures, which had been regarded as artless curios even by insistently esthetic critics. Before this time Ruskin could say in his *Political Economy of Art*, in calling for the preservation of medieval and Renaissance works, that "in Europe alone, pure and precious ancient art exists, for there is none in America, none in Asia, none in Africa." What was once considered monstrous, now became pure form and pure expression, the esthetic evidence that feeling and thought are prior to the represented world. The art of the whole world was now available on a single unhistorical and universal plane as a panorama of the formalizing energies of man.

These two aspects of abstract painting, the exclusion of natural forms and the unhistorical universalizing of the qualities of art, have a crucial importance for the general theory of art. Just as the discovery of non-Euclidian geometry gave a powerful impetus to the view that mathematics was independent of experience, so abstract painting cut at the roots of the classic ideas of artistic imitation. The analogy of mathematics was in fact present to the minds of the apologists of abstract art; they have often referred to non-Euclidian geometry in defense of their own position, and have even suggested an historical connection between them.

Today the abstractionists and their Surrealist offspring are more and more concerned with objects and the older claims of abstract art have lost the original force of insurgent convictions. Painters who had once upheld this art as the logical goal of the entire history of forms have refuted themselves in returning to the impure natural forms. The demands for liberty in art are no longer directed against a fettering tradition of nature; the esthetic of abstraction has itself become a brake on new movements. Not that abstract art is dead, as its philistine enemies have been announcing for over twenty years; it is still practiced by some of the finest painters and sculptors in Europe, whose work shows a freshness and assurance that are lacking in the newest realistic art. The conception of a possible field of "pure art"—whatever its value—will not die so soon, though it may take on forms different from those of the last thirty years; and very likely the art that follows in the countries which have known abstraction will be affected by it. The ideas underlying abstract art have penetrated deeply into all artistic theory, even of their original opponents; the language of absolutes and pure sources of art, whether of feeling, reason, intuition or the sub-conscious mind, appears in the very schools which renounce abstraction. "Objective" painters strive for "pure objectivity," for the object given in its "essence" and completeness, without respect to a viewpoint, and the Surrealists derive their images from pure thought, freed from the perversions of reason and everyday experience. Very little is written today—sympathetic to modern art—which does not employ this language of absolutes.

I

In this article I will take as my point of departure Barr's recent book,[1] the best, I think, that we have in English on the movements now grouped as abstract art. It has the special interest of combining a discussion of general questions about the nature of this art, its esthetic theories, its causes, and even the relation to political movements, with a detailed, matter-of-fact account of the different styles. But although Barr sets out to describe rather than to defend or to criticize abstract art, he seems to accept its theories on their face value in his historical exposition and in certain random judgments. In places he speaks of this art as independent of historical conditions, as realizing the underlying order of nature and as an art of pure form without content.

Hence if the book is largely an account of historical movements, Barr's conception of abstract art remains essentially unhistorical. He gives us, it is true, the dates of every stage in the various movements, as if to enable us to plot a curve, or to follow the emergence of the art year by year, but no connection is drawn between the art and the conditions of the moment. He excludes as irrelevant to its history the nature of the society in which it arose, except as an incidental obstructing or accelerating atmospheric factor. The history of modern art is presented as an internal, immanent process among the artists; abstract art arises because, as the author says, representational art had been exhausted. Out of boredom with "painting facts," the artists turned to abstract art as a pure esthetic activity. "By a common and powerful impulse they were driven to abandon the imitation of natural appearance" just as the artists of the fifteenth century "were moved by a passion for imitating nature." The modern change, however, was "the logical and inevitable conclusion toward which art was moving."

This explanation, which is common in the studios and is defended by some writers in the name of the autonomy of art, is only one instance of a wider view which embraces every field of culture and even economy and politics. At its ordinary level the theory of exhaustion and reaction reduces history to the pattern of popular views on changes in fashion. People grow tired of one color and choose an opposite; one season the skirts are long, and then by reaction they are short. In the same way the present return to objects in painting is explained as the result of the exhaustion of abstract art. All the possibilities of the latter having been explored by Picasso and Mondrian, there is little left for the younger artists but to take up the painting of objects (Neo-concretism).

The notion that each new style is due to a reaction against a preceding is especially plausible to modern artists, whose work is so often a response to another work, who consider their art a free projection of an irreducible personal feeling, but must form their style in competition against others, with the obsessing sense of the originality of their work as a mark of its sincerity. Besides, the creators of new forms in the last century had almost always to fight against those who practised the old; and several of the historical styles were formed in conscious opposition to another manner—Renaissance against Gothic, Baroque against Mannerism, Neo-classic against Rococo, etc.

The antithetic form of a change does not permit us, however, to judge a new art as a sheer reaction or as the inevitable response to the spending of all the resources of the old. No more than the succession of war and peace implies that war is due to an inherent reaction against peace and peace to a reaction against war. The energies required for the reaction, which sometimes has a drastic and invigorating effect on art, are lost sight of in such an account; it is impossible to explain by it the particular direction and force of the new movement, its specific moment, region and goals. The theory of immanent exhaustion and reaction is inadequate not only because it reduces human activity to a simple mechanical movement, like a bouncing ball, but because in neglecting the sources of energy and the condition of the field, it does not even do justice to its own limited mechanical conception. The oppositeness of a reaction is often an artificial matter, more evident in the polemics between schools or in the schemas of formalistic historians than in the actual historical change. To supply a motor force to this physical history of styles (which pretends to be anti-mechanical), they are reduced to a myth of the perpetual alternating motion of generations, each reacting against its parents and therefore repeating the motions of its grandparents, according to the "grandfather principle" of certain German historians of art. And a final goal, an unexplained but inevitable trend, a destiny rooted in the race or the spirit of the culture or the inherent nature of the art, has to be smuggled in to explain the large unity of a development that embraces so many reacting generations. The immanent purpose steers the reaction when an art seems to veer off the main path because of an overweighted or foreign element. Yet how many arts we know in which the extreme of some quality persists for centuries without provoking the corrective reaction. The "decay" of classical art has been attributed by the English critic, Fry, to its excessive cult of the human body, but this "decay" evidently lasted for hundreds of years until the moment was ripe for the Christian reaction. But even this Christian art, according to the same writer, was for two centuries indistinguishable from the pagan.

The broad reaction against an existing art is possible only on the ground of its inadequacy to artists with new values and new ways of seeing. But reaction in this internal, antithetic sense, far from being an inherent and universal property of culture, occurs only under impelling historical conditions. For we see that ancient arts, like the Egyptian, the work of anonymous craftsmen, persist for thousands of years with relatively little change, provoking few reactions to the established style; others grow slowly and steadily in a single direction, and still others, in the course of numerous changes, foreign intrusions and reactions preserve a common traditional character. From the mechanical theories of exhaustion, boredom and reaction we could never explain why the reaction occurred when it did. On the other hand, the banal divisions of the great historical styles in literature and art correspond to the momentous divisions in the history of society.

If we consider an art that is near us in time and is still widely practised, like Impressionism, we will see how empty is the explanation of the subsequent arts by reaction. From a logical viewpoint the antithesis to Impressionism depends on how Impressionism is defined. Whereas the later schools attacked the Impressionists as mere photographers of sunshine, the contemporaries of Impressionism abused it for its monstrous unreality. The Impressionists were in fact the first painters of whom it was charged that their works made as little sense right side up as up side down. The movements after Impressionism take different directions, some toward simplified natural forms, others toward their complete decomposition; both are sometimes described as historical reactions against Impressionism, one restoring the objects that Impressionism dissolved, the other restoring the independent imaginative activity that Impressionism sacrificed to the imitation of nature.

Actually, in the 1880's there were several aspects of Impressionism which could be the starting points of new tendencies and goals of reaction. For classicist painters the weakness of Impressionism lay in its unclarity, its destruction of definite linear forms; it is in this sense that Renoir turned for a time from Impressionism to Ingres. But for other artists at the same moment Impressionism was too casual and unmethodical; these, the neo-Impressionists, preserved the Impressionist colorism, carrying it even further in an unclassical sense, but also in a more constructive and calculated way. For still others, Impressionism was too photographic, too impersonal; these, the symbolists and their followers, required an emphatic sentiment and esthetic activism in the work. There were finally artists for whom Impressionism was too unorganized, and their reaction underscored a schematic arrangement. Common to most of these movements after Impressionism was the absolutizing of the artist's state of mind or sensibility as prior to and above objects. If the Impressionists reduced things to the artist's sensations, their successors reduced them further to projections or constructions of his feelings and moods, or to "essences" grasped in a violent and tense intuition.

The historical fact is that the reaction against Impressionism came in the 1880's before some of its most original possibilities had been realized. The painting of series of chromatic variations of a single motif (the Haystacks, the Cathedral) dates from the 1890's; and the Water Lilies, with their remarkable spatial forms, related in some ways to contemporary abstract art, belong to the twentieth century. The effective reaction against Impressionism took place only at a certain moment in its history and chiefly in France, though Impressionism was fairly widespread in Europe by the end of the century. In the 1880's, when Impressionism was beginning to be accepted officially, there were already several groups of young artists in France to whom it was uncongenial. The history of art is not, however, a history of single willful reactions, every new artist taking a stand opposite the last, painting brightly if the other painted dully, flattening if the other modelled, and distorting if the other was literal. The reactions were deeply motivated in the experience of the artists, in a changing world with which they had to come to terms and which shaped their practice and ideas in specific ways.

The tragic lives of Gauguin and van Gogh, their estrangement from society, which so profoundly colored their art, were no automatic reactions to Impressionism or the consequences of Peruvian or Northern blood. In Gauguin's circle were other artists who had abandoned a bourgeois career in their maturity or who had attempted suicide. For a young man of the middle class to wish to live by art meant a different thing in 1885 than in 1860. By 1885 only artists had freedom and integrity, but often they had nothing else. The very existence of Impressionism which transformed nature into a private, unformalized field for sensitive vision, shifting with the spectator, made painting an ideal domain of freedom; it attracted many who were tied unhappily to middle class jobs and moral standards, now increasingly problematic and stultifying with the advance of monopoly capitalism. But Impressionism in isolating the sensibility as a more or less personal, but dispassionate and still outwardly directed, organ of fugitive distinctions in distant dissolving clouds, water and sunlight, could no longer suffice for men who had staked everything on impulse and whose resolution to become artists was a poignant and in some ways demoralizing break with good society. With an almost moral fervor they transformed Impressionism into an art of vehement expression, of emphatic, brilliant, magnified, obsessing objects, or adjusted its coloring and surface pattern to dreams of a seasonless exotic world of idyllic freedom.

Early Impressionism, too, had a moral aspect. In its unconventionalized, unregulated vision, in its discovery of a constantly changing phenomenal outdoor world of which the shapes depended on the momentary position of the casual or mobile spectator, there was an implicit criticism of symbolic social and domestic formalities, or at least a norm opposed to these. It is remarkable how many pictures we have in early Impressionism of informal and spontaneous sociability, of breakfasts, picnics, promenades, boating trips, holidays and vacation travel. These urban idylls not only present the objective forms of bourgeois recreation in the 1860's and 1870's; they also reflect in the very choice of subjects and in the new esthetic devices the conception of art as solely a field of individual enjoyment, without reference to ideas and motives, and they presuppose the cultivation of these pleasures as the highest field of freedom for an enlightened bourgeois detached from the official beliefs of his class. In enjoying realistic pictures of his surroundings as a spectacle of traffic and changing atmospheres, the cultivated rentier was experiencing in its phenomenal aspect that mobility of the environment, the market and of industry to which he owed his income and his freedom. And in the new Impressionist techniques which broke things up into finely discriminated points of color, as well as in the "accidental" momentary vision, he found, in a degree hitherto unknown in art, conditions of sensibility closely related to those of the urban promenader and the refined consumer of luxury goods.

As the contexts of bourgeois sociability shifted from community, family and church to commercialized or privately improvised forms—the streets, the cafés and resorts—the resulting consciousness of individual freedom involved more and more an estrangement from older ties; and those imaginative members of the middle class who accepted the norms of freedom, but lacked the economic means to attain them, were spiritually torn by a sense of helpless isolation in an anonymous indifferent mass. By 1880 the enjoying individual becomes rare in Impressionist art; only the private spectacle of nature is left. And in neo-Impressionism, which restores and even monumentalizes the figures, the social group breaks up into isolated spectators, who do not communicate with each other, or consists of mechanically repeated dances submitted to a preordained movement with little spontaneity.

The French artists of the 1880's and 1890's who attacked Impressionism for its lack of structure often expressed demands for salvation, for order and fixed objects of belief, foreign to the Impressionists as a group. The title of Gauguin's picture—"Where do we come from? Where are we? Where are we going?"—with its interrogative form, is typical of this state of mind. But since the artists did not know the underlying economic and social causes of their own disorder and moral insecurity, they could envisage new stabilizing forms only as quasi-religious beliefs or as a revival of some primitive or highly ordered traditional society with organs for a collective spiritual life. This is reflected in their taste for medieval and primitive art, their conversions to Catholicism and later to "integral nationalism." The colonies of artists formed at this period, Van Gogh's project of a communal life for artists, are examples of this groping to reconstitute the pervasive human sociability that capitalism had destroyed. Even their theories of "composition"—a traditional concept abandoned by the Impressionists—are related to their social views, for they conceive of composition as an assembly of objects bound together by a principle of order emanating, on the one hand, from the eternal nature of art, on the other, from the state of mind of the artist, but in both instances requiring a "deformation" of the objects. Some of them wanted a canvas to be like a church, to possess a hierarchy of forms, stationed objects, a prescribed harmony, preordained paths of vision, all issuing, however, from the artist's feeling. In recreating the elements of community in their art they usually selected inert objects, or active objects without meaningful interaction except as colors and lines.

These problems are posed to some extent, though solved differently, even in the work of Seurat whose relation to the economic development was in many ways distinct from that of the painters of the Symbolist and Synthetist groups. Instead of rebelling against the moral consequences of capitalism he attached himself like a contented engineer to its progressive technical side and accepted the popular forms of lower class recreation and commercialized entertainment as the subjects of a monumentalized art. From the current conceptions of technology he drew the norms of a methodical procedure in painting, bringing Impressionism up to date in the light of the latest findings of science.

There were, of course, other kinds of painting in France beside those described. But a detailed investigation of the movement of art would show, I think, that these, too, and even the conservative, academic painting were affected by the changed conditions of the time. The reactions against Impressionism, far from being inherent in the nature of art, issued from the responses that artists as artists made to the broader situation in which they found themselves, but which they themselves had not produced. If the tendencies of the arts after Impressionism toward an extreme subjectivism and abstraction are already evident in Impressionism, it is because the isolation of the individual and of the higher forms of culture from their older social supports, the renewed ideological oppositions of mind and nature, individual and society, proceed from social and economic causes which already existed before Impressionism and which are even sharper today. It is, in fact, a part of the popular attraction of Van Gogh and Gauguin that their work incorporates (and with a far greater energy and formal coherence than the works of other artists) evident longings, tensions and values which are shared today by thousands who in one way or another have experienced the same conflicts as these artists.

II

The logical opposition of realistic and abstract art by which Barr explains the more recent change rests on two assumptions about the nature of painting, common in writing on abstract art—that representation is a passive mirroring of things and therefore essentially non-artistic, and that abstract art, on the other hand, is a purely esthetic activity, unconditioned by objects and based on its own eternal laws. The abstract painter denounces representation of the outer world as a mechanical process of the eye and the hand in which the artist's feelings and imagination have little part. Or in a Platonic manner he opposes to the representation of objects, as a rendering of the surface aspect of nature, the practice of abstract design, as a discovery of the "essence" or underlying mathematical order of things. He assumes further that the mind is most completely itself when it is independent of external objects. If he, nevertheless, values certain works of older naturalistic art, he sees in them only independent formal constructions; he overlooks the imaginative aspects of the devices for transposing the space of experience on to the space of the canvas, and the immense, historically developed, capacity to hold the world in mind. He abstracts the artistic qualities from the represented objects and their meanings, and looks on these as unavoidable impurities, imposed historical elements with which the artist was burdened and in spite of which he finally achieved his underlying, personal abstract expression.

These views are thoroughly one-sided and rest on a mistaken idea of what a representation is. There is no passive, "photographic" representation in the sense described; the scientific elements of representation in older art—perspective, anatomy, light-and-shade—are ordering principles and expressive means as well as devices of rendering. All renderings of objects, no matter how exact they seem, even photographs, proceed from values, methods and viewpoints which somehow shape the image and often determine its contents. On the other hand, there is no "pure art," unconditioned by experience; all fantasy and formal construction, even the random scribbling of the hand, are shaped by experience and by non-esthetic concerns.

This is clear enough from the example of the Impressionists mentioned above. They could be seen as both photographic and fantastic, according to the viewpoint of the observer. Even their motifs of nature were denounced as meaningless beside the evident content of romantic and classicist art.

In regarding representation as a facsimile of nature, the abstract artist has taken over the error of vulgar nineteenth century criticism, which judged painting by an extremely narrow criterion of reality, inapplicable even to the realistic painting which it accepted. If the older taste said, how exactly like the object, how beautiful!—the modern abstractionist says, how exactly like the object, how ugly! The two are not completely opposed, however, in their premises, and will appear to be related if compared with the taste of religious arts with a supernatural content. Both realism and abstraction affirm the sovereignty of the artist's mind, the first, in the capacity to recreate the world minutely in a narrow, intimate field by series of abstract calculations of perspective and gradation of color, the other in the capacity to impose new forms on nature, to manipulate the abstracted elements of line and color freely, or to create shapes corresponding to subtle states of mind. But as little as a work is guaranteed esthetically by its resemblance to nature, so little is it guaranteed by its abstractness or "purity." Nature and abstract forms are both materials for art, and the choice of one or the other flows from historically changing interests.

Barr believes that painting is impoverished by the exclusion of the outer world from pictures, losing a whole range of sentimental, sexual, religious and social values. But he supposes in turn that the esthetic values are then available in a pure form. He does not see, however, that the latter are changed rather than purified by this exclusion; just as the kind of verbal pattern in writing designed mainly for verbal pattern differs from the verbal pattern in more meaningful prose. Various forms, qualities of space, color, light, scale, modelling and movement, which depend on the appreciation of aspects of nature and human life, disappear from painting; and similarly the esthetic of abstract art discovers new qualities and relationships which are congenial to the minds that practice such an exclusion. Far from creating an absolute form, each type of abstract art, as of naturalistic art, gives a special but temporary importance to some element, whether color, surface, outline or arabesque, or to some formal method. The converse of Barr's argument, that by clothing a pure form with a meaningful dress this form becomes more accessible or palatable, like logic or mathematics presented through concrete examples, rests on the same misconception. Just as narrative prose is not simply a story added to a preexisting, pure prose form that can be disengaged from the sense of the words, so a representation is not a natural form added to an abstract design.

Even the schematic aspects of the form in such a work already possess qualities conditioned by the modes of seeing objects and designing representations, not to mention the content and the emotional attitudes of the painter.

When the abstractionist Kandinsky was trying to create an art expressing mood, a great deal of conservative, academic painting was essentially just that. But the academic painter, following older traditions of romantic art, preserved the objects which provoked the mood; if he wished to express a mood inspired by a landscape, he painted the landscape itself. Kandinsky, on the other hand, wished to find an entirely imaginative equivalent of the mood; he would not go beyond the state of mind and a series of expressive colors and shapes, independent of things. The mood in the second case is very different from the first mood. A mood which is partly identified with the conditioning object, a mood dominated by clear images of detailed objects and situations, and capable of being revived and communicated to others through these images, is different in feeling tone, in relation to self-consciousness, attentiveness and potential activity, from a mood that is independent of an awareness of fixed, external objects, but sustained by a random flow of private and incommunicable associations. Kandinsky looks upon the mood as wholly a function of his personality or some special faculty of his spirit; and he selects colors and patterns which have for him the strongest correspondence to his state of mind, precisely because they are not tied sensibly to objects, but emerge freely from his excited fantasy. They are the concrete evidences, thrown up from within, of the internality of his mood, its independence of the outer world. Yet the external objects which underly the mood may re-emerge in the abstraction in a masked or distorted form. The most responsive spectator is then the individual who is similarly concerned with himself and who finds in such pictures not only the counterpart of his own tension, but a final discharge of obsessing feelings.

In renouncing or drastically distorting natural shapes the abstract painter makes a judgment of the external world. He says that such and such aspects of experience are alien to art and to the higher realities of form; he disqualifies them from art. But by this very act the mind's view of itself and of its art, the intimate contexts of this repudiation of objects, become directing factors in art. When personality, feeling and formal sensibility are absolutized, the values which underly or which follow today from such attitudes suggest new formal problems, just as the secular interests of the later middle ages made possible a whole series of new formal types of space and the human figure. The qualities of cryptic improvisation, the microscopic intimacy of textures, points and lines, the impulsively scribbled forms, the mechanical precision in constructing irreducible, incommensurable fields, the thousand and one ingenious formal devices of dissolution, penetration, immateriality and incompleteness, which affirm the abstract artist's active sovereignty over objects, these and many other sides of modern art are discovered experimentally by painters who seek freedom outside of nature and society and consciously negate the formal aspects of perception—like the connectedness of shape and color or the discontinuity of object and surroundings—that enter into the practical relations of man in nature.

We can judge more readily the burden of contemporary experience that imposes such forms by comparing them with the abstract devices in Renaissance art, especially the systems of perspective and the canons of proportion, which are today misunderstood as merely imitative means. In the Renaissance the development of linear perspective was intimately tied to the exploration of the world and the renewal of physical and geographical science. Just as for the aggressive members of the burgher class a realistic knowledge of the geographical world and communications entailed the ordering of spatial connections in a reliable system, so the artists strove to realize in their own imaginative field, even within the limits of a traditional religious content, the most appropriate and stimulating forms of spatial order, with the extensiveness, traversability and regulation valued by their class. And similarly, as this same burgher class, emerging from a Christian feudal society, began to assert the prority of sensual and natural to ascetic and supernatural goods, and idealized the human body as the real locus of values—enjoying images of the powerful or beautiful nude human being as the real man or woman, without sign of rank or submission to authority—so the artists derived from this valuation of the human being artistic ideals of energy and massiveness of form which they embodied in robust, active or potentially active, human figures. And even the canons of proportion, which seem to submit the human form to a mysticism of number, create purely secular standards of perfection; for through these canons the norms of humanity become physical and measurable, therefore at the same time sensual and intellectual, in contrast to the older medieval disjunction of the body and the mind.

If today an abstract painter seems to draw like a child or a madman, it is not because he is childish or mad. He has come to value as qualities related to his own goals of imaginative freedom the passionless spontaneity and technical insouciance of the child, who creates for himself alone, without the pressure of adult responsibility and practical adjustments. And similarly, the resemblance to psychopathic art, which is only approximate and usually independent of a conscious imitation, rests on their common freedom of fantasy, uncontrolled by reference to an external physical and social world. By his very practice of abstract art, in which forms are improvised and deliberately distorted or obscured, the painter opens the field to the suggestions of his suppressed interior life. But the painter's manipulation of his fantasy must differ from the child's or psychopath's in so far as the very act of designing is his chief occupation and the conscious source of his human worth; it acquires a burden of energy, a sustained pathos and firmness of execution foreign to the others.

The attitude to primitive art is in this respect very significant. The nineteenth century, with its realistic art, its rationalism and curiosity about production, materials and techniques often appreciated primitive ornament, but considered primitive representation monstrous. It was as little acceptable to an enlightened mind as the fetishism or magic which these images sometimes served. Abstract painters, on the other hand, have been relatively indifferent to the primitive geometrical styles of ornament. The distinctness of motifs, the emblematic schemes, the clear order of patterns, the direct submission to handicraft and utility, are foreign to modern art. But in the distorted, fantastic figures some groups of modern artists found an intimate kinship with their own work; unlike the ordering devices of ornament which were tied to the practical making of things, the forms of these figures seemed to have been shaped by a ruling fantasy, independent of nature and utility, and directed by obsessive feelings. The highest praise of their own work is to describe it in the language of magic and fetishism.

This new responsiveness to primitive art was evidently more than esthetic; a whole complex of longings, moral values and broad conceptions of life were fulfilled in it. If colonial imperialism made these primitive objects physically accessible, they could have little esthetic interest until the new formal conceptions arose. But these formal conceptions could be relevant to primitive art only when charged with the new valuations of the instinctive, the natural, the mythical and the essentially human, which affected even the description of primitive art. The older ethnologists, who had investigated the materials and tribal contexts of primitive imagery, usually ignored the subjective and esthetic side in its creation; in discovering the latter the modern critics with an equal one-sidedness relied on feeling to penetrate these arts. The very fact that they were the arts of primitive peoples without a recorded history now made them all the more attractive. They acquired the special prestige of the timeless and the instinctive, on the level of spontaneous animal activity, self-contained, un-reflective, private, without dates and signatures, without origins or consequences except in the emotions. A devaluation of history, civilized society and external nature lies behind the new passion for primitive art. Time ceased to be an historical dimension; it became an internal psychological moment, and the whole mess of material ties, the nightmare of a determining world, the disquieting sense of the present as a dense historical point to which the individual was fatefully bound, these were automatically transcended in thought by the conception of an instinctive, elemental art above time. By a remarkable process the arts of subjugated backward peoples, discovered by Europeans in conquering the world, became esthetic norms to those who renounced it. The imperialist expansion was accompanied at home by a profound cultural pessimism in which the arts of the savage victims were elevated above the highest traditions of Europe. The colonies became places to flee to as well as to exploit.

The new respect for primitive art was progressive, however, in that the cultures of savages and other backward peoples were now regarded as human cultures, and a high creativeness, far from being a prerogative of the advanced societies of the West, was attributed to all human groups. But this insight was accompanied not only by a flight from the advanced society, but also by an indifference to just those material conditions which were brutally destroying the primitive peoples or converting them into submissive, cultureless slaves. Further, the preservation of certain forms of native culture in the interest of imperialist power could be supported in the name of the new artistic attitudes by those who thought themselves entirely free from political interest.

III

To say then that abstract painting is simply a reaction against the exhausted imitation of nature, or that it is the discovery of an absolute or pure field of form is to overlook the positive character of the art, its underlying energies and sources of movement. Besides, the movement of abstract art is too comprehensive and long-prepared, too closely related to similar movements in literature and philosophy, which have quite other technical conditions, and finally, too varied according to time and place, to be considered a self-contained development issuing by a kind of internal logic directly from esthetic problems. It bears within itself at almost every point the mark of the changing material and psychological conditions surrounding modern culture.

The avowals of artists—several of which are cited in Barr's work—show that the step to abstraction was accompanied by great tension and emotional excitement. The painters justify themselves by ethical and metaphysical standpoints, or in defense of their art attack the preceding style as the counterpart of a detested social or moral position. Not the processes of imitating nature were exhausted, but the valuation of nature itself had changed. The philosophy of art was also a philosophy of life.

1. The Russian painter Malevitch, the founder of "Suprematism," has described his new art in revealing terms. "By Suprematism I mean the supremacy of pure feeling or sensation in the pictorial arts. ... In the year 1913 in my desperate struggle to free art from the ballast of the objective world I fled to the form of the Square and exhibited a picture which was nothing more or less than a black square upon a white ground. ... It was no empty square which I had exhibited but rather the experience of object-lessness" (Barr, pp. 122–23).

Later in 1918 he painted in Moscow a series called White on White, including a white square on a white surface. In their purity these paintings seemed to parallel the efforts of mathematicians to reduce all mathematics to arithmetic and arithmetic to logic. But there is a burden of feeling underlying this "geometrical" art, which may be judged from the related paintings with the titles Sensation of Metallic Sounds, Feeling of Flight, Feeling of Infinite Space. Even in the work labelled Composition we can see how the formal character of the abstraction rests on the desire to isolate and externalize in a concrete fashion subjective, professional elements of the older practice of painting, a desire which issues in turn from the conflicts and insecurity of the artist and his conception of art as an absolutely private realm. Barr analyzes a composition of two squares as a "study in equivalents: the red square, smaller but more intense in color and more active in its diagonal axis, holds its own against the black square which is larger but negative in color and static in position." Although he characterizes this kind of painting as pure abstraction to distinguish it from geometrical designs which are ultimately derived from some representation, he overlooks the relation of this painting to a work by Malevitch reproduced in his book—The Woman With the Water Pails, dating from 1912. The peasant woman, designed in Cubist style, balances two pails hanging from a rod across her shoulders. Here the preoccupation with balance as a basic esthetic principle governing the relations of two counterpart units is embodied in an "elemental" genre subject; the objects balanced are not human, but suspended, non-organic elements, unarticulated forms. Although the human theme is merely allusive and veiled by the Cubist procedure, the very choice of the motif of the peasant woman with the water pails betrays a sexual interest and the emotional context of the artist's tendency toward his particular style of abstraction.

The importance of the subjective conditions of the artist's work in the formation of abstract styles may be verified in the corresponding relationship between Cubist and pre-Cubist art. Picasso, just before Cubism, represented melancholy circus acrobats, harlequins, actors, musicians, beggars, usually at home on the fringes of society, or rehearsing among themselves, as bohemian artists detached from the stage of public performance. He shows in one picture two acrobats balancing themselves, the one mature and massive, squared in body, seated firmly on a cubic mass of stone shaped like his own figure; the young girl, slender, an outlined, unmodelled form, balancing herself unstably on tiptoes on a spherical stone. The experience of balance vital to the acrobat, his very life, in fact, is here assimilated to the subjective experience of the artist, an expert performer concerned with the adjustment of lines and masses as the essence of his art—a formalized personal activity which estranges him from society and to which he gives up his life. Between this art and Cubism, where the figure finally disappears, giving way to small geometrical elements formed from musical instruments, drinking vessels, playing-cards and other artificial objects of private manipulation, there is a phase of negroid figures in which the human physiognomy is patterned on primitive or savage faces and the body reduced to an impersonal nudity of harsh, drastic lines. This figure-type is not taken from life, not even from the margins of society, but from art; this time, however, from the art of a savage, isolated people, regarded everywhere as inferior and valued only as exotic spectacles or entertainers, except by the painters to whom they are pure, unspoiled artists, creating from instinct or a native sensibility.

In the light of this analysis we can hardly accept Barr's account of Malevitch's step to abstraction: "Malevitch suddenly foresaw the logical and inevitable conclusion towards which European art was moving" and drew a black square on a white ground.

2. In his book *Ueber das Geistige in der Kunst*, published in 1912, the painter Kandinsky, one of the very first to create completely abstract pictures, speaks constantly of inner necessity as alone determining the choice of elements, just as inner freedom, he tells us, is the sole criterion in ethics. He does not say that representation has been exhausted, but that the material world is illusory and foreign to the spirit; his art is a rebellion against the "materialism" of modern society, in which he includes science and the socialist movement. "When religion, science and morality (the last through the strong hand of Nietzsche) are shaken, and when the outer supports threaten to fall, man turns his gaze away from, the external and towards himself." In his own time he respects, as interests parallel to his own and similarly motivated, theosophy, occultism, the cult of the primitive and experiments of synesthesia. Colored audition is important to him because perception is then blurred and localized in the perceiver rather than identified with an external source. His more esthetic comments are usually of a piece with these attitudes. "The green, yellow, red tree in the meadow is only … an accidental materialized form of the tree which we feel in ourselves when we hear the word tree." And in describing one of his first abstract pictures he says: "This entire description is chiefly an analysis of the picture which I have painted rather subconsciously in a state of strong inner tension. So intensively do I feel the necessity of some of the forms that I remember having given loud-voiced directions to myself, as for instance: 'But the corners must be heavy.' The observer must learn to look at the picture as a graphic representation of a mood and not as a representation of objects" (Barr, p. 66).

More recently he has written: "Today a point sometimes says more in a painting than a human figure. … Man has developed a new faculty which permits him to go beneath the skin of nature and touch its essence, its content. … The painter needs discreet, silent, almost insignificant objects. … How silent is an apple beside Laocoon. A circle is even more silent" *(Cahiers d'Art,* vol. VI, 1931, p. 351).

3. I will now quote a third avowal of artists tending toward abstraction, but this time of aggressive artists, the Italian Futurists, who can hardly be charged with the desire to escape from the world.

"It is from Italy that we launch … our manifesto of revolutionary and incendiary violence with which we found today il Futurismo. … Exalt every kind of originality, of boldness, of extreme violence. … Take and glorify the life of today, incesantly and tumultuously transformed by the triumphs of science. … A speeding automobile is more beautiful than the Victory of Samothrace" (Barr, p. 54).

Barr, who overlooks the moral, ideological aspect in Malevitch and Kandinsky, cannot help observing in the Italian movement relations to Bergson,

Nietzsche and even to fascism; and in analyzing the forms of Futurist art he tries to show they embody the qualities asserted in the manifestos.

But if Futurism has an obvious ideological aspect, it is not a pure abstract art for Barr. It is "near-abstraction," for it refers overtly to a world outside the canvas and still retains elements of representation.

Yet the forms of "pure" abstract art, which seem to be entirely without trace of representation or escapist morbidity—the neo-plasticist works of Mondrian and the later designs of the Constructivists and Suprematists—are admittedly influenced in their material aspect, as textures and shapes, and in their expressive qualities of precision, impersonal finish and neatness (and even in subtler informalities of design), by the current conceptions and norms of the machine.

Neither Futurism nor the "purer" mechanical abstract forma can be explained, however, as a simple reflection of the existing machines. Although machines have existed since ancient times and have had a central place in production in some countries for over a century, this art is peculiar to the last twenty-five years. In the middle of the 19th century when the machines were already hailed as the great works of modern art, superior to the paintings of the time, the taste of progressive industrialists was towards a realistic art, and Proudhon could celebrate as the real modern works the pictures of Courbet and the newest machines. Not even the personal preoccupation with machines necessarily leads by itself to a style of mechanical abstract forms; the inventors Alexander Nasmyth, Robert Fulton and Samuel Morse were fairly naturalistic painters, like Leonardo, one of the fathers of modern technology. The French art of the period of mechanistic philosophy, the 17th century, was dominated by idealized naturalistic human forms. And the conception of man as a machine current in France during the predominance of the unmechanical rococo style was identified by its defenders and critics with a matter-of-fact sensualism. The enemies of La Mettrie, the author of *Man the Machine*, were pleased to point out that he died of over-eating.

More significant, however, is the fact that in recent times the advanced industrial countries with the most developed technologies, the United States and England, did not originate styles of mechanical abstraction; they are also the most backward in functionalist abstraction of forms in architecture. On the other hand, the development of such arts takes place in Russia, Italy, Holland and France; and only later in Germany. Hence the explanation of the arts as a reflection of existing machines is certainly inadequate. It could not explain above all the differences in "machine-styles" from place to place at a moment when technology has an international character. In Detroit, the murals of machines by Rivera are realistic images of the factory as a world operated by workers; in Paris Léger decomposes the elements of machines into Cubist abstractions or assimilates living things to the typical rigid shapes of machines; the Dadaists improvise a whimsical burlesque with robots or reconstructed men; in Holland the neoplasticists construct their works of quasi-architectural units; in Germany the Constructivist-Suprematist forms ape the drawings and models of the machine designer, rather than the machines themselves. And the Futurists, in distinction from all of these, try to recapture the phenomenal aspect of moving mechanisms, of energy and speed.

These differences are not simply a matter of different local artistic traditions operating on a common modern material. For if this were the case, we should expect a Mondrian in Italy, the country of Renaissance tradition of clarified forms, and the Futurists in Holland and England, the pioneer lands of Impressionism.

A similar criticism would apply to the corresponding derivation of abstraction in art from the abstract nature of modern finance, in which bits of paper control capital and all human transactions assume the form of operations on numbers and titles. Here again we observe that the United States and England, with the most highly developed financial capitalism, are among the last countries to produce abstract art.

Mechanical abstract forms arise in modern art not because modern production is mechanical, but because of the values assigned to the human being and the machine in the ideologies projected by the conflicting interests and situation in society, which vary from country to country. Thus the modern conception of man as a machine is more economic than biological in its accent. It refers to the human robot rather than to the human animal, and suggests an efficient control of the costly movements of the body, a submission to some external purpose indifferent to the individual; unlike the older mechanistic views which concerned man's passions, explained them by internal mechanical forces, and sometimes deduced an ethics of pleasure, utility and self-interest.

Barr recognizes the importance of local conditions when he attributes the deviations of one of the Futurists to his Parisian experience. But he makes no effort to explain why this art should emerge in Italy rather than elsewhere. The Italian writers have described it as a reaction against the traditionalism and sleepiness of Italy during the rule of Umberto, and in doing so have overlooked the positive sources of this reaction and its effects on Italian life. The backwardness was most intensely felt to be a contradiction and became a provoking issue towards 1910 and then mainly in the North, which had recently experienced the most rapid industrial development. At this moment Italian capitalism was preparing the imperialist war in Tripoli. Italy, poor in resources yet competing with world empires, urgently required expansion to attain the levels of the older capitalist countries. The belated growth of industry, founded on exploitation of the peasantry, had intensified the disparities of culture, called into being a strong proletariat, and promoted imperialist adventures. There arose at this time, in response to the economic growth of the country and the rapid changes in the older historical environment, philosophies of process and utility—a militant pragmatism of an emphatic anti-traditionalist character. Sections of the middle class which had acquired new functions and modern urban interests accepted the new conditions as progressive and "modern," and were often the loudest in denouncing Italian backwardness and calling for an up-to-date, nationally conscious Italy. The attack of the intellectuals against the provincial aristocratic traditions was in keeping with the interest of the dominant class; they elevated technical progress, aggressive individuality and the relativism of values into theories favorable to imperialist expansion, obscuring the contradictory results of the latter and the conflicts between classes by abstract ideological oppositions of the old and the modern or the past and the future. Since the national consciousness of Italy had rested for generations on her museums, her old cities and artistic inheritance, the modernizing of the country entailed a cultural conflict, which assumed its sharpest form among the artists. Machines as the most advanced instruments of modern production had a special attraction for artists exasperated by their own merely traditional and secondary status, their mediocre outlook in a backward provincial Italy. They were devoted to machines not so much as instruments of production as the sources of mobility in modern life. While the perception of industrial processes led the workers, who participated in them directly, toward a radical social philosophy, the artists, who were detached from production, like the petty bourgeoisie, could know these processes abstractly or phenomenally, in their products and outward appearance, in the form of traffic, automobiles, railroads, and new cities and in the tempo of urban life, rather than in their social causes. The Futurists thus came to idealize movement as such, and they conceived this movement or generalized mobility mainly as mechanical phenomena in which the forms of objects are blurred or destroyed. The dynamism of an auto, centrifugal motion, the dog in movement (with twenty legs), the autobus, the evolution of forms in space, the armored train in battle, the dance hall—these were the typical subjects of Futurist art. The field of the canvas was charged with radiating lines, symbolic graphs of pervading force, colliding and interpenetrating objects. Whereas the mobility in Impressionism was a spectacle for relaxed enjoyment, in Futurism it is urgent and violent, a precursor of war.

Several of the Futurist devices, and the larger idea of abstract and interpenetrating forms, undoubtedly come from Cubism. But, significantly, the Italians found Cubism too estheticized and intellectual, lacking a principle of movement; they could accept, however, the Cubist dissolution of stable, clearly bounded forms. This had a direct ideological value, though essentially an esthetic device, for the stable and clear were very definitely identified with the older Italian art as well as with the past as such.

Outside Italy, and especially after the World War, the qualities of the machine as a rigid constructed object, and the qualities of its products and of the engineer's design suggested various forms to painters, and even the larger expressive characters of their work. The older categories of art were translated into the languge of modern technology; the essential was identified with the efficient, the unit with the standardized element, texture with new materials, representation with photography, drawing with the ruled or mechanically traced line, color with the flat coat of paint and design with the model or the instructing plan. The painters thus tied their useless archaic activity to the most advanced and imposing forms of modern production; and precisely because technology was conceived abstractly as an independent force with its own inner conditions, and the designing engineer as the real maker of the modern world, the step from their earlier Expressionist, Cubist or Suprematist abstraction to the more technological style was not a great one. (Even Kandinsky and Malevitch changed during the 1920's under the influence of these conceptions.) In applying their methods of design to architecture, printing, the theatre and the industrial arts they remained abstract artists. They often looked upon their work as the esthetic counterpart of the abstract calculations of the engineer and the scientist. If they admitted an alternative art of fantasy—in some ways formally related to their own—it was merely as a residual field of freedom or as a hygienic relaxation from the rigors of their own efficiency. Unlike the Futurists, whose conception of progress was blindly insurgent, they wished to reconstruct culture through the logic of sober technique and design; and in this wish they considered themselves the indispensable esthetic prophets of a new order in life. Some of them supported the Bolshevik revolution, many more collaborated with the social-democratic and liberal reformist architects of Germany and Holland. Their conception of technology as a norm in art was largely conditioned, on the one hand, by the stringent rationalization of industry in post-war Europe in the drive to reduce costs and widen the market as the only hope of a strangling capitalism threatened by American domination, and, on the other hand, by the reformist illusion, which was especially widespread in the brief period of post-war prosperity during this economic impasse, that the technological advance, in raising the living standards of the people, in lowering the costs of housing and other necessities, would resolve the conflict of classes, or at any rate form in the technicians habits of efficient, economic planning, conducive to a peaceful transition to socialism. Architecture or Revolution! That was in fact one of the slogans of Le Corbusier, the architect, painter and editor of the magazine *L'Esprit Nouveau*.

With the approach of the crisis of the 1930's critics like Elie Faure called on painters to abandon their art and become engineers; and architects, in America as well as Europe, sensitive to the increasing economic pressure, though ignorant of its causes, identified architecture with engineering, denying the architect any conscious esthetic function. In these extreme views, which were shared by reformists of technocratic tendency, we can see the debacle of the optimistic machine-ideologies in modern culture. As production is curtailed and living standards reduced, even art is renounced in the name of technical progress.

During the crisis the mechanical abstract styles have become secondary. They influence very few young artists, or they tend toward what Barr calls "biomorphic abstraction," of a violent or nervous calligraphy, or with amoeboid forms, a soft, low-grade matter pulsing in an empty space. An anti-rationalist style, Surrealism, which had issued from the Dadaist art of the 1917–23 period, becomes predominant and beside it arise new romantic styles, with pessimistic imagery of empty spaces, bones, grotesque beings, abandoned buildings and catastrophic earth formations.

Note

1. Alfred H. Barr, Jr., *Cubism and Abstract Art* (New York 1936). 248 pages, 223 illustrations. It was published by the Museum of Modern Art as the guide and catalogue of its great exhibition held in the spring of 1936.

12
Clement Greenberg (1909–1994)
Avant-Garde and Kitsch (1939)

Editor's Introduction

Clement Greenberg was born in the Bronx of Lithuanian parents. After earning his bachelor's degree in 1930 from Syracuse University he tried his father's business and then worked for the federal government in New York City. Finally, he found himself in Manhattan in the waning years of the Depression taking art classes sponsored by the Works Progress Administration and listening to the ideas of modernist painters such as Arshile Gorky, Willem de Kooning and Hans Hofmann. He began writing art criticism, and in the next few years saw his essays and reviews published in *Partisan Review*, the *Nation* and other magazines. Greenberg was an anti-Stalinist socialist, like those at *Partisan Review*, and in 1940 the magazine offered him a position as an editor. In 1944 he took a position as managing editor for *Commentary*.

Greenberg's signature essay, "Avant-Garde and Kitsch," appeared in *Partisan Review* in 1939. In it he argued that the artists with the greatest vision and foresight needed to detach themselves from society, work as a vanguard group, an avant-garde, and "to keep culture *moving*" instead of allowing it to stagnate into repetitive commercial renditions of easily digestible "kitsch." Modernist painting, for example, was an avant-garde approach, always working to explore new forms or expressions. Ignoring representation and embracing abstraction, modernist painting wanted "to imitate God by creating something valid solely on its own terms, in the way nature itself is valid, in the way a landscape—not its picture—is aesthetically valid."

This period in the late 1930s and early 1940s found painters, novelists, and critics—particularly if they were on the anti-Stalinist political left—trying to shed the political element in art and criticism. The proletarian realism in both painting and literature in the thirties had forced what the *Partisan Review* group thought was a dull, concrete and representational predictability on young artists and critics, and many novelists, painters and critics were proclaiming their freedom from the suffocating expectations that ideology threw over them. Greenberg, like others of the New York Intellectuals, gravitated to modernism as an edifice that might shelter him from simple political recipes—although some of his detractors later in his career accused him of employing a similarly rigid recipe of abstraction.

Over the course of the next several decades Greenberg was known as a supporter of modernist artists who painted in styles ranging from abstract expressionism to color-field painting, and his greatest sponsorship was of the work of Jackson Pollock. Greenberg felt great enthusiasm for flat-canvas painting. The history of painting was a succession of painters trying to impart a three-dimensional depth to a canvas, Greenberg said, and he believed it inauthentic. Painting, in his opinion, was not to create a recognizable image or depth of field, but to show a skill, a talent for the use of paint on a surface, an aesthetic. Unlike Meyer Schapiro, Greenberg did not embrace a multiplicity of periods and styles. He resisted the decline of abstract art and he turned his back on later trends such as the conceptual art of Andy Warhol, the pop art of Roy Lichtenstein, and the postmodernist wave that washed over the final quarter of the century. In return, many members of the younger generation scorned Greenberg late in his life and disparaged the elitist idea of an avant-garde.

Source

Clement Greenberg, "Avant-Garde and Kitsch," *Partisan Review* vol. 1, no. 5, Fall 1939.

Selected Readings

Alice Goldfarb, *Art Czar* (Boston: MFA Publications, 2006).
Clement Greenberg, *Art and Culture* (Boston: Beacon Press, 1961).

* * * * *

One and the same civilization produces simultaneously two such different things as a poem by T. S. Eliot and a Tin Pan Alley song, or a painting by Braque and a *Saturday Evening Post* cover. All four are on the order of culture, and ostensibly, parts of the same culture and products of the same society. Here, however, their connection seems to end. A poem by Eliot and a poem by Eddie Guest—what perspective of culture is large enough to enable us to situate them in an enlightening relation to each other? Does the fact that a disparity such as this within the frame of a single cultural tradition, is and has been taken for granted—does this fact indicate that the disparity is a part of the natural order of things? Or is it something entirely new, and particular to our age?

The answer involves more than an investigation in aesthetics. It appears to me that it is necessary to examine more closely and with more originality than hitherto the relationship between aesthetic experience as met by the specific—not generalized—individual, and the social and historical contexts in which that experience takes place. What is brought to light will answer, in addition to the question posed above, other and perhaps more important ones.

I

A society, as it becomes less and less able, in the course of its development, to justify the inevitability of its particular forms, breaks up the accepted notions upon which artists and writers must depend in large part for communication with their audiences. It becomes difficult to assume anything. All the verities involved by religion, authority, tradition, style, are thrown into question, and the writer or artist is no longer able to estimate the response of his audience to the symbols and references with which he works. In the past such a state of affairs has usually resolved itself into a motionless Alexandrianism, an academicism in which the really important issues are left untouched because they involve controversy, and in which creative activity dwindles to virtuosity in the small details of form, all larger questions being decided by the precedent of the old masters. The same themes are mechanically varied in a hundred different works, and yet nothing new is produced: Statius, mandarin verse, Roman sculpture, Beaux Arts painting, neo-republican architecture.

It is among the hopeful signs in the midst of the decay of our present society that we—some of us—have been unwilling to accept this last phase for our own culture. In seeking to go beyond Alexandrianism, a part of Western bourgeois society has produced something unheard of heretofore: avant-garde culture. A superior consciousness of history—more precisely, the appearance of a new kind of criticism of society, an historical criticism—made this possible. This criticism has not confronted our present society with timeless utopias, but has soberly examined in the terms of history and of cause and effect the antecedents, justifications and functions of the forms that lie at the heart of every society. Thus our present bourgeois social order was shown to be, not an eternal, "natural" condition of life, but simply the latest term in a succession of social orders. New perspectives of this kind, becoming a part of the advanced intellectual conscience of the fifth and sixth decades of the nineteenth century, soon were absorbed by artists and poets, even if unconsciously for the most part. It was no accident, therefore, that the birth of the avant-garde coincided chronologically—and geographically too—with the first bold development of scientific revolutionary thought in Europe.

True, the first settlers of Bohemia—which was then identical with the avant-garde—turned out soon to be demonstratively uninterested in politics. Nevertheless, without the circulation of revolutionary ideas in the air about them, they would never have been able to isolate their concept of the "bourgeois" in order to define what they were *not*. Nor, without the moral aid of revolutionary political attitudes would they have had the courage to assert themselves as aggressively as they did against the prevailing standards of society. Courage indeed was needed for this, because the avant-garde's emigration from bourgeois society to Bohemia meant also an emigration from the markets of capitalism, upon which artists and writers had been thrown by the falling away of aristocratic patronage. (Ostensibly, at least, it meant this—meant starving in a garret—although, as will be shown later, the avant-garde remained attached to bourgeois society precisely because it needed its money.)

Yet it is true that once the avant-garde had succeeded in "detaching" itself from society, it proceeded to turn around and repudiate revolutionary politics as well as bourgeois. The revolution was left inside society, a part of that welter of ideological struggle which art and poetry find so unpropitious as soon as it begins to involve those "precious," axiomatic beliefs upon which culture thus far has had to rest. Hence it was developed that the true and most important function of the avant-garde was not to "experiment," but to find a path along which it would be possible to keep culture *moving* in the midst of ideological confusion and violence. Retiring from public altogether, the avant-garde poet or artist sought to maintain the high level of his art by both narrowing and raising it to the expression of an absolute in which all relativities and contradictions would be either resolved or beside the point. "Art for art's sake" and "pure poetry" appear, and subject-matter or content becomes something to be avoided like a plague.

It has been in search of the absolute that the avant-garde has arrived at "abstract" or "non-objective" art—and poetry, too. The avant-garde poet or artist tries in effect to imitate God by creating something valid solely on its own terms in the way nature itself is valid, in the way a landscape—not its picture—is aesthetically valid; something *given*, increate, independent of meanings, similars, or originals. Content is to be dissolved so completely into form that the work of art or literature cannot be reduced in whole or in part to anything not itself.

But the absolute is absolute, and the poet or artist, being what he is, cherishes certain relative values more than others. The very values in the name of which he invokes the absolute are relative values, the values of aesthetics. And so he turns out to be imitating, not God—and here I use "imitate" in its Aristotelian sense—but the disciplines and processes of art and literature themselves. This is the genesis of the "abstract."[1] In turning his attention away from subject-matter or common experience, the poet or artist turns it in upon the medium of his own craft. The non-representational or "abstract," if it is to have aesthetic validity, cannot be arbitrary and accidental, but must stem from obedience to some worthy constraint or original. This constraint, once the world of common, extraverted experience has been renounced, can only be found in the very processes or disciplines by which art and literature have already imitated the former. These themselves become the subject matter of art and literature. If, to continue with Aristotle, all art and literature are imitation, then what we have here is the imitation of imitating. To quote Yeats:

"Nor is there singing school but studying
Monuments of its own magnificence."

Picasso, Braque, Mondrian, Miro, Kandinsky, Brancusi, even Klee, Matisse and Cezanne, derive their chief inspiration from the medium they work in.[2] The excitement of their art seems to lie most of all in its pure preoccupation with the invention and arrangement of spaces, surfaces, shapes, colors, etc., to the exclusion of whatever is not necessarily implicated in these factors. The attention of poets like Rimbaud, Mallarmé, Valéry, Eluard, Pound, Hart Crane, Stevens, even Rilke and Yeats, appears to be centered on the effort to create poetry and on the "moments" themselves of poetic conversion rather than on experience to be converted into poetry. Of course, this cannot exclude other preoccupations in their work, for poetry must deal with words, and words must communicate. Certain poets, such as Mallarmé and Valéry,[3] are more radical in this respect than others—leaving aside those poets who have tried to compose poetry in pure sound alone. However, if it were easier to define poetry, modern poetry would be much more "pure" and "abstract." ... As for the other fields of literature—the definition of avant-garde aesthetics advanced here is no Procrustean bed. But aside from the fact that most of our best contemporary novelists have gone to school with the avant-garde, it is significant that Gide's most ambitious book is a novel about the writing of a novel, and that Joyce's *Ulysses* and *Finnegan's Wake* seem to be above all, as one French critic says, the reduction of experience to expression for the sake of expression, the expression mattering more than what is being expressed.

That avant-garde culture is the imitation of imitat*ing*—the fact itself—calls for neither approval nor disapproval. It is true that this culture contains within itself some of the very Alexandrianism it seeks to overcome. The lines quoted from Yeats above referred to Byzantium, which is very close to Alexandria; and in a sense this imitation of imitat*ing* is a superior sort of Alexandrianism. But there is one most important difference: the avant-garde moves, while Alexandrianism stands still. And this, precisely, is what justifies the avant-garde's methods and makes them necessary. The necessity lies in the fact that by no other means is it possible today to create art and literature of a high order. To quarrel with necessity by throwing about terms like "formalism," "purism," "ivory tower" and so forth is either dull or dishonest. This is not to say, however, that it is to the *social* advantage of the avant-garde that it is what it is. Quite the opposite.

The avant-garde's specialization of itself, the fact that its best artists are artists' artists, its best poets, poets' poets, has estranged a great many of those who were capable formerly of enjoying and appreciating ambitious art and literature, but who are now unwilling or unable to acquire an initiation into their craft secrets. The masses have always remained more or less indifferent to culture in the process of development. But today such culture is being abandoned by those to whom it actually belongs—our ruling class. For it is to the latter that the avant-garde belongs. No culture can develop without a social basis, without a source of stable income. And in the case of the avant-garde this was provided by an elite among the ruling class of that society from which it assumed itself to be cut off, but to which it has always remained attached by an umbilical cord of gold. The paradox is real. And now this elite is rapidly shrinking. Since the avant-garde forms the only living culture we now have, the survival in the near future of culture in general is thus threatened.

We must not be deceived by superficial phenomena and local successes. Picasso's shows still draw crowds, and T. S. Eliot is taught in the universities; the dealers in modernist art are still in business, and the publishers still publish some "difficult" poetry. But the avant-garde itself, already sensing the danger, is becoming more and more timid every day that passes. Academicism and commercialism are appearing in the strangest places. This can mean only one thing: that the avant-garde is becoming unsure of the audience it depends on—the rich and the cultivated.

Is it the nature itself of avant-garde culture that is alone responsible for the danger it finds itself in? Or is that only a dangerous liability? Are there other, and perhaps more important, factors involved?

II

Where there is an avant-garde, generally we also find a rearguard. True enough—simultaneously with the entrance of the avant-garde, a second new cultural phenomenon appeared in the industrial West: that thing to which the Germans give the wonderful name of *Kitsch:* popular, commercial art and literature with their chromeotypes, magazine covers, illustrations, ads, slick and pulp fiction, comics, Tin Pan Alley music, tap dancing, Hollywood movies, etc., etc. For some reason this gigantic apparition has always been taken for granted. It is time we looked into its whys and wherefores.

Kitsch is a product of the industrial revolution which urbanized the masses of Western Europe and America and established what is called universal literacy.

Previous to this the only market for formal culture, as distinguished from folk culture, had been among those who in addition to being able to read and write could command the leisure and comfort that always goes hand in hand with cultivation of some sort. This until then had been inextricably associated with literacy. But with the introduction of universal literacy, the ability to read and write became almost a minor skill like driving a car, and it no longer served to distinguish an individual's cultural inclinations, since it was no longer the exclusive concomitant of refined tastes. The peasants who settled in the cities as proletariat and petty bourgeois learned to read and write for the sake of efficiency, but they did not win the leisure and comfort necessary for the enjoyment of the city's traditional culture. Losing, nevertheless, their taste for the folk culture whose background was the countryside, and discovering a new capacity for boredom at the same time, the new urban masses set up a pressure on society to provide them with a kind of culture fit for their own consumption. To fill the demand of the new market a new commodity was devised: ersatz culture, kitsch, destined for those who, insensible to the values of genuine culture, are hungry nevertheless for the diversion that only culture of some sort can provide.

Kitsch, using for raw material the debased and academicized simulacra of genuine culture, welcomes and cultivates this insensibility. It is the source of its profits. Kitsch is mechanical and operates by formulas. Kitsch is vicarious experience and faked sensations. Kitsch changes according to style, but remains always the same. Kitsch is the epitome of all that is spurious in the life of our times. Kitsch pretends to demand nothing of its customers except their money—not even their time.

The pre-condition for kitsch, a condition without which kitsch would be impossible, is the availability close at hand of a fully matured cultural tradition, whose discoveries, acquisitions and perfected self-consciousness kitsch can take advantage of for its own ends. It borrows from it devices, tricks, strategems, rules of thumb, themes, converts them into a system and discards the rest. It draws its life blood, so to speak, from this reservoir of accumulated experience. This is what is really meant when it is said that the popular art and literature of today were once the daring, esoteric art and literature of yesterday. Of course, no such thing is true. What is meant is that when enough time has elapsed the new is looted for new "twists," which are then watered down and served up as kitsch. Self-evidently, all kitsch is academic, and conversely, all that's academic is kitsch. For what is called the academic as such no longer has an independent existence, but has become the stuffed-shirt "front" for kitsch. The methods of industrialism displace the handicrafts.

Because it can be turned out mechanically, kitsch has become an integral part of our productive system in a way in which true culture could never be except accidentally. It has been capitalized at a tremendous investment which must show commensurate returns; it is compelled to extend as well as to keep its markets. While it is essentially its own salesman, a great sales apparatus has nevertheless been created for it, which brings pressure to bear on every member of society. Traps are laid even in those areas, so to speak, that are the preserves of genuine culture. It is not enough today, in a country like ours, to have an inclination towards the latter; one must have a true passion for it that will give him the power to resist the faked article that surrounds and presses in on him from the moment he is old enough to look at the funny papers. Kitsch is deceptive. It has many different levels, and some of them are high enough to be dangerous to the naive seeker of true light. A magazine like the *New Yorker*, which is fundamentally high-class kitsch for the luxury trade, converts and waters down a great deal of avant-garde material for its own uses. Nor is every single item of kitsch altogether worthless. Now and then it produces something of merit, something that has an authentic folk flavor; and these accidental and isolated instances have fooled people who should know better.

Kitsch's enormous profits are a source of temptation to the avant-garde itself, and its members have not always resisted this temptation. Ambitious writers and artists will modify their work under the pressure of kitsch, if they do not succumb to it entirely. And then those puzzling border-line cases appear, such as the popular novelist, Simenon, in France, and Steinbeck in this country. The net result is always to the detriment of true culture, in any case.

Kitsch has not been confined to the cities in which it was born, but has flowed out over the countryside, wiping out folk culture. Nor has it shown any regard for geographical and national-cultural boundaries. Another mass product of Western industrialism, it has gone on a triumphal tour of the world, crowding out and defacing native cultures in one colonial country after another, so that it is now by way of becoming a universal culture, the first universal culture ever beheld. Today the Chinaman, no less than the South American Indian, the Hindu, no less than the Polynesian, have come to prefer the products of their native art magazine covers, rotogravure sections and calendar girls. How is this virulence of kitsch, this irresistible attractiveness, to be explained? Naturally, machine-made kitsch can undersell the native handmade article, and the prestige of the West also helps, but why is kitsch a so much more profitable export article than Rembrandt? One, after all, can be reproduced as cheaply as the other.

In his last article on the Soviet cinema in the *Partisan Review*, Dwight Macdonald points out that kitsch has in the last ten years become the dominant culture in Soviet Russia. For this he blames the political regime—not only for the fact that kitsch is the official culture, but also that it is actually the dominant, most popular culture; and he quotes the following from Kurt London's *The Seven Soviet Arts:* "... the attitude of the masses both to the old and new art styles probably remains essentially dependent on the nature of the education afforded them by their respective states." Macdonald goes on to say: "Why after all should ignorant peasants prefer Repin (a leading exponent of Russian academic kitsch in painting) to Picasso, whose abstract technique is at least as relevant to their own primitive folk art as is the former's realistic style? No, if the masses crowd into the Tretyakov (Moscow's museum of contemporary Russian art: kitsch) it is largely because they have been conditioned to shun 'formalism' and to admire 'socialist realism'."

In the first place it is not a question of a choice between merely the old and merely the new, as London seems to think—but of a choice between the bad, up-to-date old and the genuinely new. The alternative to Picasso is not Michelangelo, but kitsch. In the second place, neither in backward Russia nor in the advanced West do the masses prefer kitsch simply because their governments condition them towards it. Where state educational systems take the trouble to mention art, we are told to respect the old masters, not kitsch; and yet we go and hang Maxfield Parrish or his equivalent on our walls, instead of Rembrandt and Michelangelo. Moreover, as Macdonald himself points out, around 1925 when the Soviet regime was encouraging avant-garde cinema, the Russian masses continued to prefer Hollywood movies. No, "conditioning" does not explain the potency of kitsch. ...

All values are human values, relative values, in art as well as elsewhere. Yet there does seem to have been more or less of a general agreement among the cultivated of mankind over the ages as to what is good art and what bad. Taste has varied, but not beyond certain limits: contemporary connoisseurs agree with eighteenth century Japanese that Hokusai was one of the greatest artists of his time; we even agree with the ancient Egyptians that Third and Fourth Dynasty art was the most worthy of being selected as their paragon by those who came after. We may have come to prefer Giotto to Raphael, but we still do not deny that Raphael was one of the best painters of his *time*. There has been an agreement then, and this agreement rests, I believe, on a fairly constant distinction made between those values only to be found in art and the values which can be found elsewhere. Kitsch, by virtue of rationalized technique that draws on science and industry, has erased this distinction in practice.

Let us see for example what happens when an ignorant Russian peasant such as Macdonald mentions stands with hypothetical freedom of choice before two paintings, one by Picasso, the other by Repin. In the first he sees, let us say, a play of lines, colors and spaces that represent a woman. The abstract technique—to accept Macdonald's supposition, which I am inclined to doubt—reminds him somewhat of the icons he has left behind him in the village, and he feels the attraction of the familiar. We will even suppose that he faintly surmises some of the great art values the cultivated find in Picasso. He turns next to Repin's picture and sees a battle scene. The technique is not so familiar—as technique. But that weighs very little with the peasant, for he suddenly discovers values in Repin's picture which seem far superior to the values he has been accustomed to finding in icon art; and the unfamiliar technique itself is one of the sources of those values: the values of the vividly recognizable, the miraculous and the sympathetic. In Repin's picture the peasant recognizes and sees things in the way in which he recognizes and sees things outside of pictures—there is no discontinuity between art and life, no need to accept a convention and say to oneself, that icon represents Jesus because it intends to represent Jesus, even if it does not remind me very much of a man. That Repin can paint so realistically that identifications are self-evident immediately and without any effort on the part of the spectator—that is miraculous. The peasant is also pleased by the wealth of self-evident meanings which he finds in the picture: "it tells a story." Picasso and the icons are so austere and barren in comparison. What is more, Repin heightens reality and makes it dramatic: sunset, exploding shells, running and falling men. There is no longer any question of Picasso or icons. Repin is what the peasant wants, and nothing else but Repin. It is lucky, however, for Repin that the peasant is protected from the products of American capitalism, for he would not stand a chance next to a *Saturday Evening Post* cover by Norman Rockwell.

Ultimately, it can be said that the cultivated spectator derives the same values from Picasso that the peasant gets from Repin, since what the latter enjoys in Repin is somehow art too, on however low a scale, and he is sent to look at pictures by the same instincts that send the cultivated spectator. But the ultimate values which the cultivated spectator derives from Picasso are derived at a second remove, as the result of reflection upon the immediate impression left by the plastic values. It is only then that the recognizable, the miraculous and the sympathetic enter. They are not immediately or externally present in Picasso's painting, but must be projected into it by the spectator sensitive enough to react sufficiently to plastic qualities. They belong to the "reflected" effect. In Repin, on the other hand, the "reflected" effect has already been included in the picture, ready for the spectator's unreflective enjoyment.[4] Where Picasso paints *cause*, Repin paints *effect*. Repin predigests art for the spectator and spares him effort, provides him with a short cut to the pleasure of art that detours what is necessarily difficult in genuine art. Repin, or kitsch, is synthetic art.

The same point can be made with respect to kitsch literature: it provides vicarious experience for the insensitive with far greater immediacy than serious fiction can hope to do. And Eddie Guest and the *Indian Love Lyrics* are more poetic than T. S. Eliot and Shakespeare.

III

If the avant-garde imitates the processes of art, kitsch, we now see, imitates its effects. The neatness of this antithesis is more than contrived; it corresponds to and defines the tremendous interval that separates from each other two such simultaneous cultural phenomena as the avant-garde and kitsch. This interval, too great to be closed by all the infinite gradations of popularized "modernism" and "modernistic" kitsch, corresponds in turn to a social interval, a social interval that has always existed in formal culture as elsewhere in civilized society, and whose two termini converge and diverge in fixed relation to the increasing or decreasing stability of the given society. There has always been on one side the minority of the powerful—and therefore the cultivated— and on the other the great mass of the exploited and poor—and therefore the ignorant. Formal culture has always belonged to the first, while the last have had to content themselves with folk or rudimentary culture, or kitsch.

In a stable society which functions well enough to hold in solution the contradictions between its classes the cultural dichotomy becomes somewhat blurred. The axioms of the few are shared by the many; the latter believe superstitiously what the former believe soberly. And at such moments in history the masses are able to feel wonder and admiration for the culture, on no matter how high a plane, of its masters. This applies at least to plastic culture, which is accessible to all.

In the Middle Ages the plastic artist paid lip service at least to the lowest common denominators of experience. This even remained true to some extent until the seventeenth century. There was available for imitation a universally valid conceptual reality, whose order the artist could not tamper with. The subject matter of art was prescribed by those who commissioned works of art, which were not created, as in bourgeois society, on speculation. Precisely because his content was determined in advance, the artist was free to concentrate on his medium. He needed not to be philosopher or visionary, but simply artificer. As long as there was general agreement as to what were the worthiest subjects for art, the artist was relieved of the necessity to be original and inventive in his "matter" and could devote all his energy to formal problems. For him the medium became, privately, professionally, the content of his art, even as today his medium is the public content of the abstract painter's art—with that difference, however, that the medieval artist had to suppress his professional preoccupation in public—had always to suppress and subordinate the personal and professional in the finished, official work of art. If, as an ordinary member of the Christian community, he felt some personal emotion about his subject matter, this only contributed to the enrichment of the work's public meaning. Only with the Renaissance do the inflections of the personal become legitimate, still to be kept, however, within the limits of the simply and universally recognizable. And only with Rembrandt do "lonely" artists begin to appear, lonely in their art.

But even during the Renaissance, and as long as Western art was endeavoring to perfect its technique, victories in this realm could only be signalized by success in realistic imitation, since there was no other objective criterion at hand. Thus the masses could still find in the art of their masters objects of admiration and wonder. Even the bird who pecked at the fruit in Zeuxes' picture could applaud.

It is a platitude that art becomes caviar to the general when the reality it imitates no longer corresponds even roughly to the reality recognized by the general. Even then, however, the resentment the common man may feel is silenced by the awe in which he stands of the patrons of this art. Only when he becomes dissatisfied with the social order they administer does he begin to criticize their culture. Then the plebeian finds courage for the first time to voice his opinions openly. Every man, from Tammany aldermen to Austrian house-painters, finds that he is entitled to his opinion. Most often this resentment towards culture is to be found where the dissatisfaction with society is a reactionary dissatisfaction which expresses itself in revivalism and puritanism, and latest of all, in fascism. Here revolvers and torches begin to be mentioned in the same breath as culture. In the name of godliness or the blood's health, in the name of simple ways and solid virtues, the statue-smashing commences.

IV

Returning to our Russian peasant for the moment, let us suppose that after he has chosen Repin in preference to Picasso, the state's educational apparatus comes along and tells him that he is wrong, that he should have chosen Picasso—and shows him why. It is quite possible for the Soviet state to do this. But things being as they are in Russia—and everywhere else—the peasant soon finds that the necessity of working hard all day for his living and the rude, uncomfortable circumstances in which he lives do not allow him enough leisure, energy and comfort to train for the enjoyment of Picasso. This needs, after all, a considerable amount of "conditioning." Superior culture is one of the most artificial of all human creations, and the peasant finds no "natural" urgency within himself that will drive him towards Picasso in spite of all difficulties. In the end the peasant will go back to kitsch when he feels like looking at pictures, for he can enjoy kitsch without effort. The state is helpless in this matter and remains so as long as the problems of production have not been solved in a socialist sense. The same holds true, of course, for capitalist countries and makes all talk of art for the masses there nothing but demagogy.[5]

Where today a political regime establishes an official cultural policy, it is for the sake of demagogy. If kitsch is the official tendency of culture in Germany, Italy and Russia, it is not because their respective governments are controlled by philistines, but because kitsch is the culture of the masses in these countries, as it is everywhere else. The encouragement of kitsch is merely another of the inexpensive ways in which totalitarian regimes seek to ingratiate themselves with their subjects. Since these regimes cannot raise the cultural level of the masses—even if they wanted to—by anything short of a surrender to international socialism, they will flatter the masses by bringing all culture down to their level. It is for this reason that the avant-garde is outlawed, and not so much because a superior culture is inherently a more critical culture. (Whether or not the avant-garde could possibly flourish under a totalitarian regime is not pertinent to the question at this point.) As matter of fact, the main trouble with avant-garde art and literature, from the point of view of Fascists and Stalinists, is not that they are too critical, but that they are too "innocent," that it is too difficult to inject effective propaganda into them, that kisch is more pliable to this end. Kitsch keeps a dictator in closer contact with the "soul" of the people. Should the official culture be one superior to the general mass-level, there would be a danger of isolation.

Nevertheless, if the masses were conceivably to ask for avant-garde art and literature, Hitler, Mussolini and Stalin would not hesitate long in attempting to satisfy such a demand. Hitler is a bitter enemy of the avant-garde, both on doctrinal and personal grounds, yet this did not prevent Goebbels in 1932–33 from strenuously courting avant-garde artists and writers. When Gottfried Benn, an Expressionist poet, came over to the Nazis he was welcomed with a great fanfare, although at that very moment Hitler was denouncing Expressionism as *Kulturbolschewismus*. This was at a time when the Nazis felt that the prestige which the avant-garde enjoyed among the cultivated German public could be of advantage to them, and practical considerations of this nature, the Nazis being the skilful politicians they are, have always taken precedence over Hitler's personal inclinations. Later the Nazis realized that it was more practical to accede to the wishes of the masses in matters of culture than to those of their paymasters; the latter, when it came to a question of preserving power, were as willing to sacrifice their culture as they were their moral principles, while the former, precisely because power was being withheld from them, had to be cozened in every other way possible. It was necessary to promote on a much more grandiose style than in the democracies the illusion that the masses actually rule. The literature and art they enjoy and understand were to be proclaimed the only true art and literature and any other kind was to be suppressed. Under these circumstances people like Gottfried Benn, no matter how ardently they support Hitler, become a liability; and we hear no more of them in Nazi Germany.

We can see then that although from one point of view the personal philistinism of Hitler and Stalin is not accidental to the political roles they play, from another point of view it is only an incidentally contributory factor in determining the cultural policies of their respective regimes. Their personal philistinism simply adds brutality and double-darkness to policies they would be forced to support anyhow by the pressure of all their other policies—even were they, personally, devotees of avant-garde culture. What the acceptance of the isolation of the Russian Revolution forces Stalin to do, Hitler is compelled to do by his acceptance of the contradictions of capitalism and his efforts to freeze them. As for Mussolini—his case is a perfect example of the *disponibilité* of a realist in these matters. For years he bent a benevolent eye on the Futurists and built modernistic railroad stations and government-owned apartment houses. One can still see in the suburbs of Rome more modernistic apartments than almost anywhere else in the world. Perhaps Fascism wanted to show its up-to-datedness, to conceal the fact that it was a retrogression; perhaps it wanted to conform to the tastes of the wealthy élite it served. At any rate Mussolini seems to have realized lately that it would be more useful to him to please the cultural tastes of the Italian masses than those of their masters. The masses must be provided with objects of admiration and wonder; the latter can dispense with them. And so we find Mussolini announcing a "new Imperial style." Marinetti, Chirico, et al. are sent into the outer darkness, and the new railroad station in Rome will not be modernistic. That Mussolini was late in coming to this only illustrates again the relative hesitancy with which Italian fascism has drawn the necessary implications of its role. ...

Capitalism in decline finds that whatever of quality it is still capable of producing becomes almost invariably a threat to its own existence. Advances in culture no less than advances in science and industry corrode the very society under whose aegis they are made possible. Here, as in every other question today, it becomes necessary to quote Marx word for word. Today we no longer look towards socialism for a new culture—as inevitably as one will appear, once we do have socialism. Today we look to socialism *simply* for the preservation of whatever living culture we have right now.

Notes

1. The example of music, which has long been an abstract art, and which avant-garde poetry has tried so much to emulate, is interesting. Music, Aristotle said curiously enough, is the most imitative and vivid of all the arts because it imitates its original—the state of the soul—with the greatest immediacy. Today this strikes us as the exact opposite of the truth, because no art seems to us to have less reference to something outside itself than music. However, aside from the fact that in a sense Aristotle may still be right, it must be explained that ancient Greek music was closely associated with poetry, and depended upon its character as an accessory to verse to make its imitative meaning clear. Plato, speaking of music, says: "For when there are no words, it is very difficult to recognize the meaning of the harmony and rhythm, or to see that any worthy object is imitated by them" At far as we know, all music originally served such an accessory function. Once, however, it was abandoned, music was forced to withdraw into itself to find a constraint or original. This it found in the various means of its own composition and performance.
2. I owe this formulation to a remark made by Hans Hofmann, the art-teacher, in one of his lectures. From the point of view of this formulation surrealism in plastic art is a reactionary tendency which is attempting to restore "outside" subject matter. The chief concern of a painter like Dali is to represent the processes and concepts of his consciousness, not the processes of his medium.
3. See Valery's remarks about his own poetry.
4. T. S. Eliot said something to the same effect in accounting for the shortcoming of English Romantic poetry. Indeed the Romantics can be considered the original sinners whose guilt kitsch inherited. They showed kitsch how. What does Keats write about mainly, if not the effect of poetry upon himself?
5. It will be objected that such art for the masses as folk art was developed under rudimentary conditions of production—and that a good deal of folk art is on a high level. Yes, it is—but folk art is not Athene, and it's Athene whom we want: formal culture with its infinity of aspects, its luxuriance, its large comprehension. Besides, we are now told that most of what we consider good in folk culture is the static survival of dead formal, aristocratic, cultures. Our old English ballads, for instance, were not created by the "folk," but by the post-feudal squirearchy of the English countryside, to survive in the mouths of the folk long after those for whom the ballads were composed had gone on to other forms of literature. ... Unfortunately, until the machine age culture was the exclusive prerogative of a society that lived by the labor of serfs or slaves. They were the real symbols of culture. For one man to spend time and energy creating or listening

to poetry meant that another man had to produce enough to keep himself alive and the former in comfort. In Africa today we find that the culture of slave-owning tribes is generally much superior to that of the tribes which possess no slaves.

13
Dwight Macdonald (1906–1982)
Homage to Twelve Judges (1949)

Editor's Introduction

Dwight Macdonald was the most colorful of the New York Intellectuals. Tall, lean, with a goatee and glasses, he looked like a European intellectual. Dwight also was the rare member of the group who used humor liberally to tweak others and himself. If most members of the *Partisan* circle were raised by poor immigrant families, he was raised the son of a lawyer and attended privileged schools such Phillips Exeter Academy and Yale. After flirting with an executive training program at Macy's, he opted instead to work at the new *Fortune* magazine, but the Depression turned him radical and in 1936 he quit *Fortune* and soon began writing and editing for *Partisan Review*.

Like many members of the group, Dwight was a specialist at defending moral positions that weren't especially popular. He tossed his support to those positions that were morally and intellectually principled instead of simply politically advantageous to the country. As an early editor of *Partisan Review*, he left when he failed to convince Philip Rahv to support a mass socialist revolution instead of American entry into World War II. In 1944, Macdonald began his highly moral journal *politics*, which lasted only five years but remains one of the important and unusual magazines in the history of American culture.

"Homage to Twelve Judges" could hardly be more characteristic of Macdonald's principled iconoclasm. His support for the award of the 1948 Bollingen Prize to Ezra Pound's *The Pisan Cantos* brought him denunciations from across the political spectrum. Pound, who Americans knew as a fascist and anti-Semitic traitor to the Allied cause in World War II, wrote his poems in an American Army prison. Macdonald celebrated the poetry award to Pound as evidence of how a non-totalitarian society operated. The Bollingen judges, all good poets, were able to separate literature from politics and treason—which could never have been done at the time in fascist Germany or the Stalinist Soviet Union. If many in his own country howled that Macdonald was thus a traitor too, it only showed that Americans needed to learn more from the Bollingen committee about freedom. This short essay is a classic of both Macdonald and *politics* magazine.

Source

Dwight Macdonald, "Homage to Twelve Judges," *politics* vol. 6, no. 1, Winter, 1949.

Selected Readings

Michael Wreszin, *A Rebel in Defense of Tradition* (New York: Basic Books, 1994).
Gregory D. Sumner, *Dwight Macdonald and the* politics *Circle* (Ithaca: Cornell University Press, 1996).

* * * * *

An Editorial

"The Fellows are aware that objections may be made to awarding a prize to a man situated as is Mr. Pound. In their view, however, the possibility of such objection did not alter the responsibility assumed by the jury of selection. ... To permit other considerations than that of poetic achievement to sway the decision would destroy the significance of the award and would in principle deny the validity of that objective perception of value on which any civilized society must rest."

This seems to me the best political statement made in this country for some time, just as the action of the Fellows in awarding the 1948 Bollingen Prize to Ezra Pound's *The Pisan Cantos* (New Directions, $2.75) is the brightest political act in a dark period. Let me explain why, despite the disclaimers of the Fellows themselves, I consider their award a political, as well as a literary, event.

As is well known, Mr. Pound's situation is disreputable and hopeless to a dramatic degree. For many years, he has articulated fascistic and anti-semitic sentiments; during the war, he made radio propaganda from Italy for Mussolini's regime and against his native country; he is now under arrest in a Washington mental hospital and will be tried for treason when and if he is pronounced mentally competent. The very book for which he is now honored was mostly written in a U.S. Army prison in Pisa, nor is it by any means free of its author's detestable social and racial prejudices.

The prize committee is a distinguished one. Its members are: Conrad Aiken, W. H. Auden, Louise Bogan, T. S. Eliot, Paul Green, Robert Lowell, Katherine Anne Porter, Karl Shapiro, the late Theodore Spencer, Allen Tate, Willard Thorp, and Robert Penn Warren. These constitute the Fellows in American Literature, a board appointed by Luther Evans, the Librarian of Congress. Thus we have a committee composed of eminent American writers and appointed by a high Government official, giving an important literary prize to a man under arrest for treason. I think there are not many other countries today, and certainly none East of the Elbe, where this could happen, and I think we can take some pride as Americans in having as yet preserved a society free and "open" enough for it to happen.

Whether *The Pisan Cantos* is the best poetry published by an American last year or not, I am incompetent to judge. Nor is this the point considered here, which is rather that by some miracle the Bollingen judges were able to consider Mr. Pound the poet apart from Mr. Pound the fascist, Mr. Pound the antisemite, Mr. Pound the traitor, Mr. Pound the funny-money crank, and all the other Mr. Pounds whose existence has properly nothing to do with the question of whether Mr. Pound the poet had or had not written the best American poetry of 1948.

"That objective perception of value on which any civilized society must rest"—this seems to me a formulation difficult to improve. Is not one of the most repellent aspects of the present Soviet system—or, for that matter, of the fascist system which Mr. Pound was so foolish as to admire—precisely that any "objective perception of value" is impossible under it? For such a perception is possible only under two closely related conditions. The first is that no one sphere of human activity is exalted over the rest. The second is that clear distinctions be maintained between the various spheres, so that the value of an artist's work or a scientist's researches is not confused with the value of their politics.

The horror of Soviet communism, of course, is that it reduces the individual to one aspect, the political. The consequence is the obliteration of the boundary lines between the various aspects of culture—or better, the imperialist conquest of all the rest by politics—so that the fifteen members of the Politburo decide, *ex cathedra*, literally all questions, including the most abstruse problems of esthetics and science. ... Is not the literal meaning of "totalitarianism" just this pretension of the political power to control the *totality* of human life?

Such imperfect democracy as we of the West still possess depends on our continuing ability to make the kind of discrimination the Bollingen committee made, to evaluate each sphere of human activity separate from the rest instead of enslaving them all to one great reductive tyrant, whether it be The Church, The Proletariat, People's Democracy, The Master Race, or American Patriotism. Such limping justice as our courts produce likewise rests on their ability to distinguish the defendant's total behavior and personality from the specific action he is accused of having committed. And such cultural achievement as we are still capable of is nourished by "that objective perception of value on which any civilized society must rest."

The wave of the future is rolling in the other direction, as the warmaking centralized State becomes more powerful. It is ironical that it is precisely those who are misnamed "liberals" and even "socialists" who seem to be least enthusiastic about the Pound award. What bothers them is the very thing that is healthiest, politically, about it: the fact that Pound's treason and fascism were not taken into account in honoring him as a poet.

An extreme reaction was that of Albert Deutsch (whose liberalism has a Stalinoid tinge) writing in the liberal *N. Y. Post* of February 28. After a virulent column, in which he denounces Lowell and Eliot as "friends of the turncoat poet" and criticises them because they have not turned *their* coats ("they have been faithful visitors to Pound's ward in St. Elizabeth's"), Deutsch concludes: "There is something unholy in the act. To bestow honor in any form on the man who broadcast Fascist propaganda under the auspices of the Fascist enemy of his native land smacks, to me, like Benedict Arnold's American contemporaries awarding him a medal for his undoubted military ability—after his betrayal of West Point. ... Regardless of the protestations of the prize committee, the prize given to the turncoat poet is likely to be regarded not only as a literary event but as a political act in many parts of our World."

On which: (1) such a medal to Benedict Arnold would have been, in my opinion, a noble gesture; (2) the award is indeed, as argued above, a "political act"—and one which should demonstrate to "many parts of our world" that at least some Americans have a right to oppose Soviet totalitarianism in the name of freedom.[1]

Note

1. Let us not, however, become puffed-up with righteousness. On February 11 last, John Tsourakis, a Jehovah's witness who for reasons of conscience had refused military service, was executed at Larissa, Greece. About a month later, I am informed, a second conscientious objector was tried and executed in Larissa. The government which committed these acts of barbarism is dependent for its existence on the government of this country. The State Department has not expressed any objection to executions.

14
Lionel Trilling (1905–1975)
Reality in America (1950)

Editor's Introduction

In the 1940s Lionel Trilling began an evaluation of liberalism that he continued occasionally for the next thirty years. His central essays in this endeavor
were published in *The Liberal Imagination* (1950) and *Beyond Culture* (1965).
It was not the liberalism of Franklin Roosevelt or Harry Truman that interested him, but the temper, values, and commitments of American imaginative
culture, the stories and myths Americans tell each other. Like many historians
and literary critics at midcentury—Henry Steele Commager, Richard Hofstadter, Henry Nash Smith—Trilling was interested in the American mind,
which he associated with liberalism. Every new generation of intellectuals and
scholars imaginatively attacks and eliminates the generation before them in
an act of parricide. In the final quarter of the twentieth century the baby boom
generation took the knife to the generation of Trilling and the New York Intellectuals (and Commager, Hofstadter and Smith) whose use of large terms such
as the American mind were felt to slight subcultural identities and didn't fit
with the micro-histories of the period.

No sympathy was due the New York Intellectuals because they had been
involved, in the forties and fifties, in a similar parricide of the progressive-era
thinkers. In particular, some members of the *Partisan* circle began to recon-
sider the clumsy and confining dualistic thinking of the progressive generation from the 1890s to the 1940s. For example, the progressive literary critic
Van Wyck Brooks had separated culture simply into highbrow and lowbrow.
The progressive historian Frederick Jackson Turner saw American values
created by the interplay between the civilized East and the frontier West.
Another progressive historian, Vernon Parrington, divided all of American
history between the conflicting forces of good liberal democrats and over-
bearing conservative merchants.

The reason the dualistic thinking of progressives early in the century bothered the New York Intellectuals is that it reminded them uncomfortably of
the simplicities of the mass ideologies of the thirties and forties—the absolutist doctrines fought by Hannah Arendt, Sidney Hook, Arthur Koestler and

163

Philip Rahv. Even after World War II, many of the *Partisan* circle encountered Stalinist either-or thinking by some in the American left, particularly in New York. But the New York Intellectuals knew a different world. It was not all good or all bad, they argued, and imagining a world in such stark dualistic terms led to fanatical and messianic solutions of the righteous. Useful thinkers, then, should see around them the world as it really is, complete with all of the inevitable contradictions. It is a world of complexity, nuance and chance, writers such as Trilling and Hofstadter maintained. It is capricious. The world operates on the principles of irony, accident and variousness. Knowledge and understanding then is tentative. One needs to approach it with moderation, antenna tuned to paradox and contradiction, to ambivalence, subtlety and balance. The work of historian Richard Hofstadter, who also spent his career at Columbia University, shared many of the same concerns as Trilling. (This is one of the traits that separated Henry Steele Commager from the outlook of the New York Intellectuals. Unlike Trilling and Hofstadter, Commager was all too willing to judge people on the either-or basis of the progressives, a tendency of Commager's about which his son-in-law, historian Christopher Lasch, criticized him.)

In this present essay, Trilling sees too much either-or political predictability in Parrington to consider him a good literary historian. Parrington accounted for the ideas of novelists by "the economic and social determination" of their thought, so he was clumsy explaining a writer such as Nathaniel Hawthorne. Because Hawthorne wasn't enough of a reformer, Parrington cast him as a conservative: either-or. Instead, Trilling saw important and useful complexities in Hawthorne, "who could dissent from the orthodoxies of dissent," and who was nuanced enough, like most great writers, to contain "both the yes and the no of their culture." Similarly, most progressive critics clumsily acclaimed Theodore Dreiser because of his reformist politics and disparaged Henry James because of his lack of those qualities. But to judge a work of literature by the politics of its author not only misses the subtleties of the art, but it also is bad politics, too, as Dwight Macdonald pointed out in the preceding essay "Homage to Twelve Judges."

Not all members of the *Partisan Review* circle endorsed Trilling's criticism of liberalism. Alfred Kazin later said in his *New York Jew* (1978), "Trilling, with his strong sense of history and his exquisite sense of accommodation, was the most successful leader of deradicalization—which was conducted in the name of the liberal 'imagination' against those who lacked it or had the wrong kind." Kazin concluded, "Arnold smote the philistines: Trilling the liberals. In his America there were not workers, nobody suffering from a lack of cash; no capitalists, no corporations, no Indians, no blacks. And, on the whole, neither were there any Jews."*

---

* Alfred Kazin, *New York Jew* (New York: Knopf, 1978), 192.

Source

Lionel Trilling, "Reality in America," *The Liberal Imagination* (New York, Harcourt, 1950), 3–20. The first part of this essay Trilling drew from "Parrington, Mr. Smith and Reality," *Partisan Review* vol. 7, no. 1, January–February 1940. The second part he published earlier in a different form as "Dreiser and the Liberal Mind" *The Nation*, vol. 162, no. 16, April 20, 1946.

Selected Readings

John Rodden, ed., *Lionel Trilling and the Critics* (Lincoln: University of Nebraska Press, 1999), chapters 19–34.
Mark Krupnick, *Lionel Trilling and the Fate of Cultural Criticism* (Evanston: Northwestern University Press, 1986).
Richard Hofstadter, *The Progressive Historians* (New York: Knopf, 1969).
Henry Steele Commager, *The American Mind* (New Haven: Yale, 1950).
Vernon L. Parrington, *Main Currents of American Thought* (New York: Harcourt, Brace, 1930).

* * * * *

I

It is possible to say of V. L. Parrington that with his *Main Currents in American Thought* he has had an influence on our conception of American culture which is not equaled by that of any other writer of the last two decades. His ideas are now the accepted ones wherever the college course in American literature is given by a teacher who conceives himself to be opposed to the genteel and the academic and in alliance with the vigorous and the actual. And whenever the liberal historian of America finds occasion to take account of the national literature, as nowadays he feels it proper to do, it is Parrington who is his standard and guide. Parrington's ideas are the more firmly established because they do not have to be imposed—the teacher or the critic who presents them is likely to find that his task is merely to make articulate for his audience what it has always believed, for Parrington formulated in a classic way the suppositions about our culture which are held by the American middle class so far as that class is at all liberal in its social thought and so far as it begins to understand that literature has anything to do with society.

Parrington was not a great mind; he was not a precise thinker or, except when measured by the low eminences that were about him, an impressive one. Separate Parrington from his informing idea of the economic and social determination of thought and what is left is a simple intelligence, notable for its generosity and enthusiasm but certainly not for its accuracy or originality. Take him even with his idea and he is, once its direction is established, rather too predictable to be continuously interesting; and, indeed, what we dignify with the name of economic and social determinism amounts in his use of it to not much more than the demonstration that most writers incline to stick to their own social class. But his best virtue was real and important—he had what we like to think of as the saving salt of the American mind, the lively sense of the practical, workaday world, of the welter of ordinary undistinguished things and people, of the tangible, quirky, unrefined elements of life. He knew what so many literary historians do not know, that emotions and ideas are the sparks that fly when the mind meets difficulties.

Yet he had after all but a limited sense of what constitutes a difficulty. Whenever he was confronted with a work of art that was complex, personal and not literal, that was not, as it were, a public document, Parrington was at a loss. Difficulties that were complicated by personality or that were expressed in the language of successful art did not seem quite real to him and he was inclined to treat them as aberrations, which is one way of saying what everybody admits, that the weakest part of Parrington's talent was his aesthetic judgment. His admirers and disciples like to imply that his errors of aesthetic judgment are merely lapses of taste, but this is not so. Despite such mistakes as his notorious praise of Cabell, to whom in a remarkable passage he compares Melville, Parrington's taste was by no means bad. His errors are the errors of understanding which arise from his assumptions about the nature of reality.

Parrington does not often deal with abstract philosophical ideas, but whenever he approaches a work of art we are made aware of the metaphysics on which his aesthetics is based. There exists, he believes, a thing called *reality;* it is one and immutable, it is wholly external, it is irreducible. Men's minds may waver, but reality is always reliable, always the same, always easily to be known. And the artist's relation to reality he conceives as a simple one. Reality being fixed and given, the artist has but to let it pass through him, he is the lens in the first diagram of an elementary book on optics: Fig. 1, Reality; Fig. 2, Artist; Fig. 1′, Work of Art. Figs. 1 and 1′ are normally in virtual correspondence with each other. Sometimes the artist spoils this ideal relation by "turning away from" reality. This results in certain fantastic works, unreal and ultimately useless. It does not occur to Parrington that there is any other relation possible between the artist and reality than this passage of reality through the transparent artist; he meets evidence of imagination and creativeness with a settled hostility the expression of which suggests that he regards them as the natural enemies of democracy.

In this view of things, reality, although it is always reliable, is always rather sober-sided, even grim. Parrington, a genial and enthusiastic man, can understand how the generosity of man's hopes and desires may leap beyond reality; he admires will in the degree that he suspects mind. To an excess of desire and energy which blinds a man to the limitations of reality he can indeed be very tender. This is one of the many meanings he gives to *romance* or *romanticism,* and in spite of himself it appeals to something in his own nature. The praise of Cabell is Parrington's response not only to Cabell's elegance—for Parrington loved elegance—but also to Cabell's insistence on the part which a beneficent self-deception may and even should play in the disappointing fact-bound life of man, particularly in the private and erotic part of his life.[1]

The second volume of *Main Currents* is called *The Romantic Revolution in America* and it is natural to expect that the word romantic should appear in it frequently. So it does, more frequently than one can count, and seldom with the same meaning, seldom with the sense that the word, although scandalously vague as it has been used by the literary historians, is still full of complicated but not wholly pointless ideas, that it involves many contrary but definable things; all too often Parrington uses the word romantic with the word romance close at hand, meaning *a* romance, in the sense that *Graustark* or *Treasure Island* is a romance, as though it signified chiefly a gay disregard of the limitations of everyday fact. Romance is refusing to heed the counsels of experience (p. iii); it is ebullience (p. iv); it is utopianism (p. iv); it is individualism (p. vi); it is self-deception (p. 59)—"romantic faith … in the beneficent processes of trade and industry" (as held, we inevitably ask, by the romantic Adam Smith?); it is the love of the picturesque (p. 49); it is the dislike of innovation (p. 50) but also the love of change (p. iv); it is the sentimental (p. 192); it is patriotism, and then it is cheap (p. 235). It may be used to denote what is not classical, but chiefly it means that which ignores reality (pp. ix, 136, 143, 147, and *passim*); it is not critical (pp. 225, 235), although in speaking of Cooper and Melville, Parrington admits that criticism can sometimes spring from romanticism.

Whenever a man with whose ideas he disagrees wins from Parrington a reluctant measure of respect, the word romantic is likely to appear. He does not admire Henry Clay, yet something in Clay is not to be despised—his romanticism, although Clay's romanticism is made equivalent with his inability to "come to grips with reality." Romanticism is thus, in most of its signfications, the venial sin of *Main Currents*; like carnal passion in the *Inferno*, it evokes not blame but tender sorrow. But it can also be the great and saving virtue which Parrington recognizes. It is ascribed to the transcendental reformers he so much admires; it is said to mark two of his most cherished heroes, Jefferson and Emerson: "they were both romantics and their idealism was only a different expression of a common spirit." Parrington held, we may say, at least two different views of romanticism which suggest two different views of reality. Sometimes he speaks of reality in an honorific way, meaning the substantial stuff of life, the ineluctable facts with which the mind must cope, but sometimes he speaks of it pejoratively and means the world of established social forms; and he speaks of realism in two ways: sometimes as the power of dealing intelligently with fact, sometimes as a cold and conservative resistance to idealism.

Just as for Parrington there is a saving grace and a venial sin, there is also a deadly sin, and this is turning away from reality, not in the excess of generous feeling, but in what he believes to be a deficiency of feeling, as with

Hawthorne, or out of what amounts to sinful pride, as with Henry James. He tells us that there was too much realism in Hawthorne to allow him to give his faith to the transcendental reformers: "he was too much of a realist to change fashions in creeds"; "he remained cold to the revolutionary criticism that was eager to pull down the old temples to make room for nobler." It is this cold realism, keeping Hawthorne apart from his enthusiastic contemporaries, that alienates Parrington's sympathy—"Eager souls, mystics and revolutionaries, may propose to refashion the world in accordance with their dreams; but evil remains, and so long as it lurks in the secret places of the heart, Utopia is only the shadow of a dream. And so while the Concord thinkers were proclaiming man to be the indubitable child of God, Hawthorne was critically examining the question of evil as it appeared in the light of his own experience. It was the central fascinating problem of his intellectual life, and in pursuit of a solution he probed curiously into the hidden, furtive recesses of the soul," Parrington's disapproval of the enterprise is unmistakable.

Now we might wonder whether Hawthorne's questioning of the naïve and often eccentric faiths of the transcendental reformers was not, on the face of it, a public service. But Parrington implies that it contributes nothing to democracy, and even that it stands in the way of the realization of democracy. If democracy depends wholly on a fighting faith, I suppose he is right. Yet society is after all something that exists at the moment as well as in the future, and if one man wants to probe curiously into the hidden furtive recesses of the contemporary soul, a broad democracy and especially one devoted to reality should allow him to do so without despising him. If what Hawthorne did was certainly nothing to build a party on, we ought perhaps to forgive him when we remember that he was only one man and that the future of mankind did not depend upon him alone. But this very fact serves only to irritate Parrington; he is put out by Hawthorne's loneliness and believes that part of Hawthorne's insufficiency as a writer comes from his failure to get around and meet people. Hawthorne could not, he tells us, establish contact with the "Yankee reality," and was scarcely aware of the "substantial world of Puritan reality that Samuel Sewall knew."

To turn from reality might mean to turn to romance, but Parrington tells us that Hawthorne was romantic "only in a narrow and very special sense." He was not interested in the world of, as it were, practical romance, in the Salem of the clipper ships; from this he turned away to create "a romance of ethics." This is not an illuminating phrase but it is a catching one, and it might be taken to mean that Hawthorne was in the tradition of, say, Shakespeare; but we quickly learn that, no, Hawthorne had entered a barren field, for although he himself lived in the present and had all the future to mold, he preferred to find many of his subjects in the past. We learn too that his romance of ethics is not admirable because it requires the hard, fine pressing of ideas, and we are told that "a romantic uninterested in adventure and afraid of sex is likely to become somewhat graveled for matter." In short, Hawthorne's mind was a thin one, and Parrington puts in evidence his use of allegory and symbol and the very severity and precision of his art to prove that he suffered from a sadly limited intellect, for so much fancy and so much art could scarcely be needed unless the writer were trying to exploit to the utmost the few poor ideas that he had.

Hawthorne, then, was "forever dealing with shadows, and he knew that he was dealing with shadows." Perhaps so, but shadows are also part of reality and one would not want a world without shadows, it would not even be a "real" world. But we must get beyond Parrington's metaphor. The fact is that Hawthorne was dealing beautifully with realities, with substantial things. The man who could raise those brilliant and serious doubts about the nature and possibility of moral perfection, the man who could keep himself aloof from the "Yankee reality" and who could dissent from the orthodoxies of dissent and tell us so much about the nature of moral zeal, is of course dealing exactly with reality.

Parrington's characteristic weakness as a historian is suggested by the title of his famous book, for the culture of a nation is not truly figured in the image of the current. A culture is not a flow, nor even a confluence; the form of its existence is struggle, or at least debate—it is nothing if not a dialectic. And in any culture there are likely to be certain artists who contain a large part of the dialectic within themselves, their meaning and power lying in their contradictions; they contain within themselves, it may be said, the very essence of the culture, and the sign of this is that they do not submit to serve the ends of any one ideological group or tendency. It is a significant circumstance of American culture, and one which is susceptible of explanation, that an unusually large proportion of its notable writers of the nineteenth century were such repositories of the dialectic of their times—they contained both the yes and the no of their culture, and by that token they were prophetic of the future. Parrington said that he had not set up shop as a literary critic; but if a literary critic is simply a reader who has the ability to understand literature and to convey to others what he understands, it is not exactly a matter of free choice whether or not a cultural historian shall be a literary critic, nor is it open to him to let his virtuous political and social opinions do duty for percipience. To throw out Poe because he cannot be conveniently fitted into a theory of American culture, to speak of him as a biological sport and as a mind apart from the main current, to find his gloom to be merely personal and eccentric, "only the atrabilious wretchedness of a dipsomaniac," as Hawthorne's was "no more than the skeptical questioning of life by a nature that knew no fierce storms," to judge Melville's response to American life to be less noble than that of Bryant or of Greeley, to speak of Henry James as an escapist, as an artist similar to Whistler, a man characteristically afraid of stress—this is not merely to be mistaken in aesthetic judgment; rather it is to examine without attention and from the point of view of a limited and essentially arrogant conception of reality the documents which are in some respects the most suggestive testimony to what America was and is, and of course to get no answer from them.

Parrington lies twenty years behind us, and in the intervening time there has developed a body of opinion which is aware of his inadequacies and of the inadequacies of his coadjutors and disciples, who make up what might be called the literary academicism of liberalism. Yet Parrington still stands at the center of American thought about American culture because, as I say, he expresses the chronic American belief that there exists an opposition between reality and mind and that one must enlist oneself in the party of reality.

II

This belief in the incompatibility of mind and reality is exemplified by the doctrinaire indulgence which liberal intellectuals have always displayed toward Theodore Dreiser, an indulgence which becomes the worthier of remark when it is contrasted with the liberal severity toward Henry James. Dreiser and James: with that juxtaposition we are immediately at the dark and bloody crossroads where literature and politics meet. One does not go there gladly, but nowadays it is not exactly a matter of free choice whether one does or does not go. As for the particular juxtaposition itself, it is inevitable and it has at the present moment far more significance than the juxtaposition which once used to be made between James and Whitman. It is not hard to contrive factitious oppositions between James and Whitman, but the real difference between them is the difference between the moral mind, with its awareness of tragedy, irony, and multitudinous distinctions, and the transcendental mind, with its passionate sense of the oneness of multiplicity. James and Whitman are unlike not in quality but in kind, and in their very opposition they serve to complement each other. But the difference between James and Dreiser is not of kind, for both men addressed themselves to virtually the same social and moral fact. The difference here is one of quality, and perhaps nothing is more typical of American liberalism than the way it has responded to the respective qualities of the two men.

Few critics, I suppose, no matter what their political disposition, have ever been wholly blind to James's great gifts, or even to the grandiose moral intention of these gifts. And few critics have ever been wholly blind to Dreiser's great faults. But by liberal critics James is traditionally put to the ultimate question: of what use, of what actual political use, are his gifts and their intention? Granted that James was devoted to an extraordinary moral perceptiveness, granted too that moral perceptiveness has something to do with politics and the social life, of what possible practical value in our world of impending disaster can James's work be? And James's style, his characters, his subjects, and even his own social origin and the manner of his personal life are adduced to show that his work cannot endure the question. To James no quarter is given by American criticism in its political and liberal aspect. But in the same degree that liberal criticism is moved by political considerations to treat James with severity, it treats Dreiser with the most sympathetic indulgence. Dreiser's literary faults, it gives us to understand, are essentially social and political virtues. It was Parrington who established the formula for the liberal criticism of Dreiser by calling him a "peasant": when Dreiser thinks stupidly, it is because he has the slow stubbornness of a peasant; when he writes badly, it is because he is impatient of the sterile literary gentility of the bourgeoisie. It is as if wit, and flexibility of mind, and perception, and knowledge were to be equated with aristocracy and political reaction, while dullness and stupidity must naturally suggest a virtuous democracy, as in the old plays.

The liberal judgment of Dreiser and James goes back of politics, goes back to the cultural assumptions that make politics. We are still haunted by a kind of political fear of the intellect which Tocqueville observed in us more than a century ago. American intellectuals, when they are being consciously American or political, are remarkably quick to suggest that an art which is marked by perception and knowledge, although all very well in its way, can never get us through gross dangers and difficulties. And their misgivings become the more intense when intellect works in art as it ideally should, when its processes are vivacious and interesting and brilliant. It is then that we like to confront it with the gross dangers and difficulties and to challenge it to save us at once from disaster. When intellect in art is awkward or dull we do not put it to the test of ultimate or immediate practicality. No liberal critic asks the question of Dreiser whether *his* moral preoccupations are going to be useful in confronting the disasters that threaten us. And it is a judgment on the proper nature of mind, rather than any actual political meaning that might be drawn from the works of the two men, which accounts for the unequal justice they have received from the progressive critics. If it could be conclusively demonstrated—by, say, documents in James's handwriting—that James explicitly intended his books to be understood as pleas for co-operatives, labor unions, better housing, and more equitable taxation, the American critic in his liberal and progressive character would still be worried by James because his work shows so many of the electric qualities of mind. And if something like the opposite were proved of Dreiser, it would be brushed aside—as his doctrinaire anti-Semitism has in fact been brushed aside—because his books have the awkwardness, the chaos, the heaviness which we associate with "reality." In the American metaphysic, reality is always material reality, hard, resistant, unformed, impenetrable, and unpleasant. And that mind is alone felt to be trustworthy which most resembles this reality by most nearly reproducing the sensations it affords.

In *The Rise of American Civilization*, Professor Beard uses a significant phrase when, in the course of an ironic account of James's career, he implies that we have the clue to the irrelevance of that career when we know that

James was "a whole generation removed from the odors of the shop." Of a piece with this, and in itself even more significant, is the comment which Granville Hicks makes in *The Great Tradition* when he deals with James's stories about artists and remarks that such artists as James portrays, so concerned for their art and their integrity in art, do not really exist: "After all, who has ever known such artists? Where are the Hugh Verekers, the Mark Ambients, the Neil Paradays, the Overts, Limberts, Dencombes, Delavoys?" This question, as Mr. Hicks admits, had occurred to James himself, but what answer had James given to it? "If the life about us for the last thirty years refused warrant for these examples," he said in the preface to volume XII of the New York Edition, "then so much the worse for that life. ... There are decencies that in the name of the general self-respect we must take for granted, there's a rudimentary intellectual honor to which we must, in the interest of civilization, at least pretend." And to this Mr. Hicks, shocked beyond argument, makes this reply, which would be astonishing had we not heard it before: "But this is the purest romanticism, this writing about what ought to be rather than what is!"

The "odors of the shop" are real, and to those who breathe them they guarantee a sense of vitality from which James is debarred. The idea of intellectual honor is not real, and to that chimera James was devoted. He betrayed the reality of what is in the interests of what ought to be. Dare we trust him? The question, we remember, is asked by men who themselves have elaborate transactions with what ought to be. Professor Beard spoke in the name of a growing, developing, and improving America. Mr. Hicks, when he wrote *The Great Tradition,* was in general sympathy with a nominally radical movement. But James's own transaction with what ought to be is suspect because it is carried on through what I have called the electrical qualities of mind, through a complex and rapid imagination and with a kind of authoritative immediacy. Mr. Hicks knows that Dreiser is "clumsy" and "stupid" and "bewildered" and "crude in his statement of materialistic monism"; he knows that Dreiser in his personal life—which is in point because James's personal life is always supposed to be so much in point—was not quite emancipated from "his boyhood longing for crass material success," showing "again and again a desire for the ostentatious luxury of the successful business man." But Dreiser is to be accepted and forgiven because his faults are the sad, lovable, honorable faults of reality itself, or of America itself—huge, inchoate, struggling toward expression, caught between the dream of raw power and the dream of morality.

"The liability in what Santayana called the genteel tradition was due to its being the product of mind apart from experience. Dreiser gave us the stuff of our common experience, not as it was hoped to be by any idealizing theorist, but as it actually was in its crudity." The author of this statement certainly cannot be accused of any lack of feeling for mind as Henry James represents it; nor can Mr. Matthiessen be thought of as a follower of Parrington—indeed, in the preface to *American Renaissance* he has framed one of the sharpest and most cogent criticisms of Parrington's method. Yet Mr. Matthiessen, writing in the *New York Times Book Review* about Dreiser's posthumous novel, *The Bulwark,* accepts the liberal cliché which opposes crude experience to mind and establishes Dreiser's value by implying that the mind which Dreiser's crude experience is presumed to confront and refute is the mind of gentility.

This implied amalgamation of mind with gentility is the rationale of the long indulgence of Dreiser, which is extended even to the style of his prose. Everyone is aware that Dreiser's prose style is full of roughness and ungainliness, and the critics who admire Dreiser tell us it does not matter. Of course it does not matter. No reader with a right sense of style would suppose that it does matter, and he might even find it a virtue. But it has been taken for granted that the ungainliness of Dreiser's style is the only possible objection to be made to it, and that whoever finds in it any fault at all wants a prettified genteel style (and is objecting to the ungainliness of reality itself). For instance, Edwin Berry Burgum, in a leaflet on Dreiser put out by the Book Find Club, tells us that Dreiser was one of those who used—or, as Mr. Burgum says, utilized—"the diction of the Middle West, pretty much as it was spoken, rich in colloquialism and frank in the simplicity and directness of the pioneer tradition," and that this diction took the place of "the literary English, formal and bookish, of New England provincialism that was closer to the aristocratic spirit of the mother country than to the tang of everyday life in the new West." This is mere fantasy. Hawthorne, Thoreau, and Emerson were for the most part remarkably colloquial—they wrote, that is, much as they spoke; their prose was specifically American in quality, and, except for occasional lapses, quite direct and simple. It is Dreiser who lacks the sense of colloquial diction—that of the Middle West or any other. If we are to talk of bookishness, it is Dreiser who is bookish; he is precisely literary in the bad sense; he is full of flowers of rhetoric and shines with paste gems; at hundreds of points his diction is not only genteel but fancy. It is he who speaks of "a scene more distingué than this," or of a woman "artistic in form and feature," or of a man who, although "strong, reserved, aggressive, with an air of wealth and experience, was *soidisant* and not particularly eager to stay at home." Colloquialism held no real charm for him and his natural tendency is always toward the "fine":

> ... Moralists come and go; religionists fulminate and declare the pronouncements of God as to this; but Aphrodite still reigns. Embowered in the festal depths of the spring, set above her altars of porphyry, chalcedony, ivory and gold, see her smile the smile that is at once the texture and essence of delight, the glory and despair of the world! Dream on, oh Buddha, asleep on your lotus leaf, of an undisturbed Nirvana! Sweat, oh Jesus, your last agonizing drops over an unregenerate world! In the forests of Pan still ring the cries of the worshippers of Aphrodite! From her

altars the incense of adoration ever rises! And see, the new red grapes dripping where votive hands new-press them!

Charles Jackson, the novelist, telling us in the same leaflet that Dreiser's style does not matter, remarks on how much still comes to us when we have lost by translation the stylistic brillance of Thomas Mann or the Russians or Balzac. He is in part right. And he is right too when he says that a certain kind of conscious, supervised artistry is not appropriate to the novel of large dimensions. Yet the fact is that the great novelists have usually written very good prose, and what comes through even a bad translation is exactly the power of mind that made the well-hung sentence of the original text. In literature style is so little the mere clothing of thought—need it be insisted on at this late date?—that we may say that from the earth of the novelist's prose spring his characters, his ideas, and even his story itself.[2]

To the extent that Dreiser's style is defensible, his thought is also defensible. That is, when he thinks like a novelist, he is worth following—when by means of his rough and ungainly but no doubt cumulatively effective style he creates rough, ungainly, but effective characters and events. But when he thinks like, as we say, a philosopher, he is likely to be not only foolish but vulgar. He thinks as the modern crowd thinks when it decides to think: religion and morality are nonsense, "religionists" and moralists are fakes, tradition is a fraud, what is man but matter and impulses, mysterious "chemisms," what value has life anyway? "What, cooking, eating, coition, job holding, growing, aging, losing, winning, in so changeful and passing a scene as this, important? Bunk! It is some form of titillating illusion with about as much import to the superior forces that bring it all about as the functions and gyrations of a fly. No more. And maybe less." Thus Dreiser at sixty. And yet there is for him always the vulgarly saving suspicion that maybe, when all is said and done, there is Something Behind It All. It is much to the point of his intellectual vulgarity that Dreiser's anti-Semitism was not merely a social prejudice but an idea, a way of dealing with difficulties.

No one, I suppose, has ever represented Dreiser as a masterly intellect. It is even commonplace to say that his ideas are inconsistent or inadequate. But once that admission has been made, his ideas are hustled out of sight while his "reality" and great brooding pity are spoken of. (His pity is to be questioned: pity is to be judged by kind, not amount, and Dreiser's pity—*Jennie Gerhardt* provides the only exception—is either destructive of its object or it is self-pity.) Why has no liberal critic ever brought Dreiser's ideas to the bar of political practicality, asking what use is to be made of Dreiser's dim, awkward speculation, of his self-justification, of his lust for "beauty" and "sex" and "living" and "life itself," and of the showy nihilism which always seems to him so grand a gesture in the direction of profundity? We live, understandably enough, with the sense of urgency; our clock, like Baudelaire's, has had the hands removed and bears the legend, "It is later than you think." But with us it is always a little too late for mind, yet never too late for honest stupidity; always a little too late for understanding, never too late for righteous, bewildered wrath; always too late for thought, never too late for naïve moralizing. We seem to like to condemn our finest but not our worst qualities by pitting them against the exigency of time.

But sometimes time is not quite so exigent as to justify all our own exigency, and in the case of Dreiser time has allowed his deficiencies to reach their logical, and fatal, conclusion. In *The Bulwark* Dreiser's characteristic ideas come full circle, and the simple, didactic life history of Solon Barnes, a Quaker business man, affirms a simple Christian faith, and a kind of practical mysticism, and the virtues of self-abnegation and self-restraint, and the belief in and submission to the hidden purposes of higher powers, those "superior forces that bring it all about"—once, in Dreiser's opinion, so brutally indifferent, now somehow benign. This is not the first occasion on which Dreiser has shown a tenderness toward religion and a responsiveness to mysticism. *Jennie Gerhardt* and the figure of the Reverend Duncan McMillan in *An American Tragedy* are forecasts of the avowals of *The Bulwark*, and Dreiser's lively interest in power of any sort led him to take account of the power implicit in the cruder forms of mystical performance. Yet these rifts in his nearly monolithic materialism cannot quite prepare us for the blank pietism of *The Bulwark*, not after we have remembered how salient in Dreiser's work has been the long surly rage against the "religionists" and the "moralists," the men who have presumed to believe that life can be given any law at all and who have dared to suppose that will or mind or faith can shape the savage and beautiful entity that Dreiser liked to call "life itself." Now for Dreiser the law may indeed be given, and it is wholly simple—the safe conduct of the personal life requires only that we follow the Inner Light according to the regimen of the Society of Friends, or according to some other godly rule. And now the smiling Aphrodite set above her altars of porphyry, chalcedony, ivory, and gold is quite forgotten, and we are told that the sad joy of cosmic acceptance goes hand in hand with sexual abstinence.

Dreiser's mood of "acceptance" in the last years of his life is not, as a personal experience, to be submitted to the tests of intellectual validity. It consists of a sensation of cosmic understanding, of an overarching sense of unity with the world in its apparent evil as well as in its obvious good. It is no more to be quarreled with, or reasoned with, than love itself—indeed, it is a kind of love, not so much of the world as of oneself in the world. Perhaps it is either the cessation of desire or the perfect balance of desires. It is what used often to be meant by "peace," and up through the nineteenth century a good many people understood its meaning. If it was Dreiser's own emotion at the end of his life, who would not be happy that he had achieved it? I am not even sure that our civilization would not be the better for more of us knowing and desiring this emotion of grave felicity. Yet granting the personal validity of the emotion, Dreiser's exposition of it fails, and is, moreover, offensive. Mr. Matthiessen has warned us of the attack that will be made on the doctrine of *The Bulwark* by "those who believe that any renewal of Christianity marks a new 'failure of nerve.'" But Dreiser's religious avowal is not a failure of nerve—it is a failure of mind and heart. We have only to set his book beside any work in which mind and heart are made to serve religion to know this at once. Ivan Karamazov's giving back his ticket of admission to the "harmony" of the universe suggests that *The Bulwark* is not morally adequate, for we dare not, as its hero does, blandly "accept" the suffering of others; and the Book of Job tells us that it does not include enough in its exploration of the problem of evil, and is not stern enough. I have said that Dreiser's religious affirmation was offensive; the offense lies in the vulgar ease of its formulation, as well as in the comfortable untroubled way in which Dreiser moved from nihilism to pietism.[3]

The Bulwark is the fruit of Dreiser's old age, but if we speak of it as a failure of thought and feeling, we cannot suppose that with age Dreiser weakened in mind and heart. The weakness was always there. And in a sense it is not Dreiser who failed but a whole way of dealing with ideas, a way in which we have all been in some degree involved. Our liberal, progressive culture tolerated Dreiser's vulgar materialism with its huge negation, its simple cry of "Bunk!," feeling that perhaps it was not quite intellectually adequate but certainly very *strong,* certainly very *real.* And now, almost as a natural consequence, it has been given, and is not unwilling to take, Dreiser's pietistic religion in all its inadequacy.

Dreiser, of course, was firmer than the intellectual culture that accepted him. He *meant* his ideas, at least so far as a man can mean ideas who is incapable of following them to their consequences. But we, when it came to his ideas, talked about his great brooding pity and shrugged the ideas off. We are still doing it. Robert Elias, the biographer of Dreiser, tells us that "it is part of the logic of [Dreiser's] life that he should have completed *The Bulwark* at the same time that he joined the Communists." Just what kind of logic this is we learn from Mr. Elias's further statement. "When he supported left-wing movements and finally, last year, joined the Communist Party, he did so not because he had examined the details of the party line and found them satisfactory, but because he agreed with a general program that represented a means for establishing his cherished goal of greater equality among men." Whether or not Dreiser was following the logic of his own life, he was certainly following the logic of the liberal criticism that accepted him so undiscriminatingly as one of the great, significant expressions of its spirit. This is the liberal criticism, in the direct line of Parrington, which establishes the social responsibility of the writer and then goes on to say that, apart from his duty of resembling reality as much as possible, he is not really responsible for anything, not even for his ideas. The scope of reality being what it is, ideas are held to be mere "details," and, what is more, to be details which, if attended to, have the effect of diminishing reality. But ideals are different from ideas; in the liberal criticism which descends from Parrington ideals consort happily with reality and they urge us to deal impatiently with ideas—a "cherished goal" forbids that we stop to consider how we reach it, or if we may not destroy it in trying to reach it the wrong way.

Notes

1. See, for example, how Parrington accounts for the "idealizing mind"—Melville's—by the discrepancy between "a wife in her morning kimono" and "the Helen of his dreams." Vol. 11, p. 259.

2. The latest defense of Dreiser's style, that in the chapter on Dreiser in the *Literary History of the United States*, is worth noting: "Forgetful of the integrity and power of Dreiser's whole work, many critics have been distracted into a condemnation of his style. He was, like Twain and Whitman, an organic artist; he wrote what he knew—what he was. His many colloquialisms were part of the coinage of his time, and his sentimental and romantic passages were written in the language of the educational system and the popular literature of his formative years. In his style, as in his material, he was a child of his time, of his class. Self-educated, a type or model of the artist of plebeian origin in America, his language, like his subject matter, is not marked by internal inconsistencies." No doubt Dreiser was an organic artist in the sense that he wrote what he knew and what he was, but so, I suppose, is every artist; the question for criticism comes down to *what* he knew and *what* he was. That he was a child of his time and class is also true, but this can be said of everyone without exception; the question for criticism is how he transcended the imposed limitations of his time and class. As for the defense made on the ground of his particular class, it can only be said that liberal thought has come to a strange pass when it assumes that a plebeian origin is accountable for a writer's faults through all his intellectual life.

3. This ease and comfortableness seem to mark contemporary religious conversions. Religion nowadays has the appearance of what the ideal modern house has been called, "a machine for living," and seemingly one makes up one's mind to acquire and use it not with spiritual struggle but only with a growing sense of its practicability and convenience. Compare *The Seven Storey Mountain*, which Monsignor Sheen calls "a twentieth-century form of the *Confessions* of St. Augustine," with the old, the as it were original, *Confessions* of St. Augustine.

15

Alfred Kazin (1915–1998)
The Historian as Reporter: Edmund Wilson and the 1930s (1958)

Editor's Introduction

Edmund Wilson was much admired by the New York Intellectuals and served as a role model for many of them, especially the literary critics. His "Flaubert's Politics" in *Partisan Review* in 1937 was an early and influential pronouncement that the nature of art should not be dictated by political ideology, a point that the young Lionel Trilling seconded the following year in his essay "The America of John Dos Passos." Wilson was older and more established than members of the *Partisan Review* crowd, having held the literary editorship of the *New Republic* in the late 1920s. Alfred Kazin once wrote of Trilling, who was older than himself, "Those ten years between us reinforced my impression of Trilling as a writer who had absorbed the casual, more gentlemanly style of the twenties much as Bellow and I had absorbed the social angers of the abrasive lower-class thirties."*

Kazin is the member of the *Partisan Review* circle who most approximated Wilson's style and function, so it is fitting that he reviewed Wilson's *American Earthquake*. Neither Kazin nor any other of the New York Intellectuals would have thought to travel the United States to look into the faces and towns of Depression America in the 1930s, from Michigan to New York to Tennessee to New Mexico, as Wilson did. Kazin, however, was acutely interested in the cultural and built environment of greater New York City, and there he showed his Wilsonian side. In New York he heard "the screech of the trolley cars on Rockaway Avenue" and saw on Pitkin Avenue "all the self-conscious confusion of Brownsville's show street" with "banks, Woolworth's, classy shops, loan companies, Loew's Pitkin, the Yiddish theater, the Little Oriental restaurant ... the left wing–right wing arguments around the tables in Hoffman's Cafeteria." But the *Partisan* crowd would hardly have imagined leaving New York's boroughs, not to mention traversing the South, and they had neither the reporter's interest in the actuality of America nor the proprietary sense of belonging deeply to the country, both of which motivated Wilson.

---

* Alfred Kazin, *New York Jew* (New York: Knopf, 1978), 43.

Wilson, Kazin and the rest of the *PR* circle, however, were bound by a love of the literary and cultural life and a respect for the vocation of book reviewing. A review by this recipe evaluates the book as a work of art and logical contention. Further, it tries to situate the art and intellectual claim in a historical context by describing the antecedents of the debate, the reason for the argument, the biography and politics of the author, and its potential impact on the culture. The review itself then is a work of interpretive history and literature. It is, in a heavily freighted word, criticism, and it is the task in which all members of the New York Intellectuals believed themselves employed.

Source

Alfred Kazin, "The Historian as Reporter: Edmund Wilson and the 1930's," *The Reporter* vol. 18, no. 6, March 20, 1958.

Selected Readings

Edmund Wilson, *The American Earthquake* (Garden City: Doubleday, 1958). Alfred Kazin, *Alfred Kazin's America*, ed. Ted Solotaroff (New York: Harper-Collins, 2003); *New York Jew* (New York: Knopf, 1978).

* * * * *

One of the many things that I miss in American writing today is the frankly "literary" reportage of national events that used to be done by writers like Theodore Dreiser, H. L. Mencken, John Dos Passos, Edmund Wilson. One reason for the decline of this kind of journalism is the assumption by writers that there is nothing to investigate, that ours is the dead calm that comes after or between wars, that the literary man on a news story belongs only to a blazing time of troubles. The younger writers complain that they are too far from the peaks of power to be able to say what is really happening. Some of the writers who came out of the 1930's have reacted so sharply against their youthful radicalism that they now have a vested interest in contentment. The only Victorians left in the world today are the exhausted, guilt-ridden, tediously accommodating ex-radicals who want peace at any price. Some years ago an English magazine edited by such intellectuals announced in its very first issue that the mood of the present period could be summed up as "After the Apocalypse." This was on the eve of the H-bomb, the revolts in Eastern Germany, Poland, Hungary, and the intercontinental ballistic missile; but veterans of the 1930's, as we know from the example of Whittaker Chambers and how many other ex-revolutionaries, project their sense of depletion into the world itself.

Still, it cannot be denied that writers turn to reportage in times that are warlike—times when issues are wholly on the surface, when society is visibly in flux, when there are disturbing social tensions which everyone feels in his own life. The 1930's, an era of incessant social violence, depression, revolution, war, lent themselves to reporting because writers felt themselves carried along by history. So much happened in the 1930's, from the depression to another world war, from Roosevelt to Hitler, from the Japanese attack on Manchuria to the Spanish Civil War, that it can be said of a great many writers that nothing has happened to them since. If the nineteenth century did not end until 1914, the twentieth did not fully begin until the 1930's, for it was then that we began to see even in our innocent and long-protected country the onset of the all-powerful state, the security police, the governmental manipulation of mass opinion, the establishment of the "common man" as an absolute good—all of which have become so much part of our lives, especially since 1945, that we no longer recognize how much we have changed. But in the 1930's all these things emerged out of the unexpressed admission that the crisis was permanent and uncontrollable; in America, virtually the last symbol of pure capitalism, one could see the old order of ideas actually disintegrating, while millions of people sought salvation from the welfare state, Communism, Father Coughlin, Dr. Townsend, Huey Long. And if this continuing ferment made so many writers turn to reportage, so there arose, under the whiplash of now unbelievable despair, that dependence on the state which by now has made the state the only loyalty that people profess.

But we are all wise after the event. The 1930's were not only a fearful beginning to our characteristic mid-century world but an immediate shock; while a great many people understandably lost their heads, no one now can admit it—one is supposed to have looked at fifteen millions unemployed, the country desperate, Hitlerism and fascism overriding Europe, without feeling anything. The tragedy of so many radicals of the 1930's is precisely that they believed in justice, in freedom, in co-operation. They were not prepared for politics as tragedy; Americans so rarely are. It is easier to rewrite history now, to portray Franklin Roosevelt as more calculating than he really was. So the New Deal appears, in the works of John T. Flynn, Whittaker Chambers, James Burnham, as planned, theoretical, coherent; and the picture becomes really grotesque in the last works of Charles A. Beard, who saw Roosevelt tricking the Japanese into attacking at Pearl Harbor, so that the United States would have an excuse for coming to the aid of the British Empire.

Such interpretations of the New Deal show a remarkable forgetfulness both of the mass suffering which no government during the 1930's could entirely have overlooked and of the actual confusion, amazement, and powerlessness of those in office. If the 1930's mark the beginning of the contemporary history—the century of mass society—it is because in the 1930's anyone could apply to society Henry Adams's saying that modern man has mounted science and is run away with. With the 1930's, one could see in force the unavailingness of intelligence and good will in a world where political order is continually flying apart under the pressure from ideological new states. Men like Roosevelt, who fundamentally lacked ideas, were able to give the impression that they were planning or plotting a new society, when actually their greatest gift was one of charismatic leadership, the ability to hold up images of stability and national tradition during the storm. It is this quality of flux, of storm, of violent change, that Edmund Wilson has summoned back so vividly in *The American Earthquake*, a literary expansion of his articles from the *New Republic* about the 1920's and his book reportage of the depression.

It may be that the impression of chaos and intellectual helplessness that Wilson ascribes to the New Deal appeals more to the literary imagination than it does to political historians. Arthur Schlesinger, Jr.'s, recent book on the background of the New Deal (*The Age of Roosevelt: The Crisis of the Old Order; 1919–1933*) presents a picture of intellectual foresight which Wilson, drawing on his actual writings in the 1930's, obviously does not share. And perhaps the gift for seizing and holding personal impressions, the capacity for swift observations and revealing contrasts, gives Wilson an oversensitized capacity for descriptions of social change. Writers like Wilson, with their instant feeling for the literary image that will convey the feeling of social crisis, for the scene that will instantly evoke an historical moment, are so strong on history as literature, on swift and brilliant passagework, that they tend to impress upon us, as Carlyle does, a picture of history as a series of picturesque accidents. The stream of time bursts into iridescent foam for a paragraph or two, then retires into brutal inconsequence again.

But on the other hand, Wilson's chronicle is so unflinchingly personal, it presents so dramatically the confrontation of the period by a mind obviously unused to social ugliness, that it catches perfectly the revolutionary and unsettling impact of the 1930's on those who were least suited to it. The shock of the times comes through in the reactions of someone like Wilson, whose instincts are always for culture and tradition, and who never ceases to think of himself as an unattached man even when he comes closest to Marxism. It is the radicals who committed themselves intellectually who now have to revise history, for it is themselves that they have to disengage from the past. Similarly, it was never the "proletarian" novelists who caught the drama of the 1930's—they lost themselves in the general hysteria. Much of the Communist writing done in the 1930's, by people who were honest enough but who gave away such brains as they had, now looks like the fever chart of a patient *in extremis*. Such writers are now wrecks of the 1930's, writers who fell to pieces under the last disillusioning blow of the Soviet pact with Hitler, precisely because they had no culture to abdicate from, no wit to surrender. The pseudo science of Marxism gave them all the ideas they ever had, worked on them like strong drink; and their personal confusion was stepped up by incessant political manipulation and propaganda. It was precisely these Communist writers, who saw the 1930's as a time when everything was breaking up and who deliriously joined in the *Götterdämmerung* of "bourgeois" values, who became the real victims of the period. It was not a lack of integrity that doomed so many of these writers. It was a lack of background and perspective, an inability to see that their movement, too, would have its natural and inevitable end. Wilson's cultural imagination saved him from this loss of perspective. If anything, he had too much of it, and his extraordinary gift for turning every assignment into a superb literary article is a symbol of his inability to lose himself, as many writers did, in a purely human situation. The reins are always tight, and the horses always go the same way. On the other hand, Wilson's detachment certainly never made him incurious. The secret of his durability as a writer is his patient, arduous effort to assimilate, to clarify for himself and for others, subjects from which he feels excluded by temperament. The same hard-won intellectual triumph that as an agnostic he gets out of the Dead Sea Scrolls Wilson used to get, also as a bystander, out of descriptions of the Ziegfeld Follies, police beating up Communist marchers at New York City Hall, the Scottsboro case, the career of Henry Ford, the miseries of depression Chicago. Amid the laziest minds in the world, he is the most Puritanical of intellectual students, the most exacting in the correctness of his language and his learning.

Unsympathetic critics like to portray Wilson as a popular writer who sacrifices the ambiguity and complexity of his subjects. In truth, all his strength comes from the fact that he seeks to understand, to know; and it is his habit of willed attention, of strained concentration, that explains the exciting luminousness and tension of his prose.

Wilson is not a reporter but a literary artist driven by historical imagination—like Henry Adams and Carlyle. Such writers are lightning-quick to see the many metamorphoses of modern man. In Europe, where the succession and contrast of different epochs can be seen on every hand, writers who appeal to the historical imagination can be read for their merit as artists. But in this country, where we are likely to overvalue single traditions as such but to overlook the beauty of history itself, the creative side of such writers is unappreciated. Wilson's sense of historical contrast is documented entirely from his own life and that of his family in relation to America. The points of the compass for him are "the old stone house" of his ancestors in upstate New York that he describes so movingly in this book; New York, the great symbol of the cosmopolitan 1920's, a city that he always describes with distrust; and the ancient greatness embodied in Lincoln.

Only someone who has read much of this old material before can recognize how fine a work of art Wilson has made out of his records of the 1920's and 1930's—based always on the overriding fact of American instability. To see this as coldly as Wilson does, without for a moment allowing oneself to become cold to America, is to have the gift of perspective. When Wilson writes about a buccaneer of the 1920's, "Sunshine Charlie" Mitchell of the National City Bank, he notes that "the boom produced its own human type, with its own peculiar characteristics." When he writes about "the old stone house" in Talcottville, New York, he writes with appreciation of the old farmers that "they were very impressive people, the survivors of a sovereign race who had owned their own pastures and fields and governed their own community."

The section on the solitaries in his family significantly ends with a tribute to Herndon's unsentimental biography of Lincoln, and when Wilson writes about Lincoln, his prose expands to an uncontrollable emotion and we understand why, in the face of much misery, so much helplessness, thinking of Lincoln inspires him "with a kind of awe—I can hardly bear the thought of Lincoln."

If the historical imagination lives on metamorphosis, it expresses itself as personal impressions. Wilson writes cultural reminiscences as novelists and dramatists write scenes and dialogue. His strong suit is never ideas as such (any more than ideas as such were the strength of Carlyle or, despite his pretensions to philosophy, of Henry Adams); the end of the book, with its halfhearted approval of Beard's thesis on the war, simply emphasizes Wilson's stubborn and romantic isolationism. What makes Wilson's reporting good is the impression of actual experience brought to white heat on the page; it is the re-creation of a scene that relates Wilson to history, not the significance of history in itself. Wilson's writing depends entirely on the strength and flexibility of his style, and its unusual quality lies in the coupling of his intellectual tense style with the lower depths, the city junk heaps and bread lines, the strikes and demonstrations, the agony of mass fear.

The subtler achievement of the book is in the rapid succession of these sketches, which are run together to create a sense of history in motion. In Wilson, reportage becomes a series of impressions united only by the writer's temperament. Like all writing that is fundamentally personal, it depends almost too much on the writer's spirits, his wit, his virtuosity of style. Once the tone flags, the whole threatens to become commonplace. This is what above all things it dare not become, since it is so close to life that only the personality of the writer keeps it from relapsing into meaninglessness. Nothing in such a book dare appear in its objective crudity; everything must be assimilated by imagination. Nothing is held too long, for when the attention is fixed so sharply on cultural detail, it may easily tire, and in any event, the essential point has usually been made swiftly. But the assembling of details, the movement of ideas—these give us the orbit, the "spread" of life in a particular time, the picture of history behaving organically, through a hundred filaments and cells of the social body, lighting up together.

16
Harold Rosenberg (1906–1978)
Twilight of the Intellectuals (1958)

Editor's Introduction

Harold Rosenberg was best known as an art critic but he also wrote essays on general cultural matters. Born in New York City, he received his bachelor's degree from City College and a law degree from Brooklyn Law School. From 1937 to 1941 he worked as national art editor of the America Guide Series of the Works Progress Administration, and he served as deputy chief of the domestic radio bureau of the Office of War Information from 1942 to 1945. An early and frequent contributor to *Partisan Review*, Rosenberg counted himself as one of the dissenters after *Dissent* began in 1954, and helped Irving Howe, Lewis Coser and others scold those at *Commentary*, such as Irving Kristol and Nathan Glazer, for allegedly being too satisfied with the new American consensus and affluence. Rosenberg's friend Saul Bellow featured him as Victor Wulpy in the story "What Kind of Day Did You Have?"

While Clement Greenberg championed modernist painting by explaining its formal properties, which he believed had firm boundaries, Rosenberg supported it by explaining the canvas as a site that recorded an event expressed by an individual painter. A modernist painting, by Greenberg's account, could be a prescribed act, while for Rosenberg it was an individual act—"action painting" he called it—explainable only in retrospect as a part of cultural history. Rosenberg worked as the art critic for *The New Yorker* from 1967 until his death, and during that same period he was a faculty member of the Committee on Social Thought at the University of Chicago.

Like many of the New York Intellectuals, it seemed as though the multidisciplinary Rosenberg could write on anything. Here stood a lawyer-turned-art-critic who wrote on sociology, political ideology and intellectual history while also writing some seriously funny passages. Irving Howe remembered that Rosenberg defined an intellectual as someone who turns answers into questions. He wrote an essay entitled "The Herd of Independent Minds." Before it became a standard practice in the 1990s, he had already written such titles as *The Tradition of the New, Discovering the Present* and *The De-definition of Art*. For a serious critic he employed a welcome irreverence.

In the essay below, Rosenberg reviewed for *Dissent* Raymond Aron's book *The Opium of the Intellectuals*, which attacked the dangers of ideology. Aron, a distinguished French intellectual and scholar who once called himself a socialist, now embraced liberalism but probably still thought of himself as a figure of the political left. Aron's argument against ideologies was part of that introduced a few years earlier by Sidney Hook. The question of the nature and advisability of ideology occupied an absolutely central place in the Cold War debates. Ideology, according to the *Partisan* circle, represented a committed and zealous adoption of a political point of view based on an act of faith. One accepted the tenets of the ideology on unproved *a priori* grounds. Ideologies by this definition usually respected ends over means, which meant that individuals who opposed the ends or the means were often eliminated. Ideologies were totalistic belief systems where people accepted the whole vision or none. These systems were not experimental and changeable. They represented societies such as Hannah Arendt described. The term *ideology* in this debate did not mean simply ideas or points of view, as they might in some definitions. Ideology to the New York Intellectuals meant something far more all-encompassing.

Aron's book was an attack on the continued presence of ideologies in the world, especially in Europe. Rosenberg's review of Aron's volume is a skewering of his ideas, sometimes humorously, as when Rosenberg purports to agree with Aron that intellectuals and ideas are no longer useful or necessary. Of course Aron never says that, and Rosenberg conflates "ideology," which is the topic of Aron's book, with intellectuals and ideas, which are not the same terms. But Rosenberg's criticism is close enough to the truth that it is a lively part of an important Cold War dispute. His charge that Aron is anti-intellectual is the same charge that was occasionally made against Irving Kristol. (See essays 29 and 33.) This conflict is relevant today as the West tries to separate what is properly or improperly ideology, religion, fanaticism, utopianism, fascism or simply nations and individuals seeking their own voice. A half-century later, the world again needs to decide what protections and immunities are due to ideas propounded in the name of religions, ideologies of historical inevitability or traditional national and tribal cultural beliefs.

Source

Harold Rosenberg, "Twilight of the Intellectuals," *Dissent* vol. 5, no. 3, Summer 1958.

Selected Readings

Raymond Aron, *The Opium of the Intellectuals*, translated by Terence Kilmartin (New York: Doubleday, 1957).
Dore Ashton, "On Harold Rosenberg," Critical Inquiry vol. 6, no. 4, Summer, 1980.

Saul Bellow, "What Kind of Day Did You Have?" *Him with his Foot in his Mouth, and Other Stories* (New York: Harper and Row, 1984).
Daniel Bell, "The End of Ideology in the West," (see essay 24 below).
Chaim Waxman, ed., *The End of Ideology Debate* (New York: Funk and Wagnalls, 1968).

* * * * *

It will be a bad night when, lacking truth itself, man suppresses the superstition of truth

—**Rene Char**

Much of the potency of contemporary attacks on socialism lies not in the points they score against Marx's ideas—since these points when valid could be made equally well, and often have been, by Marxists themselves—but in the fact that all ideas have turned out so badly. Ideas as such are suspect. A century ago Cardinal Newman thought that one might "look for a blessing through obedience even to an erroneous system, and a guidance even by means of it out of it." Today, from the truest system nothing but evil is expected, if only because it is a system. As for guidance out of it, the more systematic it is, the deeper it leads you into its trap. Once inside, the only hope is to break the system to pieces.

Given this attitude toward ideas, does it matter whether a critique of Marxism is referring to the conceptions of Marx, of Lenin or of Stalin? Any error, crudity or malice found in one may as well be attributed to the others. For they have, indisputably, one thing in common: they are "ideologies," that is, interpretations in which all events hang together. In such a coherence itself one already sees the outlines of a prison cell.

This mood is typified by Raymond Aron's *The Opium Of The Intellectuals*. Its pages gasp for the open air of a world cleared of ideologies. To him "ideology" is synonymous with "myth" and myth with a fog in the brain. The largest part of his book consists of blasts at phantasies generated by Marxism: "The Myth Of The Left," "The Myth Of The Revolution," "The Myth Of The Proletariat," "The Illusion Of Necessity." Aron knows the weak spots of Marxian theory and the nightmares connected with it in practice, though the advantage of this knowledge seems diminished by the fact that he feels obliged to reject, for example, the term "capitalism" in favor of "the West."

Beyond Marxism, *The Opium* is striking at all ideologies, and at their creators and carriers, the intellectuals, particularly the French intellectuals. From the café tables of St. Germain des Prés, Aron sees rising the image-laden fumes that make all of France giddy. Will the French intelligentsia never stop playing with the colored balloons of doctrinal solutions? Until they give up this pastime and get to work, France will not regain her balance. But, Aron prophesies, "The End Of The Ideological Age" may be approaching, and on this note *The Opium* concludes. In this Spring's *Partisan Review* ("Coexistence: The End Of Ideology") he goes further: the extinction of ideologies must come or mankind itself will be destroyed.

By the end of ideologies M. Aron means an end to an interest in political theories and of "nostalgia for a universal idea." The model for how nations shall think in the future is America—and the model intellectual for M. Aron is none other than the contemporary American, the intellectual as "expert" engaged in doing his job and suspicious of abstractions and systems. "The United States," declares Aron enthusiastically, "knows nothing of ideological conflicts in the French sense of the word. ... On the other side of the Atlantic there is no sign of either the traditions or the classes which give European ideas their meaning." (I hope our Southerners are listening.)

America has solved the problem of the intellectuals—except that, in M. Aron's view, there never was any problem here. Back in the Depression, he recalls, some radical exhalations did blow over from Europe; soon, however, our natural sobriety reasserted itself. For actually, there was nothing to lose one's head about. "In the name of what European values could the intellectual turn his back on the American reality?"

M. Aron admires us—with a vengeance. Not only don't American intellectuals have any ideas, nobody pays any attention to them in any case. How superior to the situation in France, where "writers with no authority whatsoever can obtain large audiences even when they treat of subjects about which they quite openly boast of knowing nothing—a phenomenon which is inconceivable in the United States. ..." (At least so long as we have a President to fill the bill.)

For those in America who continue to criticise, before tiny audiences naturally, M. Aron "conveniently borrows" Louis Bromfield's genial description of the American radical as "a doctrinaire supporter of Middle European socialism ... subject to the old-fashioned philosophical morality of Nietzsche which frequently leads him into jail or disgrace." Echoing our own ex-Left, M. Aron dismisses these dissidents as out of date: "There are some American intellectuals who remain faithful to the tradition of anti-conformism and who attack simultaneously digests [readers'], the trusts, McCarthyism [written in 1955 *The Opium* is also out of date, and in more ways than one] and capitalism. But this anti-conformism is not without a certain conformism itself, since it resurrects the themes of the militant liberalism of yesterday."

In part, Aron's vision of us is simply the old European stereotype of Primitive America, land of cowboys and Indians and millionaires, all of these being, of course, pragmatic people intent on specific objectives and without appetite for ideas. That Aron presents this image as an object of emulation rather than of contempt does not alter its character. "In the name of what *European* values could the intellectual turn his back on the American reality?" Any criticism of America could only be made in the name of European ideas—of themselves Americans know only *things*.

But there is more to this conception than the Old World platitude of American barbarism. Aron bases himself also upon what American intellectuals have been saying about themselves and doing during the past decade or so, as well as upon the temper of the nation that had elected Ike and was preparing to do so again. In a word, the sage of The League For Cultural Freedom is reporting America correctly, at least so far as appearances are concerned. The question is: has he understood what he is reporting? And is he correct in applying the measure of the post-war American to intellectuals elsewhere?

Let me make it clear without delay that I share M. Aron's ideal of the disappearance of the intellectuals. Who but one with a taste for priests would desire this peculiar caste to flourish? Except perhaps that portion of it that works quietly in the laboratory, the study, the classroom. The others, the ideological ones, those who want to remake the world, the revolutionists in everything from paint to politics, those who never stop talking save when someone puts to them a pertinent question, these people have proved themselves as a group more trouble than they are worth. With too few exceptions, they are false, fanatical, arrogant, greedy, emotionally unstable, morally sophistical, politically and socially untrustworthy—by nature they are traitors both to their ideas and to themselves, even without bribe or force, from an ineradicable nostalgia for community with other people, who essentially revolt them, and from sheer weariness with their aimless egos. This type has manifested the same disagreeable traits throughout the world, in the "new nations" as in the old, wherever the breakdown of authority has given prominence to ideas.[1] Is it an exaggeration to say that in no place where he has appeared is the intellectual loved? And if, besides, he now endangers the world, as M. Aron warns, that should certainly settle it.

Aside from his deplorable character which makes his presence in any society of dubious advantage, there is a deeper reason for desiring the elimination of the intellectual with his ideological carpetbag. He stands for deficiency in human life, a blank spot in being. The thought of an all-real world, from which abstractions, utopias, higher states and other projections of the mind have been banished, has charmed every true humanist, including Marx though not Aron's Marx. No ideas, no intellectuals. Only the concrete existence adequate to itself of individual men and women.

The goal of supplanting doctrines and superstitions with material profusion belongs equally to the dream of America as a paradise on earth and to the dream of Socialism as an earthly paradise. The dreams differ only with regard to when ideas are to be gotten rid of—in the American dream they can be dispensed with now; while Socialism wants to hold on as the last idea and liquidate itself only when all other ideas have been defeated.

In practice, however, both America and Socialism have tended to behave, whenever things have gone well, as if paradise had already been attained and to dispose of ideas prematurely. In response to this demand an intellectual without ideas appears, one whose function is indeed to stand guard against ideas as a disintegrating force. This "sobered" intellectual, serving society as a hired man, whether as expert or bureaucrat, is the figure of Aron's admiration in the United States and, in a reserved way, in the Soviet Union.

In believing that "the American reality" has permanently transfixed the American mind, this Frenchman is dreaming the American dream. Let us remember that this dream was a European product in the first place. "In the name of what European values could the intellectual turn his back ...?"—a typical American-dream question. It makes one think of a certain mariner-theoretician debarking on the glistening sands of the West Indies one refulgent morning. The same question could be heard booming in chorus from these shores since the onset of post-War prosperity. "Why should we not shed our European illusions ("myths")? Daily life is enough for us, not to say too much. We don't need ideas and what's more we don't want any." And M. Aron sums up this rosy condition in prose: "These intellectuals are perfectly reconciled with the United States" (whatever that means).

Given this happy conclusion, it is hard to see why Doubleday brought us M. Aron's tract unless perhaps to indicate where we could find a foreign market for our mental vacuum cleaners.

Unfortunately, Aron's liquidation of the American intellectual as the vanguard of the vanishing intellectuals of the world is no more to be depended on than the related attempt by his American friends to liquidate themselves. If, as he says, "anti-conformism is not without a certain conformism," anti-ideology is not without a certain ideology. The notion that radical criticism is a symptom of doctrinaire hangover or mental ankylosis has been pressed upon us from every source, including philistine psychiatry, ever since the ex-Left discovered it had a part to play in the Cold War, the part of penitents and "responsible" underwriters of social unanimity. But adopting this role did not result in the extinction of the American intellectual as a species—it was simply a new affirmation of his morbid character. Having raised to the level of a philosophy the old backwoods suspicion of the intellect and intellectuals, directed against the city, the intelligentsia became more active than ever. If, as M. Aron insists, the American intellectuals have had to go looking for an enemy, it was because they decided not to find him where he lives but to take on instead the enemy's enemy, that is to say, "ideology," or in our beautifully onomotopoetic synonym, the "isms"–whether it be Socialism, Fascism, Zionism or even New Dealism. Given the mood induced by the failure of ideas mentioned above, this antidoctrine overflowed our borders and reappeared as a world idea.

In his identification with the outlook of our typical "integrated" prosperity intellectual, Aron exemplifies the phenomenon, about which too little is known, of the flotage of ideas from their original mooring in historical fact and their fall-out in distant places. For almost four decades the Russian October was wafted around the globe in the form of abstract aims and illusory adventures; only since the parody of Budapest have The Ten Days That Shook The World begun to lose their hallucinatory power outside the USSR (in Russia the revolutionary charade faded much earlier). Why should not the unprecedented buildup of prosperity in the United States of the fifties, with its activation and absorption of the social premises of The New Deal—recognition for labor, pensions and benefits, G.I. rights and civil rights—win adherents outside the continent where it took place as realizing in practice advances which socialism could only promise. The Russian Revolution left a residue of dead ideas, American prosperity the idea of no-ideas.

Aron is a fellow traveler of the American fact. The immanent assumptions of United States accomplishment are the groundwork of his non-doctrinal progressivism, his trust in common sense, his impatience with theory. They are also the basis of his Utopian view of American life—e.g., as devoid of social conflict—and his journalist's contempt for cafe radicals and "talkers."

"France exalts her intellectuals, who reject and despise her; America makes no concession to hers, who nevertheless adore her," Aron marvels. The assumption is: Treat 'em rough, they like it. Though we have already seen there has been no one here to make any concessions to. Still, one could mention Congressmen who would consider the word "adore" too strong.

Adoring America or rejecting France has, of course, nothing to do with the relation between intellectuals and their country; the psychology of patriotism, if one must so remind an expert in Marxist "oversimplifications," is much too complex to summarize in a word. What caused American social criticism to slacken was total employment. With individual talents supplied with resources to work *within* society, the very definition of the intellectual underwent a change in America—from the ominous outsider of the days of the "brain truster" and the Red, he became the inferior "egghead," that is, a social type identified by his look and his vocabulary.

If America could maintain the incorporation of its intellectuals in productive labor, there might continue to be nothing to ideologize about, except perhaps the menace of ideology—in their material paradise (i.e., reality without opium) they could go on living in a state of adoration.

The Opium Of The Intellectuals fails even to consider whether the American intellectual's pre-occupation with "fact" belongs to conditions of a particular period, rather than to a fixed status within the nation. This taking for granted that our paradise is here to stay reveals the idealistic underpinning of M. Aron's skepticism. Perhaps he has forgotten how in the years following the Russian Revolution the most ideological generation in history was drawn into "socialist construction" and "reconciled with its reality." Did this yielding to fact make the Russian intellectuals similar to the practical Americans, or did their ideological motives cause them to resemble the idea-intoxicated French?

Aron's contrast of adoring Americans with rejecting Frenchmen is owing to more than the mistaken impression of a foreigner taken in by the "typical attitudes" of a moment; his error is made possible by his static definition of the intellectual according to ancient categories of employment: "clerk," "expert," "man of letters," all three being groupings within society. While the intellectual is designated socially by his occupation, no definition by occupation alone can distinguish the modern intellectual from his "non-intellectual" counterpart in the vast array of professions and crafts that constitute the organization of work in contemporary society. The same function may be performed by two "experts" seated side by side in a newspaper office or advertising agency, yet one is an intellectual and the other is not. What distinguishes one from the other is precisely his non-identification, open or veiled, with his métier and his self-separation from its values. This is strikingly apparent in a study like Whyte's *The Organization Man*, whose author, without any revolutionary intention, defines himself as an intellectual, in contrast with socially identical Orgmen, *by the sole fact of his inner dissociation* from the organizational universe.

Aron has completely ignored the composition of the intellectual caste by which it is re-defined under specific conditions as *a caste of social delinquents*. In a society that has reached a certain degree of literacy, which makes it susceptible to the formation of ideological bands, and in which, consequently, one may qualify as an intellectual in terms of social dynamics without having gone beyond the fifth grade, this re-definition on a large scale is inseparable from a "revolutionary situation."

To meet such a situation heroes are needed. But by what, except by the consciousness of a "plot" in history, that is to say, by a "myth," are men transformed into heroes? The aim of Marx's writing was that, in the predictable crises to come, a mass hero raised up out of the modern city should act in consciousness of itself and its possibilities. In it the humanitarianism of the 19th century was heightened to the pitch of world drama. Marxism offered the conception of a universal *acting of progress* to the point of universal victory. This myth has not been realized, and to Aron's mind it has stood in the way of real progress.

Suppose that Aron has his way and in a social crisis the intellectuals continue peering into their microscopes or analyzing the prosody of Virgil and nobody comes forward with the myth of a better world? (Or is such a supposition unreal, since without the ideological mists exuded by the intellectuals there would never be a crisis? Perhaps Algeria is the effect of an opium discourse that went wrong—and shop-keeping and ranch-owning colonials and poverty-stricken Moslems are only parts of the mirage.)

Be that as it may, suppose a crisis exists and no ideologist comes forward. Will the result be a calm development of wise solutions by the experienced men of affairs in whom M. Aron reposes such trust and whose hands he would have us untie by disappearing? Is that what has happened in France among, for example, the Centrist parties, whose ideologies are certainly blurred enough to satisfy anyone? Or does the absence of universals tend rather to result in a day-by-day yielding to events, until the steady erosion of principles become the accompaniment of a paralysis of the will? For what is a crisis but a situation in which the practical men of affairs, who are always the people in power, have already failed, exposing the limits of the practical intelligence.

Once a hero is needed the absence of ideologies will not save the day for the skeptic and pragmatist. Rather will a dream of unreason supply what the dream of reason could not. The anti-intellectual intellectual like Aron has no power to prevent history from going mad. In the end his common sense can have only the effect of promoting a distrust of ideas that brings capitulation to the myth of the man of action.

Since history has not achieved a steady sanity, the time for the extinction of the intellectual has not yet arrived. Unpleasant as it is to have us around, and anxious as we are to get rid of ourselves, society has no choice but to put up with us—if for no other reason than that we can at present be abolished only by other myth-makers. We are stuck with ourselves, and the world is stuck with us at the price of making itself perfect. Perhaps when everyone has defected from the common "reality," that is, when everyone has become an intellectual, the role of the intellectual will be ended, and with it that unhappy species itself.

For one who scorns ideologies Aron derives too much from the evidence of "opinion makers" and too little from the hints contained in historical analogies. He has performed the astonishing feat of writing a book on the modern intellectual without mentioning the disintegration of social classes and the estrangement of individuals—he has even forgotten to mention the Jews! Having no concept of the stranger, he misses the tension between the intellectual and his neighbors, even in a country he adores, and between one band of intellectuals and another. Hence he can only note as an oddity the vicious anti-egghead campaign of America's 1952 elections (erroneously set by Aron in '53), with its overtones of persecution for sedition and foreign alliance.

The poison of the intellectuals since World War I, the poison responsible for the catalepsy of the Third International as for other collapses, has been the ideal of practicality, of a politics and social philosophy stripped of "myth" and "ineffectiveness," of subordination to "reality," in sum, of their own disappearances as intellectuals. This is the drug that has transformed the fighting humanitarian Dr. Jekyll into the bureaucratic and "responsible" Mr. Hyde. The worst of it is that the somnambulist Hyde dreams not only that he alone is awake but that he is vigorously bringing into being the very same world that his original could only feebly imagine.

Note

1. It may be, or it may not be, that intellectuals are, as Aron says, "closely linked to the national community"—as a type they transcend nationality, as anyone may ascertain by dropping in at the U.N. building.

17

Daniel Bell (1919–)
The End of Ideology in the West (1960)

Editor's Introduction

Daniel Bell published his book The *End of Ideology* in 1960, five years after the
Future of Freedom Conference in Milan, Italy. At the meeting, the term "the
end of ideology" was the subject of several papers and was first widely discussed. Many of the best known intellectuals in Europe and the United States
attended the conference and the ideas surrounding the end of ideology were
hotly contested on both sides for a decade or more.

Although nominally a sociologist, Bell's volume contained a group of generalist essays, set in a Weberian language of ideas, that today would be called
intellectual history. The book featured pieces, for example, on the dissolution
of family capitalism; the lack of a ruling class in America; the work of Keynes,
Schumpeter and Galbraith; American national character, ideologies from the
1930s through the 1950s and the magazines that served them; Marx; the failure of socialism; and a few other related topics. Bell argued that America never
was a place where class had ruled very strongly, nor had Americans been very
ideological. Well, a few of them had, those such as the New York Intellectuals
and Bell himself, but they had broken painfully from that illusion. America
was now, at the end of the 1950s, a pragmatic place, as it mostly had been for
centuries. The intellectuals had reached an end of ideology.

The essays in the book made two main points. First, it regretted ideological
thinking because that led to dangerously total instead of tentative solutions—
and the zealous way ideas were held blocked complex and varied approaches
to ideas, blocked the nuanced estimation of an idea that Lionel Trilling suggested in his literary essays. Second, several of Bell's essays employed economic
or sociological data to suggest that life in the United States in the 1950s was
not quite as uniform and homogeneous as reports of the massified suburban
society suggested. His epilogue, reprinted here, has been denounced by some
as an arrogant or careless conceit that his group, the New York Intellectuals,
isn't ideological while others are. The argument occurred only because his
opponents misunderstood the definition of ideology used by Bell's generation.
None of the *Partisan* crowd would have denied they were ideological in the
sense of having a point of view. But the term ideological at midcentury came

to mean in addition that one held a totalistic, messianic, zealous political faith that stood as an obstacle to unimpeded thinking. The following passage from Harold Rosenberg's essay "The Heroes of Marxist Science" shows how the *Partisan* group believed that communist ideology, for example, proscribed real thought.

> The Communist belongs to an elite of the knowing. Thus he is an intellectual. But since all truth has been automatically bestowed upon him by his adherence to the Party, he is an intellectual who need not think. The Communist has often been criticized for his renunciation of independent thought. What good is mental activity if one can know more by giving it up? The Communist is contemptuous of the non-Communist intellectual. The latter goes through all the motions of thinking, but at best he can only hope to arrive at what is already known. At best. More likely his thinking will lead him into error. (Harold Rosenberg, "The Heroes of Marxist Science," *The Tradition of the New*. New York: Horizon Press, 1959, 184.)

In his youth Bell was a more conservative socialist than others in the City College lunchroom. He married Pearl Kazin, Alfred's sister, and thus Dan and Alfred were brothers-in-law. After a year at Columbia Law School Bell switched to the sociology department, but before he finished graduate school he began to work at *The New Leader* in 1940. There he met Sidney Hook, a contributor, and soon became managing editor. Five years later he was hired to teach at the University of Chicago, and then in 1948 he moved back to New York to become labor editor at *Fortune* magazine. In 1956–57 he worked for the Congress for Cultural Freedom in Paris. When he returned, he turned down the editorship of *Commentary* and went back to teaching in Columbia's sociology department in 1959. A decade later, he accepted a position at Harvard, where he finished his career. In the late 1960s he was co-founder with Irving Kristol of *The Public Interest*, a journal that used social science to study the social issues of the day.

Bell is an example of why people look to individuals in the *Partisan Review* circle as models of the public intellectual. Consider his training as an intellectual: weaving back and forth from the university to magazines to cultural organizations, from law to sociology to journalism, from labor issues to professorships to editorships and back, and a period of time in Paris working on cultural politics. Here was the formula that shaped the prototype. Because of his varied background, Bell was particularly interested in the relationships among economics, politics, technology and ideas. His books *The Coming of Post-Industrial Society* (1973) and *The Cultural Contradictions of Capitalism* (1976) addressed these "axial" principles. In a 1978 reaffirmation of his opposition to the rigidities of totalistic thinking, he famously declared himself "a socialist in economics, a liberal in politics, and conservative in culture," in itself a formula to keep rigid thinking at bay. (Daniel Bell, *The Cultural Contradictions of Capitalism*. New York: Basic Books, 1978, xi.)

Source

Daniel Bell, "The End of Ideology in the West," *The End of Ideology* (Glencoe, IL: The Free Press, 1960).

Selected Readings

Chaim Waxman, ed., *The End of Ideology Debate* (New York: Funk and Wagnalls, 1968).
Daniel Boorstin, *The Genius of American Politics* (Chicago: University of Chicago Press, 1953).
Job Dittberner, *The End of Ideology and American Social Thought, 1930–1960* (Ann Arbor: UMI Research Press, 1979).
Raymond Aron, *The Opium of the Intellectuals*, translated by Terence Kilmartin (New York: Doubleday, 1957).

* * * * *

Men commit the error of not knowing when to limit their hopes.

—Machiavelli

There have been few periods in history when man felt his world to be durable, suspended surely, as in Christian allegory, between chaos and heaven. In an Egyptian papyrus of more than four thousand years ago, one finds: "… impudence is rife … the country is spinning round and round like a potter's wheel … the masses are like timid sheep without a shepherd … one who yesterday was indigent is now wealthy and the sometime rich overwhelm him with adulation." The Hellenistic period as described by Gilbert Murray was one of a "failure of nerve"; there was "the rise of pessimism, a loss of self-confidence, of hope in this life and of faith in normal human effort." And the old scoundrel Talleyrand claimed that only those who lived before 1789 could have tasted life in all its sweetness.

This age, too, can add appropriate citations—made all the more wry and bitter by the long period of bright hope that preceded it—for the two decades between 1930 and 1950 have an intensity peculiar in written history: worldwide economic depression and sharp class struggles; the rise of fascism and racial imperialism in a country that had stood at an advanced stage of human culture; the tragic self-immolation of a revolutionary generation that had proclaimed the finer ideals of man; destructive war of a breadth and scale hitherto unknown; the bureaucratized murder of millions in concentration camps and death chambers.

For the radical intellectual who had articulated the revolutionary impulses of the past century and a half, all this has meant an end to chiliastic hopes, to millenarianism, to apocalyptic thinking—and to ideology. For ideology, which once was a road to action, has come to be a dead end.

Whatever its origins among the French *philosophes*, ideology as a way of translating ideas into action was given its sharpest phrasing by the left Hegelians, by Feuerbach and by Marx. For them, the function of philosophy was to be critical, to rid the present of the past. ("The tradition of all the dead generations weighs like a nightmare on the brain of the living," wrote Marx.) Feuerbach, the most radical of all the left Hegelians, called himself Luther II. Man would be free, he said, if we could demythologize religion. The history of all thought was a history of progressive disenchantment, and if finally, in Christianity, God had been transformed from a parochial deity to a universal abstraction, the function of criticism—using the radical tool of alienation, or self-estrangement—was to replace theology by anthropology, to substitute Man for God. Philosophy was to be directed at life, man was to be liberated from the "specter of abstractions" and extricated from the bind of the supernatural. Religion was capable only of creating "false consciousness." Philosophy would reveal "true consciousness." And by placing Man, rather than God, at the center of consciousness, Feuerbach sought to bring the "infinite into the finite."

If Feuerbach "descended into the world," Marx sought to transform it. And where Feuerbach proclaimed anthropology, Marx, reclaiming a root insight of Hegel, emphasized History and historical contexts. The world was not generic Man, but men; and of men, classes of men. Men differed because of their class position. And truths were class truths. All truths, thus, were masks, or partial truths, but the real truth was the revolutionary truth. And this real truth was rational.

Thus a dynamic was introduced into the analysis of ideology, and into the creation of a new ideology. By demythologizing religion, one recovered (from God and sin) the potential in man. By the unfolding of history, rationality was revealed. In the struggle of classes, true consciousness, rather than false consciousness, could be achieved. But if truth lay in action, one must act. The left Hegelians, said Marx, were only *littérateurs*. (For them a magazine was "practice.") For Marx, the only real action was in politics. But action, revolutionary action as Marx conceived it, was not mere social change. It was, in its way, the resumption of all the old millenarian, chiliastic ideas of the Anabaptists. It was, in its new vision, a new ideology.

Ideology is the conversion of ideas into social levers. Without irony, Max Lerner once entitled a book "Ideas Are Weapons." This is the language of ideology. It is more. It is the commitment to the consequences of ideas. When Vissarion Belinsky, the father of Russian criticism, first read Hegel and became convinced of the philosophical correctness of the formula "what is, is what ought to be," he became a supporter of the Russian autocracy. But when it was shown to him that Hegel's thought contained the contrary tendency, that dialectically the "is" evolves into a different form, he became a revolutionary overnight. "Belinsky's conversion," comments Rufus W. Mathewson, Jr., "illustrates an attitude toward ideas which is both passionate and myopic, which responds to them on the basis of their immediate relevances alone, and inevitably reduces them to tools."[185]

What gives ideology its force is its passion. Abstract philosophical inquiry has always sought to eliminate passion, and the person, to rationalize all ideas. For the ideologue, truth arises in action, and meaning is given to experience by the "transforming moment." He comes alive not in contemplation, but in "the deed." One might say, in fact, that the most important, latent, function of ideology is to tap emotion. Other than religion (and war and nationalism), there have been few forms of channelizing emotional energy. Religion symbolized, drained away, dispersed emotional energy from the world onto the litany, the liturgy, the sacraments, the edifices, the arts. Ideology fuses these energies and channels them into politics.

But religion, at its most effective, was more. It was a way for people to cope with the problem of death. The fear of death—forceful and inevitable—and more, the fear of violent death, shatters the glittering, imposing, momentary dream of man's power. The fear of death, as Hobbes pointed out, is the source of conscience; the effort to avoid violent death is the source of law. When it was possible for people to believe, really believe, in heaven and hell, then some of the fear of death could be tempered or controlled; without such belief, there is only the total annihilation of the self.[186]

It may well be that with the decline in religious *faith* in the last century and more, this fear of death as total annihilation, unconsciously expressed, has probably increased. One may hypothesize, in fact, that here is a cause of the breakthrough of the irrational, which is such a marked feature of the changed moral temper of our time. Fanaticism, violence, and cruelty are not, of course, unique in human history. But there was a time when such frenzies and mass emotions could be displaced, symbolized, drained away, and dispersed through religious devoton and practice. Now there is only this life, and the assertion of self becomes possible—for some even necessary—in the domination over others.[1] One can challenge death by emphasizing the omnipotence of a movement (as in the "inevitable" victory of communism), or overcome death (as did the "immortality" of Captain Ahab) by bending others to one's will. Both paths are taken, but politics, because it can institutionalize power, in the way that religion once did, becomes the ready avenue for domination. The modern effort to transform the world chiefly or solely through politics (as contrasted with the religious transformation of the self) has meant that all other institutional ways of mobilizing emotional energy would necessarily atrophy. In effect, sect and church became party and social movement.

A social movement can rouse people when it can do three things: simplify ideas, establish a claim to truth, and, in the union of the two, demand a commitment to action. Thus, not only does ideology transform ideas, it transforms people as well. The nineteenth-century ideologies, by emphasizing inevitability and by infusing passion into their followers, could compete with religion. By identifying inevitability with progress, they linked up with the positive values of science. But more important, these ideologies were linked, too, with the rising class of intellectuals, which was seeking to assert a place in society.

The differences between the intellectual and the scholar, without being invidious, are important to understand. The scholar has a bounded field of knowledge, a tradition, and seeks to find his place in it, adding to the accumulated, tested knowledge of the past as to a mosaic. The scholar, qua scholar, is less involved with his "self." The intellectual begins with *his* experience, *his* individual perceptions of the world, *his* privileges and deprivations, and judges the world by these sensibilities. Since his own status is of high value, his judgments of the society reflect the treatment accorded him. In a business civilization, the intellectual felt that the wrong values were being honored, and rejected the society. Thus there was a "built-in" compulsion for the free-floating intellectual to become political. The ideologies, therefore, which emerged from the nineteenth century had the force of the intellectuals behind them. They embarked upon what William James called "the faith ladder," which in its vision of the future cannot distinguish possibilities from probabilities, and converts the latter into certainties.

Today, these ideologies are exhausted. The events behind this important sociological change are complex and varied. Such calamities as the Moscow Trials, the Nazi-Soviet pact, the concentration camps, the suppression of the Hungarian workers, form one chain; such social changes as the modification of capitalism, the rise of the Welfare State, another. In philosophy, one can trace the decline of simplistic, rationalistic beliefs and the emergence of new stoic-theological images of man, e.g. Freud, Tillich, Jaspers, etc. This is not to say that such ideologies as communism in France and Italy do not have a political weight, or a driving momentum from other sources. But out of all this history, one simple fact emerges: for the radical intelligentzia, the old ideologies have lost their "truth" and their power to persuade.

Few serious minds believe any longer that one can set down "blueprints" and through "social engineering" bring about a new utopia of social harmony. At the same time, the older "counter-beliefs" have lost their intellectual force as well. Few "classic" liberals insist that the State should play no role in the economy, and few serious conservatives, at least in England and on the Continent, believe that the Welfare State is "the road to serfdom." In the Western world, therefore, there is today a rough consensus among intellectuals on political issues: the acceptance of a Welfare State; the desirability of decentralized power; a system of mixed economy and of political pluralism. In that sense, too, the ideological age has ended.

And yet, the extraordinary fact is that while the old nineteenth-century ideologies and intellectual debates have become exhausted, the rising states of

Asia and Africa are fashioning new ideologies with a different appeal for their own people. These are the ideologies of industrialization, modernization, Pan-Arabism, color, and nationalism. In the distinctive difference between the two kinds of ideologies lies the great political and social problems of the second half of the twentieth century. The ideologies of the nineteenth century were universalistic, humanistic, and fashioned by intellectuals. The mass ideologies of Asia and Africa are parochial, instrumental, and created by political leaders. The driving forces of the old ideologies were social equality and, in the largest sense, freedom. The impulsions of the new ideologies are economic development and national power.

And in this appeal, Russia and China have become models. The fascination these countries exert is no longer the old idea of the free society, but the new one of economic growth. And if this involves the wholesale coercion of the population and the rise of new elites to drive the people, the new repressions are justified on the ground that without such coercions economic advance cannot take place rapidly enough. And even for some of the liberals of the West, "economic development" has become a new ideology that washes away the memory of old disillusionments.

It is hard to quarrel with an appeal for rapid economic growth and modernization, and few can dispute the goal, as few could ever dispute an appeal for equality and freedom. But in this powerful surge—and its swiftness is amazing—any movement that instates such goals risks the sacrifice of the present generation for a future that may see only a new exploitation by a new elite. For the newly-risen countries, the debate is not over the merits of Communism—the content of that doctrine has long been forgotten by friends and foes alike. The question is an older one: whether new societies can grow by building democratic institutions and allowing people to make choices—and sacrifices—voluntarily, or whether the new elites, heady with power, will impose totalitarian means to transform their countries. Certainly in these traditional and old colonial societies where the masses are apathetic and easily manipulated, the answer lies with the intellectual classes and their conceptions of the future.

Thus one finds, at the end of the fifties, a disconcerting caesura. In the West, among the intellectuals, the old passions are spent. The new generation, with no meaningful memory of these old debates, and no secure tradition to build upon, finds itself seeking new purposes within a framework of political society that has rejected, intellectually speaking, the old apocalyptic and chiliastic visions. In the search for a "cause," there is a deep, desperate, almost pathetic anger. The theme runs through a remarkable book, *Convictions*, by a dozen of the sharpest young Left Wing intellectuals in Britain. They cannot define the content of the "cause" they seek, but the yearning is clear. In the U.S. too there is a restless search for a new intellectual radicalism. Richard Chase, in his thoughtful assessment of American society, *The Democratic Vista*, insists that the greatness of nineteenth-century America for the rest of the world consisted in its radical vision of man (such a vision as Whitman's), and calls for a new radical criticism today. But the problem is that the old politico-economic radicalism (pre-occupied with such matters as the socialization of industry) has lost its meaning, while the stultifying aspects of contemporary culture (e.g., television) cannot be redressed in political terms. At the same time, American culture has almost completely accepted the avant-garde, particularly in art, and the older academic styles have been driven out completely. The irony, further, for those who seek "causes" is that the workers, whose grievances were once the driving energy for social change, are more satisfied with the society than the intellectuals. The workers have not achieved utopia, but their expectations were less than those of the intellectuals, and the gains correspondingly larger.

The young intellectual is unhappy because the "middle way" is for the middle-aged, not for him; it is without passion and is deadening. Ideology, which by its nature is an all-or-none affair, and temperamentally the thing he wants, is intellectually devitalized, and few issues can be formulated any more, intellectually, in ideological terms. The emotional energies—and needs—exist, and the question of how one mobilizes these energies is a difficult one. Politics offers little excitement. Some of the younger intellectuals have found an outlet in science or university pursuits, but often at the expense of narrowing their talent into mere technique; others have sought self-expression in the arts, but in the wasteland the lack of content has meant, too, the lack of the necessary tension that creates new forms and styles.

Whether the intellectuals in the West can find passions outside of politics is moot. Unfortunately, social reform does not have any unifying appeal, nor does it give a younger generation the outlet for "self-expression" and "self-definition" that it wants. The trajectory of enthusiasm has curved East, where, in the new ecstasies for economic utopia, the "future" is all that counts.

And yet, if the intellectual history of the past hundred years has any meaning—and lesson—it is to reassert Jefferson's wisdom (aimed at removing the dead hand of the past, but which can serve as a warning against the heavy hand of the future as well), that "the present belongs to the living." This is the wisdom that revolutionists, old and new, who are sensitive to the fate of their fellow men, rediscover in every generation. "I will never believe," says a protagonist in a poignant dialogue written by the gallant Polish philosopher Leszek Kolakowski, "that the moral and intellectual life of mankind follows the law of economics, that is by saving today we can have more tomorrow; that we should use lives now so that truth will triumph or that we should profit by crime to pave the way for nobility."

And these words, written during the Polish "thaw," when the intellectuals had asserted, from their experience with the "future," the claims of humanism, echo the protest of the Russian writer Alexander Herzen, who, in a dialogue a hundred years ago, reproached an earlier revolutionist who would sacrifice the present mankind for a promised tomorrow: "Do you truly wish to condemn all human beings alive today to the sad role of caryatids ... supporting a floor for others some day to dance on? ... This alone should serve as a warning to people: an end that is infinitely remote is not an end, but, if you like, a trap; an end must be nearer—it ought to be, at the very least, the labourer's wage or pleasure in the work done. Each age, each generation, each life has its own fullness. ..."

Note

1. The Marquis de Sade, who, more than any man, explored the limits of self-assertion, once wrote: "There is not a single man who doesn't want to be a despot when he is excited ... he would like to be alone in the world ... any sort of equality would destroy the despotism he enjoys then." de Sade proposed, therefore, to canalize these impulses into sexual activity by opening universal brothels which could serve to drain away these emotions. de Sade, it should be pointed out, was a bitter enemy of religion, but he understood well the latent function of religion in mobilizing emotions.

18

Dwight Macdonald (1906–1982)

Masscult & Midcult (1960)

Editor's Indtroduction

Dwight Macdonald was the leader among the New York Intellectuals in the attack on those whom he and others termed "middlebrow." It was a variation on the words "highbrow" and "lowbrow" the critic Van Wyck Brooks used in his influential essay "America's Coming-of-Age" in 1915. Brooks claimed then that American culture, ever since Jonathan Edwards (highbrow) and Benjamin Franklin (lowbrow), had been riven into two irreconcilable camps and that American culture had been weakened by its writers' not being able to blend the two. Brooks might have considered the expression "middlebrow" encouraging, but most of the New York Intellectuals were distressed by the phenomenon. The highbrows in the *Partisan Review* circle enthusiastically embraced a literary and artistic modernism that depended on a vanguard of the intellectual elite, an avant-garde, to keep it far enough above those middlebrows to prevent an erosion of their values and standards.

Even in the 1940s, when many in the *Partisan Review* group were still socialists, they were cultural elitists who championed a modernist painting that only the initiated could interpret and a modernist literature that only those who read scholarly literary criticism could understand. As a few of the New York Intellectuals admitted later, they disliked mass culture partly because the working class never turned out to be as revolutionary, noble and cultured as radical intellectuals had hoped. Some of the *Partisan* group had assumed that, if unimpeded by capitalist commercial values, the mass of citizens would voluntarily seek out high culture themselves. When it became evident that would not happen, most New York Intellectuals deplored middlebrow as much as lowbrow culture. After all, the former was also a seductive threat to draw members of the educated citizenry away from high culture outlets, as low culture was not.

Macdonald led the scourge of the middlebrow. Few were safe. The book clubs were unmasked, the middle magazines such as the *Atlantic* and the *New Yorker* were left without dignity, intelligent novelists who did not frequent the avant-garde journals clutched their battered reputations. Yet Macdonald, though loud and fussy in print, was also very funny. Ironically, he later worked as a staff writer at the *New Yorker* and was *Esquire's* film critic.

Source

Dwight Macdonald, "Masscult & Midcult," (abridged) *Against the American Grain* (NY: Random House, 1962). Originally published in *Partisan Review* vol. 17, no. 2, Spring 1960 and vol. 17, no. 3, Summer 1960.

Selected Readings

Van Wyck Brooks, *America's Coming-of-Age* (New York: B.W. Huebsch, 1915).
Michael Wreszin, *A Rebel in Defense of Tradition* (New York: Basic Books, 1994).
Joan Shelley Rubin, *The Making of Middlebrow Culture* (Chapel Hill: University of North Carolina Press, 1992).

* * * * *

For about two centuries Western culture has in fact been two cultures: the traditional kind—let us call it High Culture—that is chronicled in the textbooks, and a novel kind that is manufactured for the market. This latter may be called Mass Culture, or better Masscult, since it really isn't culture at all. Masscult is a parody of High Culture. In the older forms, its artisans have long been at work. In the novel, the line stretches from the eighteenth-century "servant-girl romances" to Edna Ferber, Fannie Hurst and such current ephemera as Burdick, Drury, Michener, Ruark and Uris; in music, from Hearts and Flowers to Rock 'n Roll; in art, from the chromo to Norman Rockwell; in architecture, from Victorian Gothic to ranch-house moderne; in thought, from Martin Tupper's *Proverbial Philosophy* ("Marry not without means, for so shouldst thou tempt Providence;/But wait not for more than enough, for marriage is the DUTY of most men.") to Norman Vincent Peale. (Thinkers like H. G. Wells, Stuart Chase, and Max Lerner come under the head of Midcult rather than Masscult.) And the enormous output of such new media as the radio, television and the movies is almost entirely Masscult.

II

The question of Masscult is part of the larger question of the masses. The tendency of modern industrial society, whether in the USA or the USSR, is to transform the individual into the mass man. For the masses are in historical time what a crowd is in space: a large quantity of people unable to express their human qualities because they are related to each other neither as individuals nor as members of a community. In fact, they are not related *to each other* at all but only to some impersonal, abstract, crystallizing factor. In the case of crowds, this can be a football game, a bargain sale, a lynching; in the case of the masses, it can be a political party, a television program, a system of industrial production. The mass man is a solitary atom, uniform with the millions of other atoms that go to make up "the lonely crowd," as David Riesman well calls our society. A community, on the contrary, is a group of individuals linked to each other by concrete interests. Something like a family, each of whose members has his or her special place and function while at the same time sharing the group's economic aims (family budget), traditions (family history), sentiments (family quarrels, family jokes), and values ("That's the way we do it in *this* family!"). The scale must be small enough so that it "makes a difference" what each person does—this is the first condition for human, as against mass, existence. Paradoxically, the individual in a community is both more closely integrated into the group than is the mass man and at the same time is freer to develop his own special personality. Indeed, an individual can only be defined in relation to a community. A single person in nature is not an individual but an animal; Robinson Crusoe was saved by Friday. The totalitarian regimes, which have consciously tried to create the mass man, have systematically broken every communal link—family, church, trade union, local and regional loyalties, even down to ski and chess clubs—and have reforged them so as to bind each atomized individual directly to the center of power.

The past cultures I admire—Periclean Greece, the city-states of the Italian Renaissance, Elizabethan England, are examples—have mostly been produced by communities, and remarkably small ones at that. Also remarkably heterogeneous ones, riven by faction, stormy with passionate antagonisms. But this diversity, fatal to that achievement of power over other countries that is the great aim of modern statecraft, seems to have been stimulating to talent. (What could be more deadly than the usual post-Marx vision of socialism as equality and agreement? Fourier was far more perceptive when he based his Utopia on cabals, rivalry, and every kind of difference including what he called "innocent mania.") A mass society, like a crowd, is inchoate and uncreative. Its atoms cohere not according to individual liking or traditions or even interests but in a purely mechanical way, as iron filings of different shapes and sizes are pulled toward a magnet working on the one quality they have in common. Its morality sinks to the level of the most primitive members—a crowd will commit atrocities that very few of its members would commit as individuals—and its taste to that of the least sensitive and the most ignorant.

Yet this collective monstrosity, "the masses," "the public," is taken as a human norm by the technicians of Masscult. They at once degrade the public by treating it as an object, to be handled with the lack of ceremony of medical students dissecting a corpse, and at the same time flatter it and pander to its taste and ideas by taking them as the criterion of reality (in the case of the questionnaire-sociologists) or of art (in the case of the Lords of Masscult). When one hears a questionnaire-sociologist talk about "setting up" an investigation, one realizes that he regards people as mere congeries of conditioned reflexes, his concern being which reflex will be stimulated by which question. At the same time, of necessity, he sees the statistical majority as the great Reality, the secret of life he is trying to unriddle. Like a Lord of Masscult, he is—professionally—without values, willing to take seriously any idiocy if it is held by many people (though, of course, *personally*...). The aristocrat's approach to the masses is less degrading to them, as it is less degrading to a man to be shouted at than to be treated as nonexistent. But the *plebs* have their dialectical revenge: indifference to their human quality means prostration before their statistical quantity, so that a movie magnate who cynically "gives the public what it wants"—i.e., assumes it wants trash—sweats with anxiety if the box-office returns drop 5 per cent.

Whenever a Lord of Masscult is reproached for the low quality of his products, he automatically ripostes, "But that's what the public wants, what can I do?" A simple and conclusive defense, at first glance. But a second look reveals that (1) to the extent the public "wants" it, the public has been conditioned to some extent by his products, and (2) his efforts have taken this direction because (a) he himself also "wants" it—never underestimate the ignorance and vulgarity of publishers, movie producers, network executives and other architects of Masscult—and (b) the technology of producing mass "entertainment" (again, the quotes are advised) imposes a simplistic, repetitious pattern so that it is easier to say the public wants this than to say the truth which is that the public gets this and so wants it. The March Hare explained to Alice that "I like what I get" is not the same thing as "I get what I like," but March Hares have never been welcome on Madison Avenue.

For some reason, objections to the giving-to-the-public-what-it-wants line are often attacked as undemocratic and snobbish. Yet it is precisely because I do believe in the potentialities of ordinary people that I criticize Masscult. For the masses are not people, they are not The Man in the Street or The Average Man, they are not even that figment of liberal condescension, The Common Man. The masses are, rather, man as non-man, that is man in a special relationship to other men that makes it impossible for him to function as man (one of the human functions being the creation and enjoyment of works of art). "Mass man," as I use the term, is a theoretical construction, an extreme toward which we are being pushed but which we shall never reach. For to become wholly a mass man would mean to have no private life, no personal desires, hobbies, aspirations, or aversions that are not shared by everybody else. One's behavior would be entirely predictable, like a piece of coal, and the sociologists could at last make up their tables confidently. It is still some time to 1984 but it looks unlikely that Orwell's anti-Utopia will have materialized by then, or that it will ever materialize. Nazism and Soviet Communism, however, show us how far things can go in politics, as Masscult does in art. And let us not be too smug in this American temperate zone, unravaged by war and ideology. "It seems to me that nearly the whole Anglo-Saxon race, especially of course in America, have lost the power to be individuals. They have become social insects like bees and ants." So Roger Fry wrote years ago, and who will say that we have become less apian?

III

Like the early capitalism Marx and Engels described in *The Communist Manifesto*, Masscult is a dynamic, revolutionary force, breaking down the old barriers of class, tradition, and taste, dissolving all cultural distinctions. It mixes, scrambles everything together, producing what might be called homogenized culture, after another American achievement, the homogenization process that distributes the globules of cream evenly throughout the milk instead of allowing them to float separately on top. The interesting difference is that whereas the cream is still in the homogenized milk, somehow it disappears from homogenized culture. For the process destroys all values, since value-judgments require discrimination, an ugly word in liberal-democratic America. Masscult is very, very democratic; it refuses to discriminate against or between anything or anybody. All is grist to its mill and all comes out finely ground indeed.

Life is a typical homogenized magazine, appearing on the mahogany library tables of the rich, the glass cocktail tables of the middle class, and the oilcloth kitchen tables of the poor. Its contents are as thoroughly homogenized as its circulation. The same issue will present a serious exposition of atomic energy followed by a disquisition on Rita Hayworth's love life; photos of starving children picking garbage in Calcutta and of sleek models wearing adhesive brassières; an editorial hailing Bertrand Russell's eightieth birthday (A GREAT MIND IS STILL ANNOYING AND ADORNING OUR AGE) across from a full-page photo of a matron arguing with a baseball umpire (MOM GETS THUMB); nine color pages of Renoir paintings followed by a picture of a roller-skating horse; a cover announcing in the same size type two features: A NEW FOREIGN POLICY, BY JOHN FOSTER DULLES and KERIMA: HER MARATHON KISS IS A MOVIE SENSATION.[1] Somehow these scramblings together seem to work all one way, degrading the serious rather than elevating the frivolous. Defenders of our Masscult society like Professor Edward Shils of the University of Chicago—he is, of course, a sociologist—see phenomena like *Life* as inspiriting attempts at popular education—just think, nine pages of Renoirs! But that roller-skating horse comes along, and the final impression is that both Renoir and the horse were talented.

IV

The historical reasons for the rise of Masscult are well known. There could obviously be no mass culture until there were masses, in our modern sense. The industrial revolution produced the masses. It uprooted people from their agrarian communities and packed them into factory cities. It produced goods in such unprecedented abundance that the population of the Western world has increased more in the last two centuries than in the preceding two millennia—poor Malthus, never has a brilliantly original theorist been so speedily refuted by history! And it subjected them to a uniform discipline whose only precedent was the "slave socialism" of Egypt. But the Egypt of the Pharaohs produced no Masscult any more than did the great Oriental empires or the late Rome of the proletarian rabble, because the masses were passive, inert, submerged far below the level of political or cultural power. It was not until the end of the eighteenth century in Europe that the majority of people began to play an active part in either history or culture.

Up to then, there was only High Culture and Folk Art. To some extent, Masscult is a continuation of Folk Art, but the differences are more striking than the similarities. Folk Art grew mainly from below, an autochthonous product shaped by the people to fit their own needs, even though it often took its cue from High Culture. Masscult comes from above. It is fabricated by technicians hired by businessmen. They try this and try that and if something clicks at the box office, they try to cash in with similar products, like consumer-researchers with a new cereal, or like a Pavlovian biologist who has hit on a reflex he thinks can be conditioned. It is one thing to satisfy popular tastes, as Robert Burns's poetry did, and quite another to exploit them, as Hollywood does. Folk Art was the people's own institution, their private little kitchen-garden walled off from the great formal park of their masters.[2] But Masscult breaks down the wall, integrating the masses into a debased form of High Culture and thus becoming an instrument of domination. If one had no other data to go on, Masscult would expose capitalism as a class society rather than the harmonious commonwealth that, in election years, both parties tell us it is.

The same goes even more strongly for the Soviet Union. Its Masscult is both worse and more pervasive than ours, a fact which is often not recognized because in form Soviet Masscult is just the opposite, aiming at propaganda and pedagogy rather than distraction. But like ours, it is imposed from above and it exploits rather than satisfies the needs of the masses—though, of course, for political rather than commercial reasons: Its quality is even lower. Our Supreme Court building is tasteless and pompous but not to the lunatic degree of most Soviet architecture; post-1930 Soviet films, with a few exceptions, are far duller and cruder than our own; the primitive level of *serious* Soviet periodicals devoted to matters of art or philosophy has to be read to be believed, and as for the popular press, it is as if Hearst or Colonel McCormick ran every periodical in America. Furthermore, while here individuals can simply turn their back on Masscult and do their own work, there no such escape is possible; the official cultural bodies control all outlets and a *Doctor Zhivago* must be smuggled out for foreign publication.

X

We are now in a more sophisticated period. The West has been won, the immigrants melted down, the factories and railroads built to such effect that since 1929 the problem has been consumption rather than production. The work week has shrunk, real wages have risen, and never in history have so many people attained such a high standard of living as in this country since 1945. College enrollment is now well over four million, three times what it was in 1929. Money, leisure and knowledge, the prerequisites for culture, are more plentiful and more evenly distributed than ever before.

In these more advanced times, the danger to High Culture is not so much from Masscult as from a peculiar hybrid bred from the latter's unnatural intercourse with the former. A whole middle culture has come into existence and it threatens to absorb both its parents. This intermediate form—let us call it Midcult—has the essential qualities of Masscult—the formula, the built-in reaction, the lack of any standard except popularity—but it decently covers them with a cultural figleaf. In Masscult the trick is plain—to please the crowd by any means. But Midcult has it both ways: it pretends to respect the standards of High Culture while in fact it waters them down and vulgarizes them.[3]

The enemy outside the walls is easy to distinguish. It is its ambiguity that makes Midcult alarming. For it presents itself as part of High Culture. Not that coterie stuff, not those snobbish inbred so-called intellectuals who are only talking to themselves. Rather the great vital mainstream, wide and clear though perhaps not so deep. You, too, can wade in it for a mere $16.70 pay nothing now just fill in the coupon and receive a full year six hard-cover lavishly illustrated issues of *Horizon: A Magazine of the Arts*, "probably the most beautiful magazine in the world … seeks to serve as guide to the long cultural advance of modern man, to explore the many mansions of the philosopher, the painter, the historian, the architect, the sculptor, the satirist, the poet … to build bridges between the world of scholars and the world of intelligent readers. It's a good buy. Use the coupon *now.*" *Horizon* has some 160,000 subscribers, which is more than the combined circulations, after many years of effort, of *Kenyon, Hudson, Sewanee, Partisan, Art News, Arts, American Scholar, Dissent, Commentary,* and half a dozen of our other leading cultural-critical magazines.

Midcult is not, as might appear at first, a raising of the level of Masscult. It is rather a corruption of High Culture which has the enormous advantage over Masscult that while also in fact "totally subjected to the spectator," in Malraux's phrase, it is able to pass itself off as the real thing. Midcult is the Revised Standard Version of the Bible, put out several years ago under the aegis of the Yale Divinity School, that destroys our greatest monument of English prose, the King James Version, in order to make the text "clear and meaningful to people today," which is like taking apart Westminister Abbey to make Disneyland out of the fragments. Midcult is the Museum of Modern Art's film department paying tribute to Samuel Goldwyn because his movies are alleged to be (slightly) better than those of other Hollywood producers—though why they are called "producers" when their function is to prevent the production of art (cf., the fate in Hollywood of Griffith, Chaplin, von Stroheim, Eisenstein and Orson Welles) is a semantic puzzle. Midcult is the venerable and once venerated *Atlantic*—which in the last century printed Emerson, Lowell, Howells, James, and Mark Twain—putting on the cover of a recent issue a huge photograph of Dore Schary, who has lately transferred his high-minded sentimentality from Hollywood to Broadway and who is represented in the issue by a homily, "To A Young Actor," which synthesizes Jefferson, Polonius and Dr. Norman Vincent Peale, concluding: "Behave as citizens not only of your profession but of the full world in which you live. Be indignant with injustice, be gracious with success, be courageous with failure, be patient with opportunity, and be resolute with faith and honor." Midcult is the Book-of-the-Month Club, which since 1926 has been supplying its members with reading matter of which the best that can be said is that it could be worse, i.e., they get John Hersey instead of Gene Stratton Porter. Midcult is the transition from Rodgers and Hart to Rodgers and Hammerstein, from the gay tough lyrics of *Pal Joey*, a spontaneous expression of a real place called Broadway, to the folk-fakery of *Oklahoma!* and the orotund sentimentalities of *South Pacific*.[4] Midcult is or was, "Omnibus," subsidized by a great foundation to raise the level of television, which began its labors by announcing it would "be aimed straight at the average American audience, neither highbrow nor lowbrow, the audience that made the *Reader's Digest, Life*, the *Ladies' Home Journal*, the audience which is the solid backbone of any business as it is of America itself" and which then proved its good faith by programming Gertrude Stein and Jack Benny, Chekhov and football strategy, Beethoven and champion ice skaters. "Omnibus" failed. The level of television, however, was not raised, for some reason.

XV

This whole line of argument may be objected to as undemocratic. But such an objection is beside the point. As T. S. Eliot writes in *Notes Toward the Definition of Culture:*

> Here are what I believe to be essential conditions for the growth and for the survival of culture. If they conflict with any passionate faith of the reader—if, for instance, he finds it shocking that culture and equalitarianism should conflict, if it seems monstrous to him that anyone should have "advantages of birth"—I do not ask him to change his faith. I merely ask him to stop paying lip-service to culture. If the reader says: "The state of affairs which I wish to bring about is *right* (or is *just*, or is *inevitable*); and if this must lead to further deterioration of culture, we must accept that deterioration"—then I can have no quarrel with him.

I might even, in some circumstances, feel obliged to support him. The effect of such a wave of honesty would be that the word *culture* would cease to be absurd.

That the word now *is* absurd—priggish, unctuous, worn slick with abuse—shows how mass-ified we have become. The great cultures of the past have all been elite affairs, centering in small upper-class communities which had certain standards in common and which both encouraged creativity by (informed) enthusiasm and disciplined it by (informed) criticism.

The old avant-garde of 1870–1930, from Rimbaud to Picasso, demonstrated this with special clarity because it was based not on wealth or birth but on common tastes. "Common" didn't mean uniform—there were the liveliest, most painful clashes—but rather a shared respect for certain standards and an agreement that living art often runs counter to generally accepted ideas. The attitude of the old avant-garde, in short, was a peculiar mixture of conservatism and revolutionism that had nothing in common with the tepid agreeableness of Masscult. It was an elite community, a rather snobbish one, but anyone could join who cared enough about such odd things. Its significance was that it simply refused to compete in the established cultural marketplaces. It made a desperate effort to fence off some area within which the serious artist could still function, to erect again the barriers between the *cognoscenti* and the *ignoscenti* that had been breached by the rise of Masscult. The attempt was against the whole movement of history; and our cultural sociologists, had they been anachronistically consulted by Yeats or Stravinsky, could have proved to them with irrefutable tables and research studies that it could not possibly come to anything. For it was, sociologically speaking, absurd. Nevertheless, the attempt did in fact succeed, perhaps because artists, writers and musicians are not very good at statistics—and to it we owe most of the major creations of the last seventy years.

The old avant-garde has passed and left no successors. We continue to live off its capital but the community has broken up and the standards are no longer respected. The crisis in America is especially severe. Our creators are too isolated or too integrated. Most of them merge gracefully into Midcult, feeling they must be part of "the life of our time," whatever that means (I should think it would be ambitious enough to try to be part of one's own life), and fearful of being accused of snobbishness, cliqueism, negativism or, worst of all, practicing "art for art's sake" (though for what better sake?). Some revolt, but their work tends toward eccentricity since it lacks contact with the past and doesn't get support from a broad enough intelligentsia in the present. The two currently most prominent groups, the "action painters" and the beatnik academy of letters, differ from the old avant-garde in two interesting ways. They are cut off from tradition: the works of Joyce and Picasso, for instance, show an extraordinary knowledge of (and feeling for) the achievements of the past, while those of the beats and the actionists, for instance, do not. And they have had too much publicity too soon; the more they try to shock the Midcult's audience, the more they are written up in the Lucepapers; they are "different," that potent advertising word whose charm reveals how monotonous the landscape of Midcult has become.

The beatnik's pad is the modern equivalent of the poet's garret in every way except the creation of poetry. Our well-oiled machinery of cultural exploitation provides those who are Different with lecture dates, interviews, fellowships, write-ups, and fans of both sexes (the word's derivation from "fanatics" is clearer in these circles than among the more restrained enthusiasts of baseball, possibly because the latter have a technical knowledge rarely found among the former). The machinery tempts them to extremes since the more fantastic their efforts, the more delighted are their Midcult admirers. *"Pour épater les bourgeois"* was the defiant slogan of the nineteenth-century avant-gardists but now the bourgeoisie have developed a passion for being shocked. "If possible," Kerouac advises young authors, "write without 'consciousness' in a semi-trance," while a prominent advanced composer has written a piece for Twelve Radios that is performed by turning each to a different station, a sculptor has exhibited a dozen large beach pebbles dumped loosely on a board, a painter has displayed an all-black canvas only to be topped by another who showed simply—a canvas. At last, one hears the respectful murmurs, The Real Thing! The avant-garde of the heroic period generally drew the line between experiment and absurdity—Gertrude Stein was the chief exception. Efforts like the above were limited to the Dadaists, who used them to satirize the respectable Academic culture of their day. But the spoofs of Dada have now become the serious offerings of what one might call the lumpen-avant-garde.

XVII

In England, cultural lines are still drawn with some clarity. The B.B.C., for instance, offers three distinct programs: the Light (Masscult), the Home (Midcult) and the tactfully named Third (High Culture). It is true that the daily papers are divided about like ours: three good ones (*Times, Guardian, Telegraph*) with relatively small circulations and many bad ones with big circulations. The popular papers are not only much bigger than ours—the *Mirror* and the *Express* have about five million each, twice the circulation of the New York *Daily News*, our biggest—but also much worse. One must go to London to see how trivial and mindless the popular press can become. But if the masses have their dailies, the classes have a type of periodical for which there is no American analogue, and I think the vulgarity of the mass press and the high quality of the class press are both the result of the sharper definition of cultural lines there.

This is a magazine-reading country. When one comes back from abroad, the two displays of American abundance that dazzle one are the supermarkets and the newsstands. There are no British equivalents of our Midcult magazines like the *Atlantic* and the *Saturday Review,* or of our mass magazines like *Life* and the *Saturday Evening Post* and *Look,* or of our betwixt-&-between magazines like *Esquire* and the *New Yorker* (which also encroach on the Little Magazine area). There are, however, several big-circulation women's magazines, I suppose because the women's magazine is such an ancient and essential form of journalism that even the English dig it.

The one kind of magazine we haven't had over here since the liberal weeklies stubbed their toes on the Moscow Trials is the serious, widely read weekly. The English have at least seven: the *Spectator,* the *New Statesman,* the *Economist,* the *Times Literary Supplement,* the *Listener,* the *Observer* and the *Sunday Times.* The first four have circulations between 40,000 and 90,000. The *Listener* has, I believe, over 200,000; it is published by the B.B.C. and is made up almost wholly of broadcast material—how long would it take to accumulate a similar issue from our own radio and television? Months? Years? The *Observer* and the *Sunday Times* (no connection with the daily *Times,* which doesn't come out on Sunday) are really Sunday magazines in a newspaper format; their special articles and their extensive review sections are on the level of the other weeklies; and they have circulations of over 700,000 and 1,000,000 respectively. (They are postwar phenomena, analogous to our boom in quality paperbacks.) These British weeklies have large enough circulations to be self-supporting and to pay their contributors a living wage. Their nearest parallels here, in quality, are our Little Magazines, which come out either quarterly or bimonthly, have small circulations (5,000 is par, 15,000 prodigious), run at a chronic deficit and pay contributors and editors meagerly.

What must be done here marginally, with help from "angels" either personal or institutional, can be done there as a normal part of journalism. Although a much smaller percentage of the English population goes to college, they have a larger and more cohesive cultural community than we do. The sale of a serious nonfiction book by a writer who is not a Name, for instance, is often larger there than here despite our three or four times larger population. Here a book tends to be either a best seller or nothing, as a writer is either a Success or a Failure; there is no middle ground because there is no intellectual class. This may also be the reason more titles are published there; in 1958 it was 16,700 there, 11,000 here; it is the difference between handicraft and mass production, between a number of articulated publics and one great amorphous mass market.

England still has something of a functioning class system, culturally speaking. The angry young men are angry about it. I can't think why. An American living in London is delighted by the wide interest in art and letters, the liveliness of the intellectual atmosphere, the sense he gets constantly from the press and from conversations of a general interest in what he is interested in. It is, of course, general only to perhaps 5 per cent of the population, but in America it isn't even this much general; it is something shared only with friends and professional acquaintances. But in London one meets stockbrokers who go to concerts, politicians who have read Proust.[5]

The English amateur scholar—"just a hobby, really"—is a species little known over here. Most educated Englishmen seem to take an interest in cultural matters as a matter of course, and many of them have a personal, nonprofessional knowledge of one or two fields—a disinterested interest, so to speak—which is quite impressive. Our college graduates are not apt to "keep up" with such things unless they teach them. Their hobbies are less likely to be Jacobean madrigals than home workshops equipped with the latest in power tools and their equivalent of the British weekly is likely to be *Time* or *Newsweek*. In only one field do we match their amateur scholarship. The sports pages are our equivalent of the *Times Literary Supplement*; in each case, experts write for a sizable audience that is assumed to understand the fine points. Perhaps our closest approach to a living tradition is in sports. The recent centenaries of Poe and Melville passed without undue excitement in the press, but *Sports Illustrated* devoted four pages to the fiftieth anniversary of Fred ("Bonehead") Merkle's failure to touch second base in a World Series game.

XIX

What is to be done? Conservatives like Ortega y Gasset and T. S. Eliot argue that since "the revolt of the masses" has led to the horrors of totalitarianism and of California roadside architecture, the only hope is to rebuild the old class walls and bring the masses once more under aristocratic control. They think of the popular as synonomous with the cheap and vulgar. Marxian radicals and liberal sociologists, on the other hand, see the masses as intrinsically healthy but as the dupes and victims of cultural exploitation—something like Rousseau's "noble savage." If only the masses were offered good stuff instead of *Kitsch*, how they would eat it up! How the level of Masscult would rise! Both these diagnoses seem to me fallacious because they assume that Masscult is (in the conservative view) or could be (in the liberal view) an expression of *people*, like Folk Art, whereas actually it is, as I tried to show earlier in this essay, an expression of *masses*, a very different thing.

The conservative proposal to save culture by restoring the old class lines has a more solid historical basis than the liberal-cum-Marxian hope for a new democratic, classless culture. Politically, however, it is without meaning in a world dominated by the two great mass nations, the USA and the USSR, and a world that is becoming more industrialized and mass-ified all the time. The only practical thing along those lines would be to revive the spirit of the old avant-garde, that is to re-create a cultural—as against a social, political or economic—elite as a countermovement to both Masscult and Midcult. It may be possible, in a more modest and limited sense than in the past—I shall return to this point later—but it will be especially difficult in this country where the blurring of class lines, the lack of a continuous tradition and the greater facilities for the manufacturing and distribution of *Kitsch*, whether Masscult or Midcult, all work in the other direction. Unless this country goes either fascist or communist, there will continue to be islands above the flood for those determined enough to reach them and live on them; as Faulkner has shown, a writer can use Hollywood instead of being used by it, if his purpose be firm enough. But islands are not continents.

The alternative proposal is to raise the level of our culture in general. Those who advocate this start off from the assumption that there has already been a great advance in the diffusion of culture in the last two centuries—Edward Shils is sure of this, Daniel Bell thinks it is probably the case—and that the main problem is how to carry this even further; they tend to regard such critics of Masscult as Ernest van den Haag, Leo Lowenthal or myself as either disgruntled Left romantics or reactionary dreamers or both. Perhaps the most impressive—and certainly the longest—exposition of this point of view appears in Gilbert Seldes' *The Great Audience*. Mr. Seldes blames the present sad state of our Masscult on (1) the stupidity of the Lords of *Kitsch* (who underestimate the mental age of the public), (2) the arrogance of the intellectuals (who make the same mistake and so snobbishly refuse to try to raise the level of the mass media), and (3) the passivity of the public itself (which doesn't insist on better Masscult). This diagnosis seems to me superficial because it blames everything on subjective, moral factors: stupidity (the Lords of *Kitsch*), perversity (the intellectuals), or failure of will (the public). My own notion is that—as in the case of the "responsibility" of the German (or Russian) people for the horrors of Nazism (or of Soviet Communism)—it is unjust and unrealistic to blame large social groups for such catastrophes. Burke was right when he said you cannot indict a people. Individuals are caught up in the workings of a mechanism that forces them into its own pattern; only heroes can resist, and while one can hope that everybody will be a hero, one cannot demand it.

I see Masscult—and its recent offspring, Midcult—as a reciprocating engine, and who is to say, once it has been set in motion, whether the stroke or the counterstroke is responsible for its continued action? The Lords of *Kitsch* sell culture to the masses. It is a debased, trivial culture that avoids both the deep realities (sex, death, failure, tragedy) and also the simple, spontaneous pleasures, since the realities would be too real and the pleasures too lively to induce what Mr. Seldes calls "the mood of consent": a narcotized acceptance of Masscult-Midcult and of the commodities it sells as a substitute for the unsettling and unpredictable (hence unsalable) joy, tragedy, wit, change, originality and beauty of real life. The masses—and don't let's forget that this term includes the well-educated fans of *The Old Man and the Sea, Our Town, J.B.,* and *John Brown's Body*—who have been debauched by several generations of this sort of thing, in turn have come to demand such trivial and comfortable cultural products. Which came first, the chicken or the egg, the mass demand or its satisfaction (and further stimulation), is a question as academic as it is unanswerable. The engine is reciprocating and shows no signs of running down.

XX

"Our fundamental want today in the United States," Walt Whitman wrote in 1871, "is of a class and the clear idea of a class, of native authors, literatures, far different, far higher in grade than any yet known, sacerdotal, modern, fit to cope with our occasions, lands, permeating the whole mass of American mentality, taste, belief, breathing into it a new life, giving it decision, affecting politics far more than the popular superficial suffrage. ... For know you not, dear, earnest reader, that the people of our land may all read and write, and may all possess the right to vote—and yet the main things may be entirely lacking? ... The priest departs, the divine literatus comes."

The divine literatus is behind schedule. Masscult and Midcult have so pervaded the land that Whitman's hope for a democratic culture shaped by a sacerdotal class at once so sublime and so popular that they can swing elections—that this noble vision now seems absurd. But a more modest aspiration is still open, one adumbrated by Whitman's idea of a new cultural class and his warning that "the main things may be entirely lacking" even though everybody knows how to read, write and vote. This is to recognize that two cultures have developed in this country and that it is to the national interest to keep them separate. The conservatives are right when they say there has never been a broadly democratic culture on a high level. This is not because the ruling class forcibly excluded the masses—this is Marxist melodrama—but quite simply because the great majority of people at any given time (including most of the ruling class for the matter) have never cared enough about such things to make them an important part of their lives. So let the masses have their Masscult, let the few who care about good writing, painting, music, architecture, philosophy, etc., have their High Culture, and don't fuzz up the distinction with Midcult.

Whitman would have rejected this proposal as undemocratic, which it is. But his own career is a case in point: he tried to be a popular bard but the masses were not interested, and his first recognition, excepting Emerson's lonely voice, came from the English pre-Raphaelites, a decadent and precious group if ever there was one. If we would create a literature "fit to cope with our occasions," the only public the writer or artist or composer or philosopher or critic or architect should consider must be that of his peers. The informed, interested minority—what Stendhal called "We Happy Few." Let the majority eavesdrop if they like, but their tastes should be firmly ignored.

There is a compromise between the conservative and liberal proposals which I think is worth considering—neither an attempt to re-create the old avant-garde nor one to raise the general level of Masscult and Midcult. It is based on the recent discovery—since 1945—that there is not One Big Audience but rather a number of smaller, more specialized audiences that may still be commercially profitable. (I take it for granted that the less differentiated the audience, the less chance there is of something original and lively creeping in, since the principle of the lowest common denominator applies.) This discovery has in fact resulted in the sale of "quality" paperbacks and recordings and the growth of 'art" cinema houses, off-Broadway theatres, concert orchestras and art museums and galleries. The mass audience is divisible, we have discovered—and the more it is divided, the better. Even television, the most senseless and routinized expression of Masscult (except for the movie newsreels), might be improved by this approach. One possibility is pay-TV, whose modest concept is that only those who subscribe could get the program, like a magazine; but, also like a magazine, the editors would decide what goes in, not the advertisers; a small gain but a real one. The networks oppose this on philanthropic grounds—they don't see why the customer should pay for what he now gets free. But perhaps one would rather pay for bread than get stones for nothing.

As long as our society is "open" in Karl Popper's sense—that is unless or until it is closed by a mass revolution stimulated by the illusion of some "total solution" such as Russian-type Communism or Hitler-type Fascism, the name doesn't really matter—there will always be happy accidents because of the stubbornness of some isolated creator. But if we are to have more than this, it will be because our new public for High Culture becomes conscious of itself and begins to show some *esprit de corps*, insisting on higher standards and setting itself off—joyously, implacably—from most of its fellow citizens, not only from the Masscult depths but also from the agreeable ooze of the Midcult swamp.

In "The Present Age," Kierkegaard writes as follows:

In order that everything should be reduced to the same level it is first of all necessary to procure a phantom, a monstrous abstraction, an all-embracing something which is nothing, a mirage—and that phantom is the public. ...

The public is a concept which could not have occurred in antiquity because the people *en masse in corpore* took part in any situation which arose ... and moreover the individual was personally present and had to submit at once to applause or disapproval for his decision. Only when the sense of assocation in society is no longer strong enough to give life to concrete realities is the Press able to create that abstraction, "the pubic," consisting of unreal individuals who never are and never can be united in an actual situation or organization—and yet are held together as a whole.

The public is a host, more numerous than all the peoples together, but it is a body which can never be reviewed; it cannot even be represented because it is an abstraction. Nevertheless, when the age is reflective [i.e., the individual sees himself only as he is reflected in a collective body] and passionless and destroys everything concrete, the public becomes everything and is supposed to include everything. And … the individual is thrown back upon himself.…

A public is neither a nation nor a generation nor a community nor a society nor these particular men, for all these are only what they are through the concrete. No single person who belongs to the public makes a real commitment; for some hours of the day, perhaps, he belongs to a real public—at moments when he is nothing else, since when he really is what he is, he does not form part of the public. Made up of such individuals, of individuals at the moment when they are nothing, a public is a kind of gigantic something, an abstract and deserted void which is everything and nothing. But on this basis, any one can arrogate to himself a public, and just as the Roman Church chimerically extended its frontiers by appointing bishops *in partibus infidelium*, so a public is something which every one can claim, and even a drunken sailor exhibiting a peep-show has dialectically the same right to a public as the greatest man. He has just as logical a right to put all those noughts *in front of* his single number.

This is the essence of what I have tried to say.

Notes

1. The advertisements provide even more scope for the editors' homogenizing talents, as when a full-page photo of a ragged Bolivian peon grinningly drunk on cocoa leaves (which Mr. Luce's conscientious reporters tell us he chews to narcotize his chronic hunger pains) appears opposite an ad of a pretty, smiling, well-dressed American mother with her two pretty, smiling, well-dressed children (a boy and a girl, of course—children are always homogenized in our ads) looking raptly at a clown on a TV set, the whole captioned in type big enough to announce the Second Coming: RCA VICTOR BRINGS YOU A NEW KIND OF TELEVISION—SUPER SETS WITH "PICTURE POWER." The peon would doubtless find the juxtaposition piquant if he could afford a copy of *Life*, which, luckily for the Good Neighbor Policy, he cannot.

2. And if it was often influenced by High Culture, it did change the forms and themes into its own style. The only major form of Folk Art that still persists in this country is jazz, and the difference between Folk Art and Masscult may be most readily perceived by comparing the kind of thing heard at the annual Newport Jazz Festivals to Rock 'n Roll. The former is musically interesting and emotionally real; the latter is—not. The amazing survival of jazz despite the exploitative onslaughts of half a century of commercial entrepreneurs, is in my opinion, due to its folk quality. And as the noble and the peasant understood each other better than either understood the bourgeois, so it seems significant that jazz is the only art form that appeals to both the intelligentsia and the common people. As for the others, let them listen to *South Pacific*.

3. It's not done, of course, as consciously as this suggests. The editors of the *Saturday Review* or *Harper's* or the *Atlantic* would be honestly indignant at this description of their activities, as would John Steinbeck, J. P. Marquand, Pearl Buck, Irwin Shaw, Herman Wouk, John Hersey and others of that remarkably large group of Midcult novelists we have developed. One of the nice things about Zane Grey was that it seems never to have occurred to him that his books had anything to do with literature.

4. An interesting Midcult document is the editorial the *New York Times* ran August 24, 1960, the day after the death of Oscar Hammerstein 2nd:

> ... The theatre has lost a man who stood for all that is decent in life. ... The concern for racial respect in *South Pacific*, the sympathy and respect for a difficult though aspiring monarch in *The King and I*, the indomitable faith that runs through *Carousel* were not clever bits of showmanship. They represented Mr. Hammerstein's faith in human beings and their destiny....
>
> Since he was at heart a serious man, his lyrics were rarely clever. Instead of turning facetious phrases he made a studious attempt to write idiomatically in the popular tradition of the musical theatre, for he was a dedicated craftsman. But the style that was apparently so artless has brought glimpses of glory into our lives. "There's a bright, golden haze on the meadow," sings Curly in *Oklahoma!* and the gritty streets of a slatternly city look fresher. "June is bustin' out all over," sing Carrie and Nettie in *Carousel* and the harshness of our winter vanishes. ... To us it is gratifying that he had the character to use his genius with faith and scruple.

The contrast of faith (good) with cleverness (bad) is typical of Midcult, as is the acceptance of liberalistic moralizing as a satisfactory substitute for talent. Indeed, talent makes the midbrow uneasy: "Since he was a serious man, his lyrics were rarely clever." The death of Mr. Hart did not stimulate the *Times* to editorial elegy.

5. Actually, I *can* think why the young men are angry. The Enemy looks very different from there than from here. From there, it is too little democracy; from here, too much. They see cultural lines as relics of a snobbish past, I see them as dikes against the corruption of Masscult and Midcult. They see standards as inhibiting. I see them as defining. They see tradition as deadening, I see it as nourishing. It may be that, as an American, I idealize the British situation. But I hope not as absurdly as they idealize ours. In 1959 I gave a talk on mass culture at a *Universities & Left Review* forum in London. I expected the audience, which was much younger than I, to object to my lack of enthusiasm for socialism, though it was distressing to find them still talking about capitalism and the working class in the simplistic terms I hadn't heard since I left the Trotskyists; the problems we thought about in the 'thirties seem to be just coming up now in England; the illusions we were forced to abandon seem still current there. But what I was not prepared for was the reaction to my attacks on our mass culture. These were resented in the name of democracy. Hollywood to me was an instance of the exploitation rather than the satisfying of popular tastes. But to some of those who took the floor after my talk, Hollywood was a genuine expression of the masses. They seemed to think it snobbish of me to criticize our movies and television from a serious viewpoint. Since I had been criticizing Hollywood for some thirty years, and always with the good conscience one has when one is attacking from the Left, this proletarian defense of our peculiar institution left me rather dazed.

19

Lionel Trilling (1905–1975)
On the Teaching of Modern Literature (1961)

Editor's Introduction

By 1955 Lionel Trilling already had been teaching modern literature at Columbia University for a generation. That year he wrote in the preface to *The Opposing Self*, a collection of his essays, that at the end of the eighteenth century—the point when he felt modern literature began—a new sense of self emerged, one that employed an "intense and adverse imagination of the culture in which it has its being." This modern self possessed "certain powers of indignant perception" against the culture and struggled against the prisons of family, respectability and duty. Trilling explained that this self, revealed and rehearsed in modern literature, felt the alienation that Hegel documented. This literature portrayed characters who collectively staged a "long quarrel with the culture" that formed their and their readers' selfhood. These "opposing selves" in opposition to the culture are central to what we recognize as the modernism of art and literature.

In May of the same year, 1955, Trilling delivered a paper entitled "Freud and the Crisis of Our Culture" as The Freud Anniversary Lecture to the New York Psychoanalytical Society and the New York Psychoanalytical Institute. During that period, as we know from Diana Trilling's *The Beginning of the Journey*, both Lionel and Diana were in Freudian analysis. While few scholars would characterize Lionel Trilling's literary criticism as Freudian, he obviously maintained an interest in Freudian categories and approaches, and neither the image of opposing selves (ego, superego and id) nor an adversary relationship between individuals and their culture were foreign to Freudian thought.

As the larger history and experiences of the New York Intellectuals as a group and Lionel Trilling as an individual indicate, there is a welter of interwoven influences on their thought, including socialist politics, European sympathies, Marx, immigrant families, New York neighborhoods. The influence of Freudianism on Trilling's thought would be one of many. Yet it is consistent with his use of multiple and opposing points of view within his own critical outlook, with variability, nuance, complexity, and the recognition of an adversary relationship between the modern critical outlook and the dominant culture itself.

As he wrote in his preface to *Beyond Culture* (1965), it is a common modernist belief that a person can extricate himself from his culture and stand beyond it, outside of it. Modern literature has an adversary intention, an "actually subversive intention," to detach the reader from the values of his culture, "giving him a ground and a vantage point from which to judge and condemn, and perhaps revise, the culture that produced him." The modernist believes that "a primary function of art and thought is to liberate the individual from the tyranny of his culture in the environmental sense and to permit him to stand beyond it in an autonomy of perception and judgment." One need not be a Freudian to reach these conclusions, yet Freud himself would have seen their logic.

In the essay below, "On the Teaching of Modern Literature," Trilling uses an autobiographical staging in which he confesses to the reader that teaching modern literature to students is embarrassing for reserved professors like himself because it requires discussing texts that plumb the self. The classroom then becomes a deep discussion of cultural values and their effect. The entire class, including the normally diffident Trilling himself, had to reveal their opinion of characters in the novels by presenting parts of their own lives and choices. One had to mount an attack on the dominant values of the culture or else reject the adversary stance of modernist literature.

Trilling found this task uncomfortable. In addition, he began to wonder whether it was advisable for departments of English to inculcate an adversary culture in their students, although they must already have soaked it up enough by college age since he found them entirely comfortable with adversary values. Trilling's worry about the promotion of an adversary culture was adopted in the 1960s and later by Irving Kristol, Norman Podhoretz, Gertrude Himmelfarb and others of the New York Intellectuals who became the first of the neoconservatives.

Source

Lionel Trilling, "On the Teaching of Modern Literature," *Beyond Culture* (1965; reprint, Harcourt, Brace, Jovanovich, 1978). This first appeared in a different form in *Partisan Review* vol. 28, no. 1, January–February, 1961.

Selected Readings

Irving Howe, "The Culture of Modernism," *Commentary* vol. 44, no. 5, November, 1967.
Mark Krupnick, *Lionel Trilling and the Fate of Cultural Criticism* (Evanston: Northwestern University Press, 1986).
John Rodden, ed., *Lionel Trilling and the Critics* (Lincoln: University of Nebraska Press, 1999), Introduction, chapters 35–46, 57–70.
Thomas Bender, "Lionel Trilling and American Culture," *American Quarterly* vol. 42., no. 2, June 1990.

* * * * *

I propose to consider here a particular theme of modern literature which appears so frequently and with so much authority that it may be said to constitute one of the shaping and controlling ideas of our epoch. I can identify it by calling it the disenchantment of our culture with culture itself—it seems to me that the characteristic element of modern literature, or at least of the most highly developed modern literature, is the bitter line of hostility to civilization which runs through it. It happens that my present awareness of this theme is involved in a personal experience, and I am impelled to speak of it not abstractly but with the husks of the experience clinging untidily to it. I shall go so far in doing this as to describe the actual circumstances in which the experience took place. These circumstances are pedagogic—they consist of some problems in teaching modern literature to undergraduates and my attempt to solve these problems. I know that pedagogy is a depressing subject to all persons of sensibility, and yet I shall not apologize for touching upon it because the emphasis upon the teaching of literature and especially of modern literature is in itself one of the most salient and significant manifestations of the culture of our time. Indeed, if, having in mind Matthew Arnold's lecture, "On the Modern Element in Literature," we are on the hunt for *the* modern element in modern literature, we might want to find it in the susceptibility of modern literature to being made into an academic subject.

For some years I have taught the course in modern literature in Columbia College. I did not undertake it without misgiving and I have never taught it with an undivided mind. My doubts do not refer to the value of the literature itself, only to the educational propriety of its being studied in college. These doubts persist even though I wholly understand that the relation of our collegiate education to modernity is no longer an open question. The unargued assumption of most curriculums is that the real subject of all study is the modern world; that the justification of all study is its immediate and presumably practical relevance to modernity; that the true purpose of all study is to lead the young person to be at home in, and in control of, the modern world. There is really no way of quarreling with the assumption or with what follows upon it, the instituting of courses of which the substance is chiefly contemporary or at least makes ultimate reference to what is contemporary.

It might be asked why anyone should *want* to quarrel with the assumption. To that question I can return only a defensive, eccentric, self-depreciatory answer. It is this: that to some of us who teach and who think of our students as the creators of the intellectual life of the future, there comes a kind of despair. It does not come because our students fail to respond to ideas, rather because they respond to ideas with a happy vagueness, a delighted glibness, a joyous sense of power in the use of received or receivable generalizations, a grateful wonder at how easy it is to formulate and judge, at how little resistance language offers to their intentions. When that despair strikes us, we are tempted to give up the usual and accredited ways of evaluating education, and instead of prizing responsiveness and aptitude, to set store by some sign of personal character in our students, some token of individual will. We think of this as taking the form of resistance and imperviousness, of personal density or gravity, of some power of supposing that ideas are real, a power which will lead a young man to say what Goethe thought was the modern thing to say, "But is this really true—is it true for *me?*" And to say this not in the facile way, not following the progressive educational prescription to "think for yourself," which means to think in the progressive pieties rather than in the conservative pieties (if any of the latter do still exist), but to say it from his sense of himself as a person rather than as a bundle of attitudes and responses which are all alert to please the teacher and the progressive community.

We can't do anything about the quality of personal being of our students, but we are led to think about the cultural analogue of a personal character that is grave, dense, and resistant—we are led to think about the past. Perhaps the protagonist of Thomas Mann's story, "Disorder and Early Sorrow" comes to mind, that sad Professor Cornelius with his intense and ambivalent sense of history. For Professor Cornelius, who is a historian, the past is dead, is death itself, but for that very reason it is the source of order, value, piety, and even love. If we think about education in the dark light of the despair I have described, we wonder if perhaps there is not to be found in the past that quiet place at which a young man might stand for a few years, at least a little beyond the competing attitudes and generalizations of the present, at least a little beyond the contemporary problems which he is told he can master only by means of attitudes and generalizations, that quiet place in which he can be silent, in which he can *know* something—in what year the Parthenon was begun, the order of battle at Trafalgar, how Linear B was deciphered: almost anything at all that has nothing to do with the talkative and attitudinizing present, anything at all but variations on the accepted formulations about *anxiety,* and *urban society,* and *alienation,* and *Gemeinschaft* and *Gesellschaft,* all the matter of the academic disciplines which are founded upon the modern self-consciousness and the modern self-pity. The modern self-pity is certainly not without its justification; but, if the circumstances that engender it are ever to be overcome, we must sometimes wonder whether this work can be done by minds which are taught in youth to accept these sad conditions of ours as the only right objects of contemplation. And quite apart from any practical consequences, one thinks of the simple aesthetic personal pleasure of having to do with young minds, and maturing minds, which are free of cant, which are, to quote an old poet, "fierce, moody, patient, venturous, modest, shy."

This line of argument I have called eccentric and maybe it ought to be called obscurantist and reactionary. Whatever it is called, it is not likely to impress a Committee on the Curriculum. It was, I think, more or less the line of argument of my department in Columbia College, when, up to a few years ago, it would decide, whenever the question came up, not to carry its courses beyond the late nineteenth century. But our rationale could not stand against the representations which a group of students made to our Dean and which he communicated to us. The students wanted a course in modern literature—very likely, in the way of students, they said that it was a scandal that no such course was being offered in the College. There was no argument that could stand against this expressed desire: we could only capitulate, and then, with pretty good grace, muster the arguments that justified our doing so. Was not the twentieth century more than half over? Was it not nearly fifty years since Eliot wrote "Portrait of a Lady"? George Meredith had not died until 1909, and even the oldest among us had read one of his novels in a college course—many American universities had been quick to bring into their purview the literature of the later nineteenth century, and even the early twentieth century; there was a strong supporting tradition for our capitulation. Had not Yeats been Matthew Arnold's contemporary for twenty-three years?

Our resistance to the idea of the course had never been based on an adverse judgment of the literature itself. We are a department not only of English but of comparative literature, and if the whole of modern literature is surveyed, it could be said—and we were willing to say it—that no literature of the past surpassed the literature of our time in power and magnificence. Then too, it is a difficult literature, and it is difficult not merely as defenders of modern poetry say that all literature is difficult. We nowadays believe that Keats is a very difficult poet, but his earlier readers did not. We now see the depths and subtleties of Dickens, but his contemporary readers found him as simply available as a plate of oysters on the half shell. Modern literature, however, shows its difficulties at first blush; they are literal as well as doctrinal difficulties—if our students were to know their modern literary heritage, surely they needed all the help that a teacher can give?

These made cogent reasons for our decision to establish, at long last, the course in modern literature. They also made a ground for our display of a certain mean-spirited, last-ditch vindictiveness. I recall that we said something like, "Very well, if they want the modern, let them have it—let them have it, as Henry James says, full in the face. We shall give the course, but we shall give it on the highest level, and if they think, as students do, that the modern will naturally meet them in a genial way, let them have their gay and easy time with Yeats and Eliot, with Joyce and Proust and Kafka, with Lawrence, Mann, and Gide."

Eventually the course fell to me to give. I approached it with an uneasiness which has not diminished with the passage of time—it has, I think, even increased. It arises, this uneasiness, from my personal relation with the works that form the substance of the course. Almost all of them have been involved with me for a long time—I invert the natural order not out of lack of modesty but taking the cue of W. H. Auden's remark that a real book reads us. I have been read by Eliot's poems and by *Ulysses* and by *Remembrance of Things Past* and by *The Castle* for a good many years now, since early youth. Some of these books at first rejected me; I bored them. But as I grew older and they knew me better, they came to have more sympathy with me and to understand my hidden meanings. Their nature is such that our relationship has been very intimate. No literature has ever been so shockingly personal as that of our time—it asks every question that is forbidden in polite society. It asks us if we are content with our marriages, with our family lives, with our professional lives, with our friends. It is all very well for me to describe my course in the College catalogue as "paying particular attention to the role of the writer as a critic of his culture"—this is sheer evasion: the questions asked by our literature are not about our culture but about ourselves. It asks us if we are content with ourselves, if we are saved or damned—more than with anything else, our literature is concerned with salvation. No literature has ever been so intensely spiritual as ours. I do not venture to call it actually religious, but certainly it has the special intensity of concern with the spiritual life which Hegel noted when he spoke of the great modern phenomenon of the secularization of spirituality.

I do not know how other teachers deal with this extravagant personal force of modern literature, but for me it makes difficulty. Nowadays the teaching of literature inclines to a considerable technicality, but when the teacher has said all that can be said about formal matters, about verse-patterns, metrics, prose conventions, irony, tension, etc., he must confront the necessity of bearing personal testimony. He must use whatever authority he may possess to say whether or not a work is true; and if not, why not; and if so, why so. He can do this only at considerable cost to his privacy. How does one say that Lawrence is right in his great rage against the modern emotions, against the modern sense of life and ways of being, unless one speaks from the intimacies of one's own feelings, and one's own sense of life, and one's own wished-for way of being? How, except with the implication of personal judgment, does one say to students that Gide is perfectly accurate in his representation of the awful boredom and slow corruption of respectable life? Then probably one rushes in to say that this doesn't of itself justify homosexuality and the desertion of one's dying wife, certainly not. But then again, having paid one's *devoirs* to morality, how does one rescue from morality Gide's essential point about the supreme rights of the individual person, and without making it merely historical, academic?

My first response to the necessity of dealing with matters of this kind was resentment of the personal discomfort it caused me. These are subjects we usually deal with either quite unconsciously or in the privacy of our own conscious minds, and if we now and then disclose our thoughts about them, it is to friends of equal age and especial closeness. Or if we touch upon them publicly, we do so in the relative abstractness and anonymity of print. To stand up in one's own person and to speak of them in one's own voice to an audience which each year grows younger as one grows older—that is not easy, and probably it is not decent.

And then, leaving aside the personal considerations, or taking them merely as an indication of something wrong with the situation, can we not say that, when modern literature is brought into the classroom, the subject being taught is betrayed by the pedagogy of the subject? We have to ask ourselves whether in our day too much does not come within the purview of the academy. More and more, as the universities liberalize themselves, and turn their beneficent imperialistic gaze upon what is called Life Itself, the feeling grows among our educated classes that little can be experienced unless it is validated by some established intellectual discipline, with the result that experience loses much of its personal immediacy for us and becomes part of an accredited societal activity. This is not entirely true and I don't want to play the boring academic game of pretending that it *is* entirely true, that the university mind wilts and withers whatever it touches. I must believe, and I do believe, that the university study of art is capable of confronting the power of a work of art fully and courageously. I even believe that it can discover and disclose power where it has not been felt before. But the university study of art achieves this end chiefly with works of art of an older period. Time has the effect of seeming to quiet the work of art, domesticating it and making it into a classic, which is often another way of saying that it is an object of merely habitual regard. University study of the right sort can reverse this process and restore to the old work its freshness and force—can, indeed, disclose unguessed-at power. But with the works of art of our own present age, university study tends to accelerate the process by which the radical and subversive work becomes the classic work, and university study does this in the degree that it is vivacious and responsive and what is called non-academic. In one of his poems Yeats mocks the literary scholars, "the bald heads forgetful of their sins," "the old, learned, respectable bald heads," who edit the poems of the fierce and passionate young men.

> Lord, what would they say
> Did their Catullus walk this way?

Yeats, of course, is thinking of his own future fate, and no doubt there is all the radical and comical discrepancy that he sees between the poet's passions and the scholars' close-eyed concentration on the text. Yet for my part, when I think of Catullus, I am moved to praise the tact of all those old heads, from Heinsius and Bentley to Munro and Postgate, who worked on Codex G and Codex O and drew conclusions from them about the lost Codex V—for doing only this and for not trying to realize and demonstrate the true intensity and the true quality and the true cultural meaning of Catullus's passion and managing to bring it somehow into eventual accord with their respectability and

230 • The New York Intellectuals Reader

baldness. Nowadays we who deal with books in universities live in fear that the World, which we imagine to be a vital, palpitating, passionate, reality-loving World, will think of us as old, respectable, and bald, and we see to it that in our dealings with Yeats (to take him as the example) his wild cry of rage and sexuality is heard by our students and quite thoroughly understood by them as—what is it that we eventually call it?—*a significant expression of our culture*. The exasperation of Lawrence and the subversiveness of Gide, by the time we have dealt with them boldly and straightforwardly, are notable instances of the *alienation of modern man as exemplified by the artist*. "Compare Yeats, Gide, Lawrence, and Eliot in the use which they make of the theme of sexuality to criticize the deficiencies of modern culture. Support your statement by specific references to the work of each author. [Time: one hour.]" And the distressing thing about our examination questions is that they are not ridiculous, they make perfectly good sense—such good sense that the young person who answers them can never again know the force and terror of what has been communicated to him by the works he is being examined on.

Very likely it was with the thought of saving myself from the necessity of speaking personally and my students from having to betray the full harsh meaning of a great literature that I first taught my course in as *literary* a way as possible. A couple of decades ago the discovery was made that a literary work is a structure of words: this doesn't seem a surprising thing to have learned except for its polemical tendency, which is to urge us to minimize the amount of attention we give to the poet's social and personal will, to what he wants to happen outside the poem as a result of the poem; it urges us to fix our minds on what is going on inside the poem. For me this polemical tendency has been of the greatest usefulness, for it has corrected my inclination to pay attention chiefly to what the poet *wants*. For two or three years I directed my efforts toward dealing with the matter of the course chiefly as structures of words, in a formal way, with due attention paid to the literal difficulty which marked so many of the works. But it went against the grain. It went against my personal grain. It went against the grain of the classroom situation, for formal analysis is best carried on by question-and-answer, which needs small groups, and the registration for the course in modern literature in any college is sure to be large. And it went against the grain of the authors themselves—structures of words they may indeed have created, but these structures were not pyramids or triumphal arches, they were manifestly contrived to be not static and commemorative but mobile and aggressive, and one does not describe a quinquereme or a howitzer or a tank without estimating how much *damage* it can do.

Eventually I had to decide that there was only one way to give the course, which was to give it without strategies and without conscious caution. It was not honorable, either to the students or to the authors, to conceal or disguise my relation to the literature, my commitment to it, my fear of it, my ambivalence toward it. The literature had to be dealt with in the terms it announced for itself. As for the students, I have never given assent to the modern saw about "teaching students, not subjects"—I have always thought it right to teach subjects, believing that if one gives his first loyalty to the subject, the student is best instructed. So I resolved to give the course with no considerations in mind except my own interests. And since my own interests lead me to see literary situations as cultural situations, and cultural situations as great elaborate fights about moral issues, and moral issues as having something to do with gratuitously chosen images of personal being, and images of personal being as having something to do with literary style, I felt free to begin with what for me was a first concern, the animus of the author, the objects of his will, the things he wants or wants to have happen.

My cultural and non-literary method led me to decide that I would begin the course with a statement of certain themes or issues that might especially engage our attention. I even went so far in non-literariness as to think that my purposes would best be served if I could contrive a "background" for the works we would read—I wanted to propose a history for the themes or issues that I hoped to discover. I did not intend that this history should be either very extensive or very precise. I wanted merely to encourage a *sense* of a history, some general intuition of a past, in students who, as it seems to me, have not been provided with any such thing by their education and who are on the whole glad to be without it. And because there is as yet no adequate general work of history of the culture of the last two hundred years, I asked myself what books of the age just preceding ours had most influenced our literature, or, since I was far less concerned with showing influence than with discerning a tendency, what older books might seem to fall into a line the direction of which pointed to our own literature and thus might serve as a prolegomenon to the course.

It was virtually inevitable that the first work that should have sprung to mind was Sir James Frazer's *The Golden Bough*, not, of course, the whole of it, but certain chapters, those that deal with Osiris, Attis, and Adonis. Anyone who thinks about modern literature in a systematic way takes for granted the great part played in it by myth, and especially by those examples of myth which tell about gods dying and being reborn—the imagination of death and rebirth, reiterated in the ancient world in innumerable variations that are yet always the same, captivated the literary mind at the very moment when, as all accounts of the modern age agree, the most massive and compelling of all the stories of resurrection had lost much of its hold upon the world.

Perhaps no book has had so decisive an effect upon modern literature as Frazer's. It was beautifully to my purpose that it had first been published ten years before the twentieth century began. Yet forty-three years later, in 1933, Frazer delivered a lecture, very eloquent, in which he bade the world be of good hope in the face of the threat to the human mind that was being offered by the Nazi power. He was still alive in 1941. Yet he had been born in 1854, three years before Matthew Arnold gave the lecture "On the Modern Element in Literature." Here, surely, was history, here was the past I wanted, beautifully connected with our present. Frazer was wholly a man of the nineteenth century, and the more so because the eighteenth century was so congenial to him—the lecture of 1933 in which he predicted the Nazi defeat had as its subject Condorcet's *Progress of the Human Mind*; when he took time from his anthropological studies to deal with literature, he prepared editions of Addison's essays and Cowper's letters. He had the old lost belief in the virtue and power of rationality. He loved and counted on order, decorum, and good sense. This great historian of the primitive imagination was in the dominant intellectual tradition of the West which, since the days of the pre-Socratics, has condemned the ways of thought that we call primitive.

It can be said of Frazer that in his conscious intention he was a perfect representative of what Arnold meant when he spoke of a modern age. And perhaps nothing could make clearer how the conditions of life and literature have changed in a hundred years than to note the difference between the way in which Arnold defines the modern element in literature and the way in which we must define it.

Arnold used the word *modern* in a wholly honorific sense. So much so that he seems to dismiss all temporal idea from the word and makes it signify certain timeless intellectual and civic virtues—his lecture, indeed, was about the modern element in the ancient literatures. A society, he said, is a modern society when it maintains a condition of repose, confidence, free activity of the mind, and the tolerance of divergent views. A society is modern when it affords sufficient material well-being for the conveniences of life and the development of taste. And, finally, a society is modern when its members are intellectually mature, by which Arnold means that they are willing to judge by reason, to observe facts in a critical spirit, and to search for the law of things. By this definition Periclean Athens is for Arnold a modern age, Elizabethan England is not; Thucydides is a modern historian, Sir Walter Raleigh is not.

I shall not go into further details of Arnold's definition or description of the modern.[1] I have said enough, I think, to suggest what Arnold was up to, what he wanted to see realized as the desideratum of his own society, what ideal he wanted the works of intellect and imagination of his own time to advance. And at what a distance his ideal of the modern puts him from our present sense of modernity, from our modern literature! To anyone conditioned by our modern literature, Arnold's ideal of order, convenience, decorum, and rationality might well seem to reduce itself to the small advantages and excessive limitations of the middle-class life of a few prosperous nations of the nineteenth century. Arnold's historic sense presented to his mind the long, bitter, bloody past of Europe, and he seized passionately upon the hope of true civilization at last achieved. But the historic sense of our literature has in mind a long excess of civilization to which may be ascribed the bitterness and bloodiness both of the past and of the present and of which the peaceful aspects are to be thought of as mainly contemptible—its order achieved at the cost of extravagant personal repression, either that of coercion or that of acquiescence; its repose otiose; its tolerance either flaccid or capricious; its material comfort corrupt and corrupting; its taste a manifestation either of timidity or of pride; its rationality attained only at the price of energy and passion.

For the understanding of this radical change of opinion nothing is more illuminating than to be aware of the doubleness of mind of the author of *The Golden Bough*. I have said that Frazer in his conscious mind and in his first intention exemplifies all that Arnold means by the modern. He often speaks quite harshly of the irrationality and the orgiastic excesses of the primitive religions he describes, and even Christianity comes under his criticism both because it stands in the way of rational thought and because it can draw men away from intelligent participation in the life of society. But Frazer had more than one intention, and he had an unconscious as well as a conscious mind. If he deplores the primitive imagination, he also does not fail to show it as wonderful and beautiful. It is the rare reader of *The Golden Bough* who finds the ancient beliefs and rituals wholly alien to him. It is to be expected that Frazer's adduction of the many pagan analogues to the Christian mythos will be thought by Christian readers to have an adverse effect on faith, it was undoubtedly Frazer's purpose that it should, yet many readers will feel that Frazer makes all faith and ritual indigenous to humanity, virtually biological; they feel, as DeQuincey put it, that not to be at least a *little* superstitious is to lack generosity of mind. Scientific though his purpose was, Frazer had the effect of validating those old modes of experiencing the world which modern men, beginning with the Romantics, have sought to revive in order to escape from positivism and common sense.

The direction of the imagination upon great and mysterious objects of worship is not the only means men use to liberate themselves from the bondage of quotidian fact, and although Frazer can scarcely be held accountable for the ever-growing modern attraction to the extreme mental states—to rapture, ecstasy, and transcendence, which are achieved by drugs, trance, music and dance, orgy, and the derangement of personality—yet he did provide a bridge to the understanding and acceptance of these states, he proposed to us the idea that the desire for them and the use of them for heuristic purposes is a common and acceptable manifestation of human nature.

This one element of Frazer's masterpiece could scarcely fail to suggest the next of my prolegomenal works. It is worth remarking that its author was in his own way as great a classical scholar as Frazer himself—Nietzsche was Professor of Classical Philology at the University of Basel when, at the age of twenty-seven, he published his essay *The Birth of Tragedy*. After the appearance of this stunningly brilliant account of Greek civilization, of which Socrates is not the hero but the villain, what can possibly be left to us of that rational and ordered Greece, that modern, that eighteenth-century, Athens that Arnold so entirely relied on as the standard for judging all civilizations? Professor Kaufmann is right when he warns us against supposing that Nietzsche exalts Dionysus over Apollo and tells us that Nietzsche "emphasizes the Dionysiac only because he feels that the Apollonian genius of the Greeks cannot be fully understood apart from it." But no one reading Nietzsche's essay for the first time is likely to heed this warning. What will reach him before due caution intervenes, before he becomes aware of the portentous dialectic between Dionysus and Apollo, is the excitement of suddenly being liberated from Aristotle, the joy of finding himself acceding to the author's statement that "art rather than ethics constitutes the essential metaphysical activity of man," that tragedy has its source in the Dionysiac rapture, "whose closest analogy is furnished by physical intoxication," and that this rapture, in which "the individual forgets himself completely," was in itself no metaphysical state but an orgiastic display of lust and cruelty, "of sexual promiscuity overriding every form of tribal law." This sadic and masochistic frenzy, Nietzsche is at pains to insist, needs the taming hand of Apollo before it can become tragedy, but it is the primal stuff of the great art, and to the modern experience of tragedy this explanation seems far more pertinent than Aristotle's, with its eagerness to forget its origin in its achievement of a state of noble imperturbability.

Of supreme importance in itself, Nietzsche's essay had for me the added pedagogic advantage of allowing me to establish a historical line back to William Blake. Nothing is more characteristic of modern literature than its discovery and canonization of the primal, non-ethical energies, and the historical point could be made the better by remarking the correspondence of thought of two men of different nations and separated from each other by a good many decades, for Nietzsche's Dionysian orgy and Blake's Hell are much the same thing.

Whether or not Joseph Conrad read either Blake or Nietzsche I do not know, but his *Heart of Darkness* follows in their line. This very great work has never lacked for the admiration it deserves, and it has been given a kind of canonical place in the legend of modern literature by Eliot's having it so clearly in mind when he wrote *The Waste Land* and his having taken from it the epigraph to "The Hollow Men." But no one, to my knowledge, has ever confronted in an explicit way its strange and terrible message of ambivalence toward the life of civilization. Consider that its protagonist, Kurtz, is a progressive and a liberal and that he is the highly respected representative of a society which would have us believe it is benign, although in fact it is vicious. Consider too that he is a practitioner of several arts, a painter, a writer, a musician, and into the bargain a political orator. He is at once the most idealistic and the most practically successful of all the agents of the Belgian exploitation of the Congo. Everybody knows the truth about him which Marlow discovers—that Kurtz's success is the result of a terrible ascendancy he has gained over the natives of his distant station, an ascendancy which is derived from his presumed magical or divine powers, that he has exercised his rule with an extreme of cruelty, that he has given himself to unnamable acts of lust. This is the world of the darker pages of *The Golden Bough.* It is one of the great points of Conrad's story that Marlow speaks of the primitive life of the jungle not as being noble or charming or even free but as being base and sordid—and for *that* reason compelling: he himself feels quite overtly its dreadful attraction. It is to this devilish baseness that Kurtz has yielded himself, and yet Marlow, although he does indeed treat him with hostile irony, does not find it possible to suppose that Kurtz is anything but a hero of the spirit. For me it is still ambiguous whether Kurtz's famous deathbed cry, "The horror! The horror!" refers to the approach of death or to his experience of savage life. Whichever it is, to Marlow the fact that Kurtz could utter this cry at the point of death, while Marlow himself, when death threatens him, can know it only as a weary grayness, marks the difference between the ordinary man and a hero of the spirit. Is this not the essence of the modern belief about the nature of the artist, the man who goes down into that hell which is the historical beginning of the human soul, a beginning not outgrown but established in humanity as we know it now, preferring the reality of this hell to the bland lies of the civilization that has overlaid it?

This idea is proposed again in the somewhat less powerful but still very moving work with which I followed *Heart of Darkness*, Thomas Mann's *Death in Venice.* I wanted this story not so much for its account of an extravagantly Apollonian personality surrendering to forces that, in his Apollonian character, he thought shameful—although this was certainly to my purpose—but rather for Aschenbach's fevered dreams of the erotic past, and in particular that dream of the goat-orgy which Mann, being the kind of writer he is, having the kind of relation to Nietzsche he had, might well have written to serve as an illustration of what *The Birth of Tragedy* means by religious frenzy, the more so, of course, because Mann chooses that particular orgiastic ritual, the killing and eating of the goat, from which tragedy is traditionally said to have been derived.

A notable element of this story in which the birth of tragedy plays an important part is that the degradation and downfall of the protagonist is not represented as tragic in the usual sense of the word—that is, it is not represented as a great deplorable event. It is a commonplace of modern literary thought that the tragic mode is not available even to the gravest and noblest of our writers. I am not sure that this is the deprivation that some people think it to be and a mark of our spiritual inferiority. But if we ask why it has come about, one reason may be that we have learned to think our way back through tragedy to the primal stuff out of which tragedy arose. If we consider the primitive forbidden ways of conduct which traditionally in tragedy lead to punishment by death, we think of them as being the path to reality and truth, to an ultimate self-realization. We have always wondered if tragedy itself may not have been saying just this in a deeply hidden way, drawing us to think of the hero's sin and death as somehow conferring justification, even salvation of a sort—no doubt this is what Nietzsche had in mind when he said that "tragedy denies ethics." What tragedy once seemed to hint, our literature now is willing to say quite explicitly. If Mann's Aschenbach dies at the height of his intellectual and artistic powers, overcome by a passion that his ethical reason condemns, we do not take this to be a defeat, rather a kind of terrible rebirth: at his latter end the artist knows a reality that he had until now refused to admit to consciousness.

Thoughts like these suggested that another of Nietzsche's works, *The Genealogy of Morals*, might be in point. It proposes a view of society which is consonant with the belief that art and not ethics constitutes the essential metaphysical activity of man and with the validation and ratification of the primitive energies. Nietzsche's theory of the social order dismisses all ethical impulse from its origins—the basis of society is to be found in the rationalization of cruelty: as simple as that. Nietzsche has no ultimate Utopian intention in saying this, no hope of revising the essence of the social order, although he does believe that its pain can be mitigated. He represents cruelty as a social necessity, for only by its exercise could men ever have been induced to develop a continuity of will: nothing else than cruel pain could have created in mankind that memory of intention which makes society possible. The method of cynicism which Nietzsche pursued—let us be clear that it is a method and not an attitude—goes so far as to describe punishment in terms of the pleasure derived from the exercise of cruety: "Compensation," he says, "consists in a legal warrant entitling one man to exercise his cruelty on another." There follows that most remarkable passage in which Nietzsche describes the process whereby the individual turns the cruety of punishment against himself and creates the bad conscience and the consciousness of guilt which manifests itself as a pervasive anxiety. Nietzsche's complexity of mind is beyond all comparison, for in this book which is dedicated to the liberation of the conscience, Nietzsche makes his defense of the bad conscience as a decisive force in the interests of culture. It is much the same line of argument that he takes when, having attacked the Jewish morality and the priestly existence in the name of the health of the spirit, he reminds us that only by his sickness does man become interesting.

From *The Genealogy of Morals* to Freud's *Civilization and Its Discontents* is but a step, and some might think that, for pedagogic purposes, the step is so small as to make the second book supererogatory. But although Freud's view of society and culture has indeed a very close affinity to Nietzsche's, Freud does add certain considerations which are essential to our sense of the modern disposition.

For one thing, he puts to us the question of whether or not we want to *accept* civilization. It is not the first time that the paradox of civilization has been present to the mind of civilized people, the sense that civilization makes men behave worse and suffer more than does some less developed state of human existence. But hitherto all such ideas were formulated in a moralizing way—civilization was represented as being "corrupt," a divagation from a state of innocence. Freud had no illusions about a primitive innocence, he conceived no practicable alternative to civilization. In consequence, there was a unique force to the question he asked: whether we wished to accept civilization, with all its contradictions, with all its pains—pains, for "discontents" does not accurately describe what Freud has in mind. He had his own answer to the question—his tragic, or stoic, sense of life dictated it: we do well to accept it, although we also do well to cast a cold eye on the fate that makes it our better part to accept it. Like Nietzsche, Freud thought that life was justified by our heroic response to its challenge.

But the question Freud posed has not been set aside or closed up by the answer that he himself gave to it. His answer, like Nietzsche's, is essentially in the line of traditional humanism—we can see this in the sternness with which he charges women not to interfere with men in the discharge of their cultural duty, not to claim men for love and the family to the detriment of their free activity in the world. But just here lies the matter of Freud's question that the world more and more believes Freud himself did not answer. The pain that civilization inflicts is that of the instinctual renunciation that civilization demands, and it would seem that fewer and fewer people wish to say with Freud that the loss of instinctual gratification, emotional freedom, or love, is compensated for either by the security of civilized life or by the stern pleasures of the masculine moral character.

With Freud's essay I brought to a close my list of prolegomenal books for the first term of the course. I shall not do much more than mention the books with which I introduced the second term, but I should like to do at least that. I began with *Rameau's Nephew*, thinking that the peculiar moral authority which Diderot assigns to the envious, untalented, unregenerate protagonist was peculiarly relevant to the line taken by the ethical explorations of modern literature. Nothing is more characteristic of the literature of our time than the replacement of the hero by what has come to be called the anti-hero, in whose indifference to or hatred of ethical nobility there is presumed to lie a special authenticity. Diderot is quite overt about this—he himself in his public character is the deuteragonist, the "honest consciousness," as Hegel calls him, and he takes delight in the discomfiture of the decent, dull person he is by the Nephew's nihilistic mind.

It seemed to me too that there was particular usefulness in the circumstance that this anti-hero should avow so openly his *envy*, which Tocqueville has called the ruling emotion of democracy, and that, although he envied any-

238 • The New York Intellectuals Reader

one at all who had access to the creature-comforts and the social status which he lacked, what chiefly animated him was envy of men of genius. Ours is the first cultural epoch in which many men aspire to high achievement in the arts and, in their frustration, form a dispossessed class which cuts across the conventional class lines, making a proletariat of the spirit.

Although *Rameau's Nephew* was not published until fairly late in the century, it was known in manuscript by Goethe and Hegel; it suited the temper and won the admiration of Marx and Freud for reasons that are obvious. And there is ground for supposing that it was known to Dostoevski, whose *Notes from Underground* is a restatement of the essential idea of Diderot's dialogue in terms both more extreme and less genial. The Nephew is still on the defensive—he is naughtily telling secrets about the nature of man and society. But Dostoevski's underground man shouts aloud his envy and hatred and carries the ark of his self-hatred and alienation into a remorseless battle with what he calls "the good and the beautiful," mounting an attack upon every belief not merely of bourgeois society but of the whole humanist tradition. The inclusion of *Notes from Underground* among my prolegomenal books constituted something of a pedagogic risk, for if I wished to emphasize the subversive tendency of modern literature, here was a work which made all subsequent subversion seem like affirmation, so radical and so brilliant was its negation of our traditional pieties and its affirmation of our new pieties.

I hesitated in compunction before following *Notes from Underground* with Tolstoi's *Death of Ivan Ilyitch*, which so ruthlessly and with such dreadful force destroys the citadel of the commonplace life in which we all believe we can take refuge from ourselves and our fate. But I did assign it and then two of Pirandello's plays which, in the atmosphere of the sordidness of the commonplace life, undermine all the certitudes of the commonplace, common-sense mind.

From time to time I have raised with myself the question of whether my choice of these prolegomenal works was not extravagant, quite excessively tendentious. I have never been able to believe that it is. And if these works do indeed serve to indicate in an accurate way the nature of modern literature, a teacher might find it worth asking how his students respond to the strong dose.

One response I have already described—the readiness of the students to engage in the process that we might call the socialization of the anti-social, or the acculturation of the anti-cultural, or the legitimization of the subversive. When the term-essays come in, it is plain to me that almost none of the students have been taken aback by what they have read: they have wholly contained the attack. The chief exceptions are the few who simply do not comprehend, although they may be awed by, the categories of our discourse. In their papers, like poor hunted creates in a Kafka story, they take refuge first in misunderstood large phrases, then in bad grammar, then in general incoherence. After my pedagogical exasperation has run its course, I find that I am sometimes moved to give them a queer respect, as if they had stood up and said what in fact they don't have the wit to stand up and say: "Why do you harry us? Leave us alone. We are not Modern Man. We are the Old People. Ours is the Old Faith. We serve the little Old Gods, the gods of the copybook maxims, the small, dark, somewhat powerful deities of lawyers, doctors, engineers, accountants. With them is neither sensibility nor *angst*. With them is no disgust—it is they, indeed, who make ready the way for 'the good and the beautiful' about which low-minded doubts have been raised in this course, that 'good and beautiful' which we do not possess and don't want to possess but which we know justifies our lives. Leave us alone and let us worship our gods in the way they approve, in peace and unawareness." Crass, but—to use that interesting modern word which we have learned from the curators of museums—authentic. The rest, the minds that give me the A papers and the B papers and even the C+ papers, move through the terrors and mysteries of modern literature like so many Parsifals, asking no questions at the behest of wonder and fear. Or like so many seminarists who have been sytematically instructed in the constitution of Hell and the ways to damnation. Or like so many *readers*, entertained by moral horror stories. I asked them to look into the Abyss, and, both dutifully and gladly, they have looked into the Abyss, and the Abyss has greeted them with the grave courtesy of all objects of serious study, saying: "Interesting, am I not? And *exciting*, if you consider how deep I am and what dread beasts lie at my bottom. Have it well in mind that a knowledge of me contributes materially to your being whole, or well-rounded, men."

In my distress over the outrage I have conspired to perpetrate upon a great literature, I wonder if perhaps I have not been reading these papers too literally. After all, a term-essay is not a diary of the soul, it is not an occasion for telling the truth. What my students might reveal of their true feelings to a younger teacher they will not reveal to me; they will give me what they conceive to be the proper response to the official version of terror I have given them. I bring to mind their faces, which are not necessarily the faces of the authors of these unperturbed papers, nor are they, not yet, the faces of fathers of families, or of theatergoers, or of buyers of modern paintings: not yet. I must think it possible that in ways and to a degree which they keep secret they have responded directly and personally to what they have read.

And if they have? And if they have, am I the more content?

What form would I want their response to take? It is a teacher's question that I am asking, not a critic's. We have decided in recent years to think of the critic and the teacher of literature as one and the same, and no doubt it is both possible and useful to do so. But there are some points at which the functions of the two do not coincide, or can be made to coincide only with great difficulty. Of criticism we have been told, by Arnold, that "it must be apt to study and praise elements that for fulness of spiritual perfection are wanted, even though they belong to a power which in the practical sphere may be maleficent." But teaching, or at least undergraduate teaching, is not given the same licensed mandate—cannot be given it because the teacher's audience, which stands before his very eyes, as the critic's audience does not, asks questions about "the practical sphere," as the critic's audience does not. For instance, on the very day that I write this, when I had said to my class all I could think of to say about *The Magic Mountain* and invited questions and comments, one student asked, "How would you generalize the idea of the educative value of illness, so that it would be applicable not only to a particular individual, Hans Castorp, but to young people at large?" It makes us smile, but it was asked in all seriousness, and it is serious in its substance, and it had to be answered seriously, in part by the reflection that this idea, like so many ideas encountered in the books of the course, had to be thought of as having reference only to the private life; that it touched the public life only in some indirect or tangential way; that it really ought to be encountered in solitude, even in secrecy, since to talk about it in public and in our academic setting was to seem to propose for it a public practicality and thus to distort its meaning. To this another student replied; he said that, despite the public ritual of the classroom, each student inevitably experienced the books in privacy and found their meaning in reference to his own life. True enough, but the teacher sees the several privacies coming together to make a group, and they propose—no doubt the more because they come together every Monday, Wednesday, and Friday at a particular hour—the idea of a community, that is to say, "the practical sphere."

This being so, the teacher cannot escape the awareness of certain circumstances which the critic, who writes for an ideal, uncircumstanced reader, has no need to take into account. The teacher considers, for example, the social situation of his students—they are not of patrician origin, they do not come from homes in which stubbornness, pride, and conscious habit prevail, nor are they born into a culture marked by these traits, a culture in which other interesting and valuable things compete with and resist ideas; they come, mostly, from "good homes" in which authority and valuation are weak or at least not very salient and bold, so that ideas have for them, at their present stage of development, a peculiar power and preciousness. And in this connection the teacher will have in mind the special prestige that our culture, in its upper reaches, gives to art, and to the ideas that art proposes—the agreement, ever growing in assertiveness, that art yields more truth than any other intellectual activity. In this culture what a shock it is to encounter Santayana's acerb skepticism about art, or Keats's remark, which the critics and scholars never take notice of, presumably because they suppose it to be an aberration, that poetry is "not so fine a thing as philosophy—For the same reason that an eagle is not so fine a thing as a truth." For many students no ideas that they will encounter in any college discipline will equal in force and sanction the ideas conveyed to them by modern literature.

The author of *The Magic Mountain* once said that all his work could be understood as an effort to free himself from the middle class, and this, of course, will serve to describe the chief intention of all modern literature. And the means of freedom which Mann prescribes (the characteristic irony notwithstanding) is the means of freedom which in effect all of modern literature prescribes. It is, in the words of Clavdia Chauchat, *"se perdre et même ... se laisser dépérir,"* and thus to name the means is to make plain that the end is not merely freedom from the middle class but freedom from society itself. I venture to say that the idea of losing oneself up to the point of self-destruction, of surrendering oneself to experience without regard to self-interest or conventional morality, of escaping wholly from the societal bonds, is an "element" somewhere in the mind of every modern person who dares to think of what Arnold in his unaffected Victorian way called "the fulness of spiritual perfection." But the teacher who undertakes to present modern literature to his students may not allow that idea to remain in the *somewhere* of his mind; he must take it from the place where it exists habitual and unrealized and put it in the conscious forefront of his thought. And if he is committed to an admiration of modern literature, he must also be committed to this chief idea of modern literature. I press the logic of the situation not in order to question the legitimacy of the commitment, or even the propriety of expressing the commitment in the college classroom (although it does seem odd!), but to confront those of us who do teach modern literature with the striking actuality of our enterprise.

Note

1. I leave out of my summary account the two supreme virtues that Arnold ascribes to the most successful examples of a "modern" literature. One is the power of effecting an "intellectual deliverance," by which Arnold means leading men to comprehend the "vast multitude of facts" which make up "a copious and complex present, and behind it a copious and complex past." The other is "adequacy," the ability to represent the complex high human development of a modern age "in its completest and most harmonious" aspect, doing so with "the charm of that noble serenity which always accompanies true insight."

20
Susan Sontag (1933–2004)
Against Interpretation (1964)

Editor's Introduction

As Susan Sontag knew, even essays against interpretation are subject to interpretation. This early essay, published in the *Evergreen Review* in 1964, is heavy and unsure of itself, not written with the grace of normal *Partisan Review* fare, but it is bold and challenging enough to warrant the attention it received. The point of the essay, related closely to what Clement Greenberg had been saying about painting for a quarter of century, is that form—and the formalistic qualities of paint, texture and skill—is more important than the content and its meaning. But Sontag expanded this suggestion to literature, film and other arts than painting. In addition, she advised, pieces of art shouldn't have to prove how they fit into a history of interpretation for them to have standing in the culture, because that inverts the importance between a work and interpreters. We need to appreciate, even love a work, more than fit it into a historical category. This is the meaning of her notorious pronouncement that, "In place of a hermeneutics we need an erotics of art." This dictum is understood well in relation to the previous sentence in her essay: "The function of criticism should be to show *how it is what it is*, even *that it is what it is*, rather than to show *what it means*." (Her emphasis.) Sontag's insistence on the authenticity of the immediate work, and her claim that meaning should arise from a work rather than be imposed on it, is consistent with the outlook of the 1960s.

She was born Susan Rosenblatt in New York in 1933 of Jewish American parents. For her first five years she and her younger sister spent much of their time in the care of their grandparents while their parents were in China trading furs. When her father, Jack Rosenblatt, died of tuberculosis in China, her mother took the girls to live in Miami, then Tucson, and finally Los Angeles. There her mother, an alcoholic, married Nathan Sontag when Susan was twelve, and the girl took his last name. As a child, Susan skipped three grades and graduated from North Hollywood High School when she was fifteen. After a semester at Berkeley she was admitted to the University of Chicago at sixteen, where she became close to Kenneth Burke and Leo Strauss, but even closer yet to the young professor Philip Rieff, whom she married when she was seventeen and he was twenty eight. Sontag earned a master's in philosophy at

Harvard and then received a fellowship in 1957 to study at St. Anne's College, Oxford. Not caring for Oxford's sexism, she spent the second semester of her fellowship studying in Paris, where she learned the names and books of the European intellectuals who dotted her essays for the rest of her life. When she returned to the United States she divorced Rieff, taught courses at City College and Sarah Lawrence, published her first novel, *The Benefactor* (1963), with Farrar Strauss, and then taught in the Columbia University religion department for two years, from 1964 to 1966.

During these same years she also told William Phillips she wanted to publish an essay in *Partisan Review*, a magazine she first looked through at age fifteen. "Notes on Camp" appeared in *PR* in 1964, the same year that "Against Interpretation" appeared in *Evergreen Review*. She was part of the third "generation" of *Partisan Review* contributors, along with those such as Norman Podhoretz, who were born in the 1930s. Although many of her interests—in literature, painting and cultural politics—were consistent with the tradition of *Partisan Review*, many of her subjects and values represented those of the 1960s generation who encamped to the other side of an important cultural divide. Many of her works represented early whispers of postmodernism, different values about multiculturalism and meritocracy, newer views about gender and different convictions about international power than those held earlier by the New York Intellectuals.

Source

Susan Sontag, "Against Interpretation," *Evergreen Review* vol. 8, December, 1964.

Selected Readings

Susan Sontag, *A Susan Sontag Reader* (New York: Farrar Straus, Giroux, 1982).
Sohnya Sayres, *Susan Sontag: The Elegiac Modernist* (New York: Routledge, 1990).

* * * * *

Content is a glimpse of something, an encounter like a flash. It's very tiny—very tiny, content.

Willem De Kooning, in an interview

It is only shallow people who do not judge by appearances. The mystery of the world is the visible, not the invisible.

Oscar Wilde, in a letter

1

The earliest *experience* of art must have been that it was incantatory, magical; art was an instrument of ritual. (Cf. the paintings in the caves at Lascaux,

Altamira, Niaux, La Pasiega, etc.) The earliest *theory* of art, that of the Greek philosophers, proposed that art was mimesis, imitation of reality.

It is at this point that the peculiar question of the *value* of art arose. For the mimetic theory, by its very terms, challenges art to justify itself.

Plato, who proposed the theory, seems to have done so in order to rule that the value of art is dubious. Since he considered ordinary material things as themselves mimetic objects, imitations of transcendent forms or structures, even the best painting of a bed would be only an "imitation of an imitation." For Plato, art is neither particularly useful (the painting of a bed is no good to sleep on), nor, in the strict sense, true. And Aristotle's arguments in defense of art do not really challenge Plato's view that all art is an elaborate *trompe l'oeil*, and therefore a lie. But he does dispute Plato's idea that art is useless. Lie or no, art has a certain value according to Aristotle because it is a form of therapy. Art is useful, after all, Aristotle counters, medicinally useful in that it arouses and purges dangerous emotions.

In Plato and Aristotle, the mimetic theory of art goes hand in hand with the assumption that art is always figurative. But advocates of the mimetic theory need not close their eyes to decorative and abstract art. The fallacy that art is necessarily a "realism" can be modified or scrapped without ever moving outside the problems delimited by the mimetic theory.

The fact is, all Western consciousness of and reflection upon art have remained within the confines staked out by the Greek theory of art as mimesis or representation. It is through this theory that art as such—above and beyond given works of art—becomes problematic, in need of defense. And it is the defense of art which gives birth to the odd vision by which something we have learned to call "form" is separated off from something we have learned to call "content," and to the well-intentioned move which makes content the main thing and form accessory.

Even in modern times, when most artists and critics have discarded the theory of art as representation of an outer reality in favor of the theory of art as subjective expression, the main feature of the mimetic theory persists. Whether we conceive of the work of art on the model of a picture (art as a picture of reality) or on the model of a statement (art as the statement of the artist), content still comes first. The content may have changed. It may now be less figurative, less lucidly realistic. But it is still assumed that a work of art *is* its content. Or, as it's usually put today, that a work of art by definition *says* something. ("What X is saying is …," "What X is trying to say is …," "What X said is …" etc., etc.)

2

None of us can ever retrieve that innocence before all theory when art knew no need to justify itself, when one did not ask of a work of art what it *said* because one knew (or thought one knew) what it *did*. From now to the end of consciousness, we are stuck with the task of defending art. We can only quarrel with one or another means of defense. Indeed, we have an obligation to overthrow any means of defending and justifying art which becomes particularly obtuse or onerous or insensitive to contemporary needs and practice.

This is the case, today, with the very idea of content itself. Whatever it may have been in the past, the idea of content is today mainly a hindrance, a nuisance, a subtle or not so subtle philistinism.

Though the actual developments in many arts may seem to be leading us away from the idea that a work of art is primarily its content, the idea still exerts an extraordinary hegemony. I want to suggest that this is because the idea is now perpetuated in the form of a certain way of encountering works of art thoroughly ingrained among most people who take any of the arts seriously. What the over-emphasis on the idea of content entails is the perennial, never consummated project of *interpretation*. And, conversely, it is the habit of approaching works of art in order to *interpret* them that sustains the fancy that there really is such a thing as the content of a work of art.

3

Of course, I don't mean interpretation in the broadest sense, the sense in which Nietzsche (rightly) says, "There are no facts, only interpretations." By interpretation, I mean here a conscious act of the mind which illustrates a certain code, certain "rules" of interpretation.

Directed to art, interpretation means plucking a set of elements (the X, the Y, the Z, and so forth) from the whole work. The task of interpretation is virtually one of translation. The interpreter says, Look, don't you see that X is really—or, really means—A? That Y is really B? That Z is really C?

What situation could prompt this curious project for transforming a text? History gives us the materials for an answer. Interpretation first appears in the culture of late classical antiquity, when the power and credibility of myth had been broken by the "realistic" view of the world introduced by scientific enlightenment. Once the question that haunts post-mythic consciousness—that of the *seemliness* of religious symbols—had been asked, the ancient texts were, in their pristine form, no longer acceptable. Then interpretation was summoned, to reconcile the ancient texts to "modern" demands. Thus, the Stoics allegorized away the rude features of Zeus and his boisterous clan in Homer's epics to accord with their view that the gods had to be moral. What Homer really designated by the adultery of Zeus with Leto, they explained, was the union between power and wisdom. In the same vein, Philo of Alexandria interpreted the literal historical narratives of the Hebrew Bible as spiritual paradigms. What the story of the exodus from Egypt, the wandering in the desert for 40 years, and the entry into the promised land really was, said Philo, was an allegory of the individual soul's emancipation, tribulations, and final deliverance. Interpretation thus presupposes a discrepancy between the clear meaning of the text and the demands of (later) readers. It seeks to resolve that discrepancy. The situation is, that for some reason a text has become unacceptable; yet it cannot be discarded. Interpretation is a radical strategy for conserving an old text, which is thought too precious to repudiate, by revamping it. The interpreter *is* altering the text, without actually erasing or rewriting it. But he can't admit to doing this. He claims to be only making it intelligible, by disclosing its true meaning. However far the interpreters alter the text (another notorious example is the Rabbinic and Christian "spiritual" interpretations of the clearly erotic Song of Songs), they must claim to be reading off a sense that is already there.

Interpretation in our own time, however, is even more complex. For the contemporary zeal for the project of interpretation is often prompted not by piety toward the troublesome text (which may conceal an aggression), but by an open aggressiveness, an overt contempt for appearances. The old style of interpretation was insistent, but respectful; it erected another meaning on top of the literal one. The modern style of interpretation excavates, and as it excavates, destroys; it digs "behind" the text, to find a sub-text which is the true one. The most celebrated and influential modern doctrines, those of Marx and Freud, actually amount to elaborate systems of hermeneutics, aggressive and impious theories of interpretation. All observable phenomena are bracketed, in Freud's phrase, as *manifest content*. This manifest content must be probed and pushed aside to find the true meaning—the *latent content*—beneath. For Marx, social events like revolutions and wars; for Freud, the events of individual lives (like neurotic symptoms and slips of the tongue) as well as texts (like a dream or a work of art)—all are treated as occasions for interpretation. These events only *seem* to be intelligible, according to Marx and Freud. Actually, it is argued, they have no meaning without interpretation. To understand *is* to interpret. And to interpret is to restate the phenomenon, in effect to find an equivalent for it.

Thus, interpretation is not (as most people assume) an absolute value, a gesture of mind situated in some timeless realm of capabilities. Interpretation must itself be evaluated, within a historical view of human consciousness. In some cultural contexts, interpretation is a liberating act. It is a means of revising, of transvaluing, of escaping the dead past. In other cultural contexts, it is reactionary, impertinent, cowardly, stifling.

4

Today is such a time, when the project of interpretation is largely reactionary, stifling. Like the fumes of the automobile and of heavy industry which befoul the urban atmosphere, the effusion of interpretations of art today poisons our sensibilities. In a culture whose already classical dilemma is the hypertrophy of the intellect at the expense of energy and sensual capability, interpretation is the revenge of the intellect upon art.

Even more. It is the revenge of the intellect upon the world. To interpret is to impoverish, to deplete the world—in order to set up a shadow world of "meanings." It is to turn *the* world into *this* world. ("This world"! As if there were any other.)

The world, our world, is depleted, impoverished enough. Away with all duplicates of it, until we again experience more immediately what we have.

5

In most modern instances, interpretation amounts to the philistine refusal to leave the work of art alone. Real art has the capacity to make us nervous. By reducing the work of art to its content and then interpreting *that,* one tames the work of art. Interpretation makes art manageable, conformable.

This philistinism of interpretation is more rife in literature than in any other art. For decades now, literary critics have understood it to be their task to translate the elements of the poem or play or novel or story into something else. Sometimes a writer will be so uneasy before the naked power of his art that he will install within the work itself—albeit with a little shyness, a touch of the good taste of irony—the clear and explicit interpretation of it. Thomas Mann is an example of such an over-cooperative author. In the case of more stubborn authors, the critic is only too happy to perform the job.

The work of Kafka, for example, has been subjected to a mass ravishment by no less than three armies of interpreters. Those who read Kafka as a social allegory see case studies of the frustrations and insanity of modern bureaucracy and its ultimate issuance in the totalitarian state. Those who read Kafka as a psychoanalytic allegory see desperate revelations of Kafka's fear of his father, his castration anxieties, his sense of his own impotence, his thralldom to his dreams. Those who read Kafka as a religious allegory explain that K. in *The Castle* is trying to gain access to heaven; that Joseph K. in *The Trial* is being judged by the inexorable and mysterious justice of God.... Another *oeuvre* that has attracted interpreters like leeches is that of Samuel Beckett. Beckett's delicate dramas of the withdrawn consciousness—pared down to essentials, cut off, often represented as physically immobilized—are read as a statement about modern man's alienation from meaning or from God; or as an allegory of psychopathology.

One could go on, citing author after author: Proust, Joyce, Faulkner, Rilke, Lawrence, Gide; the list is endless of those around whom thick encrustations of interpretation have taken hold. But it should be noted that interpretation is not simply the compliment that mediocrity pays to genius. It is, indeed, *the* modern way of understanding something, and is applied to works of every quality. Take, as a final example, the notes that Elia Kazan published on his production of *A Streetcar Named Desire*. In order to direct the play, Kazan had to discover that Stanley Kowalski represented the sensual and vengeful barbarism that was engulfing our culture, while Blanche Du Bois was Western civilization, poetry, delicate apparel, dim lighting, refined feelings and all, though a little the worse for wear to be sure. Tennessee Williams' forceful psychological melodrama now became intelligible: it was *about* something, about the decline of Western civilization. Apparently, were it to go on being a play about a voluptuous piece of rough trade named Stanley Kowalski and a faded mangy belle named Blanche Du Bois, it would not be manageable.

6

It doesn't matter whether artists intend, or don't intend, for their works to be interpreted. Perhaps Tennessee Williams thinks *Streetcar* is about what Kazan thinks it to be about. It may be that Cocteau in *The Blood of a Poet* and in *Orpheus* wanted the elaborate readings which have been given these films, in terms of Freudian symbolism and social critique. But the merit of these works certainly lies elsewhere than in their "meanings." Indeed, it is precisely to the extent that Williams' plays and Cocteau's films do suggest these portentous meanings that they are defective, false, contrived, lacking in conviction.

From interviews, it appears that Resnais and Robbe-Grillet consciously designed *Last Year at Marienbad* as a toy for multiple interpretations. But it is just those elements of *Marienbad* which make complex interpretation plausible that are weak. What succeeds artistically in *Marienbad* is the pure, untranslatable, sensuous immediacy of some of its images.

Again, Ingmar Bergman may have meant the tank rumbling down the empty night street in *The Silence* as a phallic symbol. But if he did, it was a foolish thought. ("Never trust the teller, trust the tale," said Lawrence.) Taken as a brute object, as an immediate sensory equivalent for the mysterious abrupt armored happenings going on inside the hotel, that sequence with the tank is the most striking moment in the film. Those who reach for a Freudian interpretation of the tank are only expressing their lack of response to what is there on the screen.

It is always the case that interpretation of this type indicates a dissatisfaction (conscious or unconscious) with the work, a wish to replace it by something else.

Interpretation, based on the highly dubious theory that a work of art is composed of items of content, violates art. It makes art into an article for use, for arrangement into a mental scheme of categories.

7

Interpretation does not, of course, always prevail. In fact, a great deal of today's art may be understood as motivated by a flight from interpretation. To avoid interpretation, art may become parody. Or it may become abstract. Or it may become ("merely") decorative. Or it may become non-art.

The flight from interpretation seems particularly a feature of modern painting. Abstract painting is the attempt to have, in the ordinary sense, no content;

since there is no content, there can be no interpretation. Pop Art works by the opposite means to the same result; using a content so blatant, so "what it is," it, too, ends by being uninterpretible.

A great deal of modern poetry, too, starting from the great experiments of French poetry (including the movement that is misleadingly called Symbolist) to put silence into poems and to reinstate the *magic* of the word, has escaped from the rough grip of interpretation. The most recent revolution in contemporary taste in poetry—the revolution that has deposed Eliot and elevated Pound—represents a turning away from content in poetry in the old sense, an impatience with what made modern poetry prey to the zeal of interpreters.

I am speaking mainly of the situation in America, of course. Interpretation runs rampant here in those arts with a feeble and negligible avant garde: fiction and the drama. Most American novelists and playwrights are really either journalists or gentlemen sociologists and psychologists. They are writing the literary equivalent of program music. And so rudimentary, uninspired, and stagnant has been the sense of what might be done with *form* in fiction and drama that even when the content isn't simply information, news, it is still peculiarly visible, handier, more exposed. To the extent that novels and plays (in America), unlike poetry and painting and music, don't reflect any interesting concern with changes in their form, these arts remain prone to assault by interpretation.

But avant-gardism—which has meant, mostly, experiments with form at the expense of content—is not the only defense against the infestation of art by interpretations. At least, I hope not. For this would be to commit art to being perpetually on the run. (It also perpetuates the very distinction between form and content which is, ultimately, an illusion.) Ideally, it is possible to elude the interpreters in another way, by making works of art whose surface is so unified and clean, whose momentum is so rapid, whose address is so direct that the work can be … just what it is. Is this possible now? It does happen in films, I believe. This is why cinema is the most alive, the most exciting, the most important of all art forms right now. Perhaps the way one tells that a particular art form is most alive is that it gives a wide latitude for making mistakes in it, and still being good. Thus, many of the films of Bergman and Fellini—though crammed with lame messages about the modern spirit, thereby inviting interpretations—still triumph over the pretentious intentions of their directors. In *Winter Light* and *The Silence*, and in *8½*, the beauty and visual sophistication of the images subverts before our eyes the callow pseudo-intellectuality of the story and some of the dialogue. (The most remarkable example of this sort of discrepancy is the work of one of the greatest of all directors, D. W. Griffith.) In the very best films, there is always a directness that entirely frees us from the itch to interpret. Many old Hollywood films, like *The Maltese Falcon* and countless others, have this wonderful, positively anti-symbolic quality, no less than the best work of the new European directors, like Truffaut's *Four Hundred Blows, Shoot the Piano Player,* and *Jules and Jim*; Godard's *Breathless* and

Vivre Sa Vie; Antonioni's *Le Amiche* and *L'Avventura*; and Olmi's *Il Posto* and *The Fiancés*.

The fact that films have not been over-run by interpreters is in part due simply to the newness of cinema as an art. It also owes to the happy accident that films for such a long time were just movies; in other words, that they were understood to be part of mass, as opposed to high, culture, and were left alone by most people with minds. Then, too, there is always something other than content in the cinema to grab hold of, for those who want to analyze. For the cinema, unlike the novel, possesses a crude equivalent of a vocabulary of forms—the explicit, complex, and discussable technology of camera movements, cutting, montage, and so forth that go into the making of a film.

8

What kind of criticism, of commentary on the arts, is desirable today? For I'm not saying that works of art are ineffable, that they can't be described or paraphrased. They can be. The question is how. What would criticism look like that would serve the work of art, not usurp its place?

What is needed, first, is more attention to form in art. If excessive stress on *content* provokes the arrogance of interpretation, more extended and more thorough descriptions of *form* would silence. What is needed is a vocabulary—a descriptive, rather than prescriptive, vocabulary—for forms.[1] The best criticism, and it's uncommon, is of this sort that dissolves considerations of content into those of form. On film, drama, and painting respectively, I can think of Erwin Panofsky's essay, "Style and Medium in the Motion Pictures," Northrup Frye's essay "A Conspectus of Dramatic Genres," Pierre Francastel's essay "The Destruction of a Plastic Space." An example of formal analysis applied to the work of a single author is Roland Barthes' brilliant book, *Sur Racine*. (The best essays in Eric Auerbach's *Mimesis*, like "The Scar of Odysseus," are also of this type.) An example of formal analysis applied simultaneously to genre and author is Walter Benjamin's great essay, "The Story Teller: Reflections on the Works of Nicolai Leskov."

Equally valuable would be acts of criticism which would give us a more really accurate, sharp, loving description of the appearance of a work of art. This seems even harder to do than formal analysis. Some of Manny Farber's film criticism, Dorothy Van Ghent's essay "The Dickens World: A View from Todgers'," Randall Jarrell's essay on Walt Whitman are among the rare examples of what I mean. These are essays which reveal the sensuous surface of art without mucking about in it.

9

Transparence is the highest, most liberating value in art—and in criticism—today. Transparence means experiencing the luminousness of the thing in itself, of things being what they are. This is the greatness of, for example, the films of Bresson and Renoir and Truffaut and Godard.

Once upon a time (say, for Dante), it must have been a revolutionary and creative move to design works of art so that they might be experienced on several levels. Now it is not. It reinforces the principle of redundancy that is the principal affliction of modern life.

Once upon a time (a time when high art was scarce), it must have been a revolutionary and creative move to interpret works of art. Now it is not. What we decidedly do not need now is further to assimilate Art into Thought, or (worse yet) Art into Culture.

Interpretation takes the sensory experience of the work of art for granted, and proceeds from there. This cannot be taken for granted, now. Think of the sheer multiplication of works of art available to every one of us, superadded to the conflicting tastes and odors and sights of the urban environment that bombard our senses. Ours is a culture based on excess, on overproduction; the result is a steady loss of sharpness in our sensory experience. All the conditions of modern life—its material plenitude, its sheer crowdedness—conjoin to dull our sensory faculties. And it is in the light of the condition of our senses, our capacities (rather than those of another age) that the task of the critic, the commentator on art must be assessed.

What is important now is to recover our senses. We must learn to *see* more, to *hear* more, to *feel* more.

Our problem is not to find the maximum amount of content in a work of art, much less to squeeze more content out of the work than is already there. Our problem is to cut back content so that we can see the thing at all.

The aim of all commentary on art now should be to make works of art— and, by analogy, our own experience—more, rather than less, real to us. The function of criticism should be to show *how it is what it is*, even *that it is what it is*, rather than to show *what it means*.

10

In place of a hermeneutics we need an erotics of art.

Note

1. One of the difficulties is that our idea of form is spatial (the Greek metaphors for form are all derived from notions of space). This is why we have a more ready vocabulary of forms for the spatial than for the temporal arts. The exception among the temporal arts, of course, is the drama; perhaps this is because the drama is a narrative (i.e. temporal) form that extends itself visually and pictorially, upon a stage .... What we don't have yet is a poetics of the novel, any clear notion of the forms of narration. Perhaps film criticism will be the occasion of a breakthrough here, since films are primarily a visual form, yet they are also a new mode of the drama.

IV
The Cold War

21
Paul Goodman (1911–1972)
To Young Resisters (1949)

Editor's Introduction

Paul Goodman was born in New York City and raised by his bohemian mother and aunts. He graduated from City College in 1931 and received his Ph.D. from the University of Chicago in literature in 1954. While a graduate student and instructor in English at Chicago, he lost his job as a result of homosexual activities. Early in life he worked primarily as a novelist and poet, while later he wrote essays on anarchism, pacifism and human development. On the latter subject he wrote his most famous book, *Growing Up Absurd* (1960), about the difficulty of adolescence in a conformist and repressive society. A bisexual who lived with his common-law wife for decades, Goodman willingly transgressed the sexual ethics of the period, which made even some of his politically radical friends uncomfortable.

Like Dwight Macdonald, whose *politics* he wrote for, Goodman was creative, morally principled and outspoken. But more of an artist than Macdonald, who was essentially a critic, Goodman more closely approximated the literary vision and conscience of Thoreau. Like the Concord philosopher, Goodman also wrote perceptively about the interaction between towns and their surroundings, about material culture and technology, about the duty to remain true to one's convictions in the face of widespread opposition, and about the need to oppose wars. In Goodman's advice to draft resisters one hears echoes of Thoreau's opposition to the Mexican War and his refusal to pay taxes for it.

Goodman, even more than Dwight Macdonald, had one foot in the Old Left of the New York Intellectuals and the other foot in the moralistic, anti-technological, antiwar idealism of the 1960s New Left. He wrote for *Partisan Review* in the 1940s and *Dissent* in the 1950s, both headquarters of the Old Left. But in Goodman's 1949 advice to draft resisters, in his willingness to enlarge gender categories publicly, and in his opposition to the conformist Cold War American society in *Growing Up Absurd*, one finds the roots of the New Left values. Yet, by 1969, Goodman believed that the New Left had abandoned politics for a utopian future. "I had imagined," he wrote, "that the worldwide student protest had to do with changing political and moral institutions, to which I was sympathetic, but I now saw that we had to do with a religious crisis of the magnitude of the Reformation in the fifteen-hundreds." Alienation and religion, he acknowledged, were useful in prompting unrest and "new sacraments to give life meaning. But it is a poor basis for politics, including revolutionary politics." (Paul Goodman, "The New Reformation," in Irving Howe, ed., *Beyond the New Left* (New York: McCall Publishing, 1970), 86–87, 89.

Source

Paul Goodman, "To Young Resisters," *Resistance* vol. 7, no. 4, March 1949.

Selected Readings

Paul Goodman, *Drawing the Line: The Political Essays of Paul Goodman*, ed. Taylor Stoehr (New York: Free Life Editions, 1977).
Percival and Paul Goodman, *Communitas: Means of Livelihood, Ways of Life* (New York: Columbia University Press, 1990).
Peter Parisi, ed., *Artist of the Actual: Essays on Paul Goodman* (Metuchen, NJ: Scarecrow Press, 1986).
Kingsley Widmer, *Paul Goodman* (Boston: Twayne, 1980).

* * * * *

Dear friends,
Let me make a few personal remarks to you young men in the throes of deciding *how* to resist the war and the draft. (That we must resist them is not in question.) A friend of mine has just again been put in jail for avowed nonregistration, and I am concerned about you others who are likewise set on "enlisting in jail," as it seems to me—as if you approved more highly of penal institutions than of the army. I have heard the arguments for such public affirmation of principle, but they do not strike home to me. Now the alternative modes of resistance are devious and flexible and do not thrive on publicity. What I say here is not about the alternatives, nor about any objective political or historical advantages or disadvantages; it is addressed to you personally. You may find these remarks presumptuous and offensive, but I do not have the right not to proffer them. I am ashamed to have to discuss in a newspaper, however, what should be discussed individually.

You are set on willingly accepting heavy penalties because of principle. Most of you, I think, do not have the right to hold such hard principles nor willingly to accept such heavy penalties. Right principles are the statements of deep impulses, intuitions, insights into our underlying natures; they come from deeper than our ordinary practice, and therefore we conform our practice to principles to help us realize our deeper natures. Now young men like yourselves have not had the chance to mature and test the principles to live by. It is only independent accomplishment that tests one's principles (the test is, "are they working in me?")—you have not had the time to accomplish enough of your own. What you take to be your principles are largely borrowed ideas, or the expression of various passionate attitudes towards your elders and teachers, or at best the fruit of reasoning. Excuse me, these are harsh sentences, but you will agree it is not a sweet subject.

On the other hand, willingly accepting heavy penalties, *you are violating your primary duty as young people: to seek for animal and social satisfactions and to plunge with youthful enthusiasm into work interesting to you.* You do not have the right to postpone these satisfactions and explorations. To the extent that the State or anything else tries to make you postpone them, you must fight for them by force, cunning, recalcitrance, camouflage, playing dead, flight, etc., like any other healthy creatures we observe in nature.

Again, you prematurely assume a public role. In your "principles" there is always, is there not, a guess at a certain public expectation of you: what people think of you and by reflection what you therefore think of yourselves. This public opinion is disastrous: it gives you a false assurety of rightness and courage when your hearts are really torn by doubt and fear. In general, when in doubt the wise course is delay, avoidance, not to have to make a commitment on the doubtful issue; but on the contrary, to throw oneself all the more into good activities that are not at all doubtful, one's life-work, or love, or the quest for them. Now what is the case at present? The vast States of the entire world are embarked on obvious folly, long proved calamitous to mankind. This we must resist. But how possibly can untried young citizens know with inner conviction how to cope with such colossal problems? You do not know; you know you must resist (this a child can grasp) but you do not know how; therefore, to avoid the tension, you embrace "principles" that give you a public picture of yourselves, that let you know what is expected of you as resisters. Then you throw yourselves in jails as sacrifices. No no, go softly; since you are torn by doubt, first rather exhaust every possibility of delay, avoidance, non-commitment; and meanwhile, to relieve the tension, throw yourselves fervently into what you are sure of, interesting work, sociality, love. *It is not necessary for you to be verbally consistent as yet: do not allow yourselves to be public figures. Your own kind of consistency can only emerge with experience and accomplishment; your public force will exert itself with the realization of your inward powers.* Therefore, loosely follow every positive impulse, avoid cooperating with obvious stupidity and evil, and postpone other issues. Have the courage to say to yourselves, "I don't know; I am afraid."

The penalties you think of willingly accepting are disproportionate to your actions as yet; you do not have the right to them. If a young man is a fiery revolutionary, a great champion, then such heavy penalties (one, three, five years in jail) have a certain fitness and beauty: he is a grave offender, a great champion, he runs great dangers, he suffers grave penalties. But most of you have so far done little, you have struck only weak blows for freedom against stupidity and authority. When you are penalized, the feeling is not noble, but ugly: a sense of pity for you, a sense of insensate cruelty of the oppressor. To give color and proportion to its blind fury, the State's attorney tries to elevate you into public enemies, symbols, examples. Do not lend yourselves to this convenient lie. *You are yourselves, not symbols. Your fact is that in our society there are horrible difficulties and obstacles, threats to your joy and creativity; this is your fact, act with your eyes on this.* Certainly there are deep causes underlying this fact, causes to be faced with principled behavior, the principles you live by and may die for as great champions, but you do not yet know them as your own. Do not let either your enemies or your friends prematurely assign "your" principles to you. Stubbornly work for the personal goods that you do know and desire, and your underlying principles will emerge: then will be the time to stand witness to principles.

I have been basing this personal argument on moral considerations of "rights"—your rights to hard principles, to accept punishment, to deserve such heavy penalties—because these considerations are obviously very important to you. I am passing by the considerations of practical effects—whether your mode or other modes of resistance would be most effective for peace—because I do not know how to estimate these quantities: it seems likely to me that the way of symbolic publicized witnessing and suffering fits more with the present character of people and therefore could have a wider superficial effect, but that the mode of fighting for real (millennial) satisfactions can effect a deeper change. But I cannot omit, finally, the most important matter of all, the state of your feelings.

In feeling, your position and your decision are enviable (I envy them); tho doubtful and fearful, you have occasion to be nearly bursting with pride and joy: and this is the wonderful flooding of life. For you can perform a definite act in a crisis, with justification: approved by your good conscience, cutting loose from the prudential ego that drags us down, and by-passing the animal desires that, as we are brought up, are freighted with guilt. Rarely indeed does the life we lead give us a moment of tears, dread, and glory! Then what kind of envious and spiteful moralist am I to try to dullen your definite act and tarnish your justification?

Good, I challenge you! You are prepared for jail and for worse (the history of other young men proves it). Is it not then just you who, not turning away from your resolution but going beyond it, is it not *just* you who can act with unexampled freedom, energy, and daring in our society that never sees these things and is hungry to be moved by them? Your crisis is the means of releasing wonderful powers of nature, because you have faced what is awful. (What is there now to fear; say lightly, "We are living on velvet!") To use these powers, releasing still new powers in yourselves and us, not in the infertile place of a jail, but in our general world productive of opportunities for life.

Whichever way, may you thrive in the creation of the heavens and the earth.

Paul Goodman

22
Irving Kristol (1920–)
"Civil Liberties," 1952—A Study in Confusion (1952)

Editor's Introduction

In the anxious decade following the end of World War II in 1945 there was considerable debate in American society about how dangerous foreign and domestic communism were to American safety. Figures such as Senator Joseph McCarthy and his aides rode to power by cynically manipulating public fear, but part of the public's anxiety—particularly about Soviet rather than domestic communism—was justified. In retrospect it is easy to dismiss some of the worry, but in the teeth of a totalitarian threat, particularly coming on the heels of the Nazi threat a decade earlier, who knew confidently what would happen without vigilance?

Within the New York Intellectuals during the McCarthy period in the early 1950s there were important differences along the ideological spectrum from left to right, and even small differences were extremely important to one's identity and political reputation. Consider where the *Partisan Review* group stood, politically. On the far left were communists, a tiny minority in the country although not such a tiny portion of New York City. Next on the spectrum was the left, with varieties of democratic socialists and left Democrats, and this is where *Dissent* stood, along with Irving Howe, Harold Rosenberg, Lewis Coser and others. Next was the center, made up of a mix of liberals and conservatives, Democrats and Republicans and here *Commentary* situated itself, along with Sidney Hook, Irving Kristol, Nathan Glazer and others. Further along was the right, peopled by Billy Graham, Joseph McCarthy (an especially irresponsible member of this group) and others. And finally there was the far right, the very most extreme of anti-government, anti-integration, anticommunist sentiment, including the John Birch Society.

When Irving Kristol wrote the essay below he was managing editor of *Commentary* magazine. During the McCarthy period, both *Commentary* and *Dissent* were strongly anticommunist, but because *Commentary's* position on the political spectrum was slightly closer to McCarthy's, the *Dissenters* castigated it for being insufficiently anti-McCarthy. In return, *Commentary* charged that the *Dissenters*, by being too far left, were too outside the American mainstream to be adequately anticommunist. Most simply, it was an argument within the

New York Intellectuals (and within the nation) about which was a greater danger to the country: domestic communists or McCarthy supporters. Those at *Commentary*, who found McCarthy distasteful but thought he might also be doing some good, knew that *Dissent* and the American left was not pro-Soviet, so they couldn't call them communists. Instead, the centrists at *Commentary* called the left anti-anticommunists, implying that the American left was against the strong anticommunism represented in American centrism. That is, the "anti-antis" were those such as the *Dissent*ers, or figures such as Henry Steele Commager or those at *The Nation*, who thought that both the Soviets and McCarthy were dangerous but that we should at least have some dialogue with the Soviet Union to prevent nuclear war.

In the essay below, Kristol scolded the *Dissenters*, those at *The Nation* and *The New Republic*, those Commagers and William O. Douglases who were so hard on McCarthy, it seemed to Kristol, that they were more concerned about maintaining a perfect record of civil liberties than actually fighting the domestic communists. "For there is one thing that the American people know about Senator McCarthy: he, like them, is unequivocally anti-Communist," Kristol wrote in his article. "About the spokesmen for American liberalism, they feel they know no such thing. And with some justification." It was a charge that the *Dissenters* and left liberals resented, and it was decades before Kristol's antagonists let him forget it. Those who believe it should have been easy to find a correct and comfortable position on McCarthy and communism in 1952 might have found a half century later that it was, in fact, no easier in their own conflicts.

Source

Irving Kristol, "'Civil Liberties,' 1952—A Study in Confusion," *Commentary* vol. 13, no. 3, March 1952.

Selected Readings

Henry Steele Commager, *Freedom, Loyalty, Dissent* (New York: Oxford University Press, 1954).
Sidney Hook, *Heresy Yes—Conspiracy No!* (New York, John Day, 1953).
Ellen Schrecker, *Many Are the Crimes* (Boston: Little, Brown, 1998).
Albert Fried, ed., *McCarthyism, the Great Scare: A Documentary History* (New York: Oxford University Press, 1997).

* * * * *

Do We Defend Our Rights by Protecting Communists?

Heard ye not lately of a man
That went beside his witt,

> And naked through the citty rann
> Wrapt in a frantique fiit?

The above tantalizing bit of 17th-century verse was quoted recently in the London *Times Literary Supplement,* in the same issue in which there appeared, elsewhere in its pages, a review of the English edition of Alan Barth's *The Loyalty of Free Men.* This fortuitous juxtaposition was not without its ironic relevance, Mr. Barth's book having been provoked by the "frantique fitt" of McCarthyism, beneath which he saw a cool and calculating assault on the American democracy, and his defense being couched in a cool and calculating eloquence that turns out, upon close examination, to be not nearly the exercise in pure reason it seems.

A close examination, however, Mr. Barth's book and others of its kind have not received. It was hardly to be expected from Senator McCarthy and his friends, who are less famous for their habits of meticulous reading than for their preference for arguing in the large, while the more scholarly sections of American opinion have been so delighted to see the Senator get his, and so soothed by the cadences of a familiar tone, that they have not so much read these books as permitted themselves to be enchanted by them. This enchantment has had its political sequel, for as a result of it there has been drawn a line of battle. On the one side are the men of intellect and sensibility, fair-minded and generous-hearted and confessedly not infallible: the Alan Barths, the Henry Steele Commagers, the Zechariah Chafees, the Howard Mumford Joneses, the Ralph Barton Perrys, the William O. Douglases, and, rather more tentatively committed, the Francis Biddles. On the other side are the mindless men, the kind who get elected to office when the spirit of the age reverts to primitivism, and who wish, under cover of fighting Communism, to squeeze the nation into a Know-Nothing straitjacket.

The line is drawn—and those liberals who have rallied to their positions on the left of it find themselves ever more pressed against the outer walls of the city. The ready quotations from Jefferson about the trees of liberty and the blood of tyrants, the sonorous repetition of Justice Holmes' dissenting opinions, the schoolmaster's measured accents alternating with prophetic indignation—the whole battery has failed significantly to make an impression on the dominant American mood. Senator McCarthy remains blithely on the offensive and his critics give ground before him. It is a most exasperating and melancholy situation for liberals to be in; yet in proportion as they fail in strength, they gain in their sense of petulant righteousness.

Is it conceivable that the line was incorrectly drawn in the first place? The liberals are loath to weigh the possibility lest it give comfort to the enemy; Senator McCarthy for his part has no cause for dissatisfaction with things as they are; but those of us who are the displaced persons of this war might reflect on this question to our advantage. Perhaps it is a calamitous error to believe that because a vulgar demagogue lashes out at both Communism and liberalism as identical, it is necessary to protect Communism in order to defend liberalism. This way of putting the matter will surely shock liberals, who are convinced that it is only they who truly understand Communism and who thoughtfully oppose it. They are nonetheless mistaken, and it is a mistake on which McCarthyism waxes fat. For there is one thing that the American people know about Senator McCarthy: he, like them, is unequivocally anti-Communist. About the spokesmen for American liberalism, they feel they know no such thing. And with some justification.

With what justification, can be seen from an illustrative incident involving Professor Henry Steele Commager, a distinguished historian who never was a Communist and never will be. In the May 1947 issue of *Harper's*, Professor Commager wrote a spirited article that began as follows:

"On May 6 a Russian-born girl, Mrs. Shura Lewis, gave a talk to the students of the Western High School of Washington, D. C. She talked about Russia—its school system, its public health program, the position of women, of the aged, of the workers, the farmers, and the professional classes—and compared, superficially and uncritically, some American and Russian institutions. ... Mrs. Lewis said nothing that had not been said a thousand times, in speeches, in newspapers, magazines and books. She said nothing that any normal person could find objectionable."

What greatly disturbed Professor Commager was that this inoffensive speech did give rise to a furor in Washington. Congressmen bellowed that our schools were being subverted, the principal of the school came forward with a humble apology, the superintendent of schools for the nation's capital swore it would never happen again, and the speech itself was reprinted (after some discussion of the wisdom of exposing the public to inflammation) in the Congressional Record as a horrible example. Professor Commager saw in this a reflection of an anti-Communist hysteria that threatened to engulf all civil liberties, and he pleaded earnestly that reason control the anti-Communist passion, lest we find ourselves saddled with an anti-Communist orthodoxy no less reprehensible than the Communist one. His article was hailed as a kind of liberal manifesto, and was reprinted—alongside John Stuart Mill and John Milton—in Howard Mumford Jones' *Primer of Intellectual Freedom* (1949). Evil won a transient victory in the seats of power and Good won a permanent niche in the anthologies—a familiar tale.

Familiar, that is, until one goes to the Congressional Record and reads through this speech that no "normal person could find objectionable." Mrs. Lewis' English was broken, but her sentiments were whole:

"They call it collective farm—the peasants farm and divide up products according to work put in by each individual during the years. As a result of planning, unemployment is completely wiped out. ...

"In Russia right now people absolutely do not worry about today or tomorrow. They never think 'All of a sudden I lose a job.' That fear doesn't exist among Russian people. ...

"No matter where you live you have to work. What the Russian people have, they are more secure about this. They work. They need not worry much about losing the job. They are free to travel from one place to another, and each person must work 25 years for after that he is able to get a pension. No matter where you work—in this plant or another, 25 years and then you get 50% of your salary and live the rest of your life. ...

"I never appreciated the life in Russia until I live here. Here you have to work hard in order to live, use all your courage not to die. ...

"I read all the papers here and occasionally I go to the Library of Congress and read all papers printed in Moscow. It is very interesting, and when I read these papers always you can see here evidence of press where people talk all the time about having a war, to throw the atomic bomb on Russia, to destroy because they have a system which is very prideful. At the present time Russians are busy to restore all those houses, all those cities, all those towns. Russian people make streets, plants, produce new style of shoes, new fashion of dress, new production, and never they talk about having a war."

The echoes this awakened in Congress may have been exaggerated, but they were not factitious or beside the point. Obviously, Professor Commager can argue that it will not harm American school children to encounter an occasional Communist apologist in the flesh; one may even go further and say it would do them good. However, in the first place, Mrs. Lewis was not introduced as a Communist apologist but as an informed reporter, and, in the second place, everything she said should have been objectionable to every normal person, and especially to a historian like Professor Commager—for the good and sufficient reason that it was a tissue of lies. For Professor Commager to defend the rights of Communists to free speech is one thing, for him to assert that there is nothing objectionable in mendacious pleading in support of Communism is quite another. The conclusion "any normal person" will draw from such behavior is that, for whatever reason, his critical faculties are less alert when he looks out of the left corner of his eye.

Indeed, the heart of the matter is exactly that he looks at Communism out of the *left* corner of his eye. Professor Commager seems to be seduced by the insidious myth according to which Communism is a political trend continuous with liberalism and democratic socialism, only more impatient and inclined to the fanatical, only more "radical" than its companions who are not quite so "left." It is a myth that Senator McCarthy, for his own ends, is happy to accept, since it allows him to tag a New Dealer as being by nature an embryonic Communist. Neither the Professor nor the Senator is concerned to see that the antithesis of 'left" and "right" no longer suits the political realities; that measured by the ideals of the French or even Russian Revolution, Communism today is as counter-revolutionary as Louis XVI or Kolchak ever was; that if one wishes to defend the civil liberties of Communists (as the Senator does not), one must do so on the same grounds that one defends the civil liberties of Nazis and fascists—no more, no less.

Professor Commager might retort that he knows all this full well, and that he is for civil liberties for everyone, fascist, Communist, or what-have-you. But if a Nazi had, in 1938, addressed a high-school audience in this country, extolling the accomplishments of Hitler's regime, presenting a thoroughly fictitious account of life in Nazi Germany, never once mentioning the existence of concentration camps—would Professor Commager find in such a speech "nothing that any normal person could find objectionable"? It is doubtless an injustice to him even to conceive of the possibility.

This notion of Communism as "left" and therefore at an opposite pole from fascism, which is "right," appears to have become intrinsic to the liberal outlook. It is imbedded in the meretricious historical analogies, in the rolling phrases about "the forces of freedom and those of fear," beneath which there lies the gross metaphysic of the liberal Manichee, apportioning the universe to "forward-looking" and "backward-looking" demiurges. It helps explain how Professor Commager can permit himself to write: "After all, it is no accident that the nations dedicated to freedom won the two great wars of the 20th century and those committed to totalitarianism went under"—when it is not only no accident, it is not even a fact. The same notion is evidenced in Zechariah Chafee's explanation (in his essay in the recent symposium *Civil Liberties Under Attack)* of the origin of Communist fronts: "It is inevitable that the membership of organizations formed to bring about change should include some persons who want a great deal of change"—as if Professor Chafee and the Communists were agreed on the direction of the change, quarreling only over the measure. It is the presupposition from which Ralph Barton Perry (in his new book *The Citizen Decides)* can deduce that Communism is "democratic" by virtue of being a revolt of the "masses" against the "classes," that the Soviet regime is a government "for the people with the consent of the people" though not by the people, and that the Chinese Communist leaders are "hostages" of a popular revolution.

Moreover, after staring out of the left corner of the eye for any length of time, there comes an irrepressible inclination to wink. How else explain, for instance, the attitude Alan Barth takes toward the Hiss-Chambers affair? He can begin a sentence: "Insofar as Chambers may be credited with having told the truth. ..."; or: "whatever the guilt of Alger Hiss and whatever the utility of exposing it and punishing it a decade later. ..." About Whittaker Chambers and the Communist "informer" in general, he is no longer judiciously bland but is knowingly tart: "The ex-Communists, conscious of their betrayal of American values, wanted the comfort of company; they had to show that many others, even many who were highly respected, had been as recreant as they." In other words, Chambers in telling the truth is a man of malice, Hiss in denying it is his defenseless victim. Hiss's guilt is problematic and, in any case, not important; Chambers' wickedness is certain.

On Owen Lattimore, there is liberal unanimity: he got a raw deal. Professor Commager believes (in his contribution to *Civil Liberties Under Attack*) that the attack on Lattimore was an attack on "independence and non-conformity." Professor Chafee laments: "Owen Lattimore did his own thinking and look how his services were appreciated." Alan Barth is casually positive: "Dr. Lattimore's ordeal was, of course, only the most spectacular instance of legislative punishment of teachers for expressing their opinions." About the worst that can be said for such arrant nonsense is that it is uttered in all sincerity. For the incontrovertible facts of the case are, "of course," that Owen Lattimore did *not* do his own thinking; that his "ordeal" was the public demonstration of this fact; that he was a faithful and enormously influential fellow-traveler who for more than a decade followed the Communist line as if magnetized by it, including a docile zig-zag during the Stalin-Hitler pact. Is it really no legitimate concern of Congress that such a man was appointed advisor to Chiang Kaishek, that he accompanied Vice-President Wallace during his tour of Asia, that he was admired and listened to by important people in the State Department?

In his denunciation of Lattimore's pro-Communist record and in hurling unsubstantiated charges against him (chief of Soviet espionage, etc.), Senator McCarthy may well have been aiming a blow against independence of mind and nonconformity of spirit. For Messrs. Commager, Barth, and Chafee to defend Lattimore's pro-Communist record in order to defend such independence and nonconformity, is for them to play the Senator's game, on the losing side.

It is equally futile for liberals to try to match Senator McCarthy's irresponsible declamations with a crafty rhetoric of their own, especially when this rhetoric, while not designedly pro-Communist, is compelled by the logic of disingenuousness and special pleading to become so in effect. The need for disingenuousness arises out of a refusal to see Communism for what it is: a movement guided by conspiracy and aiming at totalitarianism, rather than merely another form of "dissent" or "nonconformity." Hence the liberal argument runs askew of reality and must clothe itself with neat obfuscation.

Once again, Professor Commager obliges with a superior specimen:

> The House Un-American Activities Committee has launched an attack on the Lawyers' Guild as a pro-Communist or "subversive" organization. The chief basis for this attack is, as far as we know, that the Guild has proffered its services to the defense of Communists under indictment for violation of the Smith Act. We need not inquire into the accuracy of this charge or into the degree of zeal displayed by the Lawyers' Guild. Let us ask rather what are the logical conclusions to be drawn by the position which the House Committee has adopted? They are two:

that certain criminals are so despicable that they are not entitled to counsel, and that a lawyer who defends a criminal is himself sympathetic to crime.

That phrase in the second sentence, "as far as we know," is curious. It implies strongly that the only conceivable explanation of the Committee's attitude is the action of the Guild in providing lawyers to defend indicted Communists, and that there is no public information which gives plausibility to the Committee's belief that the Guild is a "front" organization, controlled and run by Communists. On the contrary, however, "as far as we know," and we know much further than Professor Commager suggests, the Lawyers' Guild is a Communist creation that, as A. A. Berle stated when he resigned from it in 1940, "is not prepared to take any stand which conflicts with the Communist party line." Moreover, the House Committee on Un-American Activities has collected and published sufficient evidence to demonstrate this beyond cavil—which leads one to think that if Professor Commager spent nearly as much time reading the records of Congressional hearings as he does denouncing them, we should all be better off.

The entire third sentence is even more curious: "We need not inquire into the accuracy of this charge or into the degree of zeal displayed by the Lawyers' Guild." If we take "zeal" to mean pro-Communism (in the context, that is all it can mean), then the degree of this zeal and the accuracy of the charge of pro-Communism are precisely what we *do* need to inquire into. How can we know whether to sanction or condemn the Committee's investigation of the Guild as a pro-Communist organization unless we make an effort to find out if the Guild is or is not, in fact, a pro-Communist organization? Even Professor Commager surreptitiously ignores his own disclaimer, as the last two sentences of his paragraph show. Obviously, the two "logical conclusions" flow, not from the Committee's premise, but his own: namely, that the Lawyers' Guild is neither pro-Communist nor subversive. From the Committee's own premise, quite other logical conclusions may be inferred—one of them being that the Committee is engaged in showing up Communist fronts for what they are. Professor Commager's "logic" is a sleight-of-hand whereby premises that are prejudiced in favor of the Communist interpretation of affairs are made to pass for natural conclusions.

In the same vein, there is a liberal rhetoric of insinuation that works under cover of a high moral posture. Its net effect is to give a backhanded credence to the Communist assertion that it is impossible to oppose Communism vigorously without walking into the arms of Black Reaction. It is the kind of thing represented in the following observation of Alan Barth's:

In the New York trial of eleven Communist Party leaders in 1949, a number of FBI undercover operatives who had joined the party appeared as prosecution witnesses. How widely such agents have been dispersed in labor unions, in lawful voluntary associations, and in political groups is a matter of mere conjecture. But it is certainly a matter of legitimate concern to Americans who care about preservation of the traditional rights of privacy.

A noble sentiment, and the unwary reader assents—who is against the right to privacy, and who is not prepared to be concerned with its violation? Only the exceptionally attentive will note that the supposed threat to "the traditional rights of privacy" is "a matter of mere conjecture." Whose conjecture? We are not told. Is there any ground for such a conjecture? We are not told that either. Is Mr. Barth against the use of undercover agents in principle? He does not say so. Is he against the use of undercover agents in Communist organizations? He does not say this, either. He would seem to be against dispersing FBI agents in bona fide labor unions, lawful voluntary associations, and political groups, and reminds us of the consequences. But who is for it? The answer, which he does not bother to give, is: nobody—and that is why the FBI is doing no such thing and why the whole business is a "matter of mere conjecture." In the course of Mr. Barth's innuendoes, however, the onus has been neatly shifted from the Communist conspirators to the FBI agents who identified them.

The same technique of persuasion is at work in such a statement as this one by Professor Commager: "It will be useful to determine, a generation from now, whether those universities that have purged their faculties are actually stronger than they were before the purges occurred—stronger in those essentials that go to make a university." This has about it so trembling an air of bitter-sweet wisdom that it seems positively boorish to ask: just which universities would Professor Commager describe as "purged"? Surely Columbia is not one of them, for Professor Commager is not the kind of man who would retain his post on a "purged" faculty. Is it Yale? Princeton? Harvard? University of Chicago? The list could be extended indefinitely, and never provoke an affirmative response, for there is not a single university in the United States that can be said to have been, in any meaningful sense of the word, "purged." There has been no more than a handful of cases where Communist college teachers have been dismissed, and less than a handful of cases where non-Communists have been unjustly fired as "Reds." To call this a "purge"—even regardless of whether or not one thinks Communists have a right to teach in colleges—is to echo Communist propaganda.

Perhaps Professor Commager had in mind the University of California, where several dozen (out of a total of more than a thousand) teachers found the idea of a special loyalty oath—the content of which was irrelevant to their action—so offensive and intolerable that they exercised their constitutional right to refuse to swear it, and consequently had to seek other employment. Granting that the notion of a special oath for teachers is obnoxious, and even conceding that this minority was correct and courageous in its particular reaction to it—is it the part of sobriety to insist, as Professor Commager goes on to do, that the philosophy behind the actions of California's Board of Trustees does not differ "in any essentials" from the philosophy behind the totalitarian control of university teaching? One swallow does not make a spring, or one injustice an apocalypse.

Despite their fondness for clichés of Communist manufacture, all these liberal spokesmen are sincerely anti-Communist—otherwise, what they have to say would be of little interest to anyone. But their rejection of Communism has all the semblance of a preliminary gesture, a repudiation aiming to linger in the memory as a floating credential. It has little relation to all the ensuing scenes of the political drama, where bad conscience and stubborn pride join to guide the liberal through his role.

Did not the major segment of American liberalism, as a result of joining hands with the Communists in a Popular Front, go on record as denying the existence of Soviet concentration camps? Did it not give its blessing to the "liquidation" of millions of Soviet "kulaks"? Did it not apologize for the mass purges of 1936–38, and did it not solemnly approve the grotesque trials of the Old Bolsheviks? Did it not applaud the massacre of the non-Communist left by the GPU during the Spanish Civil War? All this carries no weight with Alan Barth who knows that, though a man repeat the Big Lie, so long as he is of a liberal intention he is saved. On the participation of non-Communists in Communist fronts during the 30's, he writes: "In the main, their participation, while it lasted, was not only innocent but *altogether* praiseworthy." (My italics.)

Even Francis Biddle, who is generally cautious, remarks in his book *The Fear of Freedom*: "What makes an organization subversive? If a vast majority of its members are Communists but its conduct has always been exemplary, advocating desirable social reforms which Communists usually back, it can hardly fit the description."

One surmises that Mr. Biddle is not really so politically naive as this statement, on the face of it, would lead one to believe. He must know what it means to be "subversive," since it was he who, as Attorney General, sent eighteen members of a minuscule Trotskyist sect to jail in 1942 for being just that; he must know how Communists work, how front organizations act as an ancillary to the Communist party apparatus, since this is a matter of common knowledge and Mr. Biddle is uncommonly literate and intelligent. No, it was no elevated unsophistication that urged him on, but rather a sense of shame and a cowardliness to confess that shame. Mr. Biddle, like Mr. Barth, refuses to admit what is now apparent: that a generation of earnest reformers who helped give this country a New Deal should find themselves in retrospect stained with the guilt of having lent aid and comfort to Stalinist tyranny. This is, to be sure, a truth of hindsight, an easy truth. But it is the truth nonetheless, and might as well be owned up to. If American liberalism is not willing to discriminate between its achievements and its sins, it only disarms itself before Senator McCarthy, who is eager to have it appear that its achievements *are* its sins.

There is a false pride, by which liberals persuade themselves that no matter what association a man has had with a Communist enterprise, he is absolutely guiltless of the crimes that Communism has committed so long as he was moved to this association by a generous idealism. There is a political mythology, by which liberals locate Communism over on the "left," in a zone exempt from the unsparing verdict directed against the totalitarian "right." There is also a fear, a fear that the American democracy in an excess of anti-Communism will gather its abundant energy into a wave of "conformism" that will drown all free thought. This pride, this mythology, this fear all unite for a liberal prejudgment of issues (e.g., the cases of Alger Hiss, Owen Lattimore, William Remington, Harry Dexter White) which is not easy to explain on a purely rational view. It is what stimulates a flood of irrelevant and gaudy prose about loyalty in the abstract ("like love it must be given freely," etc.) while it shuns a careful discussion of Communist disloyalty in the concrete.

Of the three factors, the fear of "conformism" or "orthodoxy" is probably the most influential in its appeal, for it is founded in some degree on objective fact. Alexis de Tocqueville and John Stuart Mill, both friendly critics of the egalitarian trend, pointed out long ago that in every democratic society there is an inherent tendency toward a "despotism of public opinion"; where the majority makes the laws, it may also wish—especially in feverish and unsettled times—to make opinion, lauding the popular and extirpating the unpopular. In America, where the people are more powerful than elsewhere, and where there is, too, a significant tradition of vigilante-ism, the danger of a despotism of public opinion is proportionately greater. When the State Department is forced to suspend an exhibition abroad of modern American art because some Congressmen denounce it as "Communistic," the danger of such a despotism seems more than academic, and many otherwise sensible people are led to reprehend any attempt to unveil Communist activities or Communist beliefs as a malignant form of "punishment by publicity," which will soon be extended to all opinions that illiterate and narrow-minded Congressmen detest.

What these people do not see is that Communism, because it is a conspiratorial movement, has not the faintest interest in any genuine resistance to the despotism of public opinion. These martyrs whose testament is—"I refuse to answer on the grounds that it might incriminate me"! These "intellectuals" of Hollywood and radio who are outraged at a Congressman's insistence that they say what they actually believe, and who wail that they are in danger of—being excluded from well-paying jobs! Is this the vibrant voice of "nonconformity" and "dissent"? Are these the American rebels of today? Oddly enough, the majority of American liberals seem to think so: they have been moved to indignation by the questions, but never moved to disgust by the answers. Presumably, this is what they think a dissenter looks like, and no sadder commentary is possible on the corruption they have inflicted on themselves. And not only on themselves—for this image of a dissenter happens to coincide with the image held by Joseph McCarthy and Pat McCarran, for whom the dissenter is *per se* a scheming subversive. No greater spur to the despotism of public opinion can be imagined than this identification of free thought with underground conspiracy.

There is only one way the despotism of public opinion can be resisted. That is for a person with unpopular views to express himself, loudly, brazenly, stubbornly, in disregard of the consequences. Such a person may have to suffer for his convictions, as others have suffered before him, and as others will suffer after. But the responsibility for the mind's freedom in a democracy lies with the intransigent thinker, with his courage to shout the truth in the face of the mob, with his faith that truth will win out, and with his maddening commitment to the truth, win or lose. Yet, during all the occasions of the past several years, not a single liberal voice was to say to these strange "victims": "Speak up and damn the consequences! Let them take your job—as they certainly will anyway; tell the truth—you have nothing to lose and honor to gain!" Instead, there were erudite essays on the "right to a job" that would have corroborated William James in his mournful conviction that "the prevalent fear of poverty among our educated classes is the worst moral disease from which our civilization suffers."

Still, unworthy as these "victims" are, may they not, despite themselves, represent the right of the individual to hold whatever opinions he pleases without having to give a public accounting of them? Even if these Communists and Communist sympathizers are despicable, don't they have the right to believe privately anything they please? This is the way the question is frequently put, and it reveals a total misapprehension as to what Communism really is.

Communism is an idea, beyond question. Indeed, it is an Idea, and it is of the essence of this Idea that it is also a conspiracy to subvert every social and political order it does not dominate. It is, furthermore, an Idea that has ceased to have any intellectual status but has become incarnate in the Soviet Union and the official Communist parties, to whose infallible directives unflinching devotion is owed. A person who is captive to this Idea can, at any time, in any place, be called upon to do whatever the Idea, i.e., the Party, thinks necessary. Since this is so, it is of considerably more than private interest if a person is held by the Idea—he is, all appearances to the contrary, a person with different loyalties, and with different canons of scrupulousness, from ours. To grant him an "immunity by silence" is to concede the right to conspiracy, a concession no government ever has made or ever will make.

This sounds exaggerated, as it must, being so foreign to the nature of American political experience. Many of us have known Communists, and most of them conveyed no impression of being conspirators. But then, some of us have known Nazis too, and they conveyed no immediate association with gas chambers. It is quite impossible to judge a political movement by the personality of an individual member. Roosevelt certainly didn't see in Stalin any symptoms of blood lust. Hermann Goering in jail struck one as a clever clown. And there are still plenty of people who can't believe that Alger Hiss ever did any such thing.

No doubt there are some present members of the Communist party who would, in a showdown, break free of the Idea and rally to the democratic cause. Unfortunately, we have no way of knowing who they are. No doubt there are some present members and fellow-travelers of the Communist party who would sooner or later get disillusioned with Communism if they were permitted to hold down their present jobs as teachers, civil service workers, etc., whereas they are likely to harden in the face of persecution. Unfortunately, it is quite as impossible to tell the citizens of Oshkosh, some of whom have suffered personal loss as a result of the war in Korea, that there is no harm in having their children taught the three R's by a Communist, as it would have been to persuade the citizens of Flatbush in 1939 that there was no cause for excitement in their children being taught by a Nazi, or to convince a businessman that it is smart practice for him to pay a handsome salary to someone pledged to his "liquidation." No doubt some of these people became Communists after having suffered during the depression, or during a labor conflict, or as a result of race prejudice, and society must bear its share of the blame. Unfortunately, as Fitzjames Stephens remarked many decades ago: "It does not follow that because society caused a fault it is not to punish it. A man who breaks his arm when he is drunk may have to cut it off when he is sober."

The problem of fighting Communism while preserving civil liberties is no simple one, and there is no simple solution. A prerequisite for any solution, however, is, firstly, a proper understanding of Communism for what it is, and secondly, a sense of proportion. So long as liberals agree with Senator McCarthy that the fate of Communism involves the fate of liberalism, and that we must choose between complete civil liberties for everyone and a disregard for civil liberties entirely, we shall make no progress except to chaos. So long as one is either for or against "guilt by association," it is hopeless to try to distinguish between a sober and silly definition of that concept—sober when it is taken to mean, as for instance the Canwell Committee of the State of Washington took it to mean, that anyone who is a member of three or more organizations officially declared subversive is to be considered a Communist; silly when it is taken to mean, as many government loyalty boards take it to mean, that if you have a friend or a relation who is sympathetic to Communism, you are a "bad security risk." So long as Senator McCarthy and the liberals agree that the right of a Communist to teach or be a government employee is a matter of principle, we shall remain distant from that intelligent discrimination between one case and another, and one situation and another, which alone can give us our true bearings. And so long as Senator McCarthy and the liberals are enmeshed in this confusion, the Senator will grow the stronger, for such confusion is the sap of his political life.

Inevitably, liberals will disagree among themselves about the appropriateness of specific actions with regard to Communism and Communists. Inevitably, too, there will always be a basic division and antagonism between liberalism (which is solicitous of freedom) and McCarthyism (which is not). But if a liberal wishes to defend the civil liberties of Communists or of Communist fellow-travelers, he must enter the court of American opinion with clean hands and a clear mind. He must show that he knows the existence of an organized subversive movement such as Communism is a threat to the consensus on which civil society and its liberties are based. He must bluntly acknowledge Communists and fellow-travelers to be what they are, and then, if he so desires, defend the expediency in particular circumstances of allowing them the right to be what they are. He must speak as one of *us*, defending *their* liberties. To the extent he insists that they are on our side, that we can defend our liberties only by uncritically defending theirs, he will be taken as speaking as one of them.

23

Sidney Hook (1902–1989) and Bertrand Russell (1872–1970)

A Foreign Policy for Survival: An Exchange (1958)

Editor's Introduction

From early in his life Sidney Hook admired the British philosopher, mathematician and social activist Bertrand Russell. Even at age twenty-one, Hook was more interested in Russell than in Marx, and Russell was one of the people he most wanted to meet. Although they did not expound the same philosophy (Russell was not a pragmatist), Hook later said that Russell was "the one I have come closest to hero-worshiping." (Hook, *Out of Step*, chapter 23.)

It is an understatement to say that Russell's career was interesting. Born into an aristocratic English family and with John Stuart Mill as his godfather, he became the third Earl Russell and was elected a Fellow of the Royal Society. He earned his way into the front rank of philosophers of his time yet also wrote popular books that widely extended his fame. In addition, Russell was an exceedingly controversial figure. He married four times and was a sexual libertine who did not hide his practices. A liberal socialist of a mild sort, he denounced communism for its absolutism and its destruction of individual thought and action. Opposed to World War I, in 1916 Russell lost his teaching position at Trinity College, Cambridge for his antiwar activism under the Defence of the Realm Act, and two years later he was imprisoned for five months on similar charges. In 1949, a public outcry about his politics and lifestyle prevented him from accepting a position at the City University of New York, despite a great effort from Hook and others to help him. In the same year, Russell was awarded the Order of Merit and the next year was given the Nobel Prize for Literature. In 1958 Russell became the founding president of the Campaign for Nuclear Disarmament, and three years later he was again imprisoned for his part in anti-nuclear protests.

Hook acknowledged that Russell was a pacifist who made exceptions to the rule. He knew, for example, that Russell believed Hitler had to be opposed militarily because fighting the Nazis would prevent even greater dangers. What bothered Hook most was his belief that Russell began to tip against the United States by the mid-1950s. Russell, according to Hook, slowly became convinced during this time that Senator Joe McCarthy's point of view was taking over the U.S. and transforming it into a more repressive and aggressive nation. In Hook's view, Russell saw the Cold War tensions as deriving more from U.S. than Soviet actions, and the Vietnam War confirmed Russell's suspicions.

Source

Sidney Hook and Bertrand Russell, "A Foreign Policy for Survival," (abridged) *New Leader* vol. 41, no. 14, April 7, 1958; *New Leader* vol. 41, no. 21, May 26, 1958.

Selected Readings

Sidney Hook, *Sidney Hook on Pragmatism, Democracy, and Freedom*, Robert B. Talisse and Robert Tempio, eds. (Amherst, NY: Prometheus Books, 2002). Sidney Hook, *Out of Step* (New York: Carroll and Graf, 1987), chapter 23. Eduard S. Shapiro, ed., *Letters of Sidney Hook: Democracy, Communism, and the Cold War* (Armonk, NY: M.E. Sharpe, 1995).

* * * * *

A Foreign Policy for Survival

Sidney Hook

American foreign policy has been in a state of crisis ever since the end of World War II. The crises have been partly of this country's own making. It has made error upon error, all based on a failure to understand the nature of the Communist threat. It sacrificed essential political principles in the military struggle against Nazi totalitarianism. It demobilized its troops in Europe too soon. It failed to use its monopoly of atomic power to effect world disarmament and international control of nuclear weapons. It withdrew American troops from Korea, practically inviting Communist aggression. It fought the Korean War against the Chinese under self-imposed limitations. It liquidated the war short of victory when the Communist Chinese were in retreat. It stood idly by when Soviet troops slaughtered the Hungarian freedom-fighters, who were actually the allies of the West.

Whatever these tragic errors, and however disastrous their consequences, it seems indisputable that they have all flowed from the American desire for peace in a divided world. The simple truth is that the United States, and the concert of powers of which it is a part, has accepted the principle of peaceful coexistence and faithfully tried to live by it. This is to its eternal credit. Yet, despite the concessions, the meetings, the restraints, the United States today, together with its uncertain and uneasy allies, is relatively weaker *vis-à-vis* the Communist world than it was ten years ago. This is evidenced not only by the development of Soviet intercontinental weapons and the Soviet technological strength symbolized by the sputniks but by the expansion of Communist power in Asia and Africa, and the increase of neutralist and pacifist sentiment throughout the world.

Even those who disagree with this reading of the past and present must admit that American foreign policy, with the exception of the Marshall Plan and some other aid programs, has been largely a matter of improvisation, of reaction to moves taken on the initiative of the Communist world. The U.S. has never really taken the psychological or political offensive. It has always contented itself with defending the *status quo* even when the *status quo* was changing. Its policy of containment did not contain and its policy of liberation did not liberate. The rhetoric of the Democratic and Republican Administrations has differed, but the strategic principles of U.S. foreign policy from Roosevelt to Eisenhower seem to me to have been essentially the same (and equally mistaken) with respect to the Soviet Union, alternating between weakness and bluster.

The most crucial mistakes can be easily stated. The first was the underestimation of the significance of Communist ideology as a determinant of Soviet behavior. This ideology accounts for the implacable hostility, the incessant war of nerves, war of words, and, wherever it seemed safe, war of weapons waged by the Kremlin against the free world. This ideology explains the fact that the Communist slogan of "peaceful coexistence" is a deception masking the myriad campaigns of infiltration and propaganda by which Moscow seeks to undermine free cultures.

The second mistake was the failure to understand that, despite this unappeasable fanaticism, the Soviet Union really did not desire a general war—that, although it moved in wherever there was a vacuum of power or an opportunity to create mischief, it moved out wherever there was a danger of its being completely embroiled. Its belief that the processes of history were on its side, the evidence of disunion and weakness in the free world, the uncertainties of survival in any all-out struggle against the West reinforced its fear of a general conflict.

This meant (and it should have been clear from Soviet history from the beginning) that the Communist leadership, short of a direct attack upon its territories, *cannot be provoked into war*. After all, Japanese and Soviet armies fought on the banks of the Amur, Hitler challenged the Soviet Union for years with naked threats without a general war being unleashed. Stalin's quarrel with Tito began with the latter's demand that Stalin help him take Trieste; Stalin refused because of his fear that this would result in world war.

Bolshevism is the greatest movement of secular fanaticism in human history. The only thing that can tame a secular fanaticism is a fear of failure, of defeat in the only world it knows. Unless it is certain of victory, or unless it fears certain defeat, it will not venture everything upon a war in which, although it may defeat the enemy, it cannot itself survive.

Of course, there are those who maintain that Bolshevism has changed its spots, that the internal terror of the Soviet regime has eased, and that, just as

Stalin revised Lenin for the worse, Khrushchev is revising Stalin for the better. Even if Khrushchev's policies really did represent a return to Leninism, this would hardly be a cause for rejoicing. For Leninism in international affairs was even more intransigent than Stalinism, which originally was the ideology of socialism-in-one-country. Lenin placed greater emphasis on the extension of Bolshevik power throughout the world than on its retention in the Soviet system.

There have been changes in the Soviet Union since Stalin died. The reign of internal terror has somewhat moderated, purges are fewer and not so bloody—these domestic effects of the transition from Stalin to Khrushchev are not to be denied. Khrushchev's speech at the 20th Party Congress has had irreversible consequences. All this, nonetheless, leaves the monolithic structure of political power within the Soviet Union unaffected. More important, it has led to no basic reorientation in Soviet foreign policy. The propaganda of the big lie has been continued. The techniques of infiltration and penetration in non-Communist countries have been intensified. Soviet power has moved into the Middle East and rattled atomic weapons at England and France for purposes of diplomatic blackmail. By his cunning in Poland and ruthless brutality in Hungary, Khrushchev has shown himself a worthy successor of Stalin, who trained him and raised him to power.

Whatever changes in American foreign policy are indicated, they do not follow from any changes in the basic Soviet strategy for world conquest by subversion and aggression.

I wish to defend a course for American foreign policy in Europe which will not be popular with either the defenders or most critics of our foreign policy. It is not the position of the British Labor party, of the German Social Democratic party, of George Kennan's Reith lectures, but it is in the same quarter of the compass. This policy is designed to preserve peace, defend the free world, and roll back the Iron Curtain in Europe to the prewar borders, if possible, of the Soviet Union.

The most explosive area in Europe today is Central Europe—Germany and the Soviet satellite states. It is the most explosive area because the last two years have shown that the overwhelming majority of the population in these countries is anti-Communist, that even the Communist parties in most of the satellite countries are probably more nationalist than Communist, and that, to the extent they are Communist, they would, if they could, seek political independence of the Kremlin. George Kennan was grievously wrong when he declared early in 1956 that "there is a finality for better or for worse about what has now occurred in Eastern Europe." If the Red Army were withdrawn from East Germany and Eastern Europe today, these countries would soon, without any intervention from the West, rewin their political freedom.

If, however, the Soviet Army remains astride their lands, then the free nations of the world are in the intolerable moral position of either having to encourage the people of these countries to accept their bonds of tyranny or standing idly by and seeing them slaughtered, as in Hungary. In effect, we become the unwitting allies of the Kremlin in holding down the countries of Eastern Europe—at the very time when the Eastern European satellites have become an *economic* liability to the Soviet Union, and at a time when, since Hungary, they are a *moral* liability to the Soviet Union. (The myth that Soviet troops are in Central and Eastern Europe at the invitation of the peoples of those countries is now in everyone's eyes a blood-stained fiction. And for the moment the Soviet Union seems to have more appetizing fish to fry in Asia and Africa.)

The present time seems to provide appropriate opportunity to help liberate Eastern Europe from the threat of the Red Army. It is obvious that we cannot do this unless we offer a *quid pro quo* to the Kremlin, a concession which would test the sincerity of its professions for a settlement before the entire world.

It seems to me therefore that the NATO nations should offer publicly a phased withdrawal of their military forces from West Germany on condition that Soviet troops withdraw from East Germany and Eastern Europe and that the Soviet Government assent to unification of Germany by free elections. Further, this offer should be coupled with a proposal to keep Germany and Eastern Europe militarily neutral.

The advantages of establishing this neutralized area are many. First, the satellite powers would liberate themselves from Soviet rule. Second, the spectacle of this development may accelerate the processes of democratization—at least, the processes of dissent and dissatisfaction—within the Soviet Union itself. Third, under the umbrella of a Western guarantee of its neutrality, the resources of Central Europe could be diverted in large measure to raising its standard of living and reinforcing, by the contrast in living conditions and cultural freedom, the discontent in the Soviet Union. Fourth, if the neutralization is effective in this area of the world it could be extended to other areas—perhaps the Middle East, perhaps the Far East.

There are, of course, certain dangers in this plan for the neutralization of East and Central Europe.

How can we trust the Kremlin to live up to its pledge in view of the long history of its violation of its pledged word? In the event that Communist regimes are over thrown in the satellite countries, what is to prevent the Soviet Army from marching in and violating the neutrality of these countries? To the last question, I reply by asking another: What is to prevent the Kremlin, in the event that a satellite regime changes its character *now*, from acting in the same way as it did in Hungary? Nothing that *we* are pledged to do.

Once neutralization is agreed upon, these countries should be entrusted with sufficient weapons, conventional and perhaps nuclear, to prevent the Kremlin from overrunning them without some opposition. I make a distinction between neutralization and demilitarization. More important, I believe that the NATO countries should publicly declare in advance that a violation of the neutrality of these nations would be a *casus belli*. To be sure, the history of Korea is instructive on this point; undoubtedly, Dean Acheson's bitter criticism of George Kennan is the result of his memory of the Korean incident, in which, after the American troops marched out, North Korean Communists marched in. But I am confident that, had the Kremlin been convinced that we would resist aggression in Korea and resist it by taking the struggle beyond Korean borders, there would have been no Korean invasion. Had not Mr. Acheson declared that Korea was outside the interests of American policy, there would have been no Korean War.

As Henry Kissinger and others have pointed out, uncertainty in these matters represents the greatest danger of all to peace. It is questionable whether even a psychotic like Hitler would have moved when he did had he been convinced that it meant war with England and the United States as well. After he was permitted his triumphs at Munich and at Prague, Hitler complained that he was "tricked" into war, since he had every reason to believe that, if England would not fight to preserve the Czech borders, she certainly would not fight to preserve the integrity of the Polish frontiers.

A second danger of neutralization is that the Kremlin might move to recapture control of the satellite countries not by outright aggression but by subversion or by a coup. This seems to be not a very formidable threat. Internal subversive movements can be handled by domestic military forces with conventional weapons if they are sufficiently alert to the possibilities.

A third danger of neutralization is that the West, and particularly the United States, might not risk the destruction of its cities and its very survival in order to defend Poland or East Germany. This is a very real danger, strong enough in my eyes to make the withdrawal of all American troops from Europe (as Kennan proposes) far too premature. To some extent, the problem can be met by using measures of graduated deterrence ranging from conventional weapons to tactical atomic weapons. Retaliation would be a function of the kind of weapons the enemy himself used. We would say to the Kremlin, in the words of Denis Healey: "If you move, we will hit you so hard that it will hurt you more to keep on fighting than you can possibly gain by persisting in aggression."

No one knows whether the use of tactical atomic weapons can be limited and the use of the ultimate weapons with thermonuclear warheads avoided. During the last war, despite all the prewar Cassandras, poison gas was not used because of the certainty that it would be employed by the other side in retaliation. The same might be true for hydrogen bombs in the next war. Nonetheless, it seems to me to be true that the ultimate weapon can be a deterrent only if the Kremlin believes it will be used. *This means that the ultimate weapon of the West is not the hydrogen bomb or any other super-weapon but the passion for freedom and the willingness to die for it if necessary.* Once the Kremlin is convinced that we will use this weapon to prevent it from subjugating the world to its will, we will have the best assurance of peace. Once the Kremlin believes that this willingness to fight for freedom at all costs is absent, that it has been eroded by neutralist fear and pacifist wishful thinking, it will blackmail the free countries of the world into capitulation and succeed where Hitler failed.

Shortly after the first atomic bomb was exploded, Elmer Davis responded to the call for one world with the retort: "No world is better than some worlds." It is possible to panic the West by a picture of the universal holocaust a nuclear world war would bring, to panic the West to a point where survival on any terms seems preferable to the risks of resistance. The pages of history show that moral integrity in extreme situations is often the highest political wisdom. The struggle against totalitarianism is not only a political struggle but also a moral one, which limits the extent to which we can carry appeasement. If Hitler had commanded the weapon resources of the Soviet Union, would we have yielded to one Munich after another until the world was one vast concentration camp? I hardly think so. Those who are prepared to sacrifice freedom for peace and for mere life will find after such sacrifice no genuine peace and a life unfit for man. Paradoxical as it may sound, life itself is not a value. What gives life value is not its mere existence but its quality.

Whoever proclaims that life is worth living under any circumstances has already written for himself an epitaph of infamy. For there is no principle or human being he will not betray; there is no indignity he will not suffer or compound.

Sometimes those who should know better seem to ignore this. Bertrand Russell recently declared in an interview with Joseph Alsop that, if the Communists could not be induced to agree to reasonable proposals for controlled nuclear disarmament, he would be in favor of unilateral disarmament even if this meant Communist domination of the entire world. Althought he stated this view as only his own, the fact that he made it public is tantamount to an advocacy of a policy sure to be widely interpreted both in the West and in the Kremlin as one of complete capitulation to Communist intransigence.

It is with a feeling of great personal sadness that I observe Bertrand Russell urge that, to avoid the risk of war, we in effect haul down the colors of freedom and moral decency to save mankind for Communist rule. After all, we cannot be certain that, if we have to defend ourselves by nuclear weapons, they will inevitably destroy the entire human race; nor can we be certain that the terror of Communism will not endure or be followed by something worse. "Oh! what a noble mind is here o'erthrown!" The man who in *The Free Man's Worship* was prepared to defy the very cosmos and "the trampling march of unconscious power," in order to sustain the ideals of human freedom come what may, now sinks on unwilling but still bended knees before Khrushchev at the thought of the danger of universal destruction.

Bertrand Russell's career as a counselor to mankind, here as in some of his observations about the United States as a police state, proves that all the mathematical logic in the world is not a substitute for common sense. In so many words, he says: "I am for controlled nuclear disarmament, but, if the Communists cannot be induced to agree to it, then I am for unilateral disarmament even if it means the horrors of Communist domination." When they listen to sentiments like this, why *should* the Soviets consent to controlled nuclear disarmament? All they need do is wait and the world will be given to them on a platter to do with as they will. *Why should* they compromise? Not knowing whether they will survive *our* resolution to fight if necessary for freedom, they may be tempted to accept reasonable proposals. But words like Russell's tell them that all they need do is sit tight, make threats and wait for us to come crawling to them disarmed. It is like saying to a ruffian or burglar: "You let me alone and I'll let you alone, but if you insist on not letting me alone you can have your way with me. If you find my lock too difficult to force, be patient and I shall remove it." This is almost a provocation to the burglar to make the most extreme demands and reject any reasonable settlement. Russell's words express a dubious political morality and a bad strategy. They bring about the very intransigence among the Communists which he uses as the justification for capitulation.

We do not, however, need to strike an heroic stance in shaping a viable foreign policy. Intelligence must be our guide. If we can keep the free world from falling into the trap set by the Kremlin and preserve peace by increasing the power and readiness of the free world, we can then rely upon the processes of education, the force of example, the contagion of free ideas, the cultural osmosis of the great traditions of the West gradually to soften, to liberalize, to round off the edges of the totalitarian regimes of the world until their own peoples rally their energies to overthrow their oppressors and establish the democratic governments necessary to establish one free world republic.

I conclude that our foreign policy in Western Europe must be based on a proposal for cautious, vigilant military withdrawal—not political disengagement, for European affairs are our affairs—in order to win more elbow room for free culture in Eastern Europe.

In Asia and Africa, our task is more difficult and complex. The emphasis on economic aid on the order of a new Marshall Plan is good as far as it goes. But more important than economic aid is the effective use of it. The foreign-aid program, if it is spread universally, is too thin. Waste is enormous. What we must do here is concentrate on massive aid to some key countries or develop some public projects in which adjacent countries can join.

All the economic aid in the world will not win us friends and allies unless the U.S. regains for itself it reputation as an anti-imperialist power. Here we have followed French policy and sometimes British policy with disastrous consequences. The policy of France in Indo-China and now in North Africa, the adventure of Suez, the repressions in Cyprus have alienated large sections of the uncommitted peoples of the earth from the cause of the free world. They have made it difficult for us to put Soviet Russia on the spot as the chief colonial power in the world. From the North Sea to the Pacific Ocean, from the Arctic to Turkestan, the Communists have imposed their rule by force on a score of non-Russian peoples. But instead of the Soviet Union being the target of Asian-African scorn, it is the U.S., because of our allies' sins of commission and omission, which is widely regarded as imperialistic.

I do not underestimate the difficulties of a coalition of powers, but, as the strongest member of the NATO group, we are called upon to give leadership. Our greatest mistake is that we followed the lead of France and Britain too long. It is alleged that our abrupt reversal on the Aswan Dam, which led to fateful developments in Egypt, was taken at the request of Great Britain— which didn't prevent our British friends from criticizing the action after its consequences were clear. We would be more respected by our allies if we took a strong stand against colonialism and made bold and imaginative proposals to counteract Communism politically, diplomatically and economically. Many people scoff at the idea of a war of propaganda despite the fact that the Kremlin has been winning the cold war mostly by its propaganda. The war of weapons is much more likely to break out when we lose the war of words and the war of ideas. And it is our *ideas*, the common ideas of the free world, the heritage of the Atlantic democracies and their allies, which can inspire a continuing offensive against Communism all along the line. To us, much more important than a cultural exchange of technicians, metallurgists and farmers with the Soviet Union should be an exchange of philosophers, historians, literary critics, economists and sociologists. We can open our gates safely to thousands of Soviet students and teachers, no matter how indoctrinated they are, provided they permit thousands of our students and teachers to study and travel in the Soviet Union.

It is often said that democracies cannot successfully wage cold wars. They are not geared for it. They are too self-critical. And the factions of normal political life sometimes regard each other with more hostility than the enemy at the gate. All this is true. But a democracy also possesses the virtues of its defects. Once it is informed, its voluntary discipline can accomplish more than columns that are dragooned into goosesteps. It is tougher in crisis than its totalitarian enemies, but this will not avail for victory or even for survival unless it follows the lead of intelligence.

World Communism and Nuclear War

Bertrand Russell

Dr. Sidney Hook's article, "A Foreign Policy for Survival" contains much with which I am in agreement—more, I think, than Dr. Hook realizes. Before embarking upon controversial matters, I will emphasize the extent of agreement by repeating a statement, the first three paragraphs of which were originally made to the American Nobel Anniversary Committee and subsequently published, with the addition of the last paragraph, in many countries on both sides of the Iron Curtain:

> Negotiations between East and West with a view to finding ways of peaceful coexistence are urgently desirable. Certain principles should govern such negotiations: (1) Any agreement arrived at should as a whole be not advantageous to either party; (2) it should be such as to diminish causes of friction; (3) it should be such as to diminish the danger of a more or less inadvertent outbreak of nuclear warfare.

> The procedure I should wish to see adopted would be, first, a meeting at the highest level between the governments of the U.S. and the USSR, not intended to reach binding agreements but to explore the possibility of a compromise which both powers would accept. The negotiations involved should be secret until the possibility of such compromise had been established. If such a compromise seems feasible, it should be recommended by both parties to the other powers of NATO and the Warsaw Pact.

> If an agreement is to be successful in averting the risk of nuclear warfare, it must provide for the destruction of nuclear weapons and the cessation of their manufacture under the guarantee of inspection by an agreed neutral authority. It must also provide for the removal of all alien troops from agreed territory including, as minimum, East and West Germany, Czechoslovakia, Poland and Hungary—Germany not to remain in NATO or the above satellites in the Warsaw Pact. The countries in Eastern and Western Europe must be free to adopt whatever form of government and whatever economic system they may prefer.

> I have been dealing with measures that are imminently necessary if the risk of a great war is to be diminished. But in the long run the only solution which will make the world safe is the establishment of a World Government with a monopoly of the major weapons of war. The world is not yet ready for such an institution, but it may be hoped that experience will gradually convince men of its necessity.

It will be seen that this statement is very similar to the first part of Dr. Hook's article. Where he and I disagree is as to the advisability of an ultimate resort to nuclear war if the Communist powers cannot be contained by anything less. Both Dr. Hook and I are concerned with possibilities which we respectively think improbable. Dr. Hook maintains that, even if his policy led to the extinction of human life, it would still be better than a Communist victory. I maintain, on the contrary, that a Communist victory would not be so great a disaster as the extinction of human life. He admits that his policy *might* lead to the one disaster, though he does not think that it would. I admit that the policy which I advocate *might* lead to the other disaster, though I, again, do not think that it would do so. We are agreed that both these extreme consequences are somewhat hypothetical, and we are also agreed that both of them would be disasters. We differ only as to which of them would be the greater disaster.

Before arguing this question in impersonal terms, there are some observations of a more personal kind that may help to clear the ground. Those who oppose the policy which I advocate insinuate that it is inspired by personal cowardice. A moment's reflection would show them that such a supposition is absurd. Neither universal Communist domination nor the extinction of the human race is likely to occur before I die a natural death. I do not, therefore, have to consider whether I should most fear my nuclear disintegration or my slow torture in an Arctic labor camp. At my age, views as to the not immediate future are necessarily impersonal.

Another thing which is insinuated is that I am surreptitiously favorable to Communism. One might as well accuse Dr. Hook of wishing to see the human race exterminated. Obviously, he does not wish the one and I do not wish the other. We both admit that both would be disasters. We differ only, I repeat, as to which would be the greater disaster.

I cannot but deplore the passage in which Dr. Hook laments my supposed moral downfall. It is not by such arguments that difficult issues can be decided. He does not seem aware that it would be easy to make a retort in kind and to accuse him of being a super-Caligula. But argumentation in this vein is an obstacle to rationality. I shall, therefore, abstain from it, and I wish that he would do likewise.

I come now to an impersonal consideration of the issue. There are here two quite distinct matters to be discussed: First, what is the likelihood that the policy which I advocate would lead to the universal domination of Communism? And, second, if it did, would this be worse than the ending of human life? It is the second question that I wish to examine, since the first involves difficult political and psychological considerations as to which differences of opinion will inevitably persist.

Dr. Hook asserts that "Bolshevism is the greatest movement of secular fanaticism in human history." I will not dispute this, but is there not also fanaticism in the attitude of Dr. Hook and of the powerful men who agree with him? Human history abounds in great disasters. One civilization after another has been swept away by hordes of barbarians. The Minoan-Mycenaean civilization was destroyed by savage warriors whose descendants, after a few centuries, became the Greeks whom we still revere. When the Mohammedans swept over the greater part of the Eastern Roman Empire, it seemed to Christian contemporaries that the civilization of the regions which they conquered was being destroyed, and yet, before long, it was the Arabs who mainly preserved the heritage of antiquity. Genghis Khan was quite as bad as Stalin at his worst, but his grandson Kublai Khan was a highly civilized monarch under whom Chinese culture flourished.

The men who think as Dr. Hook does are being un-historical and are displaying a myopic vision to which future centuries are invisible. A victory of Communism might be as disastrous as the barbarian destruction of the Roman Empire, but there is no reason to think that it would be more disastrous than that event. While the human race survives, humaneness, love of liberty, and a civilized way of life will, sooner or later, prove irresistibly attractive. The progress of mankind has always been a matter of ups and downs. The downs have always seemed final to contemporaries, and the ups have always given rise to unfounded optimism. Western Europe in the year 1000 gave no promise of the renaissance that began some centuries later. The human spirit throughout Western Christendom was as narrowly imprisoned as it was in Russia under Stalin. Any person who supposes that the evils of Communism, if it achieved a supremacy, would last forever is allowing himself to be so limited by the heat of present controversies as to be unable to see their similarity to equally virulent controversies in the past or to realize that a dark age, if it is upon us, like the dark ages of the past will not last forever.

Dr. Hook says quite truly that life, in itself, is not of value. It gives, however, the only possibility of any value. I cannot applaud the arrogance of those who say: "If the next century or so is to be such as I (if I were alive) would find unpleasant, I shall decide that not only this period but all future time shall be destitute of life." Nor can I wholly admire the kind of "courage" which is advocated by Dr. Hook and others who think like him, which has, in large part, a vicarious character somewhat detracting from its nobility. I have nothing to say against the man who commits suicide rather than live under a regime which he thinks evil, but I do not feel much approval of the man who condemns everybody else to death because he himself does not find life worth living.

I have tried to keep this discussion on a rational rather than an emotional plane, but I cannot resist giving expression to my final judgment, which is that to risk the end of human life because we regard Communism as evil is fanatical, defeatist and pusillanimous in the highest possible degree.

A Free Man's Choice

Sidney Hook

It is a debater's stratagem, unworthy of Bertrand Russell's great gifts, to assert that I called his personal courage into question in criticizing the policy he advocates as one of surrender to Communism. It was his political judgment I criticized, not his character. Indeed, despite his praiseworthy declaration that arguments in the impersonal mode will best clarify our disagreements, it is he who descends to the use of personal epithets. I shall not follow him. I ask only that he stop pretending that anyone is charging him with cowardice or that any politically literate person believes he favors Communism. He no more favors Communism than the democratic Western statesmen who appeased Hitler out of fear of war favored Fascism. Nonetheless they were the assisting architects of the ruin of millions.

The issues between us are two. The first Russell wholly avoids, even though it is my main point and by far of greater political weight. Russell has declared to the entire world that, if the Soviet Union refuses to accept reasonable proposals for international disarmament, the West should disarm unilaterally— even at the cost of the universal reign of Communist terror. I criticized this view as helping to produce the very situation in which we may have to choose between capitulation to Communist tyranny or war.

I find bewildering Russell's claim that the four paragraphs he cites in his rejoinder are "very similar" to the first part of my article. These paragraphs are worth precisely nothing when coupled with his present advice. They flatly contradict it. The first principle he recommends to govern negotiations between East and West is: "Any agreement arrived at should as a whole be not advantageous to either party." Excellent! Then he broadcasts to the world: If the Kremlin refuses to make such an agreement, the West should disarm unilaterally. Why, then, should the Kremlin enter into any such agreement or abide by it if it does? Russell's position today constitutes positive encouragement to the Communist leaders to be unreasonable and thus inherit the world without a struggle.

Let us not deceive ourselves: It is obvious that the leaders of the Soviet Union are keeping a sensitive watch on the pulse of public opinion in Western countries. It is not for nothing that the man whom they called "the running dog of imperialism," and who still despises their tyranny, is now built up in their controlled press as the "true friend of peace." Throughout the world, Communists are infiltrating into the pacifist movement whose non-pacific demonstrations they often spark. I am convinced that the growth of pacifist and neutralist sentiment in the West was at least partly responsible for the Soviet Union's withdrawal from the sessions of the UN Disarmament Commission, where reasonable proposals along the lines of Russell's paragraphs could be considered; its hardening attitude along the political front; its repudiation of the Geneva agreement on Germany; its recent UN veto of the proposal for Arctic inspection. Such actions may also be based on the hope that a position like Russell's will undermine the West's resolution to resist aggression.

Arguments from history are rarely decisive, but I think it is fairly well established that the appeasement of Hitler—not only Munich but the mood that nothing could be worse than war—encouraged Hitler in his aggression. I go further. Even if in my heart I agreed with Russell (as I do not) that in the ultimate event, capitulation to Communism was a lesser evil than the risks of war, I should regard it as a piece of unmitigated political foolishness to proclaim it. We live in a contingent world. What we do, even sometimes what we say, counts. Especially important are the policies we advocate. For, to the extent that they influence human action, they influence future events. Russell's proposal is tantamount to playing with all cards face up against a shrewd and ruthless gambler with a hidden hand. When the stakes are human freedom, it is irresponsible to play a game which invites the Kremlin to bluff us into submission with threats of atomic blackmail. The Soviets are just as vulnerable to us as we are to them.

The Soviet leaders belong to the human race, too. For them, survival is an even more important value than for many in the West. That is why I am convinced that ultimately they are more likely to consent to reasonable proposals for a peaceful settlement once they are persuaded that we will fight rather than surrender, than if they are persuaded by Russell and others that we will surrender rather than fight. *This* is the crucial point which Russell has completely ignored.

Santayana somewhere defines a fanatic as one who, having forgotten his goal, redoubles his efforts. Among my goals are freedom *and* peace. That is why I believe that all nations should freely choose their economic and political systems. That is why I have never advocated a preventive war for the sake of peace, as Russell did in 1948, when the West had a monopoly of atomic power. He was wrong then in urging that the Soviet Union be forced, by atomic bombs if necessary, to yield to a world government. (Many A-bombs could have the effect of a few H-bombs.) He is wrong now in urging capitulation on the West because the Soviet Union has the hydrogen bomb. He went too far in one direction; he now goes too far in the other, as if he were atoning for his early extremism. In both cases, he underestimated the political and psychological elements in the situation and overestimated the technological ones.

I do not see why a policy which seeks to confine the fanaticism of Bolshevism by taming it with the fear of failure should be called fanatical. As well say that a man who believes in tolerance and is therefore intolerant of those who manifest intolerance is himself intolerant. On the contrary, assuming belief to be a habit of action, a person who is tolerant of a show of intolerance does not really believe in tolerance. If the West follows the foreign policy I have advocated, it will not have to choose between capitulation to Communism or war. This is the choice Russell's proposal forces us into. It seems to me today that the probability of Communism destroying human liberty everywhere is considerably greater than the probability, if it comes to war, of human life being destroyed everywhere—particularly if we keep up scientific inquiry into defense.

After all, just a few short years ago, Russell declared that the destruction of the whole of Europe was not too great a price to pay in order that "Communism be wiped out." There were some who regarded this position as "fanatical, defeatist and pusillanimous," since such a war if prolonged might have had a disastrous effect on the human race. It may be that today, if the scientists of the free world rally to the cause of freedom's defense and not to the cause of Russell and unilateral Western disarmament, discoveries will be made which will counteract some of the lethal after-effects of weapons. In that case, even if the Kremlin forces a war on the West, it may be repelled without the destruction of all human life or even the whole of Western Europe. It is an error to assume that a balance of armaments or even an armaments race inevitably makes for war. Else we would never be at peace. Unpreparedness also may lead to war. There is a risk, of course. The important thing, therefore, is to see to it that the potential aggressor never is certain that he can win. But this is precisely what Russell's policy prevents us from doing.

Suppose now we were confronted with the limiting case: choice between the horror of Communism for some hundreds of years and the end of human life. Here every lover of freedom and of life is on uncertain and tragic ground. One cannot be sure that at the decisive moment the situation will look the same. Yet every compassionate person, including Russell, feels that there is a limit in suffering and ignominy beyond which the whole human enterprise comes into moral question. The problem is where to draw the limit. At present, I cannot, like Russell, find grounds in history for reconciling myself to the first of the above alternatives. Some of my reasons are:

1. In the past, the triumphs of barbarism were local, not universal. Today, a Communist world would be a tightly knit despotism of fear without sanctuaries, without interstices to hide, without possibilities for anonymity.

2. In the past, tyrants ruled with a primitive technology. The possession today of refined scientific techniques increases immeasurably the extent and intensity of terror ruthless men can impose on those they rule. A Communist world could easily become a scientific Gehenna—some thing incomparably worse than the destruction of the Roman Empire by the barbarians.

3. I cannot regard the achievement which in the past has sometimes followed the triumph of cruel tyrants as worth the price in torture and agony that preceded it. To me, the splendor and glory of the Court of Kublai Khan were not worth even one of the many pyramids of human skulls his grandfather, Genghis Khan, heaped up in carving out his empire. And a few years ago I believe Bertrand Russell would have agreed with me. If the triumph of Hitler were a necessary condition for a new renaissance, what anti-Fascist would be willing to pay the price?

4. It is not at all unlikely that factional struggle will break out again either at the Communist center or periphery among the political gangsters who rule the Communist world. In such an event, thermonuclear weapons of even more destructive power than those we know may be used to end men's miserable lives, and all the additional agony and terror would have been in vain.

5. It is no arrogance on my part to propose to the generation of the free that they follow a policy of resistance rather than of surrender, any more than it is arrogant for Russell to propose surrender rather than resistance. But perhaps he means it is arrogant for any generation of men to make a decision which

will prevent the future generations of the yet unborn to have their chance and make their choice. I must confess that I have some difficulty with this notion of obligation, as if it implied there were millions of souls extending into eternity waiting to be born. I do not share this theology. If there are such souls, they may perhaps become embodied elsewhere.

Communists have always argued that it is justified to bury several generations, if necessary, in order to fertilize the soil of history for a glorious future to be enjoyed by the still unborn. In some respects, Russell's argument is similar except that, as an opponent of Communism, he puts the glory much further into the future. Cosmic optimism, however, seems no more credible to me than historical optimism.

Morally, those who are unborn cannot reproach us for denying them the bliss of birth in a Communist world but those who already exist, our children and grandchildren, may curse us for turning them over to the jailors of a Communist 1984 in which, brainwashed and degraded, they are not even free to die until their masters give them leave. There are more horrors in the Communist heaven or hell than Russell seems aware of.

There is an air of unreality about this phase of the discussion. It is improbable that Englishmen who refused to knuckle under to Hitler and his V-2 bombs will seriously consider doing so to Khrushchev and his more powerful bombs. If they did, the United States and Canada would still remain staunchly opposed to Communist tyranny. The discussion seems fanciful, almost bizarre, because only if we accept Russell's position or one similar to it will the enemies of freedom be emboldened to confront us with the momentous *choice* of total surrender or total war. Human life may be destroyed by accident or by the maniacal whim of a dictator, against which there is no safeguard—even by surrender. But, if it is destroyed by war, it will be because our foolishness will tempt the enemy to forget his mortality.

In conclusion, I wish to repeat that nothing I have written is intended in any way as a personal reflection on Bertrand Russell, a man and philosopher whom I have usually admired even when I have strongly disagreed with him. I impugn only his political intelligence in this grave crisis of human freedom. I lament the fact that he has capped a lifetime of gallant opposition to despotism with the unsound recommendation that we unconditionally surrender to the cruelest tyranny in human history.

24

C. Wright Mills (1916–1962) and Irving Howe (1920–1993)

Intellectuals and Russia: An Exchange (1959)

Editor's Introduction

Both Irving Howe and C. Wright Mills were critics of 1950s America and Mills was attracted to *Dissent* and those skeptical democratic socialists who wrote for it. Mills, however, was known as someone irascible enough to have trouble getting along even with his friends, a trait that made him a sharp surveyor of the habits of mass suburban America but also enforced his natural loner tendencies. Mills, who taught at sociology at Columbia after earning a Ph.D. at the University of Texas and teaching briefly at the University of Maryland, knew the New York Intellectuals relatively well. It was Mills who suggested the name for Dwight Macdonald's magazine *politics*, and he knew Richard Hofstadter, Lionel Trilling, and others in the group. He also knew fellow sociologist Lewis Coser, who taught at Brandeis and, as an editor of *Dissent*, brought Mills into the magazine. Yet, because Howe, another editor of *Dissent*, could sting like a hornet in a debate, Mills and Howe were unlikely to have a smooth relationship.

If one reads Mills' *White Collar* (1951) and *The Power Elite* (1956) and also Howe's *Partisan Review* essay "This Age of Conformity" (1954) it is clear how much the two authors shared in their criticism of the United States at midcentury. At just the point when America was becoming the first post-industrial society, Mills was appalled by the rush to build a war machine, detested the way the white collar society was suffocating any live ideas in its corporate uniformity, and hated the evisceration of political free-thinking as industrial workers donned ties and were led into offices and then into middle class suburbs where populism died. (Kevin Phillips, of course, discovered the roots of populism in those same suburbs a decade later.) In his essay Howe found many of the same problems: a culture content to live by the advice of corporate advertising and capitalist consumerism; a society willing to watch television instead of involving itself in political issues; and intellectuals happy to be bought out by Madison Avenue, Wall Street, university positions, middlebrow culture, and the seductions of the suburbs. Both Mills and Howe wondered where intelligent dissatisfaction had gone.

But a political and cultural fault line, one that helped explain their animosity so evident in this exchange over foreign policy, ran between Howe and Mills at the time. It was one of the first sparks of the battle between the Old Left Howe and the New Left Mills. The latter's "Letter to the New Left" was a spur to its formation. Mills was a radical in culture as well as politics, a James Dean who rode a motorcycle. His attitude differed from Howe's. Like the New Left later, he wanted to be done with the haggling over the relative benefits of communism vs. socialism vs. capitalism and thought the real question had to do with power elites and white collar corporations—whether publicly or privately owned.

In this exchange with Mills, Howe tasted what would return *en masse* to confront him in the following decade. The occasion for the exchange was Howe's review in *Dissent* of Mills' book *The Causes of World War III*, in which Mills suggested that two enormous mass societies, the Soviet Union and the United States, were drifting toward war with each other. Howe, given his background writing about the differences between American liberal culture and the Soviet communist life and ideas, did not appreciate Mills' suggestion that the Soviet Union and the U.S. had more similarities than most people thought. In addition, Mills wondered how *Dissent's* anticommunist foreign policy differed from the State Department's. It was a preview of Howe's interaction with the New Left in the 1960s, when student radicals also saw similarities between the centralization and bureaucracy in the Soviet Union and the U.S., and in addition wondered whether the cold war was worth fighting in Vietnam.

Source

C. Wright Mills and Irving Howe, "Intellectuals and Russia," (abridged) *Dissent* vol. 6, no. 2, Spring 1959, 191-196; *Dissent*, Summer 1959, vol. 6, no. 3.

Selected Readings

Irving Howe, "On the Career and Example of C. Wright Mills," *Steady Work* (New York: Harcourt, Brace, 1966).

Irving Louis Horowitz, *C. Wright Mills: An American Utopian* (New York: The Free Press, 1983).

Todd Gitlin, "C. Wright Mills, Free Radical," *The Intellectuals and the Flag* (New York, Columbia University Press, 2006).

* * * * *

Irving Howe: "Intellectuals and Russia

That *The Causes of World War III* has been written by C. Wright Mills, author of *Power Elite* and a man who in recent years has made a notable contribution to democratic radicalism in America, is reason enough for taking it seriously. The pamphlet itself—it would be unfair to treat it as a book—is not a good one. It is characterized by a relentless thrust of assertion and a bludgeoning style, neither of which is much affected by complexity of argument or thoroughness of evidence. But it is an important pamphlet because at the present moment, when there is a general and justified weariness with the sterility of the cold war and an incipient sentiment that at almost any cost a deal must be worked out with the Russians, it expresses certain views and moods.

Surely there are few things we need more than a sharply-articulated proposal for a democratic foreign policy that can be counterposed to the Dulles stance. But I think it is this very sense of urgency, which all intelligent men share, that has led to the analytic carelessness and moral disequilibrium of Mill's pamphlet. Many of his specific proposals are fine, many of his specific observations valid; but the mode or style of thought to which he has recently turned seems to me unacceptable for the democratic left.

Most of *The Causes* is devoted to a description of the power mechanics of the Cold War; the way the accumulation of armaments has led to the "idiot's strategy" of amassing weapons powerful enough to destroy humanity; the way the power blocs have worked each other into a paralysis of "semi-organized stalemate"; the way both sides, through stupidity, fear and callousness, help perpetuate this stalemate.

Mills restates this familiar description with his characteristic forcefulness, though also with some serious faults. But what needs first to be noticed is that such a description does not answer the question implicitly posed in this title: what are the *causes* of World War III? Within which political-intellectual framework does he wish to present his argument? I do not mean that he should provide a full-scale academic or Marxist thesis; not at all. But a writer of his sophistication ought to distinguish between a description of the present state of the cold war and an analysis of the historical causes that have led us to this state.

Is the cold war primarily the result of traditional imperialist rivalries? Is it due to a clash between two divergent world-outlooks, democracy and totalitarianism? Should it be regarded mainly in terms of conflicting national interests? Or are we now to see it as a clash between a decadent capitalism and a vibrant new Communism?

These are possibilities; there are others. Political wisdom does not consist simply in taking one's pick or contriving a synthesis. But if one is going to talk about the *causes* of World War III, it would seem necessary to say something substantial about these, or other, ways of dealing with the problem. And this Mills does not do.

Perhaps, however, like some of us in *Dissent*, he tries to approach the problem piece-meal, without elaborate theories? Were he writing about a particular issue like the Berlin crisis or the mid-East, this might be satisfactory. But if one is writing a book called *The Causes of World War III*, there is really some obligation to offer generalized statements about the causes. Otherwise, you succumb to the danger of arguing as if the cold war were a blight of mysterious origin that can be eliminated by urging house holders on both sides of the street to use the proper brand of weed-killer.

The *Causes*, to be sure, does have an intellectual framework, but a framework that by its very nature cannot yield an answer to the questions I have raised. Mills advances the idea that both Russia and the U.S. are instances of a world-wide drift toward "the mass society." A polarization of power has taken place in the world, so that today there are only two effective power centers. Within each industrialized nation there is a similar centralization.

> In the two superstates ... facilities of violence are absolute ... politically each of them is increasingly a closed world; and in all these spheres their bureaucracies are world-wide.

That differences still exist between Russia and the U.S., Mills recognizes; yet "so similar are the bureaucratic facts of their industrialization ... that in their encounter we witness their parallel development." And it is upon this last notion that Mills places his main stress.

Now part of what Mills is saying here is surely true. The theory of "mass society" is indispensable, though not sufficient, for an understanding of the modern world. But to note that Russia and the U.S. are both examples of a drift toward the mass society cannot be regarded as an answer—good or bad—to the questions raised earlier concerning the *causes* of the cold war.

For if the "parallel development" and increasingly bureaucratic structures of the two superstates were really crucial, one might wonder why Russia and the U.S. did not become harmonious partners rather than bitter enemies. Surely the trend toward a parallel "massification" of the two societies cannot have been the decisive cause of so sharp and deep-going a conflict. And if tomorrow there were to be a rapprochment between the two superstates, resting perhaps upon a tacit division of the world into spheres of influence, would that be the result of a "parallel development" of the two societies? No more, I should think, than their past and present antagonisms. A rapprochement might be facilitated—though also hindered—by this "parallel development"; but if we wish to consider the operative causes of the cold war, or of its possible ending, we must inquire into other factors which have to do with social, economic and ideological *differentiations* between the two superstates.

In a word, then, the theory of "mass society," be it right or wrong, tells us very little about the causes of World War III.

There are other difficulties in Mills' approach:

1. It systematically understates the significance of political ideas and ideologies as motifs affecting the behavior of and helping to explain the differences between nations—a failing almost inevitably a consequence of his hard-boiled

stress upon "power" as a dominant factor in world politics. In terms of analysis, this leads to an underrating of the role of Communist ideology. In terms of values, it means underrating the role of democratic sentiments in the West.

2. In the name of a long-range and necessarily speculative analysis of *one* tendency in modern society, Mills severely minimizes the differences in nature and quality between the Western world and the Communist countries. Both may be headed in the same direction; but one's political-moral response is largely determined by a measurement of how far they are from the alleged goal, at what rate they are travelling, and what conditions of life they permit for the human beings forced to take these journeys. There is a crucial difference between America, a democratic country that shows some signs of drifting toward authoritarianism, and Russia, which for decades has been something considerably worse.

Mills is aware of this difference; he merely fails to take it into vital consideration; and sometimes he unaccountably minimizes its importance. In both countries, he tells us, "political struggles tend to be replaced by administrative decisions." Now in the U.S., it is true, political struggles of "articulate publics" (to use Mills' excellent phrase) have *tended* to be replaced by administrative decisions. That this remains a tendency is partly shown by our ability still to protest against it. But where in Russia during the past three decades have there been any free or open "political struggles" involving "articulate publics" that have then "*tended* to be replaced by administrative decisions?" Nor is this a quibble over phrasing, as a casual reader might assume; it involves that crucial assimilation of the U.S and Russia into one category which is close to, if not actually the heart of Mills' argument.

Again: "The ideas of freedom and rationality ... are now quite ambiguous in the new societies of the United States and of the Soviet Union." One would expect a sociologist as expert as Mills to specify which social or intellectual strata he is referring to; surely it is hazardous to assume that there exists a common attitude toward freedom shared by all groups within each society. But more important, the idea of freedom is sometimes ambiguous in the U.S.: in some ways respected, in some ways not. But I fail to see anything ambiguous about the attitude of the Soviet state or its ruling party toward the idea of freedom: they simply deny what any serious person would regard as human freedom. That there are people in Russia and the satellite countries who yearn for freedom; that communication should be established with such people—yes, of course. But surely this does not sanction so dubious a step as aligning either logically or morally the ambiguous freedom of the U.S. with the unambiguous unfreedom of Russia.

3. Mills' approach to the war danger focuses upon the "irresponsibility" of the leaders on both sides. Decisions in Russia and the U.S. are now made by small groups of powerful men; the democratic process, even when relatively genuine, affects mainly "middle-level" (that is, not crucial) issues; it is

the power elites that manage the cold war; hence, it follows, almost everything now depends on the good-will and intelligence of a handful of men. But if so, Mills has twisted his way back to the view of those soft-headed liberals whom he usually dismisses: the view that if only the leaders got together and "communicated" in prolonged conversations and were willing to be reasonable. ... And if Mills is right, then he unexpectedly does offer new comfort for this kind of approach.[1]

What I find most disturbing in *The Causes* is a certain notion it approaches concerning coexistence. Now in one obvious but important sense, coexistence is indispensable. Both superstates exist; they can at present be removed only through war; and war is unthinkable. That means that negotiations are necessary, and where there are negotiations there may have to be concessions. But what troubles me is a sentiment one finds these days which urges not merely this political coexistence but also a kind of "moral coexistence," by which I mean an accommodation not merely with Russia as a power but with Communist dictatorship as a form of society. (It may be that a Secretary of State, negotiating with the Russians, cannot always heed this distinction: all the more reason for intellectuals of the democratic left to stress it!)

Mills, to be sure, does not write as a spokesman for "moral coexistence"; but at a number of points he comes uncomfortably close to it. He seems not to feel any overwhelming urge to notice that whatever arrangements may have to be made with the Russian state, there can be no secure peace or genuine relaxation as long as totalitarianism flourishes. He writes impatiently of those who persist in dwelling on "the evil character of the enemy." Well, it is really a question of the character of Russian *society*—though I think it also important to remember that Khrushchev and Mikoyan have committed many evil acts that, to put it mildly, do call their characters into question. Mills writes that "the only realistic military view is the view that war, and not Russia, is now the enemy." No; the only realistic military (and political) view is that both the Russian regime and war are enemies, and that ways should be found to limit the power of the first while preventing the outbreak of the second. Mills writes that "as the Soviet economy is further industrialized, this kind of imperialist temptation [the temptation to "brutal conquest"] loses its strength. The reverse is the case with capitalist imperialism." Another hasty generalization that cannot bear scrutiny: Did the advanced state of Russian industrialization keep Khrushchev and Mikoyan from "brutal conquest" in Hungary? And is there not some evidence—for example, in England—that "the imperialist temptation" of the capitalist countries has decreased? The matter is complex, and I would not pretend that my two questions do more than indicate that Mills has borrowed from certain pseudo-Marxist sources a crude generalization which, at the very least, requires extensive qualifying.

One last quotation:

The Soviet intervention in Hungary might be supposed a ground for believing that agreements with the Soviet would be useless. There is of course no moral excuse for the Russian intervention, but there is a political explanation: given the armaments race, Harry Lustig has suggested, "the Russians felt they could not afford to let Hungary become at best neutral and at worst another base for American bombers and missiles.

If this be explanation, then one need hardly worry about excuses! A little too conveniently for the Russians, Harry Lustig (whoever he might be) raises the spectre of American missiles in Hungary—neither a genuine option nor a necessary consequence of the wish of the Hungarian people to achieve national freedom. There are no missile bases in Titoist Yugoslavia: why should there have been in a free Hungary? The truth is that Khrushchev and Mikoyan suppressed the Hungarian revolution because they feared the spread of freedom to other satellite countries and to their own borders. That this central fact of our time should escape Mr. Lustig is not our concern; but that C. Wright Mills should care to lean on Lustig at so crucial a moment is extremely depressing.

There remains an 18 point program which climaxes *The Causes*. It is a mixture of (1) ideas that any decent person would accept (the U.S. should abolish fingerprinting of aliens); (2) valid radical proposals (a high percentage of our national income should go to economic aid to underdeveloped countries); (3) notions so doubtful that they require both prolonged debate and separate presentation if they are not to endanger the popularization of the previous two groups of points. Mills argues, for example, that the government should "abandon all military bases and installations outside the continental domain of the United States." This proposal, like others of its kind, is put forward as a unilateral one, though there later appears an after-thought that the Russians should be "invited and reinvited to join in each of these efforts." But it is clear that, for Mills, American action in this respect should not be contingent upon Russian acceptance of our "invitation." At no point, however, does he trouble seriously to consider the possible consequences of such a step for, say, the political situation in Europe. Does his program mean, for example, that the West should now withdraw from Berlin? One might suppose that such questions would be confronted in a somewhat sustained way; they are not.

My point is not so much that I disagree with a few of Mills' 18 points, but that his book is guilty of a high-handed carelessness as to the possible consequences of their adoption. Something can perhaps be said for unilateral disarmament or for unilateral withdrawal from Europe. But it is distressing to see a man like Mills advance these highly problematic notions in tidy little paragraphs without a serious and sustained discussion of possible repercussions, which is to say, their extreme riskiness. It is a procedure that may stir some readers—generally those already prepared for such responses—to emotions of indignant certitude; but I doubt that it will contribute to their political education.

Intellectuals and Russia

The following letter has been written as a reply to a review by Irving Howe of C. Wright Mills' *The Causes of World War Three*, which appeared in the last *Dissent*. A rejoinder by Howe follows.

—Editors

Dear Irving:

No doubt there are others, but I have seen only three "negative" U. S. reviews of my essay, *The Causes of World War Three*. In the *Wall Street Journal*, William H. Chamberlain wrote—as expected; in the N. Y. *Post*, Arthur Schlesinger Jr. wrote—as expected; and in *Dissent*, you wrote—unexpectedly. I had thought that you had abandoned the foot-dragging mood of the Cold War and were trying to make a new beginning. I had thought that an editor of *Dissent* would have taken due note of differences, and then gone on to build a new left, taking into account the changed state of the world and the sorry condition of U. S. foreign policy. But no. Why waste time with lib-lab apologists and fanatical anti-Communists? But you are supposed to be in some way or another "left." So I feel the need to make a few points and to ask you a few questions.

The major questions with which your review leaves me are: Just how does your basic view of the world confrontation today differ from the line expressed by the work of Dulles-Adenauer? I suppose there are differences, but just how far do they extend? What do *you* want the United States government to do, tomorrow, next week, next year? In my essay I have tried to answer such questions, positively. Moreover, I have tried to do so in terms open to intellectuals. What, if anything, do you propose that leftward intellectuals in the USA now do? Just how do your proposals differ from those that I have offered?

I

As for your gimcrackery about causation: I think you have missed the political strategy of my essay. You don't seem to understand that to seek causes is to seek those factors that are at once strategic to the course of events and possibly open to our political will—or at least to our political demands. Nor do you see that I have always made clear for whom the programs and demands outlined are intended: they are for you and me; they are for intellectuals. (There isn't much political sense in talking to people who can't be "reached.") That is why I find so altogether curious your assertion that I understate "the significance of political ideas and ideologies." On the contrary: probably I have overstated them, both in analysis and in program. You seem to recognize this yourself, in your comments on "soft-headed liberals." Anyway: what do *you* think is the function of "ideologies" in the world confrontation today?

What you seem to want by way of a general statement of causes you indicate by stereotypes: "imperialist rivalries," "democracy vs. totalitarianism," "capitalism vs. communism," etc. My view of the state of the world is not so black-and-white. I've tried to cut beneath such tired slogans. As most literate reviewers have understood, my statement of causes rests upon the theory of history-making outlined in part one of *The Causes*, elaborated from. *The Power Elite*. I don't think the strategic causes now making for World War III are to be found in some magic key; what you call my "description of the mechanics of the cold war," I think a statement of its strategic causes. If you believe it is not, then: What do *you* think are the major causes?

II

In your comments about the parallel developments of the U. S. and the USSR, you ask: Why, then, haven't they become "harmonious partners"? First answer: What a curious expectation! The parallel developments of western indus- trial nations have not seemed to make them "harmonious partners." Second answer: Wait a while; it is not inconceivable that they will. In the meantime, I do not "assimilate" the U. S. and the USSR "into one category." One writes in a context in which the two are regularly presented as polar opposites, one good, the other evil. Therefore: I state differences, but I stress parallels. From these, by the way, I do not draw optimistic conclusions. But what do *you* think are the most significant differences and parallels?

What disturbs you most is my attitude towards the Soviet Bloc and the balance of blame I try to draw between Russian and American policies and practices. We differ, I suppose, in two evaluations: You do not take as seriously as I do the new beginnings in the Soviet Bloc since the death of Stalin. You no longer take as seriously as I do the lack of new beginnings and the disuse of formal freedom in the USA since World War Two. Probably these are the real issues between us. I suspect that you take a more or less standard view. I don't. The truth is I've not yet worked out an assessment that really satisfies me; 1 am very much at work on it these days. I wish you'd try to break out of the weary old beliefs you seem to hold about it and help me, and others, formulate a fresh view. I am not dogmatic about it: persuade me.

In the meantime, I am coming to believe that the Soviet Bloc is changing very fast indeed, that some of these changes are "liberalizing" in a firm sense of the word, that there are signs that these are going to continue, and that what *we* do will affect their chances to be more fully realized.

In *The Causes*—as well as elsewhere (see the BBC's *Listener*, 12 March, 16 March, 2 April 1959)—I have drawn many parallels between the USA and the USSR. I have also noted that I do not "wish to minimize the important differences between the establishment of culture, and of cultural workmen, in the Soviet Union and in the United States. I wish neither to excuse the brutal facts of Soviet cultural tyranny, nor to celebrate the formal freedom of cultural workmen in the West. Surely there is enough such celebration of self and denunciation of enemy.

"The formal freedom of the West rests upon cultural traditions of great force; it is very real—this freedom; it has been and it is immensely valuable. But must we not now ask to what extent the continuation of this freedom today is due to the fact that it is *not* being exercised? And that it has little or no effect of public consequence? Certainly in America today there is much more celebration and 'defense' of civil liberties than insurgent and effective use of them."

But how about *you*? Do you believe that the Soviet Bloc and the Soviet Union itself is a monolithic and unchanging piece of evil? If not, what are the five or six most significant changes in the Soviet Union since the death of Stalin? What are the most hopeful? The most depressing?

III

You do seem to feel that the Soviet Union is absolutely evil; "morally" you do not want to co-exist with it. But you take the curiously expedient view that amoral co-existence is OK, necessary, etc. I do not believe the Soviet system is absolutely evil. In my own reflection I certainly do not make the curiously expedient distinction which you suggest between moral and political co-existence, I am for co-existing, period. Given the means of violence and the facts of their distribution, this is only to say that I am for living and against dying. Also I am against subordinating morality to "politics" or political policy to "military strategy."

I do not believe the Soviet Bloc is a total lie, and the American alliance a half-truth. Both are full of lies; both are full of truths; the cold war they wage—the *New Statesman* has recently observed—is primarily "a conflict of hypocrisies." Do you deny that? *The Causes* is not an attempt to draw up an overall balance of blame. Nor is it a full-scale book of ideals. It is about war and the arms race. In both of these systems the one big lie that concerns me in this book, is the military: the lie that war is still a means of any conceivably human policy. On this point, the balance, of blame is very difficult to draw up. This difficulty, I suspect from your review, you are too ready to ignore by old slogans rooted in old political emotions; my concern is that we confront it carefully with full awareness of the meaning of World War III. Recently you have written of a collapse of "cold war moods"; in your review, however, you do not display much of this "collapse." You write like the cold warriors.

To dissent is lovely. But Irving, as regards foreign policy, from what, tell me, do you dissent? I think probably what you may need—if you'll forgive my saying so—is a big dose of new fact. Don't you alternate between intake and output? I do. Just now—in fact for about two years now—I've been organizing materials-of-fact about each of the world's regions. I find it all quite different than it was when you probably last looked at it closely—which I suppose to have been sometime in the forties. Could it be that you have set your mind in terms of what-was-what some time ago? What have you recently read—apart from rumors filed from Hong Kong—about China? Why not give yourself a big dose of new fact? By the way, don't you think Stuart Hughes' review of my essay in *Commentary* (Feb. 1959 issue) ever so much more politically intelligent than your weary hesitations?

You say nothing that intellectually or politically breaks through what you acknowledge to be the "sterility" of cold war ideology. So far as program goes, all you say is: Matters are very complex; let us not be careless; there are great risks. Indeed there are: The greatest is World War III. Why don't you take the risk of nuclear war seriously enough to pick up from this essay what you agree with and go on from there to set forth alternative programs for the USA, and for intellectuals of the "democratic left"? It would be a welcome relief from the general "sterility"—the boredom and the "balance"—of *Dissent*'s recent pages having to do with the world scene. Why do you not really take stock of where you stand, and try to make a new beginning? Until you do, I'll stick to the assessments and proposals I've outlined in my essay and continue to elaborate them with the help of those who have not yet joined The Old Futilitarians of the dead American left.

Yours truly,
C. Wright Mills

Irving Howe replies:

Let me confess that I have small appetite for answering Mills' "letter." I enjoy open and forthright polemics, and don't mind being roughed up a little: one must expect to take as well as give. But I find profoundly distasteful—it offends my view of polemic as an art form—a Pecksniffian strategy that can begin with "dear Irving" and end with a death notice. Nothing is more characteristic of mass culture in America than maintaining a surface of "friendliness" in order to leak out a dribble of innuendo. (As Dwight Macdonald remarked in a recent *Dissent*: "'Brother' is used by Americans to express hostility and contempt.")

Yes, the essential disagreement concerns the Communist dictatorships. That there have been important changes, some due to an inner stabilization of totalitarian society, others to a desire by the rulers to lead more relaxed lives, still others to fear of pressures from long-suffering peoples (to mention only a few possible causes)—all this is quite familiar and has been discussed frequently in *Dissent*. That some of these changes have resulted in an easing of the immediate living conditions of the people subjected to Communist regimes, is also familiar to everyone. The crucial fact remains, however, that the Communist states are still monolithic one-party dictatorships which deprive their people of the most elementary rights; and that anyone, especially an intellectual, who values freedom must continue to be a principled moral-political opponent of these regimes. Does Mills agree with this or not? This is the heart of the matter, and he cannot evade it by airy references to "tired slogans" or to his dislike of "black and white" formulas.

When Mills quotes himself as not wishing "to excuse the brutal facts of Soviet cultural tyranny," I recognize the man I have known through many years of intellectual and personal association; the man, if I may say so, who learned something, though perhaps not enough, from "the Old Futilitarians of the dead American left." But when Mills writes in his book as he does about Hungary, when he systematically does minimize the differences between totalitarian and democratic societies (differences that extend far beyond the bounds of "culture"), and when in his "letter" he writes about Soviet society in terms that I find distressing and shall note in a moment—then it is a new Mills. There is obviously an inner conflict here, and one can only hope for a fruitful resolution.

Is "the Soviet Bloc and the Soviet Union itself ... a monolithic and unchanging piece of evil?" Words like good and evil may not be the most satisfactory categories for analyzing political phenomena; but never mind. The answer is: No, the kinds and forms of totalitarian Communism have changed. But more: there are many signs of good in the Communist countries. The Hungarian revolutionists who proclaimed the idea of a free socialist society and now rot in jail under the "liberalizing" dispensation, are good. The Polish "revisionists," largely silenced by Gomulka, are good. Milovan Djilas is good. So too is Boris Pasternak. And so too are the Chinese "right deviationist" intellectuals. Everything in the totalitarian world which helps to crumble the party's monopoly of power and thereby disintegrate the rule of the regime, is good. But the regime itself is evil. And only by ceaselessly attacking it—in *our* ways, the ways of democrats and socialists—can we give some little aid to our comrades, known and unknown, in the east. This means for example that if one were to visit Poland today one would instinctively solidarize oneself with the defeated and harassed "revisionists"—the dissenters of the east—rather than with, say, a "cultural spokesman" for Gomulka.

Is it, in any case, to beliefs like these that Mills refers when he speaks of "old slogans rooted in old political emotions?" How old is old, anyway? Let us assume, just for the moment, that my main "political emotion" in regard to the Russian regime is the consequence of its bloody suppression of the Hungarian revolution. That happened only two and a half years ago! Now Americans have a notorious incapacity for remembering, but are the lessons of Hungary and the intense responses they aroused to be dismissed as "old political emotions"? An intellectual should have a memory lasting a bit longer than two and a half years; he should remember the purges and the slave camps and the terror, not merely out of piety toward their victims, though that too, but because the kind of society that made these possible still flourishes. I, for one, choose to remember: *everything*. Does that make me "an Old Futilitarian of the Dead American left"? So be it. Better an "old Futilitarian of the dead American left" than a surf-rider on the Wave of the Future.

War is unthinkable. The Western powers, tied to the interests and out-looks of capitalism, have usually shown themselves unable to cope politically with the Communist thrust. This is the dilemma and tragedy of our moment (which cannot even be apprehended, let alone met, through the neat list of 18 points which Mills drew up in his book and of which, like a middle-aged man come late to pleasurable vices, he is so proud). Because that is the dilemma and tragedy of our moment, we must accept the coexistence of the two power blocs. That means, to quote a few words from my review of Mills' book, "that negotiations are necessary, and where there are negotiations there may have to be concessions. But what troubles me is a sentiment one finds these days which urges not merely this political coexistence but also a kind of 'moral coexistence,' by which I mean an accommodation not merely with Russia as a power *but with Communist dictatorship as a form of society. ...*"

Mills wishes to know whether my objection to "moral coexistence" implies a preference for amoral coexistence: a question that shows he hasn't begun to function seriously as a political man. My objection implies, first of all, as I wrote in my review, the realization that "there can be no secure peace or genu-ine relaxation as long as totalitarianism flourishes" (does Mills disagree?) and second, that, no matter what arrangements are or have to be made by the power blocs, the intellectuals, though not they alone, must continue their fundamen-tal opposition to and criticism of Communist totalitarianism. There may be no choice but to put up with (that's what coexist means) societies that systemati-cally suppress freedom; but let us not learn to find virtues in their vices. It *may* be necessary for the U. S. government to recognize the Pankow regime; but let us not, as independent intellectuals, behave like American businessmen when they are introduced to Mikoyan or American tourists on a guided journey. Our supreme task is to continue to speak and fight for freedom: which means, among other things, to oppose the Communist dictatorships. That, in a word, is what I urge in my opposition to "moral coexistence."

Mills, however, seems impatient with these qualifications. He wants "coexistence, period." The innocence that a sophisticated man can force himself into! Can he not see that the whole agonizing political problem is how to "coexist with commas, semi-colons and dashes," that is, how to shape the terms of coexistence, which can vary from catastrophic rigidity to cata-strophic appeasement. Simply to cry "coexistence, period" is to abandon the right to political judgment.

In any case, what does all of it—the "coexistence, period," the "program," the "18 points"—come to in practice? Here we are before a crucial problem: Berlin. In my review I asked Mills what his program and his points signify in regard to Berlin; but he has not troubled to answer this question. At one point in his book he advocates that the government "abandon all military bases and installations outside the continental domain of the United States." Is he then prepared to urge a unilateral withdrawal from Berlin, leaving its two million people to the mercies of the "liberalizing" Khrushchev? If he says "no," then his program is not to be taken seriously; if he says "yes," then it is all too serious.

As for his rhetorical compost—the American executive, a Cyrus Eaton of the intellectuals, who in an expansive belly-patting mood lets us in on his Methods of Work (and the big revelation?—that he alternates between "intake and output"—which, if you translate it into English, means between reading and writing); the disingenuous questions, really "questions," advanced with a sort of TV abundance (is he really so incapable of intellectual distinctions as to be unable to tell the difference between me and "Dulles-Adenauer"?); the patronizing *chutzpah* with which he asks whether I don't agree that Stuart Hughes is politically more intelligent than I am (let me inform Mills that Hughes and I, as good friends, have discussed this problem at some length and have come to a definitive answer); and his new role of the one-man political sect, beguiled at having his "program," though ready, in his largeness of spirit, to allow one to make modifications in it—all this I find tedious.

Sometimes, however, a phrase will reveal a spirit. "What," asks Mills, "have you recently read—apart from rumors filed from Hong Kong–about China?" Anyone with political sensitiveness will have no trouble in recognizing the nature, the bent, the tone of that question. Well, let me say that I've read a good deal about the recent "liberalizing" of Tibet. And I've read the richly detailed report in *Dissent* (Autumn 1958) based on official Communist sources, which shows how Chinese intellectuals were beaten down after the 100 Flowers. But this apart, I am struck by the echoes that Mills' question raises. For the last time I heard something like *that* it was 20 years ago, when certain intellectuals were denouncing "slander factories" in Riga. It seems these "factories" were spreading rumors that there was slave labor in Russia.

Note

1. Mills is somewhat less than clear as to what he believes the attitudes of the two power elites are toward war. On page 88: "I assume that there have been and are in the U.S.A. and in the U.S.S.R. 'war parties,' men who want war; and also 'peace parties,' men who do not want war ... Most of those who consciously want war and accept it, and so help create its 'inevitability,' want it in order to shift the locus of their problems' [their problems, that is, as members of the U.S. power elite having to deal with an intractable world.–I.H.]

    Twelve pages later: "Do the Russian elite recognize that World War III would not be to Russia's advantage? ... The answer is yes every bit as much for the Russian elite as it is for the American elite."

V
Cultures and Countercultures

25
Norman Podhoretz (1930–)
The Know-Nothing Bohemians (1958)

Editor's Introduction

Norman Podhoretz was raised in the Brownsville section of Brooklyn, and later wrote, "one of the longest journeys in the world is the journey from Brooklyn to Manhattan—or at least from certain neighborhoods in Brooklyn to certain parts of Manhattan." In 1950, he graduated from Columbia College, where he was a student and protégé of Lionel Trilling. After Columbia he won fellowships to attend Cambridge, where he studied under F. R. Leavis, the Trilling of England. A left liberal when he began, Podhoretz was the editor-in-chief of *Commentary* from 1960 to 1995. He later wrote in *Breaking Ranks* (1979) that in the early years at the magazine he and Nathan Glazer were to the left of Trilling. "He [Trilling], after all, had at first strongly resisted the ideas that led to the new radicalism, whereas by developing and spreading those ideas we had done everything in our power to bring the new radicalism into being." (Norman Podhoretz, *Breaking Ranks*, New York: Harper and Row, 1979, 208.)

Podhoretz's well-known early essay on the Beats marks an important divide within the intellectual community in the late fifties. Traces of the counterculture that would divide America in half beginning in the mid-sixties had already been around for a decade. Early influences on the counterculture can be traced to the writing of Dwight Macdonald, Paul Goodman and others in *politics* magazine in the late 1940s, and to critics such as C. Wright Mills in the 1950s. The Beats themselves appeared as undergraduates in the late 1940s at Columbia University in New York (Jack Kerouac, Allen Ginsberg) and Reed College in Portland, Oregon (Gary Snyder, Philip Whalen, Lew Welch). A few years later, both contingents met Kenneth Rexroth, Lawrence Ferlinghetti and others in San Francisco. By 1958, when Podhoretz's article appeared, the first stirrings of a wider counterculture had been energized by the civil rights movement and the 1957 creation of the Committee for a Sane Nuclear Policy (SANE).

Podhoretz was one of the first critics to wade into the initial writings of the Beat counterculture and begin to delineate the border between the New York Intellectuals and the younger generation on matters of culture and politics. The counterculture rejected middle-class American values, particularly those concerning industry, consumerism, sobriety, responsibility, sexual propriety, respect for elders and other symbols of authority, rationality and traditional religion. The Beats, a post-World War II counterculture differed from the earlier post-World War I counterculture, the Lost Generation. Both rejected bourgeois values, but the Beats were essentially romantic, while the Lost Generation was not. Unlike the Lost Generation, the Beats endorsed nature, intuition, a religion of the spirit derived from the anthropological (American Indians, Hinduism, Buddhism) and a search for enlightenment. This put the Beats close to such nineteenth-century transcendentalists as Ralph Waldo Emerson, Henry David Thoreau and, most of all, Walt Whitman.

Emerson and Whitman were not American figures the New York Intellectuals, including Podhoretz, were drawn to. Members of the *Partisan* circle appreciated modernist figures who had something to say about individual alienation in a wasteland world, an orientation that arose with the industrial revolutions and the ideological wars of industrializing societies. The New York Intellectuals, consequently, found themselves aggravated by the counterculture. Podhoretz, firmly tied to the culture of middle-class ambition so evident in his book *Making It*, vented his hostility at the countercultural members of his generation who rebelled against middle-class ethics. In addition, Podhoretz used the literary skills learned at Columbia and Cambridge to attack the Beats' writing.

In essence, this was the beginning of the fight that lasted a couple of decades and helped define some of the generational hostilities of the second half of the twentieth century in American culture. It was a fight between two different outlooks on the liberal left. The New York Intellectuals, members of the Old Left, agreed with Marx that the bourgeoisie had done a great service in producing wealth and now simply had to redistribute that wealth and power more equally. The counterculture, however, resented the *culture* of the bourgeoisie. At one point the New York Intellectuals, first as socialists and then as modernists, also were hostile to the bourgeoisie, but by the time of Podhoretz's article this was behind the group. This disagreement over middle-class values was an early fissure in the dam, and when it broke a few years later the flood produced the great cultural watershed. By the 1980s, many of the inheritors of what was left of the counterculture—as in Doonesbury—were satisfied to live with the monetary rewards of the bourgeoisie while feeling themselves radically anointed by their slightly counter cultural values.

Source

Norman Podhoretz, "The Know-Nothing Bohemians," *Partisan Review* vol. 25, no. 2, Spring 1958.

Selected Readings

Norman Podhoretz, "The Beat Generation," *Partisan Review,* Summer 1958, 476–479; "My War with Allen Ginsberg," *Commentary* vol. 104, no. 2, August 1997; *Doings and Undoings* (New York: Farrar, Straus, 1964).
Thomas L. Jeffers, "A Literary Filiation," *Columbia,* Spring 2006.

* * * * *

Allen Ginsberg's little volume of poems, *Howl,* which got the San Francisco renaissance off to a screaming start a year or so ago, was dedicated to Jack Kerouac ("new Buddha of American prose, who spit forth intelligence into eleven books written in half the number of years ... creating a spontaneous bop prosody and original classic literature"), William Seward Burroughs ("author of *Naked Lunch,* an endless novel which will drive everybody mad"), and Neal Cassady ("author of *The First Third,* an autobiography ... which enlightened Buddha"). So far, everybody's sanity has been spared by the inability of *Naked Lunch* to find a publisher, and we may never get the chance to discover what Buddha learned from Neal Cassady's autobiography, but thanks to the Viking and Grove Presses, two of Kerouac's original classics, *On the Road* and *The Subterraneans,* have now been revealed to the world. When *On the Road* appeared last year, Gilbert Milstein commemorated the event in the New York *Times* by declaring it to be "a historic occasion" comparable to the publication of *The Sun Also Rises* in the 1920's. But even before the novel was actually published, the word got around that Kerouac was the spokesman of a new group of rebels and Bohemians who called themselves the Beat Generation, and soon his photogenic countenance (unshaven, of course, and topped by an unruly crop of rich black hair falling over his forehead) was showing up in various mass-circulation magazines, he was being interviewed earnestly on television, and he was being featured in a Greenwich Village nightclub where, in San Francisco fashion, he read specimens of his spontaneous bop prosody against a background of jazz music.

Though the nightclub act reportedly flopped, *On the Road* sold well enough to hit the best-seller lists for several weeks, and it isn't hard to understand why. Americans love nothing so much as representative documents, and what could be more interesting in this Age of Sociology than a novel that speaks for the "young generation?" (The fact that Kerouac is-thirty-five or thereabouts was generously not held against him.) Beyond that, however, I think that the unveiling of the Beat Generation was greeted with a certain relief by many people who had been disturbed by the notorious respectability and "maturity" of post-war writing. This was more like it—restless, rebellious, confused youth living it up, instead of thin, balding, buttoned-down instructors of English composing ironic verses with one hand while changing the baby's diapers with the other. Bohemianism is not particularly fashionable nowadays, but the image of Bohemia still exerts a powerful fascination—nowhere more so than in the suburbs, which are filled to overflowing with men and women who uneasily think of themselves as conformists and of Bohemianism as the heroic road. The whole point of *Marjorie Morningstar* was to assure the young marrieds of Mamaroneck that they were better off than the apparently glamorous *luftmenschen* of Greenwich Village, and the fact that Wouk had to work so hard at making this idea seem convincing is a good indication of the strength of prevailing doubt on the matter.

On the surface, at least, the Bohemianism of *On the Road* is very attractive. Here is a group of high-spirited young men running back and forth across the country (mostly hitch-hiking, sometimes in their own second-hand cars), going to "wild" parties in New York and Denver and San Francisco, living on a shoe-string (GI educational benefits, an occasional fifty bucks from a kindly aunt, an odd job as a typist, a fruit-picker, a parking-lot attendant), talking intensely about love and God and salvation, getting high on marijuana (but never heroin or cocaine), listening feverishly to jazz in crowded little joints, and sleeping freely with beautiful girls. Now and again there is a reference to gloom and melancholy, but the characteristic note struck by Kerouac is exuberance:

> We stopped along the road for a bite to eat. The cowboy went off to have a spare tire patched, and Eddie and I sat down in a kind of homemade diner. I heard a great laugh, the greatest laugh in the world, and here came this rawhide oldtimes Nebraska farmer with a bunch of other boys into the diner; you could hear his raspy cries clear across the plains, across the whole gray world of them that day. Everybody else laughed with him. He didn't have a care in the world and had the hugest regard for everybody. I said to myself, Wham, listen to that man laugh. That's the West, here I am in the West. He came booming into the diner, calling Maw's name, and she made the sweetest cherry pie in Nebraska, and I had some with a mountainous scoop of ice cream on top. "Maw, rustle me up some grub afore I have to start eatin myself or some damn silly idee like that." And he threw himself on a stool and went hyaw hyaw hyaw hyaw. "And throw some beans in it." It was the spirit of the West sitting right next to me. I wished I knew his whole raw life and what the hell he'd been doing all these years besides laughing and yelling like that. Whooee, I told my soul, and the cowboy came back and off we went to Grand Island.

Kerouac's enthusiasm for the Nebraska farmer is part of his general readiness to find the source of all vitality and virtue in simple rural types and in the dispossessed urban groups (Negroes, bums, whores). His idea of life in New York is "millions and millions hustling forever for a buck among themselves ... grabbing, taking, giving, sighing, dying, just so they could be buried in those awful cemetery cities beyond Long Island City," whereas the rest of America is populated almost exclusively by the true of heart. There are intimations here of a kind of know-nothing populist sentiment, but in other ways this attitude resembles Nelson Algren's belief that bums and whores and junkies are more interesting than white-collar workers or civil servants. The difference is that Algren hates middle-class respectability for moral and political reasons—the middle class exploits and persecutes—while Kerouac, who is thoroughly unpolitical, seems to feel that respectability is a sign not of moral corruption but of spiritual death. "The only people for me," says Sal Paradise, the narrator of *On the Road,* "are the mad ones, the ones who are mad to live, mad to talk, mad to be saved, desirous of everything at the same time, the ones who never yawn or say a commonplace thing, but burn, burn, burn like fabulous yellow roman candles exploding like spiders across the stars. ..." This tremendous emphasis on emotional intensity, this notion that to be hopped-up is the most desirable of all human conditions, lies at the heart of the Beat Generation ethos and distinguishes it radically from the Bohemianism of the past.

The Bohemianism of the 1920's represented a repudiation of the provinciality, philistinism, and moral hypocrisy of American life—a life, incidentally, which was still essentially small-town and rural in tone. Bohemia, in other words, was a movement created in the name of civilization: its ideals were intelligence, cultivation, spiritual refinement. The typical literary figure of the 1920's was a midwesterner (Hemingway, Fitzgerald, Sinclair Lewis, Eliot, Pound) who had fled from his home town to New York or Paris in search of a freer, more expansive, more enlightened way of life than was possible in Ohio or Minnesota or Michigan. The political radicalism that supplied the characteristic coloring of Bohemianism in the 1930's did nothing to alter the urban, cosmopolitan bias of the 1920's. At its best, the radicalism of the 1930's was marked by deep intellectual seriousness and aimed at a state of society in which the fruits of civilization would be more widely available—and ultimately available to all.

The Bohemianism of the 1950's is another kettle of fish altogether. It is hostile to civilization; it worships primitivism, instinct, energy, "blood." To the extent that it has intellectual interests at all, they run to mystical doctrines, irrationalist philosophies, and left-wing Reichianism. The only art the new Bohemians have any use for is jazz, mainly of the cool variety. Their predilection for bop language is a way of demonstrating solidarity with the primitive vitality and spontaneity they find in jazz and of expressing contempt for coherent, rational discourse which, being a product of the mind, is in their view a form of death. To be articulate is to admit that you have no feelings (for how can real feelings be expressed in syntactical language?), that you can't respond to anything (Kerouac responds to everything by saying "Wow!"), and that you are probably impotent.

At the one end of the spectrum, this ethos shades off into violence and criminality, main-line drug addiction and madness. Allen Ginsberg's poetry, with its lurid apocalyptic celebration of "angel-headed hipsters," speaks for the darker side of the new Bohemianism. Kerouac is milder. He shows little taste for violence, and the criminality he admires is the harmless kind. The hero of *On the Road*, Dean Moriarty, has a record: "From the age of eleven to seventeen he was usually in reform school. His specialty was stealing cars, gunning for girls coming out of high school in the afternoon, driving them out to the mountains, making them, and coming back to sleep in any available hotel bathtub in town." But Dean's criminality, we are told, "was not something that sulked and sneered; it was a wild yea-saying overburst of American joy; it was Western, the west wind, an ode from the Plains, something new, long prophesied, long a-coming (he only stole cars for joy rides)." And, in fact, the species of Bohemian that Kerouac writes about is on the whole rather law-abiding. In *The Subterraneans*, a bunch of drunken boys steal a pushcart in the middle of the night, and when they leave it in front of a friend's apartment building, he denounces them angrily for "screwing up the security of my pad." When Sal Paradise (in *On the Road*) steals some groceries from the canteen of an itinerant workers' camp in which he has taken a temporary job as a barracks guard, he comments, "I suddenly began to realize that everybody in America is a natural-born thief"—which, of course, is a way of turning his own stealing into a bit of boyish prankishness. Nevertheless, Kerouac is attracted to criminality, and that in itself is more significant than the fact that he personally feels constrained to put the brakes on his own destructive impulses.

Sex has always played a very important role in Bohemianism: sleeping around was the Bohemian's most dramatic demonstration of his freedom from conventional moral standards, and a defiant denial of the idea that sex was permissible only in marriage and then only for the sake of a family. At the same time, to be "promiscuous" was to assert the validity of sexual experience in and for itself. The "meaning" of Bohemian sex, then, was at once social and personal, a crucial element in the Bohemian's ideal of civilization. Here again the contrast with Beat Generation Bohemianism is sharp. On the one hand, there is a fair amount of sexual activity in *On the Road* and *The Subterraneans*. Dean Moriarity is a "new kind of American saint" at least partly because of his amazing sexual power: he can keep three women satisfied simultaneously and he can make love any time, anywhere (once he mounts a girl in the back seat of a car while poor Sal Paradise is trying to sleep in front). Sal, too, is always on the make, and though he isn't as successful as the great Dean, he does pretty well: offhand I can remember a girl in Denver, one on a bus, and another in New York, but a little research would certainly unearth a few more. The heroine of *The Subterraneans*, a Negro girl named Mardou Fox, seems to have switched from one to another member of the same gang and back again ("This has been an incestuous group in its time"), and we are given to understand that there is nothing unusual about such an arrangement. But the point of all this hustle and bustle is not freedom from ordinary social restrictions or defiance of convention (except in relation to homosexuality, which is Ginsberg's preserve: among "the best minds" of Ginsberg's generation who were destroyed by America are those "who let themselves be ——— in the —— by saintly motorcyclists, and screamed with joy, / who blew and were blown by those human seraphim, the sailors, caresses of Atlantic and Caribbean love"). The sex in Kerouac's books goes hand in hand with a great deal of talk about forming permanent relationships ("although I have a hot feeling sexually and all that for her," says the poet Adam Moorad in *The Subterraneans*, "I really don't want to get any further into her not only for these reasons but finally, the big one, if I'm going to get involved with a girl now I want to be permanent like permanent and serious and long termed and I can't do that with her"), and a habit of getting married and then duly divorced and re-married when another girl comes along. In fact, there are as many marriages and divorces in *On the Road* as in the Hollywood movie colony (must be that California climate): "All those years I was looking for the woman I wanted to marry," Sal Paradise tells us. "I couldn't meet a girl without saying to myself, What kind of wife would she make?" Even more revealing is Kerouac's refusal to admit that any of his characters ever make love wantonly or lecherously—no matter how casual the encounter it must always entail sweet feelings toward the girl. Sal, for example, is fixed up with Rita Bettencourt in Denver, whom he has never met before. "I got her in my bedroom after a long talk in the dark of the front room. She was a nice little girl, simple and true [naturally], and tremendously frightened of sex. I told her it was beautiful. I wanted to prove this to her. She let me prove it, but I was too impatient and proved nothing. She sighed in the dark. 'What do you want out of life?' I asked, and I used to ask that all the time of girls." This is rather touching, but only because the narrator is really just as frightened of sex as that nice little girl was. He is frightened of failure and he worries about his performance. For *performance* is the point—performance and "good orgasms," which are the first duty of man and the only duty of woman. What seems to be involved here, in short, is sexual anxiety of enormous proportions—an anxiety that comes out very clearly in *The Subterraneans*, which is about a love affair between the young writer, Leo Percepied, and the Negro girl, Mardou Fox. Despite its protestations, the book is one long agony of fear and trembling over sex:

> I spend long nights and many hours making her, finally I have her, I pray
> for it to come, I can hear her breathing harder, I hope against hope it's
> time, a noise in the hall (or whoop of drunkards next door) takes her
> mind off and she can't make it and laughs—but when she does make it
> I hear her crying, whimpering, the shuddering electrical female orgasm
> makes her sound like a little girl crying, moaning in the night, it lasts a
> good twenty seconds and when it's over she moans, "O why can't it last

longer," and "O when will I when you do?"—"Soon now I bet," I say, "you're getting closer and closer"—

Very primitive, very spontaneous, very elemental, very beat.

For the new Bohemians interracial friendships and love affairs apparently play the same role of social defiance that sex used to play in older Bohemian circles. Negroes and whites associate freely on a basis of complete equality and without a trace of racial hostility. But putting it that way understates the case, for not only is there no racial hostility, there is positive adulation for the "happy, true-hearted, ecstatic Negroes of America."

> At lilac evening I walked with every muscle aching among the lights of 27th and Welton in the Denver colored section, wishing I were a Negro, feeling that the best the white world had offered was not enough ecstasy for me, not enough life, joy, kicks, darkness, music, not enough night. ... I wished I were a Denver Mexican, or even a poor overworked Jap, anything but what I was so drearily, a "white man" disillusioned. All my life I'd had white ambitions. ... I passed the dark porches of Mexican and Negro homes; soft voices were there, occasionally the dusky knee of some mysterious sensuous gal; and dark faces of the men behind rose arbors. Little children sat like sages in ancient rocking chairs.

It will be news to the Negroes to learn that they are so happy and ecstatic; I doubt if a more idyllic picture of Negro life has been painted since certain Southern ideologues tried to convince the world that things were just as fine as fine could be for the slaves on the old plantation. Be that as it may, Kerouac's love for Negroes and other dark-skinned groups is tied up with his worship of primitivism, not with any radical social attitudes. Ironically enough, in fact, to see the Negro as more elemental than the white man, as Ned Polsky has acutely remarked, is "an inverted form of keeping the nigger in his place." But even if it were true that American Negroes, by virtue of their position in our culture, have been able to retain a degree of primitive spontaneity, the last place you would expect to find evidence of this is among Bohemian Negroes. Bohemianism, after all, is for the Negro a means of entry into the world of the whites, and no Negro Bohemian is going to cooperate in the attempt to identify him with Harlem or Dixieland. The only major Negro character in either of Kerouac's two novels is Mardou Fox, and she is about as primitive as Wilhelm Reich himself.

The plain truth is that the primitivism of the Beat Generation serves first of all as a cover for an anti-intellectualism so bitter that it makes the ordinary American's hatred of eggheads seem positively benign. Kerouac and his friends like to think of themselves as intellectuals ("they are intellectual as hell and know all about Pound without being pretentious or talking too much about it"), but this is only a form of newspeak. Here is an example of what

Kerouac considers intelligent discourse—"formal and shining and complete, without the tedious intellectualness":

> We passed a little kid who was throwing stones at the cars in the road. "Think of it," said Dean. "One day he'll put a stone through a man's windshield and the man will crash and die—all on account of that little kid. You see what I mean? God exists without qualms. As we roll along this way I am positive beyond doubt that everything will be taken care of for us—that even you, as you drive, fearful of the wheel ... the thing will go along of itself and you won't go off the road and I can sleep. Furthermore we know America, we're at home; I can go anywhere in America and get what I want because it's the same in every corner, I know the people, I know what they do. We give and take and go in the incredibly complicated sweetness zigzagging every side."

You see what he means? Formal and shining and complete. No tedious intellectualness. Completely unpretentious. "There was nothing clear about the things he said but what he meant to say was somehow made pure and clear." *Somehow.* Of course. If what he wanted to say had been carefully thought out and precisely articulated, that would have been tedious and pretentious and, no doubt, *somehow* unclear and clearly impure. But so long as he utters these banalities with his tongue tied and with no comprehension of their meaning, so long as he makes noises that come out of his soul (since they couldn't possibly have come out of his mind), he passes the test of true intellectuality.

Which brings us to Kerouac's spontaneous bop prosody. This "prosody" is not to be confused with bop language itself, which has such a limited vocabulary (Basic English is a verbal treasure-house by comparison) that you couldn't write a note to the milkman in it, much less a novel. Kerouac, however, manages to remain true to the spirit of hipster slang while making forays into enemy territory (i.e., the English language) by his simple inability to express anything in words. The only method he has of describing an object is to summon up the same half-dozen adjectives over and over again: "greatest," "tremendous," "crazy," "mad," "wild," and perhaps one or two others. When it's more than just mad or crazy or wild, it becomes "really mad" or "really crazy" or "really wild." (All quantities in excess of three, incidentally, are subsumed under the rubric "innumerable," a word used innumerable times in *On the Road* but not so innumerably in *The Subterraneans*.) The same poverty of resources is apparent in those passages where Kerouac tries to handle a situation involving even slightly complicated feelings. His usual tactic is to run for cover behind cliché and vague signals to the reader. For instance: "I looked at him; my eyes were watering with embarrassment and tears. Still he stared at me. Now his eyes were blank and looking through me. ... Something clicked in both of us. In me it was suddenly concern for a man who was years younger than I, five years, and whose fate was wound with mine across the passage of the recent years; in him it was a matter that I can ascertain only from what he did afterward." If you can ascertain what this is all about, either beforehand, during, or afterward, you are surely no square.

In keeping with its populistic bias, the style of *On the Road* is folksy and lyrical. The prose of *The Subterraneans,* on the other hand, sounds like an inept parody of Faulkner at his worst, the main difference being that Faulkner usually produces bad writing out of an impulse to inflate the commonplace while Kerouac gets into trouble by pursuing "spontaneity." Strictly speaking, spontaneity is a quality of feeling, not of writing: when we call a piece of writing spontaneous, we are registering our impression that the author hit upon the right words without sweating, that no "art" and no calculation entered into the picture, that his feelings seem to have spoken themselves, seem to have sprouted a tongue at the moment of composition. Kerouac apparently thinks that spontaneity is a matter of saying whatever comes into your head, in any order you happen to feel like saying it. It isn't the *right* words he wants (even if he knows what they might be), but the first words, or at any rate the words that most obviously announce themselves as deriving from emotion rather than cerebration, as coming from "life" rather than "literature," from the guts rather than the brain. (The brain, remember, is the angel of death.) But writing that springs easily and "spontaneously" out of strong feelings is *never* vague; it always has a quality of sharpness and precision because it is in the nature of strong feelings to be aroused by specific objects. The notion that a diffuse, generalized, and unrelenting enthusiasm is the mark of great sensitivity and responsiveness is utterly fantastic, an idea that comes from taking drunkenness or drug-addiction as the state of perfect emotional vigor. The effect of such enthusiasm is actually to wipe out the world altogether, for if a filling station will serve as well as the Rocky Mountains to arouse a sense of awe and wonder, then both the filling station and the mountains are robbed of their reality. Kerouac's conception of feeling is one that only a solipsist could believe in—and a solipsist, be it noted, is a man who does not relate to anything outside himself.

Solipsism is precisely what characterizes Kerouac's fiction. *On the Road* and *The Subterraneans* are so patently autobiographical in content that they become almost impossible to discuss as novels; if spontaneity were indeed a matter of destroying the distinction between life and literature, these books would unquestionably be It. "As we were going out to the car Babe slipped and fell flat on her face. Poor girl was overwrought. Her brother Tim and I helped her up. We got in the car; Major and Betty joined us. The sad ride back to Denver began." Babe is a girl who is mentioned a few times in the course of *On the Road*; we don't know why she is overwrought on this occasion, and even if we did it wouldn't matter, since there is no reason for her presence in the book at all. But Kerouac tells us that she fell flat on her face while walking toward a car. It is impossible to believe that Kerouac made this detail up, that his imagination was creating a world real enough to include wholly gratuitous elements; if that were the case, Babe would have come alive as a human being. But she is only a name; Kerouac never even describes her. She is in the book because the sister of one of Kerouac's friends was there when he took a trip to Central City, Colorado, and she slips in *On the Road* because she slipped that day on the way to the car. What is true of Babe who fell flat on her face is true of virtually every incident in *On the Road* and *The Subterraneans*. Nothing that happens has any dramatic reason for happening. Sal Paradise meets such-and-such people on the road whom he likes or (rarely) dislikes; they exchange a few words, they have a few beers together, they part. It is all very unremarkable and commonplace, but for Kerouac it is always the greatest, the wildest, the most. What you get in these two books is a man proclaiming that he is *alive* and offering every trivial experience he has ever had in evidence. Once I did this, once I did that (he is saying) and by God, it *meant* something! Because I *responded*! But if it meant something, and you responded so powerfully, why can't you explain what it meant, and why do you have to insist so?

I think it is legitimate to say, then, that the Beat Generation's worship of primitivism and spontaneity is more than a cover for hostility to intelligence; it arises from a pathetic poverty of feeling as well. The hipsters and hipster-lovers of the Beat Generation are rebels, all right, but not against anything so sociological and historical as the middle class or capitalism or even respectability. This is the revolt of the spiritually underprivileged and the crippled of soul—young men who can't think straight and so hate anyone who can; young men who can't get outside the morass of self and so construct definitions of feeling that exclude all human beings who manage to live, even miserably, in a world of objects; young men who are burdened unto death with the specially poignant sexual anxiety that America—in its eternal promise of erotic glory and its spiteful withholding of actual erotic possibility—seems bent on breeding, and who therefore dream of the unattainable perfect orgasm, which excuses all sexual failures in the real world. Not long ago, Norman Mailer suggested that the rise of the hipster may represent "the first wind of a second revolution in this century, moving not forward toward action and more rational equitable distribution, but backward toward being and the secrets of human energy." To tell the truth, whenever I hear anyone talking about instinct and being and the secrets of human energy, I get nervous; next thing you know he'll be saying that violence is just fine, and then I begin wondering whether he really thinks that kicking someone in the teeth or sticking a knife between his ribs are deeds to be admired. History, after all—and especially the history of modern times—teaches that there is a close connection between ideologies of primitivistic vitalism and a willingness to look upon cruelty and blood-letting with complacency, if not downright enthusiasm. The reason I bring this up is that the spirit of hipsterism and the Beat Generation strikes me as the same spirit which animates the young savages in leather jackets who have been running amuck in the last few years with their switch-blades and zip guns. What does Mailer think of those wretched kids, I wonder? What does he think of the gang that stoned a nine-year-old boy to death in Central Park in broad daylight a few months ago, or the one that set fire to an old man drowsing on a bench near the Brooklyn waterfront one summer's day, or the one that pounced on a crippled child and orgiastically stabbed him over and over and over again even after he was good and dead? Is that what he means by the liberation of instinct and the mysteries of being? Maybe so. At least he says somewhere in his article that two eighteen-year-old hoodlums who bash in the brains of a candy-store keeper are murdering an institution, committing an act that "violates private property"—which is one of the most morally gruesome ideas I have ever come across, and which indicates where the ideology of hipsterism can lead. I happen to believe that there is a direct connection between the flabbiness of American middle-class life and the spread of juvenile crime in the 1950's, but I also believe that juvenile crime can be explained partly in terms of the same resentment against normal feeling and the attempt to cope with the world through intelligence that lies behind Kerouac and Ginsberg. Even the relatively mild ethos of Kerouac's books can spill over easily into brutality, for there is a suppressed cry in those books: Kill the intellectuals who can talk coherently, kill the people who can sit still for five minutes at a time, kill those incomprehensible characters who are capable of getting seriously involved with a woman, a job, a cause. How can anyone in his right mind pretend that this has anything to do with private property or the middle class? No. Being for or against what the Beat Generation stands for has to do with denying that incoherence is superior to precision; that ignorance is superior to knowledge; that the exercise of mind and discrimination is a form of death. It has to do with fighting the notion that sordid acts of violence are justifiable so long as they are committed in the name of "instinct." It even has to do with fighting the poisonous glorification of the adolescent in American popular culture. It has to do, in other words, with being for or against intelligence itself.

Editor's Introduction

Irving Howe was already one of the prominent intellectual leaders of the Old Left by the 1950s. That was a position of frustration rather than power, however, as the left was decidedly weak in the fifties. Howe and his friend the sociologist Lewis Coser, with whom he taught at Brandeis, worked hard to forge a democratic left in a decade in which Americans were fatigued with ideologies and settled comfortably into a safe and prosperous center. In this inhospitable setting in 1954, Howe, Coser and a handful of other democratic leftists began *Dissent*, a magazine of liberal socialism.

Thus, when the New Left rose in the early 1960s Howe was keenly interested in its ideas and plans. At first he found its members utopian. But, by the mid-sixties, he had become more discouraged as he saw, in the New Left, radical elements he considered illiberal. In the 1960s, he was pulled between wanting to encourage the expansion of left liberalism in the country but also fighting against many of its young practitioners with his demands that they be appropriately democratic and liberal. He insisted that they be aware of the dangers his generation fought in the Stalinism of the 1930s and 1940s and be vigilant not to repeat the mistakes of the American communist sympathizers of those decades.

The New Left, however, was not so easily corralled and instructed as Howe hoped. The New Left was antinomian, Emersonian, Whitmanesque. It did not depend mainly on rationality and theory, but on intuition and the action of the moment. It believed that ideology arose and was explained by action, not that ideology should direct action. It believed that the world should be made anew, and was convinced this wouldn't be done by simply falling in step with the previous generation. Many members of the New Left rejected the idea of studying the radical tradition to find the best path for them because it would simply entangle them in the struggles of the past. As a result, Howe and the New York Intellectuals accused the young of being anti-intellectual.

The Vietnam War further complicated the New York Intellectuals' relationship with the young radicals. New Leftists believed that the anticommunism of thinkers like Howe had produced the war, and of course that was true.

How, the young wanted to know, could the New York Intellectuals' anticommunism and support of the Vietnam War be consistent with being radicals? Yet Howe and others felt the relevant history was more complicated than the New Left supposed, and realized the young could not know its complexities without reading the history of the ideological conflicts from the 1930s to the present. Again, most of the young weren't interested. But the New York group could no more give up their anticommunism than they could their identities as intellectuals.

Source

Irving Howe, *A Margin of Hope* (New York: Harcourt Brace Jovanovich, 1982), pp. 291–299, 314–315.

Selected Readings

Irving Howe, ed., *Beyond the New Left* (New York: McCall, 1970). "The Young Radicals: A Symposium," *Dissent* vol. 9, no. 2, Spring 1962.

＊ ＊ ＊ ＊ ＊

In 1962, several leading figures from Students for a Democratic Society, then a tiny, obscure organization, paid a visit to the *Dissent* editorial board. I remember among them Paul Potter, Tom Hayden, and Paul Booth, bright and eager young men who would become important in the politics of the sixties. At this meeting two generations sat facing each other, fumbling to reach across the spaces of time. We were scarred, they untouched. We bore marks of "corrosion and distrust," they looked forward to clusterings of fraternity. We had grown skeptical of Marxism, they were still unchained to system. We had pulled ourselves out of an immigrant working class, an experience not likely to induce romantic views about the poor; they, children of warm liberals and cooled radicals, were hoping to find a way into the lives and wisdom of the oppressed. ("I live in Newark among the rats," said Tom Hayden proudly to a fourteen-year-old stepson of mine, who looked up to Hayden with awe, as at a decorated hero.)

Both sides in this encounter favored social criticism, both had no taste for Marxist-Leninist vanguards, both held to a vision of socialism as a society of freedom. It seemed at first as if there might be a joining of two generations of the Left.

The SDS visitors kept using the term "participatory democracy," by which they meant a society in which masses of people wouldn't just vote once every few years but would become active and articulate citizens, thereby endowing the democratic "forms" with popular substance. That seemed fine with us, until they started juxtaposing this envisaged "participatory democracy" with the "representative democracy" in which we lived, as if somehow the two were contraries. We winced. It sounded a little too much like the fecklessness of our youth, when Stalinists and even a few Socialists used to put down "mere" bourgeois democracy. At least as troubling was the readiness of SDS people to excuse the lack of freedom in Cuba, a country that seemed to them the home of a better or more glamorous kind of communism. They, in turn, made quite clear their distaste for our "rigid anticommunism" and our lack of responsiveness to the new moods of the young.

Wise after the event, I now see that we mishandled this meeting badly. Unable to contain our impatience with SDS susceptibility to charismatic dictators like Castro, several *Dissent* people, I among them, went off on long, windy speeches. Might it not have been better to be a little more tactful, a little readier to engage in give-and-take rather than just to pronounce opinions? No doubt; yet a clash was inevitable. We simply could not remain quiet about our deepest and costliest conviction: that if socialism still has any meaning, it must be set strictly apart from all dictatorships, whether by frigid Russians or hot Cubans. There is the value of tact, but also the value of candor.

I liked the evident sincerity of the young SDSers, and still more the gentleness of some of them. As our talk continued, it turned into polemic and it soon became clear that the most brilliant among them was a boy named Tom Hayden. But also the most rigid, perhaps even fanatical. Pinched in manner, holding in some obscure personal rage, he spoke as if he were already an experienced, canny "political"; after the meeting a number of *Dissenters* remarked spontaneously that in Hayden's clenched style—that air of distance suggesting reserves of power—one could already see the beginnings of a commissar. All through the sixties I kept encountering Hayden, each time impressed by his gifts yet also persuaded that some authoritarian poisons of this century had seeped into the depths of his mind.

The meeting broke up, our relations broke down; but one kept hoping. Something good, an undogmatic native radicalism, might yet blossom in this new student movement. The early SDS statement adopted at Port Huron still strikes me as a fresh exposition of an American democratic radicalism. And equally attractive were the new radicals' sense of style, their feeling for community, their readiness to take risks.

I attended one or two SDS board meetings, sitting through interminable and structureless sessions. Two ideas were being tested here: that decisions be reached not by vote but consensus, and that the role of leaders be kept to a strict minimum. Attractive as these notions were, it soon became clear they had not been thought through. In the blur of fraternity nothing was thought through.

For some of the SDS people the ideal polity seemed to be a community without or beyond rules, an anarchy of pals, in which anyone dropping in at a meeting could speak as long as they wished, whether upon the topic of the moment or not; then, out of this chaos of good feeling, concord would emerge. But to me it all seemed a chaos favoring manipulation by tight sects and grandiose charismatic leaders; the SDS theory of organization did not take enough account of people as they actually are and are likely to remain. To talk out differences endlessly was all very well; but what if the differences persisted, as in the frailty of the human condition they always do? Didn't the SDS procedure put an improper kind of pressure on minorities to give way, so that all might end in public ceremonies of affection and harmony?[1]

Friends who had gone South in organizing drives reported that an attractive "movement" leader named Bob Moses refused on principle to sit up front at meetings: he wished to avoid the arrogant postures of the *apparatchik*. An admirable motive; yet some of us argued that what Moses was doing had an undemocratic potential. There is good reason for putting leaders up front: to position them as targets for criticism.

Still, the SDS was brushing against important matters in its talk about "participatory democracy." The malaise it wished to treat had earlier been designated as the "mass society," one in which populations grow passive and atomized, coherent publics based on clear interests fall apart, and man tends to shrink to a consumer, mass-produced like the products, diversions, and values he takes in. No serious advocate of this theory would have claimed it was more than an alarming possibility, but as popularized by the New Left this view of modern society ("one-dimensional man," in Herbert Marcuse's phrase) tended to treat the cartoon as if it were an actual photograph. The early SDS style—a mixture of student bull session, Quaker meeting, and group therapy—had its uses for young people with lots of time and no pressing need for sleep; but it could seldom contribute to solving problems of democracy in societies where the sheer number of citizens and the complexity of clashing interests require some system of representation.

In 1965, after I had given a lecture in New York, a young writer named Sally Kempton came up and with all good will asked whether I favored representative or participatory democracy. I started to stammer that choosing between the two would be foolish, but suddenly fell into depressed silence. I thought I knew how to cope with error, but innocence left me baffled. Ms. Kempton must have thought me rude.

Suppose the United States had not become so deeply embroiled in the Vietnam war—how might this have affected the New Left? Probably toward a more gradual and harmonious development. Its growth would have been less rapid, but it might have found a path to a democratic radicalism suitable to the American temper. We will never know, for the Vietnam war soon eclipsed everything else in American life.

If the fifties had been marked by a contagion of repressiveness soon infecting large portions of official society, then the years of the Vietnam war constituted a time of structured deceit. Lying now became a systematic "necessity" of the war—lying about the nature of the regime we were propping up in South Vietnam, lying about the attitudes of the Vietnamese people, lying about the methods used by American troops. For the poisonous atmosphere blanketing the country, the Johnson and Nixon administrations were mainly responsible. They knew the puppet regimes in Saigon neither enjoyed nor merited much support among the Vietnamese. They knew the scare talk about "falling dominoes"—let Vietnam go communist and Malaysia will fall soon, to be followed by Indonesia and India—was at best a speculative notion, at worst a cheap intimidation. They knew that some methods used by government agencies to infiltrate and incite antiwar movements were illegal. No one in power told the truth.

What gave these years a special aura of sleaziness was that the language of liberalism was often employed to justify the war. Rhetoric from the days of the Marshall Plan was reheated for Vietnam. The economic aid to Western Europe after the Second World War had been a major achievement of American policy: it really helped save democratic societies. But no one could argue seriously that helping the corrupt dictatorships of Diem, Ky, and Thieu formed a legitimate continuation of that earlier policy. When liberals like Hubert Humphrey tried to justify the Vietnam war by recalling a strategy that had been beneficial to European freedom, they caused grave damage to American liberalism. Young people outraged by the war tended to identify the liberal idea with liberal politicians, and liberal politicians with American policy in Vietnam; it was impossible to persuade them this was a simplification almost as gross as those of the people in power.

Within the antiwar movement, the simplest opinion was that a victory of Hanoi and the Vietcong would advance the "progressive" cause. Or a shade less simply, that only a leftist authoritarian government could be both radical and ruthless enough to further national independence and capital accumulation in Third World countries. The assumption here—a curse of our age—was that political liberty is a luxury that developing nations can, or must, do without.

A more authentic response was that of people, mostly non-political, who felt morally repelled by the war. The war seemed to them unjust because it constituted an attempt by a great power to impose its will on an oppressed people. This was a strong judgment, but it needed to be buttressed by a political analysis of the struggle in Vietnam. That our side committed atrocities was cause for shame; but could it really be argued that the other side did not? Was there a reliable measure with which to compare magnitudes of atrocity? (Communist atrocities in Indochina reached their culmination only after the war was over.) That nonintervention should be a strong moral principle or disposition is certainly true; but could it be an absolute principle, an unqualified premise in a century that saw the rise of expansive totalitarian states? The moral argument against the war was strongest when it rested on considerations specific to *this* war, and did not merely invoke a generalized pacifist sentiment. But it was an argument that could be secured only through a strong link to political analysis.

As the war dragged on, wearying and depressing everyone, many people, especially in Washington, who cared little about either moral issues or political analysis came to the "pragmatic" conclusion that the cost of continuing it was simply too great. No national interest, they hastened to say, required a victory in Vietnam. Even conservatives, at least those not drugged with ideology, came to see the point.

As for liberal and socialist opponents of the war, by the mid-sixties we had concluded that the most to be hoped for was a negotiated truce enabling American troops to leave Vietnam and delaying somewhat the impending communist victory. That victory now seemed certain, and the more America plunged into the war, the less likely was even an appearance of compromise. We saw the war as partly an inherited colonial struggle, with the United States taking over the imperial role of France; partly a civil war between two orders of society within Vietnam; and partly a reflection of the worldwide conflict between the two superpowers. As early as the mid-fifties it had become clear that the conflict in Vietnam had acquired an all-but-irreversible political character that precluded the Saigon government's winning mass support among the Vietnamese people. The Communists had appropriated the historical energies of Vietnamese nationalism; they were superbly organized; they were ready—and inspired a readiness among their followers—to fight hard and risk death. About few other Vietnamese could this be said.

By, say, 1965 or 1966 there was consequently no real choice but to accept a communist victory or keep the war going endlessly, with terrible consequences both in Vietnam and, in lesser ways, at home. This political judgment lent a sad sort of cogency to the moral argument against the war, since it helped explain why the American intruders, in themselves neither more nor less moral than other people, were often guilty of outrages during their "pacification" campaigns. What they could not do politically, they tried to do through sheer military weight—and of course failed.

It never was necessary to defend the communist regime in Hanoi or the Vietcong guerrillas in order to oppose American intervention. Some of us had hoped during the mid-fifties for the emergence of a Vietnamese "third force," capable of rallying the people through land reform in the countryside and democratization in the cities. This now appears to have been a vain hope: there simply were no political forces strong or coherent enough to move in this direction. Vietnam had been fiercely polarized by the French who, unlike the British in India, allowed almost no freedom for the early Vietnamese nationalists. This, in turn, made it virtually certain that moderate or liberal tendencies among these nationalists would be rendered helpless and that the better-organized, more combative Communists would take over leadership of the nationalist movement.

Working for a measure of freedom in Third World countries does not strike me as futile, even though authoritarians of Left and Right often take a peculiar delight in sneering at the idea. But it is, I admit, difficult. The policies of the United States, usually tilted toward support of old-style autocrats, constitute one major reason for the difficulty. Soon the Vietnam war would settle into a struggle between the totalitarian government of Hanoi, skilled at exploiting nationalist traditions and peasant needs, and the authoritarian government of Saigon, precariously kept in power by foreign money, arms, and troops. Even if one judged the Saigon regime to be a "lesser evil," the reality in Vietnam was that once the civil war began, support to Saigon meant assuring the victory of Hanoi. And so it did.

All through the late sixties antiwar demonstrations were mounting in size and intensity, and for the democratic Left this posed some perplexing choices. We too thought it calloused to prolong the war. We too wanted to demonstrate against it. But we took the trouble to read the materials issued by the organizers of the antiwar demonstrations, and what we saw dismayed us. Always a double standard: harsh criticism of Saigon and either silence about or approval of Hanoi. The tens of thousands who came to these demonstrations paid about as much attention to the manifestoes as most citizens to the platforms of the major parties; but for Socialists to have yielded to this American nonchalance would have been to break with all our training, all our habits.

Segments of the antiwar movement were starting to talk about proposals for forcible resistance: stopping troop trains, blocking induction centers, "storming" the Pentagon. This was mostly talk, but of a kind that could easily become dangerous, inducing delusions of revolutionary coups, providing government provocateurs with opportunities to incite violence, and leading to confrontations with the government that the movement could not win.

Here is Staughton Lynd, one of the cooler New Left leaders, writing about an antiwar demonstration in Washington: "It was unbearably moving to watch the sea of banners move out toward the Capitol....Still more poignant was the perception that ... our forward movement was irresistibly strong....Nothing could have stopped that crowd from taking possession of its government. Perhaps next time we should keep going, occupying for a time the rooms from which orders came." Under whose mandate, some of us asked Lynd, were the marchers to "occupy" the government? And if "next time" they did manage a coup, even if only for five playful minutes, how did he propose to keep other crowds, other causes, equally moving and sincere, from doing the same "perhaps the time after next"?

A strong case could be made out for conscientious objection and civil disobedience to the war. Many people felt the usual methods of political protest were no longer adequate. But what was not legitimate was to use tactics that looked like civil disobedience yet really constituted "uncivil" and prerevolutionary acts. "Stopping" troop trains—I leave aside the question of whether anyone could—is a basic challenge to the authority of the state, and it makes sense only if undertaken as part of a revolutionary sequence. Otherwise, it must seem ineffectual playacting. The rhetoric of the New Left escalated, and there was plenty of provocation from a government that kept lying about the war. For that very reason it was important that the methods used in opposing the war not give enemies of liberty a plausible excuse for destroying both the protest and democratic procedures. So at least my friends and I argued, though with little success.

We were stuck, those of us who opposed American involvement in Vietnam yet did not favor a communist victory. We had no happy ending to offer. By the mid-sixties, and probably for some time before then, no happy ending was possible. If our protest did not seem quite as single-minded as that of others, it was because we were caught in a trap: we thought it would be good to end the war, but knew that no good was likely to follow in Vietnam. Our opinions, perhaps too shaded to be effective, were swept aside. The tacit or open allies of Hanoi prevailed, their slogans captivating a good many of the young. The truth seems to be that in moments of crisis those who try to speak with some awareness of complexity are likely to be disabled politically. A depressing thought. ...

In the late sixties I felt politically beleaguered, intellectually isolated. I kept throwing myself into conflicts with New Left spokesmen, but with very little profit or success. Why didn't I simply pull away and wait for time to sort things out? Whatever common ground there had once been for debate was steadily shrinking, and after a while political encounters took on a predictably ritualistic character. Yet something within me—sentimentality, conscience, stubbornness—kept murmuring that I had an obligation to speak. And I felt genuine sadness at seeing the early idealism of the New Leftist youth turn sour.

Part of what had gone wrong with the New Left seemed an extreme instance of what had always been wrong with American radicalism. Their mistakes were not new; some I had participated in a few decades earlier. The trap in which I found myself was this: if the New Left registered victories I couldn't share in them, but when it suffered defeats I would probably have to bear at least some of the consequences. True, with the passage of time there occurred a growing dissociation, and for the fascistic Weathermen I felt nothing but hostility. Yet there were still a number of young New Leftists sparked by a genuine idealism, and they stirred in me painfully mixed and thwarted feelings.

There was something peculiarly wounding in the New Left attacks on older liberals and radicals. I felt that some of its spokesmen wanted not just to refute my opinions—that would have been entirely proper—but also to erase, to eliminate, to "smash" people like me. They wanted to deny our past, annul our history, wipe out our integrity, and not as people mistaken or even pusillanimous but as people who were "finished," "used up." (Lenin in 1907 explained his attacks on the Socialists: "That tone ... is not designed to convince but to break ranks, not to correct a mistake of the opponent but to annihilate him, to wipe him off the face of the earth.") When New Left students painted the slogan "Up against the wall, motherfuckers!" on campus buildings, they had in mind not just the corporate state or the Pentagon or the CIA; they had in mind the only "enemy" they knew at first hand, their liberal and socialist teachers; they had in mind parents of the New Deal generation who had raised them on the deplorable doctrine of "repressive tolerance."

But before someone else does, I had better put to myself the question: wasn't all this a case of unrequited love? Hadn't middle-aged Socialists like you set for yourselves the role of mentor to the young, and weren't you now reeling from blows of rejection?

Yes; I see no reason to deny that this is part of the truth. We had, after all, been waiting a long time, almost as long as Beckett's pair for Godot. If all we had wanted was the admiration of the young, we could easily have chosen the paths Marcuse and Chomsky took, and for a while Paul Goodman. We need only have said, at some expense to our convictions, what the New Left wanted to hear. Goodman had been a guru to the Berkeley students, though in 1969, as soon as he published an essay criticizing his disciples, they thrust him aside with contempt, another "used-up" intellectual.

Perhaps I should not have gotten so emotionally entangled in disputes with the New Left. But I did. Perhaps I should have eased my way into the paternalism that some intellectuals adopted. But I could not. I overreacted, becoming at times harsh and strident. I told myself that I was one of the few people who took the New Left seriously enough to keep arguing with it. Cold comfort.

Friends began to hint in the kindliest way that I was becoming a little punch-drunk. I found myself wondering why Michael Harrington, who expressed criticisms of the New Left close to mine, was not regarded as so dastardly an opponent. The generous-hearted Harrington was a Christian of sorts, while I was a polemicist in the old style. So, in a conversation painful to both of us, Michael Walzer gently told me. Couldn't I make my criticisms more temperate? Someone should, I could not.

The truth is that the "kids," as the phrase goes, "got to me." I might score in polemic, but they scored in life.

Note

1. George Orwell writes in his essay about *Gulliver's Travels*: "In a society in which there is no law, and in theory no compulsion, the only arbiter of behavior public opinion. But public opinion, because of the tremendous urge to conformity in gregarious animals, is less tolerant than any system of law. When human beings are governed by 'thou shalt not,' the individual can practice a certain amount of eccentricity; when they are supposedly governed by 'Love' or 'Reason,' he is under continuous pressure to make him behave and think in exactly the same way as everyone else."

27

Norman Podhoretz (1930–)
My Negro Problem—and Ours (1963)

Editor's Introduction

Norman Podhoretz contributed his thoughts to the problem of race half a year before the famous 1963 March on Washington where Martin Luther King gave his "I Have a Dream" speech. Consequently, Podhoretz's ideas and instincts reflect the integrationist, color blind, meritocratic, assimilationist mindset that preceded the days of Black Power, the Black Panthers and the multicultural society—a change of mood and ethic that started only two years after his essay appeared. It is a candid essay in which he bares his soul in an attempt to help envision a path to change. His description of the animosity between blacks and Jews had already been discussed by James Baldwin fifteen years earlier in "The Harlem Ghetto" in *Commentary* in a similar spirit of honest acknowledgment, and Baldwin continued with a series of essays after that in *Partisan Review, The New Leader, The Reporter* and other publications.

For much of the twentieth century blacks and Jews had felt an alliance as targets of discrimination in the United States, and Jews had extended help to blacks as lawyers and union bosses. But under the patina of this partnership there had been resentment on both sides. Jews, as Baldwin wrote, were businessmen and landlords, "they operate in accordance with the American business tradition of exploiting Negroes, and they are therefore identified with oppression and are hated for it." (Baldwin, *Notes of a Native Son*, 68.) Podhoretz tells the other side of the story, admitting that the Jews had it better in the long run but that as children they felt physically threatened by blacks. This mutual antagonism exploded in the Ocean Hill–Brownsville argument in Brooklyn in 1967 in which the predominantly Jewish teachers and union opposed the new community control of schools by black parents in those neighborhoods. This painful fight is usually acknowledged as the point at which black–Jewish relations disintegrated to a point of mutual contempt. Podhoretz was raised in Brownsville.

Thirty years later, Podhoretz admitted there might be, as one critic had said, something in his article to offend everyone. But he emphasized that, though he had written as a Jew, he had intended it to be a statement of "a white liberal … about liberal feeling in general, rather than about Jewish feeling in particular." (Podhoretz, "Postscript" (1993) to "My Negro Problem and Ours," in Paul Berman, ed., *Blacks and Jews: Alliances and Arguments*, New York: Delacorte Press, 1994.) Podhoretz ends his essay with the suggestion that, through intermarriage for all in America, blacks and Jews can become one and live in peace. This ethic of assimilation runs directly counter to the multicultural celebration of ethnicity, race and culture that began shortly after his essay, yet it also was notably brave for a Jew to suggest. In light of his proposal for intermarriage, there is little question that Podhoretz meant his essay as a genuine attempt to address the painful racial problems of his time.

Source

Norman Podhoretz, "My Negro Problem—And Ours," *Commentary* vol. 35, no. 2, February 1963.

Selected Readings

James Baldwin, *Notes of a Native Son* (Boston: Beacon Press, 1955).
Paul Berman, ed., *Blacks and Jews: Alliances and Arguments* (New York: Delacorte Press, 1994).
Jonathan Rieder, *Canarsie* (Cambridge: Harvard University Press, 1985).
David Hollinger, *Post-Ethnic America* (New York: Basic, 1995).

* * * * *

If we—and ... I mean the relatively conscious whites and the relatively conscious blacks, who must, like lovers, insist on, or create, the consciousness of the others—do not falter in our duty now, we may be able, handful that we are, to end the racial nightmare, and achieve our country, and change the history of the world.

—James Baldwin

Two ideas puzzled me deeply as a child growing up in Brooklyn during the 1930's in what today would be called an integrated neighborhood. One of them was that all Jews were rich; the other was that all Negroes were persecuted. These ideas had appeared in print; therefore they must be true. My own experience and the evidence of my senses told me they were not true, but that only confirmed what a day-dreaming boy in the provinces—for the lower-class neighborhoods of New York belong as surely to the provinces as any rural town in North Dakota—discovers very early: *his* experience is unreal and the evidence of his senses is not to be trusted. Yet even a boy with a head full of fantasies incongruously synthesized out of Hollywood movies and English novels cannot altogether deny the reality of his own experience—especially when there is so much deprivation in that experience. Nor can he altogether gainsay the evidence of his own senses—especially such evidence of the senses as comes from being repeatedly beaten up, robbed, and in general hated, terrorized, and humiliated.

And so for a long time I was puzzled to think that Jews were supposed to be rich when the only Jews I knew were poor, and that Negroes were supposed to be persecuted when it was the Negroes who were doing the only persecuting I knew about—and doing it, moreover, to *me.* During the early years of the war, when my older sister joined a left-wing youth organization, I remember my astonishment at hearing her passionately denounce my father for thinking that Jews were worse off than Negroes. To me, at the age of twelve, it seemed very clear that Negroes were better off than Jews—indeed, than *all* whites. A city boy's world is contained within three or four square blocks, and in my world it was the whites, the Italians and Jews, who feared the Negroes, not the other way around. The Negroes were tougher than we were, more ruthless, and on the whole they were better athletes. What could it mean, then, to say that they were badly off and that we were more fortunate? Yet my sister's opinions, like print, were sacred, and when she told me about exploitation and economic forces I believed her. I believed her, but I was still afraid of Negroes. And I still hated them with all my heart.

It had not always been so—that much I can recall from early childhood. When did it start, this fear and this hatred? There was a kindergarten in the local public school, and given the character of the neighborhood, at least half of the children in my class must have been Negroes. Yet I have no memory of being aware of color differences at that age, and I know from observing my own children that they attribute no significance to such differences even when they begin noticing them. I think there was a day—first grade? second grade?—when my best friend Carl hit me on the way home from school and announced that he wouldn't play with me any more because I had killed Jesus. When I ran home to my mother crying for an explanation, she told me not to pay any attention to such foolishness, and then in Yiddish she cursed the *goyim* and the *schwartzes,* the *schwartzes* and the *goyim.* Carl, it turned out, was a *schwartze,* and so was added a third to the categories into which people were mysteriously divided.

Sometimes I wonder whether this is a true memory at all. It is blazingly vivid, but perhaps it never happened: can anyone really remember back to the age of six? There is no uncertainty in my mind, however, about the years that followed. Carl and I hardly ever spoke, though we met in school every day up through the eighth or ninth grade. There would be embarrassed moments of catching his eye or of his catching mine—for whatever it was that had attracted us to one another as very small children remained alive in spite of the fantastic barrier of hostility that had grown up between us, suddenly and out of nowhere. Nevertheless, friendship would have been impossible, and even if it had been possible, it would have been unthinkable. About that, there was nothing anyone could do by the time we were eight years old.

Item: The orphanage across the street is torn down, a city housing project begins to rise in its place, and on the marvelous vacant lot next to the old orphanage they are building a playground. Much excitement and anticipation as Opening Day draws near. Mayor LaGuardia himself comes to dedicate this great gesture of public benevolence. He speaks of neighborliness and borrowing cups of sugar, and of the playground he says that children of all races, colors, and creeds will learn to live together in harmony. A week later, some of us are swatting flies on the playground's inadequate little ball field. A gang of Negro kids, pretty much our own age, enter from the other side and order us out of the park. We refuse, proudly and indignantly, with superb masculine fervor. There is a fight, they win, and we retreat, half whimpering, half with bravado. My first nauseating experience of cowardice. And my first appalled realization that there are people in the world who do not seem to be afraid of anything, who act as though they have nothing to lose. Thereafter the playground becomes a battleground, sometimes quiet, sometimes the scene of athletic competition between Them and Us. But rocks are thrown as often as baseballs. Gradually we abandon the place and use the streets instead. The streets are safer, though we do not admit this to ourselves. We are not, after all, sissies—that most dreaded epithet of an American boyhood.

Item: I am standing alone in front of the building in which I live. It is late afternoon and getting dark. That day in school the teacher had asked a surly Negro boy named Quentin a question he was unable to answer. As usual I had waved my arm eagerly ("Be a good boy, get good marks, be smart, go to college, become a doctor") and, the right answer bursting from my lips, I was held up lovingly by the teacher as an example to the class. I had seen Quentin's face—a very dark, very cruel, very Oriental-looking face—harden, and there had been enough threat in his eyes to make me run all the way home for fear that he might catch me outside.

Now, standing idly in front of my own house, I see him approaching from the project accompanied by his little brother who is carrying a baseball bat and wearing a grin of malicious anticipation. As in a nightmare, I am trapped. The surroundings are secure and familiar, but terror is suddenly present and there is no one around to help. I am locked to the spot. I will not cry out or run away like a sissy, and I stand there, my heart wild, my throat clogged. He walks up, hurls the familiar epithet ("Hey, mo'f---r"), and to my surprise only pushes me. It is a violent push, but not a punch. A push is not as serious as a punch. Maybe I can still back out without entirely losing my dignity. Maybe I can still say, "Hey, c'mon Quentin, whaddya wanna do *that* for. I dint do nothin' to *you*," and walk away, not too rapidly. Instead, before I can stop myself, I push him back—a token gesture—and I say, "Cut that out, I don't wanna fight, I ain't got nothin' to fight about." As I turn to walk back into the building, the corner of my eye catches the motion of the bat his little brother has handed him. I try to duck, but the bat crashes colored lights into my head.

The next thing I know, my mother and sister are standing over me, both of them hysterical. My sister—she who was later to join the "progressive" youth organization—is shouting for the police and screaming imprecations at those dirty little black bastards. They take me upstairs, the doctor comes, the police come. I tell them that the boy who did it was a stranger, that he had been trying to get money from me. They do not believe me, but I am too scared to give them Quentin's name. When I return to school a few days later, Quentin avoids my eyes. He knows that I have not squealed, and he is ashamed. I try to feel proud, but in my heart I know that it was fear of what his friends might do to me that had kept me silent, and not the code of the street.

Item: There is an athletic meet in which the whole of our junior high school is participating. I am in one of the seventh-grade rapid-advance classes, and "segregation" has now set in with a vengeance. In the last three or four years of the elementary school from which we have just graduated, each grade had been divided into three classes, according to "intelligence." (In the earlier grades the divisions had either been arbitrary or else unrecognized by us as having anything to do with brains.) These divisions by IQ, or however it was arranged, had resulted in a preponderance of Jews in the "1" classes and a corresponding preponderance of Negroes in the "3's," with the Italians split unevenly along the spectrum. At least a few Negroes had always made the "1's," just as there had always been a few Jewish kids among the "3's" and more among the "2's" (where Italians dominated). But the junior high's rapid-advance class of which I am now a member is overwhelmingly Jewish and entirely white—except for a shy lonely Negro girl with light skin and reddish hair.

The athletic meet takes place in a city-owned stadium far from the school. It is an important event to which a whole day is given over. The winners are to get those precious little medallions stamped with the New York City emblem that can be screwed into a belt and that prove the wearer to be a distinguished personage. I am a fast runner, and so I am assigned the position of anchor man on my class's team in the relay race. There are three other seventh-grade teams in the race, two of them all Negro, as ours is all white. One of the all-Negro teams is very tall—their anchor man waiting silently next to me on the line looks years older than I am, and I do not recognize him. He is the first to get the baton and crosses the finishing line in a walk. Our team comes in second, but a few minutes later we are declared the winners, for it has been discovered that the anchor man on the first-place team is not a member of the class. We are awarded the medallions, and the following day our home-room teacher makes a speech about how proud she is of us for being superior athletes as well as superior students. We want to believe that we deserve the praise, but we know that we could not have won even if the other class had not cheated.

That afternoon, walking home, I am waylaid and surrounded by five Negroes, among whom is the anchor man of the disqualified team. "Gimme my medal, mo'f---r," he grunts. I do not have it with me and I tell him so. "Anyway, it ain't yours," I say foolishly. He calls me a liar on both counts and pushes me up against the wall on which we sometimes play handball. "Gimme my mo'f---n' medal," he says again. I repeat that I have left it home. "Le's search the li'l mo'f---r," one of them suggests, "he prolly got it *hid* in his mo'f---n' *pants*." My panic is now unmanageable. (How many times had I been surrounded like this and asked in soft tones, "Len' me a nickle, boy." How many times had I been called a liar for pleading poverty and pushed around, or searched, or beaten up, unless there happened to be someone in the marauding gang like Carl who liked me across that enormous divide of hatred and who would therefore say, "Aaah, c'mon, le's git someone else, *this* boy ain't got no money on 'im.") I scream at them through tears of rage and self-contempt, "Keep your f---n' filthy lousy black hands offa me! I swear I'll get the cops." This is all they need to hear, and the five of them set upon me. They bang me around, mostly in the stomach and on the arms and shoulders, and when several adults loitering near the candy store down the block notice what is going on and begin to shout, they run off and away.

I do not tell my parents about the incident. My team-mates, who have also been waylaid, each by a gang led by his opposite number from the disqualified team, have had their medallions taken from them, and they never squeal either. For days, I walk home in terror, expecting to be caught again, but nothing happens. The medallion is put away into a drawer, never to be worn by anyone.

Obviously experiences like these have always been a common feature of childhood life in working-class and immigrant neighborhoods, and Negroes do not necessarily figure in them. Wherever, and in whatever combination, they have lived together in the cities, kids of different groups have been at war, beating up and being beaten up: micks against kikes against wops against spicks against polacks. And even relatively homogeneous areas have not been spared the warring of the young: one block against another, one gang (called in my day, in a pathetic effort at gentility, an "S.A.C.," or social-athletic club) against another. But the Negro-white conflict had—and no doubt still has—a special intensity and was conducted with a ferocity unmatched by intramural white battling.

In my own neighborhood, a good deal of animosity existed between the Italian kids (most of whose parents were immigrants from Sicily) and the Jewish kids (who came largely from East European immigrant families). Yet everyone had friends, sometimes close friends, in the other "camp," and we often visited one another's strange-smelling houses, if not for meals, then for glasses of milk, and occasionally for some special event like a wedding or a wake. If it happened that we divided into warring factions and did battle, it would invariably be half-hearted and soon patched up. Our parents, to be sure, had nothing to do with one another and were mutually suspicious and hostile. But we, the kids, who all spoke Yiddish or Italian at home, were Americans, or New Yorkers, or Brooklyn boys: we shared a culture, the culture of the street, and at least for a while this culture proved to be more powerful than the opposing cultures of the home.

Why, *why* should it have been so different as between the Negroes and us? How was it borne in upon us so early, white and black alike, that we were enemies beyond any possibility of reconciliation? Why did we hate one another so?

I suppose if I tried, I could answer those questions more or less adequately from the perspective of what I have since learned. I could draw upon James Baldwin—what better witness is there?—to describe the sense of entrapment that poisons the soul of the Negro with hatred for the white man whom he knows to be his jailer. On the other side, if I wanted to understand how the white man comes to hate the Negro, I could call upon the psychologists who have spoken of the guilt that white Americans feel toward Negroes and that turns into hatred for lack of acknowledging itself as guilt. These are plausible answers and certainly there is truth in them. Yet when I think back upon my own experience of the Negro and his of me, I find myself troubled and puzzled, much as I was as a child when I heard that all Jews were rich and all Negroes persecuted. How could the Negroes in my neighborhood have regarded the whites across the street and around the corner as jailers? On the whole, the whites were not so poor as the Negroes, but they were quite poor enough, and the years were years of Depression. As for white hatred of the Negro, how could guilt have had anything to do with it? What share had these Italian and Jewish immigrants in the enslavement of the Negro? What share had they—downtrodden people themselves breaking their own necks to eke out a living—in the exploitation of the Negro?

No, I cannot believe that we hated each other back there in Brooklyn because they thought of us as jailers and we felt guilty toward them. But does it matter, given the fact that we all went through an unrepresentative confrontation? I think it matters profoundly, for if we managed the job of hating each other so well within out benefit of the aids to hatred that are supposedly at the root of this madness everywhere else, it must mean that the madness is not yet properly understood. I am far from pretending that I understand it, but I would insist that no view of the problem will begin to approach the truth unless it can account for a case like the one I have been trying to describe. Are the elements of any such view available to us?

At least two, I would say, are. One of them is a point we frequently come upon in the work of James Baldwin, and the other is a related point always stressed by psychologists who have studied the mechanisms of prejudice. Baldwin tells us that one of the reasons Negroes hate the white man is that the white man refuses to *look* at him: the Negro knows that in white eyes all Negroes are alike; they are faceless and therefore not altogether human. The psychologists, in their turn, tell us that the white man hates the Negro because he tends to project those wild impulses that he fears in himself onto an alien group which he then punishes with his contempt. What Baldwin does *not* tell us, however, is that the principle of facelessness is a two-way street and can operate in both directions with no difficulty at all. Thus, in my neighborhood in Brooklyn, *I* was as faceless to the Negroes as they were to me, and if they hated me because I never looked at them, I must also have hated them for never looking at *me*. To the Negroes, my white skin was enough to define me as the enemy, and in a war it is only the uniform that counts and not the person.

So with the mechanism of projection that the psychologists talk about: it too works in both directions at once. There is no question that the psychologists are right about what the Negro represents symbolically to the white man. For me as a child the life lived on the other side of the playground and down the block on Ralph Avenue seemed the very embodiment of the values of the street—free, independent, reckless, brave, masculine, erotic. I put the word "erotic" last, though it is usually stressed above all others, because in fact it came last, in consciousness as in importance. What mainly counted for me about Negro kids of my own age was that they were "bad boys." There were plenty of bad boys among the whites—this was, after all, a neighborhood with a long tradition of crime as a career open to aspiring talents—but the Negroes were *really* bad, bad in a way that beckoned to one, and made one feel inadequate. *We* all went home every day for a lunch of spinach-and-potatoes; *they* roamed around during lunch hour, munching on candy bars. In winter *we* had to wear itchy woolen hats and mittens and cumbersome galoshes; *they* were bare-headed and loose as they pleased. *We* rarely played hookey, or got into serious trouble in school, for all our street-corner bravado; *they* were defiant, forever staying out (to do what delicious things?), forever making disturbances in class and in the halls, forever being sent to the principal and returning uncowed. But most important of all, they were *tough;* beautifully, enviably tough, not giving a damn for anyone or anything. To hell with the teacher, the truant officer, the cop; to hell with the whole of the adult world that held *us* in its grip and that we never had the courage to rebel against except sporadically and in petty ways.

This is what I saw and envied and feared in the Negro: this is what finally made him faceless to me, though some of it, of course, was actually there. (The psychologists also tell us that the alien group which becomes the object of a projection will tend to respond by trying to live up to what is expected of them.) But what, on his side, did the Negro see in me that made me faceless to *him?* Did he envy me my lunches of spinach-and-potatoes and my itchy woolen caps and my prudent behavior in the face of authority, as I envied him his noon-time candy bars and his bare head in winter and his magnificent rebelliousness? Did those lunches and caps spell for him the prospect of power and riches in the future? Did they mean that there were possibilities open to me that were denied to him? Very likely they did. But if so, one also supposes that he feared the impulses within himself toward submission to authority no less powerfully than I feared the impulses in myself toward defiance. If I represented the jailer to him, it was not because I was oppressing him or keeping him down: it was because I symbolized for him the dangerous and probably pointless temptation toward greater repression, just as he symbol-ized for me the equally perilous tug toward greater freedom. I personally was to be rewarded for this repression with a new and better life in the future, but how many of my friends paid an even higher price and were given only gall in return.

We have it on the authority of James Baldwin that all Negroes hate whites. I am trying to suggest that on their side all whites—all American whites, that is—are sick in their feelings about Negroes. There are Negroes, no doubt, who would say that Baldwin is wrong, but I suspect them of being less honest than he is, just as I suspect whites of self-deception who tell me they have no spe-cial feeling toward Negroes. Special feelings about color are a contagion to which white Americans seem susceptible even when there is nothing in their background to account for the susceptibility. Thus everywhere we look today in the North, we find the curious phenomenon of white middle-class liberals with no previous personal experience of Negroes—people to whom Negroes have always been faceless in virtue rather than faceless in vice—discovering that their abstract commitment to the cause of Negro rights will not stand the test of a direct confrontation. We find such people fleeing in droves to the suburbs as the Negro population in the inner city grows; and when they stay in the city we find them sending their children to private school rather than to the "integrated" public school in the neighborhood. We find them resist-ing the demand that gerrymandered school districts be re-zoned for the pur-pose of overcoming de facto segregation; we find them judiciously considering whether the Negroes (for their own good, of course) are not perhaps push-ing too hard; we find them clucking their tongues over Negro militancy; we find them speculating on the question of whether there may not, after all, be something in the theory that the races are biologically different; we find them saying that it will take a very long time for Negroes to achieve full equality, no matter what anyone does; we find them deploring the rise of black nationalism and expressing the solemn hope that the leaders of the Negro community will discover ways of containing the impatience and incipient violence within the Negro ghettos.[1]

But that is by no means the whole story; there is also the phenomenon of what Kenneth Rexroth once called "crow-jimism." There are the broken-down white boys like Vivaldo Moore in Baldwin's *Another Country* who go to Harlem in search of sex or simply to brush up against something that looks like primitive vitality, and who are so often punished by the Negroes they meet for crimes that they would have been the last ever to commit and of which they themselves have been as sorry victims as any of the Negroes who take it out on them. There are the writers and intellectuals and artists who romanticize Negroes and pander to them, assuming a guilt that is not prop-erly theirs. And there are all the white liberals who permit Negroes to black-mail them into adopting a double standard of moral judgment, and who lend themselves—again assuming the responsibility for crimes they never committed—to cunning and contemptuous exploitation by Negroes they employ or try to befriend.

And what about me? What kind of feelings do I have about Negroes today? What happened to me, from Brooklyn, who grew up fearing and envying and hating Negroes? Now that Brooklyn is behind me, do I fear them and envy them and hate them still? The answer is yes, but not in the same proportions and certainly not in the same way. I now live on the upper west side of Manhattan, where there are many Negroes and many Puerto Ricans, and there are nights when I experience the old apprehensiveness again, and there are streets that I avoid when I am walking in the dark, as there were streets that I avoided when I was a child. I find that I am not afraid of Puerto Ricans, but I cannot restrain my nervousness whenever I pass a group of Negroes standing in front of a bar or sauntering down the street. I know now, as I did not know when I was a child, that power is on my side, that the police are working for me and not for them. And knowing this I feel ashamed and guilty, like the good liberal I have grown up to be. Yet the twinges of fear and the resentment they bring and the self-contempt they arouse are not to be gainsaid.

But envy? Why envy? And hatred? Why hatred? Here again the intensities have lessened and everything has been complicated and qualified by the guilts and the resulting over-compensations that are the heritage of the enlightened middle-class world of which I am now a member. Yet just as in childhood I envied Negroes for what seemed to me their superior masculinity, so I envy them today for what seems to me their superior physical grace and beauty. I have come to value physical grace very highly, and I am now capable of aching with all my being when I watch a Negro couple on the dance floor, or a Negro playing baseball or basketball. They are on the kind of terms with their own bodies that I should like to be on with mine, and for that precious quality they seem blessed to me.

The hatred I still feel for Negroes is the hardest of all the old feelings to face or admit, and it is the most hidden and the most overlarded by the conscious attitudes into which I have succeeded in willing myself. It no longer has, as for me it once did, any cause or justification (except, perhaps, that I am constantly being denied my right to an honest expression of the things I earned the right as a child to feel). How, then, do I know that this hatred has never entirely disappeared? I know it from the insane rage that can stir in me at the thought of Negro anti-Semitism; I know it from the disgusting prurience that can stir in me at the sight of a mixed couple; and I know it from the violence that can stir in me whenever I encounter that special brand of paranoid touchiness to which many Negroes are prone.

This, then, is where I am; it is not exactly where I think all other white liberals are, but it cannot be so very far away either. And it is because I am convinced that we white Americans are—for whatever reason, it no longer matters—so twisted and sick in our feelings about Negroes that I despair of the present push toward integration. If the pace of progress were not a factor here, there would perhaps be no cause for despair: time and the law and even the international political situation are on the side of the Negroes, and ultimately, therefore, victory—of a sort, anyway—must come. But from everything we have learned from observers who ought to know, pace has become as important to the Negroes as substance. They want equality and they want it *now*, and the white world is yielding to their demand only as much and as fast as it is absolutely being compelled to do. The Negroes know this in the most concrete terms imaginable, and it is thus becoming increasingly difficult to buy them off with rhetoric and promises and pious assurances of support. And so within the Negro community we find more and more people declaring—as Harold R. Isaacs recently put it in these pages[2]—that they want *out*: people who say that integration will never come, or that it will take a hundred or a thousand years to come, or that it will come at too high a price in suffering and struggle for the pallid and sodden life of the American middle class that at the very best it may bring.

The most numerous, influential, and dangerous movement that has grown out of Negro despair with the goal of integration is, of course, the Black Muslims. This movement, whatever else we may say about it, must be credited with one enduring achievement: it inspired James Baldwin to write an essay[3] which deserves to be placed among the classics of our language. Everything Baldwin has ever been trying to tell us is distilled here into a statement of overwhelming persuasiveness and prophetic magnificence. Baldwin's message is and always has been simple. It is this: "Color is not a human or personal reality; it is a political reality." And Baldwin's demand is correspondingly simple: color must be forgotten, lest we all be smited with a vengeance "that does not really depend on, and cannot really be executed by, any person or organization, and that cannot be prevented by any police force or army: historical vengeance, a cosmic vengeance based on the law that we recognize when we say, 'Whatever goes up must come down.'" The Black Muslims Baldwin portrays as a sign and a warning to the intransigent white world. They come to proclaim how deep is the Negro's disaffection with the white world and all its works, and Baldwin implies that no American Negro can fail to respond somewhere in his being to their message: that the white man is the devil, that Allah has doomed him to destruction, and that the black man is about to inherit the earth. Baldwin of course knows that this nightmare inversion of the racism from which the black man has suffered can neither win nor even point to the neighborhood in which victory might be located. For in his view the neighborhood of victory lies in exactly the opposite direction: the transcendence of color through love.

Yet the tragic fact is that love is not the answer to hate—not in the world of politics, at any rate. Color is indeed a political rather than a human or a personal reality and if politics (which is to say power) has made it into a human and a personal reality, then only politics (which is to say power) can unmake it once again. But the way of politics is slow and bitter, and as impatience on the one side is matched by a setting of the jaw on the other, we move closer and closer to an explosion and blood may yet run in the streets.

Will this madness in which we are all caught never find a resting-place? Is there never to be an end to it? In thinking about the Jews I have often wondered whether their survival as a distinct group was worth one hair on the head of a single infant. Did the Jews have to survive so that six million innocent people should one day be burned in the ovens of Auschwitz? It is a terrible question and no one, not God himself, could ever answer it to my satisfaction. And when I think about the Negroes in America and about the image of integration as a state in which the Negroes would take their rightful place as another of the protected minorities in a pluralistic society, I wonder whether they really believe in their hearts that such a state can actually be attained, and if so *why* they should wish to survive as a distinct group. I think I know why the Jews once wished to survive (though I am less certain as to why we still do): they not only believed that God had given them no choice, but they were tied to a memory of past glory and a dream of imminent redemption. What does the American Negro have that might correspond to this? His past is a stigma, his color is a stigma, and his vision of the future is the hope of erasing the stigma by making color irrelevant, by making it disappear as a fact of consciousness.

I share this hope, but I cannot see how it will ever be realized unless color does *in fact* disappear: and that means not integration, it means assimilation, it means—let the brutal word come out—miscegenation. The Black Muslims, like their racist counterparts in the white world, accuse the "so-called Negro leaders" of secretly pursuing miscegenation as a goal. The racists are wrong, but I wish they were right, for I believe that the wholesale merging of the two races is the most desirable alternative for everyone concerned. I am not claiming that this alternative can be pursued programmatically or that it is immediately feasible as a solution; obviously there are even greater barriers to its achievement than to the achievement of integration. What I am saying, however, is that in my opinion the Negro problem can be solved in this country in no other way.

I have told the story of my own twisted feelings about Negroes here, and of how they conflict with the moral convictions I have since developed, in order to assert that such feelings must be acknowledged as honestly as possible so that they can be controlled and ultimately disregarded in favor of the convictions. It is *wrong* for a man to suffer because of the color of his skin. Beside that clichéd proposition of liberal thought, what argument can stand and be respected? If the arguments are the arguments of feeling, they must be made to yield; and one's own soul is not the worst place to begin working a huge social transformation. Not so long ago, it used to be asked of white liberals, "Would you like your sister to marry one?" When I was a boy and my sister was still unmarried, I would certainly have said no to that question. But now I am a man, my sister is already married, and I have daughters. If I were to be asked today whether I would like a daughter of mine "to marry one," I would have to answer: "No, I wouldn't *like* it at all. I would rail and rave and rant and tear my hair. And then I hope I would have the courage to curse myself for raving and ranting, and to give her my blessing. How dare I withhold it at the behest of the child I once was and against the man I now have a duty to be?"

Notes

1. For an account of developments like these, see "The White Liberal's Retreat" by Murray Friedman in the January 1963 *Atlantic Monthly*.
2. "Integration and the Negro Mood," December 1962.
3. Originally published last November in the *New Yorker* under the title "Letter From a Region in My Mind," it has been reprinted (along with a new introduction) by Dial Press under the title *The Fire Next Time*.

28

Nathan Glazer (1923–)
Negroes & Jews: The New Challenge to Pluralism (1964)

Editor's Introduction

Nathan Glazer was born and raised in New York City in a mildly socialist household in which his moderate family culture rejected "an intense commitment to communism, Orthodoxy, freethinking, anarchism, Yiddish." When he began City College in 1940 he majored in history and became editor of the *Avukah Student Action*, the paper for a Zionist organization he described as "in most ways left sectarian." Members of the *Avukah* crowd read *Partisan Review*, where they became familiar with Sidney Hook, Dwight Macdonald and others. Glazer's newspaper was allowed to borrow cartoons from *The New Leader*, and in *The New Leader's* office he met the managing editor, Daniel Bell. From Bell and from Glazer's college friend Seymour Martin Lipset, he began to think of sociology as his scholarly identity. He switched his major at City College and finished in 1944 with a sociology degree, and soon after he earned a master's degree from the University of Pennsylvania in social anthropology. As a youth he was a social democrat, but by 1947 his study of social science left no room for a belief in socialism and it dropped from his writing.

In 1944 Glazer began as an editor at the *Contemporary Jewish Record*, and the next year when it changed to *Commentary* he was on the staff of the new magazine. He took a year's leave in the late forties to work on *The Lonely Crowd* with David Riesman, and still at *Commentary* in the fifties he took courses occasionally toward a Ph.D. in sociology at Columbia, where he studied with Robert Merton and Paul Lazarsfeld, and helped C. Wright Mills gather and analyze interview data for *White Collar*. Glazer received his doctorate in 1962. He was always a collegial, centrist liberal, a polite person whether or not he agreed with someone. Interestingly, in 1954, he wrote the first criticism of the new magazine *Dissent* from *Commentary*, partly because he believed that Howe and the marauders at *Dissent* had been attacking *Commentary* for years. In 1954 he left *Commentary* and worked first for Anchor Books, then taught in several one-year jobs. Beginning in 1959, he wrote *Beyond the Melting Pot*, for which Daniel Patrick Moynihan wrote a chapter on the Irish, and later Moynihan helped him get a job in Washington at the Housing and Home Finance Agency. From there Berkeley hired him to teach sociology, and in 1969 Harvard gave him a position in the School of Education and the Department of Sociology. In 1973 he replaced Daniel Bell as co-editor of *The Public Interest,* where he served alongside Irving Kristol.

A major feature of Glazer's work has been on immigrant groups and the subject of race and ethnicity in America. He has argued that the United States, as it has showed in the past, can continue to absorb arriving ethnic groups. In his books he suggested that this capacity is not reserved for white ethnics, as the American inclusion of Asians demonstrates. But he has worried that blacks have been resistant to cultural assimilation, partly because they have wanted to keep a separate identity, and he has feared their example might prompt other ethnic groups to claim their own separateness that needs special compensation. His critics have claimed that he imposed the mobility assumptions of white ethnicity, which were "voluntary" in that they could be erased or declined, on those for whom ethnicity was not a choice. His main critics were multiculturalists who were angered by his opposition to much of the multicultural agenda.

When Glazer wrote *We Are All Multiculturalists Now* in 1997 it prompted a debate about whether he had changed his mind and had switched camps. Written by a centrist liberal, Glazer's new book disappointed everyone but the contingent of liberals who supported the old integrationist liberalism before 1964. He was denounced by members of the right such as Dinesh D'Souza for giving up the fight against affirmative action and was attacked by those on the left such as Stephen Steinberg for not giving up the fight against multiculturalism despite the title of his book. It was a defense of liberalism, the midcentury liberalism that Americans had once liked, where outsiders had worked their way up. Glazer now admitted that maybe Americans wouldn't let blacks succeed by the old model, or perhaps that they were somehow a different case. When the ethic of multiculturalism, part of which was using unfairness to fight previous unfairness, arose among younger liberals in the 1970s, liberals as a whole lost the allegiance of American voters and have never really regained it. Yet it is hard to identify an area of public policy that has done more for the basic unity of America than laws to promote diversity.

Source

Nathan Glazer, "Negroes & Jews: The New Challenge to Pluralism," *Commentary* vol. 38, no. 6, December 1964.

Selected Readings

James Traub, "I Was Wrong," *Slate*, May 15, 1997.
Stephen Steinberg, "Nathan Glazer and the Assassination of Affirmative Action," *New Politics*, vol. 9, no. 3 (new series), Summer 2003.
Richard Williams, "Review of Nathan Glazer, *We Are All Multiculturalists Now,*" *H-Pol, H-Net Reviews*, March, 1999.

* * * * *

If today one re-reads the article by Kenneth Clark on Negro-Jewish relations that was published in *Commentary* almost nineteen years ago,[1] one will discover that tension between Negroes and Jews is neither of recent origin nor a product of the civil rights revolution. In that article Dr. Clark described the bitter feelings of the masses of Northern Negroes toward Jews. Not that these feelings hampered cooperation between Negro and Jewish leaders—an effective cooperation which was to play an important role in the following years in bringing fair-employment, fair-housing, and fair-education legislation to many communities, and indeed to most of the large Northern and Western states. But whatever the relationships were at the top, the fact was that down below, the Negro's experience of the Jew was not as a co-worker or friend or ally, but, in a word, as an exploiter.

As Dr. Clark wrote: "Some Negro domestics assert that Jewish housewives who employ them are unreasonably and brazenly exploitative. A Negro actor states in bitters terms that he is being flagrantly underpaid by a Jewish producer. A Negro entertainer is antagonistic to his Jewish agent, who, he is convinced, is exploiting him.... Antagonism to the 'Jewish landlord' is so common as to become almost an integral part of the folk culture of the Northern urban Negro." And, of course, one would have to add to this catalogue the Jewish merchants in the Negro business districts, believed by their customers to be selling them inferior goods at high prices and on poor credit terms (a charge the merchants might answer by explaining that they were simply covering the greater financial costs—through payment delinquency and robbery—of doing business in a Negro area, plus compensation for the physical danger involved).

In any case, long before many of those Negro youths were born who took part last summer in the destruction and looting of Jewish businesses in Harlem and Bedford-Stuyvesant and Philadelphia, Dr. Clark explained clearly enough the basis for the anti-Semitism prevalent in the Negro ghettos. It was, he said, a special variant of anti-white feeling, encouraged by the more direct and immediate contact that Negroes had with Jews than with other whites, and encouraged as well by the inferior position of Jews in American society, which permitted the Negro to find in the luxury of anti-Jewishness one of his few means of identifying with the American majority. Two years later, also in *Commentary*, the young James Baldwin told the same story in one of his first published articles,[2] underlining the point with his elegant acidity: "But just as a society must have a scapegoat, so hatred must have a symbol. Georgia has the Negro and Harlem has the Jew." One still feels the shock of that cold ending: is *that* what the Jew was to Harlem in 1948?

If, however, we knew decades ago that the ironic historic confrontation of Jew (as landlord, merchant, housewife, businessman) with Negro (as tenant, customer, servant, and worker) in the North had produced hatred on the part of many poor and uneducated Negroes, we now have to record two new developments in this confrontation. First, the well of ill-feeling has moved upward to include a substantial part of the Negro leadership, mainly some of the newer leaders thrown up in the North by the civil rights revolution; and second, Jewish feeling toward the Negro has undergone changes of its own.

There is little question that this feeling has never been hatred. It has ranged from passionate advocacy of Negro rights by Jewish liberals (and Communists and Socialists too), through friendly cooperation on the part of Jewish leaders who saw Negroes as allies in the fight for common goals, to a less effective but fairly widespread good will on the part of ordinary Jews. The hatred of poor Negroes for Jews was not reciprocated by Jews; in the way that Harlem "needed" the Jew, the Lower East Side, Brownsville, and Flatbush perhaps needed the *goy,* but they never needed the Negro. If there was prejudice against Negroes (and, of course, there was), it was part of the standard Jewish ethnocentrism which excluded all outsiders. The businesslike adoption of the norms of behavior of the white world (in refusing to rent to Negroes in New York, or serve them in department stores in the South) was just that—businesslike rather than the reflection of a deeply held prejudice. The Irish had had experiences which had taught many of them to dislike or hate Negroes: their competition with Negroes for the worst jobs in the early days of immigration, their antagonism to a Civil War draft that forced them to fight—as they thought—for Negroes. But the Jews had never come into direct competition with Negroes, in North or South. The tenant or customer might hate the landlord or storekeeper—the feeling was not mutual.

In the North, then, in the late 40's and 50's, well-staffed and well-financed Jewish organizations usually had the support of much more poorly staffed and poorly financed Negro organizations in fighting for legislation that advanced the interests of both groups, even though they stood on very different steps in the economic and occupational ladder. For the same law permitted a Jew to challenge exclusion from a Fifth Avenue cooperative apartment and a Negro to challenge exclusion from a much more modest apartment building.

This situation is now changing. As the Negro masses have become more active and more militant in their own interests, their feelings have become more relevant, and have forced themselves to the surface; and Jewish leaders—of unions, of defense and civil rights organizations—as well as businessmen, housewives, and home-owners, have been confronted for the first time with demands from Negro organizations that, they find, cannot serve as the basis of a common effort. The new developments feed each other, and it would be impossible to say which came first. The resistance of Jewish organizations and individual Jews to such demands as preferential union membership and preferential hiring, and to the insistence on the primacy of integration over all other educational objectives, breeds antagonism among former Negro allies. The "white liberal," who is attacked as a false friend unwilling to support demands which affect him or his, and as probably prejudiced to boot, is generally (even if this is not spelled out) the white *Jewish* liberal—and it could hardly be otherwise, in view of the predominance of Jews among liberals, particularly in major cities like New York, Chicago, Philadelphia, and Los Angeles. This Jewish resistance, however, is often based not only on the demands themselves, but on a growing awareness of the depths of Negro antagonism to the world that Jewish liberalism considers desirable.

One important new element in the situation, then, is that the feelings of the Negro masses have become politically relevant and meaningful in a way that they were not in 1935 or 1943. In those years, too, the Negroes of Harlem rioted, and broke the show windows of the Jewish-owned stores, and looted their contents. But these earlier outbreaks—which in terms of the feelings involved were very similar to the outbreaks of last summer—were not tied up with a great civil rights movement. While the Negro leaders of today could deny all responsibility for such outbreaks, and could point out that this kind of hoodlumism had been endemic in the Negro ghettos since the depression, the growing tendency toward militancy in the civil rights movement meant that the leadership would inevitably be charged with responsibility—as they were not in 1935 and 1943 (except for Communists and race radicals). Moreover, the feelings of the Negro masses were now in greater measure *shared* by middle-class and white-collar and leadership groups. And this is also strikingly new.

For the Negro no longer confronts the Jew only as tenant, servant, customer, worker. The rise of Negro teachers, social workers, and civil servants in considerable numbers means another kind of confrontation. Once again, the accidents of history have put the Jew just ahead of the Negro, and just above him. Now the Negro teacher works under a Jewish principal, the Negro social worker under a Jewish supervisor. When HARYOU [Harlem Youth Opportunities Unlimited] issued its huge report, *Youth in the Ghetto,* last summer, only one of some 800 school principals in the New York system was a Negro, and only four of the 1,200 top-level administrative positions in the system were filled by Negroes! But as significant as these ridiculously tiny percentages is the fact that most of the *other* principalships and administrative positions are filled by Jews who poured into the educational system during the 30's and are now well advanced within it, while thousands of Negroes, comparative latecomers, have inferior jobs. And what makes the situation even worse is that part of the blame for the poor education of Negro children can be placed on this white (but concretely Jewish) dominance. As the HARYOU report states (though indicating that this is only one possible point of view):

Public school teachers in New York City come largely from the city colleges, which have a dominant pupil population from a culture which prepares the child from birth for competition of a most strenuous type. These students are largely white, middle-class, growing up in segregated white communities where, by and large, their only contact with the Negro finds him in positions of servitude .... Responsible positions, even within the neighborhood schools, are in the main held by people who perceivably differ from [the Negro pupils]. The dearth of Negro principals, assistants and supervisors is a most glaring deficit and one which leaves a marked, unwholesome effect upon the child's self-image. ...The competitive culture from which the bulk of the teachers come, with the attendant arrogance of intellectual superiority of its members, lends itself readily to the class system within the school ... which in effect perpetuates the academic pre-eminence of the dominant group.

This new confrontation of middle-class Negroes, recently arrived at professional status, and middle-class Jews, who got there earlier and hold the superior positions, is most marked in New York, because of its huge Jewish population. It is there that the animus against the white liberal reaches its peak, and where the white liberal tends most often to be a Jew. But the confrontation is only somewhat less sharp in Philadelphia, Detroit, Chicago, Los Angeles, and other cities with substantial Jewish populations. Perhaps the only place where the term "white liberal" is not used to mean the "Jewish liberal" is in San Francisco. The reason is that radicalism in San Francisco has a peculiarly non-Jewish base in Harry Bridges's International Longshoreman's and Warehouseman's Union; moreover, the Jewish group there contains many early settlers who are closely identified with San Franciscans of the same class and origin. Indeed, in San Francisco, there was never even a Jewish ghetto available to become transformed into a Negro ghetto; yet the fragment of a Jewish ghetto that did exist is now part of a Negro ghetto.

And this brings us to yet another new twist in the historic confrontation of Jew and Negro. I do not know why in so many American cities Negro settlement has concentrated in the very areas that originally harbored Jewish immigrants. There are possibly three reasons. First, Jews have on the whole favored apartment-house living, and apartments provide cheap quarters for newcomers. Second, Jews have been economically and geographically more mobile than other immigrant groups who arrived around the same time (for example, Italians and Poles), and consequently their neighborhoods opened up to Negroes more rapidly. And finally, Jews have not resorted to violence in resisting the influx of new groups—in any case, most of them were already moving away.

But as Jews kept retreating to the edges of the city and beyond, the Negroes, their numbers and in some measure their income rising, followed— in recent years, as far as the suburbs. This is a problem, of course, for the same reasons that it is a problem for any white property-owner or homeowner: fear of the declining real-estate values that can be occasioned by a flight of panicky white residents; fear of changes in the neighborhood affecting the schools and the homogeneity of the environment. Obviously, Jews are not the only people caught up in such concerns; but since migrating urban groups generally follow radial paths outward (a pattern that is not so marked in New York, broken up as it is by rivers and bays, but that is very clear in inland cities like Detroit, Chicago, Cleveland, and Cincinnati), this new Negro middle class has moved into Jewish areas far more often than statistical probability alone would lead one to expect. Here again, therefore, a novel type of tension—specifically involving middle-class groups and home-owners— has been introduced.

In a number of suburbs Jewish home-owners of liberal outlook have banded together in an effort to slow down the outflow of whites and thus create an integrated community (which, of course, also helps to maintain the value of their homes). But to create an integrated community not only means slowing down the outflow of whites; it also means reducing the influx of Negroes. In some cases these good—from the Jewish point of view—intentions (and they usually *are* good) have looked, from the Negro point of view, like just another means of keeping Negroes *out,* but this time using the language of liberalism instead of race prejudice. We are all acquainted with the paranoia of persecuted minorities, and many jokes that used to be told of Jews (for example, the one about the stutterer who could not get a job as a radio announcer because of "anti-Semitism") could now be told of Negroes—and would be just as true.

All this forms part of the background of Negro-Jewish relations today. But in the immediate foreground are the new demands that have come to be made in the North and West by the civil rights movement. Negroes are acutely aware of how few of their young people even now get into the good colleges, and they see as a critical cause of this the small proportion of Negroes in good public elementary and high schools; they are acutely aware that their large-scale entry into the ranks of the clerks and typists of our huge public bureaucracies has not been accompanied by any equivalent entry into the higher positions of the civil service; they know that their new junior executive trainees in the large corporations are matched by hardly any Negroes higher up in these great private bureaucracies. And since political pressure and organized group pressure have been effective in breaching segregation in the South, and in bringing about some of these entries in the North, they see no reason why similar pressures should not be equally effective in making good the deficiencies that continue to be apparent. If whites say, "But first you must earn your entry—through grades, or examinations," Negroes, with a good deal more knowledge of the realities of American society than foreign immigrants used to have, answer, "But we know how *you* got ahead—through political power, and connections, and the like; therefore, we won't accept your pious argument that merit is the only thing that counts."

There is some truth to this rejoinder; there is, I believe, much less truth when it is made to Jews. For the Jews have, indeed, put their faith in the abstract measures of individual merit—marks and examinations. Earlier, before school grades and civil-service test scores became so important, they depended on money: it, too, could be measured, and the man who had it could manage without any ties of blood or deep organic connection to the ruling elite of the land. In addition to this, the reason merit and money have been the major Jewish weapons in overcoming discrimination, rather than political power and pressure, is that only in exceptional cases (New York City is one of them) have they had the numbers to make these latter means of advancement effective. As a result, their political skills are poor (where are the master Jewish politicians in America?), but their ability to score the highest grades in examinations and to develop money-getting competence still shows no sign of declining.

The ideologies that have justified the principle of measurable individual merit and the logic of the market place, where one man's money is equal to any other man's, have always appeared to Jews, even more than to other Americans, almost self-evidently just and right. And the New York *Times,* which most of the newer Negro leaders dislike intensely, expresses this liberal ideology in its purest form. The *Times* has never been tolerant toward the accommodations that others have sometimes seen as necessary in our mixed and complex society—the balanced ticket, for example, which has nothing to do with the abstract principles of merit.

But the liberal principles—the earlier ones arguing the democracy of money, the newer ones arguing the democracy of merit—that have been so congenial to Jews and so much in their interest are being increasingly accepted by everyone else nowadays under the pressures of a technological world. We are moving into a diploma society, where individual merit rather than family and connections and group must be the basis for advancement, recognition, achievement. The reasons have nothing directly to do with the Jews, but no matter—the Jews certainly gain from such a grand historical shift. Thus Jewish interests coincide with the new rational approaches to the distribution of rewards.

It is clear that one cannot say the same about Negro interests. And so the Negroes have come to be opposed to these approaches. But when Negroes challenge—as they do in New York—the systems of testing by which school principals and higher officials in the educational bureaucracy are selected and promoted, they are also challenging the very system under which Jews have done so well. And when they challenge the use of grades as the sole criterion for entry into special high schools and free colleges, they challenge the system which has enabled Jews to dominate these institutions for decades.

But there is another and more subtle side to the shift of Negro demands from abstract equality to group consideration, from color-blind to color-conscious. The Negroes press these new demands because they see that the abstract color-blind policies do not lead rapidly enough to the entry of large numbers of Negroes into good jobs, good neighborhoods, good schools. It is, in other words, a group interest they wish to further. Paradoxically, however, the ultimate basis of the resistance to their demands, I am convinced—certainly among Jews, but not Jews alone—is that they pose a serious threat to the ability of other groups to maintain *their* communities.

In America we have lived under a peculiar social compact. On the one hand, publicly and formally and legally, we recognize only individuals; we do not recognize groups—whether ethnic, racial, or religious. On the other hand, these groups exist in actual social fact. They strongly color the activities and lives of most of our citizens. They in large measure determine an individual's fate through their control of social networks which tend to run along ethnic, racial, and religious lines. Even more subtly, they determine a man's fate by the culture and values they transmit, which affect his chances in the general competition for the abstract signs of merit and money.

This is not an easy situation to grasp. On the one hand (except for the South) there is equality—political equality, equal justice before the law, equal opportunity to get grades, take examinations, qualify for professions, open businesses, make money. This equality penetrates deeper and deeper into the society. The great private colleges now attempt to have nationally representative student bodies, not only geographically, but socially and economically and racially. The great private corporations reluctantly begin to accept the principle that, like a government civil service, they should open their selection processes and their recruiting procedures so that all may be represented. On the other hand, these uniform processes of selection for advancement, and the pattern of freedom to start a business and make money, operate not on a homogeneous mass of individuals, but on individuals as molded by a range of communities of different degrees of organization and self-consciousness, with different histories and cultures, and with different capacities to take advantage of the opportunities that are truly in large measure open to all.

Here we come to the crux of the Negro anger and the Jewish discomfort. The Negro anger is based on the fact that the system of formal equality produces so little for them. The Jewish discomfort is based on the fact that Jews discover they can no longer support the newest Negro demands, which may be designed from the Negro point of view to produce equality for all, but which are also designed to break down this pattern of communities. We must emphasize again that Jewish money, organizational strength, and political energy have played a major role in most cities and states in getting effective law and effective administration covering the rights to equal opportunity in employment, housing, and education. But all this past cooperation loses its relevance as it dawns on Jews, and others as well, that many Negro leaders are now beginning to expect that the pattern of their advancement in American society will take quite a different form from that of the immigrant ethnic groups. This new form may well be justified by the greater sufferings that have been inflicted on the Negroes by slavery, by the loss of their traditional culture, by their deliberate exclusion from power and privilege for the past century, by the new circumstances in American society which make the old pattern of advance (through formal equality plus the support of the group) less effective today. But that it *is* a new form, a radically new one, for the integration of a group into American society, we must recognize.

In the past, the established groups in American society came to understand, eventually, that the newer groups would not push their claims for equality to the point where the special institutions of the older groups would no longer be able to maintain their identity. There were certainly delicate moments when it looked as if the strongly pressed and effectively supported Jewish demand for formal equality, combined with Jewish wealth and grades, would challenge the rights of vacation resorts, social clubs, and private schools of the old established white Protestant community to serve as exclusive institutions of that community. But after a time the established Protestant community realized there were limits to the demands of the Jews, as there were limits to the demands of the Catholics. They realized that Jews and Catholics could not demand the complete abolition of lines between the communities because they too wanted to maintain communities of their own. Most Jews wanted to remain members of a distinctive group, and regardless of how consistent they were in battering against the walls of privilege, they always implicitly accepted the argument that various forms of division between people, aside from those based on the abstract criteria of money and achievement, were legitimate in America. Thus, when John Slawson of the American Jewish Committee argued against the discriminatory practices of various social clubs, he did not, I believe, attack the right of a group to maintain distinctive institutions. He argued rather that Jews in banking or high politics could not conduct their *business* if they were not accepted as members of these clubs. He did not attack social discrimination as such—he attacked it because of its political and economic consequences and suggested it was abetting economic and political discrimination. The grounds he chose for his attack are revealing, for they indicate what he felt were the legitimate claims that one group in American society could raise about the way the other groups conducted their social life.

Now it is my sense of the matter that with the Negro revolution there has been a radical challenge to this pattern of individual advancement within an accepted structure of group distinctiveness. The white community into which the Negro now demands full entrance is not actually a single community—it is a series of communities. And all of them feel threatened by the implications of the new Negro demand for full equality. They did not previously realize how much store they set by their power to control the character of the social setting in which they lived. They did not realize this because their own demands generally did not involve or imply the dissolution of the established groups: they never really wanted to mingle too closely with these established groups. They demanded political representation—which assumed that the group continued. They demanded the right to their own schools, or (like the Catholics today) support for their own schools—which again proceeded from the assumption of group maintenance. They demanded equal rights in employment, in education, in housing. But as a matter of fact many of their jobs were held in business enterprises or in trades controlled by members of their own group. Many of them set up their own educational institutions to create the kind of higher education they thought desirable for their young people. If freedom of housing became an issue on occasion, such freedom was nevertheless used as much to create voluntary new concentrations of the group as to disperse it among other people.

The new Negro demands challenge the right to maintain these sub-communities far more radically than the demands of any other group in American history. As Howard Brotz has pointed out, the exclusion of the Negro from his legitimate place in American society was so extreme, so thoroughgoing, so complete, that all the political energy of the Negro has been directed toward beating down the barriers. The corollary of this exclusive focus is that most Negroes see nothing of value in the Negro group whose preservation requires separate institutions, residential concentration, or a ban on intermarriage. Or rather, the only thing that might justify such group solidarity is the political struggle itself—the struggle against all barriers. What other groups see as a value, Negroes see as a strategy in the fight for equal rights.

We have become far more sophisticated in our understanding of the meaning of equality, far more subtle in our understanding of the causes of inequality. As a result, political equality alone— which the Negro now enjoys in most parts of the country—is considered of limited importance. The demand for economic equality is now not the demand for equal opportunities for the equally qualified: it is the demand for equality of economic *results*—and it therefore raises such questions as why some businesses succeed and others fail, and how people are selected for advancement in large organizations. When we move into areas like that, we are not asking for abstract tolerance, or a simple desisting from discrimination. We are involving ourselves in the complex relationships between people, and we are examining the kinds of ties and judgments that go to make up our American sub-communities. Or consider the demand for equality in education, which has also become a demand for equality of *results, of outcomes.* Suppose one's capacity to gain from education depends on going to school with less than a majority of one's own group? Or suppose it depends on one's home background? Then how do we achieve equality of results? The answers to this question and many similar ones suggest that the deprived group must be inserted into the community of the advantaged. For otherwise there is no equality of outcome.

The force of present-day Negro demands is that the sub-community, because it either protects privileges or creates inequality, *has no right to exist.* That is why these demands pose a quite new challenge to the Jewish community, or to any sub-community. Using the work of Oscar Handlin and Will Herberg, the Jewish community has come up with a convenient defense of Jewish exclusiveness—namely, that everyone else is doing it, too. The thrust of present-day Negro demands is that everyone should *stop* doing it. I do not interpret Jewish discomfort over this idea as false liberalism—for Jewish liberalism, even if it has never confronted the question directly, has always assumed that the advancement of disadvantaged groups, both Jews and others, would proceed in such a way as to respect the group pattern of American life. But the new Negro leaders believe Negroes cannot advance without a modification of this pattern. The churches, one of the major means by which group identities maintain themselves, are challenged by the insistent Negro demand for entry into every church. And if the Jews, because their church is so special, are for the moment protected against this demand, they are not protected against demands for entry on equal footing into other institutions which are the true seats of Jewish exclusiveness—the Jewish business, for example, the Jewish union, or the Jewish (or largely Jewish) neighborhood and school. Thus Jews find their interests and those of formally less liberal neighbors becoming similar: they both have an interest in maintaining an area restricted to their own kind; an interest in managing the friendship and educational experiences of their children; an interest in passing on advantages in money and skills to them.

The Negro now demands entry into a world, a society, that does not exist, except in ideology. In that world there is only one American community, and in that world, heritage, ethnicity, religion, race are only incidental and accidental personal characteristics. There may be many reasons for such a world to come into existence—among them the fact that it may be necessary in order to provide full equality for the Negroes. But if we do move in this direction, we will have to create communities very different from the kinds in which most of us who have already arrived—Protestants, Catholics, Jews—now live.

Notes

1. "Candor on Negro-Jewish Relations," February 1946.
2. "The Harlem Ghetto: Winter 1948," February 1948.

VI
Legacies

29

Michael Walzer (1935–)
In Defense of Equality (1973)

Editor's Introduction

As an undergraduate in the mid-1950s Michael Walzer took a class from Irving Howe at Brandeis University. Howe's new publication *Dissent* was less than two years old, and as editor he constantly expected it to fail, as did so many little magazines—not to mention little socialist magazines. More than a half-century later, *Dissent* is still very much alive, now with Michael Walzer as editor.

After Walzer graduated summa cum laude from Brandeis in 1956 with a degree in history, he studied for a year at Cambridge University on a Fulbright Fellowship and then received a Ph.D. in government at Harvard in 1961. Walzer taught at Princeton until 1966, when he accepted a job at Harvard. In 1980 he joined the faculty of social science at the Institute for Advanced Study at Princeton. During his career he has taught such subjects as modern political thought and philosophy, socialist thought, nationalism, means and ends, obligations, and just war. Among his more than two dozen books, many of them compilations of his essays, are *Radical Principles* (1977), *Just and Unjust Wars* (1977), *Spheres of Justice* (1983) and *On Toleration* (1997). His essay "In Defense of Equality" is an example of the democratic socialist thought for which *Dissent* is known.

Immediately following the attacks on the World Trade Towers and the Pentagon in 2001 Walzer complained that a portion of the left in the United States and Europe lived in "a political culture of excuses" for terrorist organizations such as the Irish Republican Army and the Palestine Liberation Organization, and he detested "the exaggerated and distorted descriptions of American wickedness that underpin these excuses." Terrorism, he warned, was, "like rape or murder," an attack on innocents. (Walzer, "Excusing Terror," *The American Prospect*, October 22, 2001.) Walzer characterized part of the left as harboring "festering resentment, ingrown anger, and self-hate," and he asked, "can there be a decent left in a superpower?" (Walzer, "Can There Be a Decent Left?") *Dissent*, Spring 2002. Several ideological commitments, Walzer proposed, had led to the anti-Americanism of part of the left. It was, he said, still influenced by the Marxist theory of imperialism and the third-worldism of the 1960s and 1970s. Some leftists thought if they blamed the U.S. for everything, it would erase the taint of American imperialism. Allied to this, leftists felt that by living in American privilege they had no right to criticize other countries. "The left," he wrote solemnly, "needs to begin again." (Walzer, "Can There Be a Decent Left?")

None of this was evidence that Walzer was giving up on the left. It showed instead that he was trying to nudge the left to oppose religious authoritarianism and urging it to support the important values of liberalism, values that are part of democratic socialism. Walzer was simply pushing for a responsible and intelligent left, and he was joined in this suggestion by other intelligent figures of the liberal left such as Paul Berman (*Terror and Liberalism*, 2003) and Todd Gitlin (*The Intellectuals and the Flag*, 2006) Their point of view captures the best sense of the New York Intellectuals of old, and perhaps exceeds it by employing a greater sense of American humility and a desire to balance the rights of Americans with the rights of others. Walzer, Berman and Gitlin were updating the important liberal anti-absolutism covered in section two of this volume with a newer liberal spirit.

Source

Michael Walzer, "In Defense of Equality," *Dissent* vol. 20, no. 4, Fall 1973.

Selected Readings

Irving Kristol, "About Equality," *Neoconservatism: The Autobiography of an Idea* (New York: Free Press, 1995).
Michael Walzer, "Excusing Terror," *The American Prospect*, October 22, 2001; "Can There Be a Decent Left?" *Dissent*, Spring 2002; *On Toleration* (New Haven: Yale University Press, 1997).
Paul Berman, *Terror and Liberalism* (*New York*: Norton, 2003).
Todd Gitlin, *The Intellectuals and the Flag* (New York: Columbia University Press, 2006).

* * * * *

I

At the very center of conservative thought lies this idea: that the present division of wealth and power corresponds to some deeper reality of human life. Conservatives don't want to say merely that the present division is what it ought to be, for that would invite a search for some distributive principle—as if it were possible to *make* a distribution. They want to say that whatever the division of wealth and power is, it naturally is, and that all efforts to change it, temporarily successful in proportion to their bloodiness, must be futile in the end. We are then invited, as in Irving Kristol's recent *Commentary* article, to reflect upon the perversity of those who would make the attempt.[1] Like a certain sort of leftist thought, conservative argument seems quickly to shape itself around a rhetoric of motives rather than one of reasons. Kristol is especially adept at that rhetoric and strangely unconcerned about the reductionism it involves. He aims to expose egalitarianism as the ideology of envious and resentful intellectuals. No one else cares about it, he says, except the "new class" of college-educated, professional, most importantly, professorial men and women, who hate their bourgeois past (and present) and long for a world of their own making.

I suppose I should have felt, after reading Kristol's piece, that the decent drapery of my socialist convictions has been stripped away, that I was left naked and shivering, small-minded and self-concerned. Perhaps I did feel a little like that, for my first impulse was to respond in kind, exposing anti-egalitarianism as the ideology of those other intellectuals—"they are mostly professors, of course"—whose spiritual course was sketched some years ago by the editor of *Commentary*. But that would be at best a degrading business, and I doubt that my analysis would be any more accurate than Kristol's. It is better to ignore the motives of these "new men" and focus instead on what they say: that the inequalities we are all familiar with are inherent in our condition, are accepted by ordinary people (like themselves), and are criticized only by the perverse. I think all these assertions are false; I shall try to respond to them in a serious way.

Kristol doesn't argue that we can't possibly have greater equality or greater inequality than we presently have. Both communist and aristocratic societies are possible, he writes, under conditions of political repression or economic underdevelopment and stagnation. But insofar as men are set free from the coerciveness of the state and from material necessity, they will distribute themselves in a more natural way, more or less as contemporary Americans have done. The American way is exemplary because it derives from or reflects the real inequalities of mankind. Men don't naturally fall into two classes (patricians and plebeians) as conservatives once thought; nor can they plausibly be grouped into a single class (citizens or comrades) as leftists still believe. Instead, "human talents and abilities ... distribute themselves along a bell-shaped curve, with most people clustered around the middle, and with much smaller percentages at the lower and higher ends." The marvels of social science!—this distribution is a demonstrable fact. And it is another "demonstrable fact that in all modern bourgeois societies, the distribution of income is also along a bell-shaped curve. ..." The second bell echoes the first. Moreover, once this harmony is established, "the political structure—the distribution of political power—follows along the same way. ..." At this point, in Kristol must add, "however slowly and reluctantly," since he believes that the Soviet economy is moving closer every year to its natural shape, and it is admittedly hard to a find evidence that nature is winning out in the political realm. But in the United States, nature is triumphant: we are perfectly bell-shaped.

The first bell is obviously the crucial one. The defense of inequality reduces to these two propositions: that talent is distributed unequally and that talent will out. Clearly, we all want men and women to develop and express their talents, but whenever they are able to do that, Kristol suggests, the bell-shaped curve will appear or reappear, first in the economy, then in the political system. It is a neat argument but also a peculiar one, for there is no reason to think that "human talents and abilities" in fact distribute themselves along a *single* curve, although income necessarily does. Consider the range and variety of human capacities: intelligence, physical strength, agility and grace, artistic creativity, mechanical skill, leadership, endurance, memory, psychological insight, the capacity for hard work—even, moral strength, sensitivity, the ability to express compassion. Let's assume that with respect to all these, most people (but different people in each case) cluster around the middle of whatever scale we can construct, with smaller numbers at the lower and higher ends. Which of these curves is actually echoed by the income bell? Which, if any, ought to be?

There is another talent that we need to consider: the ability to make money, the green thumb of bourgeois society—a secondary talent, no doubt, combining many of the others in ways specified by the immediate environment, but probably also a talent which distributes, if we could graph it, along bell-shaped curve. Even this curve would not correlate exactly with the income bell because of the intervention of luck, that eternal friend of the untalented, whose most important social expression is the inheritance of property. But the correlation would be close enough, and it might also be morally plausible and satisfying. People who are able to make money ought to make money, in the same way that people who are able to write books ought to write books. Every human talent should be developed and expressed.

The difficulty here is that making money is only rarely a form of self-expression, and the money we make is rarely enjoyed for its intrinsic qualities (at least, economists frown upon that sort of enjoyment). In a capitalist world, money is the universal medium of exchange; it enables the men and women who possess it to purchase virtually every other sort of social good; we collect it for its exchange value. Political power, celebrity, admiration, leisure, works of art, baseball teams, legal advice, sexual pleasure, travel, education, medical care, rare books, sailboats—all these (and much more) are up for sale. The list is as endless as human desire and social invention. Now isn't it odd, and morally implausible and unsatisfying, that all these things should be distributed to people with a talent for making money? And even odder and more unsatisfying that they should be distributed (as they are) to people who have money, whether or not they made it, whether or not they possess any talent at all?

Rich people, of course, always look talented—just as princesses always look beautiful—to the deferential observer. But it is the first task of social science, one would think, to look beyond these appearances. "The properties of money," Marx wrote, "are my own (the possessor's) properties and faculties. What I *am* and *can do* is, therefore, not at all determined by my individuality. I *am* ugly, but I can buy the most beautiful woman for myself. Consequently, I am not ugly, for the effect of ugliness, its power to repel, is annulled by money. … I am a detestable, dishonorable, unscrupulous, and stupid man, but money is honored and so also is its possessor."[2]

It would not be any better if we gave men money in direct proportion to their intelligence, their strength, or their moral rectitude. The resulting distributions would each, no doubt, reflect what Kristol calls "the tyranny of the bell-shaped curve," though it is worth noticing again that the populations in the lower, middle, and upper regions of each graph would be radically different. But whether it was the smart, the strong, or the righteous who enjoyed all the things that money can buy, the oddity would remain: why them? Why anybody? In fact, there is no single talent or combination of talents which plausibly entitles a man to every available social good—and there is no single talent or combination of talents that necessarily must win the available goods of a free society. Kristol's bell-shaped curve is tyrannical only in a purely formal sense. Any particular distribution may indeed be bell-shaped, but there are a large number of possible distributions. Nor need there be a single distribution of all social goods, for different goods might well be distributed differently. Nor again need all these distributions follow this or that talent curve, for in the sharing of some social goods, talent does not seem a relevant consideration at all.

Consider the case of medical care: surely it should not be distributed to individuals because they are wealthy, intelligent, or righteous, but only because they are sick. Now, over any given period of time, it may be true that some men and women won't require any medical treatment, a very large number will need some moderate degree of attention, and a few will have to have intensive care. If that is so, then we must hope for the appearance of another bell-shaped curve. Not just any bell will do. It must be the right one, echoing what might be called the susceptibility-to-sickness curve. But in America today, the distribution of medical care actually follows closely the lines of the income graph. It's not how a man feels, but how much money he has that determines how often he visits a doctor. Another demonstrable fact! Does it require envious intellectuals to see that something is wrong?

There are two possible ways of setting things right. We might distribute income in proportion to susceptibility-to-sickness, or we might make sure that medical care is not for sale at all, but is available to those who need it. The second of these is obviously the simpler. Indeed, it is a modest proposal and already has wide support, even among those ordinary men and women who are said to be indifferent to equality. And yet, the distribution of medical care solely for medical reasons would point the way toward an egalitarian society, for it would call the dominance of the income curve dramatically into question.

II

What egalitarianism requires is that many bells should ring. Different goods should be distributed to different people for different reasons. Equality is not a simple notion, and it cannot be satisfied by a single distributive scheme—not even, I hasten to add, by a scheme which emphasizes need. "From each according to his abilities, to each according to his needs" is a fine slogan with regard to medical care. Tax money collected from all of us in proportion to our resources (these will never correlate exactly with our abilities, but that problem I shall leave aside for now) must pay the doctors who care for those of us who are sick. Other people who deliver similar sorts of social goods should probably be paid in the same way—teachers and lawyers, for example. But Marx's slogan doesn't help at all with regard to the distribution of political power, honor and fame, leisure time, rare books, and sailboats. None of these things can be distributed to individuals in proportion to their needs, for they are not things that anyone (strictly speaking) needs. They can't be distributed in equal amounts or given to whoever wants them, for some of them are necessarily scarce, and some of them can't be possessed unless other people agree on the proper name of the possessor. There is no criteria, I think, that will fit them all. In the past they have indeed been distributed on a single principle: men and women have possessed them or their historical equivalents because they were strong or well-born or wealthy. But this only suggests that a society in which any single distributive principle is dominant cannot be an egalitarian society. Equality requires a diversity of principles, which mirrors the diversity both of mankind and of social goods.

Whenever equality in this sense does not prevail, we have a kind of tyranny, for it is tyrannical of the well-born or the strong or the rich to gather to themselves social goods that have nothing to do with their personal qualities. This is an idea beautifully expressed in a passage from Pascal's *Pensées,* which I am going to quote at some length, since it is the source of my own argument.[3]

> The nature of tyranny is to desire power over the whole world and outside its own sphere.
>
> There are different companies—the strong, the handsome, the intelligent, the devout—and each man reigns in his own, not elsewhere. But sometimes they meet, and the strong and the handsome fight for mastery—foolishly, for their mastery is of different kinds. They misunderstand one another, and make the mistake of each aiming at universal dominion. Nothing can win this, not even strength, for it is powerless in the kingdom of the wise. ...
>
> *Tyranny.* The following statements, therefore, are false and tyrannical: "Because I am handsome, so I should command respect." "I am strong, therefore men should love me. ..." "I am ... etc."

Tyranny is the wish to obtain by one means what can only be had by another. We owe different duties to different qualities: love is the proper response to charm, fear to strength, and belief to learning.

Marx makes a very similar argument in one of the early manuscripts; perhaps he had this *pensée* in mind.

Let us assume man to be man, and his relation to the world to be a human one. Then love can only be exchanged for love, trust for trust, etc. If you wish to enjoy art you must be an artistically cultivated person; if you wish to influence other people, you must be a person who really has a stimulating and encouraging effect upon others. ... If you love without evoking love in return, i.e., if you are not able, by the manifestation of yourself as a loving person, to make yourself a beloved person, then your love is impotent and a misfortune.[4]

The doctrine suggested by these passages is not an easy one, and I can expound it only in a tentative way. It isn't that every man should get what he deserves—as in the old definition of justice—for desert is relevant only to some of the exchanges that Pascal and Marx have in mind. Charming men and women don't deserve to be loved: I may love this one or that one, but it can't be the case that I ought to do so. Similarly, learned men don't deserve to be believed: they are believed or not depending on the arguments they make. What Pascal and Marx are saying is that love and belief can't rightly be had in any other way—can't be purchased or coerced, for example. It is wrong to seek them in any way that is alien to their intrinsic character. In its extended form, their argument is that for all our personal and collective resources, there are distributive reasons that are somehow *right,* that are naturally part of our ideas about the things themselves. So nature is reestablished as a critical standard, and we are invited to wonder at the strangeness of the existing order.

This new standard is egalitarian, even though it obviously does not require an equal distribution of love and belief. The doctrine of right reasons suggests that we pay equal attention to the "different qualities," and to the "individuality" of every man and woman, that we find ways of sharing our resources that match the variety of their needs, interests, and capacities. The clues that we must follow lie in the conceptions we already have, in the things we already know about love and belief, and also about respect, obedience, education, medical care, legal aid, all the necessities of life—for this is no esoteric doctrine, whatever difficulties it involves. Nor is it a panacea for human misfortune, as Marx's last sentence makes clear: it is only meant to suggest a humane form of social accommodation. There is little we can do, in the best of societies, for the man who isn't loved. But there may be ways to avoid the triumph of the man who doesn't love—who buys love or forces it—or at least of his parallels in the larger social and political world: the leaders, for example, who are obeyed because of their coercive might or their enormous wealth. Our goal should be an end to tyranny, a society in which no man is master outside his sphere. That is the only society of equals worth having.

But it isn't readily had, for there is no necessity implied by the doctrine of right reasons. Pascal is wrong to say that "strength is powerless in the kingdom of the wise"—or rather, he is talking of an ideal realm and not of the intellectual world as we know it. In fact, wise men (at any rate, smart men) have often in the past defended the tyranny of the strong, as they still defend the tyranny of the rich. Sometimes, of course, they do this because they are persuaded of the necessity or the utility of tyrannical rule; sometimes for other reasons. Kristol suggests that whenever intellectuals are not persuaded, they are secretly aspiring to a tyranny of their own: they too would like to rule outside their sphere. Again, that's certainly true of some of them, and we all have our own lists. But it's not necessarily true. Surely it is possible, though no doubt difficult, for an intellectual to pay proper respect to the different companies of men. I want to argue that in our society the only way to do that, or to begin to do it, is to worry about the tyranny of money.

III

Let's start with some things that money cannot buy. It can't buy the American League pennant: star players can be hired, but victories presumably are not up for sale. It can't buy the National Book Award: writers can be subsidized, but the judges presumably can't be bribed. Nor, it should be added, can the pennant or the award be won by being strong, charming, or ideologically correct—at least we all hope not. In these sorts of cases, the right reasons for winning are built into the very structure of the competition. I am inclined to think that they are similarly built into a large number of social practices and institutions. It's worth focusing again, for example, on the practice of medicine. From ancient times, doctors were required to take an oath to help the sick, not the powerful or the wealthy: That requirement reflects a common understanding about the very nature of medical care. Many professionals don't share that understanding, but the opinion of ordinary men and women, in this case at least, is profoundly egalitarian.

The same understanding is reflected in our legal system. A man accused of a crime is entitled to a fair trial simply by virtue of being an accused man; nothing else about him is a relevant consideration. That is why defendants who cannot afford a lawyer are provided with legal counsel by the state: otherwise justice would be up for sale. And that is why defense counsel can challenge particular jurors thought to be prejudiced: the fate of the accused must hang on his guilt or innocence, not on his political opinions, his social class, or his race. We want different defendants to be treated differently, but only for the right reasons.

The case is the same in the political system, whenever the state is a democracy. Each citizen is entitled to one vote simply because he is a citizen. Men and women who are ambitious to exercise greater power must collect votes, but they can't do that by purchasing them; we don't want votes to be traded in the marketplace, though virtually everything else is traded there, and so we have made it a criminal offense to offer bribes to voters. The only right way to collect votes is to campaign for them, that is, to be persuasive, stimulating, encouraging, and so on. Great inequalities in political power are acceptable only if they result from a political process of a certain kind, open to argument, closed to bribery and coercion. The freely given support of one's fellow citizens is the appropriate criteria for exercising political power and, once again, it is not enough, or it shouldn't be, to be physically powerful, or well-born, or even ideologically correct.

It is often enough, however, to be rich. No one can doubt the mastery of the wealthy in the spheres of medicine, justice, and political power, even though these are not their own spheres. I don't want to say, their unchallenged mastery, for in democratic states we have at least made a start toward restricting the tyranny of money. But we have only made a start: think how different America would have to be before these three companies of men—the sick, the accused, the politically ambitious—could be treated in strict accordance with their individual qualities. It would be immediately necessary to have a national health service, national legal assistance, the strictest possible control over campaign contributions. Modest proposals, again, but they represent so many moves toward the realization of that old socialist slogan about the abolition of money. I have always been puzzled by that slogan, for socialists have never, to my knowledge, advocated a return to a barter economy. But it makes a great deal of sense if it is interpreted to mean *the abolition of the power of money outside its sphere.* What socialists want is a society in which wealth is no longer convertible into social goods with which it has no intrinsic connection.

But it is in the very nature of money to be convertible (that's all it is), and I find it hard to imagine the sorts of laws and law enforcement that would be necessary to prevent monied men and women from buying medical care and legal aid over and above whatever social minimum is provided for everyone. In the U.S. today, people can even buy police protection beyond what the state provides, though one would think that it is the primary purpose of the state to guarantee equal security to all its citizens, and it is by no means the rich, despite the temptations they offer, who stand in greatest need of protection. But this sort of thing could be prevented only by a very considerable restriction of individual liberty—of the freedom to offer services and to purchase them. The case is even harder with respect to politics itself. One can stop overt bribery, limit the size of campaign contributions, require publicity, and so on. But none of these things will be enough to prevent the wealthy from exercising power in all sorts of ways to which their fellow citizens have never consented.

Indeed, the ability to hold or spend vast sums of money is itself a form of power, permitting what might be called preemptive strikes against the political system. And this, it seems to me, is the strongest possible argument for a radical redistribution of wealth. So long as money is convertible outside its sphere, it must be widely and more or less equally held so as to minimize its distorting effects upon legitimate distributive processes.

IV

What is the proper sphere of wealth? What sorts of things are rightly had in exchange for money? The obvious answer is also the right one: all those economic goods and services, beyond what is necessary to life itself, which men find useful or pleasing. There is nothing degraded about wanting these things; there is nothing unattractive, boring, debased, or philistine about a society organized to provide them for its members. Kristol insists that a snobbish dislike for the sheer productivity of bourgeois society is a feature of egalitarian argument. I would have thought that a deep appreciation of that productivity has more often marked the work of socialist writers. The question is, how are the products to be distributed? Now, the right way to possess useful and pleasing things is by making them, or growing them, or somehow providing them for others. The medium of exchange is money, and this is the proper function of money and, ideally, its only function.

There should be no way of acquiring rare books and sailboats except by working for them. But this is not to say that men deserve whatever money they can get for the goods and services they provide. In capitalist society, the actual exchange value of the work they do is largely a function of market conditions over which they exercise no control. It has little to do with the intrinsic value of the work or with the individual qualities of the worker. There is no reason for socialists to respect it, unless it turns out to be socially useful to do so. There are other values, however, which they must respect, for money isn't the only or necessarily the most important thing for which work can be exchanged. A lawyer is surely entitled to the respect he wins from his colleagues and to the gratitude and praise he wins from his clients. The work he has done may also constitute a good reason for making him director of the local legal aid society; it may even be a good reason for making him a judge. It isn't, on the face of it, a good reason for allowing him an enormous income. Nor is the willingness of his clients to pay his fees a sufficient reason, for most of them almost certainly think they should be paying less. The money they pay is different from the praise they give, in that the first is extrinsically determined, the second freely offered.

In a long and thoughtful discussion of egalitarianism in the *Public Interest*, Daniel Bell worries that socialists today are aiming at an "equality of results" instead of the "just meritocracy" (the career open to talents) that he believes was once the goal of leftist and even of revolutionary politics.[5] I confess that I am tempted by "equality of results" in the sphere of money, precisely because it is so hard to see how a man can merit the things that money can buy. On the other hand, it is easy to list cases where merit (of one sort or another) is clearly the right distributive criteria, and where socialism would not require the introduction of any other principle.

- Six people speak at a meeting, advocating different policies, seeking to influence the decision of the assembled group.
- Six doctors are known to aspire to a hospital directorship.
- Six writers publish novels and anxiously await the reviews of the critics.
- Six men seek the company and love of the same woman.

Now, we all know the right reasons for the sorts of decisions, choices, judgments that are in question here. I have never heard anyone seriously argue that the woman must let herself be shared, or the hospital establish a six-man directorate, or the critics distribute their praise evenly, or the people at the meeting adopt all six proposals. In all these cases, the personal qualities of the individuals involved (as these appear to the others) should carry the day.

But what sorts of personal qualities are relevant to owning a $20,000 sailboat? A love for sailing, perhaps, and a willingness to build the boat or to do an equivalent amount of work. In America today, it would take a steelworker about two years to earn that money (assuming that he didn't buy anything else during all that time) and it would take a corporation executive a month or two. How can that be right, when the executive also has a rug on the floor, air-conditioning, a deferential secretary, and enormous personal power? He's being paid as he goes, while the steelworker is piling up a kind of moral merit (so we have always been taught) by deferring pleasure. Surely there is no meritocratic defense for this sort of difference. It would seem much better to pay the worker and the executive more or less the same weekly wage and let the sailboat be bought by the man who is willing to forgo other goods and services, that is, by the man who really wants it. Is this "equality of result"? In fact, the results will be different, if the men are, and it seems to me that they will be different for the right reasons.

Against this view, there is a conventional but also very strong argument that can be made on behalf of enterprise and inventiveness. If there is a popular defense of inequality, it is this one, but I don't think it can carry us very far toward the inequalities that Kristol wants to defend. Consider the case of the man who builds a better mousetrap, or opens a restaurant and sells delicious blintzes, or does a little teaching on the side. He has no air-conditioning, no secretary, no power; probably his reward has to be monetary. He has to have a chance, at least, to earn a little more money than his less enterprising neighbors. The market doesn't guarantee that he will in fact earn more, but it does make it possible, and until some other way can be found to do that, market relations are probably defensible under the doctrine of right reasons.

Here in the world of the petty-bourgeoisie, it seems appropriate that people able to provide goods or services that are novel, timely, or particularly excellent should reap the rewards they presumably had in mind when they went to work. And which they were right to have in mind: no one would want to feed blintzes to strangers, day after day, merely to win their gratitude.

But one might well want to be a corporation executive, day after day, merely to make all those decisions. It is precisely the people who are paid or who pay themselves vast sums of money who reap all sorts of other rewards too. We need to sort out these different forms of payment. First of all, there are rewards, like the pleasure of exercising power, which are intrinsic to certain jobs. An executive must make decisions—that's what he is there for—and even decisions seriously affecting other people. It is right that he should do that, however, only if he has been persuasive, stimulating, encouraging, and so on, and won the support of a majority of those same people. That he owns the corporation or has been chosen by the owners isn't enough. Indeed, given the nature of corporate power in contemporary society, the following statement (to paraphrase Pascal) is false and tyrannical: because I am rich, so I should make decisions and command obedience. Even in corporations organized democratically, of course, the personal exercise of power will persist. It is more likely to be seen, however, as it is normally seen in political life—as the chief attraction of executive positions. And this will cast a new light on the other rewards of leadership.

The second of these consists in all the side-effects of power: prestige, status, deference, and so on. Democracy tends to reduce these, or should tend that way when it is working well, without significantly reducing the attractions of decision-making. The same is true of the third form of reward, money itself, which is owed to work, but not necessarily to place and power. We pay political leaders much less than corporation executives, precisely because we understand so well the excitement and appeal of political office. Insofar as we recognize the political character of corporations, then, we can pay their executives less too. I doubt that there would be a lack of candidates even if we paid them no more than was paid to any other corporation employee. Perhaps there are reasons for paying them more—but not meritocratic reasons, for we give all the attention that is due to their merit when we make them our leaders.

We don't give all due attention to the restaurant owner, however, merely by eating his blintzes. Him we have to pay, and he can ask, I suppose, whatever the market will bear. That's fair enough, and no real threat to equality so long as he can't amass so much money that he becomes a threat to the integrity of the political system and so long as he does not exercise power, tyrannically, over other men and women. Within his proper sphere, he is as good a citizen as any other. His activities recall Dr. Johnson's remark: "There are few ways in which man can be more innocently employed than in getting money."

V

The most immediate occasion of the conservative attack on equality is the reappearance of the quota system—newly designed, or so it is said, to move us closer to egalitarianism rather than to maintain old patterns of religious and racial discrimination. Kristol does not discuss quotas, perhaps because they are not widely supported by professional people (or by professors): the disputes of the last several years do not fit the brazen simplicity of his argument. But almost everyone else talks about them, and Bell worries at some length, and rightly, about the challenge quotas represent to the "just meritocracy" he favors. Indeed, quotas in any form, new or old, establish "wrong reasons" as the basis of important social decisions, perhaps the most important social decisions: who shall be a doctor, who shall be a lawyer, and who shall be a bureaucrat. It is obvious that being black or a woman or having a Spanish surname (any more than being white, male, and Protestant) is no qualification for entering a university or a medical school or joining the civil service. In a sense, then, the critique of quotas consists almost entirely of a series of restatements and reiterations of the argument I have been urging in this essay. One only wishes that the critics would apply it more generally than they seem ready to do. There is more to be said, however, if they consistently refuse to do that.

The positions for which quotas are being urged, are, in America today, key entry points to the good life. They open the way, that is, to a life marked above all by a profusion of goods, material and moral: possessions, conveniences, prestige, and deference. Many of these goods are not in any plausible sense appropriate rewards for the work that is being done. They are merely the rewards that upper classes throughout history have been able to seize and hold for their members. Quotas, as they are currently being used, are a way of redistributing these rewards by redistributing the social places to which they conventionally pertain. It is a bad way, because one really wants doctors and (even) civil servants to have certain sorts of qualifications. To the people on the receiving end of medical and bureaucratic services, race and class are a great deal less important than knowledge, competence, courtesy, and so on. I don't want to say that race and class are entirely unimportant: it would be wrong to underestimate the distortions introduced by an inegalitarian society into these sorts of human relations. But if the right reason for receiving medical care is being sick, then the right reason for giving medical care is being able to help the sick. And so medical schools should pay attention, first of all and almost exclusively, to the potential helpfulness of their applicants.

But they may be able to do that only if the usual connections between place and reward are decisively broken. Here is another example of the doctrine of right reasons. If men and women wanted to be doctors primarily because they wanted to be helpful, they would have no reason to object when judgments were made about their potential helpfulness. But so long as there are extrinsic reasons for wanting to be a doctor, there will be pressure to choose doctors (that is, to make medical school places available) for reasons that are similarly extrinsic. So long as the goods that medical schools distribute include more than certificates of competence, include, to be precise, certificates of earning power, quotas are not entirely implausible. I don't see that being black is a worse reason for owning a sailboat than being a doctor. They are equally bad reasons.

Quotas today are a means of lower-class aggrandizement, and they are likely to be resolutely opposed, opposed without guilt and worry, only by people who are entirely content with the class structure as it is and with the present distribution of goods and services. For those of us who are not content, anxiety can't be avoided. We know that quotas are wrong, but we also know that the present distribution of wealth makes no moral sense, that the dominance of the income curve plays havoc with legitimate distributive principles, and that quotas are a form of redress no more irrational than the world within which and because of which they are demanded. In an egalitarian society, however, quotas would be unnecessary and inexcusable.

VI

I have put forward a difficult argument in very brief form, in order to answer Kristol's even briefer argument—for he is chiefly concerned with the motives of those who advocate equality and not with the case they make or try to make. He is also concerned, he says with the fact that equality has suddenly been discovered and is now for the first time being advocated as the *chief* virtue of social institutions: as if societies were not complex and values ambiguous. I don't know what discoverers and advocates he has in mind.[6] But it is worth stressing that equality as I have described it does not stand alone, but is closely related to the idea of liberty. The relation is complex, and I cannot say very much about it here. It is a feature of the argument I have made, however, that the right reason for distributing love, belief, and, most important for my immediate purposes, political power is the freely given consent of lovers, believers, and citizens. In these sorts of cases, of course, we all have standards to urge upon our fellows: we say that so and so should not be believed unless he offers evidence or that so and so should not be elected to political office unless he commits himself to civil rights. But clearly credence and power are not and ought not to be distributed according to my standards or yours. What is necessary is that everyone else be able to say yes or no. Without liberty, then, there could be no rightful distribution at all. On the other hand, men are not free, not politically free at least, if *his* yes, because of his birth or place or fortune, counts seventeen times more heavily than *my* no. Here the case is exactly as socialists have always claimed it to be: liberty and equality are the two chief virtues of social institutions, and they stand best when they stand together.

Notes

1. "About Equality," *Commentary,* November 1972.
2. *Early Writings,* trans. T. B. Bottomore (London: Watts, 1963), p. 191.
3. I am also greatly indebted to Bernard Williams, in whose essay "The Idea of Equality" (first published in Laslett and Runciman, *Philosophy, Politics and Society,* second series [Oxford: Blackwell, 1962]) a similar argument is worked out. The example of medical care, to which I recur, is suggested by him. The Pascal quote is from J. M. Cohen's translation of *The Pensées* (London and Baltimore: Penguin Classics, 1961), no. 244.
4. *Early Writings,* pp. 193–94.
5. "On Meritocracy and Equality," *Public Interest,* Fall 1972.
6. The only writer he mentions is John Rawls, whose *Theory of Justice* Kristol seems entirely to misunderstand. For Rawls explicitly accords priority to the "liberty principle" over those other maxims that point toward greater equality.

30
Irving Howe (1920–1993)
Socialism and Liberalism: Articles of Conciliation? (1977)

Editor's Introduction

From the time Irving Howe was in his mid-thirties, as *Dissent* began in 1954, he slowly initiated a personal crusade to fashion an outlook that intertwined the socialism of his youth with the liberal values he increasingly cherished as he approached middle age. Even as he was chiding his fellow New York Intellectuals in 1954, complaining in *Partisan Review* that they had exchanged their leftism for what Philip Rahv called their *"embourgeoisement,"* Howe asserted his "hope that any revival of American radicalism will acknowledge not only its break from, but also its roots in, the liberal tradition." (Irving Howe, "This Age of Conformity," *Partisan Review* vol. 21, no. 1, January–February, 1954. Philip Rahv, "Our Country and Our Culture," *Partisan Review*, vol. 19, no. 3, May–June, 1952.) It was a departure from the Howe of the 1930s and 1940s. The change from socialism to democratic socialism to liberalism occurred at different times for different members of the group. Lionel Trilling, for example, became a liberal by 1940s, if not earlier, while Howe moved from socialism to democratic socialism in the 1950s.

In the late 1950s *Dissent* began to envision what shape a distinctly liberal socialism might take. Ben B. Seligman, professor of economics at the University of Massachusetts, addressing this question, wrote a series of articles for the magazine, one of which outlined the idea of market socialism. Social thinkers in the 1890s in Austria began discussing market socialism, but the conversation wasn't imported to the United States until Oskar Lange and Fred Taylor wrote their *On the Economic Theory of Socialism* (1938). The articles on market socialism in *Dissent* underlined the magazine's conviction that democratic socialists needed to incorporate the liberal values of individual choice and a basic element of decentralization in the economy. Although Seligman was not speaking for everyone at *Dissent*, his series of essays indicated that Howe wanted the issues discussed. Seligman concluded that "the way in which a socialist economy works must be in consonance with the moral and political aims that socialists seek to attain. In such a framework the competitive solution of market socialism seems be far the more desirable objective." The market, that is, the symbol of liberal thought since Adam Smith, should be at the center of a democratic socialist system. It would be, as Seligman cast it, "socialism without Marx." (Ben B. Seligman, "Socialism Without Marx," *Dissent* vol. 6, no. 3, Summer 1959. See also Neil Jumonville, *Critical Crossings*, 90–101.)

It is clear in "Socialism and Liberalism: Articles of Conciliation?" that Howe was an adept political thinker. In his youth, in meetings and on street corners, he was trained in politics long before he ever thought of becoming a literary critic. It was a grueling training, an intellectual warfare, among his ambitious and disputatious socialist friends. In this essay Howe provides another example of the wide-ranging interdisciplinary interests of the *Partisan Review* circle that have made its members popular examples of the public intellectual.

Source

Irving Howe, "Socialism and Liberalism: Articles of Conciliation?" *Dissent* vol. 24, no. 1, Winter 1977.

Selected Readings

Ben B. Seligman, "Socialism Without Marx," *Dissent* vol. 6, no. 3, Summer 1959.
Irving Howe, "This Age of Conformity," *Partisan Review* vol. 21, no. 1, January-February, 1954.
Oskar Lange and Fred Taylor, *On the Economic Theory of Socialism* (Minneapolis: University of Minnesota Press, 1938).
Henry D. Dickinson, *Economics of Socialism* (London: Oxford University Press, 1939).

* * * * *

I

It will surprise none of my readers to learn that after a reasonably diligent search I have not been able to find a serious attempt to bring together systematically the usual socialist criticisms of liberalism. The socialist criticisms of liberalism, though familiar enough in their general features, appear in the literature mainly through occasional passages, unquestioned references, rude dismissals, and, during the last few decades, a few wistful beckonings for reconciliation. What I propose to do here is to construct a synthesis, necessarily open to the charge that it is ahistorical, of the criticisms socialists have traditionally leveled against liberalism, and then to offer some remarks about possible future relations.

Socialists, who are they? and liberalism, what is it? I shall choose here to signify as socialist those thinkers and spokesmen who cannot be faulted as tender toward authoritarian regimes: I shall exclude Communists, Maoists, Castroites, as well as their hybrids, cousins, and reticent wooers. I shall assume that with regard to liberalism there has been some coherence of outlook among the various shades of socialist (and Marxist) opinion. But in talking about liberalism I shall be readier to acknowledge the complexities and confusions of historical actuality. And this for two reasons: first, that liberalism is our main interest today; and second, that since a surplus of variables can paralyze analysis (eight kinds of socialism matched against six of liberalism yield how many combinations/confrontations?), I would justify taking one's sights from a more-or-less fixed position as a way of grasping a range of shifting phenomena.

In the socialist literature, though not there alone, liberalism has taken on at least the following roles and meanings:

1. Especially in Europe, liberalism has signifed those movements and currents of opinion that arose toward the end of the 18th century, seeking to loosen the constraints traditional societies had imposed on the commercial classes and proposing modes of government in which the political and economic behavior of individuals would be subjected to a minimum of regulation. Social life came to be seen as a field in which an equilibrium of desired goods could be realized if individuals were left free to pursue their interests.[1] This, roughly, is what liberalism has signified in Marxist literature, starting with Marx's articles for the *Rheinische Zeitung* and extending through the polemics of Kautsky, Bernstein, and Luxemburg. In short: "classical" liberalism.

2. Both in Europe and America, liberalism has also been seen as a system of beliefs stressing such political freedoms as those specified in the U.S. Bill of Rights. Rising from the lowlands of interest to the highlands of value, this view of liberalism proposes a commitment to "formal" freedoms—speech, assembly, press, etc.—so that in principle, as sometimes in practice, liberalism need have no necessary connection with, or dependence upon, any particular way of organizing the economy.

3. Especially in 20th-century America but also in Europe, liberalism has come to signify movements of social reform seeking to "humanize" industrial-capitalist society, usually on the premise that this could be done sufficiently or satisfactorily without having to resort to radical/socialist measures—in current shorthand: the welfare state. At its best, this social liberalism has also viewed itself as strictly committed to the political liberalism of #2 above.

4. In America, sometimes to the bewilderment of Europeans, liberalism has repeatedly taken on indigenous traits that render it, at one extreme, virtually asocial and anarchic and, at the other extreme, virtually chiliastic and authoritarian. Perhaps because the assumptions of a liberal polity were so widely shared in 19th-century America (the slaveocracy apart), "liberal" as a term of political designation can hardly be found in its writings. When liberalism as a distinctive modern politics or self-designated ideological current begins to emerge in America—first through the high-minded reforming individualism of Edward Godkin, editor of the *Nation* during the 1880s and 1890s, and

then through the social-nationalist progressivism of Herbert Croly, editor of the *New Republic* when it was founded in 1914—it becomes clear that it cannot escape a heritage of native individualism, utopianism, and "conscience-politics." Nor can it escape the paradisial vision that is deeply lodged in the American imagination, going back to Emerson and Thoreau, and further back, perhaps, to the Puritans. Nor can it escape a heritage of Protestant self-scrutiny, self-reliance, and self-salvation. Consequently American liberalism has a strand of deep if implicit hostility to politics *per se*—a powerful kind of moral absolutism, a celebration of conscience above community, which forms both its glory and its curse.

5. Meanwhile, through the decades, liberalism has encompassed a *Weltanschauung*, a distinctive way of regarding the human situation. Despite some recent attempts to render it profound through a gloomy chiaroscuro, liberalism has customarily been an expression of that view of man which stresses rationality, good nature, optimism, and even "perfectibility" (whatever that may mean). Whether or not there is a necessary clash between the Christian and liberal views of man, and despite some strains of continuity that may coexist with the differences, there can hardly be any question that historically, in its effort to gain its own space, liberalism has emerged as a competitor to traditional religious outlooks.

II

That there are other significant usages of the term "liberalism" I do not doubt; but for today these should be quite enough. Let me now schematically note some—by no means all—of the major socialist criticisms of at least some of these variants of liberalism:

• The socialist criticism of "classical" liberalism (joined at points by that of conservative iconoclasts like Carlyle) seems by now to have been largely absorbed in our political culture—with the exception of such ideological eccentrics and utopians as Ayn Rand, Milton Friedman, and the current President of the United States. That the historical conditions of early capitalist society made a mockery of any notion of free and equal competitors entering into free and equal exchange, with each employing his gifts and taking his risks; that large masses of people were excluded from the very possibility of significant social choice; that even "liberal" governments never quite practiced the noninterventionist principles of "classical" liberalism but in fact were actively engaged in furthering the growth of bourgeois economy; of that the notion "entitlement," with its premise of some early point of fair beginnings, is mostly ideological—these have been the kinds of criticisms that socialists, and especially Marxists, have made of early liberalism.[2] The very world we live in—irreversible if inconvenient, and open to almost every mode of criticism except nostalgia for the alleged bliss of pure capitalism—testifies to the cogency of these socialist criticisms.

Yet that is by no means the whole story. One of the strengths of Marxist historiography (I shall come to weaknesses) has been that even while assaulting capitalism it saw the vitality of its early phases, and that even in the course of ridiculing "classical" liberalism as an ideological rationale for bourgeois ascendency, it honored its liberating role in behalf of humanity at large. The early Marx—he who could write that "laws are positive and lucid universal norms in which freedom has attained an impersonal, theoretical existence independent of any arbitrary individual. A statute book is the people's Bible of freedom"; or who could write that "without parties there is no development, without division, no progress"—this early Marx clearly recognized his ties to, or descent from, the liberalism he subjected to attack and sought to "transcend."

Socialists—let us be honest: some socialists—have recognized that in its heroic phase liberalism constituted one of the two or three greatest revolutionary experiences in human history. The very idea of "the self or "the individual," quintessential to modern thought and sensibility, simply could not have come into being without the fructifying presence of liberalism. The liberalism that appears in 18th-century Europe promises a dismissal of intolerable restraints; speaks for previously unimagined rights; declares standards of sincerity and candor; offers the vision that each man will have his voice and each voice be heard. It would be making things too easy (at least for me) to say that socialism emerges unambiguously out of this tradition. Obviously, there have been authoritarian alloys in the socialist metals; but when the socialist imagination is at its most serious, it proposes a dialectical relationship to "classical" liberalism: a refusal, on the one hand, of quasi-Benthamite rationales for laissez-faire economics and a pact in behalf of preserving and enlarging the boundaries of freedom.

•   Both in some early efforts at Marxist scholarship and in recent academic revivals, socialists have charged against liberalism that its defenders elevate it to a supra-historical abstraction, an absolute value presumably untainted by grubby interests or bloodied corruptions, whereas in actuality liberalism, like all other modes of politics, arose as a historically conditioned and thereby contaminated phenomenon, and hence must be regarded as susceptible to historical decay and supercession.

Now, if we see this matter mainly as one of historiography, there is a point to the socialist criticism. No political movement, not even liberalism, likes to have the time of its origins deglamorized, yet there is sufficient reason for subjecting all movements to that chastening procedure. But with regard to a living politics, this criticism is dangerous and has done a share of mischief.

The tendency of some Marxists to regard liberal ideas as mainly or merely epiphenomena of a historical moment always runs the risk of declining into an absolutist relativism, that is, a historicism that acknowledges no fixed point of premise other than its own strategies of deflation. A sophisticated analogue is the "sociology of knowledge"; a vulgar reduction, the habit of speaking about "*mere* bourgeois democracy." This mode of historical analysis ignores the possibility that even movements and currents of thought conditioned by class interest can yield ideas, traditions, methods, customs that will seem of permanent value to future generations. There may not be unimpeded progress in history, but there do seem to be a few permanent conquests. To show that the principles of a liberal polity did not descend from Mount Sinai but arose together with social classes whose dominance we would like to see ended or curtailed is not at all to deny that those liberal principles are precious both to newly ascending classes and humanity at large. To show that the Founding Fathers of the United States represented commercial interests or kept slaves or, when in office, violated some of their own precepts is not at all to diminish the value of the Bill of Rights for people who despise commercial interests, abhor slavery, and propose, if in power, never to violate their own precepts. Criticism of Jefferson's inadequacies is made possible by the adequacy of Jeffersonian principles.

If these remarks seem excessively obvious, we might remember that the history of 20th-century politics, as also that of the 20th-century intelligentsia, offers scant ground for resting securely in a common devotion to liberal values. Quite the contrary! We are living through a century of counterrevolution, one in which the liberal conquests of the 19th century, inadequate as these might have been, have been systematically destroyed by left-and-right authoritarian dictatorships. "Vulgar Marxism," with its quick reduction of ideas to ideology and its glib ascription of ideology to interest, has become the mental habit of lazy and half-educated people throughout the world.[3] In general, by now we ought to be extremely wary of all statements featuring the word "really"—as in "Mill's ideas really represent the interests of the British, etc., etc." and "Freud's ideas really reflect the condition of the Viennese, etc., etc." Statements of this kind are, no doubt, unavoidable and sometimes fruitful, but they have too often come to be damaging to both the life of the mind and a polity of freedom.

Insofar, then, as the socialist criticism of liberalism has furthered an element of historical reductionism—unavoidable, I suspect, in the context of a mass movement—it has weakened the otherwise valid insistence that liberalism be treated as part of mundane history and thereby subject to mundane complications.

• A powerful socialist criticism of liberalism has been that it has detached political thought and practice from the soil of shared, material life, cutting politics off from the interplay of interests, needs, and passions that constitutes the collective life of mankind. A linked criticism has been that liberalism lacks an adequate theory of power, failing to see the deep relationships between political phenomena and alignments of social class. (Kenneth Minogue makes the point vividly: "The adjustment of interest conception [intrinsic to contemporary liberalism] … omits the crunch of truncheon on skull which always lies just in the background of political life…") Still another linked criticism, in the line of Rousseau, proposes that modern man is torn apart by a conflict between the liberal acceptance of bourgeois institutions, which sanction the pursuit of selfish-interest without regard to a larger community, and the liberal doctrine of popular sovereignty, which implies that the citizen must set aside private interests and concern himself with the common welfare.

Here, surely, it must be acknowledged that the socialist criticism—in fairness it has also been made by nonsocialists—has all but completely conquered, indeed taken effect so strongly as to become absorbed into the thought even of those who oppose socialism and/or Marxism. Almost every sophisticated (and thereby, soon enough, unsophisticated) analysis of society now takes it for granted that politics must be closely related to, and more or less seen as a reflection of, social interest; that society forms a totality in which the various realms of activity, though separable analytically, are intertwined in reality; that no segment of the population can be assumed any longer to be mute or passive, and that there has appeared a major force, the working class, which must be taken into historical account; and that the rationalism of most liberal theory, though not (one hopes) simply to be dismissed, must be complicated by a recognition of motives and ends in social behavior that are much richer, more complicated, and deeply troubling.[4]

• Both in our efforts to understand history and affect politics, there has occurred a "thickening" of our sense of society—indeed, the very idea of society, itself largely a 19th-century invention, testifies to that "thickening." We might even say that as a result of Marx there has occurred a recreation of social reality. (The Christian historian Herbert Butterfield praises the Marxist approach to history in a vivid phrase: "it hugs the ground so closely"—which in his judgment does not prevent it from surveying what occurs in the upper reaches.) It is very hard—though some people manage—still to see politics as a mere exercise for elites, or an unfolding of first principles; it is very hard still to see politics apart from its relation to the interaction of classes, levels of productivity, modes of socioeconomic organization, etc. Writing in 1885 about his early work Engels says:

> While I was in Manchester, it was tangibly brought home to me that the economic facts, which have so far played no role or only a contemptible one in the writing of history, are, at least in the modern world, a decisive historical force; that they form the basis of the origination of

the present-day class antagonisms; that these class antagonisms, in the countries where they have become fully developed, thanks to large-scale industry, hence especially in England, are in their turn the basis of the formation of political parties and party struggles, and thus of all political history.

If the germs of reductionism can be detected in such a passage, so too can the possibilities for complication and nuance: all depends on which clause one chooses to stress. These possibilities for complication and nuance were seized only a dozen years later by Emile Durkheim:

> I consider extremely fruitful the idea that social life should be explained, not by the notions of those who participate in it, but by more profound causes which are unperceived by consciousness, and I think also that these causes are to be sought mainly in the manner according to which the associated individuals are grouped.

Anyone wishing to trace the development of modern thought—among other things, from socialism to sociology—could do worse than start with gloss on these passages from Engels and Durkheim.

The "economism," real or apparent, of the Engels passage was followed by a vulgarization in popular Marxist writings, but there is also present in the Marxist tradition another—and for our time crucial—view of the relation between state and society. In his earlier and middle years especially, Marx saw that the state could possess or reach an autonomy of its own, rising "above" classes as a kind of smothering Leviathan. (The state in Louis Napoleon's France, wrote Marx, is "an appalling parasitic body, which enmeshes the body of French society like a net and chokes all its pores.") This perception could be crucial for a reconciliation between socialists and liberals—we shall come back to it.

• Yet, from the vantage point of the late 20th century, it ought to be possible for socialists to be self-critical enough to admit that the victory over liberalism with regard to such matters as the relationship between politics and society, state and economy, has by no means been an unambiguous one, certainly not a victory to bring unqualified satisfaction. Apart from reductionism, I would raise a point that seems to me increasingly important but for which my own tradition offers an inadequate vocabulary. I have in mind what might be called the body of traditional political wisdom, or the reflections of thoughtful men on the "perennial" problems of politics. To speak of "perennial" problems, I want to insist, is to locate them within a historical continuum rather than to elevate them "above" history.

In its historicist relativizing, its absorption with a particular social circumstance, the socialist tradition has given rather short shrift to this body of traditional political reflection. A pity! Marx might have been unsympathetic to Madison's reflections in *The Federalist Papers* regarding the dynamics of faction in a republic; perhaps he would have seen them as excessively abstract or as a rationale for class interest. Yet both of these criticisms could have been cogent without necessarily undermining the value of what Madison said. The socialist movement has sinned and suffered from its impatience with the accumulated insights of the centuries regarding political life. As a result, despite its prolonged attention to politics and its often brilliant analyses of political strategy (from Marx in the *18th Brumaire* to Trotsky on pre-Hitler Germany), the socialist tradition has lacked, or refused, a theory of politics as an autonomous or at least distinct activity. It has had little or nothing to say about such matters as necessary delimitations of power, the problems of representation, the uses or misuses of a division of authority, the relation between branches of government, etc.

Let me cite a fascinating example. In late 1874 and early 1875 Marx read Bakunin's book *Statism and Anarchy*, made extended extracts and attached to these his own sharply polemical comments. Bakunin was anticipating one of the questions endlessly rehearsed by writers of the nonauthoritarian left: how to prevent the bureaucratization of a "workers' state," whether exworkers raised to power would become corrupted, etc., etc. Bakunin writes that

> … universal suffrage—the right of the whole people—to elect its so-called representatives and rulers of the State—this is the last word of the Marxists as well as of the democratic school. And this is a falsehood behind which lurks the despotism of a governing minority…. But this minority, say the Marxists, will consist of workers. Yes, indeed, of *ex-workers, who, once they become rulers or representatives of the people, cease to be workers* ….

At which point Marx interrupts: "No more than does a manufacturer today cease to be a capitalist on becoming a city councilman." Continues Bakunin: "From that time on they [the ex-workers] represent not the people but themselves and their own claims to govern the people. Those who doubt this know precious little about human nature."

One need not acquiesce in Bakunin's hostility to democratic institutions in order to see that, in his own way, he has hit upon one of the "perennial" problems in political thought—the problem of representation, how the elected representative of a group or class can become corrupted or bureaucratized upon acquiring power. Marx's answer seems to me unsatisfactory: the manufacturer representing his class in a city council, though obviously susceptible to corruption, is not expected to help usher in a new, socialist era, he need only defend particularistic interests—while the worker elected to office in a "worker's state" is burdened, according to the Marxist prescription, with great historical and moral responsibilities, thereby rendering the problems of corruption and bureaucratism all the more acute. Surely Marx was able to understand this!—but what made it hard for him to respond to such matters with sufficient seriousness was a historical method, an ideological bent, a political will.

Yet, hidden within the class analyses of the Marxists there have remained— a Marxist analysis of Marxism might suggest that there *must* remain—elements of traditional political thinking. Lenin, the one Marxist writer most impatient with talk about "perennial" problems, seems nevertheless to recognize in *State and Revolution* that a theory focusing upon change must also take into account continuity. He writes:

> Men ... liberated from capitalist exploitation will gradually become accustomed to abide by the elementary rules of social life which have been known from time immemorial and have been set out for thousands of years in all regulations, and they will follow these rules without force, compulsion, subservience, and the special apparatus of compulsion which is known as the state.

One wants to reply: but if there are "elementary rules of social life ... known from time immemorial," rules which can be fully realized only in a classless society, then it must follow that in earlier, class-dominated societies those rules became manifest in some way, otherwise we could not recognize their existence. There are, then, "perennial" problems of politics, by no means so "elementary" either—considering the fact that they have never been solved, nor seem likely ever to be entirely solved. And these problems cannot be dismissed by references to class or historical contexts, though obviously class or historical contexts give them varying shape and significance. They are problems, it might be acknowledged, that have been discussed with greater depth, because more genuine interest, by conservatives and liberals than by socialists.

The Marxist/socialist criticism of liberalism regarding the relation of politics to society now seems less cogent, or at least requires greater complication, than it did half a century ago. And this for an additional reason: with the growth of the modern industrial state, in both its Western and Eastern versions, politics takes on a new primacy, indeed, a kind of "independence," vis-à-vis the institutions and mechanisms of the economy. In the Communist countries, what happens to the economy, what is done with one or another segment of the working class, how the peasants are treated in the kolkhoz: all stem from political decision. Far from the ruling Party bureaucracy being a mere agency of, or even (as Trotsky believed) a parasite upon, one of the social classes, the Party bureaucracy is the decisive sociopolitical force in the country, akin to, even if not quite like, a ruling class. State and society tend to merge in totalitarian countries, so that traditional discriminations between politics and economics come to seem of little use.

In advanced capitalist countries, the state increasingly takes over crucial functions of the market, while still allowing a considerable measure of autonomy to corporations and private business. These developments have been noted frequently and need not be elaborated here; suffice it to say that insofar as they persist, some of the apparently sealed conclusions from the long debate between liberalism and socialism need to be reopened. The traditional liberal notions of politics cannot, of course, be exhumed, but neither can the traditional socialist objections to them be repeated with confidence. What can be said, tentatively, is that the liberal insistence upon politics as a mode of autonomous human action with "laws" and "rules" of its own has come to have a new persuasiveness and, not least of all, within socialist thought.

•   There is a criticism of liberal politics and thought that runs through the whole of the socialist literature but, by now, can also be heard at many points to the right and left of liberalism: among "organicist" conservatives, followers of the young Marx, Christian socialists, syndicalists, communitarian New Leftists. This criticism is most often expressed as a defense of the values of community—human fellowship, social grouping—against egotism, competition, private property. Necessarily, it raises questions about the quality of life in bourgeois society: the failure of a common culture, the burdens placed upon the family when people lack alternative spheres of cooperative activity, the breakdown of social discipline that follows from laissez faire. This criticism also takes a political form: the argument that democracy requires public life, that it cannot be successfully maintained in a society of privatized persons whose interests are confined to their families and businesses, and that public life depends upon a sharing of political and economic goods. Does it not seem likely that some of the ills of American society follow from the situation described in this attack upon classical liberalism?

The idea of economic man is declared to be a libel upon humanity; the vision of extreme individualism, an impoverishment of social possibility; and the kind of life likely to emerge from a society devoted to such ideas, a terrible drop from traditional humanist and Christian standards.

Most thoughtful liberals have by now acknowledged the force of this criticism. Indeed, there is rather little in it that cannot be found in John Stuart Mill's essays on Bentham and Coleridge. In the long run, then, freedom of criticism does seem to yield some benefits: does seem to prompt spokesmen for major political-intellectual outlooks to complicate and modify their thought. Liberal criticism has made a difference in socialism; socialist criticism, in liberalism.

Still, who does not feel the continued poignancy in the yearning for community, which seems so widespread in our time? Who does not respond, in our society, to the cry that life is poor in shared experiences, vital communities, free brother (sister) hoods?

Yet precisely the pertinence and power of this attack upon traditional liberalism must leave one somewhat uneasy. For we must remember that we continue to live in a time when the yearning for community has been misshaped into a gross denial of personal integrity, when the desire for the warmth of social bonds—marching together, living together, huddling together, complaining in concert—has helped to betray a portion of the world into the shame of the total state.

One hears, these days, celebrations of the fact that in Communist China large masses of people actively "participate" in the affairs of state. They do. And it is not necessary to believe they always do so as a response to terror or force in order to be persuaded that the kind of "participation" to which they yield themselves is a denial of human freedom.

Let us be a little more cautious, then, in pressing the attack upon liberalism that invokes an image of community—a little more cautious if only because this attack is so easy to press. There is indeed an element of the paltry in the more extreme versions of liberal individualism; but the alienation that has so frequently, and rightly, been deplored in recent decades may have its sources not only in the organization of society but in the condition of mankind. Perhaps it is even to be argued that there is something desirable in recognizing that, finally, nothing can fully protect us from the loneliness of our selves.

A social animal, yes; but a solitary creature too. Socialists and liberals have some areas of common interest in balancing these two stresses, the communal and the individual, the shared and the alone. It is a balance that will tilt; men and women must be free to tilt it.

• Functioning for a good many decades as an opposition movement, and one, moreover, that could not quite decide whether it wished to be brought into society or preferred to seek a "total" revolutionary transformation, the socialist movement systematically attacked liberalism for timidity, evasiveness, vacillation, "rotten compromise," etc. It charged that liberalism was weak, that it never dared to challenge the socioeconomic power of the bourgeoisie, that it was mired in what Trotsky called "parliamentary cretinism," etc.

The historical impact of this criticism can hardly be overestimated. A major source of the "welfare state," insofar as we have one, has surely been the pressure that socialist movements have exerted upon a liberalism that has long gone past its early elan. Insofar as the socialist criticism served to force liberalism into awareness of and militancy in coping with social injustice, the results have been for the better.

But also—for the worse. For the socialist criticism (as the rise of bolshevism and its various offshoots make clear) contained at least two strands: one that disdained liberalism for its failure to live up to its claims and one that disdained liberalism for its success in living up to its claims. We touch here upon a great intellectual scandal of the age: the tacit collaboration of right and left in undermining the social and moral foundations of liberalism. In the decades between the Paris Commune and World War II both right- and left-wing intellectuals were gravely mistaken, and morally culpable, in their easy and contemptuous dismissal of liberalism. That the society they saw as the tangible embodiment of bourgeois liberalism required scathing criticism I do not doubt. But they failed utterly to estimate the limits of what was historically possible in their time, as they failed, even more importantly, to consider what the consequences might be of their intemperate attacks upon liberalism. It was all very well to denounce liberalism as what Ezra Pound called—Lenin would have agreed—"a mess of mush"; but to assault the vulnerable foundations of liberal democracy meant to bring into play social forces the intellectuals of both right and left could not foresee. There were, as it turned out, far worse things in the world than "a mess of mush."

Bourgeois Europe was overripe for social change by the time of World War I. But the assumptions that such change required a trampling on liberal values in the name of hierarchical order or proletarian dictatorship and that liberal values were inseparable from cultural decadence and capitalist economy—these assumptions proved a disaster. In the joyful brutality of their verbal violence many intellectuals, at both ends of the political spectrum, did not realize how profound a stake they had in preserving the norms of liberalism. They felt free to sneer at liberalism because, in a sense, they remained within its psychological orbit; they could not really imagine its destruction and took for granted that they would continue to enjoy its shelter. Even the most authoritarian among them could not foresee a situation in which *their* freedom would be destroyed. Dreaming of natural aristocrats or sublime proletarians, they helped pave the way for maniac *lumpen.*

• Still another socialist/radical criticism of liberalism, familiar from polemics of the '30s but urgently revived during the last decade by the New Left, is that the structure of liberties in democratic society rests on a shared acquiescence in the continued power of the bourgeoisie; that these liberties survive on condition they not be put to the crucial test of basic social transformation—and that they might well be destroyed by the bourgeoisie or its military agencies if a serious effort were made by a democratically elected government to introduce socialist economic measures. The overthrow of the Allende regime in Chile has been cited as a telling confirmation.

It is an old problem. Marx and Engels suggested that a socialist transition in such countries as England and Holland, with their deep-rooted democratic traditions, might be peaceful. Most other European countries not yet having completed the "bourgeois revolution" by the mid-19th century, it seemed reasonable to the founders of "scientific socialism" that revolutionary methods might be necessary on the continent—though we also know that later, when the German Social Democracy became a mass party, Engels accepted the parliamentary course. The standard Bolshevik gloss would soon be that since the time Marx and Engels had written, the bourgeois state in England and Holland had grown more powerful, developing a traditional apparatus of repression. Thereby, the expectation of peaceful transition had become obsolete.

I think it would be an error to dismiss the Marxist criticism on this point as outmoded or irrelevant. Changes in class rule have in the past rarely come about without one or another quantity of violence, and as I remember hearing and saying in my youth, ruling classes don't just fold up their tents and slink away. By the same token, I now reply to my younger self, past changes in class rule have rarely, if ever, taken place within established democratic societies, hence could not be said to provide a test of the socioeconomic strains democratic societies can be expected to sustain.

To insist that liberalism and/or liberties must collapse under a serious effort to introduce socialist measures signifies

(a) an unfortunate concession to those right-wing ideologues who insist that political liberty is inseparable from and could not survive the destruction of private property; or

(b) a vision of socialist transformation so "total" and apocalyptic that the collapse of political liberties in such circumstances could as readily be the work of revolutionary insurgents as of a resistant bourgeoisie. (To concede, after all, that liberalism could not survive a "dictatorship of the proletariat" in the Leninist or Leninist-Stalinist versions is hardly very damaging to the claim that liberalism can coexist with more than one form of economy.)

As for the historical evidence, it seems inconclusive and mixed. A very great deal, perhaps everything, depends on the strength of attachment among a people to democratic values; only a bit less, on the ability of a given society to avoid the kind of economic cataclysms that would put this attachment under excessive strain. If, say, the social democratic governments of Scandinavia and England, ruling with substantial majorities and elected as parties pledged to go considerably beyond welfare-state measures, were to introduce extensive socialist measures, there is not much reason to expect major extra-legal efforts to undo their policies.[5] For the tradition of pacific social life and "playing by the rules" seems strong enough in such countries to allow one to envisage a major onslaught against the power of corporations and large business without risking the survival of democracy.

(I referred a few sentences back to governments with substantial majorities. It seems reasonable, after all, that a government that squeaks into office with a narrow margin should exercise restraints in any effort to introduce major social change.)

At least in some "advanced" European countries, the problem would not seem to be the bourgeoisie itself—by now a class without an excess of self-confidence. Socialist anxiety as to the ability of a liberal society to absorb major change might more appropriately be directed toward the middle classes and the army, which can no longer be assumed to act (if ever they did) as mere pliant agents and accomplices of the bourgeoisie. It is by no means clear that the Chilean experiences "prove" that a democratic path to socialism is impossible. What it may prove is

(a) that a left-wing government trying to maintain democratic norms while introducing major social change must be especially sensitive to the interests and sentiments of the middle class; and

(b) that the army, acting out of its own interests and sentiments, can become an independent political force, establishing a dictatorial regime that it might well be a mistake to see as a mere creature of bourgeois restoration.

The role of armies in contemporary politics is a fascinating problem, beyond discussion here. Except for this: in a variety of circumstances, but especially where a mutual weakening of antagonistic classes has occurred, the army (like the state) can take on an unexpected autonomy. Nor is it clear that this follows the traditional Marxist expectation that the army would be employed by the ruling class to save its endangered interests. Even if that was true in Chile, it was not in Peru. And in sharply different ways, it is not true either in Portugal or Greece. In Asian and African countries, the role of the army is evidently that of a makeshift power compensating for the feebleness of all social classes. There is, then, something new here, not quite anticipated in liberal or socialist thought.

The question whether a liberal democratic regime can peacefully sustain major social or socialist changes remains open. If a categorical negative is unwarranted, so too is an easy reassurance. Given the probable configuration of politics in the Western democracies, there is some reason to conclude that even left-socialist regimes staying within democratic limits would have to proceed more cautiously, with greater respect for the multiplicity of group interests, than the usual leftist expectations have allowed. And the anxiety provoked by a possible effort to combine liberal polity with socialist economy remains a genuine anxiety, shared by both liberals and socialists.

• If we confine ourselves to the "advanced" countries, one criticism socialists have come increasingly to make of liberalism is that it fails to extend sufficiently its democratic concerns from the political to the economic realm.[6] Early in the century the distinguished British liberal writer L.T. Hobhouse put the matter elegantly: "liberty without equality is a name of noble sound and squalid result." I will not linger on this point except to note:

(a) It suggests that the difference between social liberalism and democratic socialism keeps growing smaller, so that at some point it may become no more than incremental. Both traditional liberal thinkers and Marxist theoreticians would deny this; a good many social democrats, in effect, believe it.

(b) It leaves aside what in a fuller consideration could not be left aside: that there remain serious liberal criticisms of socialist proposals, e.g., that efforts to legislate greater equality of wealth, income, and power in economic life will seriously impair political liberty, and that the statist version of socialism (the only realistic one, say some liberal critics) would bring about a fearful concentration of power.

(c) We may be ready to subscribe to the socialist criticism that modern liberalism fails sufficiently to extend its democratic concerns to economic life—e.g., the governance of corporations; we may also share the socialist desire for greater participation of the masses in political and economic decision-making; but, to turn things around, I would largely accept the liberal dislike for schemes involving "mass" or "direct" democracy. Such schemes, insofar as they would brush aside representative institutions (elections, parliaments, etc.) in favor of some sort (but which sort?) of "direct" or "participatory" rule, are likely to end up as hopelessly vague or as prey to demagogic techniques for manipulating those who "participate" in movements, meetings, plebiscites, etc. If the survival of democracy depends on greater popular participation, greater popular participation by no means insures or necessarily entails the survival of democracy. Under modern conditions representative institutions are indispensable to democratic societies; any proposals for "transcending" them, even if they come through socialist goodwill, should be regarded with suspicion.

• There is, finally, the plenitude of attacks directed against liberalism along a spectrum of positions ranging from the reactionary to the revolutionary, most of them chastising its "deeper" failures as a philosophical outlook. So copious is this literature, there is hardly a need to cite texts or authorities.

Liberalism, we are told, accepts an egalitarianism that a day or two spent with open eyes in our mass society shows to be insupportable—while a sage like Professor Leo Strauss makes clear the traditional warrants and esoteric virtues of hierarchy. Liberalism proposes a belief in rational harmony, the "illusion" (to quote Kenneth Minogue) "of ultimate agreement" among men, "and perhaps most central of all, the idea that will and desire can ultimately be sovereign in human affairs"—while a sage like Professor Michael Oakeshott tells us that life is muddle, efforts at rational structuring of our affairs are likely to lead to still greater muddle, even, perhaps, to tyranny. Liberalism congeals into the simplistic notion, as Lionel Trilling has written, "that the life of man can be nicely settled by correct social organization, or short of that, by the election of high moral attitudes." Liberalism, focusing obsessively upon change, distracts us from the essentials of existence largely beyond the grasp of mere reason or public agency. Liberalism has a false view of the human situation, refusing to take into account the irrationalities and aggressions of our nature. (How can a liberal cope with the realities of the Hobbesian jungle? What can a good-hearted liberal make of the Freudian view of the human heart?) Liberalism ignores or dispatches the tragic sense of life, turning people away from that suffering which is unavoidable (perhaps even good?) in our experience. Liberalism replaces the warming cohesion of traditional communities with a rootless anonymity. Liberalism cannot cope with the mysteries of death, as Christianity does through its myth of resurrection, or existentialism tries, through its unblinking gaze into the void.

What is one to say of these criticisms? That often they confuse the historical genesis of liberalism, accompanied as it was by excessive claims, with later and more realistic versions of liberalism; that the alleged rootlessness of liberal man, though clearly surrounded with difficulties, also has brought unprecedented freedoms and opportunities, indeed, entire new visions of the personal self; that the increasing stress of modern liberal thought upon a pluralist society indicates at least some recognition of clashing interests, irreconcilable needs, confrontations of class; that a recognition of the irrational and aggressive components of human conduct can become an argument in favor of limitations upon power favored by liberalism; that we may recognize weaknesses and limitations in liberalism as a *Weltanschauung*—indeed, refuse to see it as a *Weltanschauung*—while still fervently believing that a liberal polity allows for the best realization of human diversity and freedom; that there is no necessary conflict between "dark" views of the human condition and an acceptance of the liberal style in public life.

Let us grant, then, some of the criticism made of liberal afflatus (usually in the past) and liberal smugness (usually in the present), and admit, as well, the probability that insofar as men need religious myths and rites to get through their time on earth, liberalism is not likely to offer enough satisfaction. What needs to be stressed, all the same, is that a commitment to the liberal style in politics does not necessarily imply a commitment to a total world view claiming to include all experience from private fantasy to public authority. (Perhaps we would all be better off to live, for a time, without total world views.)

Toward these and similar exchanges between liberalism and its critics, socialists have shown a very wide range of responses. The more extreme leftist tendencies, verging on the authoritarian and chiliastic, have been tempted to borrow some of the arguments of the right, especially those releasing contempt for the flaccid moderation of liberalism, its alleged failures to confront painful realities of social life and human nature. But for those socialists who largely accept the premises of a liberal polity, there are other problems, notably the disconcerting fact that the bulk of the philosophical-existential criticism directed against liberalism can be brought to bear with equal cogency against social democracy.

III

Unavoidably, this leads to the question: apart from whatever capacity both liberalism and social democracy show for handling our socioeconomic difficulties, how well can they cope with—I choose deliberately a portentous term—the crisis of civilization that many people feel to be encompassing our lives? The crisis of civilization that besets the 20th century has to do, in part, with a breakdown in the transmission and common acceptance of values—which may also be a way of saying, with residual but powerful yearnings toward transcendence. Insofar as this occurs, there follows a pervasive uncertainty as to the "meanings" and ends of existence. One sign of this crisis is the resurgence in Western society of a strident contempt for the ethic of liberal discourse and the style of rationality. Partly this arises from the mixed failings and successes of the welfare state, but partly from an upswell of ill-understood religious sentiments that, unable to find a proper religious outlet, become twisted into moral-political absolutism, a hunger for total solutions and apocalyptic visions. Impatience with the sluggish masses, burning convictions of righteousness, the suffocations of technological society, the boredom of overcrowded cities, the yearning for transcendent ends beyond the petty limits of group interest, romantic-sinister illusions about the charismatic virtues of dictatorship in underdeveloped countries—all these tempt intellectuals and semi-intellectuals into apolitical politics registering an amorphous revulsion from civilization itself.

The customary rationalism of earlier generations of socialists (and liberals too) could hardly grasp such a development. Yet, no matter how distant we may be from the religious outlook, we must ask ourselves whether the malaise of our time isn't partly a consequence of that despairing emptiness which has followed the breakup of traditional religious systems in the 19th century; whether the nihilism that sensitive people feel to be seeping through their lives may not itself testify to a kind of inverted religious aspiration; whether the sense of moral disorientation that afflicts us isn't due to the difficulties of keeping alive a high civilization without a sustaining structure of belief.

Perhaps, in honesty, there really is no choice but to live with the uncomfortable aftereffects of this disintegration of religious belief, which has brought not only the positive consequences some of us hoped for but also others that leave us discomfited. In any case, nothing seems more dubious than the impulse I detect these days among rightward-moving intellectuals: a willing of faith in behalf of alleged social-moral benefits. Here, finally, liberals and democratic socialists find themselves in the same boat, even if at opposite ends of it. The Fabian course to which some of us are committed seems to me politically good and perhaps even realistic, but we ought to acknowledge that this course fails to stir the passions or speak to the needs of many people. We ought to acknowledge that between the politics we see as necessary and the expressive-emotional needs that break out recurrently in Western society there are likely to be notable gaps. I think, by way of homely instance, of a remark made to me a few years ago by a very decent and intelligent liberal professor: "But the politics of social democracy [he might also have said liberalism] are so boring!" It is a troubling remark, and one that may help explain why cultivated people of liberal training can be drawn to illiberal causes and impulses. We can only worry about this matter, recognizing that it may be one of those instances where virtue entails formidable deficits.

But let me end on a somewhat more hopeful note. Half a century from now, one fact about our time may come to be seen as the most crucial. Whatever the separate or linked failures of liberalism and democratic socialism may be, there have come to us these past 20 or 25 years voices from the East superbly reasserting the values of freedom, tolerance, openness of discourse. These men and women have, thus far, "failed"; they have been destroyed, imprisoned, humiliated, isolated. Yet their very appearance signifies an enormous moral triumph for both liberalism and democratic socialism. Beneath the snow, the seed has lived.

Notes

1. The philosophical underpinning is provided by Kant: "everyone is entitled to seek happiness in whatever manner seems best to him, provided that he does not interfere with the freedom of others to strive toward the same objective, which can coexist with the freedom of everyone else under a conceivable general law."

2. In *Capital*, 1, Marx applies his powers of sarcasm to such assumptions of "classical" liberalism: "The sphere of circulation and exchange of commodities within which labor is bought and sold was in reality a paradise of innate human rights—governed entirely by freedom, equality, property, and Bentham! Freedom! Because the buyers and sellers of a commodity, such as labor-power, are constrained only according to their own free will. They enter into a contract as free and legally equal free agents. The contract is the final result in which their common free will is given common legal expression. Equality! Because their relationships with one another are purely those of the owners of commodities and they exchange like for like. Property! Because each individual makes use only of what belongs to him. Bentham! Because each of the two thinks only of himself. The only power that holds them together and establishes a relationship between them is their egotism, personal advantage, and private interest. And precisely because each individual thinks of himself and never of anyone else, they all work toward their mutual advantage, the general good and common interest, in accordance with a preestablished harmony of things or under the auspices of a cunning knowing providence."

3. Occasionally, there are counterinstances suggesting that "vulgar Marxism" may meet with correction from within traditions it has debased. A leader of the Spanish Comunist party, one Luis, is quoted in the *New York Times* of October 29, 1975. saying: "We do not renounce a single one of the bourgeois liberties. If the bourgeoisie can dominate in freedom we want to provide more profound, more real liberties, not less. Socialism can provide the economic base for more complete liberty, without restricting a single aspect of bourgeois liberty." How much credence, if any, to give to this man's claim to democratic belief I do not know; but the fact that he speaks as he does must be regarded as significant.

4. A word about the role of the working class in socialist thought, as it contrasts with the frequent claims of liberalism to rise "above" mere class interest. Granted the common criticism that Marxism has overestimated the revolutionary potential of the workers; granted that socialist rhetoric has sometimes romanticized the workers. It nevertheless remains that a major historical and moral conquest of the socialist movement, especially in the 19th century, was to enable the same passion—the masses of the lowly to enter the stage of history and acquire a historical consciousness. Few developments in the last two centuries have so decisively helped the consolidation of democratic institutions; few have so painfully been exploited to violate democratic norms. It would be foolish to say that socialism alone should take credit for the entry of "the masses" into political life; but it was the socialists who gave this entry a distinct moral sanction. At its best, socialism enabled the formation of that impressive human type we know as the self-educated worker in the late 19th century. That the rise of the working class to articulation and strength could, nevertheless, be exploited for authoritarian ends is surely a major instance of the tragedy of progress.

5. Harold Laski, in his *Parliamentary Government in England*, questioned whether democracy could survive if a Labor government came to power and legislated a socialist program. In 1945 a Labor government did come to power and legislated, if not a socialist program, then a huge welfare-state program decidedly akin to, or at least pointing the way toward, socialism. And democracy did not collapse. This does not yet "prove" that Laski was wrong; only that it would be unwise to assume that he was right.

6. A criticism anticipated in general terms by the early Marx: "Political emancipation is indeed a great step forward. It is not, to be sure, the final form of universal human emancipation, but it is the final form *within* the prevailing order of things…. Where the political state has achieved its full development, man leads a double life, a heavenly and an earthly life, not only in thought or consciousness but in *actuality*. In the *political community* he regards himself as a *communal being*; but in *civil society* he is active as a *private individual*, treats other men as means, reduces himself to a means, and becomes the plaything of alien powers."

31

Nathan Glazer (1923–)
On Being Deradicalized (1970)

*c+i ··
5+·ynn
c·unp+n (3)*

Editor's Introduction

Neoconservatism began in the late 1960s among some of the New York Intellectuals most associated with *Commentary* and *The Public Interest*. Prompted in part by the unintended consequences of reform measures in the Great Society, neoconservative ideas also grew from a hostility toward the radicalism of the New Left and counterculture. In addition, it was fueled in the 1970s by the liberal abandonment of color-blind and meritocratic approaches to race problems. Affirmative action, part of the groundswell of cultural change produced by the civil rights movement, profoundly reoriented the world the New York Intellectuals inhabited like a change of the compass. Integration and pluralism creaked, wobbled and then gave way to multiculturalism, new gender roles, a shift of authority from the old to the young—in a flood that changed the national values and created the ensuing culture wars. When liberals, attempting to preserve many of their midcentury liberal values intact, opposed some of these changes in support of the longstanding liberal commitments of old they became neoconservatives. At the border between liberalism and neoconservatism the two shade into each other, of course. In the 1970s when neoconservatism first appeared, many neocons continued to support liberal values, endorsed many liberal reforms, stood with liberals on civil rights and civil liberties issues and backed liberal politicians such as Henry "Scoop" Jackson.

In the essay below, Nathan Glazer swiped at what he considered the utopianism of the young, and his distaste for the illiberal character of New Left thinking is obvious. He accused the young of using "absolute thinking," of employing "the kind of undifferentiated blanket issue that radicals of the Left and Right have always favored," of adopting rigid and apocalyptic positions where "there could be no neutrality, no objectivity." The battle against absolutist thinking in the name of liberal possibility and variability remained a central element of the New York Intellectuals' world view throughout their lives. Glazer also hoped for a more pragmatic liberal reform in the wake of Lyndon Johnson's presidency. Social improvements should be viewed through the lens of social science and should be tempered by experience, what has worked in the past. He recounts how in his time in Washington, DC he learned that government policies were crafted for multiple constituencies on the basis of what had worked in the past "in a world of infinite complexity," a world where radical changes were difficult to introduce but pragmatic changes based on tests and empirical evidence were welcome and useful.

Source

Nathan Glazer, "On Being Deradicalized," *Commentary* vol. 50, no. 4, October 1970.

Selected Readings

Richard M. Scammon and Ben J. Wattenberg, *The Real Majority* (New York: Coward-McCann, 1970).
Samuel G. Freedman, *The Inheritance* (New York: Simon and Schuster, 1996).
Nicholas Lemann, *The Promised Land* (New York: Knopf, 1991).

* * * * *

I

How does a radical—a mild radical, it is true, but still someone who felt closer to radical than to liberal writers and politicians in the late 1950's—end up by early 1970 a conservative, a mild conservative, but still closer to those who now call themselves conservative than to those who call themselves liberal? I seem to have moved from a position in which I was a bit embarrassed to be considered liberal (surely I was a degree further to the Left than that!) to a position where I am again embarrassed, but from the other side: surely I am not so "Establishmentarian" as that!

One way of explaining this change is to describe what it was to be a mild radical in the late 1950's. Consider the writers who, in those days before and just after the Cuban revolution, were thought of as radical: Paul Goodman, Dwight Macdonald, Irving Howe, Michael Harrington, C. Wright Mills. Consider the kinds of actions that radicals engaged in then. One demonstrated—if one lived in New York—against civil defense in City Hall park, applauded Castro's speech in Central Park (applauding Castro more than his speech: who knew what he was saying?), joined with Jane Jacobs in her attacks on urban renewal, supported the organization of public-housing tenants and other groups of the poor and dismissed New Deal political orientations in their current liberal Democratic phase as outdated and insufficiently farreaching.

All of us who stood in these ways to the Left of the liberals shared, of course, in a complete disdain of apologists for Russian and Chinese oppression: the least we could agree on was free speech, civil liberties, and democratic procedures. The division between "liberal" and "radical" in those days did not run along the line of more or less sympathy with Communist states, as it so often seems to do today. After the exposure of Stalin's ferocity, Russian anti-Semitism, Communist suppression of all originality in the arts, those who still saw some virtues in the Communist version of socialism had simply grown silent. In the area of international affairs, the division was between the "mainstream" liberals who tended to find America's foreign policy—NATO, nuclear deterrence, the maintenance of Berlin's special status—basically sound and those of us, standing further to the Left, who were convinced that the nuclear arms race would lead inexorably to a final disaster. We were unimpressed or horrified by the new strategic thinking involving game theory and nuclear deterrence, not that we were very clear about what we would put in its place. We believed that there were more opportunities for negotiation with Russia and for détente with the Communist world than American foreign policy supposed. We did not like the frozen stance of the United States on Berlin: were there not more imaginative solutions? The *Correspondent*, a newsletter created by David Riesman and Erich Fromm, and which I edited for a short time, reflected some of these views.

In domestic affairs the radical position was skeptical of the intelligence and capacities of large bureaucracies, whether in education, welfare, urban renewal, housing, or government in general. Having found nothing in particular in Marx to explain either what was wrong with modern society or what might help (certainly not the monstrous state bureaucracies of Russia and its imitators), radicals in those days were in a condition of peculiar openness. When Norman Podhoretz became editor of *Commentary* in 1960, his quest for something which would mark a departure from old and rigid positions and would suggest the direction in which we might now move led him to seize on Paul Goodman's manuscript, *Growing Up Absurd*, most of which he published in the first few issues of *Commentary* he turned out. Jason Epstein, at Random House, trying to find something that expressed his own blocked radical instincts, also seized upon the same talisman: this was fresh, new, radical. Goodman, thus restored to prominence, began to publish like a flowing stream. All his books emphasized the anti-bureaucratic, the small and immediate, the human-scale as the salvation of a society grown too large, too highly organized and articulated, too suppressive of instinct and feeling.

Many rivulets of the late 1950's fed the radicalism of the early 1960's. There was the fight against urban renewal and other overblown programs such as Mobilization for Youth on the Lower East Side of New York. There was the beginning of campus political activity—in Berkeley in 1957–58, where students organized the first campus party, Slate, a distant premonition of what was to come; and on a number of other campuses where chapters of the Student Peace Union came into being and where publications like *New University Thought* and *Studies on the Left* (taking their inspiration from the English *New Left Review*, which gave the name "New Left" to the New Left) began to appear. The organizing impulse was taken over by SDS. Its Port Huron statement of 1962, a model of humanist radicalism, even stopped short of socialism in its refusal of any commitment to a developed Marxist political position or analysis. SDS would go to the people and learn from them, and so it did in the early organizing projects in the Newark slums, in the poor white areas of Chicago, and elsewhere.

All these various developments then seemed of a piece—criticism of American foreign policy, of the strategy of nuclear deterrence, of homegrown bureaucracies; the emphasis on humanism, on going to the roots, on the small-scale and the immediate. This was the radicalism of the late 1950's, and holding to it was sufficient to distinguish one from liberalism. John F. Kennedy meant little to us: he was just another liberal politician, though the fact that some of our friends worked for him did make a difference.

This was a radicalism that had a good deal in common with conservatism—the bias against government intervention in various areas, the willingness to let people decide for themselves how to spend their money, the belief that the theoretical and political structures reared by liberals to control policy in the foreign and domestic realms would no longer work, the allergy to Communist repression, the attraction toward the small. Paul Goodman and Norman Mailer express this affinity when, on various occasions, they call themselves "conservative"—indeed, in some respects they are, and for this among other reasons they do not go along with those developments that place so much of the radicalism of the late 1960's squarely in the succession to the simple-minded, grotesque, freedom-denying radicalism of the Leninists and Stalinists of the 1930's.

Thus, one explanation of my own move from a mild radicalism to a mild conservatism is that the character of radicalism changed over the course of the decade. But it would be incomplete to leave it at that. I changed too, and perhaps the largest influence in that change was a year spent in Washington, in the Housing and Home Finance Administration. I learned, to my surprise, that most of the radical ideas my friends and I were suggesting had already been thought of, considered, analyzed, and had problems in their implementation that we had never dreamed of. I learned to respect many of the men who worked in the huge bureaucracies, who limited their own freedom, and who made it possible occasionally for the radical ideas of others to be implemented. I learned that the difficulty with many radical ideas lay in the fact that so many varied interests played a role in government, and that most of them were legitimate interests. It was a big country, and it contained more kinds of people than were dreamed of on the shores of the Hudson. I learned, in quite strictly conservative fashion, to develop a certain respect for what was; in a world of infinite complexity some things had emerged and survived, and if the country was in many ways better than it might be or had been (just as in many ways it was much worse than it might be or would be), then something was owed to its political institutions and organizational structures.

My experience at the University of California in Berkeley, where I went to teach in 1963, carried a similar lesson. Many interests were represented in that strange and inefficient amalgam—students, their parents, professors, taxpayers, business, and even unions—and yet each of these interests, in its narrow-mindedness, saw the institution as properly expressing only its own desires. I did not share some of my colleagues' views of administrators; I believed they were doing necessary and difficult things in reconciling these complex interests, and I appreciated the additional freedom I possessed by virtue of their work. I did not believe universities should be run for the pleasure and convenience of the faculty alone, as—with faculty bargaining power so great by 1964—in large measure they were. Neither, however, did I believe that it was good or wise or possible for them to be run for the pleasure and convenience of the students—let alone a particular element of the student body. So I changed, finding it harder to participate in a casual attack on existing institutions without considering what would replace them and whether it would mark any improvement.

Radicalism certainly spread as the 1960's moved on, but many radicals also fell away. One must consider to what extent it was they who changed, to what extent it was they who gave up on positions they had once considered humane and rational, and even more seriously to what extent they gave up on these positions simply because the fight for them turned out to demand a far more intense and fierce and violent opposition to the conservative institutions of society than they had originally expected. One asks oneself, having agreed in some measure with Mario Savio about the nature of the "machine" upon whose gears he asked the students of Berkeley to throw themselves, why one withdrew when the opposition to bureaucracy escalated from discourse, petitions, and debates to the whole sequence of actions, including violent actions, with which we are by now all too familiar.

One is reminded of the paths away from Communism. When did the break come and why? What action finally seemed insupportable? There is no point in pushing the parallel too far. One thing that was the same was the bitter division that developed among intellectuals. It was impossible for those of us who were alive and conscious during World War II and Korea to take the same easy path as the radical youth. We had known the country and its army in different times and in different wars. The United States had defeated Hitler and had turned back the brutal invasion of a small country by its better organized, better armed, and infinitely more repressive neighbor. Even as the cloud over Vietnam grew, even as the reports of the horrors came through (and no one can say the reporting was not full or adequate or immediate), we were torn between the old style of political action and the new. We valued the country, the role it had played in international affairs, its ability to handle complex domestic problems, its stability in the maintenance of democratic procedures, its capacity for change and correction.

And some of us were affected similarly by developments on the racial scene. Having lived before the Supreme Court decision of 1954, the Montgomery bus strike, the Birmingham movement of 1963, we had seen significant change— the registration of Negroes in the South; the election of hundreds of Negro officials; the growing role of Negroes in the mass media, the universities, government; the solid hope for a greater role in business and the unions. Yet along with these changes—some, of course, in response to pressure and even violence, but many, too, that represented the inexorable movement toward equality that was proceeding on many fronts and for many reasons—came increasing radicalization, increasing vituperation, increasing disaffection with the country and its institutions.

It was impossible for many of us to accept the easy and frequent equations of the United States with Nazi Germany, of Johnson with Hitler. At first one signed ads against the Vietnam war. Later the ads became fiercer: they not only called for ending the war and getting out, they accused the country's leaders of the same crimes for which Germany had been condemned at Nuremberg. Then people took their stand and divided, and it sometimes seemed that one of the key factors determining the division was a capacity for hatred. Did you hate Johnson enough—or Rusk, or Rostow, or the police, or the leaders of South Vietnam? Did you hate the Southerners enough, or the Northern white middle classes, or the Northern white workers, or the Jewish school-teachers of New York? It was not pleasant then, and it is not pleasant now.

Thus, more and more people who had been radicals at the start of the decade fell away, and new radicals were made to replace them, the replacements eventually far outnumbering the fallen away, as the student revolt which began at Berkeley in 1964 spread to encompass universities and colleges of every kind and in every part of the country. But if this revolt made radicals of many who had previously considered themselves liberals, the course it took also served to deepen the estrangement from radicalism of others like myself who saw it as a threat to the very existence of the university and to the values of which the university, with all its faults, was a unique and precious embodiment.

II

I was from the beginning convinced of the importance of the student revolt. I did not see it as an expression of youthful high spirits, or of earnest youth insisting on a better education, or of committed youth demanding the right of political activity and participation on the campus, or of passionate youth insisting that the institutions of higher education abandon hypocrisy and the support of evil public policies. It was all these things of course, in some measure. But if I had felt that they were the dominant factors, I would have joined all those faculty members, intellectuals, and political leaders—there were so many of them all during this period, and there are so many of them now, in the year 1970, as the fires and dynamite charges are set—who welcomed the student revolt because, they said, it brought a breath of fresh air to the stale universities, because it forced them to become responsive to the needs of their students and the society, because it insisted that the universities take the lead in solving society's critical problems, because these were the best-educated youth in American society, the most morally committed, the most concerned with injustice. I could see some evidence for all this, but from the beginning I saw something else, too, and that was a passion for immediate action, for confrontation, for the humiliation of others, for the destruction of author-ity—any authority, whether necessary and worthwhile or not—and finally, for the destruction of what was most distinctive and most valuable about the universities—their ability to distance themselves from immediate crises, their concern with the heritage of culture and science, their encouragement of indi-viduality and even eccentricity.

From the beginning I believed that it did not get us to the heart of the mat-ter to analyze the revolt primarily in terms of such issues as faculty-student relations, the nature of administration, the growth and subsequent bureau-cratization of the university, the impact of research and government grants on teaching, the relevance of curriculum. All these things were important. All concerned me. But when student discontent broke into forceful action at Berkeley, it bore very little relation to these grave developments in higher education. And in time, as the revolt spread to such very different colleges and universities as Chicago, Columbia, Wisconsin, San Francisco State, Har-vard, the City College of New York, it became clearer that the causes did not lie in the special character of a given college or university. Berkeley had an enormous undergraduate college that received little attention from the senior faculty; Chicago and Columbia had the smallest undergraduate colleges, with perhaps the greatest commitment to undergraduate teaching, of any major university; Harvard did not have classified research; some places did not have much research of any kind; some had favorable faculty-student ratios, and some unfavorable. None of these differences mattered.

In particular, to see the student revolt as directed at educational inade-quacy, or as a movement that could be satisfied by educational change, was sentimental. Educational reform was a rather low priority of the Berkeley Free Speech Movement and its heirs, important as it may have been to individual leaders, and to a good number of followers. The objective of the student revolt quite clearly became not that of transforming the universities and colleges from the point of view of their proper ends—that is, as institutions devoted to teaching and research—but rather of transforming them so that they could realize quite other, and directly political, ends. The thrust of the student revolt in situation after situation was to bend the universities and colleges to the political orientation and outlook of the radical students, who saw the univer-sity as a potential recruiting ground, and then as an active participant in the political struggles of society.

The position of the critics of the student movement—certainly of this critic—became a peculiar and difficult one. I shared the ostensible concern with university and college reform. All the issues raised were in one way or another real, and in one way or another important—free political activity on the campus, the parental role of the college or university, its involvement with the state, its inability to order its various functions properly. I also shared the growing horror at the consequences of public policy, principally in Vietnam but also in other areas—nuclear and biological warfare, the bloated military expenditures starving other needs, the mechanical resort to technology to solve problems regardless of their human complexity. And yet, with all these elements of agreement, on one point I stuck, and that point made me an enemy: yes, let us reform the university, and let us, if we can, save the world, but let us not sacrifice the university on either altar, because there is no need that we should.

I was willing to concede that academic freedom often looked like—and often was—academic irrelevance, academic exoticism, academic self-seeking, academic status-striving, academic arrogance, and for that matter a cover for political action, too. On the whole, the share that all these played in the academic enterprise had not, I thought, increased in recent times, even as the academic enterprise itself had undergone such enormous expansion (here I accepted the judgment of analysts of the academic scene like Christopher Jencks and David Riesman). All these excrescences on the academic enterprise could be reduced without endangering what was after all one of the most remarkable products of civilization. The willingness of government (and in this country, private interests) to support scholars in freedom to pursue research and teaching with very minor interference and constraint should not, I thought, be taken for granted: it would be all too easy to arrange matters so that this rare development should come to an end, as it did for a time in Nazi Germany, Soviet Russia, and elsewhere.

The student radicals and their allies, both inside and outside the universities, argued that it was hypocritical to speak of defending academic freedom. Were the universities not already directly involved in political activities? Were they not engaged in defense research, research in support of American foreign policy, research in support of private economic interests? Did their teaching not reflect their interests, did they not train the ROTC, not to mention employees of government and private business? Parts of this critique had force. As it was extended, however, all critical distinctions were lost, and uncompromising styles of thinking and analysis emerged. When this happened—and it happened regularly as we can see by comparing the rhetoric of the beginning of each phase of the movement with that of its later phases—the issue shifted from the question of whether this movement would reform the university or turn public policy around to whether it would destroy the university. I argued from the start that the new tactics, the new violence of language, and the new joy in confrontation and political combat contained more of a threat to what remained valuable within the universities than a hope either of changing them or of changing public policy.

As the criticism of the universities came to be cast in the current radical rhetoric, one saw again the rise of the doctrine that there could be no neutrality, no objectivity, not even partial neutrality or objectivity: in the famous words of Eldridge Cleaver, "If you are not part of the solution [that is, if you are not actively with us], you are part of the problem [that is, you are against us]." If this doctrine were to become widely accepted, or acted upon, there would be no function for the universities and they would be as good as dead.

A real issue—the degree to which the universities had become embroiled in the disastrous foreign policies of the United States government—was translated into the kind of undifferentiated blanket issue that radicals of the Left and Right have always favored. The Peace Corps became as bad as the CIA (I leave aside the question of how bad *that* was—the CIA became an issue which could barely be raised with physical safety in the universities), innocuous research on government contracts as bad as direct research in support of military tactics, studying the characteristics of developing countries morally equivalent to plotting to overthrow them. These are not extravagant statements: they will only sound extravagant to those who have not had direct experience with university campuses. To radicals, those of us who believed that these differences were still important became "part of the problem."

This style of absolute thinking, which characterized so many different things as all being in the service of "imperialism," "racism," and "capitalism," also served to obscure the distinctive characteristics of the colleges and universities: their commitment to free inquiry, free discussion, free teaching—characteristics that were valuable whatever the disasters of American policy, foreign, military, or domestic, might be. But these virtues were not obscured only by the idea which insisted that the colleges and universities must be enlisted in radical social change (a belief which became surprisingly influential among many who were not themselves radical); they had already been considerably obscured by developments within the universities and in the relationships among universities and government and other outside authorities. Thus, a good part of the support that was needed for the enormous expansion of the universities and colleges was granted on the basis of the argument that these institutions provided trained employees for business and government, did valued research for them, and added to the gross national product. I have always doubted that this argument can really be substantiated. When economists assert that a certain investment in higher education will do more for the economic development of a poor country than a steel mill or a dam, they may have a point, but a point that is commonly exaggerated to a grotesque degree. As David Riesman has often said, we veil our idealistic and altruistic and playful impulses in pragmatic and self-interested guise, and by "we," I mean all kinds of people in all countries. Higher education has always had a role as simply a consumption good; this must have been more obvious when it was reserved for the upper and upper-middle classes, and there were clear distinctions between those who were trained to practice some useful profession (doctors, engineers, lawyers), and those who were being "finished" to take up a life in a particular social milieu. Colleges and universities also have a role in providing a "liberal" education, whose economic or practical value is undeterminable. And they have a role, of equally uncertain value economically, in maintaining and extending knowledge of the arts and sciences: it was in this connection that the idea of academic freedom developed, and that universities became to some extent centers of social criticism.

As the growth of universities was increasingly justified in terms of service and contribution to economic growth, the simple fact that they exist also to provide liberal education and to protect knowledge, speculation, and criticism, tended to get overlooked. Argument rarely took account of these functions of the university, even though in reality they grew along with the professional schools and the more practical parts of the physical and social sciences. When the situation called for radical social criticism, the universities and colleges, despite their development in the direction of service, direct professional qualification, and research for clients, had great reserves of it in store—more than any other part of society could provide.

For this and other reasons, then, many of us continued to regard the university as precious. To the degree that radicalism in the latter part of the 60's wished to destroy the university or even refused to acknowledge its right to distance itself from the world, to remain free to be foolish or irrelevant or outrageous no matter how great the horrors of the world outside, to that degree were we further estranged from the radicalism with which we had begun.

III

There was, finally, one other large consideration which entered into my transformation from mild radical to mild conservative, and this was the conviction which grew upon me as the decade progressed that we are entering a world in which various forms of new social control will become necessary. They will become necessary not because some men want to control others, or because organizations want to shape men to their will, or because social institutions inevitably turn men into their servants (though all these things are true), but because human demands, demands that most of us consider good and proper, and that the radicals among us support most enthusiastically, cannot be satisfied without highly developed organizations and some limits on human freedom.

This is a position that is easy to misunderstand, and radicals—and not they alone—regularly misunderstand it. The democratic and egalitarian revolution means that people do not accept tradional limits on their standards of living, on their desire for material goods, on their demand for political participation and for control of their own lives. Most of us generally see all this as leading ultimately to a better society, a society in which every person receives varied and nutritious food, good housing, adequate clothing, proper medical care, access to higher education, opportunities for travel and for wider experience and for playing more active political and social roles. If we are to be truly equal, such goods and services cannot be denied to anyone; if we are democratic, people will insist on a higher and higher level of governmental responsibility to provide these goods and services; if our systems of communication are such that everyone is aware of the level of goods and services that prevail in some places, and the deficiencies that still obtain in others, then a democratic people, in an egalitarian society, will know what to demand.

To meet such demands inevitably means greater social control. It means heavy taxation, to pay the cost; it means setting limits on the building of houses and on the growth of towns to maintain some measure of amenity as population and production expand; it means stricter regulation not only of industry in its disposal of waste but of ordinary people who may wish to burn refuse or discard litter ("Alice's Restaurant" deals with larger issues than Arlo Guthrie perhaps knows, and the heroes may well turn out to be the officer and the judge). In the end it may mean the control of such intimate human functions as the right to bring children into the world. The expansion of human freedom in some directions, one can demonstrate, must ultimately mean the limitation of human freedom in others. Young people, wishing to divest themselves of a corrupt civilization, take to what they conceive to be the wilderness, to live with freedom and without restraint. But if they litter the wilderness, pollute the streams, and abandon cars in the forest, their freedom to seek what they consider the good life will have to be restrained so that some aspect of the good life can be retained for others. Some day we may get tickets to visit Yosemite—one visit to a lifetime, and perhaps they will be sold and bought on the stock market—just as licenses to bear and raise one's quota of children may be bought and sold on the stock market. How else can one reconcile the expansion of human desires and the insistence on equality with the growth of population?

This incapacity of the earth, as nature and God left it to us, to support the rising human demands that are now encouraged by every social force, justified by every major philosophy and ideology, accepted as legitimate by every major government, will inevitably mean that a society of freedom, plenty, equality, and loose or no organization cannot come into being, whatever the passionate convictions of young radicals.

Obviously, within the large general perspective I have presented, there are many alternatives, from Sweden on down. But neither to our young radicals nor to theirs does Sweden seem to be the way of the future. Yet even Sweden is better off today than it will be, as immigration brings more people into the country, and as it seeks to share its wealth with poorer countries like North

Vietnam. And even Sweden today demands, and must demand, stronger controls than the United States does, in order to maintain its advanced social and physical environment. It takes more in taxes, limits the freedom of its citizens to build houses, more systematically regulates their educational and occupational choices, records all the facts about them in a national computerized system.

Some of us have called the student rebels "Luddites"—machine smashers—and have been answered: the Luddites of the early Industrial Revolution smashed machines that were good for life; the students smash the machines that bring death. This simple retort will not carry us very far. Even in the United States, engaged in an awful war, less than 10 per cent of the gross national product goes to the military, and a good part of that provides education, medical care, housing, food, and clothing for some millions of people.

The radicals answer that much of the remaining 90 per cent is also life-denying, going to such unnecessary or harmful products as cars, roads, and television sets. But the vast majority of the population sees in these things the essence of the good life. Human wants can be met in many ways, but they cannot be met by dismantling the machinery, physical and institutional, of modern society. Only a drastic reduction in standards of living—and radicals are the first to insist that standards are already too low for large numbers of our people—or a drastic reduction in the total number of people is compatible with the degree of freedom from organization, control, discipline, and responsibility for the support of others that seems to be the special demand of contemporary radicals.

The young radical guerrillas now engaged in the sabotage of social organization take it for granted that they will be provided with complex means of transportation and communication, and with food, clothing, shelter, and medical care. The easy availability of these things is based on a system they deride and which in their confusion they want to bring down, not realizing that they themselves and all those they wish to help would thereby be reduced to misery. The arduous and necessary discipline of Cuba and China does not deter them from taking those countries as models, or perhaps really only as symbols, since they know almost nothing about them. The mild discipline of free countries, which makes it possible for large numbers to withdraw into nonproductive styles of life, they experience as more chafing.

This argument is often mistaken as simply a moral argument: "Since the radical youth benefit from modern capitalist society, they have no right to attack it, just as Marx and Engels, since they benefited from capitalism and led a life based (in their theory) on the exploitation of others, placed themselves in an insupportable moral position."

Perhaps there is some justice in the moral argument; I am not sure. But in any case I am not making a moral argument, I am making a logical one, based on empirical reality. What I am asserting is that to dismantle the structures of modern society will mean a radical reduction in the general standard of living. Rather than weakening these structures, we must alas strengthen them. In other words, we cannot insist on giving more people the opportunity to maintain a high standard of living and simultaneously demand that they be given a greater freedom from control, from work, from family discipline. More and better food will mean more people working on food production and distribution. Better housing will mean more people working on the production and maintenance of housing. Better medical care will mean more people working in health services. Access to better communication and transportation will mean more people working on these systems. The belief that the introduction of new machinery and technology makes possible the release from labor was an illusion in Marx's day, and is an illusion in ours. The rising level of human demand and human expectations steadily outstrips the productivity of machines, and by now the ecological damage caused by many kinds of machines means that we must find ways of containing the rise of these demands and expectations. Rich countries have severer shortages of labor than poor countries, and countries like Sweden, West Germany, and Japan which spend little on arms or on other life-denying products have the worst shortages.

It is only in literary utopias that there is less work to do. In real societies which attempt to improve themselves, whether by reform or revolution, whether it be England or Sweden or Yugoslavia or Cuba or China, there is a continual demand for more work, and more and more people are drawn into the work force. First the rural population is driven from its life of following the seasons, with its periods of leisure; then the women are recruited into the work force; finally foreign labor is imported from those countries in which progress is not yet so far advanced. Nor can we simply place quotation marks around the word "progress": what we are talking about is the kind of change, after all, that revolutionaries, as well as reformers and conservatives, encourage and promise to the people of the world.

It was considerations such as these which led me to believe that the radical thinking of the late 1960's was almost completely misguided, based on an amazing ignorance of the lineaments of modern society and an almost equally amazing arrogance. One saw formulations by Marxist activists and scholars of the 1890's or 1930's served up again as an adequate explanation of contemporary America or the capitalist world in general, and one could only sputter in response. The second time around, the views of Rosa Luxemburg or of Lenin not only seemed irrelevant, but had been cheapened and vulgarized. Nevertheless, the passions which leaned upon their theories for support were as fierce as ever. Capitalism, imperialism, and colonialism had all undergone immense changes, but hatred of the free world (and I insist on using that designation without quotation marks as well, for despite the combination of ignorance and intimidation which has forced its abandonment in recent years, it still points to the largest *single* distinction between the Communist and the non-Communist countries) was as fierce in 1970 as hatred of the unreformed capitalism of forty or eighty years ago.

I will not pretend to possess any full understanding of why this hatred should be so fierce or why those who feel it most keenly should now come predominantly from the upper-middle class. But whatever its sources, it served as an additional factor in the estrangement of people like myself from the radicalism of the late 60's. I for one, a indeed, have by now come to feel that this radicalism is so beset with error and confusion that our main task, if we are ever to mount a successful assault on our problems, must be to argue with it and to strip it ultimately of the pretension that it understands the causes of our ills and how to set them right.

32

Norman Podhoretz (1930–)

Between Nixon and the New Politics (1972)

Editor's Introduction

American politics were changing noticeably in the late 1960s. History is complex, and the transformation had its roots in many different soils: the civil
rights movement and the resentment it prompted in lower-class whites, the
baby boom and post World War II affluence that created a youth culture and
its rejection of the bourgeoisie, the invention of television that quickened and
magnified cultural trends, the rise of the sunbelt and the conservative Republican strategy of Kevin Phillips that Richard Nixon employed enthusiastically,
and the war in Vietnam that had been brewing since the early 1960s. In 1962,
Democrats drove pickup trucks and worked in manufacturing jobs. They
drank beer at the bar down the street. They liked cowboys and cops and family. It was the Republicans who knew fine wine, drove nice cars, subscribed to
good magazines and vacationed in Europe. Between 1968 and 1980, the parties
traded constituencies, and in the aftermath the Democrats drove Volvos, knew
the wines and ran the culture. Republicans either owned businesses large or
small, or they worked for those businesses. Now they drove the pickup trucks.

In June 1970, Norman Podhoretz began a monthly column in *Commentary*, and in this series of essays Podhoretz worked out the beginning of his
own neoconservatism. He began to vent his dissatisfaction with the change
he saw in liberalism, a change beginning with youthful radicals who then
infected susceptible adults who should have known better. In a column written a few months before the Nixon–McGovern contest in 1972, he showed
that he understood some of the political forces changing the country. When
Podhoretz typed this essay, the two parties were in the beginning stages of
altering their traditional constituencies, a pattern that had been in place for
forty years.

Although the process had not advanced enough for him to articulate it
precisely, Podhoretz did a good job of describing the frustrations of neoconservatives and identifying a resentment in the middle- to lower-middle-class
Democrats that would lead them to leave the party and become Republicans.
As he pointed out, Jews and others were leaving the Democrats because of
more than McGovern. They left because a new kind of liberalism was suf-

fusing the former party of the middle class. The New Politics was the name of the outlook peopled by younger activists inspired by the sixties' student movement, who (or so it seemed to the middle class) championed the poor but not the working class; who admired African Americans but not the white lower-middle class; who believed in education and equality but not the trials of home ownership and playing by the rules; who believed in a new cultural agenda but not the family; who believed in an upper-middle-class bohemianism but none of the values of the simple bourgeoisie. In the 1950s and 1960s Americans had happily voted for liberals. Now, in the early 1970s, normal Democratic voters no longer recognized the party's liberalism as standing for values they could endorse.

Near the end of his essay, Podhoretz warned that if the McGovern-New Politics constituency happened to beat Nixon "*despite* the defection of traditionally Democratic groups like the Jews," then a major political realignment might occur. While McGovern didn't win, his New Politics forces and their attitudes saturated the party and, as Podhoretz predicted, a realignment occurred. Since that time, the Democrats, divided over the meaning of liberalism, have lost their power both at the national and state levels. Some members of the New York Intellectuals, critical of the New Politics and the cultural change in the sixties, by the mid to late seventies were happy to call themselves neoconservatives, and were quick in the 1980s to endorse Reagan's policies.

Source

Norman Podhoretz, "Between Nixon and the New Politics," *Commentary* vol. 54, no. 3, September 1972.

Selected Readings

Norman Podhoretz, *Breaking Ranks* (New York: Harper and Row, 1979.)

* * * * *

Although Nathan Glazer is for McGovern and Milton Himmelfarb is against him, they both expect that Jews will give a smaller majority of their vote to the Democratic candidate this year than they have ever given to a Democratic candidate in any recent Presidential election. The normal pattern has been for Jews to give between 80 and 90 per cent of their vote to the Democratic Presidential candidate; this year the figure is widely expected to go below 70 per cent and could even, some say, go below 60. One also hears that a certain number of wealthy Jews who have contributed heavily to Democratic Presidential candidates in the past are either planning to sit this election out or to throw their financial support to Nixon.

Does all this mean that the Jews are beginning to move into the Republican party? I think not—or at least not necessarily. In my opinion, the turn away from McGovern has been caused not by a sudden access of Jewish enthusiasm for Nixon or his party, but by a steadily mounting Jewish uneasiness over McGovern. I think, moreover, that to understand this uneasiness fully, one has to look not only at the two issues of Israel and quotas which Mr. Glazer and Mr. Himmelfarb between them so exhaustively discuss, but also at the character of the "McGovern phenomenon" as a whole. For everything in this discussion depends on whether the forces led by McGovern will retain control of the Democratic party or whether they will indeed prove to be, as many people have predicted, the Gold-waterites of the Left.

That Richard Nixon inspires dislike among liberals and even hatred is hardly news, and it is hardly necessary to show in detail that in the course of his pre-Presidential career he generally spoke and acted in such a way as to deserve this response. Even as President he has done many things calculated to infuriate liberals. He has unleashed Agnew, he has taken a tough line on civil disobedience and direct-action protest, he has invaded Cambodia, he has intensified the air war in North Vietnam, he has appointed conservatives to the Supreme Court, he has come out against busing.

Yet it is also true that in the course of his career as President he has done more and more to deserve, if not the affection of liberals, then at least a diminution of their dislike. He has proposed a guaranteed annual income, he has instituted wage-and-price controls, he has withdrawn half-a-million men from Vietnam, he has enunciated a foreign-policy doctrine involving a lesser degree of American intervention in international disputes, he has visited Communist China, he has negotiated an arms limitation treaty with the Soviet Union and possibly also (if such surprising developments as the move toward unification of the two Koreas and the departure of Soviet troops from Egypt are anything more than coincidence) the beginnings of a long-range political settlement. On balance, surely, it makes more sense for Nixon's old supporters in the conservative camp like William F. Buckley, Jr. and Richard J. Whalen to feel betrayed (which indeed they seem to do) than it does for liberals to go on hating him as much as *they* seem to do. Nevertheless liberals do go on hating him, less perhaps than they used to but still much more than, on the record, they rationally should.

And if this is the case with liberals in general, it is also the case with Jews, who are still one of the most liberal groups in the country (for even if the most wildly pessimistic forecasts from the Democratic point of view were to prove accurate, it would mean that "only" 60 per cent of Jewish voters were going for McGovern—a higher percentage than he is likely to get from any other group except perhaps the blacks). Jews as liberals share in the general liberal dislike of Nixon, and Jews as Jews, often with an even lesser degree of rationality, dislike him on their own. The Israelis say that Nixon has done more for them than any American President before him, and yet in speaking before Jewish audiences I have repeatedly been asked what I think makes the Nixon administration "anti-Israel." More Jews have been appointed to powerful positions within the Nixon administration—one has only to mention the names of Henry Kissinger, Arthur Burns, and Herbert Stein—than has probably ever happened before, and yet I have repeatedly been asked by these same Jewish audiences whether the "fact" that there are no Jews in the Nixon administration means that the President is anti-Semitic. For just as blacks seem not to realize that it is under the Nixon administration that the dual school systems of the South have finally been abolished, and that the concept of "affirmative action" has been turned into a means of instituting a quota system mainly in the black behalf, so Jews seem not to realize that the Nixon administration has been friendly in a variety of important ways to them.

To complicate matters even further, those Jews who worry about quotas and who oppose McGovern because he appears to favor them, seem not to realize that it is under the *Nixon* administration that quotas have become a threat. But this is only one of many indications that the Jewish uneasiness over McGovern is not to be fully explained with reference to specific issues, any more than the probable loss he will suffer of normally Democratic Jewish votes is to be explained by a newfound Jewish fondness for Nixon. The specific issues are certainly real and the concern over them is certainly genuine, but there is, I believe, something larger and more difficult to define for which they serve as a manageably concrete, though not altogether satisfactory, stand-in. This something is the New Politics.

By the New Politics I mean the insurgency within the Democratic party which came out of the antiwar movement and which, having lost its chance to capture the party in 1968 either through Eugene McCarthy or through Robert Kennedy, found a second chance in the reforms developed by the McGovern Commission and then seized it through the candidacy of McGovern himself. The nature of the New-Politics movement is easy enough to describe in sociological terms. The movement is made up largely of educated, prosperous people, members of the professional and technical intelligentsia and their wives and children, academics and their students: the group, in short, as Michael Novak reminds us, that David T. Bazelon presciently identified as a New Class long before it came to consciousness of itself as a class and as a potential political force. Thus for all the self-gratulatory speeches about the unprecedented "representativeness" of the 1972 Democratic convention, a survey by Haynes Johnson of the Washington *Post* showed that fully 39 per cent of the delegates—as compared with 4 per cent of the population as a whole—held postgraduate degrees, and that 31 per cent had incomes of more than $25,000 a year, whereas only 5 per cent of the population as a whole is in so high an economic bracket.

But if the sociological character of the New-Politics movement is clear, its political or ideological character has been obscured somewhat in the process of its transformation into the McGovern "populist" movement. Lately the talk has all been of tax reform and the redistribution of wealth, but this was not an issue indigenous to the New Politics or to the "McGovern phenomenon"; it was taken over from George Wallace, and the carelessness with which the McGovern proposals have been thought out is perhaps a sign of the fundamental indifference to such matters which the New-Politics movement until so recently felt. For what this movement really cares about is not the distribution of economic power but the distribution of political power. It wishes to "participate in the decisions that affect our lives" and it wishes to govern, but it has no clear idea of what, in addition to participating and governing, it wishes to do. Consequently it has *itself* become the issue. Why has the AFL-CIO, which until the nomination of McGovern obsessively kept declaring that its main political priority was the defeat of Nixon, refused to endorse McGovern? Asked this question, George Meany and I. W. Abel and the other anti-McGovern labor leaders fish for unconvincing explanations in McGovern's voting record, when what is actually bothering them is the hostility of the New Politics toward organized labor ("It isn't worth the powder it would take to blow it up," I once heard a leading McGovern strategist say of the labor movement) and the contempt of the New-Politics people for the ordinary workingman and the "racism" and vulgar materialism which allegedly define his character.

So too with those Jews who are bothered by McGovern. They are bothered in my judgment much more by the general attitudes of the New-Politics movement than by McGovern's stand on Israel—which, after all, as Nathan Glazer points out, is by now as fervent as any friend of Israel could wish—or by his stand on quotas: after all, the Nixon administration has done more to further quotas by deeds than McGovern could possibly yet have done by words. But the Jews who are bothered by McGovern sense that the movement of which he is presently the head represents the entry into the political mainstream of that widespread antagonism toward the Center and its "middle-class" values which grew into so vivid a presence in American life and culture over the course of the 60's; and they see in that antagonism not only a denigration of them, of their achievements and their aspirations, but a threat to their future position. This is why a relatively large number of Jews will almost certainly refuse to vote for McGovern, even if—as will surely happen in many instances—they should decide not to vote for Nixon either.

In other words, if there should be a large-scale defection of Jews from the Democratic ticket this year, it would not necessarily signify the birth of a permanently substantial Jewish Republican vote. If the McGovern candidacy should indeed turn out to be a counterpart of the Goldwater candidacy of 1964, with the electorate severely punishing the Democrats now for challenging the Centrist consensus from the Left as it punished the Republicans then for challenging it from the Right, the Democrats would no doubt do in their catastrophic defeat what the Republicans did after theirs in 1964. They would move once again toward the Center, politely overriding their now discredited and demoralized insurgents in the process (just as Nixon has quietly ignored the protests of the Goldwater Right against many of his foreign and domestic policies), and renewing their appeal to groups like the Jews whose repudiation of the insurgents would have contributed to the size of the defeat.

If, on the other hand, the projections of the McGovern strategists should be vindicated and McGovern, carried along by a new coalition of blacks, youth, and women, should win *despite* the defection of traditionally Democratic groups like the Jews, there might then very well come about one of those periodic realignments which C. Vann Woodward and other historians tell us is long overdue, with a sizable number of Jews and other former Democrats now turning to the Republican party in the hope of finding or creating a reconstituted Center there. For if America should "come home" to the Democrats under McGovern, many whose home is the Center would no longer be at home with the Democrats.

In either case, we would all know better than anyone knows today where the country is, how it feels, what it wants. In the event of a McGovern victory, even a narrow one, we would know that the McGovernites are right when they say, in the words of Arthur Schlesinger, Jr., that "disgust with the way things have been recently managed in this country, the recoil against the Establishment, the pessimism about the national future, the desire for unspecified ... change ... infect every bloc in the nation." By contrast, in the event of a catastrophic McGovern defeat, we would know that the anti-McGovern forces, both Republican and Democratic, are right when they say that such feelings are still confined to an ideologically passionate minority (what the *Wall Street Journal* sometimes calls the "mass intelligentsia" and sometimes the "modernist-academic elite"); that most other people, if they are really infected with disgust, are disgusted not with the "Establishment" in general but precisely with that wing of it dominated by the New Class and the New Politics; and that the great majority of Americans believes the country is already "home," that the structure of the house is sound, and that what it mainly needs is patching and sprucing up to a greater (if they are liberals) or lesser (if they are conservatives) extent.

If, however, the Democrats under McGovern should neither win nor be decisively defeated—if, that is, Nixon should be re-elected by a very close margin—everything would remain uncertain, unsettled, and bitterly polarized, for the Jews and for everyone else.

33
Irving Kristol (1920–)
The Adversary Culture of Intellectuals (1979)

Editor's Introduction

By the end of the 1970s some members of the New York Intellectuals were ready—actually eager—to accept that they were conservatives of some type, and by then the term *neoconservative* became a nationally recognized name for them. There had been a long gestation of at least mildly conservative attitudes in the group. The strong satisfaction with American culture evident in Irving Kristol's "The Adversary Culture of Intellectuals" was found in essays in *Commentary* nearly from its beginning in the mid-forties, and it was the focus of *Dissent's* frequent fusillades against *Commentary* from the *Dissent's* first issue. The New York Intellectuals, in fact, could easily be divided into *affirmers* and *dissenters* after World War II. Norman Podhoretz and others were already worried about affirmative action by the mid-sixties, and by 1972 many at *Commentary* worried about whether the "New Politics" in the Democratic party would create a battle over the term *liberalism*. Midge Decter had not entirely given up on the term liberal in 1976, but she had by 1980. In 1979, the title of Podhoretz's book *Breaking Ranks* announced his relationship with his liberal colleagues. In that same year, Kristol published "Confessions of a True, Self-Confessed—Perhaps the Only—Neoconservative," and if that title was not sufficiently proprietary about Kristol's relationship to the movement, his 1995 book was titled *Neoconservatism: The Autobiography of an Idea*.

What did Kristol believe neoconservatism to be at the moment of its inception? It originated, he said, in the universities in a disillusionment with the liberalism of the moment. It opposed utopianism and romanticism, both of which were code words for the New Left radicalism. Neocons admired the classical and other premodern values, and Kristol claims they were influenced by Leo Strauss's defense of those commitments—although in the decades of their writing it's hard to think of an essay of the New York Intellectuals that mentions Strauss, let alone analyzes his work. Perhaps Kristol, like so many Americans before him, was creating a usable intellectual past for his tradition when in fact it had none. Finally, Kristol wrote, neocons endorsed the economic market, economic growth, a state, even "a conservative welfare state," to "elevate" society, and held that family and religion helped reconcile liberty and community among the people. (Irving Kristol, "Confessions of a True, Self-Confessed—Perhaps the Only—Neoconservative.")

One of the central convictions of neoconservatives that Kristol did not mention, but one that became synonymous with neoconservative essays, including his, is that intellectuals who dealt with art, culture and ideas (economic intellectuals, who defend the commercial class, were exempt) were a cancerous presence in society—an assumption that is part of the essay below. This disparagement of intellectuals is one of the traits *Dissent* criticized about *Commentary* when Kristol was a major figure in the magazine in the 1950s. "Has there ever been, in all of recorded history," Kristol inquired near the beginning of his essay, "a civilization whose culture was at odds with the values and ideals of that civilization itself?" The answer, of course, is yes. The better question might be in what culture has it ever been absent: in the United States, Latin America, Asia, the Muslim world, Russia? It is so important for the functioning of a people that without it a society is near death.

Kristol's criticism of academic intellectuals was not a new invention. It followed the observation of economist Joseph Schumpeter, who wrote in his *Capitalism, Socialism and Democracy* (1942) that "capitalism creates a critical frame of mind which, after having destroyed the moral authority of so many other institutions [the monarchy, hereditary privileges], in the end turns against its own." It's called intellectual freedom and independence. "Unlike any other type of society," Schumpeter concluded, "capitalism inevitably and by virtue of the very logic of its civilization creates, educates and subsidizes a vested interest in social unrest." (Joseph Schumpeter, *Capitalism, Socialism and Democracy*, Third edition,1942; revised, New York: Harper and Row, 1950, 143, 146.) That fresh air has kept the nation alive and free. Kristol's habit of attacking cultural intellectuals has prompted *Dissent*ers such as Michael Walzer (essay 29) and Irving Howe to point out the irony of Kristol, an intellectual, campaigning as an anti-intellectual. It is reminiscent of Harold Rosenberg's article (essay 16) in which he notices the same anti-intellectualism in the French intellectual Raymond Aron.

Part of the reason Kristol was so bothered by cultural intellectuals is that he understands that ideas have consequences, and, as he admitted, he saw that liberals at one point dominated the national discourse. In the mid-seventies he took it as his responsibility to convince business leaders they needed to be serious about ideas. Conservatives, he said in the *Wall Street Journal*, should invest in thinkers. Foundations, mostly funded by the money of past business figures, he urged, should stop financing "social change," and instead should fund "the survival of the corporation itself as a relatively autonomous institution in the private sector." Moreover, he suggested, "if you decide to go exploring for oil, you find a competent geologist. Similarly, if you wish to make a productive investment in the intellectual and educational worlds, you find competent intellectuals and scholars to offer guidance." (Irving Kristol,

"On Corporate Philanthropy," *Two Cheers for Capitalism* (New York: Basic Books, 1978), 144–45.)

But Kristol was more than simply an intelligent and articulate voice of business conservatism. He scolded business leaders for their philistinism and indifference to values in society. Yes, "what rules the world is ideas," but what makes a good and worthy society are the important values to which we commit ourselves. Religion and "the bourgeois ethos" formerly gave capitalism its moral element, but both of those have collapsed. Kristol, wanting more than commerce from society, believed conservatism must add "its own moral and intellectual substance to its idea of liberty" in order to make capitalism worthy. (Irving Kristol, "On Conservatism and Capitalism," *Neoconservatism: The Autobiography of an Idea*, 1995; reprint, Chicago: Ivan Dee, 1999, 233–34.) During the same period, Kristol, in his cleverly named essay "Of Decadence and Tennis Flannels," sounding very much like the moral premoderns he admires, argued that if the major benefit of capitalism is allowing people the leisure to play tennis, it's not worth it, and it would only show "our spiritual inability to cope with affluence." Kristol endorses a difficult instead of easy capitalism, a system of hard work, moral behavior and high ideals, church, school, family, and corporation—the old ethic of the bourgeoisie.

Source

Irving Kristol, "The Adversary Culture of Intellectuals," *Encounter* vol. 53, no. 4, October 1979.

Selected Readings

Irving Kristol, "Confessions of a True, Self-Confessed—Perhaps the Only—Neoconservative," *Public Opinion* vol. 2, no. 5, October/November 1979; "On Corporate Philanthropy" and "Of Decadence and Tennis Flannels," *Two Cheers for Capitalism* (New York: Basic Books, 1978); "On Conservatism and Capitalism," *Neoconservatism: The Autobiography of an Idea* (New York: Free Press, 1995).

* * * * *

No sooner did the late Lionel Trilling coin the phrase "adversary culture" than it became part of the common vocabulary. This is because it so neatly summed up a phenomenon that all of us, vaguely or acutely, had observed. It is hardly to be denied that the culture that educates us—the patterns of perception and thought our children absorb in their schools, at every level—is unfriendly (at the least) to the commercial civilization, the bourgeois civilization, within which most of us live and work. When we send our sons and daughters to college, we may expect that by the time they are graduated they are likely to have a lower opinion of our social and economic order than when they entered. We know this from opinion poll data; we know it from our own experience.

We are so used to this fact of our lives, we take it so for granted, that we fail to realize how extraordinary it is. Has there ever been, in all of recorded history, a civilization whose culture was at odds with the values and ideals of that civilization itself? It is not uncommon that a culture will be critical of the civilization that sustains it—and always critical of the failure of this civilization to realize perfectly the ideals that it claims as inspiration. Such criticism is implicit or explicit in Aristophanes and Euripides, Dante and Shakespeare. But to take an adversary posture toward the ideals themselves? That is unprecedented. A few writers and thinkers of a heretical bent, dispersed at the margins of the culture, might do so. But culture as a whole has always been assigned the task of, and invariably accepted responsibility for, sustaining and celebrating those values. Indeed, it is a premise of modern sociological and anthropological theory that it is the essence of culture to be "functional" in this way.

Yet ours is not. The more "cultivated" a person is in our society, the more disaffected and malcontent he is likely to be—a disaffection, moreover, directed not only at the actuality of our society but at the ideality as well. Indeed, the ideality may be more strenuously opposed than the actuality. It was, I think, Oscar Wilde who observed that, while he rather liked the average American, he found the ideal American contemptible. Our contemporary culture is considerably less tolerant of actuality than was Oscar Wilde. But there is little doubt that if it had to choose between the two, it would prefer the actual to the ideal.

The average "less cultivated" American, of course, feels no great uneasiness with either the actual or the ideal. This explains why the Marxist vision of a radicalized working class erupting into rebellion against capitalist society has turned out to be so erroneous. Radicalism, in our day, finds more fertile ground among the college-educated than among the high-school graduates, the former having experienced more exposure to some kind of adversary culture, the latter—until recently, at least—having its own kind of "popular" culture that is more accommodating to the bourgeois world that working people inhabit. But this very disjunction of those two cultures is itself a unique phenomenon of the bourgeois era, and represents, as we shall see, a response to the emergence, in the nineteenth century, of an "avant-garde," which laid the basis for our adversary culture.

Bourgeois society is without a doubt the most prosaic of all possible societies. It is prosaic in the literal sense. The novel written in prose, dealing with the (only somewhat) extraordinary adventures of ordinary people, is its original and characteristic art form, replacing the epic poem, the lyric poem, the poetic drama, the religious hymn. These latter were appropriate to societies formally and officially committed to transcendent ideals of excellence—ideals that could be realized only by those few of exceptional nobility of character—or to transcendent visions of the universe wherein human existence on earth is accorded only a provisional significance. But bourgeois society is uninterested in such transcendence, which at best it tolerates as a private affair, a matter for individual taste and individual consumption, as it were. It is prosaic, not only in form, but in essence. It is a society organized for the convenience and comfort of common men and common women, not for the production of heroic, memorable figures. It is a society interested in making the best of this world, not in any kind of transfiguration, whether through tragedy or piety.

Because this society proposes to make the best of this world, for the benefit of ordinary men and women, it roots itself in the most worldly and common of human motivations: self-interest. It assumes that, though only a few are capable of pursuing excellence, everyone is capable of recognizing and pursuing his own self-interest. This "democratic" assumption about the equal potential of human nature, in this limited respect, in turn justifies a market economy in which each individual defines his own well-being, and illegitimates all the paternalistic economic theories of previous eras. One should emphasize, however, that the pursuit of excellence by the few—whether defined in religious, moral, or intellectual terms—is neither prohibited nor inhibited. Such an activity is merely interpreted as a special form of self-interest, which may be freely pursued but can claim no official status. Bourgeois society also assumes that the average individual's conception of his own self-interest will be sufficiently "enlightened"—that is, sufficiently far-sighted and prudent—to permit other human passions (the desire for community, the sense of human sympathy, the moral conscience, etc.) to find expression, albeit always in a voluntarist form.

It is characteristic of a bourgeois culture, when it exists in concord with bourgeois principles, that we are permitted to take "happy endings" seriously ("… and they lived happily ever after"). From classical antiquity through the Renaissance, happy endings—worldly happy endings—were consigned to the genre of Comedy. "Serious" art focused on a meaningful death, in the context of heroism in battle, passion in love, ambition in politics, or piety in religion. Such high seriousness ran counter to the bourgeois grain, which perceived human fulfillment—human authenticity, if you will—in terms of becoming a good citizen, a good husband, a good provider. It is, in contrast to both pre-bourgeois and postbourgeois *Weltanschauungen*, a *domestic* conception of the universe and of man's place therein.

This bourgeois ideal is much closer to the Old Testament than to the New—which is, perhaps, why Jews have felt more at home in the bourgeois world than in any other. That God created this world and affirmed its goodness; that men ought confidently to be fruitful and multiply; that work (including that kind of work we call commerce) is elevating rather than demeaning; that the impulse to "better one's condition" (to use a favorite phrase of Adam Smith's) is good because natural—these beliefs were almost perfectly congruent with the world view of postexilic Judaism. In this world view, there was no trace of aristocratic bias: Everyman was no allegorical figure but, literally, every common person.

So it is not surprising that the bourgeois world view—placing the needs and desires of ordinary men and women at its center—was (and still is) also popular among the common people.[1] Nor is it surprising that, almost from the beginning, it was an unstable world view, evoking active contempt in a minority, and a pervasive disquiet among those who, more successful than others in having bettered their condition, had the leisure to wonder if life did not, perhaps, have more interesting and remote possibilities to offer.

The emergence of romanticism in the middle of the eighteenth century provided an early warning signal that, within the middle class itself, a kind of nonbourgeois spiritual impulse was at work. Not antibourgeois; not yet. For romanticism—with its celebration of noble savages, *Weltschmerz*, passionate love, aristocratic heroes and heroines, savage terrors confronted with haughty boldness and courage—was mainly an escapist aesthetic mode as distinct from a rebellious one. It provided a kind of counterculture that was, on the whole, safely insulated from bourgeois reality, and could even be tolerated (though always uneasily) as a temporary therapeutic distraction from the serious business of living. A clear sign of this self-limitation of the romantic impulse was the degree to which it was generated, and consumed, by a particular section of the middle class: women.

One of the less happy consequences of the women's liberation movement of the past couple of decades is the distorted view it has encouraged of the history of women under capitalism. This history is interpreted in terms of repression—sexual repression above all. That repression was real enough, of course; but it is absurd to regard it as nothing but an expression of masculine possessiveness, even vindictiveness. Sexual repression—and that whole code of feminine conduct we have come to call Victorian—was imposed and enforced by women, not men (who stand to gain very little if *all* women are chaste). And women insisted on this code because, while sexually repressive, it was also liberating in all sorts of other ways. Specifically, it liberated women, ideally if not always actually, from their previous condition as sex objects or work objects. To put it another way: All women were now elevated to the aristocratic status of *ladies*, entitled to a formal deference, respect, consideration. (Even today, some of those habits survive, if weakly—taking off one's hat when greeting a female acquaintance, standing up when a woman enters the room, etc.) The "wench," as had been portrayed in Shakespeare's plays, was not dead. She was still very much to be found in the working and lower classes. But her condition was not immutable; she, too, could become a lady—through marriage, education, or sheer force of will.

The price for this remarkable elevation of women's status was sexual self-restraint and self-denial, which made them, in a sense, owners of valuable (if intangible) property. It is reasonable to think that this change in actual sexual mores had something to do with the rise of romanticism, with its strong erotic component, in literature—the return of the repressed, as Freud was later to call it. For most of those who purchased romantic novels, or borrowed them (for a fee) from the newly established circulating libraries, were women. Indeed they still are, even today, two centuries later, though the romantic novel is now an exclusively popular art form, which flourishes outside the world of "serious" writing.

This extraordinary and ironical transformation of the novel from a prosaic art form—a tradition that reached its apogee in Jane Austen—to something radically different was itself a bourgeois accomplishment. It was made possible by the growing affluence of the middle classes that provided not only the purchasing power but also the leisure and the solitude ("a room of one's own"). This last point is worth especial notice.

It is a peculiarity of the novel that, unlike all previous art forms, it gains rather than loses from becoming a private experience. Though novels were still occasionally read aloud all during the romantic era, they need not be and gradually ceased to be. Whereas Shakespeare or Racine is most "enchanting" as part of a public experience—on a stage, in daylight—the novel gains its greatest power over us when we "consume" it (or it consumes us) in silence and privacy. Reading a novel then becomes something like surrendering oneself to an especially powerful daydream. The bourgeois ethos, oriented toward prosaic actualities, strongly disapproves of such day dreaming (which is why, even today, a businessman will prefer not to be known as an avid reader of novels, and few in fact are). But bourgeois women very soon discovered that living simultaneously in the two worlds of nonbourgeois "romance" and bourgeois "reality" was superior to living in either one.

The men and women who wrote such novels (or poems—one thinks of Byron) were not, however, simply responding to a market incentive. Writers and artists may have originally been receptive to a bourgeois society because of the far greater individual freedoms that it offered them; and because, too, they could not help but be exhilarated by the heightened vitality and quickened vivacity of a capitalist order with its emphasis on progress, economic growth, and liberation from age-old constraints. But, very quickly, disillusionment and dissent set in, and the urge to escape became compelling.

From the point of view of artists and of those whom we have come to call "intellectuals"—a category itself created by bourgeois society, which converted philosophers into *philosophes* engaged in the task of critical enlightenment—there were three great flaws in the new order of things.

First of all, it threatened to be very boring. Though the idea of ennui did not become a prominent theme in literature until the nineteenth century, there can be little doubt that the experience is considerably older than its literary expression. One can say this with some confidence because, throughout history, artists and writers have been so candidly contemptuous of commercial activity between consenting adults, regarding it as an activity that tends to coarsen and trivialize the human spirit. And since bourgeois society was above all else a commercial society—the first in all of recorded history in which the commercial ethos was sovereign over all others—their exasperation was bound to be all the more acute. Later on, the term "philistinism" would emerge to encapsulate the object of this sentiment.

Second, though a commercial society may offer artists and writers all sorts of desirable things—freedom of expression especially, popularity and affluence occasionally—it did (and does) deprive them of the status that they naturally feel themselves entitled to. Artists and writers and thinkers always have taken themselves to be Very Important People, and they are outraged by a society that merely tolerates them, no matter how generously. Bertolt Brecht was once asked how he could justify his Communist loyalties when his plays could neither be published nor performed in the USSR, while his royalties in the West made him a wealthy man. His quick rejoinder was: "Well, there at least they take me seriously!" Artists and intellectuals are always more respectful of a regime that takes their work and ideas "seriously." To be placed at a far distance from social and political power is, for such people, a deprivation.

Third, a commercial society, a society whose civilization is shaped by market transactions, is always likely to reflect the appetites and preferences of common men and women. Each may not have much money, but there are so many of them that their tastes are decisive. Artists and intellectuals see this as an inversion of the natural order of things, since it gives "vulgarity" the power to dominate where and when it can. By their very nature "elitists" (as one now says), they believe that a civilization should be shaped by an *aristoi* to which they will be organically attached, no matter how perilously. The consumerist and environmentalist movements of our own day reflect this aristocratic impulse, albeit in a distorted way: Because the democratic idea is the only legitimating political idea of our era, it is claimed that the market does not truly reflect people's preferences, which are deformed by the power of advertising. A minority, however, is presumed to have the education and the will to avoid such deformation. And this minority then claims the paternalist authority to represent "the people" in some more authentic sense. It is this minority which is so appalled by America's "automobile civilization," in which everyone owns a car, while it is not appalled at all by the fact that in the Soviet Union only a privileged few are able to do so.

In sum, intellectuals and artists will be (as they have been) restive in a bourgeois-capitalist society. The popularity of romanticism in the century after 1750 testifies to this fact, as the artists led an "inner emigration" of the spirit—which, however, left the actual world unchanged. But not all such restiveness found refuge in escapism. Rebellion was an alternative route, as the emergence of various socialist philosophies and movements early in the nineteenth century demonstrated.

Socialism (of whatever kind) is a romantic passion that operates within a rationalist framework. It aims to construct a human community in which *everyone* places the common good—as defined, necessarily, by an intellectual and moral elite—before his own individual interests and appetites. The intention was not new—there is not a religion in the world that has failed to preach and expound it. What was new was the belief that such self-denial could be realized, not through a voluntary circumscription of individual appetites (as Rousseau had, for example, argued in his *Social Contract*) but even while the aggregate of human appetites was being increasingly satisfied by ever-growing material prosperity. What Marx called "utopian" socialism was frequently defined by the notion that human appetites were insatiable, and that a self-limitation on such appetites was a precondition for a socialist community. The trouble with this notion, from a political point of view, was that it was not likely to appeal to more than a small minority of men and women at any one time. Marxian "scientific" socialism, in contrast, promised to remove this conflict between actual and potentially ideal human nature by creating an economy of such abundance that appetite as a social force would, as it were, wither away.

Behind this promise, of course, was the profound belief that modern science—including the social sciences, and especially including scientific economics—would gradually but ineluctably provide humanity with modes of control over nature (and human nature, too) that would permit the modern world radically to transcend all those limitations of the human condition previously taken to be "natural." The trouble with implementing this belief, however, was that the majority of men and women were no more capable of comprehending a "science of society," and of developing a "consciousness" appropriate to it, than they were of practicing austere self-denial. A socialist elite, therefore, was indispensable to mobilize the masses for their own ultimate self-transformation. And the techniques of such mobilization would themselves of necessity be scientific—what moralists would call "Machiavellian"—in that they had to treat the masses as objects of manipulation so that eventually they would achieve a condition where they could properly be subjects of their own history making.

Michael Polanyi has described this "dynamic coupling" of a romantic moral passion with a ruthlessly scientific conception of man, his world, and his history as a case of "moral inversion." That is to say, it is the moral passion that legitimates the claims of scientific socialism to absolute truth, while it is the objective necessities that legitimate every possible form of political immorality. Such a dynamic coupling characterized, in the past, only certain religious movements. In the nineteenth and twentieth centuries, it became the property of secular political movements that sought the universal regeneration of mankind in the here and now.

The appeal of any such movement to intellectuals is clear enough. As intellectuals, they are qualified candidates for membership in the elite that leads such movements, and they can thus give free expression to their natural impulse for authority and power. They can do so, moreover, within an ideological context, which reassures them that, any superficial evidence to the contrary notwithstanding, they are disinterestedly serving the "true" interests of the people.

But the reality principle—*la force des choses*—will, in the end, always prevail over utopian passions. The fate of intellectuals under socialism is disillusionment, dissent, exile, silence. In politics, means determine ends, and socialism everywhere finds its incarnation in coercive bureaucracies that are contemptuously dismissive of the ideals that presumably legitimize them, even while establishing these ideals as a petrified orthodoxy. The most interesting fact of contemporary intellectual life is the utter incapacity of so-called socialist countries to produce socialist intellectuals—or even, for that matter, to tolerate socialist intellectuals. If you want to meet active socialist intellectuals, you can go to Oxford or Berkeley or Paris or Rome. There is no point in going to Moscow or Peking or Belgrade or Bucharest or Havana. Socialism today is a dead end for the very intellectuals who have played so significant a role in moving the modern world down that street.

In addition to that romantic-rationalist rebellion we call socialism, there is another mode of "alienation" and rebellion that may be, in the longer run, more important. This is romantic antirationalism, which takes a cultural rather than political form. It is this movement specifically that Trilling had in mind when he referred to the adversary culture.

Taking its inspiration from literary romanticism, this rebellion first created a new kind of "inner emigration"—physical as well as spiritual—in the form of "bohemia." In Paris, in the 1820s and 1830s, there formed enclaves of (mostly) young people who displayed *in nuce* all the symptoms of the counterculture of the 1960s. Drugs, sexual promiscuity, long hair for men and short hair for women, working-class dress (the "jeans" of the day), a high suicide rate—anything and everything that would separate them from the bourgeois order. The one striking difference between this bohemia and its heirs of a century and a quarter later is that to claim membership in bohemia one had to be (or pretend to be) a producer of "art," while in the 1960s to be a consumer was sufficient. For this transition to occur, the attitudes and values of bohemia had to permeate a vast area of bourgeois society itself. The engine and vehicle of this transition was the "modernist" movement in the arts, which in the century after 1850 gradually displaced the traditional, the established, the "academic."

The history and meaning of this movement are amply described and brilliantly analyzed by Daniel Bell in his *The Cultural Contradictions of Capitalism* (1976). Suffice it to say here that modernism in the arts can best be understood as a quasi-religious rebellion against bourgeois sobriety, rather than simply as a series of aesthetic innovations. The very structure of this movement bears a striking resemblance to that of the various gnostic-heretical sects within Judaism and Christianity. There is an "elect"—the artists themselves—who possess the esoteric and redeeming knowledge *(gnosis)*; then there are the "critics," whose task it is to convey this gnosis, as a vehicle of conversion, to potential adherents to the movement. And then there is the outer layer of "sympathizers" and "fellow travelers"—mainly bourgeois "consumers" of the modernist arts—who help popularize and legitimate the movement within the wider realms of public opinion.

One can even press the analogy further. It is striking, for instance, that modernist movements in the arts no longer claim to create "beauty" but to reveal the "truth" about humanity in its present condition. Beauty is defined by an aesthetic tradition that finds expression in the public's "taste." But the modern artist rejects the sovereignty of public taste, since truth can never be a matter of taste. This truth always involves an indictment of the existing order of things, while holding out the promise, for those whose sensibilities have been suitably reformed, of a redemption of the spirit (now called "the self"). Moreover, the artist himself now becomes the central figure in the artistic enterprise—he is the hero of his own work, the sacrificial redeemer of us all, the only person capable of that transcendence that gives a liberating meaning to our lives. The artist—painter, poet, novelist, composer—who lives to a ripe old age of contentment with fame and fortune strikes us as having abandoned, if not betrayed, his "mission." We think it more appropriate that artists should die young and tormented. The extraordinarily high suicide rate among modern artists would have baffled our ancestors, who assumed that the artist—like any other *secular* person—aimed to achieve recognition and prosperity in this world.

Our ancestors would have been baffled, too, by the enormous importance of critics and of criticism in modern culture. It is fascinating to pick up a standard anthology in the history of literary criticism and to observe that, prior to 1800, there is very little that we would designate as literary criticism, as distinct from philosophical tracts on aesthetics. Shakespeare had no contemporary critics to explain his plays to the audience; nor did the Greek tragedians, nor Dante, Racine, and so forth. Yet we desperately feel the need of critics to understand, not only the modern artist, but, by retrospective reealuation, all artists. The reason for this odd state of affairs is that we are looking for something in these artists—a redeeming knowledge of ourselves and our human condition—which in previous eras was felt to lie elsewhere, in religious traditions especially.

The modernist movement in the arts gathered momentum slowly, and the first visible sign of its success was the gradual acceptance of the fact that bourgeois society had within it two cultures: the "avant-garde" culture of modernism, and the "popular culture" of the majority. The self-designation of modernism as avant-garde is itself illuminating. The term is of military origin, and means not, as we are now inclined to think, merely the latest in cultural or intellectual fashion, but the foremost assault troops in a military attack. It was a term popularized by Saint-Simon to describe the role of his utopian-socialist sect vis-à-vis the bourgeois order, and was then taken over by modernist innovators in the arts. The avant-garde is, and always has been, fully self-conscious of its hostile intentions toward the bourgeois world. Until 1914, such hostility was as likely to move intellectuals and artists toward the romantic Right as toward the romantic Left. But Right or Left, the hostility was intransigent. This is, as has been noted, a cultural phenomenon without historical precedent.

And so is the popular culture of the bourgeois era, though here again we are so familiar with the phenomenon that we fail to perceive its originality. It is hard to think of a single historical instance where a society presents us with two cultures, a "high" and a "low," whose values are in opposition to one another. We are certainly familiar with the fact that any culture has its more sophisticated and its more popular aspects, differentiated by the level of education needed to move from the one to the other. But the values embodied in these two aspects were basically homogeneous: The sophisticated expression did not *shock* the popular, nor did the popular incite feelings of revulsion among the sophisticated. Indeed, it was taken as a mark of true artistic greatness for a writer or artist to encompass both aspects of his culture. The Greek tragedies were performed before all the citizens of Athens; Dante's *Divine Comedy* was read aloud in the squares of Florence to a large and motley assemblage; and Shakespeare's plays were enacted before a similarly mixed audience.

The popular culture of the bourgeois era, after 1870 or so, tended to be a culture that educated people despised, or tolerated contemptuously. The age of Richardson, Jane Austen, Walter Scott, and Dickens—an age in which excellence and popularity needed not to contradict one another, in which the distinction between "highbrow" and "lowbrow" made no sense—was over. The spiritual energy that made for artistic excellence was absorbed by the modernist, highbrow movement, while popular culture degenerated into a banal reiteration—almost purely commercial in intent—of "wholesome" bourgeois themes.

In this popular literature of romance and adventure, the "happy ending" not only survived but became a standard cliché. The occasional unhappy ending, involving a sinful action (e.g., adultery) as its effectual cause, always concluded on a note of repentance, and was the occasion for a cathartic "good cry." In "serious" works of literature in the twentieth century, of course, the happy ending is under an almost total prohibition. It is also worth making mention of the fact that popular literature remained very much a commodity consumed by women, whose commitments to the bourgeois order (a "domestic" order, remember) has always been stronger than men's. This is why the women's liberation movement of the past two decades, which is so powerfully moving the female sensibility in an antibourgeois direction, is such a significant cultural event.

In the last century, the modernist movement in the arts made constant progress at the expense of the popular. It was, after all, the only serious art available to young men and women who were inclined to address themselves to solemn questions about the meaning of life (or "the meaning of it all"). The contemporaneous evolution of liberal capitalism itself encouraged modernism in its quest for moral and spiritual hegemony. It did this in three ways.

First, the increasing affluence that capitalism provided to so many individuals made it possible for them (or, more often, for their children) to relax their energetic pursuit of money, and of the goods that money can buy, in favor of an attention to those nonmaterial goods that used to be called "the higher things in life." The antibourgeois arts in the twentieth century soon came to be quite generously financed by restless, uneasy, and vaguely discontented bourgeois money.

Second, that spirit of worldly rationalism so characteristic of a commercial society and its business civilization (and so well described by Max Weber and Joseph Schumpeter) had the effect of delegitimizing all merely traditional beliefs, tasks, and attitudes. The "new," constructed by design or out of the passion of a moment, came to seem inherently superior to the old and established, this latter having emerged "blindly" out of the interaction of generations. This mode of thinking vindicated the socialist ideal of a planned society. But it also vindicated an anarchic, antinomian, "expressionist" impulse in matters cultural and spiritual.

Third, the tremendous expansion—especially after World War II—of post-secondary education provided a powerful institutional milieu for modernist tastes and attitudes among the mass of both teachers and students. Lionel Trilling, in *Beyond Culture,* poignantly describes the spiritual vitality with which this process began in the humanities—the professors were "liberated" to teach the books that most profoundly moved and interested them—and the vulgarized version of modernism that soon became the mass counterculture among their students who, as consumers, converted it into a pseudo-bohemian life-style.

Simultaneously, and more obviously, in the social sciences, the antibourgeois socialist traditions were absorbed as a matter of course, with "the study of society" coming quickly and surely to mean the management of social change by an elite who understood the verities of social structure and social trends. Economics, as the science of making the best choices in a hard world of inevitable scarcity, resisted for a long while; but the Keynesian revolution—with its promise of permanent prosperity through government management of fiscal and monetary policy—eventually brought much of the economics profession in line with the other social sciences.

So utopian rationalism and utopian romanticism have, between them, established their hegemony as adversary cultures over the modern consciousness and the modern sensibility.

But, inevitably, such victories are accompanied by failure and disillusionment. As socialist reality disappoints, socialist thought fragments into heterogeneous conflicting sects, all of them trying to keep the utopian spark alive while devising explanations for the squalid nature of socialist reality. One is reminded of the experience of Christianity in the first and second centuries, but with this crucial difference: Christianity, as a religion of transcendence, of *other-worldly* hope, of faith not belief, was not really utopian, and the Church Fathers were able to transform the Christian rebellion against the ancient world into a new, vital Christian orthodoxy, teaching its adherents how to live virtuously, that is, how to seek human fulfillment in this world even while waiting for their eventual migration into a better one. Socialism, lacking this transcendent dimension, is purely and simply trapped in this world, whose realities are for it nothing more than an endless series of frustrations. It is no accident, as the Marxists would say, that there is no credible doctrine of "socialist virtue"—a doctrine informing individuals how actually to live "in authenticity" as distinct from empty rhetoric about "autonomous self-fulfillment"—in any nation (and there are so many!) now calling itself socialist. It is paradoxically true that other-worldly religions are more capable of providing authoritative guidance for life in this world than are secular religions.

The utopian romanticism that is the impulse behind modernism in the arts is in a not dissimilar situation. It differs in that it seeks transcendence—all of twentieth-century art is such a quest—but it seeks such transcendence within the secular self. This endeavor can generate that peculiar spiritual intensity that characterizes the antibourgeois culture of our bourgeois era, but in the end it is mired in self-contradiction.

The deeper one explores into the self, without any transcendental frame of reference, the clearer it becomes that nothing is there. One can then, of course, try to construct metaphysics of nothingness as an absolute truth of the human condition. But this, too, is self-contradictory: If nothingness is the ultimate reality, those somethings called books, or poems, or paintings, or music are mere evasions of truth rather than expressions of it. Suicide is the only appropriate response to this vision of reality (as Dostoevski saw long ago) and in the twentieth century it has in fact become the fate of many of our artists: self-sacrificial martyrs to a hopeless metaphysical enterprise. Those who stop short of this ultimate gesture experience that *tedium vitae,* already mentioned, which has made the "boringness" of human life a recurrent theme, since Baudelaire at least, among our artists.

This modern association of culture and culture heroes with self-annihilation and ennui has no parallel in human history. We are so familiar with it that most of us think of it as natural. It is, in truth, unnatural and cannot endure. Philosophy may, with some justice, be regarded as a preparation for dying, as Plato said—but he assumed that there would never be more than a handful of philosophers at any time. The arts, in contrast, have always been life-affirming, even when dealing with the theme of death. It is only when the arts usurp the role of religion, but without the transcendence that assures us of the meaning of apparent meaninglessness, that we reach our present absurd (and *absurdiste*) condition.

Moreover, though utopian rationalism and utopian romanticism are both hostile to bourgeois society, they turn out to be, in the longer run, equally hostile to one another.

In all socialist nations, of whatever kind, modernism in the arts is repressed—for, as we have seen, this modernism breeds a spirit of nihilism and antinomianism that is subversive of *any* established order. But this repression is never entirely effective, because the pseudo-orthodoxies of socialism can offer no satisfying spiritual alternatives. It turns out that a reading of Franz Kafka can alienate from socialist reality just as easily as from bourgeois reality, and there is no socialist Richardson or Fielding or Jane Austen or Dickens to provide an original equipoise. Who are the "classic" socialist authors or artists worthy of the name? There are none. And so young people in socialist lands naturally turn either to the high modernist culture of the twentieth century or to its debased, popularized version in the counterculture. Picasso and Kafka, blue jeans and rock and roll may yet turn out to be the major internal enemies of socialist bureaucracies, uniting intellectuals and the young in an incorrigible hostility to the status quo. Not only do socialism and modernism end up in blind alleys—their blind alleys are pointed in radically different directions.

Meanwhile, liberal capitalism survives and staggers on. It survives because the market economics of capitalism does work—does promote economic growth and permit the individual to better his condition while enjoying an unprecedented degree of individual freedom. But there is something joyless, even somnambulistic, about this survival.

For it was the Judeo-Christian tradition which, as it were, acted as the Old Testament to the new evangel of liberal, individualistic capitalism—which supplied it with a moral code for the individual to live by, and which also enabled the free individual to find a transcendental meaning in life, to cope joyfully or sadly with all the *rites de passage* that define the human condition. Just as a victorious Christianity needed the Old Testament in its canon because the Ten Commandments were there—along with the assurance that God created the world *"and it was good,"* and along, too, with its corollary that it made sense to be fruitful and multiply on this earth—so liberal capitalism needed the Judeo-Christian tradition to inform it authoritatively about the use and abuse of the individual's newly won freedom. But the adversary culture, in both its utopian-rationalist and utopian-romantic aspects, turns this Judeo-Christian tradition into a mere anachronism. And the churches, now themselves a species of voluntary private enterprise, bereft of all public support and sanction, are increasingly ineffectual in coping with its antagonists.

Is it possible to restore the spiritual base of bourgeois society to something approaching a healthy condition?

One is tempted to answer no, it is not possible to turn back the clock of history. But this answer itself derives from the romantic-rationalist conception of history, as elaborated by Saint-Simon and Hegel and Marx. In fact, human history, read in a certain way, can be seen as full of critical moments when human beings deliberately turned the clock back. The Reformation, properly understood, was just such a moment, and so was the codification of the Talmud in postexile Judaism. What we call the "new" in intellectual and spiritual history is often nothing more than a novel way of turning the clock back. The history of science and technology is a cumulative history, in which new ways of seeing and doing effectively displace old ones. But the histories of religion and culture are not at all cumulative in this way, which is why one cannot study religion and culture without studying their histories, while scientists need not study the history of science to understand what they are up to.

So the possibility is open to us—but, for better or worse, it is not the only possibility. All we can say with some certainty, at this time, is that the future of liberal capitalism may be more significantly shaped by the ideas now germinating in the mind of some young, unknown philosopher or theologian than by any vagaries in annual GNP statistics. Those statistics are not unimportant, but to think they are all-important is to indulge in the silly kind of capitalist idolatry that is subversive of capitalism itself. It is the ethos of capitalism that is in gross disrepair, not the economics of capitalism—which is, indeed, its saving grace. But salvation through this grace alone will not suffice.

Note

1. This generalization, skimming over differences in national traditions and religious cultures (especially Protestant vs. Catholic cultures), is obviously an oversimplification But it is only an oversimplification, not a distortion.

Permission Acknowledgments

Alfred Kazin, *Starting Out in the Thirties*. 1962; reprint, New York: Vintage, 1980. Reprinted with permission of Judith Dunford and the Estate of Alfred Kazin.

Irving Howe, "A Memoir of the Thirties," *Steady Work* (New York: Harcourt, Brace & World, 1966). Reprinted by permission of *Dissent* and Nicholas Howe, Literary Executor of Irving Howe.

Irving Kristol, "Memoirs of a Trotskyist," *New York Times Magazine*, Jan 23, 1977. Reprinted courtesy of Irving Kristol.

Mary McCarthy, "Philip Rahv, 1908-1973," *New York Times Book Review,* February 17, 1974. Reprinted courtesy of the Mary McCarthy Literary Trust.

"Editorial Statement," *Partisan Review*, vol. 1, no. 1, February-March 1934. From the Partisan Review Collection, Howard Gotlieb Archival Research Center at Boston University.

Editorial Statement," *Partisan Review*, vol. 4, no. 1, December 1937. From the Partisan Review Collection, Howard Gotlieb Archival Research Center at Boston University.

Dwight Macdonald, "I Choose the West," reprinted from *Memoirs of a Revolutionist* (NY: Farrar, Straus and Cudahy, 1957).

Sidney Hook, "The New Failure of Nerve," *Partisan Review* vol. 10, no. 1, January-February 1943. Reprinted courtesy of Ernest B. Hook.

Hannah Arendt, "Total Domination," from *The Origins of Totalitarianism*, copyright © 1973, 1968, 1966, 1958, 1951, 1948 by Hannah Arendt and renewed by Lotte Kohler and Mary McCArthy West. Reprinted by permission of Harcourt, Inc.

Philip Rahv, "The Sense and Nonsense of Whitaker Chambers,"*Partisan Review* vol.19, no. 4, July-August 1952, 472-482. Reprinted courtesy of Betty Rahv.

Meyer Schapiro, "Nature of Abstract Art," reprinted from *Marxist Quarterly*, vol. 1, January 1937, 77-98. Reprinted with the permission of George Braziller, Inc.

Clement Greenberg, "Avant-Garde and Kitsch," *Partisan Review* vol. 1, no. 5, Fall 1939. Reprinted courtesy of Janice Van Horne and the Estate of Clement Greenberg.

Dwight Macdonald, "Homage to Twelve Judges," reprinted from *politics* vol. 6, no. 1, Winter, 1949.

Lionel Trilling, "Reality in America" from *The Moral Obligation to Be Intelligent*. Reprinted by permission of Farrar, Straus, and Giroux, LLC. Copyright © 2000 by Lionel Trilling.

Alfred Kazin, "The Historian as Reporter: Edmund Wilson and the 1930s," *The Reporter* vol. 18, no. 6, March 20, 1958. Reprinted with the permission of Judith Dunford and the Estate of Alfred Kazin.

Harold Rosenberg, "Twilight of the Intellectuals," from *Discovering the Present*. Reprinted courtesy of University of Chicago Press.

Daniel Bell, "The End of Ideology in the West," reprinted by permission of the publisher from *The End of Ideology*, pp. 393-407, Cambridge, Mass.: Harvard University Press, Copyright ©1960, 1961, 1962, 1988, 2000, by Daniel Bell.

Dwight Macdonald, "Masscult & Midcult," from *Against the American Grain* (NY: Random House, 1962). Originally published in *Partisan Review* vol. 17, no. 2, Spring 1960 and vol. 17, no. 3, Summer 1960. From the Partisan Review Collection, Howard Gotlieb Archival Research Center at Boston University.

Lionel Trilling, "On the Teaching of Modern Literature," *Beyond Culture* (1965; reprint, Harcourt, Brace, Jovanovich, 1978) © 1965 by Lionel Trilling, reprinted with the permission of the Wylie Agency.

Susan Sontag, "Against Interpretation," from *Against Interpretation*. Reprinted by permission of Farrar, Straus, and Giroux, LLC. Copyright © 1964, 1966, renewed 1994 by Susan Sontag.

Paul Goodman, "To Young Resisters," *Resistance* vol. 7, no. 4, March 1949. Reprinted with permission of Sally Goodman.

Irving Kristol, "'Civil Liberties,' 1952—A Study in Confusion," *Commentary* vol. 13, no. 3, March 1952. Reprinted courtesy of Irving Kristol.

Sidney Hook and Bertrand Russell, "A Foreign Policy for Survival," (abridged) *New Leader* vol. 41, no. 14, April 7, 1958; *New Leader* vol. 41, no. 21, May 26, 1958. Reprinted with permission of *The New Leader*.

C. Wright Mills and Irving Howe, "Intellectuals and Russia," *Dissent* vol. 6, no. 2, Spring 1959, 191-196; *Dissent*, Summer 1959, vol. 6, no. 3. Reprinted courtesy of *Dissent*.

Norman Podhoretz, "The Know-Nothing Bohemians," *Partisan Review* vol. 25, no. 2, Spring 1958. From the Partisan Review Collection, Howard Gotlieb Archival Research Center at Boston University. Reprinted courtesy of Norman Podhoretz.

Irving Howe, "Problems in the 1960s" reprinted from *A Margin of Hope*: An Intellectual Autobiography, copyright © 1982 by Irving Howe, reprinted by permission of Nicholas Howe, Literary Executor of Irving Howe and Harcourt, Inc.

Norman Podhoretz, "My Negro Problem—And Ours," *Commentary* vol. 35, no. 2, February 1963. Reprinted from *Commentary*, February 1963, by permission; all rights reserved.

Nathan Glazer, "Negroes & Jews: The New Challenge to Pluralism," *Commentary* vol. 38, no. 6, December 1964. Reprinted from *Commentary*, December 1964, by permission; all rights reserved.

Michael Walzer, "In Defense of Equality," *Dissent* vol. 20, no. 4, Fall 1973. Reprinted courtesy of *Dissent*.

Irving Howe, "Socialism and Liberalism: Articles of Conciliation?" *Dissent* vol. 24, no. 1, Winter 1977. Reprinted by permission of *Dissent* and Nicholas Howe, Literary Executor of Irving Howe.

Nathan Glazer, "On Being Deradicalized," *Commentary* vol. 50, no. 4, October 1970

Norman Podhoretz, "Between Nixon and the New Politics," *Commentary* vol. 54, no.3 September 1972. Reprinted from *Commentary*, September 1972, by permission; all rights reserved.

Irving Kristol, "The Adversary Culture of Intellectuals," *Encounter* vol. 53, no. 4, October 1979. Reprinted courtesy of Irving Kristol.

Index